ECONOGUIDE® SERIES

ECONOGUIDE® LAS VEGAS

Also Includes Reno, Lake Tahoe, and Laughlin

Fifth Edition

COREY SANDLER

INSIDERS' GUIDE®

GUILFORD, CONNECTICUT
AN IMPRINT OF THE GLOBE PEQUOT PRESS

To Janice, my fellow traveler

The prices and rates listed in this guidebook were confirmed at press time. We recommend, however, that you call establishments to obtain current information before traveling.

To buy books in quantity for corporate use or incentives, call **(800) 962–0973** or e-mail **premiums@GlobePequot.com**.

INSIDERS' GUIDE®

Copyright © 2003, 2004, 2005, 2006, 2007 by Word Association, Inc.

All rights reserved. No part of this book may be reproduced or transmitted in any form by any means, electronic or mechanical, including photocopying and recording, or by any information storage and retrieval system, except as may be expressly permitted by the 1976 Copyright Act or by the publisher. Requests for permission should be made in writing to The Globe Pequot Press, P.O. Box 480, Guilford, Connecticut 06437.

Insiders' Guide is a registered trademark of Morris Book Publishing, LLC.
Econoguide is a registered trademark of Word Association, Inc.

All photos by the author unless otherwise specified.
Text design: Lesley Weissman-Cook
Maps by XNR Productions, Inc. © Morris Book Publishing, LLC

ISSN 1544-8436
ISBN-13: 978-0-7627-4168-7
ISBN-10: 0-7627-4168-6

Manufactured in the United States of America
Fifth Globe Pequot Press Edition/First Printing

CONTENTS

PART IV: ABOUT GAMBLING

ACKNOWLEDGMENTS

DOZENS OF HARDWORKING and creative people helped move my words from the keyboard to the book you're now reading.

Thanks to Mary Luders Norris and Elizabeth Taylor along with the editors and production staff at Globe Pequot Press, including Lynn Zelem, Gia Manalio, Heather Carreiro, and Joanna Beyer.

Gene Brissie has been a believer for more than a decade; Ed Claflin has signed on for the next round of voyages.

As always, thanks to Janice Keefe for running the office and putting up with me, a pair of major assignments.

We appreciate our friends at hotels, casinos, restaurants, and attractions who opened their doors to us.

And thanks to you for buying this book. We all hope you find it of value; please let us know how we can improve the book in future editions.

Corey Sandler
Econoguide® Travel Books

You can receive a free subscription to the *Econoguide Newsletter* for updates, announcements, and special offers. To subscribe, go to our Web page at www.econoguide.com and click on the newsletter subscription link.

You can also subscribe by sending an e-mail with your name and e-mail address to: newsletter@econoguide.com.

To contact the author, please send an e-mail to the following address:

info@econoguide.com

I hope you'll also consider other books in the Econoguide series. You can find them at bookstores, or ask your bookseller to order them. All are written by Corey Sandler.

Econoguide® Walt Disney World®, Universal Orlando®
Econoguide® Disneyland® Resort, Universal Studios Hollywood®
Econoguide® Cruises
Econoguide® Buying or Leasing a Car
Econoguide® Buying and Selling a Home

INTRODUCTION

I MADE MY FIRST VISIT to Las Vegas as a teenager forty years ago, when the place was very raw: gambling, sex, and the desert. The best thing about Las Vegas (and much of the rest of Nevada), in fact, is everything that has grown up around these three things.

Since then I've been back more times than I can count—as a tourist, as a conventioneer, as a newspaper journalist, and as a travel writer. I've put fingers to keyboard numerous times to write about Las Vegas, Reno, Lake Tahoe, and Laughlin.

In some ways, Las Vegas is the same as it was the first time I saw it: It is still an oasis in the desert devoted to adult vices (some call them entertainment). But over the past few decades, Las Vegas has made a silk purse out of a sow's ear: The gambling pits are surrounded and supported by a fantasy world made up of the skyscrapers of Manhattan, Excalibur's castle, the canals of Venice, the bacchanals of Caesar, the riches of Paris, and so much more.

From its start, Las Vegas has been most closely associated with gambling and sex, but over the years it has also become a mecca for entertainment and dining. And today shopping is the new sex: The Strip is becoming populated with some of the most attractive shopping districts on the planet. There are massive monuments to consumerism at the Fashion Show Mall, Caesars Forum Shops, Mandalay Bay, the Miracle Mile, and elsewhere.

I hope you'll join me in treating Las Vegas as a gigantic buffet of things to see and do: Few places on Earth have so many options for dining, entertainment, shopping, and sights to see.

FOREVER FRONTIER

Nevada will probably always be the frontier. It is a place where things are different, where old assumptions are challenged, and where new ideas are tried. That is, after all, why people come to Nevada. Although legal gambling has spread across the nation, there is still nothing like Las Vegas in Chicago or Los Angeles or Boston. There is no Lake Mead in New Jersey. There are no snowcapped mountains with ski runs that careen down to an alpine lake in Kansas. And although Nevada is a relatively young state, there are few places I know that are as imbued with living history as Virginia City.

But before we go too far, let's start with what this book is not:

■ It is not a rose-colored view of the world endorsed by the chamber of commerce. Not everything in Nevada is wonderful, a good value, or a worthwhile use of your vacation time. I'll try to help you get the most from your trip.

■ It is not a guide for the cheapskate interested in sleeping in bus terminals (or motels that look like bus terminals) and eating exclusively at restaurants that use plastic forks. What we mean by *Econoguide* is this: helpful information to help

NEVADA HIGHWAYS

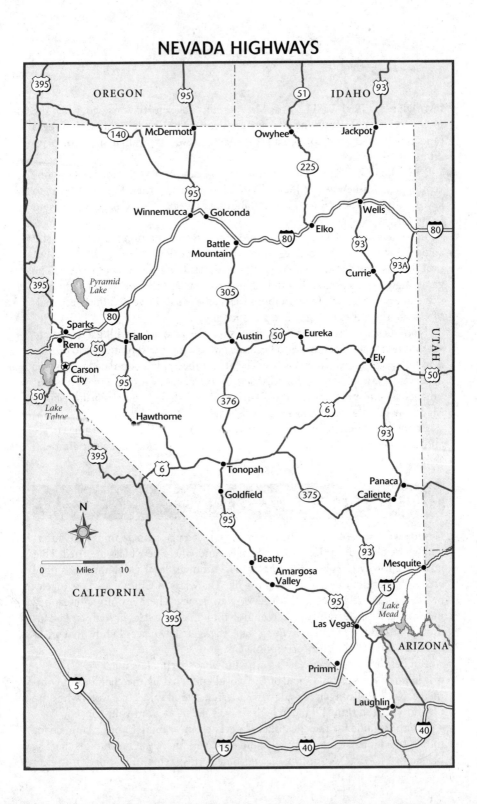

you get the most out of your trip to Nevada. I'll show you how to save time and money on travel, hotels, restaurants, and entertainment. Even if you choose to go for first-class airfare, luxury hotels, and the most expensive restaurants in town, I'll help you spend your money wisely.

■ It is not a guide to making money at the gambling tables. I will, though, offer a cautious guide to casinos, concentrating on how to have fun and not lose more money than you are prepared to donate in the name of entertainment.

Let's think a bit about the state of Nevada, a place of huge contrasts. According to the National Census Bureau, Nevada has been the country's fastest-growing state for the past two decades, growing by 3.5 percent in 2005. According to Census and state numbers, the Las Vegas metropolitan area (sprawling Clark County—bigger than the state of Massachusetts—includes Las Vegas, North Las Vegas, Henderson, Boulder City, and Laughlin) was home to about 1.6 million people in mid-2005; to the north, the state's second-largest city, Reno, was home to about 252,000 residents.

The seventh-largest state in the union, Nevada is only in thirty-fifth place when it comes to population (but Utah, Arkansas, and Kansas may find their places shuffled in the coming decade). In any case, though, it is still very sparsely populated with its total of about 2.6 million people spread across 110,540 square miles—and almost all of the residents are concentrated around the urban areas of Las Vegas and Reno.

Winters are extremely cold in the north and west; summers in the south are ovenlike. Nevada's highest point is a lofty 13,143 feet at Boundary Peak on the snowy border with California; the lowest is along the Colorado River as it enters the hot and dry desert in the southern tip of the state.

Nevada's economy is focused on mining: mining minerals out of the earth and mining gold and silver out of the pockets of tourists who come to visit in great droves—a record total of 38.6 million people visited Las Vegas in 2005, up by 1.2 million over the year before. Another eleven million or so went to other areas of the state, including Reno, Lake Tahoe, and Laughlin. Many of the growing number of visitors were conventioneers: about 6.2 million in 2005, an increase of about half a million over 2004.

Fully half of the workers in the state are in the service trades, with 25 percent directly employed by casinos or hotels. In Las Vegas alone, casinos provide more than 100,000 jobs.

In 2005, "gaming win" income at Nevada casinos topped $11 billion across the state, with more than $9.1 billion raked in at Clark County establishments including the Strip and downtown Las Vegas. In Washoe County, which includes Reno, Sparks, and Lake Tahoe, the "win" was more than $1 billion.

Let's put that "winnings" number in perspective: We're talking about the gross revenues of the casinos. The gross "handle," which is the amount of money that crosses back and forth across the table and in and out of machines, was about $160 billion in 2005. That means that about 7 percent of the money gambled in Nevada was kept as profit by the casinos.

That's a decent but not spectacular profit on the investments made in the fabulous resorts of Nevada . . . until you also consider the money earned from

New York–New York Hotel & Casino at night

hotel rooms, restaurants, shops, and entertainment. At one time casinos commonly all but gave away room and board to lure gamblers; that is no longer true for most of Las Vegas, but you'll still find $19.00 hotel rooms and 99-cent shrimp cocktails and $1.99 steaks at sawdust joints most everywhere else in the state.

Over the years receipts have declined on baccarat, twenty-one, craps, and roulette. The growth areas are slot machines and video poker. Reports also show that there is a huge amount of money to be made on nickel slots, perhaps indicating that the visitors who come to Las Vegas are looking for less expensive ways to lose money, or just the sheer volume of small bettors.

In the United States Nevada holds on to the largest single share of gambling revenues. In second place, a billion dollars or so behind, is Atlantic City, New Jersey. The third-biggest regional market is the Midwest, including Illinois, Indiana, Michigan, and Iowa.

One of the great, uncelebrated things about Nevada's tourist centers of Las Vegas, Reno, Laughlin, and Lake Tahoe is that you can find a restroom, telephone, change booth, or restaurant at any hour of the day or night, any day of the year. You can also find a casino open at any time. Usually in the same place, of course.

Let's head out on an exploration of all sides of Nevada, from the oasis in the desert at Laughlin to the mirage at Las Vegas to the great western rest stop at Reno to the honeycombed mountains of Virginia City and the Comstock Lode to the breathtaking beauty of Lake Tahoe.

PART I

NEVADA BOUND

CHAPTER ONE

A SHORT AND IRREVERENT HISTORY OF NEVADA

WHEN THEY SPOKE OF THE "WILD WEST," it was often Nevada they had in mind.

Wild, as in a nearly virgin land when the first white explorers set foot there about the time of the American Revolution.

Wild, as in the extremes of weather from the arid deserts of the eastern part of the state to the high, snowy mountains of the Sierra Nevada in the west.

Wild, as in the heady days of the 1850s and 1860s, when gold and then silver were discovered south of Reno, and when for a short period of time Virginia City was the richest place on Earth.

Wild, as in the early days of Las Vegas at the start of the twentieth century, when the "anything goes" atmosphere of the railroad town laid the foundation for what would become Glitter Gulch and then the Strip.

Wild, as in the state of Nevada of today, a place that is just slightly ahead of—or behind or off to one side of—anywhere else we know. (As comedian Rita Rudner, a cultural icon on the Strip, told us, "I don't care where you come from; Las Vegas is the opposite of it.")

Throughout its history Nevada has been looked upon as a colony for outside interests to exploit. First came the Spanish and then the British and their Canadian surrogates. When the land came under the control of the young United States, Nevada was considered little more than a rest stop on the highway to California. When gold and silver were discovered in great quantities in and around Virginia City, much of the wealth was exported out of the state to California and even as far away as England.

The interests that developed much of the early commercial properties of Nevada were the railroads, and they, too, sent their money west and east. And finally there was gambling, Nevada's one major homegrown industry. The casinos took off in the 1940s only after organized-crime capitalists from New York, Chicago, Miami, Los Angeles, and elsewhere came in and exerted their control.

Today the gangsters are mostly gone, and control of nearly all major casinos and hotels rests in the hands of huge stateless corporations.

THE RIVER TO THE PACIFIC

The region that would one day be Nevada was originally part of the Spanish Empire in the New World. Father Francisco Garcés is believed to have entered the Las Vegas Valley in 1776. Garcés and other priest-explorers were expanding the Old Spanish Trail, which led from the commercial centers of Santa Fe (now in New Mexico) to the Spanish missions in southern California. Along the way they sought to make converts if they could; more than a few Native Americans were killed in skirmishes and by disease.

There was, of course, a significant problem faced by the Spanish: getting through the deserts and high mountain passes that stood between New Mexico and California. *Sierra Nevada* is a Spanish phrase meaning "snowy mountains." Garcés and others of his time followed the Colorado River into Nevada but did not fully explore the region geologists now call the Great Basin. Consequently they made some significant errors on their maps and created the myth of what they called the "San Buenaventura River," a great waterway that was supposed to cross the Great Basin and empty into the Pacific Ocean. In other words, they claimed there was an easy route from east to west that did not require crossing the high mountains. For much of the next half century, trappers and explorers searched in vain for the San Buenaventura.

In 1825 Peter Skene Ogden explored parts of Nevada from the other direction, south from Canada. Working for the Hudson's Bay Company, he discovered the Humboldt River in northwest Nevada in that year. A year later Jedediah Strong Smith, an explorer and fur trader, followed the Colorado River into southern Nevada—the same entry Garcés took fifty years earlier—and soon thereafter the 1,200-mile-long Spanish Trail became firmly established.

Smith, born in 1798 in Bainbridge, New York, went to the West as a young fur trapper and became one of the great pathfinders of our country. His group of seventeen set out from the Great Salt Lake in 1826 looking for fur trade routes to California and the Northwest. He crossed the Mojave Desert to Mission San Gabriel, California, near what is today San Diego, and may have been the first nonnative to enter California from the East. Returning eastward the next year, he crossed the Great Salt Lake Desert on an epic journey through the inhospitable, waterless sands.

Another group of explorers was seeking a way to link the Mormon settlements of Salt Lake City with California, and the trailblazers sought a way to avoid the highest of the Sierra Nevada mountain passes by going south.

In 1829 Rafael Rivera, a young scout for Spanish traders, entered a valley that had a patch of tall grass about 2 miles long and half a mile wide—a desert oasis that offered a small amount of drinkable water. That valley, called *las vegas* (Spanish for "the meadows"), became a regular stopping-off point for travelers on the westward trail.

John C. Frémont, a U.S. Army officer, conducted extensive explorations in 1843 and 1845. In 1848 at the end of the Mexican War, the territory that included what would become Nevada was acquired by the United States from Mexico for $15 million in the Treaty of Guadalupe Hidalgo.

But it took the discovery of gold in 1847 in the American Fork River at Sutter's Mill near Sacramento, California, to begin mass migration to the West Coast, and much of the traffic passed through Nevada. During the next seven years, the population of California grew from about 15,000 to 300,000.

In 1849 Mormon settlers established a trading post at Mormon Station (now known as Genoa) near Lake Tahoe in the Carson River Valley, at the base of the Sierra Nevada. In 1855 a colony of Mormon evangelists arrived in the Las Vegas Valley to establish the Las Vegas Mission, attempting to bring their religion and knowledge to the Paiute Indians. They built a fort—importing some of the wood from mountains as far as 20 miles away—and planted crops. Although they apparently had some success in their assignments, in 1857 the settlers were recalled to Salt Lake City by Brigham Young after the church government had a dispute with the U.S. government, and the mission was abandoned.

In the late 1850s the area in and around Virginia City, Carson City, and Genoa served as a staging area for settlers about to head over the Sierra Nevada to California. The Mormon Station had become a thriving commercial operation after a simple log-cabin store was erected in 1851. Genoa was also the first home of the *Territorial Enterprise* newspaper, which was to become an important element of the developing Western culture.

The relatively quiet status of Nevada as a rest stop on the highway west changed mightily around this time. There had been some minor gold finds in Gold Canyon in about 1850, but the quantity was so relatively small as to be lost in the excitement over the California discoveries.

But in January of 1859 gold and then silver—the Great Comstock Lode—were found on the slopes of Mount Davidson between Reno and Carson City. By the spring of 1860, a full boom was under way at Virginia City. (One of the miners, James "Old Virginny" Finney, bestowed his name on the rough settlement of tents and cave dwellings of the first miners.)

The mines in and around Virginia City had a lasting impact on the nation when Nevada Territory entered the Union as a source of wealth at the start of the Civil War in 1861. Many local mine owners were opposed to statehood, fearing their riches would be taxed to support the war; President Lincoln, who sought Nevada's support in Congress, pushed its statehood, which took place in 1864. Along the way the riches of the Comstock Lode provided much of the capital for the development of San Francisco.

After the Mormons abandoned their fort in Las Vegas in 1857, a local farmer, Octavius Decatur Gass, acquired the water rights in the valley and moved into the old Mormon fort. Gass, who went on to become a major political force in the area, had come from Ohio in search of gold. The 640-acre site, now referred to as the Las Vegas Ranch, occupied what is currently the entire downtown area. A section of the old fort still stands in a city museum.

The next driving force in Nevada was the coming of the railroads. In 1862 the

U.S. Congress granted a charter to the Union Pacific Railroad to build the first transcontinental railroad, stretching from near Sacramento, California, to Missouri, where it would connect to eastern systems. Though the Civil War held most of the attention of a war-weary America at this time, citizens also watched as the Central Pacific (CP) and Union Pacific (UP) Railroads raced east and west toward each other. The CP began on January 1, 1863, in Sacramento, California; the UP broke ground on December 2 of the same year in Omaha, Nebraska. The CP tracks passed through northern Nevada (Reno, Winnemucca, and Elko) to the meeting point at Promontory Point, Utah, where the Golden Spike was driven on May 10, 1869.

The main line lured more railroad construction to the state. The Virginia & Truckee Railroad, which served the silver and gold mines of Virginia City, was extended from Carson City to the east-west tracks at Reno. At the start of 1905, the final spike connecting a southern railroad route between Los Angeles and Salt Lake City was driven into the desert floor about 20 miles south of what would become Las Vegas. The Tonopah & Las Vegas Railroad sprang up to link mining and ranching operations to the southern tracks.

Following Octavius Gass, the former Mormon fort came into the ownership of the Stewart family in 1882. Twenty years later they sold the property for $55,000 to copper and railroad magnate William Clark, who was also a U.S. senator from Montana. He decided to make Las Vegas a division point for his San Pedro, Los Angeles, and Salt Lake Railroad and not incidentally drive up the value of his landholdings. And so, on the morning of May 15, 1905, Clark's railroad and the closely linked Las Vegas Land and Water Company banged the opening gavel for an auction of the Las Vegas Ranch and surrounding lands. The sale was conducted from a temporary structure near the railroad station; the site today is roughly the location of the Union Plaza Hotel at the head of Fremont Street in downtown Las Vegas.

A crowd of more than 1,000 bid feverishly on some 1,200 lots; the auction continued into a second day. Spots considered prime property brought as much as $1,750, and the total net was about $265,000.

THE LAS VEGAS REST STOP

The first train from Salt Lake City to Los Angeles passed through the growing town of Las Vegas in 1906, and a year later a second railroad line was installed from Las Vegas northwest to Tonopah. For most of the next quarter century, the town thrived as a rest stop for travelers on the railroads and also as a commercial center for outlying mining operations.

The wants and needs of the miners were by most sensibilities a bit on the rough side. Many visited what passed for a town to buy basic supplies, obtain a hot bath, visit a saloon for some drinking and gambling, and find a woman for sex; the priorities were not necessarily in that order, either.

As a frontier town Las Vegas included its share of illegal gaming parlors and a red-light district almost from the start. When the planners for the San Pedro,

Los Angeles, and Salt Lake Railroad divvied up the Las Vegas Ranch, they named the area that is now between First and Second and Ogden and Stewart Streets (1 block in from the main drag of Fremont Street) Block 16. It was here that the first saloons—many with "cribs" out back—were located.

The Arizona Club was one of the first brick buildings in town and was generally considered the class of Las Vegas. An old photograph shows the tiny saloon along a rough dirt road with a 50-foot-long boardwalk. Its sign reads ARIZONA CLUB. HEADQUARTERS FOR FULLY MATURED REIMPORTED STRAIGHT WHISKEY.

Town officials and the police turned a blind eye to the drinking, entertainment, prostitution, and gambling that took place in Block 16, which soon became known more simply as "the Block." These vices were not exactly legal, existing in a political netherworld for decades. In fact, the operators of the whorehouses were required to purchase an annual license for their operations, and the employees were subject to weekly medical examinations.

Gambling had been legal in Nevada from the time of its statehood until 1911, when the legislature, reacting to a developing conservatism in the country, outlawed betting. Eight years later, the U.S. Congress instituted Prohibition, outlawing consumption of alcoholic beverages nationwide.

But that seemed to matter very little in the Wild West of Las Vegas, particularly in Block 16. Bootleggers supplied alcohol, prostitution flourished, and unregulated games of chance continued for the next twenty years.

A DAM SITE

The next important event in local history came courtesy of the Federal Bureau of Reclamation when it authorized the construction of the Boulder Dam on the Colorado River about 30 miles southeast of Las Vegas. The dam was deemed necessary to control the Colorado, which regularly flooded the Imperial Valley in California and the Yuma Valley in Arizona when mountain snows melted each spring and dried to a near trickle in the summer. Bureau of Reclamation engineers investigated more than seventy sites along the Colorado River before choosing the site of Black Canyon.

The dam was to create the 110-mile-long Lake Mead reservoir upstream and allow the controlled release of water down the Colorado River. (During the construction period, the Colorado River was diverted around the site by four huge tunnels, each 50 feet in diameter.) Construction began in 1930 and took five years to complete. More than 5,000 workers, many of them with families, moved to the area, and Las Vegas once more was the attractive rest stop in the desert.

Not at all coincidentally the Nevada legislature reestablished casino gambling in 1931, and small casinos began catering to the construction workers. Approved in the same session was a liberalization of divorce laws, requiring a short six-week residency for out-of-staters seeking to cast asunder their marriage vows.

Also not incidentally the huge generators at the dam—renamed Hoover Dam—produced plentiful, cheap electricity that was essential to the neon signs of Glitter Gulch and the Strip and the air-conditioning within the huge hotels.

Nevada, which entered the Union on October 31, 1864, as the thirty-sixth state, covers 110,540 square miles, the seventh-largest state in the country. As big as Nevada is, consider the fact that 86 percent of the land area is owned by the federal government.

The first Las Vegas gaming license was issued in 1931 to the Northern Club at 15 East Fremont Street. Two years later Prohibition was officially ended throughout the nation, and the consumption of alcohol became legal again.

Block 16, which continued to thrive even when most of its vices became legal, was finally killed off by a different sort of national urgency: World War II. The commander of the Las Vegas Aerial and Gunnery Range, where many thousands of soldiers were training, feared outbreaks of disease and lack of discipline among his troops. Las Vegas officials were informed that unless they cracked down on the Block, the Army would declare the whole city off-limits to servicemen. Almost immediately the liquor and slot machine licenses of the Block were revoked. Organized prostitution, which operated as an adjunct to the other forms of entertainment, died off soon afterward.

Prostitution receded into the underworld again for the next few decades, reemerging as a legal industry in 1973 when the Nevada Supreme Court upheld the right of the state's counties to permit the activity. Today brothels are legal in several Nevada counties, and several legal and relatively large businesses operate outside of Las Vegas, Reno, and Carson City. Prostitution is not legal in the big cities themselves, which is not to say that it doesn't go on.

The first major casinos were established in downtown Las Vegas along Fremont Street, which eventually became known as Glitter Gulch. Joining the Northern Club in 1932 was the Hotel Apache, with a hundred rooms and the first elevator in town. With the exception of the dam workers—most of whom departed by 1936—the attraction of the casinos was almost entirely regional.

The war contributed to the growth of the area with the establishment of the Aerial Gunnery School and a huge magnesium-processing plant, Basic Magnesium, that brought 10,000 workers to Pittman (now Henderson) between Las Vegas and Boulder City. Magnesium is a component of incendiary bombs.

It was in the 1940s, however, that Las Vegas gained international notoriety; much of the impetus came from organized crime led by Benjamin "Bugsy" Siegel, Charles "Lucky" Luciano, Meyer Lansky, and others. Clever businessmen, the gangsters forged links right from the start with Hollywood. This is not to say that the movie stars of the era were directly involved with the gangsters, but there was a synergy between the needs of the stars and the operators of the casinos.

Clara Bow (the "It girl") and Rex Bell, film stars of the 1920s and 1930s, were early adopters of Las Vegas glitz. They built a ranch and were hosts of the town; they brought many later stars, including Clark Gable, Errol Flynn, the Barrymores, and others, to town for visits.

GAMBLERS GET OUT OF TOWN

The El Rancho Vegas was founded miles south of downtown in 1941, on U.S. Highway 91, then called the Los Angeles Highway. The hotel had sixty-three bungalow-like rooms, riding stables, a showroom, and, of course, a casino.

The famous Flamingo hotel opened five years later on this major highway (renamed Las Vegas Boulevard and soon to become known as the Strip), and the seeds of modern Las Vegas were sown.

If there is a true civic father to Las Vegas, it would be Benjamin Siegel; you didn't call him "Bugsy" to his face. Born in Brooklyn, Siegel was a major operator in East Coast organized crime. He was sent out West in the 1930s to run a bookmaking wire service and to look after other interests there; among other things, he also owned and operated a fleet of offshore gambling ships that served Californians.

The Flamingo was Siegel's lavish dream; at its opening on December 26, 1946 (with Jimmy Durante and Abbott & Costello as opening acts), it was the southernmost hotel on the Strip. Siegel saw that such an expensive pleasure palace would draw rich—and unprofessional—gamblers. Siegel was martyred for his cause, too. He was executed by business associates in 1947, allegedly because of claims he siphoned money from the building fund for the Flamingo.

The second big resort out of town was the Last Frontier, which featured an Old West theme; guests were picked up at the airport in a stagecoach. The Last Frontier, only slightly updated, became the New Frontier. (In any case, the resort may have reached the final frontier, as plans were announced in 2006 for its demolition and replacement by a new megaresort.)

One after another, hotels and casinos were built on the Strip, moving farther southward, away from downtown.

The Desert Inn opened in 1950 and made its mark with its showrooms featuring some of the biggest stars of the time. The Stardust brought another staple of Las Vegas in 1958, the fancified girlie show. The *Lido de Paris* was a spectacular stage show that (almost) incidentally included a stage full of topless dancers.

In 1966 Caesars Palace opened and launched the era of the opulent gambling palace, and Las Vegas as we know it was born. The idea of Las Vegas as a "family" resort accelerated in 1993 and 1994 with the opening of the MGM Grand Adventures theme park and hotel (with a casino, of course), as well as the spectacular Luxor and Treasure Island.

Today the race is on to create the most luxurious, most phantasmagoric pleasure palaces. At the front of this very expensive pack are Mandalay Bay, the Venetian, Paris Las Vegas, Bellagio, and the Wynn Las Vegas.

Nearly all of the originals are gone: The Desert Inn lies beneath the Wynn, and the New Frontier and the Stardust are both scheduled to be demolished and replaced with multibillion-dollar modern fantasies.

A section of the unique Las Vegas skyline

THE BIGGEST LITTLE SECOND CITY OF NEVADA

Across the state, Reno began as a tollbooth over the Truckee River, a private bridge known as Lake's Crossing. And, of course, it became a rest stop for travelers heading somewhere else—to California over the Sierra Nevada and to the wild mining towns of Virginia City and the rest of the Comstock.

Today, although Reno depends upon casinos and tourism for much of its income, it has a more diversified economy than Las Vegas.

And by the way, not all the gold mined in Nevada comes from the pockets of unlucky gamblers. Today the state itself is the world's third-largest producer of gold. It mines about 80 percent of the gold in the United States, more than $2.7 billion per year. Other minerals, including silver, copper, gypsum, and a bit of oil, bring in another billion or so.

CHAPTER TWO

FINDING LOW-COST AIRLINE TICKETS

AND AVOIDING THE UNCERTAINTIES OF MODERN TRAVEL

I LOVE TO TRAVEL, but I hate to waste time and money. It all but kills me to know that I spent $200 more than I should have for an airline ticket, or that the next guy over has a nicer hotel room at a better price. Put another way, my goal is to take more vacations and spend more time in wondrous places than most people and to have a better time while I'm at it.

Let's get something straight here, though: This book is not a guide for the cheapskate who wants a $10-a-night tour of dreadful dives and uninspiring-but-free sights. I'm perfectly willing to spend a reasonable amount of money for good value. In this book I'll help you make the same sort of good use of your own money and time.

AIR TRAVEL

The way I figure it, one major airline is pretty much like another. Sure, one company may offer a larger bag of peanuts while the other promises its flight attendants have more accommodating smiles. Me, I'm much more interested in other things:

1. safety
2. the most convenient schedule
3. the lowest price

Although I'm sometimes willing to trade price for convenience, I'll never risk my neck for a few dollars. But that doesn't mean I don't try my hardest to get the very best price on airline tickets. I watch the newspapers for seasonal sales and price wars, clip coupons from the usual and not-so-usual sources, consult the burgeoning world of Internet travel agencies, and happily play one airline against the other.

Here are some things to look for when shopping for airline tickets:

■ **A new airline.** In recent years we have seen the arrival of carriers like JetBlue and the growth of no-frills discount carriers like Southwest. Almost all the new carriers make a big splash with low fares and extra amenities.

■ **New service.** When airlines come into a market, they often offer "introductory" prices. I've seen prices as low as $19 in fare wars; in recent years there have been several periods during which you could buy cross-country tickets for $79 to $99 each way.

■ **The right airport.** When one airline dominates a particular airport, chances are prices are not as competitive as they should be. You'll get the best prices at an airport where two or more airlines fly between the same pairs of cities; even better, when one of the low-cost carriers (including Southwest and JetBlue) offers tickets, the major airlines generally match their prices on some or all flights, at a huge cost to their own bottom line.

■ **The best time.** The busiest travel days of the year are usually the days before Thanksgiving, Christmas, and school holidays. You can bet that deep-discount tickets will be rare at those times of the year, and seats themselves will be in short supply. On the other hand you can expect the best prices and availability during slack periods that include the time between Thanksgiving and Christmas and in the dead of winter.

In this book we're exploring vacation trips, and in theory, you can make some adjustments to your plans to get the best possible rate.

Let's start with a real-life scenario. I want to get away from New England to Las Vegas. I know to stay away from the busiest and most expensive times of the year: the Christmas–New Year's holiday, the Presidents' Week vacation, and the heart of the summer (yes, I know it can be unbearably hot, but the desert vacationland still draws millions). I've also checked to make sure I'm not planning to visit during one of the huge national conventions (by calling the visitor bureau to obtain the schedule or by asking one of the major hotels). The availability of online reservation systems from the hotels and from travel portals makes it easy to see when rates are high or low.

It is also usually less expensive to fly during the middle of the week—Tuesday through Thursday instead of on Monday or Friday; Saturday is sometimes a good day to travel, too. And most important, in this example, I am willing to consider saving some money by driving a bit farther to the airport.

Here are some real prices I found for round-trip flights to Las Vegas in the summer: I could fly early in the morning, arriving in Las Vegas in time for dinner and a show, for as little as $203 from Providence, $303 from Boston, or $269 to $303 from New York's LaGuardia Airport. Or, according to the suggestion made by a Web site, I could save the most by flying from Manchester, New Hampshire, for a mere $171.

If it doesn't make a difference to you, check for the lowest fares by time of day. Sometimes the least expensive flights are the first ones out in the morning and the most expensive is the final trip of the night, but travel patterns can reverse that order. The advantage of an early-morning flight is that you may gain part of a day at your destination; night flights might save you the cost of a night in a hotel.

Most airlines have eliminated or reduced the price differential for business flyers who travel within a single week, but in general you will still get the best price on a ticket by booking ahead of time and by including a weekend in your plans.

The businessman across the aisle, who is flying out on a Monday and back on a Friday, will suffer through the same plastic baggie of fried something or other, watch the same crummy movie, and arrive in Las Vegas at the same millisecond I do. The only difference will be the fact that he may have paid nearly $1,000 for his ticket. And in first class, someone who (in my humble opinion) has more money than sense has paid an astounding $1,332 for a slightly wider, slightly plusher seat and an airline meal. (I'd rather spend just some of that money on a better place to sleep and a meal at a restaurant where half the meal doesn't end up in your lap.)

Somewhere else on this same plane is a couple who were bumped off a previous flight because of overbooking. They are happily discussing where to use the two free round-trip tickets they received in compensation.

And up front in first class, where you arrive a millisecond earlier, a family of four is traveling on free tickets earned through Mom's frequent-flyer plan.

Me, I'm perfectly happy with that cut-rate ticket. I use some of the money I saved to buy a bag lunch to eat on the plane, and I daydream about where to use

Funny-Hat Fares

If you are traveling to a convention, you may be able to get in on an airline discount negotiated by the group. In fact you may not need any affiliation with a convention group to take advantage of special rates, if offered. All the airline will ask is the name or number of the discount plan for the convention; that information is often listed on convention materials or available through sponsoring organizations. The reservationist is almost certainly not going to ask to see your union card or funny hat.

Call convention bureaus or check their Web sites to see if any large groups are traveling when you plan to fly. Is this sneaky and underhanded? Perhaps. But I think it is sneaky and underhanded for an airline to charge hundreds of dollars more for the seats to the left and right of the one I am sitting in.

Off-Peak Travel

Low season in most of Nevada is generally the late fall to early spring. The quietest times of the year are the weeks around Christmas and New Year's, not including the holidays themselves. Watch out, however, for the huge conventions that descend on Las Vegas and grab the premium rooms and drive up the prices of all the rest.

Other busy times are during major sporting events such as the Super-bowl, the NCAA Final Four, or a championship boxing match. Tens of thousands of gamblers—from casual to very serious—come to casino sports books to watch the events . . . and place their bets.

In Reno the winter is the offest of off-seasons with the exception of occasional massive bowling-tournament crowds. The ski-oriented resorts around Lake Tahoe are busy in the winter and sometimes sold out on weekends and holidays, but rooms are usually available during the week, except in holiday periods.

the frequent-flyer miles I'm earning on the airfare, hotel, and car rental. And on my trip back home, depending on how busy the season and the prevailing security climate, I might try to get on the flight I really wanted to take instead of the less-convenient reservation I was forced to sign up for when I bought that cut-rate ticket.

ALICE IN AIRLINELAND

In today's strange world of air travel, there is a lot of room for the dollarwise and clever traveler to wiggle. You can pay an inflated full price, you can take advantage of the lowest fares, or you can play the ultimate game and parlay tickets into free travel.

Should you use a travel agent? If an agent can save you money or offer you some service you cannot obtain by doing it yourself, go ahead. The fact is, though, that very few traditional travel agencies are still in the business of selling airline tickets and hotel reservations. Most airlines have severely cut or eliminated commissions on tickets, and there's not much money to be made on hotels, either. The surviving traditional travel agencies instead concentrate on big-ticket items such as cruises or all-in-one airline, hotel, car rental, and entertainment packages. If you were to ask a travel agent to sell you an airline ticket, he or she might slap a service charge on the price. And there is a built-in major conflict of interest here. Under the traditional arrangement the agent was paid by the seller not the buyer, and an agent would usually make more commission on a $500 ticket than a $250 ticket.

The modern replacement for travel agencies is the online travel portal where you can compare prices, departure times, and other considerations. Here you can find computerized travel agencies that offer airline, hotel, car, cruise, and package reservations. You don't receive personal assistance, but you are able to make as many price checks and itinerary routings as you'd like without apology. Several services feature special deals, including companion fares and rebates you cannot find elsewhere.

At an online travel Web site, your purchase is charged to your credit card (which adds a layer of protection for you), and in most cases you receive an electronic confirmation code instead of a paper ticket, which speeds the whole process and cuts costs.

There are three golden rules when it comes to saving hundreds of dollars on travel: Be flexible, be flexible, and be flexible. Here's how to translate that flexibility into extra dollars in your pocket:

- Shop around. Consult several online travel Web sites for the best availabile fares and connections, and then check the airline's Web site to see if an even better fare is available there. You can also call the airline; although prices online are usually less than those quoted by a reservations agent, you can ask questions for free. And in some cases, the reservations agent will match the online price quote if you make that specific request. It doesn't hurt to ask.
- Be flexible about when you choose to travel. Go during the off-season or low season when airfares, hotel rooms, cruises, and attractions are offered at substantial discounts. Try to avoid school vacations, spring break, and the prime summer travel months of July and August, unless you enjoy a lot of company.
- Be flexible about the day of the week you travel. In many cases you can save hundreds of dollars by bumping your departure date one or two days in either direction. Ask the airline reservations agent (or read the fine print on the Web site) about current fare rules and restrictions. The days of lightest air travel are generally midweek, Saturday afternoon, and Sunday morning. The busiest days are Sunday evening, Monday morning, and Friday afternoon and evening. In many cases you will receive the lowest possible fare if your stay includes all day Saturday; this class of ticket is sold as an excursion fare. It used to be standard practice by airlines to use this as a way to exclude business travelers from the cheapest fares, assuming that businesspeople want to be home by Friday night. Most airlines have been forced by economic conditions to end this discrimination against business travelers, but you may still run into price differentials.
- Know the prevailing rates and look for up-and-down fluctuations. The day of the week on which you *buy* your tickets may also make a price difference. Airlines often test out higher fares over the relatively quiet weekends. They're looking to see if their competitors will match their higher rates; if the other carriers don't bite, the fares often float back down by Monday morning.
- Buy round-trip tickets. In general, you will receive the lowest fare if you buy a round-trip ticket, and if the flights on the itinerary are all on the same airline or on codeshare partners. However, in certain circumstances, you may find it less expensive to buy one-way tickets in each direction. Some of the low-fare airlines, including JetBlue and Southwest, usually allow you to buy an outbound and return ticket separately without additional cost. There is no reason I can think of not to choose different carriers for different directions if you can save cash in the process.
- Take advantage of frequent-flyer programs only when they make economic sense. If you need to accumulate 50,000 miles to earn a ticket worth between $350 and $500—a fairly typical equation—your miles are worth somewhere between a penny and a penny-and-a-half each. So if you are buying a 6,000-mile round-trip transcontinental ticket, the miles could be worth between $60 and $90—if you end up using them. But if you could find a fare on a different air-

The Best Policy

Consider buying trip-cancellation insurance from a travel agency or tour operator or directly from an insurance company (ask your insurance agent for advice). The policies are intended to reimburse you for any lost deposits or prepayments if you must cancel a trip because you or certain specified members of your family become ill. Read the policy carefully to understand the circumstances under which the company will pay.

Take care not to purchase more coverage than you need; if your tour package costs $5,000 but you would lose only $1,000 in the event of a cancellation, then the amount of insurance required is just $1,000. Some policies will cover you for health and accident benefits while on vacation, excluding any preexisting conditions.

And be sure you understand your contract with your airline. You may be able to reschedule a flight or even receive a refund after payment of a service charge; some airlines will give full refunds or free rescheduling if you can prove a medical reason for the change.

line priced $200 less, it doesn't make sense to pay more for a ticket with frequent-flyer mileage. (One possible exception: You need just a few hundred or a thousand miles to reach a free-ticket plateau. But before you buy a more expensive ticket just for that reason, check to see if you can purchase miles directly from the airline or earn them in other ways such as through affinity credit card programs.)

■ Be flexible about the hour of your departure. There is generally lower demand—and therefore lower prices—for flights that leave in the middle of the day or very late at night. The highest rates are usually assigned to breakfast-time (7:00 to 11:00 A.M.) and cocktail-hour (4:00 to 7:00 P.M.) departures.

■ Be flexible on the route you will take and be willing to put up with a change of plane or stopover. Once again you are putting the law of supply and demand in your favor. For example, a nonstop flight from Boston to Las Vegas for a family of four may cost hundreds more than a flight from Boston that includes a change of planes in Chicago (a United hub) before proceeding on to Nevada. (Sometimes, though, it works the other way: On a popular route the nonstop may be less expensive than a connecting flight.)

(You should also understand that in airline terminology, a "direct" flight does not mean a "nonstop" flight. Nonstop means the plane goes from Point A to Point B without stopping anywhere else. A direct flight may go from Point A to Point B, but it may include a stopover at Point C or at more than one airport along the way. A connecting flight means you must get off the plane at an airport en route and change to another plane. And just to add one more level of confusion, some airlines have "direct" flights that involve a change of plane along the way—the flight number stays the same but passengers have to get off at an intermediate stop, dragging all their carry-on luggage to another gate and aircraft. Go figure.)

Consider flying on one of the newer, deep-discount airlines, but don't let economy cloud your judgment. Some carriers are simply better run than others. Read the newspapers, check with a trusted fellow traveler, and use common sense. As far as I'm concerned, the best thing about the cheapo airlines is the pressure they put on the established carriers to lower prices or even to match fares on certain flights. Look for the cheapest fare you can find and then call your favorite big airline and see if it will sell you a ticket at the same price—it just might work.

■ Don't overlook the possibility of flying out of a different airport either. For example, metropolitan New Yorkers can find domestic flights from LaGuardia, Newark, White Plains, and a developing discount mecca at Islip. Suburbanites of Boston might want to consider flights from Providence or Manchester as possibly cheaper alternatives to Logan Airport. Chicago has O'Hare and Midway. From southern California, there are major airports at Los Angeles, Orange County, Burbank, and San Diego.

■ Plan way ahead of time and purchase the most deeply discounted advance tickets, which usually are nonrefundable. Most carriers limit the number of discount tickets on any particular flight. Although there may be plenty of seats left on the day you want to travel, they may be offered at higher rates.

■ Understand the difference between nonrefundable and noncancelable. Most airlines interpret nonrefundable to mean that they can keep all of your money if you cancel a reservation or fail to show up for a flight. You can, though, apply the value of the ticket (minus a fee of as much as $150) toward the purchase of another ticket. A noncancelable fare means that you have bought a specific seat on a specific flight. If your plans change or you are forced to cancel your trip, you lose the value of the ticket. (Think of it as missing a concert performance. You can't use the ticket another day.) Of course if the airline cancels your flight or makes a schedule or routing change you find does not meet your needs, you are entitled to a refund of your fare.

■ If you're feeling adventurous, you can take a big chance and wait for the last possible moment, keeping in contact with charter tour operators and accepting a bargain price on a leftover seat and hotel reservation. You may also find that some airlines will reduce the prices on leftover seats within a few weeks of your departure date; don't be afraid to check with the airline regularly or ask your travel agent to do it for you. In fact some travel agencies have automated computer programs that keep a constant electronic eagle eye on available seats and fares.

■ Take advantage of special discount programs such as senior citizens' clubs, military discounts, or offerings from other organizations to which you may belong. If you are in the broadly defined "senior" category, you may not even have to belong to a group such as AARP; simply ask the airline ticket agent if there is a discount available. You may have to prove your age or show a membership card when you pick up your ticket or boarding pass.

■ Consider doing business with discounters or ticket brokers, known in the industry as consolidators or, less flatteringly, as bucket shops. These companies buy the airlines' slow-to-sell tickets in volume and resell them to consumers at rock-bottom prices. Search the Internet for listings; you may also find ads in the classified listings of many Sunday newspaper travel sections. Be sure to weigh the savings on the ticket price against any restrictions attached to the tickets; for example, they may not be changeable, which could be a big problem, and they usually don't accrue frequent-flyer mileage, which is a less important issue.

■ Shop online through one of the Internet travel sites or the Web sites of individual airlines. You can expect to receive the lowest possible airfares—usually a few percent below the best prices offered if you call the airline directly—but little assistance in choosing among the offerings. Be sure to pay close attention to details such as the number of connections required between origin and destination. Note, too, that tickets sold in this way may have severe restrictions on changes and cancellations.

Some of the best Internet agencies include:
Microsoft Expedia, www.expedia.com
Orbitz, www.orbitz.com
Travelocity, www.travelocity.com

Among the airlines that offer online booking are:
American Airlines, www.aa.com
Continental Airlines, www.continental.com
Delta Airlines, www.delta.com
JetBlue, www.jetblue.com
Northwest Airlines, www.nwa.com
Southwest, www.southwest.com
United Airlines, www.united.com
US Airways (now combined with **America West**), www.usairways.com

■ Consider, very carefully, buying tickets from an online travel auction site such as www.priceline.com or www.hotwire.com. These sites promise to match your travel plans with available seats on major airlines at deep-discount prices; you will not be able to choose departure or arrival times or a particular airline. The way to use these sites is to do your research beforehand on one of the regular Web sites to find the best price you can; compare that to the "blind" offerings from the auction sites. Although the auction sites can often deliver the best prices, the tickets come with some detractions: You cannot time your arrival for a particular time of the day; it may be impossible to make changes or obtain a refund if your plans change; and you may not be permitted to stand by for another flight with your limited ticket. And read the fine print carefully: Prices may not include taxes and fees, and the sites may tack on a service charge. Be sure to compare the true bottom line to the price quoted on other Web sites or from a travel agent.

These auction sites have also begun offering a more traditional form of ticket booking, where the airline and flight times are displayed before you make your purchase. Be sure to check the prices against another Web travel site to make sure you are receiving a real discount from the regular fare.

■ Use an electronic ticket when it is to your advantage. Most major airlines have dispensed with their former practice of producing an individualized ticket for your travel and mailing it to you; instead you are given a confirmation number (sometimes called a record locator) and asked to show up at the airport with proper identification and receive your ticket and boarding pass there. If you absolutely insist on receiving an actual ticket in advance of your flight, some airlines charge as much as $50 per ticket for their trouble.

In general, electronic ticketing works well. At many major airports airlines have begun installing automated check-in machines, similar in operation to a bank's ATM. You'll be asked to insert a credit card or a frequent-flyer ID card just for the purposes of identification, and the device will print out your ticket and boarding pass there. A nearby attendant will take your bags and attach luggage tags.

OTHER MONEY-SAVING STRATEGIES

Airlines are forever weeping and gnashing their teeth about huge losses due to cutthroat competition. And then they regularly turn around and drop their prices radically with major sales. I don't waste time worrying about the bottom line of the airlines; it's my own wallet I want to keep full. Therefore, the savvy traveler keeps an eye out for airline fare wars all the time. Read the ads in newspapers and keep an ear open for news broadcasts that often cover the outbreak of price drops. If you have a good relationship with a travel agent, you can ask to be notified of any fare sales.

The most common times for airfare wars are in the weeks leading up to the quietest seasons for carriers, including the period from mid-May to mid-June (except Memorial Day weekend), between Labor Day and Thanksgiving, and again in the winter, with the exception of Christmas, New Year's, and Presidents' Day holiday periods.

Study the fine print on discount coupons distributed by the airlines or third parties such as supermarkets, catalog companies, and direct marketers. In my experience these coupons are often less valuable than they seem. Read the fine print carefully and be sure to ask the reservationist if the price quoted with the coupon is higher than another fare for which you qualify.

Don't be afraid to ask for a refund on previously purchased tickets if fares go down for the period of your travel. The airline may refund the difference, or you may be able to reticket your itinerary at the new fare, paying a penalty of about $100 for cashing in the old tickets. Be persistent: If the difference in fare is significant, it may be worth making a visit to the airport to meet with a supervisor at the ticket counter.

YOUR RIGHTS AS A CONSUMER

The era of airline deregulation has been a mixed blessing for the industry and the consumer. After an era of wild competition based mostly on price, we now are left with fewer but larger airlines and a dizzying array of confusing rules.

The U.S. Department of Transportation and its Federal Aviation Administration (FAA) still regulate safety issues. Almost everything else is between you and the airline.

Policies on fares, cancellations, reconfirmation, check-in requirements, and compensation for lost or damaged baggage or for delays all vary by airline. Your rights are limited and defined by the terms of the contract you make with an airline when you buy your ticket. You may find the contract included with the ticket you purchase, or the airlines may "incorporate terms by reference" to a separate document that you will have to request to see.

Whether you are buying your ticket through a travel Web site or a travel agent or dealing directly with the airline, here are some important questions to determine:

- Is the price guaranteed, or can it change from the time of the reservation until you actually purchase the ticket?
- Can the price change between the time you buy the ticket and the date of departure?
- Is there a penalty for cancellation of the ticket?
- Can the reservation be changed without penalty or for a reasonable fee? Be sure you understand the sort of service you are buying.
- Is this a nonstop flight, a direct flight (an itinerary where your plane will make one or more stops en route to its destination), or a flight that requires you to change planes one or more times?
- What seat has been issued? Do you really want the center seat in a three-seat row, between two strangers?

And a savvy traveler also pays attention to the newspapers and consults others to consider the following:

- Is there anything I should know about the short-term financial health of this airline that might affect my flight?
- Are there any threats of work stoppages or legal actions that could ruin my trip?

Your best protection against bankruptcies, strikes, and fraud is to use a major credit card to purchase your tickets and enlist the aid of that company in disputing charges for services not delivered.

BEATING THE AIRLINES AT THEIR OWN GAME

In my opinion, the airlines deserve all the headaches we travelers can give them because of the costly pricing schemes they throw at us—deals such as take-it-or-leave-it fares of $350 to fly 90 miles between two cities where they hold a monopoly and $198 bargain fares to travel 3,000 miles across the nation. Or round-trip fares of $300 if you leave on a Thursday and return on a Monday, but $1,200 if you leave on Monday and return the next Thursday.

But a creative traveler can find ways to work around most of these roadblocks. Nothing I'm going to suggest here is against the law; some of the tips, though, are against the rules of some airlines. Here are a couple of strategies:

Round-Trip Ticket for a One-Way Flight. Some airlines offer their very best fares for round-trip bookings, with prices often considerably less than the cost of a one-way ticket. For example, a promotional round-trip from New York to Las Vegas may cost $198 while a one-way ticket is priced at $279.

If you find yourself in a situation where you need only a one-way ticket—for example, a complex multileg trip, or if you plan to drive or take a train in one direction—consider buying a round-trip ticket and throwing away the return coupon. In theory this violates airline policies, but that doesn't mean savvy travelers don't use this technique. The airline is not likely to object unless it detects a large number of such no-shows in a short period of time.

Nested Tickets. This scheme generally works in either of two situations: where regular fares are more than twice as high as excursion or special fares, or in situations where you plan to fly between two locations twice in less than a year.

Let's say you want to fly from Boston to Las Vegas. Buy two sets of tickets in your name. The first is from Boston to Las Vegas and back. This set has the return date for when you want to come back from your second trip. The other set of tickets is from Las Vegas to Boston and back to Las Vegas, this time making the first leg of the ticket for the date you want to come back from the first trip, and the second leg of the trip the date you want to depart for the second trip.

If this sounds complicated, that's because it is. It will be up to you to keep your tickets straight when you travel. Some airlines have threatened to crack down on such practices by searching their computer databases for multiple reservations. I have seen no evidence of this, though.

One solution: Buy one set of tickets on one airline and the other set on another carrier.

Split Tickets. Fare wars sometimes result in supercheap fares through a connecting city. For example, an airline seeking to boost traffic through a hub in Cincinnati creates a situation in which it is less expensive to get from New York to Las Vegas by buying a round-trip ticket from New York to Cincinnati and then a separate round-trip ticket from Cincinnati to Las Vegas.

Be sure to book a schedule that allows enough time between flights; if you miss your connection, you could end up losing time and money.

STANDING UP FOR STANDING BY

One of the little-known secrets of air travel on most airlines and most types of tickets is the fact that travelers with valid tickets may be allowed to stand by for flights other than the ones for which they have reservations; if there are empty seats on the flight, standby ticket holders are permitted to board.

Some airlines are very liberal in their acceptance of standbys within a few days of the reserved flight, while others will charge a fee for changes in itinerary. And some airline personnel are stricter about regulations than others.

Here's what I do know: If I can't get the exact flight I want for a trip, I make the closest acceptable reservations available after that flight and then show up early at the airport and head for the check-in counter for the flight I really want to take. Unless you are seeking to travel during an impossibly overbooked holiday period or arrive on a bad-weather day when flights have been canceled, your chances of successfully standing by for a flight are usually pretty good.

One trick is to call the airline the day before the flight and check on the availability of seats for the flight for which you want to try. Some reservation clerks are very forthcoming with information; many times I have been told something like, "There are seventy seats open on that flight."

Be careful with standby maneuvers if your itinerary requires a change of plane en route; you'll need to check the availability of seats on all of the legs of your journey.

Some deep-discount fares may include prohibitions against standing by for other flights; read the fine print, especially if you are booking your own flight over the Internet.

The fly in the ointment in today's strict security environment is this: Airlines are required to match bags to passengers before a flight takes off. It is difficult, if not impossible, to stand by for a flight other than the one for which you hold a ticket if you have checked a bag. Your chances are much better if you limit yourself to carry-on bags.

And security screeners may not let you into the concourse for flights more than two hours before scheduled departure. Consult with the ticket agents at check-in counters *outside* of the security barriers for advice.

And a final note: Be especially careful about standing by for the very last flight of the night. If you somehow are unable to get on that flight, you're stuck for the night.

OVERBOOKING

Overbooking is a polite industry term for the legal business practice of selling more than an airline can deliver. It all stems, alas, from the rudeness of many travelers who neglect to cancel flight reservations that will not be used. Airlines study the patterns on various flights and city pairs and apply a formula that allows them to sell more tickets than there are seats on the plane in the expectation that a certain percentage of ticket holders will not show up.

But what happens if all passengers holding a reservation do show up? Obviously the result will be more passengers than seats, and some will have to be left behind.

The involuntary bump list will begin with passengers who check in late. Airlines must ask for volunteers before bumping any passengers who have followed the rules on check-in.

Now, assuming that no one is willing to give up his or her seat just for the fun of it, the airline will offer some sort of compensation—either a free ticket or cash, or both. It is up to the passenger and the airline to negotiate a deal.

Some air travelers, including this author, look forward to an overbooked flight when their schedules are flexible. My most profitable score: $4,000 in vouchers on a set of four $450 international tickets. The airline was desperate to clear a large block of seats, and it didn't matter to us if we arrived home a few hours late. We received the equivalent of three tickets for the price of one, and we went on to earn some more free travel on future tickets purchased with those vouchers.

The U.S. Department of Transportation's consumer protection regulations set some minimum levels of compensation for passengers who are bumped from a flight due to overbooking.

- If you are bumped involuntarily, the airline must provide a ticket on its next available flight. Unfortunately there is no guarantee there will be a seat on that plane or that it will arrive at your destination at a convenient time.

- If the airline can get you on another flight that will get you to your destination within one hour of the original arrival time, no compensation need be paid. If you are scheduled to get to your destination more than one hour but less than two hours late, you're entitled to receive an amount equal to the one-way fare of the oversold flight, up to $200. If the delay is more than two hours, the bumpee will receive an amount equal to twice the one-way fare of the original flight, up to $400.

- It is not considered bumping if a flight is canceled because of weather, equipment problems, or the lack of a flight crew. You are also not eligible for compensation if the airline substitutes a smaller aircraft for operational or safety reasons, or if the flight involves an aircraft with sixty seats or fewer.

HOW TO GET BUMPED

Why in the world would you want to be bumped? Well perhaps you'd like to look at missing your plane as an opportunity to earn a little money for your time instead of an annoyance. Is a two-hour delay worth $100 an hour to you? For the inconvenience of waiting a few hours on the way home, a family of four might receive a voucher for $800—that could pay for a week's hotel plus a heck of a meal at the airport.

If you're not in a rush to get to your destination—or to get back home—you might want to volunteer to be bumped. We wouldn't recommend doing this on the busiest travel days of the year or if you are booked on the last flight of the day, unless you are also looking forward to a free night in an airport motel.

BAD WEATHER, STRIKES, AND OTHER HEADACHES

You don't want pilots to fly into weather they consider unsafe, of course. You also don't want them to take up a plane with a mechanical problem. No matter how you feel about unions, you probably don't want to cross a picket line to board a plane piloted by strikebreakers. And so, you should accept an airline's cancellation of a flight for any of these legitimate reasons.

Here's the bad news, though: If a flight is canceled for an "act of God" such as bad weather, an earthquake, or a plague of locusts, or because of a strike or labor dispute, the airline isn't required to do anything for you except refund your money. In practice, carriers will usually make a good effort to find another way to get you to your destination more or less on time, which could mean rebooking on another flight on the same airline or on a different carrier. But you could be facing a delay of a day or more in the worst situations, such as a major snowstorm.

Here is a summary of your rather limited rights as an air passenger:

■ An airline is required to compensate you above the cost of your ticket only if you're bumped from an oversold flight against your will.

■ If you volunteer to be bumped, you can negotiate for the best deal with the ticket agent or a supervisor; for your inconvenience, you can generally expect to be offered a free round-trip ticket on the airline.

■ If your scheduled flight is unable to deliver you directly to the destination on your ticket, and alternate transportation such as a bus or limousine is provided, the airline is required to pay you twice the amount of your one-way fare if your arrival on the alternate transportation will be more than two hours later than the original airline ticket promised.

■ If you purchased your ticket with a credit card, the airline must credit your account within seven days of receiving an application for a refund.

All that said, in many cases you will be able to convince an agent or a supervisor to go beyond the letter of the law. I've found that the best strategy is to politely but firmly stand your ground. Ask the ticket clerk for another flight, for a free night in a hotel and a flight in the morning, or for any other reasonable accommodation. Don't take no for an answer but remain polite and ask for a supervisor if necessary. Sooner or later they'll do something to get you out of the way.

And then there are labor problems such as those that have faced airlines including American Airlines and US Airways in recent years. Your best defense against a strike is to anticipate it before it happens; keep your ears open for labor problems when you make a reservation. Then keep in touch with your travel agent or the airline itself in the days leading up to any strike deadline. It is often easier to make alternate plans or seek a refund in the days immediately before a strike; wait until the last minute and you're going to be joining a very long line of upset people.

In the face of a strike, a major airline will attempt to reroute you on another airline if possible; if you buy your own ticket on another carrier, you're unlikely to be reimbursed. If your flight is canceled, you'll certainly be able to claim a full refund of your fare or obtain a voucher in its value without paying any penalties.

AIRLINE SAFETY

There are no guarantees in life, but in general, flying on an airplane is considerably safer than the drive to the airport. All the major air carriers have very good safety records; some are better than others. I pay attention to news reports about Federal Aviation Administration (FAA) inspections and rulings and then make adjustments. And although I love to squeeze George Washington until he yelps, I avoid start-up and super–cut-rate airlines because I have my doubts about how much money they can afford to devote to maintenance.

Among major airlines, the fatal-accident rate during the last twenty-five years stands somewhere between 0.3 and 0.74 incidents per million flights. Not included in these listings are small commuter airlines (except those that are affiliated with major carriers). Put another way, if you were to take one flight per day—randomly selected—chances are it would be about 22,000 years before you would end up as a statistic on a fatal crash.

The very low numbers over such a long period of time, experts say, make them poor predictors of future incidents. Instead you should pay more attention to reports of FAA or National Transportation Safety Board (NTSB) rulings on maintenance and training problems.

■ THE NEW WORLD OF AIRPORT SECURITY

Travel has become more complicated and less convenient in the wake of the terrorist attacks of 2001. The bottom line for well-meaning, nonviolent business and pleasure travelers is this: You'll need to add an hour or more to the check-in process, and your options to stand by for a different flight or make other changes to your itinerary are severely limited.

Here are some things you can do to lessen the pain:

■ Consult with the airline or your travel agent about current policies regarding check-in times.

■ Consider your departure time; lines for check-in and security clearance are longest during peak travel times—early morning and late afternoon.

■ An alternate airport may have shorter lines. Some major hubs may, by necessity, be more efficient at processing huge crowds; at the same time, smaller airports with fewer crowds may be easier to navigate.

■ Try to avoid carrying unnecessary metallic items on your person. Choose a belt with a small buckle rather than the one with the three-pound world-championship steer-wrestling medallion. Put your cell phone, keys, coins, and wristwatch in a plastic bag and place it in your carry-on bag as you approach the magnetometer; this will speed your passage and reduce the chances of losing items.

■ Travel in a pair of simple sneakers instead of heavy boots or high heels; you are less likely to have to remove your shoes.

■ Be cooperative and remember that the screening is intended to keep you safe, and hope that the guards do their job well.

TOUR PACKAGES AND CHARTER FLIGHTS

Tour packages and flights sold by tour operators or travel agents may look similar, but the consumer may end up with significantly different rights.

What you end up with is greatly dependent on

Don't Wait to Drop a Card

If you have booked a trip through a travel agent or tour operator, keep in touch. In many cases they can anticipate major changes before departure time and will let you know. And many operators will try hard to keep you from demanding a refund if you find a major change unacceptable. They may offer a discount or upgrade on a substitute trip or adjust the price of the changed tour.

If you have booked a flight directly through an airline, make sure they have your phone number in case of a change in the schedule. Call the airline a few days before your first flight to confirm your reservation and check for any changes.

whether the flight is a scheduled or nonscheduled flight. A scheduled flight is one that is published in the Official Airline Guide and available to the general public through a travel agent or from the airline. This doesn't mean that a scheduled flight will necessarily be on a major carrier or that you'll be flying on a 747 jumbo jet; it could just as easily be the propeller-driven pride of Hayseed Airlines. In any case, though, a scheduled flight does have to meet stringent federal government certification requirements.

A nonscheduled flight is also known as a "charter flight." The term is sometimes also applied to a complete package that includes a nonscheduled flight, hotel accommodations, ground transportation, and other elements. Charter flights are generally a creation of a tour operator who will purchase all the seats on a specific flight to a specific destination or who will rent an airplane and crew from an air carrier.

Charter flights and charter tours are regulated by the federal government, but your rights as a consumer are much more limited than those afforded to scheduled flight customers. You wouldn't buy a hamburger without knowing the price and specifications (two all-beef patties on a sesame seed bun, etc.). Why, then, would you spend hundreds or even thousands of dollars on a tour and not understand the contract that underlies the transaction?

When you purchase a charter flight or a tour package, you should review and sign a contract that spells out your rights. This contract is sometimes referred to as the "Operator Participant Contract" or the "Terms and Conditions." Look for this contract in the booklet or brochure that describes the packages; ask for it if one is not offered.

Remember that the contract is designed mostly to benefit the tour operator, and each contract may be different from others you have agreed to in the past. The basic rule here is this: If you don't understand it, don't sign it.

■ HOW TO BOOK A PACKAGE OR CHARTER FLIGHT

For charter flights and packages, consider using a travel agent, preferably one you know and trust. The tour operator usually pays the agent's commission. Some tour packages, however, are available only from the operator who organized the tour; in certain cases, you may be able to negotiate a better price by dealing directly with the operator, although you are giving up one layer of protection for your rights.

Pay for your ticket with a credit card; I consider this a cardinal rule for almost any situation in which you're paying in advance for a service or product. If you end up in a dispute with the travel provider or a travel agency, you should be able to enlist the assistance of the credit card issuer on your behalf.

Keep in mind that charter airlines don't have fleets of planes available as substitutes in the event of a me-

Second Chance

Most tour operators, if forced to cancel, will offer another package or other incentives as a goodwill gesture. If a charter flight or charter tour is canceled, the tour operator must refund your money within fourteen days.

chanical problem or an extensive weather delay. They may not be able to arrange for a substitute plane from another carrier.

If you're still willing to try a charter after all of these warnings, make one more check of the bottom line before you sign the contract.

Lug It Yourself

If you are connecting between a charter and a scheduled airline, your bags will likely not be transferred "interline"—you will have to pick them up and deliver them between counters.

- First of all, is the air travel significantly less expensive than the lowest nonrefundable fare available from a scheduled carrier? (Remember that you are, in effect, buying a nonrefundable fare with most charter flight contracts.)

- Have you included taxes, service charges, baggage transfer fees, or other charges the tour operator may put into the contract?

- Are the savings significantly more than the 10 percent the charter operator may (typically) boost the price without your permission? Do any savings come at a cost of time? Put a value on your time.

- Finally, don't buy a complete package until you have compared it to the a la carte cost of such a trip. Call the hotels offered by the tour operator, or similar ones in the same area, and ask them a simple question: "What is your best price for a room?" Be sure to mention any discount programs that are applicable, including the American Automobile Association (AAA) or other organizations. Do the same for car rental agencies, and place a call to any attractions you plan to visit to get current prices.

If you miss a flight because of a problem with an unrelated carrier, you could forfeit nonrefundable tickets. Try to avoid such combinations; if you can't, allow extra hours between connections.

Some tour operators offer travel insurance that pays for accommodations or alternate travel costs made necessary by certain types of delays.

CHAPTER THREE

HOW TO SLEEP FOR LESS

MARBLE AND CRYSTAL AND RISING PRICES

Spending a night at one of the fabulous palaces along the Las Vegas Strip is more expensive than ever . . . some of the time, for some people. You can, if you choose, spend hundreds or even thousands of dollars for a room. That said, the careful shopper can also find some of the best bargains anywhere.

According to state tourism surveys, in 2005 the average cost of a night's stay in a hotel resort on the Strip was $125.38, up from $113.02 in 2004. In 2000 the average price was $96.92. Prices were also on the rise in the surrounding area: The average nightly rate in 2005 off the Strip was $103.00, up from $90.00 the year before.

But what lies beneath those numbers? Among the tens of thousands of rooms on the Strip are thousands that rent for $300 to $500 per night; that means there are many more that sell for well below $100. And even those pricey suites have rates that swing wildly between the basement and the penthouse levels depending on the time of year you visit.

Just as an example I took a look at two resorts on the Strip: The same rooms that sell for $150 to $200 or more during holiday periods or major sporting events were available for as little as $40 for a midweek visit in a slow time of the year. One of the hotels even included about $40 in "free" meals, drinks, and entertainment tickets.

And unless you are absolutely determined to close your eyes and go to sleep within a replica of an Egyptian pyramid, a Parisian landmark, or a golden pleasuredome, you can usually save hundreds of dollars by taking a room a few blocks or a few miles away from the Strip. You can still visit the fancy places—there is no requirement that you are a guest at a resort in order to enter a casino.

The same principle holds for other places in Nevada, although the rise in room rates has not been anywhere near as precipitous in Laughlin (off-season rooms are sometimes priced below $20, with slightly higher rates in the summer), in Primm (the highest prices there end below the lowest range in Las Vegas), in Reno (prices are firmly in the moderate range), and even in Lake Tahoe (except for peak winter ski or summer lake seasons.)

NEGOTIATING FOR A ROOM

Notice the title of this section: I don't call it "buying" a room, I call it "negotiating." The fact of the matter is that hotel rooms, like almost everything else, are subject to negotiation and change.

Here is how to pay the highest possible price for a hotel room: Walk up to the front desk without a reservation and say, "I'd like a room." Unless the NO VACANCY sign is lit, you may have to pay the "rack rate," which is the published maximum nightly charge.

Here are a few ways to pay the lowest possible price:

1. Before you head for your vacation, spend an hour on the phone and call directly to a half-dozen hotels that seem to be in the price range in which you'd like to spend. (I recommend membership in AAA and use of their annual tour books as starting points for your research. If you are of a certain age, consider joining AARP; many hotels will accept a driver's license as proof of age and not require actual membership in a particular association.)

Start by asking for the room rate. Then ask them for their best rate. Does that sound like an unnecessary second request? It's not; many hotels will offer their promotional rates only if you hesitate at paying the list price. Keep asking for lower rates until the agent reaches bottom.

When you feel you've negotiated the best deal you can obtain over the phone, make a reservation at the hotel of your choice. Be sure to go over the dates and prices one more time, and obtain the name of the person you spoke with and a confirmation number if available.

2. When you show up at your hotel on the first night, check to see if the hotel is offering a discount rate. Walk up to the desk as if you did not have a reservation and ask the clerk: "What is your best room rate for tonight?" If the rate quoted is less than the rate in your reservation, you are now properly armed to ask for a reduction in your room rate.

Similarly, if the room rate drops during your stay, don't be shy about asking that your charges be reduced. Just be sure to ask for the reduction before you spend another night at the old rate and obtain the name of the clerk who promises a change. If the hotel tries a lame excuse like, "That's only for new check-ins," you can offer to check out and then check back in again. That will usually work; you can always check out and go to the hotel across the road.

3. Are you planning to stay for a full week? Ask for a weekly rate. If the room clerk says there is no such rate, ask for the manager. The manager may be willing to shave a few dollars per day off the rate for a long-term stay.

BOOKING ON THE INTERNET

In many ways the Wild West still lives on the Internet. Someday the laws of economics will apply—the day when Internet companies and e-commerce outposts of traditional businesses will actually have to show a profit. Until then, though, the focus of most Web sites is to generate traffic and market share, even as they lose millions of dollars.

There are some tremendous deals available to the careful shopper. At the least you'll be able to easily compare rates from several chains or major casino-hotels; you'll also find some special deals offered only on the Internet. Check the Web page listings for casinos at the end of each write-up in this book.

Here are some travel agency Web sites worth checking for hotels, car rentals, and airline flights:

1-800-USA-HOTELS.COM, www.1800usahotels.com

Expedia, www.expedia.com

Hotels.com, www.hotels.com

Hotel Reservations Network, www.hotelreservations.com

Orbitz, www.orbitz.com

Travelocity, www.travelocity.com

You can also shop for hotel rooms on Web sites from a number of companies specializing in Las Vegas. Be sure to compare prices between sites and pay special attention to cancellation fees and other charges that may be applied.

LasVegas.com, www.lasvegas.com

Las Vegas Hotel Central, www.lasvegashotelcentral.com

Las Vegas Tourism, www.lasvegastourism.com

Vegas.com, www.vegas.com

What's On Magazine, www.ilovevegas.com

Here's how I use these sites: I look for their best rates, and then before I make a reservation, I go directly to the Web site of the individual hotel I have chosen. The hotel may save its very best rates—especially for last-minute bookings—for its own site. And you can make a phone call to the hotels and ask for last-minute rates.

And with the increasing trend toward hotel groups, you may be able to go (as an example) to the MGM Grand site and be directed to a great rate at New York–New York, the Mirage, or the Luxor.

Drop-off Child Care

Station Casinos offer Kids Quest babysitting for customers. Call for details:

▶ **Boulder Station**
(702) 432–7569

▶ **Sunset Station**
(702) 547–7773

▶ **Texas Station**
(702) 631–1000

WELCOME, CONVENTIONEERS

Not all visitors to Las Vegas come to recreate. Each year millions are drawn to the spectacular facilities of the Las Vegas Convention Center, the Sands Expo & Convention Center, or smaller facilities at many major hotels. In 2005, 6.2 million of the 38.6 million

Las Vegas visitors wore little plastic badges around their necks.

The conventioneers come to town because of the lure of the casinos and entertainment, but even more important, they come because Las Vegas is one of the few places in the country with a huge capacity for shows as well as an available bank of hotel rooms for attendees.

There are conventions all through the year, but the busiest time of year runs from fall through spring. In 2007 among the whoppers is the Consumer Electronics Show in early January, which draws about 150,000 conventioneers; another 35,000 are in town for the Adult Entertainment Expo held that same week . . . with more than a bit of crossover traffic between the two. The Automotive Aftermarket Products Expo and the Specialty Equipment Market Association claim 250,000 attendees between them (again with some duplication) in early November. The National Association of Broadcasters makes regular appearances in mid-April, usually bringing in more than 110,000 members.

Showing Your Card

Membership in AAA brings some important benefits for the traveler, although you may not always be able to apply the club's usual 10 percent discount on top of whatever hotel rate you negotiate. (It doesn't hurt to ask, though.) Be sure to request a tour book and Nevada maps from AAA even if you plan to fly there; they are much better than the rental car agency maps.

A big convention soaks up most of the rooms on the Strip and drives up prices all through Clark County. You can call the Las Vegas Convention and Visitors Authority at (877) 847–4858 or visit www.lasvegas24hours.com to inquire about big events that could affect your cost.

Of course there are dozens of smaller gatherings, from class reunions to groups like the National Pizza and Pasta Association, the Coca-Cola Collectors Club International, the International Carwash Association, and the American Ostrich Association, which in past years has drawn 2,000 people (and, I presume, a few big birds).

Should you come to Las Vegas during the time when a big convention is in town? On the downside you can expect rooms on and near the Strip to be scarce and priced at the high end of the rate card; the higher rates sometimes extend to outlying, lesser hotels. And it will be difficult to obtain tickets to popular shows and reservations at the hottest restaurants. On the plus side it's exciting to be in town when the casinos, showrooms, and the Strip itself are jumping with visitors.

The leading convention facility is the Las Vegas Convention Center at 3150 Paradise Road, about 3 blocks east of the Strip and adjacent to the huge Las Vegas Hilton Hotel. The convention center is the largest single-level convention and meeting facility in the United States.

In 2006 Las Vegas had about 9 million square feet of convention and meeting space, including the convention center, Mandalay Bay's 1.5 million-square-foot conference center, and the 1.8-million-square-foot Sands Expo Convention Center.

Another facility used for smaller conventions and for occasional special events from the megagatherings is the Cashman Field Center on Las Vegas Boulevard North, just below downtown Las Vegas.

HOW TO GET A ROOM DURING A CONVENTION

For most of the year, finding a place to stay in Las Vegas is not difficult. However, the very largest of the conventions will soak up most of the rooms at the major hotels.

If you are coming to Las Vegas as part of a convention, check with the organizers for hotels that have promised space. Or the convention may use the services of the Las Vegas Convention and Visitors Authority to book rooms.

The advantages of using a group's services include these: They may hold a block of discounted rooms. And the "official" hotel may be the location of the convention itself or on the bus route for shuttle service to the convention hall.

However, there are times when you can obtain a less expensive or more convenient place to stay by booking directly. Most major conventions, for example, reserve blocks of rooms only at the largest hotels. Although a convention's housing bureau may report a sellout of its available rooms at a particular hotel, you may still be able to obtain a room there by contacting the hotel directly. Additionally, smaller hotels right near the convention halls are sometimes overlooked.

When the town is completely packed because of a convention, you may be able to sweet-talk your way into a room by contacting the lodging bureau handling the group. You don't have to be so bold as to lie, but you may be able to allow them to assume you are with the convention and in dire need of a room.

On the other hand don't always assume that convention groups will be offered the lowest prices at hotels. On more than one occasion I have obtained a cheaper price by calling a hotel directly to book a room rather than going through the lodging bureaus.

In addition, although the official hotels for a convention may be packed and may be charging peak or even above-peak rates, nonconvention hotels may have rooms at low-season bargain rates. For example, during one of the research trips for this book, all the major official hotels were sold out for a huge construction equipment show, and the few others that had rooms were asking $150 to $200 per night. Yet the huge Circus Circus hotel, which was not affiliated with the convention, had plenty of rooms at $39; ten minutes out of town, hotels on Boulder Highway offered ordinary but acceptable rooms for about the same price.

One safe bet in Las Vegas is that downtown hotels will often have available rooms even during major conventions. Of course all bets are off during peak Christmastime and other holiday times.

CHAPTER FOUR

PLANES, CARS, AND BUSES

MCCARRAN INTERNATIONAL AIRPORT

Las Vegas's airport is within a chip's throw of the Strip, about a mile from the top end of the casino district, and 5 miles from downtown. And, as only Las Vegas could offer: Its street address is 5757 Wayne Newton Boulevard.

In 2005 McCarran was the fifth busiest airport in North America and the twelfth busiest in the world, receiving more than 840 flights per day and providing service to more than forty-four million passengers per year—an average of more than 121,315 per day. The leading carrier at the airport is Southwest Airlines, which brought in or took away 12.7 million passengers in 2005; in second place was America West with about seven million seats sold. The airport includes a shopping mall and restaurants . . . and a set of slot machines in the gate areas.

In my experience the airport is pretty efficient at processing incoming flights—by the time passengers make the long walk (and tram ride) from outlying gates, checked luggage is usually arriving in the huge baggage room. During busy times taxicabs are usually lined up outside the terminal to take guests to their hotels.

When it comes time to leave Las Vegas, though, the airport can become quite crowded with lengthy lines for check-in and especially for security screening. This is one airport where you should plan to arrive at least ninety minutes to two hours ahead of your departure time on weekends and at peak times of the day; if your flight is early in the morning you may be able to get away with sixty minutes of lead time. Check with your airline for current conditions and advice.

The airport is named after U.S. Senator Patrick A. McCarran, who was an early advocate of government regulation of airlines. In 1938 he was principal sponsor of the Civil Aeronautics Act, the predecessor of today's Federal Aviation Administration and National Transportation Safety Board.

McCARRAN AIRPORT

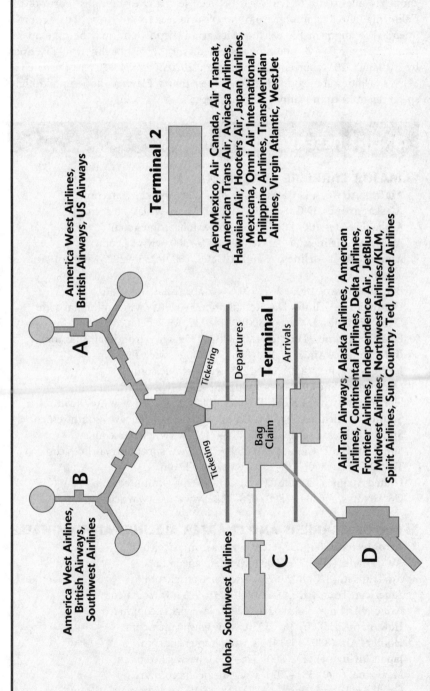

America West Airlines, British Airways, US Airways

America West Airlines, British Airways, Southwest Airlines

Aloha, Southwest Airlines

A

B

C

D

Ticketing

Ticketing

Departures

Terminal 1

Arrivals

Bag Claim

Terminal 2

AeroMexico, Air Canada, Air Transat, American Trans Air, Aviacsa Airlines, Hawaiian Air, Hooters Air, Japan Airlines, Mexicana, Omni Air International, Philippine Airlines, TransMeridian Airlines, Virgin Atlantic, WestJet

AirTran Airways, Alaska Airlines, American Airlines, Continental Airlines, Delta Airlines, Frontier Airlines, Independence Air, JetBlue, Midwest Airlines, Northwest Airlines/KLM, Spirit Airlines, Sun Country, Ted, United Airlines

Plans are under way for the design of a new airport in the Ivanpah Valley, about 25 miles south of Las Vegas between Jean and Primm, just north of the California state line, not far from the existing casinos at Primm. The airport is intended to augment the existing McCarran Airport and may become operational . . . some day. At one time it seemed as if the new facility would be open by 2010, then 2014; current hopes are for a 2020 opening, well past the date Las Vegas's facilities are expected to be at their limits. Planners hope to add high-speed rail links from Ivanpah into Las Vegas.

AIRLINE RESERVATION NUMBERS

■ MAJOR CARRIERS AT TERMINAL 1

AirTran Airways, D Gates. (800) 247–8726. www.airtran.com.
Alaska Airlines, D Gates. (800) 426–0333. www.alaskair.com.
Aloha, C Gates. (800) 367–5250. www.alohaairlines.com.
American Airlines, D Gates. (800) 433–7300. www.aa.com.
America West Airlines, A and B Gates. (800) 235–9292. www.americawest
.com.
British Airways. (800) 247–9297. www.britishairways.com.
Continental Airlines, D Gates. (800) 525–0280. www.continental.com.
Delta Air Lines, D Gates. (800) 221–1212. www.delta.com.
Frontier Airlines, D Gates. (800) 432–1359. www.frontierairlines.com.
Independence Air, D Gates. (800) 359–3594. www.flyi.com.
JetBlue, D Gates. (800) 538–2583. www.jetblue.com.
Midwest Airlines, D Gates. (800) 452–2022. www.midwestairlines.com.
Northwest Airlines/KLM, D Gates. (800) 225–2525. www.nwa.com.
Southwest Airlines, B and C Gates. (800) 435–9792. www.southwest.com.
Spirit Airlines, D Gates. (800) 772–7117. www.spiritair.com.
Sun Country, D Gates. (800) 359–6786. www.suncountryairlines.com.
Ted, D Gates. (800) 225–5833. www.flyted.com.
United Airlines, D Gates. (800) 241–6522. www.united.com.
US Airways, A Gates. (800) 428–4322. www.usairways.com.

■ MAJOR CARRIERS AND CHARTER AIRLINES AT TERMINAL 2

AeroMexico. (800) 237–6639. www.aeromexico.com.
Air Canada. (800) 776–3000. www.aircanada.ca.
Air Transat. (877) 872–6728. www.airtransat.com.
American Trans Air (ATA). (800) 435–9282. www.ata.com.
Aviacsa Airlines. (888) 528–4227. www.aviacsa.com.mx.
Hawaiian Air. (800) 367–5320. www.hawaiianair.com.
Hooters Air. (800) 359–4668. www.hootersair.com.
Japan Airlines (JAL). (800) 525–3663. www.jal.co.jp/en.
Mexicana. (800) 531–7921. www.mexicana.com.mx.
Omni Air International. (877) 718–8901. www.omniairintl.com.
Philippine Airlines. (800) 435–9725. www.philippineair.com.

TransMeridian Airlines. (866) 435–9862. www.iflytma.com.
Virgin Atlantic. (800) 862–8621. www.virgin-atlantic.com.
WestJet. (888) 937–8538. www.westjet.com.

AIRPORT PHONE DIRECTORY

Main number, (702) 261–5211. www.mccarran.com.
Parking information, (702) 261–5121.
Flight information, (702) 261–4636.
Paging, (702) 261–5733.
Lost and found, (702) 261–5134.

FROM THE AIRPORT TO THE STRIP AND DOWNTOWN

You'll know you're in Las Vegas the moment you get off your plane. Yep, those are slot machines in the airport lounge waiting to suck up your first (or last) quarters.

McCarran International Airport is just over a mile from the top of the Strip and about 5 miles from downtown Las Vegas.

Taxis cost about $8.00 to $12.00 to the Strip or $12.00 to $18.00 to downtown, plus tip. Cabs are usually plentiful outside the baggage area of the airport.

An alternative is to take one of the shuttle services. For about $5.00 to $6.00 to the Strip or $6.00 to $7.00 to downtown per person, you'll share the minibus with as many as a dozen or so others, and the driver will choose the order of the stops. The shuttle service may be appropriate if you are traveling alone and are not in a hurry; otherwise, a taxi makes more sense.

You can also hop a ride on one of the CAT (Citizens Area Transport) buses, although between airport pickups and traffic on the Strip, they are painfully slow. The private shuttles or taxis are much better alternatives.

SHOULD YOU RENT A CAR?

Do you need to rent a car? If you are planning to fly into Las Vegas and stay on the Strip, you can do without a rental car and use taxis, monorails, and your feet instead.

Personally I find it mind-boggling that a visitor to Las Vegas who will ogle the Mirage or the Luxor or Excalibur can come and go without seeing even more amazing sights such as Hoover Dam or Red Rock Canyon. (And as you'll find later in this book, I cannot imagine a trip to Reno that does not include a visit to Lake Tahoe and Virginia City.) There are bus trips to attractions, but it is just as easy—and less expensive for a group—to rent a car and do it on your own.

■ CAR RENTAL STRATEGIES

All the major car rental agencies, and a selection of smaller ones, have offices in Las Vegas.

Except when demand way outstrips supply—such as during a major convention—car rentals in Las Vegas represent a great deal. Think of the deal as borrowing $15,000 for a $35 daily fee to put things in perspective.

In general you'll get the best deals on car rentals by booking in advance. Rental companies, like airlines and hotels, usually publish a limited number of deep-discount rates that they use to lure customers, and when those are gone, you may end up paying a higher rate than the guy next to you at the counter for the same class of car.

However, as you fly across the country, read the airline's magazine in the seat's back pocket. There are often special car rental rates advertised for destinations served by the airline. It may be worthwhile to take the ad with you to the rental counter and ask for a better rate than the one you've reserved.

Your travel agent may be of assistance in finding the best rates; make a few phone calls by yourself, too. Sometimes you'll find significant variations in prices from one agency to another. Be sure to check Web sites as well; sites such as www.expedia.com and www.travelocity.com allow you to directly compare rates from several rental agencies for the dates and locations you specify.

You may also find lower rental rates at the Web sites of the rental car companies themselves. Join the agencies' priority clubs—usually free—to receive special offers.

In Las Vegas all the major rental car companies and many smaller agencies have booths near the baggage pickup hall; you'll need to catch a shuttle bus from the terminal to their lots and return the car to the outlying area at the end of your trip. This may add about twenty to thirty minutes to your arrival and departure schedule.

Car rental companies will try—with varying levels of pressure—to convince you to purchase special insurance coverage. They'll tell you it's "only" $7.00 or $9.00 per day. What a deal! That works out to about $2,500 or $3,330 per year for a set of rental wheels. Of course the coverage is intended primarily to protect the rental company, not you.

Before you travel, check with your insurance agent to determine how well your personal automobile policy will cover a rental car and its contents. I strongly recommend you use a credit card that offers rental car insurance; such insurance usually covers the deductible below your personal policy. The extra auto insurance by itself is usually worth an upgrade to a gold card or other extra-service credit card.

The only sticky area comes for those visitors who have a driver's license but no car and therefore no insurance. Again, consult your credit card company and your insurance agent to see what kind of coverage you have or what kind you need.

Pay attention, too, when the rental agent explains the gas policy. The most common plan says you must return the car with a full tank; if the agency must refill the tank, you will usually be billed a very high per-gallon rate and sometimes a service charge as well.

Other optional plans include one where the rental agency sells you a full tank when you first drive away and takes no note of how much gas remains when you return the car. Unless you somehow manage to return the car with the engine running on fumes, you are in effect making a gift to the agency with every gallon you bring back.

I prefer the first option, which requires making it a point to refill the tank on the way to the airport on getaway day.

Although it is theoretically possible to rent a car without a credit card, you will find it to be an inconvenient process. If the rental agency can't hold your credit card account hostage, it will most often require a large cash deposit—perhaps as much as several thousand dollars—before it will give you the keys.

And finally, check with the rental company about its policies on taking the car out of the state. Some companies will charge you extra if you're planning to take the car across a state line; if you visit Hoover Dam, be aware that the dam straddles the state line with Arizona. Similarly, in Laughlin the bridge across the Colorado River begins in Nevada and ends in Arizona. In Reno the California state line is nearby on the west side of the Sierra Nevada, and the popular destination of Lake Tahoe is on the line; restrictions on interstate travel are less common there.

The following are among companies serving McCarran Airport, the Strip, and downtown; check with them for the most convenient office.

Alamo/National, (702) 261–5391; (800) 227–7368 for National, (800) 462–5266 for Alamo. www.nationalcar.com or www.alamo.com.

Avis Rent A Car, (702) 261–5595, (800) 367–2847. www.avis.com.

Budget Car & Truck Rental, (702) 736–1212, (800) 922–2899. www.budget.com or www.budgetvegas.com.

Dollar Rent-a-Car, (702) 739–9507. www.dollar.com.

Enterprise Rent-a-Car, (702) 261–4435, (800) 736–8222. www.enterprise.com.

Hertz Rent A Car, (702) 736–4900, (800) 654–3131. www.hertz.com.

Payless, (702) 736–6147. www.paylesscarrental.com.

Thrifty Car Rental, (702) 896–7600, (800) 367–2277. www.thrifty.com.

GETTING AROUND IN LAS VEGAS

Navigating in Las Vegas is pretty simple. Almost every major hotel and casino is found along Las Vegas Boulevard (better known as the Strip), along Fremont Street in downtown Las Vegas, or on a cross street to one of those two roads.

Except when there is a large convention in town, taxis are plentiful at the airport and along the Strip, and bus service is adequate. And although it is not as common as it should be, it is quite possible to walk between and among the clusters of casino-hotels on the Upper Strip and Center Strip.

THE LAS VEGAS MONORAIL

Here's your chance to get taken for a ride on the Strip: After several years of technical delays, the Las Vegas Monorail is now in regular operation on a 4-mile track from the Sahara to the MGM Grand.

The new Las Vegas Monorail

The privately owned and operated system includes seven stations in its first phase: Sahara, Las Vegas Hilton, Las Vegas Convention Center, Harrah's/Imperial Palace, Flamingo/Caesars Palace, Bally's/Paris, and MGM Grand. The trains move along an elevated track about 50 feet above the ground; by night, the interiors of the cars are dimmed so that visitors can enjoy the neon skyline. Designers took into account the possibility that some visitors may be in mid-celebration as they travel from casino to casino; each stop is walled off with glass, and the doors only open when the train is ready for boarding.

The system, the nation's longest urban monorail system, began with nine four-car trains, each capable of hauling as many as 300 people at speeds of as much as 50 mph. The trains are an urbanized version of the Mark VI monorail used at Walt Disney World in Orlando, Florida.

Plans call for eventual extension of the track another 3 miles north to downtown Las Vegas, with stations at the Stratosphere, Charleston Boulevard, Bonneville, and Fremont Street. And there are dreams of extending it a few miles south to connect to McCarran Airport.

Tickets for the monorail cost $5.00 per person for a single ride, or $9.00 for a two-ride pass. Other passes include an unlimited day pass for $15.00, a three-day pass for $40.00, or a ten-ride ticket for $35.00.

The Las Vegas Monorail operates daily from 7 A.M. to 2 A.M. during the week, and until 3 A.M. from Friday through Sunday. High-tech dreams include the possibility of allowing tourists to bill tickets to their hotel room charge.

Several casinos on the west side of Las Vegas Boulevard South have their own short systems; these include a system from Excalibur to Mandalay Bay, with a stop at Luxor, and a system between Treasure Island and Mirage. A line from the MGM Grand to Bally's/Paris Las Vegas was shut down and incorporated into the new Las Vegas Monorail.

For more information consult www.lvmonorail.com.

You can catch a bus, Citizens Area Transit Route 551, to connect between the north end of the monorail at the Sahara station to the Fremont Street Experience in downtown Las Vegas.

TAXI SERVICES

Cabs, cabs everywhere—except when there is a big convention in town, anytime you are in a hurry, or during one of Las Vegas's rare rainstorms. There are two major taxi companies that all but control the market: Yellow Cab and Whittlesea Blue Cab.

Taxi rates start at about $3.20 for the first mile on the meter and then rack up $2.00 per mile. There is also a $1.20 surcharge for trips beginning at the airport, and waiting time is charged at 35 cents per minute.

Taxis line up at McCarran Airport to meet most flights. During conventions taxis also arrive regularly at the front entrance to the Las Vegas Convention Center. They're usually found at the main entrances of the major hotels as well, where you are expected to grease the palm of the bellman.

As part of the expansion of McCarran Airport, a tunnel was added beneath a runway with a connection to Interstate 15. Though some drivers claim the tunnel shaves a minute or so off the trip, the fact is it also adds about 2 miles to the drive, and fares are based on odometer readings. The faster route generally adds about $3.00 to $5.00 to the typical taxi fare from the airport to much of the Strip.

If you're heading to the south end of the Strip to resorts including the Luxor and Mandalay Bay, the tunnel may make sense. Otherwise, staying out of the tunnel is the better way to go.

ANLV/Ace/Union/Vegas-Western, (702) 736–8383.
Checker/Yellow/Star, (702) 873–2000.
Desert, (702) 386–9102.
Lucky, (702) 477–7555.
Nellis, (702) 248–1111.
Western, (702) 736–8000.
Whittlesea/Henderson, (702) 384–6111.

Taxi Dancing

Here's a tip for visitors unable to get a cab from the convention center: Walk up Convention Center Drive to the Strip and wait for a car at one of the hotels there—with luck you will be able to share a ride in a taxi that has brought a rider the few blocks you walked from the LVCC.

Mileage to Las Vegas

Atlanta	1,964
Barstow	153
Boston	2,725
Boulder City	24
Carson City	430
Chicago	1,772
Dallas	1,221
Death Valley	160
Denver	777
Flagstaff	275
Grand Canyon Village	288
Grand Canyon West Rim	175
Henderson	13
Hoover Dam	25
Jackpot	488
Kingman	103
Lake Havasu City	145
Lake Tahoe	470
Laughlin	93
Los Angeles	282
New York City	2,548
Palm Springs	280
Philadelphia	2,468
Phoenix	298
Primm	39
Reno	440
Salt Lake City	433
San Diego	337
San Francisco	564
Sparks	207
Washington, D.C.	2,393
Zion National Park	156

BUSING TO THE TABLES

Citizens Area Transit (CAT) operates bus routes serving much of the metropolitan area. For information call (702) 228–7433 or (800) 228–3911, or consult www.rtcsouthernnevada.com/cat. The Downtown Transportation Center, at Stewart Avenue and Casino Center Boulevard, is the transfer point for many routes; request a transfer at the time of paying the first fare. Other transfer points are at Vacation Village at the south end of the Strip and in Henderson at the Triple J Casino.

In late 2005, CAT added a distinctive high-capacity bus service up and down the Strip. The Deuce double-decker bus runs a near-continuous schedule in both directions. In 2006 one ticket cost $2.00, or you could purchase an all-day pass for $5.00.

Adult cash fare is $1.25 except for Strip routes, which are $2.00. Transfers are free. A one-day pass is $5.00.

Route 301 connects downtown to the Strip, and Route 303 goes from downtown to north Las Vegas. Route 301 runs twenty-four hours a day at ten-minute intervals until about midnight and fifteen minutes apart from midnight until 5:30 A.M. from the Downtown Transportation Center on Stewart Avenue to Vacation Village at the top of the Strip.

The Mall Hopper (Route 14) connects the west entrance of the Fashion Show Mall on the Strip to the Meadows and Boulevard Shopping Malls. The bus runs in an S-curve from the Boulevard Mall on Maryland Parkway across Twain and Sands to the Strip and the west entrance of the Fashion Show Mall, continuing north on the I–15 freeway to the Meadows Mall west of downtown.

Long-distance buses come into a terminal in downtown Las Vegas.

LAS VEGAS STRIP TROLLEY

A much less expensive alternative to a taxi is the Las Vegas Strip Trolley—slow, but convenient. The small bus on rubber tires makes its way up and down the Strip from 9:30 to 1:30 A.M. daily, from the Stratosphere at the north end to the Mandalay Bay Resort at the south.

The fare is $2.00, with exact change required; a day pass is also sold. For information call (702) 382–1404.

TRAIN SERVICE

Despite the fact that Las Vegas was born because of the railroad, the last regularly scheduled passenger train service ended in 1997; the nearest train station is in Needles, California, about 112 miles south. Greyhound bus service connects Needles to Las Vegas; Amtrak also sells tickets for direct bus service from Los Angeles to Las Vegas, about a six-hour trip.

Amtrak, state, and federal officials, together with tourism and casino interests, have been talking for many years about ways to resume conventional or high-speed train service between Las Vegas and major population centers in California.

PART II

LAS VEGAS

CHAPTER FIVE

WELCOME, PILGRIM

AS FAR AS I AM CONCERNED, there are two types of visitors to Las Vegas: (1) those who have never been there before and are anxious to see if all the strange and wonderful things they have heard are true, and (2) those who are returning to Las Vegas to see if things are really as strange and wonderful as they remember.

Either way, Las Vegas is unlike any other place on Earth, with the possible exception of those other fantasy zones, Walt Disney World and Disneyland.

In 2005, 38.6 million visitors came to Las Vegas—including more than 6.2 million conventioneers—making an annual economic impact of more than $32 billion. The average visitor was about forty-eight years old—continuing a downward trend in age—and spent 3.4 nights in town. About 20 percent of those visitors were making their first visit to Las Vegas. About 8 percent of visitors came from foreign countries, and about 29 percent came from Southern California—which may or may not qualify as a foreign country, depending on your point of view.

And the typical visitor spent about $627 on gambling, $248 on food and beverages, and $137 on shopping.

COMING INTO LAS VEGAS

The best way to approach Las Vegas is to fly in on a clear night. As your plane descends from points east, you cross hundreds of miles of barren desert that seem as lifeless as the moon. Suddenly you come upon a huge, oddly shaped lake in the desert that is held back by a tremendous dam, a pale white saucer set on end in a canyon. That's the Hoover Dam and Lake Mead.

Just minutes later you see on the horizon an island of light, an electric oasis in the desert. About the time the pilot brings down the landing gear, you should be able to pick out some of the elements of a skyline like nowhere else on Earth:

Frequently Asked Questions about Las Vegas

▶ **Do I have to gamble to enjoy Las Vegas?** Although the local economy is primarily based around the immense profits from slot machines and table games, there is no law that forces visitors to spend a dime on gambling. You can enter any casino in Nevada to enjoy the ambience or gawk at the gaudiness without making any bets.

And you can eat at one of the many buffets (with prices subsidized by the casinos in hopes of luring gamblers) without being a player. The same goes for the stage shows and concerts: Anyone can buy a ticket.

In more than two decades of visits to Las Vegas, I have never been forced to lay down a bet as I strolled through the casinos.

▶ **How do I get comped?** The casinos will go to great lengths to keep their best customers coming back to the slots or the tables. If you expect to play for a few hours, or to "invest" a fair amount of money, be sure to make your presence known to the floor managers.

If you're a slot machine player, most casinos operate slot clubs that automatically track your "action" over time. You may be issued a card to insert into a reader on the slot machine that will keep track of your gambling. Ask one of the casino workers . . . if they don't ask you first.

If your game is blackjack, poker, craps, or baccarat, catch the eye of one of the pit bosses or other personnel on the dealer's side of the table. Let them know you want to be rated for comps.

Casinos offer free drinks, free meals, free shows, and even "RFB" (room, food, and beverages) to the most dedicated gamblers. It doesn't matter whether you win or lose—the judgment is based on the amount of money you bet over time. The casino knows through experience that sooner or later, it comes out ahead.

▶ **Should I stay on the Strip, downtown, or outside of town?** The answer depends on your goals and style of travel.

If you are determined to spend the night inside an Egyptian pyramid, with a view of the Eiffel Tower, or in a phantasmagorical castle with a drawbridge, you're going to need to book a room on the Las Vegas Strip.

If you like the idea of strolling from one casino to the other without having to take a cab or consult a map, you might want to stay downtown.

And if you're looking for the absolute lowest-price room in town, you're probably going to find it downtown or off the Strip. At the quietest times of the year, though, even the best casinos on the Strip offer rock-bottom room rates.

Finally, if you plan to rent a car or are willing to ride a cab, you can stay almost anywhere in Las Vegas and commute from the pyramid to the tower to the castle. The arrival of the Las Vegas Monorail has made moving from one casino on or near the Strip to another much easier.

(continued)

▶ **When is the best time to visit?** Summer can be brutally hot—and busy. Winter can be pleasantly cool or persistently hot—and busy.

Depending on your point of view, one of the worst (or best) times to visit Las Vegas is during a major convention or sporting event that fills up every room, packs the casino floors, and builds the lines at restaurants, taxi stands, and showrooms.

The secret seasons at Las Vegas—times when crowds are smallest and room rates are usually at their lowest—include the period between Thanksgiving and Christmas and early in the year until the end of March.

▶ **Can I get tickets to any show in town?** No, and yes. The major attractions sell out days or weeks ahead of time. However, you may be able to obtain tickets—at a hefty premium—from the concierge at your hotel. And if you are a major gambler, front-row tickets to almost any event can not-so-mysteriously appear in the hands of a casino manager.

▶ **Should I bring the kids?** In the 1990s a number of casinos tried to expand their appeal by creating "family" entertainment including theme parks, rides, and shows. After expenditures of millions of dollars, they found that they were creating attractions that were diverting customers away from the real profit-making industry in town: gambling. The current emphasis is back to gambling and adult shows. In fact casinos have been showing more and more skin (or less and less costuming) in their shows; the latest trend includes a resurgence in strip clubs, burlesque shows, and other forms of girlie shows   with a bit of beefcake here and there for the women.

That said, if you do bring your kids, you'll find many things for them to do. They can gawk at the architecture, gorge themselves on the buffets, and attend many of the shows with you. Kids, though, are not allowed to touch slot machines or loiter in the casinos. The legal age for gambling and drinking in Nevada is twenty-one.

And you'll have to decide for yourself whether you want to expose children to Las Vegas; the place is designed for adult passions, desires, and sensibilities.

▶ **Do I need to rent a car?** No, or yes.

McCarran Airport is just a few miles from the Strip and a reasonable ride away from downtown. Many of the casinos on the Strip are now connected by the Las Vegas Monorail and by several smaller train links, and you can usually catch a taxicab at any time of the day. If you insist, you can also walk from one casino to another on the Strip, although most of the newer places are set well back from the road.

However, if your intention is to explore the area—visiting the Hoover Dam, Red Rock Canyon, and other worthy sites—a rental car is a good way to get there. Rates are generally very low; availability gets tight when a major convention is in town.

(continued)

And if you do rent a car, all the casinos on the Strip offer free parking. In downtown you can find free parking at some casinos, and you can have your parking ticket validated at others.

There are also many bus tours to area sites, including trips to Hoover Dam and the west rim of the Grand Canyon; someone else does the driving, but for a group of three or four people, it is probably less expensive to rent a car.

▶ **Can I take pictures in the casino?** Cameras used to be prohibited everywhere, but the rules have been loosened in recent years. Most casinos will permit you to take photos if you are discreet and do not include the faces of strangers at the tables.

▶ **Can I use a cell phone?** Casinos tried to ban the use of phones but were overwhelmed by the millions of pocket phones. Cell phones are still prohibited in sports and race books in an effort to prevent collusion.

Some casinos do manage to block cell phones, either intentionally or accidentally, because of all the electronics and radio signals bouncing around the casino.

▶ **What is the best game to play?** How about Monopoly? If you're asking about the best odds on gambling, most experts recommend twenty-one (blackjack)—but only for well-informed and careful bettors.

If you play the slot machines, the odds are generally best on video poker. On any machine the highest payouts are given to players who bet the maximum number of coins. In other words, your chances of a high payoff are better if you play five quarters at a time on a quarter machine rather than just one dollar at a time on a dollar machine.

a huge Egyptian pyramid, a Roman garden and amphitheater, a pirate ship, and a gaudy castle constructed of gigantic toy blocks.

Coming from the west, your plane passes over Death Valley before it drops over the shelf of mountains that includes 11,918-foot-high Mount Charleston and then hangs a right turn above the Stratosphere Tower at the north end of the Strip to follow the neon lights to the airport.

Welcome to Las Vegas, pilgrim.

A PLACE TO LAY YOUR HEAD

Las Vegas laid claim to the mantle as the first resort destination in America to pass the 100,000-room mark. By the end of 2007, there are expected to be about 141,597 rooms for rent—that's more than in New York, Paris, or Los Angeles. This includes massive recent additions at Bellagio, Mandalay Bay, Paris Las Vegas, and the Venetian.

The Rio

According to the Las Vegas Convention and Visitors Authority, despite the huge growth in available rooms, the average occupancy level for all hotel rooms in the Las Vegas metropolitan area is about 93 percent, nearly thirty points above the national average. (The weekend occupancy rate averages a bit above 95 percent.)

LAS VEGAS CLIMATE

Las Vegas has two basic weather patterns: sunny and mild, and sunny and hot. The area averages 320 days of sunshine per year and only 4.19 inches of rain.

In the summer (from June to September), daytime temperatures may top one hundred degrees. In the short spring and fall seasons, they usually reach the seventies during the day. In winter high temperatures may drop all the way down to the fifties.

Average high temperature in January	56 degrees
Average low temperature in January	33 degrees
Average high temperature in July	104 degrees
Average low temperature in July	75 degrees
Annual average rainfall	4.19 inches
Annual average snowfall	1.5 inches
Annual days with precipitation	26 days

CHAPTER SIX

THE BEST OF THE STRIP

Econoguide Best Casino-Hotels in Las Vegas

★★★★★ **Bellagio.** *Prodigioso!*

★★★★★ **Caesars Palace.** *Render unto Caesar . . . in high style.*

★★★★★ **Mandalay Bay.** *Shangri-la on the Strip with hidden gems within and without.*

★★★★★ **Four Seasons Hotel Las Vegas.** *High tea in Sin City.*

★★★★★ **Paris Las Vegas.** *Disneyland Paris . . . in Las Vegas.*

★★★★★ **Rio All-Suite.** *Carnival! Show us your . . . chips.*

★★★★★ **The Venetian.** *Prettier than the real thing.*

★★★★★ **Wynn Las Vegas.** *Steve Wynn's modest dream, entering Part Deux . . . with a hotel and a casino and a fews billion dollars of glitz.*

★★★★ **Hard Rock Hotel.** *Heavy metal and a casino, too.*

★★★★ **Las Vegas Hilton.** *Elvis slept here. Now the Vulcans visit.*

★★★★ **MGM Grand.** *You're not in Kansas anymore.*

★★★★ **The Mirage.** *A volcano out front and the Beatles within.*

★★★★ **Monte Carlo.** *Only in Vegas would this place seem real.*

★★★★ **New York–New York.** *Bustling, confusing. You got a problem with that?*

★★★★ **Planet Hollywood.** *Poof! From the sands of Arabia to Tinseltown glitter, Aladdin no more.*

ALSO IN THIS CHAPTER

★★★ **Circus Circus.** *Clowns, slots, jugglers, blackjack, and an indoor coaster.*

★★★ **Excalibur.** *A gaudy shrine.*

★★★ **Luxor.** *Pyramid power, in all of its strangeness.*

★★★ **Stratosphere Tower.** *P. T. Barnum would feel at home.*

★★★ **Treasure Island.** *PG-rated Sirens patrol the waters out front.*

LAS VEGAS STRIP

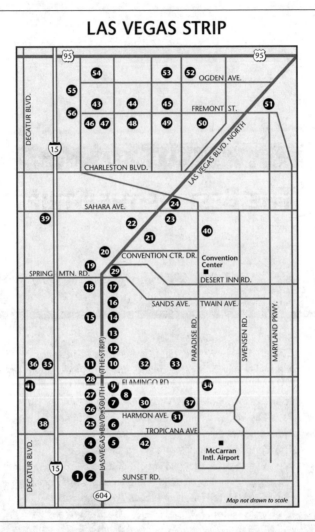

Map not drawn to scale

ECONOGUIDE ★★★★★ RESORTS

★★★★★ BELLAGIO

We already had an Arabian souk, an Egyptian pyramid, an Arthurian castle, a Roman palace, and a British man-of-war. And then there was Paris, Venice, and New York. But it was so obvious: What Las Vegas really needed was a $2 billion Italian beach resort on an artificial lake in the desert.

Bellagio spreads its massive pair of wings opposite Bally's. The hotel draws its inspiration from the tiny town of the same name that overlooks breathtaking Lake Como in Italy. The property on the Strip didn't have a lake—this is the desert, after all, and the former home of the very dry Dunes Hotel no less—and so a nine-acre pond had to be created.

LAS VEGAS STRIP

1. Four Seasons
2. Mandalay Bay
3. Luxor
4. Excalibur
5. Tropicana
6. MGM Grand
7. Planet Hollywood
8. Paris Las Vegas
9. Bally's
10. Barbary Coast
11. Caesars Palace
12. Flamingo Las Vegas
13. O'Shea's
14. Imperial Palace
15. Mirage
16. Harrah's
17. Venetian
18. Treasure Island
19. The Frontier
20. Stardust
21. Riviera
22. Circus Circus
23. Sahara
24. Stratosphere Tower
25. New York–New York
26. Monte Carlo
27. Boardwalk Hotel and Casino
28. Bellagio
29. Wynn Las Vegas

NEAR THE STRIP

30. Alexis Park
31. St. Tropez
32. Bourbon Street
33. Maxim's
34. Terrible's
35. Rio All-Suite
36. Gold Coast
37. Hard Rock
38. Orleans
39. Palace Station
40. Las Vegas Hilton
41. The Palms
42. San Rémo

DOWNTOWN

43. Vegas Club Casino
44. Binion's
45. Fremont
46. Golden Gate
47. Pioneer
48. Golden Nugget
49. Four Queens
50. Fitzgeralds
51. El Cortez
52. Gold Spike
53. Lady Luck
54. California
55. Main Street
56. Plaza

When the place opened in late 1998, the construction bill was a mere $1.6 billion; in 2005 Bellagio unveiled the $375 million Spa Tower with 928 more rooms and suites, a new restaurant, **Sensi,** and the **Jean-Philippe Pâtisserie,** a European-style pastry shop.

The new tower is alongside the south side of the hotel's main pool and courtyard with an entrance through the hotel's spectacular conservatory. All told, the resort offers more than 100,000 square feet of gaming and twice that much space for meetings and conventions. There are a total of five outdoor pools, four spas, and fifty-two private cabanas around a Mediterranean courtyard setting.

Outside the doors are the **Fountains of Bellagio,** a $30 million "choreographed water ballet." The show, inspired by the fabulous light and fountain productions once popular in Europe, includes more than 1,200 water jet heads that can shoot water as much as 460 feet into the air across a span of 1,000 feet to the

Bellagio

musical accompaniment of artists from Luciano Pavarotti and Andrea Bocelli to Gene Kelly, Frank Sinatra, and Lionel Richie. The water ballet is presented every thirty minutes from 3:00 to 8:00 P.M. on weekdays and from noon to 7:00 P.M. on weekends; from 8:00 P.M. to midnight, the show goes on every fifteen minutes. There's no charge to stand around the lake and watch the show.

Another $70 million went into *O*, from Cirque du Soleil, which has become synonomous with Las Vegas with shows up and down the Strip. At Bellagio a troupe of seventy-four performs in and above a large body of water (which gives the show its French pun of a name, *O* as in *eau*, which sounds the same and means water) within the 1,800-seat theater, which has an exterior design similar to the Paris Opera House. I haven't the slightest idea how Paris got into this mix, although Cirque du Soleil is from French Canada. Neither Montreal nor Las Vegas is anywhere near Lake Como. The show is presented twice per night, Friday to Tuesday. Tickets for the show are available three months in advance for hotel guests and two months ahead for day visitors and range in price from $93.50 to $150.00.

The ultraluxe **Via Bellagio** shopping street, set in an elegant Crystal Palace–like glass arcade, features stores including Giorgio Armani, Chanel, Gucci, Hermès, Fred Leighton, Prada, and Tiffany. Stores are open daily from 10:00 A.M. to midnight. With the opening of the Spa Tower came **Via Fiore,** with more stores including Regali, the Giardini garden store, the Chihuly Gallery, and a Cirque du Soleil shop.

The guest rooms and suites of the expanded hotel are decorated with antiques and art characteristic of southern Europe, and there's extensive use of imported marble throughout.

The bellmen out front are adorned with top hats; the concierge staff is outfitted in waistcoats. The registration desk is set within a living fantasy garden that changes with the seasons and is home to robotic and real butterflies, birds, plants, and smells.

The public areas are an elegant wash of white and gold, with flowers—real and fanciful—at every turn, including a fabulous ceiling of 1,600 blown-glass flowers by American artist Dale Chihuly. The conservatory is a spectacular private botanical garden under a 50-foot-high glass ceiling; plantings are changed four to five times each year to celebrate seasons and holidays.

The **Bellagio Gallery of Fine Art** is home to museum-caliber exhibitions selected from prestigious international collections. Soon after the acquisition of the company MGM Grand Inc. in 2002, eleven of the hotel's own treasures were sold off for a total of $124 million with three of the pieces going to former owner Stephen Wynn.

Gallery hours are 9:00 A.M. to 9:00 P.M. daily, with the last admission sold thirty minutes prior to closing; tickets are $15 per person. Reservations are recommended and can be made by calling (702) 693–7871 or (877) 957–9777.

There is, of course, a huge casino with more than a hundred table games and 2,500 slot machines. The elaborate sports and race book features a huge video screen on the wall; most tables offer private televisions with video of sporting events.

Bellagio features a wide range of specialty restaurants, including a Las Vegas version of the famed New York French restaurant Le Cirque, and the less-formal Circo, a northern Italian eatery; both were created by the Maccioni family. The Bellagio general restaurant reservation number is (888) 987–7111.

The supertrendy nightclub at the hotel is **Light,** a bottle-service lounge with just forty tables—available by reservation only. In other words, if you're not a celebrity, you've got to know someone who knows someone, or be very lucky, to get in. For reservations call (702) 693–8300. For more information consult www.lightlv.com.

Caramel at Bellagio is an informal lounge from the creators of Light, intended as the perfect preshow evening or late-night fun destination. Guests can enjoy martinis served in chilled chocolate- and caramel-coated glasses, served to the accompaniment of hip-hop, Tony Bennett, '80s hits, the Rolling Stones, and others. Consult www.caramelbar.com for details.

Le Cirque, overlooking the lake at the hotel, is among the more formal eateries with jacket and tie required for men. Specialties include *pauprette de loup-de-mer* (black sea bass in crispy potatoes) for about $34 and *dégustation d'agneau* (Colorado lamb fillet with baked cranberry beans) for $38. Appetizers are priced from about $16 to $32 and main courses from $37 to $41. There's also a five-

,asting menu for about $95. There are just eighty seats, and preference
goes to high rollers. The restaurant is open for dinner only from 5:30 to 10:00
P.M. Your best bet is to seek an early reservation by calling (702) 693–7223 or
(888) 987–7111.

Circo features home-style Tuscan food, complemented by a wine cellar that
offers more than 500 selections from around the world, and a spectacular view
of the hotel's lake. Dinner entrees are priced from about $17 to $36; many can
also be ordered as smaller-portion appetizers if you want to create your own
sampler. Specialty dishes include *costaletta di vitello* (veal cutlet), *maltagliati alla
Bolognese* (a specialty pasta), and *tartara di Branzino* (tartare of wild striped bass
in a lemon dressing). Circo is open for lunch from Wednesday to Sunday and for
dinner nightly from 5:30 to 10:30 P.M. For reservations, call (702) 693–8150 or
(888) 987–7111.

Picasso, decorated with drawings and pottery by the artist of the same name,
celebrates French and Mediterranean cuisine. Taking its inspiration from the villages of the Mediterranean, Picasso is a rough-hewn restaurant with a beam-
and-brick ceiling and gesso-covered burlap walls.

Some of the great master's colorful and delightful paintings as well as his ce-
ramics, tiles, and sculpture have been incorporated into the restaurant's decor.
Claude Picasso, the son of Pablo, designed the carpet and the furniture for the
restaurant. Entrees are priced from about $20 to $30, and there's a nightly prix
fixe menu priced from about $85 to $95 plus wine, which can add as much as
$43 per person if you accept the suggested sampling of glasses. Reservations are
recommended and can be made by calling (702) 693–7871 or (877) 957–9777.

Examples from the menu include roasted langoustines, sautéed medallion of
fallow deer, and roasted pigeon. The dress code is "casual elegance," which means
jackets are recommended. Open for dinner 6:00 to 9:30 P.M.; closed Tuesday. For
reservations call (702) 693–7223 or (888) 987–7111.

Michael Mina is a high-tone seafood fest based on a world-renowned San
Francisco favorite run by the chef of the same name. On the plates you'll find
works of art priced from about $29 to $49. Appetizers include roasted whole foie
gras for $80 and caviar varieties reaching to near $100. One menu included
Hawaiian swordfish au poivre for $31 and seared scallops with caviar for $32. A
five-course tasting menu was priced at $75 per person for the whole table, offer-
ing samples for everyone. Open daily, 5:30 to 11:00 P.M. For reservations call
(702) 693–7223 or (888) 987–7111.

Olives is a Las Vegas extension of Todd English's well-known Mediterranean
restaurant of the same name in Boston, and it is a bit less formal than the other
eateries at Bellagio. Dinner entrees are priced from about $22 to $40. On a recent visit menu items included roasted John Dory fish for $34, brick
oven–roasted rack of lamb for $44, and portobello piccata for $12. Located
within the Via Bellagio shopping arcade, the casual Mediterranean cafe is open
daily for lunch from 11:00 A.M. to 3:00 P.M. and for dinner from 5:30 to 10:00 P.M.
For reservations, call (702) 693–8181.

Prime Steakhouse is a luxury restaurant that's styled like a 1930s chophouse
and speakeasy. Entrees on recent visits included six-peppercorn aged New York

steak, crusted sea bass, rosemary garlic roasted chicken, veal chops, spiced rack of lamb, and tuna steak with lemon confit. Entrees are priced from about $25 to $69. Jackets are preferred. Open daily, 5:30 to 10:00 P.M. For reservations call (702) 693–7223 or (888) 987–7111.

Jasmine is a gourmet Chinese restaurant with European influences, decorated with authentic and replicated Chinese art. The interior design is almost French in style. Menu offerings include Imperial Peking duck, Chinoise scallops, and more ordinary dishes such as Moo Shu pork. Entrees range in price from about $24 to $80.

Jasmine also offers a tasting menu priced at about $70 per person with a minimum of two at a table. On a recent visit the menu included Imperial minced squab, honey-glazed barbecued baby back ribs, Fa Dew clam soup, Maine lobster in ginger and scallion, wok-seared beef tenderloin in black pepper sauce, and an exotic crème brûlée dessert. The restaurant is open daily, 5:30 to 10:00 P.M. For reservations call (702) 693–7223 or (888) 987–7111.

Shintaro, a most elegant (and expensive) Japanese restaurant, specializes in fresh seafood, sushi, and teppanyaki. The unusual sushi bar, with offerings from $40 to $50, appears to be floating on dazzling blocks of ice. The kaiseki seven-course meal was priced at $95 at the time of my visit; *kaiseki* means "stone in pocket," referring to an old Japanese folktale roughly equivalent to the English "stone soup" fable. Teppanyaki dinners, from 5:30 to 10:00 P.M. nightly, are priced at $50 to $90. For reservations call (702) 693–7223 or (888) 987–7111.

Noodles features regional noodle dishes from Thailand, Japan, China, and Vietnam. Entrees are priced from about $9.00 to $28.00. Chinese dim sum is available Friday, Saturday, and Sunday from 11:00 A.M. to midnight and until 2:00 A.M. on weekends. Reservations are not accepted.

Sensi mixes and melds Italian, Asian, grilled, and seafood classics for lunch and dinner. Japanese design firm Super Potato has crafted a unique, interactive culinary theater setting. **Jean-Philippe Pâtisserie** offers an indulgent selection of sweet and savory items including chocolates, cookies, cakes, crepes, salads, and sandwiches in a room with the air of a lavish jewelry salon. Chef Jean-Philippe Maury's shop features a first-of-its-kind, 27-foot-high chocolate fountain, circulating nearly two tons of dark, milk, and white melted chocolate.

Fix, a late-night American bistro adjacent to the Light nightclub, offers classic American fare, open daily for dinner from 5:00 P.M. to midnight and until 2:00 A.M. on weekends. The elegant interior is paneled and decorated almost entirely in padouk, an exotic red wood from Costa Rica.

And if you're in the mood for fine caviar, champagne, or smoked salmon, just off the lobby there's the **Petrossian Bar,** which specializes in all of the above as well as a proper afternoon tea.

Finally, the **Buffet at Bellagio** is almost as elegant as the formal dining places in the hotel, one of the *Econoguide* bests with Italian, Japanese, Chinese, and seafood specialties.

A tram connects Bellagio to its neighbor, Monte Carlo; a walkway connects Bellagio to its other neighbor, Caesars Palace.

Room rates at Bellagio range from about $159 to $899 for basic accommodations; rooms are considerably larger than the norm in Las Vegas. Expect lower prices during slow periods and premium rates during holidays and conventions. There are also nine 6,000-square-foot villas for invited guests and a floor of luxurious penthouse suites.

And for the very well-heeled golfer, there is **Shadow Creek,** one of the highest-rated—and most expensive—courses anywhere. Any guest at one of the MGM Mirage resorts (Bellagio, the Mirage, MGM Grand, Treasure Island, New York–New York, or Primm Valley Resort) can reserve a tee time for a cool $500. The fee includes, of course, limousine transportation to and from the course, a caddy, and a golf cart.

Bellagio. 3600 Las Vegas Boulevard South. 3,933 rooms. Standard room rates $159 to $899. (702) 693–7111, (888) 987–6667. www.bellagio.com.

★★★★ CAESARS PALACE

In many ways the original Caesars Palace launched the era of the megaresort on the Strip. Bits and pieces of the old place are still there, although it has grown up, out, and more extravagant over the years. More than forty years after it first opened, Caesars Palace retains its position as one of the great, unnatural wonders of the world. Caesars Palace is a must-see among must-sees.

Think of Caesars Palace as a realization of Hollywood's vision of ancient Rome as seen through the off-kilter eye of a Las Vegas decorator. With slot machines.

Everything about this place is grand. The Roman Forum casino is a riot of red and gold. The sports book set the standard for spectacular viewing rooms and is still a sight for sore eyes and unsore losers. The various restaurants include some of the most opulent settings on the Strip. And there is equal-opportunity gawking for both sexes: Although the togas have become just a bit less revealing over the years, there are still gods and goddesses at most every turn, some of them bearing drinks.

The huge casino, nearly 150,000 square feet in size, spreads out left, right, and center from every entrance. And the spectacular **Forum Shops at Caesars** features more than 160 specialty retailers and restaurants set in a re-creation of the skies of ancient Rome.

In 2005 the $289 million Augustus Tower opened, bringing the total number of rooms available at Caesars Palace to more than 3,340. Overlooking the Garden of the Gods pools on the south property perimeter, the all-suite tower includes 874 "petite" suites that range in size from 650 to 760 square feet, 29 huge luxury suites, and 23 gigantic luxury suites of 2,470 square feet apiece.

The tower's culinary jewel is named for three-star Michelin chef **Guy Savoy.** The acclaimed French chef's namesake restaurant in Paris has been ranked among the finest dining establishments in the world. The tower's highest floor was left largely unfinished to accommodate future development for more suites or facilities.

The new front door to the resort is the **Roman Plaza** at the corner of Las Vegas Boulevard and Flamingo Road, built atop a 500-space underground park-

aquarium stocked with live rock cod, Dungeness crab, lobster, and other seafood used in meals. The galley itself includes some extraordinarily hot grills used in preparation of specialties.

The Empress Court menu includes prix fixe dinners at about $55 per person, as well as a la carte offerings. One menu we sampled included crispy crab claws, minced squab in crystal wrap, seafood wonton soup, sautéed prawns, stir-fried prime sirloin and chicken with oyster sauce, and mango pudding delight. Individual entrees range from about $20 to $55.

Unusual offerings have included braised abalone with fish maw in oyster sauce, pan-fried scallops with double eggs, sautéed jellyfish, and bird's nest with bamboo fungus. Also featured are the Emperor and the Empress: extensive, multicourse, fixed-price menu alternatives, available for two persons or more. Open only for dinner from 5:00 to 11:00 P.M. on weekdays and until midnight on weekends; there is a semiformal dress code. For reservations call (702) 731–7731.

Hyakumi means "one hundred tastes," and you'll find at least that many at his attractive room. The elaborate and authentic design was inspired by traditional upscale Japanese residences, including both traditional and contemporary elements. The interior includes a teahouse, garden, and an azalea-lined dry verbed. Interior landscaping includes authentic Japanese flora.

Hyakumi features prix fixe teppanyaki feasts priced at about $60. Of course if a want to substitute Kobe beef for the prime tenderloin, the price rises to ut $199 per person. You can also order a la carte Japanese offerings such as *nabe* (seafood and vegetables in fish broth served in a paper pot with ponzu e), sea bass teriyaki, or *unaju* (barbecued freshwater eel on rice).

he bar offers at least ten varieties of sake, which are rated on a dry-to-sweet and sold in small glasses or small bottles with prices reaching $180. Dinner ved Tuesday through Sunday nights. For reservations call (702) 731–7731.

ey don't fiddle around at **Nero's**, an elegant seafood and steak house with of modern and classical themes. Open for dinner nightly from 5:00 to .M., with entrees priced from about $25 to $50, Nero offers dishes such as swordfish with pan-fried risotto cakes, roasted Sonoma squab with puree, and grilled sirloin with sautéed oyster mushrooms.

recent visit specialties included pan-roasted veal loin chop with leek and se tart and caramelized beets for $38 and grilled swordfish with sweet ree for $28. Seating capacity has expanded to 150 with the completion nal patio seating that overlooks the casino. Open nightly for dinner eservations call (702) 731–7731.

ual but very stylish twenty-four-hour eatery **Cafe Lago** overlooks the the Gods pool complex through a 13-foot-high window wall. The themed interior seats 300 for international a la carte or buffet dining; additional eighty-five seats in a private dining room and eighty-five on A stone aqueduct, pools, and two water walls surround the Frank Sin way, where a pianist and bassist play most nights.

treet Marketplace** offers nine popular cuisines at self-serve action stat ts enter the Marketplace under a modern interpretation of seven life-size California cypress trees. Visitors are given a dining passport—a "smart" card to swipe through card readers at each action station as they pick up items. At the checkout a computer reads the card and creates a bill.

Offerings range from hand-carved turkey, hot pastrami, or corned beef to Carolina-style slow-roasted pulled pork and beef brisket. An Asian section presents pot stickers, spring rolls, and other popular Asian appetizers and entrees including Mongolian beef, kung pao chicken, Japanese edamame (soybean appetizer), suomono (cucumber salad), and California rolls. Other styles include lobster and chowder, wraps, burgers, pizza, and salads.

Cypress Street Marketplace is open from 11:00 A.M. until 11:00 P.M. daily. Prices range from $2.25 for a slice of cheese pizza to $5.95 for a pint of kung pao chicken with steamed rice, and from $8.95 for a turkey dinner with all the trimmings to $12.95 for a fresh Maine lobster roll sandwich.

Dining areas in the Marketplace combine to offer 300 seats, with an additional 18 in Java Coast and 62 in Slice Bar. Seating is available in varied styles that reflect a fun "Picnic in the Marketplace" atmosphere, including picnic tables and bistro-style umbrella tables under stylized trees. In the west dining room is a Wall of Memories, which includes wall-mounted samples of art and decor formerly displayed within Caesars Palace; included are some of the original bricks used to build the resort.

Within the Roman Plaza is **Augustus Cafe,** with 230 indoor and outdoor seats for casual and more sophisticated dining. **Viale's** cuisine is contemporary Italian with a culinary nod to the specialties of Rome, serving pasta, pizza panini, focaccete, salads, and a wide array of dinner entrees. Selections of grille country bread panini include grilled summer vegetables grilled chicken with salsa verde; and fontina cheese, roasted red peppers, and wild mushroom Focaccete are available with baked mozzarella, slow-roasted Roma tomato pesto, and balsamic onions; and there is the "PLT" of pancetta, arugula, toma and herbed mayonnaise. Open daily for lunch and dinner.

And don't overlook dining possibilities at the **Forum Shops at Caes** which include Chinois, The Palm, La Salsa, Bertolini's, Planet Hollywood, Sp and the Stage Deli. You'll discover more about these restaurants in chapter

Hot Spots at the Palace

One very hot place at Caesars is **Shadow Bar,** a small nightclub just of casino floor, where the bar is flanked by thin backlit screens that are intend just barely hide the near-bare female "Shadow concierges" who gyrate b them. The bar is open twenty-four hours a day, but the show goes on evening until early morning.

The pool at Caesars Palace is appropriately sybaritic. Strolling grap desses offer chilled fruit to guests broiling on chaises; one of the pools, de to Venus, encourages topless sunbathing in relative privacy.

The two-story **PURE nightclub,** with investors including Celin Shaquille O'Neal, Andre Agassi, and Steffi Graf, grabs much of the la spotlight in Las Vegas. The 36,000-square-foot club offers several distir riences in one venue, including the Pussycat Dolls Lounge.

Adjoining pedestrian bridges that cross the Las Vegas Strip at the bustling intersection of Las Vegas Boulevard and Flamingo Road is the five-acre, open-air **Roman Plaza,** a 250-seat bar and outdoor event/entertainment amphitheatre.

Caesars Palace. 3570 Las Vegas Boulevard South. 3,340 rooms. Standard room rates $120 to $499. (702) 731–7110, (800) 634–6661. www.caesars.com.

★★★★★ MANDALAY BAY

The Road to Mandalay runs through the south end of the Las Vegas Strip.

Mandalay Bay Resort and Casino is one of the most striking hotels in Las Vegas, a surprise at the top end of the Strip. Not as ostentatious as Paris Las Vegas or the Venetian, or with its nose stuck so high in the air as Bellagio, Mandalay is merely handsome.

In a town where almost nothing is what it seems to be, or ends up like it is promised to be, Mandalay Bay stands apart. This is an attractive, fun, and, dare I say it, classy addition to Las Vegas. Set in a mythical place vaguely inspired by Kipling's poem about Mandalay, the hotel includes some of the best-looking and most enticing restaurants in any casino in the real world of Las Vegas.

The 3,700-room, $950 million Mandalay Bay occupies the former site of the Hacienda Hotel and Casino; it (along with corporate cousins Luxor, Excalibur, and Circus Circus) became part of the MGM-Mirage Company in 2005, creating the largest hotel-casino group in town. It is linked by an automated tram to Excalibur and Luxor.

On the west side of the property is **THEhotel at Mandalay Bay,** a forty-three-story-high tower with 1,117 suites, each with separate living and sleeping areas. The suites average 750 square feet each, among the largest in the Las Vegas market. The hotel and casino has a "forbidden city" theme with waterfalls, terraced gardens, and mythical statuary. The luxury hotel is connected to the main building and all its eateries and amenities.

And the top floors of the main hotel are operated as a luxury palace within the palace; you can read about the Four Seasons Hotel Las Vegas in the next section of this chapter.

The huge hotel includes more than sixteen formal and informal restaurants. Formal dining spots are small, expensive, and exclusive. For reservations at Mandalay Bay restaurants, call the general reservation line at (877) 632–5300.

Among the more unusual offerings is **Rumjungle,** located along the hotel's restaurant row and nicely isolated from the beeps and squawks of the casino. Water cascades down dramatic glass walls throughout the eatery; theatrical lighting sets the mood late at night. Live cocktail lounge entertainment starts nightly at 11:00 P.M. The menu spreads across Latin, Caribbean, and African fare; the restaurant is from the creators of China Grill.

A star offering is the Fire Pit dinner, served to everyone at the table and consisting of dish after dish of salmon roasted in a banana leaf, grilled chorizo, Martiniquan lamb skewer with green curry coconut glaze, hulihuli chicken, and more. Adults about $37.50, children $19.00.

Mandalay Bay

Individual plates are priced from $20 to $44 and include Columbian coffee–smoked baby back ribs and Cubano pork shank braised in cumin with black beans.

Fleur de Lys, from chef Hubert Keller, is located next to Aureole and is the closest fine restaurant to the casino floor. Born in France, Keller trained with Paul Bocuse and worked at restaurants in France and Brazil. In 1986 Keller became co-owner of Fleur de Lys on Sutter Street in San Francisco. Keller presents a high-tone French menu but has also contributed to a cookbook on gourmet low-fat recipes; some of those dishes were presented at a private dinner for President Clinton and his family in the White House.

In a place of $100 margaritas and $1,000 shots of whiskey, it should come as no surprise that Las Vegas has found a way to offer a hamburger that costs more than a good used car. The FleurBurger 5000 at Fleur de Lys is a Kobe beef burger topped with fois gras and black truffles, served on a brioche truffle bun and garnished with Chef Keller's special sauce consisting of more truffles. As an accompaniment guests are served a bottle of Chateau Petrus 1990 poured in Ichendorf Brunello stemware, exclusively imported from Italy. After the meal the team at Fleur de Lys ships the glasses to the guest's home at no additional charge. All this for a mere $5,000.

The ultramoderne **3950** (named after the hotel's street address) is a high-tech steak-and-seafood eatery, with entrees starting at about $30. Specialties include lobster thermidor and Tupelo honey-basted chicken. Seafood cioppino was priced at $42, grilled veal chop at $40, and lamb chop and lobster at $45. An intriguing, if rich, appetizer is seared foie gras with grilled Fuji apple. And then there is an ultimate form of macaroni and cheese made with white truffles and lobster pasta.

Across the row is Wolfgang Puck's **Trattoria del Lupo,** an upscale restaurant set within a small piazza in Milan with views of the pasta, charcuterie, and bakery production areas. The menu focuses on northern and southern Italian specialties and includes Puck's well-known exotic pizzas. Entrees include roasted Alaskan halibut with lemon and pancetta, priced around $24; rib eye diavola for $35; and braised lamb shank with caramelized onion and saffron for about $26. The 200-seat restaurant is open for lunch and dinner. (The name of the place, by the way, is a bit of wordplay: *Trattoria del Lupo* means "Restaurant of the Wolf," as in *Wolfgang*.)

A huge statue of Lenin, in headless post–cold war form, stands outside the elegant and quirky **Red Square,** an outpost of Miami's South Beach original. Decorated in Romanov splendor in red and black with onion domes and high ceilings, the restaurant's showpiece is its extensive vodka collection that includes private vodka lockers; the bar—its top a sheet of ice—offers more than a hundred varieties as well as all manner of infusions, martinis, and cocktails.

Hacienda History

The Hacienda was imploded, on national television, on New Year's Eve at the end of 1996. When it was built in 1956 near McCarran Airport, the Hacienda was miles away from the rest of the Las Vegas action. The Hacienda was a haven for low rollers. Among its pioneering efforts were some of the first gambling junkets; at one time it maintained its own fleet of thirty airplanes to bring the sheep in to be shorn.

Over the years, though, the Strip extended south to encompass the Hacienda, and eventually it found itself in the reflected gaudy glow of the Excalibur, Luxor, and the nearby MGM Grand.

A star of the menu is *kulebyaka*, a fillet of salmon filled with mushroom, egg, and fresh dill and wrapped in a puff pastry. There's also fillet Stroganoff, chicken Kiev, and Roquefort-crusted filet mignon. And there is smothered blini with crème fraiche and caviar or smoked salmon. Entrees range from about $22 to $36. The restaurant serves dinner only.

Changing tastes in dining . . . and politics . . . resulted in a pair of makeovers of the little cafe at the focal point of restaurant row. The lively Rock Lobster restaurant was remade in 2003 as Bleu Blanc Rouge, a French cafe and patisserie. By the end of that year, it had been converted once again to **Red, White, and Blue,** offering three types of American dining experiences: red for American favorites including seafood specialties and an oyster bar, blue for California-inspired sandwiches and salads, and white for familiar sweets and pastries. Entrees are priced from about $15 to $30. Sample items include turkey meat loaf, steamed Maine mussels, and San Francisco cioppino. Raw bar assortments of clams, oysters, and shellfish range in price from about $39 to $99. The restaurant is open for breakfast, lunch, and dinner.

The ultrachic **Aureole** is a cousin to Charlie Palmer's acclaimed New York restaurant, featuring seasonal American dishes. The interior of the 383-seat room was designed by the eclectic Adam Tihany and is centered around a unique four-story wine tower; wine stewards strap on harnesses and are hoisted up the tower to make selections from the "cellar in the sky." Aureole is open for dinner only; prix fixe offerings range from about $55 to $95 per person. The $55 menu included a roasted "brick" of duck, a seared ahi tuna block, and roast rack of lamb with an herbed goat-cheese crust. The $95 prix fixe offered salmon tartare, warm oysters with Sevruga caviar, oven-roasted halibut bouillabaisse, and sautéed medallions of beef.

An elegant turn to the Far East, **Shanghai Lilly** is encased in polished wood, mirrors, and glass; dishes are served on fine Limoges china. Chinese entrees, ranging from about $16 to $75, include basics like kung pao chicken and moo shu pork to unusual and pricey offerings like abalone with sea cucumber, shark's fin with Dungeness crab, or Maine lobster sashimi.

Across the row is **China Grill,** described as a China-inspired brasserie. Its broad menu reaches across Asia with offerings from China, Korea, Japan, and elsewhere. The eatery is part of a group of restaurants in New York, Miami Beach, and Beverly Hills. Entrees, ranging from about $26 to $60, include a massive two-pound porterhouse steak with kimchi and orange maple dressing, sesame-speckled skate, and Japanese veal crusted with panko bread crumbs. Open for dinner only.

Border Grill, an upscale Southwestern taqueria, is a Los Angeles favorite owned by *Too Hot Tamales* chefs Mary Sue Milliken and Susan Feniger. Gourmet fare for lunch and dinner features dishes such as grilled skirt steak with garlic and cilantro, sautéed rock shrimp with toasted ancho chilies, and grilled breast of turkey. One unusual dish is *mulitas de hongos,* which layers grilled portobello mushrooms with guacamole, manchego cheese, black beans, poblano chilies, and tomatoes. Entrees are priced from about $18 to $25; lunch prices are a bit less expensive.

Giorgio Caffe & Ristorante, another operation of chef Piero Selvaggio, offers a casual setting for traditional Italian dishes including pizza, pasta, chicken, meat, and fish. Entrees range from about $25 to $50. Open for lunch and dinner.

Located in the Mandalay Place shopping district is **restaurant rm,** an offshoot of Rick Moonen's seafood bistro in New York. Upstairs is the **r.bar.café,** offering a casual seafood experience with a bustling market atmosphere and abundant raw bar.

Just off the casino floor is the 600-seat **House of Blues,** the hotel's largest restaurant, offering down-home cooking and music. A larger concert hall is nearby. Entry to the restaurant is through a version of a Mississippi backyard with candles hung from low-hanging trees and a constant symphony of crickets.

Specialties, priced from about $14 to $20, include slow-cooked baby back ribs, crawfish and shrimp étoufée, and Creole jambalaya. The restaurant offers a gospel brunch on Sunday mornings.

The **Raffles Café** offers upscale diner food, including an interesting assortment of specialty omelets. Within its walls is the Noodle Shop, offering Chinese and Hong Kong dishes. The 504-seat Bay Side Buffet includes "action stations" for breakfast, lunch, and dinner.

The **Burger Bar at Mandalay Place** offers a menu of burgers, from the basic to the gourmet—reaching all the way up to a $60 Kobe burger with foie gras, truffles, and Madeira sauce. Also on the menu are "sweet burgers" built around donuts, including a chocolate burger filled with ganache that resembles a burger, lettuce made of mint, and tomato-shaped strawberries.

At the top of THEhotel is **Mix,** serving "world cuisine." Typical entrees include roasted lobster in curry, bison tenderloin in sauce au poivre, and caviar halibut.

In addition to world-class restaurants created by top-rated chefs, Mandalay Bay's attractions include an eleven-acre tropical lagoon featuring a sand-and-surf beach, a ¾-mile lazy river ride, and a swim-up shark tank.

A handsome section of shops occupies **Mandalay Place,** a pedestrian walkway between Mandalay Bay and Luxor. In a break from the now-standard Las Vegas painted blue sky, the mall is lorded over by an impressive skylit dome.

The 12,000-seat **Mandalay Bay Events Center** is the setting for superstar concerts and major sporting events. The Mandalay Beach Stage, over the sand and surf wave pool, is used for concerts from May through September. Concertgoers are invited to bring their blankets, sit on the beach or wade in the surf, and listen to the music. High rollers can also rent a private bungalow for the evening.

The **Mandalay Bay Theatre,** a 1,700-seat Broadway-style theater, includes a full orchestra pit. It has been used for theatrical presentations and concerts. *Mamma Mia,* a musical based on twenty-two of the songs of Abba, opened in 2003 and ran deep into 2006.

The 2,000-seat **House of Blues** is also used for musical presentations. The International House of Blues Foundation Room, located on the top floor of the hotel, is reserved for VIPs and special events.

Mandalay Bay Resort & Casino. 3950 Las Vegas Boulevard South. 3,700 rooms. Standard room rates $119 to $499. (702) 632–7777. www.mandalaybay.com.

THEhotel at Mandalay Bay. 1,117 suites. Suite rates range from about $189 to $699. (702) 632–7800. www.thehotelatmandalaybay.com

---

★★★★★ FOUR SEASONS HOTEL LAS VEGAS

The Four Seasons is a hotel within a hotel, occupying 424 rooms on the thirty-fifth through thirty-ninth floors of Mandalay Bay. The premium hotel has its own entrance, check-in, five-star dining, pool and spa, and convention area. Room rates at Four Seasons are among the highest in Las Vegas.

The showplace restaurant is the **Charlie Palmer Steak Restaurant,** a clublike space serving traditional American cuisine. Specialties include a 38-ounce rib steak for two and charcoal-grilled tuna steak with braised romaine. Main courses range in price from about $17 to $35. For information call (702) 632–5120, or consult www.charliepalmersteaklv.com.

The **Verandah Cafe** at the Four Seasons offers indoor and outdoor seating for breakfast, lunch, and dinner and serves Mexican, Californian, Italian, and Oriental food. You can indulge in high tea each afternoon, from 2:00 to 5:00 P.M., munching on scones, cakes, and tea sandwiches; tea costs about $25, or $35 with champagne. On weekends there's an extraordinary buffet brunch, also priced at about $23 per person.

Four Seasons Hotel Las Vegas. 3960 Las Vegas Boulevard South. 424 rooms. Standard room rates $250 to $500 and higher. (702) 632–5000. www.fourseasons .com/lasvegas.

★★★★★ PARIS LAS VEGAS

Ooh, la la. Paris arrived on the Las Vegas Strip with the opening of the opulent Paris Las Vegas Casino Resort on a plot south of Bally's Casino facing the Bellagio Resort.

Paris is an ambitious but cartoony Disneyland Paris. Some will appreciate the little touches like the cocktail waitresses dressed in French gendarmes caps and little else and the supports of the Eiffel Tower that poke through the ceiling of the casino. The ironwork in the casino is just for show, though; the real imitation tower stands a bit farther west, closer to the Strip.

The thirty-three-story resort re-creates Parisian landmarks including a 540-foot half-scale replica of the Eiffel Tower that has a French restaurant and an observation level. Other re-created sites include the Arc de Triomphe, Champs-Elysées, the Paris Opera House, the River Seine, and the Rue de la Paix.

Designers consulted Gustav Eiffel's original 1889 drawings to help construct their replica; unlike the original in Paris, this tower's pieces are welded together, although designers added cosmetic rivets everywhere they appear on the real thing. Three of the re-created Eiffel Tower's legs spring from the resort's casino floor, jutting through the roof of the gaming area. Guests can dine on gourmet French cuisine in the restaurant on the seventeenth level of the tower or ride an elevator to the observation deck.

Napoleon's Lounge at Paris Las Vegas has reinvented itself with the debut of dueling pianos. The casual bar offers a happy-hour special each afternoon offering a free sandwich from a carving station with the purchase of an alcoholic beverage.

The **Champagne Bar at Napoleon's** boasts a selection of more than one hundred champagnes and sparkling wines by the bottle and by the glass. There's also a full premium bar, including an impressive selection, as well as tempting champagne cocktails and specialty martinis made with the Champagne Bar's own secret recipes. To complement the drinks, the bar offers a light menu of California cuisine.

The main restaurant district lies along the Rue de la Paix under a fake blue sky and movie-set false fronts.

The **Eiffel Tower Restaurant** is an informal gourmet restaurant with one of the most exciting views in town. The menu, with entrees starting at about $20 and rising as sharply as the tower elevator, includes classical and contemporary French offerings; there's also a piano champagne bar. Appetizers include caviar, with a sampler of three ounces of Beluga, Osetra, and Sevruga for $260; roasted foie gras for $19.95; and blue cheese soufflé pudding for $16.95. Entrees include sautéed wild red snapper for $26.95, boneless duck a l'Orange for $35.95, and Tournedos Rossini with foie gras and truffle sauce for $43.95. Open nightly from 5:30 to 10:00 P.M. during the week and until 10:30 P.M. on weekends. For reservations call (702) 948–6937.

Ah Sin, described as a pan-Asian bistro, features Japanese sushi, Chinese noodle specialties, Korean barbecue, Thai satay, and Mongolian, Malay, and other tastes of the Orient. Many of the dishes are prepared at action stations. A selection of boutique wines, Japanese beers, and fine sakes complement the menu. With a nod to its Las Vegas address, you can top it all off with indulgent French desserts. The Cantonese name, by the way, means "always lucky."

Parisians fell in love with Asian culture and cuisine during the World's Fair in 1889. Accented by large exposed beams and shades of red, maroon, pink, gray, and silver, the decor inspires the feeling of an old French building that has been gutted and transformed into a contemporary establishment. Ah Sin features both indoor and outdoor patio dining. Above is a chic second-story lounge, **Risqué,** a haute nightspot offering plush couches, an intimate dance floor, and private balconies with an impressive view of the Strip.

Entrees range in price from about $11 to $25, and specialties include chosin sesame-crusted chicken, Mongolian Khorkhog lamb chops, Indian Ocean scallops, and crispy Malaysian T-bone. Appetizers include a Malaysian satay bar, dim sum, and a selection of familiar and unusual sushi and sashimi. The restaurant is open daily from 11:00 A.M. to midnight.

Les Artistes Steakhouse is an unusual two-story dining room that has an open kitchen on the first level. A pair of ornate spiral staircases ascend

Paris Las Vegas

to the balcony where there are more seats. The waitstaff, attired in traditional long white aprons, black vests, white shirts, and bow ties, offers French-style steak house entrees (priced from about $20) and desserts that include classics such as tart tatin, raspberry clafoutis, and crème brûlée. Open nightly except Monday and Tuesday from 5:30 to 10:30 P.M. For reservations call (702) 967–7999.

A stylish Parisian-style street cafe housed within the Louvre facade, **Mon Ami Gabi** offers street-level seating on the Las Vegas Strip. The eatery, originally opened in Chicago, serves lunch from 11:30 A.M. to 3:30 P.M. and dinner from 5:00 to 11:00 P.M. during the week and until midnight on weekends, with fresh-baked breads and pastries along with specialties such as gratinée of white French onion soup and a variety of quiches. By night candlelit dinners include traditional cassoulet and shallot steak; entrees start at around $18. For reservations call (702) 944–4224.

Le Provençal is an informal European village–style restaurant. Waiters and waitresses serve the French-Italian cuisine native to the Provence region; when the spirit moves, they'll break into song. Guests can also order provincial wines decanted from large barrels located in the dining area or order from an extensive list of wines that are local to Provence. Open daily from 11:30 A.M. to 10:30 P.M. For reservations call (702) 967–7999.

At the internal connection between Paris Las Vegas and Bally's is **Ortanique,** which offers an eclectic menu of world food. Specialties include Guinness Stout Black Angus strip steak for $33, jerked double porks for $28, curried free-range chicken for $21, and Caribbean bouillabaisse for $33. The restaurant serves lunch from 11:30 A.M. to 3:30 P.M. and dinner from 5:00 to 11:00 P.M. during the week and until midnight on weekends. For reservations call (702) 946–1346.

And then there is **Le Village Buffet,** an ambitious entrant in the "can you top this?" competition in Las Vegas. The buffet celebrates the five provinces of France with action stations. Chefs prepare meals that include duck braised with Riesling wine from Alsace, rock crab salad from Brittany, sautéed sea bass with artichoke crust from Provence, coq au vin from Burgundy, and fricassee of scallops with roasted forest mushrooms from Normandy. The buffet is set within a villagelike setting with tables in the indoor town square and in a casual dining room by a fireplace. The room fills quickly; you can make an approximate reservation for a seat as mealtime approaches. The buffet is attractive and relatively intimate, offering some unusual dishes. On several of my visits, the tastes were more pedestrian.

Serving stations at Le Village include La Raclette (which comes from the French word *racler,* meaning "to scrape"), which offers melted cheese accompanied by a medley of cured meats, steamed potatoes, assorted vegetables, and French bread. La Grillade (grill), displayed in the window of the buffet for passersby on Le Boulevard to see, features a selection of skewers of meat, seafood, and sausages.

Other casual dining areas include **JJ's Boulangerie,** a French bakery where guests sit near the bakers kneading dough, creating pastries, and removing racks of baguettes from the display oven. The fresh bread is delivered to other restaurants at the resort by bicycle.

Nearby, one of France's leading marketers of French fine pastry, **Lenôtre,** operates its only gourmet boutique in the United States. Delectables range from French breakfast pastries to luxurious chocolates to petite cakes to flavorful teas and cappuccinos. For visitors on the go, Lenôtre offers freshly baked French croissants and other Viennoiseries, pain au chocolat, pain aux raisins, apple turnover, briôche, and an assortment of pastries.

Le Café Île St. Louis is a twenty-four-hour Las Vegas coffee shop with a French flair located at the south end of the casino; lunch and dinner specials are priced from $9.00 to $13.00.

Paris Le Théâtre des Arts offers headliner entertainment, and **Le Cabaret Show Lounge** features live French and English entertainment.

Paris Las Vegas offers 2,916 guest rooms, 295 suites, a two-acre pool area, an 85,000-square-foot casino, 160,000 square feet of meeting and convention space, six specialty restaurants, and a 1,500-seat showroom.

Paris Las Vegas. 3655 Las Vegas Boulevard South. 2,916 rooms. Standard room rates $79 to $299. (702) 946–7000, (877) 796–2096. www.parislasvegas.com.

★★★★★ RIO ALL-SUITE HOTEL & CASINO

Hot, hot, hot! This is one fun place—a bit of Rio de Janeiro about a mile west of the Strip. It's a bright and cheery place of flowers, flowered shirts, and some of the hottest cocktail-waitress uniforms in town—more of a swimsuit than an outfit, actually. Dancers in pink thong bikinis and dancers with trained birds parade through the casino regularly.

The latest and greatest: a squad of "bevertainers" who put down their serving trays to sing and dance on ministages as they saunter in and among the slot machines and tables. Under Harrah's management, Rio has toned down the outfits of the cocktail waitresses from 11 on a scale of 10 to a more sedate 9 or so. They make up for it, though, with some of the raciest lounge shows in town.

And the hotel rooms at the Rio are among the nicest in town, spacious and attractive and offering views of the mountains or the distant Strip.

Although the Rio is only about a mile from the Strip, it's not an easy walk because of the highways in the area; you'll need to use a car, cab, or the hotel's shuttle bus to get there.

Even by Las Vegas standards, the Rio story has been a jackpot success. The original building opened in 1990 and was from the start a wild and crazy place; it was almost immediately too small. Construction of a new tower was completed in 1994, and that same year work was begun on a third suite tower and a new parking garage. In 1997 the Rio completed construction of a forty-one-story tower with 1,037 more rooms, bringing the total to 2,563.

Even the basic suite is large and impressive, but other accommodations available for rent include the Carioca Suites (1,100 square feet), the Super Suites (1,200 square feet), and the Masquerade Suites. Invited guests—the biggest spenders at the tables—may be offered a Palazzo Suite. Located in a private building, the nine suites range from 4,000 to 13,000 square feet.

Rio All-Suite Hotel

In 1998 the Rio was purchased by Harrah's Entertainment, parent company of the Harrah's casinos and resorts that now also includes Caesars. The place still rocks, although like many places in Las Vegas it has gone a bit downscale, adding a section of nickel slots to its 120,000-square-foot casino.

In 2006, as part of the rearrangements that resulted from Harrah's purchase of Binion's Horseshoe in downtown Las Vegas, the Rio is now home to the World Series of Poker. (Harrah's sold off Binion's to a third party but held on to the Horseshoe brand and the poker championship.) A renovation of the sports book added ten new tables in the heart of the Rio's sports book.

The headline-grabber in the casino is the **Masquerade Show in the Sky** in the Masquerade Village. The show is presented six or more times a day, usually between 3:00 to 9:30 P.M., with a cast of thirty dancers, musicians, aerialists, and costumed stilt walkers. Most of the performers pass by above the casino floor on floats that travel a 950-foot track. There are four different parades, each about twenty minutes long, presented on a rotating schedule through the day. Some of the acts include indoor bungee flying and singers within representations of butterflies, crabs, lobsters, and dolphins. Over the years the free show has progressed from a PG to an R rating, adding a bounteous display of cleavage and thongs . . . and a bit of beefcake for the distaff visitor. Guests can even purchase tickets to dress in Mardi Gras finery and ride on one of the floats; the privilege goes for about $10, with tickets for sale at the Play Rio ticket sales counter.

There are plenty of good places to view the Masquerade Show, including the center of the upper balcony or on the casino floor in front of the main stage. Be aware, though, that security may shoo away any children who stop on the casino level; families are better off on the upper level.

Among the many hot spots at the resort is the **I-Bar Ultra Lounge,** located in the center of the main casino pit and open from noon until late in the night. It draws its name from the famed Ipanema beach in Rio de Janeiro, with natural elements of earth, rock, and water. There are twelve signature cocktails, including Hypnosis, Peachy Keen, Exotic Spice, and Passion Pulse. And the lounge is the only known natural habitat of the I-Girls, ten carefully selected models and mixologists dressed in flesh-colored costumes, trained to move with the rhythmic sounds of I-bar.

Way up top, on the fiftieth and fifty-first floors of the Masquerade Tower, the **VooDoo Café and Lounge** offers fabulous sights, sounds, and an unusual menu that adds a Creole flavor to American favorites. Appetizers include a Witch Doctor Sampler of crab cakes, coconut-battered shrimp, andouille beignets, and voodoo hot wings. Entrees, priced from about $26 to $50, include lobster thermidor, stuffed blue crabs gratin, and Chicken Somestreetinneworleans (grilled chicken with tasso ham and pepper jack cheese).

Specialty drinks include "What the Witch Doctor Ordered," which blends four rums, peach schnapps, banana liqueur, fruit juices, and dry ice for two close friends and costs $21. And there's "Sexual Trance" in a twisted stem glass, mixing Absolut citron, Midori, Chambord, and fruit juices, at a mere $7.00.

Visitors can take the elevator to the terrace for a breathtaking view of the skyline of the Strip. (By the way, there are only some forty-one actual floors in the tower. In keeping with Japanese and American superstitions, the unlucky numbers of four and thirteen are skipped, along with a few others for marketing purposes.)

The floor show after 7:00 P.M. includes the lounge's fire-breathing, bottle-juggling bartenders. VooDoo is open nightly.

Gaylord India Restaurant is a gourmet eatery specializing in the tangy cuisine of northern India. Specialties, ranging in price from about $15 to $30, include savory biryani rice dishes; tandoori chicken, salmon, and prawns; kebabs of chicken, lamb, and fish; and a colorful spectrum of curry dishes. The restaurant also offers a wide variety of vegetarian entrees. Royal feast sampling menus range from $39.95 to $49.95. Open from 11:30 A.M. to 2:30 P.M. for lunch Monday through Thursday, with a lunch buffet on Friday and Saturday from 11:30 A.M. to 3:30 P.M.; dinner is served nightly from 5:00 to 11:00 P.M. Other Gaylord restaurants are in San Francisco, Beverly Hills, Chicago, Hong Kong, London, New Delhi, Bombay, and Kobe.

Hamada's Asiana Restaurant offers Japanese teppanyaki exhibition tableside cooking, as well as sushi, steaks, tempura, and Chinese dishes. Entrees range from about $20 to $80 (for Kobe beef specialties).

Mah Jong Chinese Noodle Bar, across from the Asian Pit, features authentic Cantonese and Chinese dishes. Specialties include beef brisket noodle soup, preserved egg and pork congee, and salt and pepper seabass and scallops with asparagus.

Sao Paulo Café spreads its focus from American to Chinese to Italian specialties—everything but Brazilian, despite its name. Open twenty-four hours a day, it is adjacent to the Rio Box Office and the Samba Theater.

Another place for quick bites is the quirky **Tilted Kilt,** which offers specialties from potato pizza to Sloppy Janes (shaved deli meats topped with coleslaw on a potato roll) and drunken clams (bivalves steamed in beer). You'll also find buffalo chicken wings, Maggie Mae's fish and chips, and chili. The Super Sundae Bar is based around three pints of ice cream served on a lazy Susan with all the basic toppings, and priced at $11.99 for someone with a huge appetite or some friends to share. Open weekdays from 4:00 P.M. to 2:00 A.M., and weekends from noon to 2:00 A.M. Entrees are priced from about $7.00 to $10.00.

Antonio's Ristorante serves northern Italian fare, complete with a strolling guitarist. Open nightly from 5:00 to 11:00 P.M., in the Ipanema Tower between the Main Cashier's Cage and Rio Java. Entrees range from about $17 to $35 and include semolina-crusted fillet of salmon, Tuscan osso buco, and filet of beef with a spinach and fontina crust.

The **Wine Cellar & Tasting Room** bills itself as the "world's largest and most extensive public collection of fine and rare wines" and features wine appreciation instruction, weekly tasting seminars that include dinner, and a complete line of tasting accessories and gifts. The collection, valued at some $6 million, includes as its centerpiece the Chateau d'Yequem with bottles from every vintage between 1855 and 1990. The cellars are open daily for tours.

The two levels of the Masquerade Village include an eclectic selection of upscale stores. The shops include a Harley Davidson clothing outlet, the Nawlins Authentic shop selling New Orleans–themed products, and Diamonds International.

And then there are the Rio's smorgasbord offerings. Quite simply, the Rio is home to not just one great buffet but the two best buffet rooms in town: the Carnival World Buffet and the upscale Village Seafood Buffet.

The **Carnival World Buffet** is a pretty, bright room just off the casino floor that offers a whole range of unusual—and unusually good selections, from cooked-to-order Brazilian stir-fry to sushi to steaks and chops.

Breakfast features made-to-order omelets, waffles, pancakes, sausage, bacon, fresh salsa, fruit, and a variety of fritters. Just when we were ready to waddle on out, we discovered the dessert section, which is the fulfillment of many a sweet tooth's wildest dream: a bakery where you can sample any food simply by pointing to it.

The buffet underwent a major renovation in 2005 that included new action stations for stir-fried Asian and Brazilian fare, as well as Mexican, Japanese, Chinese, and Italian sections. One new feature at the dessert bar: a selection of gourmet gelato selections.

The Rio's buffet is (rightfully) very popular, and long lines can build; arrive early or late to get in without waiting. On an average day the buffet serves 7,000 people; the record crowd of 11,000 arrived on a Fourth of July weekend. On a typical day diners chow down 1,000 pounds of crab legs and shrimp, 5,500 pounds of meat and poultry, 1,000 pizzas, 7,680 eggs, 40 gallons of ice cream, and 8,000 cakes and pastries. The price is $10 to $16 for breakfast, lunch, dinner, or weekend brunch.

The **Village Seafood Buffet** is, somehow, one step above its cousin at the other end of the casino. Tucked into a room at the end of the Masquerade Village, the buffet includes all-you-can-eat crab legs, shrimp, and other shellfish as well as a Japanese stir-fry counter where you can add shrimp, fish, mussels, or calamari to vegetables of your choice. And the dessert section includes some of the richest and finest cakes and sweets around.

The Village buffet is the highest-priced casino smorgasbord in town (about $34.99 per person) but still a great deal if you enjoy fresh seafood.

Another hot place at the Rio is **Buzio's Seafood Restaurant,** an oyster-and-seafood bar with an open show kitchen and a view of Ipanema Beach and swimming pools. Located near the Samba Theater, Buzio's is open for dinner from 5:00 to 11:00 P.M. Entrees range from about $17 to $40 and include roasted, broiled, and steamed lobster, halibut roasted in a corn husk, and steaks and chops.

The Rio's elegant **Fiore Steakhouse and Cigar Lounge**, near the hotel's Beach Club, is a quiet sanctuary down a glass-walled hallway; you can eat in the lovely dining room or move out onto the open-air porch. Entrees, priced from about $26 to $48, include pasta, veal, chicken, and beef dishes. Specialties include cappuccino of lobster bisque, steak au poivre, filet mignon with steamed center-cut crab, spiced citron vodka–cured salmon, and pan-seared Chilean sea bass with clams.

An interesting small cafe is the **All-American Bar and Grille,** which was extensively remodeled in 2004. Luncheon fare includes burgers for $5.00 to $7.00 and salads for $6.00 to $11.00. Dinner selections are priced from about $7.00 to $26.00 and include grilled steaks, chops, and fish and half-pound burgers with twenty different toppings and sauces. The setting is a little dark sports bar with pennants on the wall; the walls are open to the casino.

Bamboleo is an attractive Mexican cantina above Masquerade Village. Open from 5:00 to 11:00 P.M., entrees are in the range of about $10 to $28, and you can wash them down with a forty six-ounce margarita. Unusual offerings include fish tacos, polle mole negro (chicken breasts with a dried chile, sesame seed, almond, and chocolate coating), plus all manner of enchiladas, fajitas, and burritos.

Comic magicians **Penn & Teller** have taken up long-term residence in the 1,486-seat Samba Theater, performing nightly except Tuesday at 9:00 P.M., with tickets priced at about $75.

Greg Thompson's Erocktica Live! Sex, Sweat & Rock 'n' Roll opened in 2005, featuring the Mistinguett dancers and just barely enough clothing to allow the use of the term *costumes*: think fishnets, feathers, leather . . . and less. Dancers perform in front of a live band that specializes in classic rock 'n' roll from bands like Guns n' Roses, Aerosmith, Kiss, Led Zeppelin, Journey, and Foreigner. Performances are offered nightly at 10 P.M. except Tuesday; tickets are about $50.

Las Vegas stalwart **Ronn Lucas,** an edgy and funny ventriloquist, has a long gig for his afternoon show in the Masquerade Showroom, performing daily except Friday at 3 P.M. Tickets are $29.95.

And while you're in town, you might want to drop in on the wedding of Anthony Nunzio Jr. and Valentina Lynne Vitale, which happens at 7:00 P.M. Wednesday to Monday in the Calypso Room. *Tony 'n' Tina's Wedding* includes the wedding ceremony, a rowdy reception complete with an Italian buffet dinner, champagne toast, wedding cake, live dance music, and all sorts of wild goings-on. Tickets run from about $79 for basic seating to $125 for a VIP package.

If it's sex, not romance, on a woman's mind, there's also **Chippendales, The Show.** A troupe of twelve men bump and grind nightly except Wednesday at 8:00 P.M., with an additional performance at 10:30 P.M. on Friday and Saturday at Club Rio. Tickets range from $34.95 to $49.95, with a $75 Sky Lounge package also offered.

There's also the Chippendales Ultimate Girls' Night Out, featuring the **Flirt** lounge, designed by women for women, where the all-male serving staff (in Chippendales costumes) has been specially trained in flattery and flirting. Flirt is open to ticket holders to the Chippendales show from 6:30 P.M. and to the general public from 8:30 P.M. during the week, and from 10:30 P.M. on weekends.

The Rio also owns the **Rio Secco Golf Club** in Henderson, which features a 7,250-yard championship course designed by Rees Jones.

All rooms at the hotel are considered suites, with capacious 600-square-foot rooms. Standard rates start at about $130 on slow weekdays and rise to $340 and more during busy weekends; the oversize rooms include a dressing area and sofa.

You're really going to like this place. Did I remember to mention the buffet, the bevertainers, and the cocktail-waitress outfits?

Rio All-Suite Hotel & Casino. 3700 West Flamingo Road. 2,563 rooms. Standard room rates $130 to $340. (702) 252–7777, (800) 888–1808. www.harrahs .com.

★★★★★ THE VENETIAN RESORT HOTEL CASINO

The canals of Venice, complete with gondolas and gondoliers, on a spit of sand in the Las Vegas desert. Seems logical to me.

The Venetian Resort opened in 1999 on the former site of the Sands opposite the Mirage, with replicas of some of Venice's best-loved landmarks, including the Bridge of Sighs, Doge's Palace, the Rialto Bridge, and the Campanile Tower. Oh, yes: There's also a canal running along the Strip and the shopping district within, with singing gondoliers plying their trade for visitors.

And to give you a sense of the size of this place: Most of the buildings were re-created more or less in their actual size. This is no half-scale model.

And if all of that is not enough, by the end of 2007 an expansion of the Venetian will bring the $1.6 billion **Palazzo Resort Hotel Casino,** with a design intended to evoke high-end locales such as Beverly Hills and Bel Air. The Palazzo will feature more than 3,000 all-suite rooms and offer new shopping, dining, and entertainment on two luxurious levels. The Shoppes at the Palazzo will be connected to the Venetian via the Grand Canal Shoppes and will include six new restaurants and approximately eighty high-end and mid-level stores from the most recognizable brands (including Barneys New York) to hot newcomers and unique one-of-a-kind boutiques drawn from all over the world. The Palazzo will also feature a 1,800-seat theater that is expected to host a major production or Broadway show.

The construction of the new hotel, alas, took with it a bit of Las Vegas history, the Tam O'Shanter, a family-owned hotel (in its dotage shabby but full of character) that had stood at the corner of Twain Avenue and the Strip since 1959.

Gondoliers on the pond in front of the Venetian

Newspaper and government reports show that plans for the new hotel changed during the construction of nearby arch-competitor resort Wynn Las Vegas so that the Palazzo will stand 103 feet taller than Wynn Las Vegas and offer hotel rooms higher in the air than the Stratosphere Tower.

The original marketing plan was aimed at luring huge conventions during the week, augmented by tourists on the weekend. Intense competition, though, has brought new efforts to bring in high rollers from Asia and Europe.

Standard rooms are an expansive 700 square feet with private bedrooms, sunken living rooms, and oversize bathrooms constructed of Italian marble. Each room includes a private fax machine with a personal number; the machine also functions as a computer printer and copier.

The mall area features a quarter-mile Venetian streetscape with intimate "piazza"-style settings and a 630-foot "grand canal." Running its length is a fleet of functional gondolas, singing gondoliers, and waterside cafes crossed by Venetian bridges. They even release doves into the perpetually (painted) blue skies overhead.

The attention to detail in the construction of this resort is amazing. Stones have been hand-weathered to make them look old. Stop to spend the time to gawk at the amazing 65-foot-high dome at the entrance to the casino; the trompe l'oeil art on the dome is worthy of a real palace. The walls and alcoves of the hotel are filled with hand-painted frescoes and pieces of art. The Campanile includes a working set of bells; the Archangel Gabriel at its top is 11 feet tall and 6 feet wide.

The indoor gondolas are beautiful replicas of antique boats from Venice, with one minor improvement: They include a tiny electric motor and propeller, controlled by a foot pedal. Tickets for the gondola cost $12.50 for a ride outdoors on the plaza or $15.00 for a longer indoor cruise. A private two-passenger gondola ride goes for $50.00 outdoors and $60.00 under the artificial sky.

In this town of superlatives, the spectacular Grand Canal Shoppes is one of the most amazing shopping districts you will find, a more modern version of the Forum Shops at Caesars Palace. For a listing of the 140 stores along the canal, see chapter 11.

The Great Hall is a wonder of spectacular ceiling paintings, wall frescoes, ironwork, a fabulous stone floor . . . plus a Brookstone store. It almost fits in.

The resort includes an outpost of the famed Canyon Ranch Spa Club of California. Adjoining the pool deck, the spa—at 69,000 square feet, the largest on the Strip—includes massage, skin care, and body treatment rooms, a 40-foot rock-climbing wall, a movement therapy and Pilates studio, a spinning gym, therapeutic Watsu pools, and a medical center.

The **Guggenheim Hermitage Museum** is located at the front of the Venetian, adjacent to the main entrance lobby. The museum is home to exhibitions based on the collections of the famed Guggenheim Museum of New York and the Hermitage Museum in Saint Petersburg, Russia; exhibitions change approximately twice a year. The inaugural exhibition was "Masterpieces and Master Collectors," displaying impressionist and early modern paintings, including masterpieces by Cézanne, Chagall, Kandinsky, Matisse, Monet, Picasso, Renoir, and van Gogh.

Admission to the Guggenheim Hermitage Museum in 2006 was about $20 for adults, with reduced rates for students and seniors. For information consult www.guggenheimlasvegas.org.

Out front on the second and third floors of the Saint Mark's Library building, for reasons that make sense only in Las Vegas, is a branch of Madame Tussauds wax museum, a British company by way of Paris. **Madame Tussauds Las Vegas** is unusual in that it encourages visitors to touch and pose with its lifelike statues. More than a hundred celebrities are in the decidedly eclectic collection. A few random selections: Muhammad Ali, Jodie Foster, Madonna, and Ivanna Trump. Tickets for the museum are pretty pricey for a wax museum . . . about $22.95 for adults and $10.00 for children ages four to twelve. A discounted family pass for two adults and two children is also available.

In 2006 the supremely strange Blue Man Group jumped ship from the Luxor to the Venetian for a long-term stay in a new 1,760-seat theater. In the same year, the resort opened a production of Andrew Lloyd Webber's *Phantom of the Opera*. Tickets for either show are in the range of about $70 to $150.

There is, of course, a huge casino at the Venetian located within the Doge's Palace.

There are more than 3,000 restaurant seats at the Venetian. Within the re-created Ca'D'Oro Palace is an outpost of Manhattan's famed **Lutèce**, found behind a very subtly marked doorway off the casino floor near the race and sports book. The menu and prices are not posted out front, either; if you've got to ask, you may not want to know. But because you asked me, you'll find lobster, steak, and salmon dishes priced from about $30 to $60.

Lutèce takes its name from the ancient Celtic title for Paris, the birthplace of French gastronomy. The menu includes modern French delicacies and classic influences. Among the expensive highlights is a nightly prix fixe menu degustation.

Examples from the menu include a salad of lobster and mango and raw slices of Atlantic salmon with a tomato-coriander coulis. Entrees include beef short ribs slow-braised in dark beer, Maine sea scallops in a warm black-truffle vinaigrette, and roasted lobster bathed in rich cognac butter.

Lutèce, located on the casino level, has ninety-five inside seats and sixty-five out on the terrace and is open for dinner. For reservations call (702) 414–2220.

At the entrance to the Grand Canal Shoppes is **Tao Asian Bistro**, an offshoot of one of the largest and most popular upscale Asian restaurants on East Fifty-eighth Street in New York, in the old Plaza Theatre. The eatery specializes in high-tone Asian food with some French touches and outrageous decor and special effects.

Within the Venezia Tower is **Bouchon,** a classic French bistro from chef Thomas Keller. Bouchon, which means "cork," is patterned after the informal bistros of Lyon in France and Keller's famed French Laundry restaurant in California, featuring daily specials, raw seafoods, seasonal specials, and an extensive wine list; meals are served in the elegant main dining room or alongside the pool. Bouchon is open for breakfast, lunch, and dinner. For reservations call (702) 414–6200.

Most of the other eateries are on Restaurant Row off the casino floor.

Piero Selvaggio's **Valentino** offers contemporary and traditional Italian with entrees produced from about $13 to $30. Many of the ingredients in the kitchen are imports from Italy, including white truffles, fresh porcino mushrooms, burrata cheese from Puglia, and Mediterranean and Adriatic Sea fish. On a recent visit menu items included spicy chicken Paillard and a New York steak with Tuscan barbecue sauce. Selvaggio is the owner of Primi and Posto in Los Angeles. For reservations call (702) 414–3000.

At the entryway to Valentino is **The Grill at Valentino,** serving simple, quick, and lighter-styled foods and specializing in grilled pizza. And in this town of excess, there's also an eatery that seeks to keep things in reasonable control. The **Canyon Ranch Cafe,** an outpost of the ultra-luxe health resort of the same name, offers wholesome meals that use fresh, seasonal ingredients and foods free from additives, preservatives, and chemicals for breakfast and lunch.

Selections include egg-white omelets, specialty pancakes, grilled organic salmon, grass-fed natural beef, chicken stir-fry, and a variety of fresh fruits, vegetarian dishes, and healthy desserts like warm pecan pie. There's also a juice bar and . . . a martini bar. The cafe, open from early morning through 6:00 P.M., is located in the Canyon Ranch Spa Club on the fourth floor of the Venetian Tower.

Los Angeles celebrity chef Joachim Splichal's **Pinot Brasserie** offers steak, poultry, pastas, seafood, and wild game, complete with a large rotisserie and an oyster bar that sports waiters in rubber boots. Entrees (priced from about $20 to $30) include butternut-squash gnocchi and pan-seared venison loin.

A living statue at the Venetian

Most of the decor was imported from France, including the wooden French door facade from a hotel in Lyon, the copper pots, and kitchen utensils, as well as the Coq d'Or, the large weathered cast-iron rooster that stands guard at the entry. For reservations call (702) 414–8888.

Restaurateur Kevin Wu and master Hong Kong chefs Lai Lam and Chiu Kee Yung established the highly regarded Royal Star Seafood Restaurant in California. In combination with Chinese cuisine expert Theresa Lin, they created the **Royal Star** at the Venetian.

Appetizers include a variety of specialties that have their origins in various regions of China, ranging from the familiar (lettuce cups) to the exotic (giant scallops). Seafood entrees include crab, lobster, fish, prawns, shrimp, and geoduck, all taken from a live tank. There is a large offering of classic and creative meat, poultry, and vegetarian dishes. There's also a separate kitchen for dim sum, served tableside in traditional carts. The 200-seat restaurant is on Restaurant Row; meals are served from 9:00 A.M. to midnight.

The decor blends shimmering slate floors and wood accents within cool celadon walls. A silver-leafed ceiling and elegant chenille upholstery surround authentic Chinese artifacts that complete the fusion of contemporary design with traditional Chinese art.

The ultrahigh-end Asian eatery is almost hermetically sealed off from the casino floor and passersby. I watched a pair of waiters artfully carving a huge Royal Peking duck table side. Entrees range from about $18 to $60. For reservations call (702) 414–1888.

Aquaknox, an elegant seafood restaurant hidden behind walls of water and bathed in a blue glow on Restaurant Row, features a wide selection of fresh seafood flown in daily from around the world. Additional offerings include a selection of caviar with traditional garnishes, butternut-squash soup with duck confit and apple compote, grilled lobster with drawn herb butter, and pan-seared filet mignon with truffle aioli. Entrees are priced from about $28 to $40.

A chef's table and a private banquet room seating as many as eighty-five guests are also available. The restaurant is open daily from 5:30 to 11:00 P.M. during the week and until 11:30 P.M. on weekends. For reservations call (702) 414–3772.

The **Delmonico Steakhouse** is a combination of a venerable New Orleans steak house with one of today's best-known and flashiest chefs, Emeril Lagasse. The 320-seat restaurant, open for lunch and dinner, has an earthy but modern Tuscan look. Entrees, with prices beginning above $20, include traditional steak, seafood, and poultry dishes, as well as Lagasse's Creole specialties. For reservations call (702) 414–3737.

Gian Paulo "Zeffirino" Belloni, a fourth-generation chef, brings authentic Italian technique to the **Zeffirino Ristorante** at the Venetian, located on the canal at the Grand Canal Shoppes.

According to insiders the late Pope John Paul II had a secret passion for the Zeffirino family's pesto and received an annual parcel of pesto and sausages. The 450-seat restaurant, open for lunch and dinner, focuses on seafood; specialties include fillet of sole piccola, lobster tail, fresh fish, grilled fish, zuppa, and pizzarettes and pastas. Specialty oils, pastas, spices, tomatoes, and other ingredients are imported from Italy; breads and pastas are made on the premises. A $19.95 lunch special includes an appetizer, main course, dessert, and coffee. Featured items include salmon with potato topping, chicken and veal with prosciutto, or pasta of the day. For reservations call (702) 414–3500.

Tsunami Asian Grill offers appetizers such as sake-steamed mussels and blackened Ahi Tataki flash seared with red chili seasoning. Many of the dishes are prepared in unusual ways, such as smoked oolong duck slow roasted with black tea leaves and seasoned with star anise scallions, fresh ginger, and a five-spice chili plum sauce. In a haunting premonition of the real natural disaster that befell parts of Asia in late 2004, the walls display images of a woman dissolving and disappearing into waves of Asian imagery.

Within the Grand Canal Shoppes overlooking the canal, chef Wolfgang Puck created **Postrio,** comprising an informal bistro cafe on the Piazza San Marco and an elegant San Franciscan–European formal dining room serving American cuisine with Asian and Mediterranean influences. Offerings range from gourmet pizzas to a four-course experience, complete with fine wine. Entrees start at about $15.

Along with fresh daily baked breads, pastries, and pastas, the menu includes grilled quail with spinach and soft egg ravioli; foie gras terrine with fennel, haricot verts, and walnut toast; grilled lamb chops with tamarind glaze, shoestring potatoes, and peanut sauce; and Chinese-style duck with mango sauce and crispy fried scallions. For reservations call (702) 796–1110. For a peek at Puck's Web site, visit www.cooking.com/wolfgang.

Created by the founders of Il Fornaio, **Canaletto** features the food and wine of the Veneto region of northern Italy. Chef Maurizio Mazzon, a native of Venice, offers fresh seafood, beef, game, and poultry cooked on wood-fired rotisseries and grills, as well as northern Italian staples such as risotto, gnocchi, and polenta. Entrees start at about $15. The restaurant's unusual wine list spotlights the lesser-known wines of northeast Italy.

Canaletto's two-story architecture incorporates many facets of Venetian-inspired design. "Outside" tables surrounding a 40-foot-tall statue sit in the heart of Saint Mark's square, much like the cafes lining the original Piazza San Marco. Past Canaletto's elegant double-arched bar, luxurious navy-blue–striped booths under 16-foot-tall ceilings offer a more refined dining experience. Polished hardwood floors blend into terrazzo tile leading to the exhibition kitchen. Spectacular Venetian lights and chandeliers crafted by the artisans of Murano cast a flattering glow. For reservations call (702) 733–0070.

Casual diners can head for the **Grand Lux Café** from the creators of the Cheesecake Factory.

You'll find a menu of authentic Mexican dishes with an American ambience from the father of Southwestern cuisine at **Taqueria Canonita**. The menu includes authentic Mexican dishes such as tacos, tamales, tostados, gorditas, and rellenos made with grilled and roasted meats, vegetables, and seafood; entrees start at about $18. Tacos al carbon feature beef, chicken, and pork varieties served on fresh, handmade corn tortillas, accompanied by spicy, creamy slaw. Other entrees include quesadillas with shrimp and mango and *carbrito barbacoa* with black beans (spit-roasted barbecued young goat with clay pot black beans). The decor features a high ceiling and central exhibition kitchen. It is located canal side at the Grand Canal Shoppes. For reservations call (702) 414–3773.

The hotel includes its own sprawling meeting center that complements the original Sands Expo Center. The combination of the hotel, meeting center, and Sands Expo Center makes the Venetian the world's largest hotel and convention complex under one roof.

In 2003 the twelve-story Venezia hotel tower opened, adding 1,013 more luxury suites and a lavish pool deck; the resort, including the top five floors of concierge-level suites, is operated as a hotel within the hotel. Guests use a separate check-in desk and elevators. Suites average about 700 square feet in size, including a sunken living room area.

The expansion also added 150,000 square feet of meeting space, bringing the grand total to nearly 1.9 million square feet of meeting, convention, and exhibition space at the Venetian and the Sands Expo Center. Also in the building are a new restaurant and the Venetian's first wedding chapel.

A pedestrian bridge crosses the Las Vegas Strip connecting the Venetian hotel and the Mirage and Treasure Island hotels.

The Venetian Resort Hotel Casino. 3355 Las Vegas Boulevard South. 4,049 rooms. Standard room rates $129 to $999. (702) 414–1000, (877) 883–6423. www .venetian.com.

★★★★★ WYNN LAS VEGAS

Resort mogul Steve Wynn's $2.4 billion dream of a comeback opened on the Strip in the spring of 2005, adding some 2,700 guest rooms in a fifty-story tower, a 111,000-square-foot casino, eighteen restaurants, an eighteen-hole championship golf course, and a flashy and splashy watery show.

Amost every new hotel-casino-resort on the Strip is huge, but Wynn Las Vegas is monumental. Modestly named after the mogul himself, Wynn Las Vegas spreads its huge blue-gray wings across the site of the former Desert Inn. The hotel tower includes forty-five floors of hotel rooms and suites on top of a three-story structure housing the casino, eighteen restaurants, and retail outlets.

At the focal point of the building's arc is a man-made lake and a fifteen-story-high mountain with a waterfall along the Strip. The hotel arrival area features an atrium garden with a view of the lake.

In of the spring of 2006 Wynn and his wife, Elaine, broke ground on **Wynn Encore,** a 2,000-room hotel with even more flash and splash, including a pool with a retractable glass roof. Room rates at the two neighboring hotels generally begin at about $300, but Mrs. Wynn said everyone would be welcome to come gamble, dine, shop, and otherwise mingle with the glitterati. "Nobody is intending for this to be exclusive," she told resporters. People can visit the gardens and buy $28 T-shirts as souvenirs, she said.

While the hotel was being developed—with great secrecy—it was originally expected to be called Le Rêve, after a Picasso painting in Wynn's collection; *Le Rêve* is French for "the dream." Instead that name was given to the signature theatrical show at the resort, an entrancing but exceedingly strange show; think of it as Busby Berkeley meets Cirque du Soleil . . . at sea, and you'll have a sliver of an idea about what you can expect.

Standard rooms at the hotel include about 620 square feet, as much as 125 square feet more than a typical luxury hotel room. The arc design offers views that include the Strip, the lake and mountains out front, and the golf course at

Wynn Las Vegas

the back. There are also single- and multiple-bedroom luxury suites, including 270 parlor and salon suites, eighteen one- and two-bedroom fairway villas, and four two-bedroom and two four-bedroom private-entry villas averaging approximately 7,000 square feet. Luxury amenities include flat-screen televisions in both the living and bathroom areas, plush European linens and bedding; many of the luxury suites include private massage rooms. All guest rooms and suites feature high-speed Internet access.

The golf course—open only to Wynn Las Vegas guests—is an update of the former Desert Inn golf course; the design is by golfer Tom Fazio with an assist by . . . Steve Wynn. The course includes three lakes and a series of streams flowing from the west to the east end of the property, with water features on almost every hole.

The Aqua Theater showroom was designed to accommodate *Le Rêve,* a production by Franco Dragone, the creative force behind Bellagio's production of *O* and Treasure Island's *Mystère,* as well as Celine Dion's show at Caesars Palace. The showroom seats 2,087 guests, surrounding a million-gallon performance pool, with no seat farther than about 42 feet from the watery stage. In 2006, tickets ranged in price from about $80 to about $110. You're all but certain to get wet if you're seated in rows B or C of the circular theater—the designated splash zone—and soaked in row A. The show is offered twice nightly at 7:30 and 10:30 P.M., dark Tuesday and Wednesday.

A second theater, with 1,200 seats, is used for special presentations. For the first year of the hotel's operation this was the home of the wicked *Avenue Q,* a Tony Award–winning Best Musical.

Wynn filled out his showplace with some spectacular restaurants, a combination of classical cuisines and Asian fusion. Most of the restaurants are open for dinner only, from about 5:30 to 10:30 P.M. unless otherwise noted; to make reservations at any, call (702) 770–9966.

Among the new stars on the Strip is **Alex,** based on chef Alessandro Stratta's cuisine brought to Las Vegas from the French Riviera.

Wing Lei is described as a decadent twist on French-influenced Shanghai, an elegant but casual Chinese eatery.

SW Steakhouse, named after you-know-who, combines a classic American steak house with the flavors of Alsace, France. **Okada** offers teppanyaki and robata cooking as well as modern Japanese creations and sushi. It offers a view of SW's Lake of Dreams.

Restaurants that offer lunch (11:30 A.M. to 2:30 P.M.) as well as dinner include **Daniel Boulud Brasserie,** a bustling casual French eatery. **Bartolotta Ristorante di Mare** celebrates traditional Italian dishes; chef Paul Bartolotta's menu includes seafood flown in daily from fish markets throughout Europe. **Corsa Cucina** serves Stephen Kalt's contemporary Mediterranean-Italian dishes from wood-fired grilled pizza to marinated rotisserie chicken.

Chef Mark LoRusso's high-end American cuisine is offered at **Tableau,** featuring breakfast, lunch, and dinner. The **Red 8 Asian Bistro** is a casual eatery open through the day and deep into the night, serving dishes from Cantonese noodle dishes to Hong Kong–style dim sum and barbecue.

Wynn Las Vegas sits directly across the Strip from the Fashion Show Mall and nearby to the Las Vegas Convention Center and the Sands Expo and Convention Center. There's a hotel shuttle to the convention centers and a pedestrian bridge to the mall.

The original occupant of the site, the famed Desert Inn, was home base for the Rat Pack. Named after the considerably greener and officially gambling-free hotel in Palm Springs, California, the Desert Inn debuted in 1950. In typical Las Vegas fashion, the grand opening was a blast: Ceremonies were made to coincide with the test of an atomic bomb outside of town. The most famous owner of the Desert Inn was the reclusive Howard Hughes, who moved into a penthouse suite on November 23, 1966; when he was asked to leave six months later to make room for casino high rollers, he bought the place instead.

Wynn Las Vegas. 3131 Las Vegas Boulevard South. 2,700 rooms. (702) 770–7800, (877) 770–7077. www.wynnlasvegas.com.

ECONOGUIDE ★★★★ RESORTS

★★★★ HARD ROCK HOTEL AND CASINO

In Las Vegas, where the unusual is merely ordinary, the Hard Rock Hotel is heavy metal in a hard place. Welcome to the only casino with the world's largest guitar on the roof and a chandelier made from thirty-two gold saxophones.

Located 3 blocks in from the Strip on Paradise Road, the relatively small hotel opened with a loud splash in 1995. The Hard Rock unveiled its eleven-story, 330-room expansion in 2000, doubling the size of the hotel and casino. And more development may be in the offing under new owners who took over in 2006.

A jumping place at almost any hour, the restaurants are down a quiet corridor off the floor. Eateries include **Pink Taco,** a high-tone Mexican diner. The room features thoroughly new but decidedly old-looking corrugated metal, aged and distressed wood, and bare-bulb lighting fixtures. Visitors can sip ice-cold margaritas and cervezas to accompany hot enchiladas prepared in an open-air taqueria. There's a half-price happy hour weekdays from 4:00 to 7:00 P.M.

Nobu is an exotic Japanese restaurant based around the cooking of Chef Nobu Matsuhisa, who operates eateries bearing his name in London and New York. Trees line a pathway leading to the entry, while the sushi bar glows from within a curved plane of river rock.

AJ's Steakhouse is an homage to Arnie Morton, the legendary Chicago restaurateur and father of Hard Rock founder Peter Morton. Just past a '50s-style marquee advertising cocktails is a small restaurant decorated in dark woods, tufted oxblood leather, and an elevated bar that has bronze rails and a countertop of black granite. Oil paintings of legendary boxers line the walls. Entrees range from about $19 to $35.

The Counter is a small but elegant lunch counter, a place where waffle irons, blenders, and sizzling grills make a modern return.

Simon Kitchen and Bar is the trendiest eatery in the trendy hotel. Chef Kerry

Simon's friends and clientele include rock and film stars and fans of his eclectic menu, which features fancified comfort food like meat loaf, tandoori salmon, and rib eye cowboy steak. The staff is decked out in their very best blue jeans. Entrees range from about $25 to $35. For reservations call (702) 693–4440.

In mid-2006 Hard Rock cofounder Peter Morton sold the resort to New York–based Morgans Hotel Group. The $770 million transaction included the hotel and casino plus twenty-four adjacent acres for development. Morton told reporters that he was "taking his chips off the table" and leaving the Las Vegas scene after creating a rock-and-roll landmark. Morton cofounded the Hard Rock brand in 1971 and sold his chain of Hard Rock Cafes to the Rank Group for $410 million in 1996. (In late 2006, Rank sold the rest of the company, except for the Vegas property, to the Seminole Tribe of Florida.) The resort sale included most of the unique pop memorabilia on display at the Hard Rock Hotel. According to published reports, Morton kept two Jimi Hendrix items—the rocker's famous floral print jacket and his flying V guitar—for his sons.

Morgans, the new owner, was founded by Studio 54's Ian Schrager. It has a collection of trendy boutique hotels including Morgans, Royalton, and Hudson in New York; Delano and the Shore Club in Miami; Mondrian in Los Angeles and Scottsdale; Clift in San Francisco; and Sanderson and St. Martin's Lane in London. Morgans has plans to build a 600-room Delano and 1,000-room Mondrian hotel at Echelon Place, under development by Boyd Gaming at the former location of the Stardust on the Strip.

Squeezed in amongst the guitars and spangled jackets is a casino with some 800 slot and video poker machines and about forty table games. Some 250 of the slot machines have handles shaped like Fender guitars, and roulette tables are shaped like pianos. And then there are the gambling chips, which over the years have included the $5.00 Red Hot Chili Pepper "Give It Away," the $25.00 purple Jimi Hendrix "Purple Haze," and the $100.00 Tom Petty "You Got Lucky" chips. The casino cashier's counter sits beneath a large sign that reads BANK OF HARD ROCK. IN ROCK WE TRUST.

Memorabilia on display include one of Elvis's gold lamé jackets, Harley Davidson motorcycles from Guns n' Roses and Mötley Crüe, and guitars from Nirvana, Pearl Jam, ZZ Top, Aerosmith, Bruce Springsteen, Van Halen, Chris Isaak, Lenny Kravitz, and many others. An Elvis suit and guitar are on display outside the Hard Rock store. And a San Francisco Giants uniform worn by Willie Mays adorns a mannequin outside the sports book.

"The Joint" is Hard Rock's live-music theater; it seats an intimate 1,400, a relatively small room in these days of stadium concerts for 25,000 of your closest friends. **Baby's** nightclub is so hip it's hidden behind an unmarked door that leads down to the basement.

Under Morton's stewardship, although the enterprise was certainly intended to make a profit, there was an undercurrent of social consciousness beneath the glitz. Some of the machines were designated to pay their profits to the National Resources Defense Council and Conservation International. There were recycling bins and water-saving measures. And leftover restaurant food was donated to local charities.

Amenities include the Hard Rock Beach Club, where music plays underwater in the lagoonlike pool, which has a sand bottom, rock outcroppings, and a swim-up blackjack table. French doors open the rooms to the outside air, an unusual feature in Las Vegas. The walls are decorated with pictures by rock photographers.

Hard Rock Hotel and Casino. 4475 Paradise Road. 657 rooms. Standard room rates $79 to $199. (702) 693–5000, (800) 473–7625. www.hardrockhotel.com.

★★★★ LAS VEGAS HILTON

Elvis slept here! In fact this place is so large that he may still be roaming the halls somewhere, looking for the elevator. Until you find him, you can pose next to his bronze statue in the courtyard near the main entrance.

The Hilton is next to the Las Vegas Convention Center; its own 220,000-square-foot meeting rooms are often used for spillover from shows such as the Comdex computer exposition. Its hotel rooms are among the first to sell out for major conventions, too. The hotel's showroom was the site of the late-model Elvis Presley's glitter-era performances from 1969 until his reputed death in 1977.

Actually, in a perfect Las Vegas remake, Elvis has been replaced by a passel of Ferengis, Romulans, and the crew of the USS *Enterprise* at **Star Trek: The Experience at the Hilton.** The Experience is part theme park and part futuristic casino. For details about the theme park, see chapter 10. To learn more about the casino, read on, voyager.

At least until deep in 2007, the headliner at the resort will be singer Barry Manilow. The large theater is also used for other star acts at various times of the year.

A Hotel and Casino, Too

The Hilton's three thirty-story towers include 3,174 rooms and suites. The 1,500-seat showroom, used for major shows and boxing matches, has one of the largest stages in Las Vegas. Recreational facilities include a large pool (it actually sits above the ceiling of the main casino), tennis courts, a health club, and a nine-hole putting green.

The casino provides a large and attractive field in which to dream. Ongoing renovations have upgraded the chandeliers throughout. There are sixty-five game tables and more than a thousand slot machines. A sports and race book with more than fifty television monitors and projection screens is one of the most spectacular in town.

And there is also the **SpaceQuest Casino,** part of the Star Trek Experience ex-

---

Elvis Sighting Number One

Elvis Presley made 837 sold-out appearances in fifteen concert series at the Hilton from 1969 to 1977, performing before about 2.5 million people in just that one showroom. From time to time the hotel has exhibited various pieces of Elvis memorabilia.

A statue of Elvis Presley, first unveiled in 1978 about a year after the singer's death, was returned to a place of honor in the courtyard at the front of the property in 2006 after about a year in storage while the lobby was renovated.

pansion of the hotel. Here visitors can travel to the twenty-fourth century to . . . gamble. (This is Las Vegas, remember.)

The SpaceQuest Casino, though, is quite a trip, with a setting that places you aboard a futuristic space station orbiting 1,500 miles above Earth. Glance up to catch the view through three large space windows that reveal Earth below as well as space limousines picking up and delivering the highest of the high rollers.

There are more than 400 slot machines at SpaceQuest. This is the future, so instead of pulling a slot handle, you can spin the wheels by passing your hand through a light beam.

There is, of course, a gift shop and a spacey bar.

Three fabulous "sky villas" at the top of the Hilton include the 12,600-square-foot Villa Conrad, a two-story home away from home decorated in French style; the larger Villa Tuscany, which has a private garden; and the 15,400-square-foot Villa Verona, modestly modeled after the Palace of Versailles outside Paris.

As for restaurants, **Andiamo** is the home of northern Italian specialties and homemade pasta offered Tuesday to Saturday for dinner from 5:00 to 11:00 P.M.; closed Sunday and Monday. There's an impressive espresso-and-cappuccino counter at the entrance, and diners can see the chefs at work behind a glass wall. Specialties include Steak Sinatra, with tomatoes, onions, and mushrooms in wine; *pollo al porcini,* chicken with marsala wine and porcini mushrooms; fettuccine Portofino with shrimp, squid, scallops, and lobster; *medaglioni di vitello andiamo* (two veal medallions sautéed and served with creamy rosemary sauce and asparagus); and *costoletta di vitello con spagnole* (Provini veal chop sautéed with morel mushrooms and pine nuts in marsala sauce). Entrees are priced from about $15 to $30.

At **Benihana,** chefs chop, slice, and grill your food at your table. Offerings range from about $15 to $40. **Robata** offers seafood specialties prepared in Japanese fashion, priced from about $25 to $35. Dinner, from 5:00 to 11:00 P.M., is complemented by the animated musical show *Jambirdee* and a faux-fireworks display over the Benihana Musical Waters.

Within Benihana is the **888 Noodle Bar,** which features pan-Asian noodles, congee, and rice dishes. Signature dishes include roast duck, braised Mandarin beef, curry chicken, and stir-fried

Las Vegas Hilton

sea bass, with entrees priced from about $10 to $28. The eatery is open nightly for dinner. Nearby is **Teru Sushi,** offering more than forty types of sushi shipped in daily from around the world; open Tuesday through Saturday from 5:30 to 10:30 P.M.

Garden of the Dragon offers gourmet Chinese fare from 5:00 to 11:00 P.M. Thursday to Monday. In addition to basic Chinese dishes, you'll also find some unusual offerings such as sizzling lamb (tender lamb loin sliced with Chinese fresh vegetables, served sizzling at the table), steamed whole flounder (steamed in the Cantonese style and garnished with scallions, ginger, and soy sauce), and West Lake Beef Soup. Prix fixe dinners are about $22 to $27; individual entrees are also available, priced from about $15 to $28.

The **Hilton Steakhouse** offers charbroiled steak, ribs, fish, and chicken priced from about $18 to $60. Open daily 5:00 to 11:00 P.M. Offerings include several cuts of steak, such as a thirty-six-ounce double New York strip sirloin for two, priced at nearly $60; center-cut pork chops; and large-cut filet mignon. Other entrees include swordfish steak, tiger shrimp, and lemon oregano chicken.

Also available is **MargaritaGrille,** a casual Mexican restaurant. Offerings for lunch and dinner, served daily from 11:30 A.M. to 11:00 P.M., include *albondigas* (Mexican vegetable soup with meatballs), chili con queso, fajitas, chimichangas, flautas, and burritos. Entrees range in price from about $15 to $25.

> ## Elvis Sighting Number Two
>
> Elvis had his own intimate 5,000-square-foot hideaway on the thirtieth floor of the Hilton, used during his appearances there. After Elvis's death the maintenance staff at the Hilton filled in two bullet holes in the walls and actually redecorated the place! Obviously they had no sense of history.
>
> In 1994 the entire place was gutted and incorporated into one of three spectacular suites, each 10,000 to 15,000 square feet in size and costing a cool $45 million to build.

Within the SpaceQuest Casino, **Quark's Bar and Restaurant** is open daily from 11:00 A.M. to 11:00 P.M. Uniformed aliens take orders on tricorders, with specialties including chicken wings in Vulcan hot sauce, Klingon Kabob, Glop on a Stick, and Thalian Chocolate Mousse. In the bar you can order a draft of Romulan Ale . . . a galactic favorite; the bright blue beer packs a punch (and marks the lips of imbibers emerging from Quark's).

Paradise Cafe is a twenty-four-hour coffee shop. **The Buffet** is open for breakfast during the week from 7:00 to 11:00 A.M.; lunch is served from 11:00 A.M. to 2:30 P.M.; dinner is from 5:00 to 10:00 P.M. A champagne brunch is offered Saturday, Sunday, and holidays.

The Las Vegas Hilton is owned by Colony Capital, which also owns Resorts International properties.

Room rates range from about $59 to $349 but climb sharply—if rooms are available at all—during conventions.

Las Vegas Hilton. 3000 Paradise Road. 3,174 rooms. Standard room rates $59 to $349. (702) 732–5111, (800) 732–7117. www.lv-hilton.com.

★★★★ MGM GRAND

The MGM Grand is a decidedly strange and somewhat wonderful place, a Las Vegas Land of Oz for adults and children of all ages. There's a rain forest, an artsy Parisian girlie show, some spectacular restaurants, and a gigantic gilded lion facing the Strip that is as much a symbol of the promise and threat of Las Vegas as anything else in town. Oh, and it also features a huge hotel and casino and one of the widest ranges of restaurants in town. It's all spread over 115 acres of prime real estate, with 5,034 guest rooms, including 751 suites in four thirty-story towers plus a set of private villas at the Mansion at MGM Grand, a luxury hotel within the hotel.

Rising above the 100,000-pound, 45-foot-tall lion at the Strip and Tropicana Avenue is a spectacular tower of a sign, boasting an impressive video screen visible by day and night that broadcasts scenes from the hotel's shows and other events. In case that's not quite enough eye candy, there are also water fountains, statues of Atlas, and lush landscaping.

Alongside the gilded feline—the largest bronze statue in the United States—the casino has linked a set of pedestrian bridges that connect the four corners of the Strip and Tropicana Avenue; you can walk from the MGM to New York–New York or the Tropicana and connect to a bridge to the Excalibur and from there by tram to Mandalay Bay.

Speaking of cats, rooms at the hotel include a three-level lion habitat within the casino, home to about a dozen living, growling symbols of the MGM empire; about half a dozen will be on display at any one time. Among regular guests are Goldie, Metro, and Baby Lion, said to be direct descendants of the MGM Studios' original marquee lion, Metro.

The habitat is under the supervision of animal trainer Keith Evans, who cares for seventeen lions, three tigers, and two snow leopards at his Las Vegas home, known to some as "The Cat House." Admission to the area is free; you can, though, plunk down $20 for a special "photo opportunity" with some of the creatures. The habitat is open daily from 11:00 A.M. to 10:00 P.M.

Various parts of the hotel have different themes. The 700-room Emerald Tower follows an art deco design. Deluxe rooms in the main hotel showcase either a Clark Gable (dark woods and massive, masculine furnishings) or a Jean Harlow theme (blonde woods, platinum metal accents, and a curvilinear chaise lounge).

Standard hotel rooms are about 446 square feet in size; suites range in size from 675 to 6,000 square feet. (A bit of perspective here: A typical three- or four-bedroom home is 2,000 square feet or less.)

Standard rooms are decorated in *Wizard of Oz,* Hollywood, Southern, and *Casablanca* styles. They are larger than average and fairly quiet. Suites include traditional, Marrakech, Oriental, Bahamian, and Las Vegas designs.

The 752 suites at the hotel include multiroom "bungalow" designs and spectacular two-story terrace suites with an outdoor patio at the top of the hotel.

The hotel's Grand Class on the twenty-ninth floor includes fifty-two two-story suites primarily reserved for VIP guests and celebrities; three Presidential Suites include wraparound glass windows, a full kitchen with private chef and butler, and no less than twenty-one telephones, including one in the personal suite elevator. There is even a semiprivate restaurant that you have to know about and be known to before you can enter. The largest of the suites sprawl across 6,040 square feet; the three penthouse suites are located at the end of the tallest three towers and offer 180-degree views of Las Vegas through two-story glass windows.

Skylofts at MGM Grand consist of forty-one two-story lofts on the upper floors; the suites come with a concierge, butler, maid, and business services twenty-four hours a day. Guests receive complimentary Maybach limousine service to and from the airport, luggage unpacking and packing, engraved personalized stationery, and the services of spa and sleep butlers.

The **Signature** at MGM Grand is a 576-suite hotel in three separate towers. And there are also twenty-nine private villas inside the Mansion at MGM Grand.

Expansions of the core hotel include the **West Wing,** a boutique hotel of 700 rooms.

The hotel and casino are certainly grand and worth a visit, but the overall tone is down a notch from places like Bellagio, the Venetian, or the Mirage. It is also one of the few hotel complexes I know of that requires the use of a map; I suspect some of the bellhops keep copies in their back pockets, too.

At **Teatro Euro Bar,** an electronic violinist opens the night with a blend of urban rhythms; as the evening progresses the music and surroundings evolve into a global jukebox for DJs to spin a variety of music genres from around the world. **Centrifuge** is a seventy-seven-seat bar adjacent to the poker room, near Studio 54, featuring specialty fruit infusion cocktails drawn from many of the MGM Grand's signature restaurants.

The hotel goes back to the future with the resurrection of the somewhat-infamous **Studio 54,** one of the ultratrendy landmarks of New York's 1970s disco scene.

MGM Grand's Studio 54 showcases state-of-the-art sound, music, and lighting with four dance floors and bars. There is also an exclusive invited-guest area and several semiprivate lounges that can hold up to 400 people; total capacity is about 1,200. The decor of the club features artwork from New York's original dance club and techno-chic scaffolding and lighting; there is, of course, a mirrored ball over the dance floor. And, of course, showgirls swing above the crowd, dropping glitter on the dancers below.

The bartenders and host are part of the performance, and they enforce a dress code with the emphasis on flash. The sign on the door demands: DRESS SPECTACULAR. If you're allowed in, you'll have to pay a $20 cover charge on Friday and Saturday or $10 during the week. The cover charge, though, applies only to men; ladies are free.

Tuesday night is EDEN Night—Erotically Delicious Entertainers Night—which invites and indulges workers in the entertainment industry to come and party and the rest of us to watch. Thursday is Dollhouse Night, with costumed "dolls" serving as hosts and hostesses and guests bringing their own rags or borrowing from Studio 54's closet of outfits.

The club is open nightly Tuesday through Saturday from 10:00 P.M. for ages twenty-one and older, closed on Sunday and Monday. For more information call (702) 891–7254.

Zuri, a lively twenty-four-hour lobby bar, is an unusual combination of a Sinatra-based piano joint, a martini bar, and a touch of Africa; *Zuri* is Swahili for "beautiful."

The one-hundred-seat bar serves cocktails alongside fruit-infused spirits such as Granny Smith apple and cinnamon-infused vodka and frozen Woodford Reserve Bourbon infused with peaches. Zuri also features Veuve Cliquot Champagne by the glass, hard-to-find specialty beers from around the world, a cigar humidor, and a special menu for the morning after the night before that includes a variety of liquid brunch drinks and Bloody Marys.

Tabú at MGM Grand is a cosmopolitan ultra lounge that includes some truly private VIP areas with funky furniture, marble, and wood floors plus tables with reactive imagery. Open Tuesday through Sunday at 10:00 P.M. Wednesday is Boutique Night, with the lounge's hosts modeling outfits from local boutiques and other fashion houses.

For a quick cool one, you can visit **32°,** a frozen drink bar in Studio Walk. For a quick upscale sandwich, there's **'wichcraft**, Tom Colicchio's offshoot of his New York City upscale sandwich eatery, open daily from 10:00 A.M. to 6:00 P.M.

The dining buzz at the sprawling resort comes from **Joël Robuchon at the Mansion.** Legendary French chef Robuchon came out of retirement to open a fine-dining restaurant at the ultraluxe Mansion section of the MGM Grand. Prices start high and go upward from there; you may also need some special connections just to get a reservation on a busy night.

Samples from the menu include scallops cooked in the shell with lemon and seawood butter, frog-leg fritters with garlic puree and parsley sauce, sea urchin flan flavored with fennel, duck foie gras and spring vegetables in a green cabbage ravioli, and pan-fried sea bass with a lemon-grass foam. Meat dishes include confit of lamb with a Mediterranean wheat semoule, and sautéed veal chop.

If you want to sample some of the master chef's delicacies, you may be able to sidle up to a stool at **L'Atelier de Joël Robuchon.** An atelier is a workplace, and this small space offers a glimpse of the kitchen of one of the highest-tone gourmet restaurants in town. Both of Robuchon's establishments are open for dinner only.

Near the Strip entrance is an outpost of the **Rainforest Cafe** chain. The entrance to the two-story, 500-seat restaurant and store is beneath a 40-foot cascading waterfall. There is almost always a long wait to get in; make your reservation at the elephant's head and plan to dine early or late to avoid crowds.

Within the cafe, the Magic Mushroom Juice and Coffee Bar includes a playful animatronic gorilla family. There's also a robotic alligator moving back and forth in a steamy pond; he is a target for coins. Alongside the gift shop are stands for live parrots and other birds; a naturalist will answer questions from time to time. Other highlights include several huge aquariums. Take the escalator toward the sky bridge for a good view into the restaurant. Lunch and dinner entrees, which include burgers, sandwiches, salads, and pasta dishes, are generally in the range of $9.00 to $18.00. The restaurant opens at 8:00 A.M. daily and stays open until 11:00 P.M. during the week, until midnight on Friday and Saturday. Waiting lines can grow to serious lengths on busy weekends.

Shibuya combines traditional ingredients with modern techniques and offers an expansive sake cellar. The restaurant takes its name and inspiration from a neighborhood of Tokyo known for its bustling urbanism and modern lifestyle. The menu offers sushi, teppan, and a la carte specialties in adjoining dining areas. The menu features such signature creations as toro tartare with beluga caviar, miso wild salmon in a sauce of lotus root and ginger, and Kobe beef tataki with shichimi onions and lemon soy. Shibuya is open for dinner nightly from 5:00 to 10:30 P.M. weekdays and from 5:30 P.M. to 1:00 A.M. on weekends.

Diego combines traditional Mexican cuisine with sophisticated sensibility; the interior embraces Mexico's vivid cultural landscape with colors drawn from the murals and paintings of the country's extraordinary modern artists. Drink specialties include classic or strawberry margarita popsicles. Open daily for lunch from 11:30 A.M. to 2:30 P.M. weekdays and until 4:00 P.M. weekends. Dinner is offered nightly from 5:30 to 11:00 P.M. or midnight.

Wolfgang Puck's Bar & Grill offers pizzas priced from about $10 to $13, including varieties with wild mushrooms, leeks, thyme, and goat cheese or pesto, shrimp, rapini, and sun-dried tomatoes. Entrees, priced from about $13 to $32, include Prince Edward Island mussels mariniere, flatiron steak with Maytag blue cheese, and duck bratwurst sausage with mascarpone polenta. The California-simple design is very attractive, but the location is very loud, just off the floor. The cafe is open from 11:00 A.M. to 11:00 P.M. daily.

Fiamma Trattoria, an import of the three-star New York original, Fiamma Osteria, offers Italian regional specialties including yellowfin tuna carpaccio, charcoal-grilled swordfish putanesca with caperberries and black olives, and Florentine steak. An interesting offer we saw on a recent visit: raviolini stuffed with braised shortrib in Barbera wine glaze. Entrees range from about $20 to $40. Fiamma, Italian for "flame," became an instant hit on the East Coast; it first opened in Manhattan's SoHo district. Fiamma is open daily for dinner from 5:30 to 10:30 P.M.

Coming from the other coast, San Francisco chef Michael Mina opened **Seablue,** his second restaurant in the MGM Grand Hotel and his third in Las Vegas. The menu is built around "jet fresh" seafood dishes and fresh seasonal produce. Guests are welcomed by a dramatic 1,800-gallon cylindrical fish tank filled with shimmering Pacific sardines, an under-the-sea theme also seen in the walls of stone and water in the dining room. Guests can watch the preparation of dishes and peruse the "market" of fish, greens, fruits, and vegetables.

Most Seablue dishes begin on the grill, using a variety of oils and natural juices, and are finished in a *tagine* (a Moroccan clay oven) to extract flavors without further oil. None of the dishes on the menu, with the exception of desserts, are cooked with butter or cream. The restaurant specializes in "simple fish" dishes, with entrees raw, marinated, steamed, and fried. Salmon, sea bass, North Sea cod, lobster, loup de mer, daurade, and tuna are included. Entrees are priced from about $24 to $44.

The Mina Group also manages and operates Arcadia in San Jose, California, and Nobhill at the MGM Grand (see below); additionally, Michael Mina serves as the managing chef of **Michael Mina Bellagio.** The restaurant, which seats 130 people in the main dining room and 24 in the private dining room, is open weekdays at 5:00 P.M. and weekends at 5:30 P.M., closing at 10:00 P.M.

Among the hottest seats in town are the 260 available at **Craftsteak,** a New York–style steak house under the direction of chef Tom Colicchio, whose culinary approach emphasizes pure, natural ingredients with hand-selected beef, poultry, fish, lamb, pork, and veal. The menu features ingredients from small family farms, artisanal producers, and day-boat fishermen. A typical menu includes Kobe rib eye steak for about $98, grilled grass-fed strip steak for $39, and braised lamb shank for $28. As the chef and owner of two New York favorites, Gramercy Tavern and Craft, Colicchio's first restaurant outside New York City looks equally impressive. An average check totals about $75 per person. Open nightly from 5:30 to 10:00 P.M. For reservations call (702) 891–7318.

San Francisco arrived at the hotel with the opening of **Nobhill,** inspired by neighborhood restaurants of that famed city and dramatically posed behind wood and glass. Special dishes include sautéed Monterey Bay abalone, lobster potpie, and roasted rack of Hop Sang Market pork. A giant bread oven continuously yields fresh sourdough, focaccia, and other breads. On a recent visit a tasting menu, for $79, featured Avocado Alexis, Green Goddess Salad, North Beach cioppino, roasted Sonoma chicken, filet of beef Rossini, and seasonal fresh fruit tart. Other menu items included wood-grilled diver scallops for $32 and pomegranate-glazed pork chop for $28.

Typical dinner checks range from about $50 to $60. The full restaurant menu is also available at the adjacent lounge. Nobhill is open nightly from 5:30 to 10:30 P.M. For reservations call (702) 891–3110.

Pearl is an intimate gourmet eatery several cuts above your neighborhood Chinese restaurant. Typical menu items include Oregon Kobe beef and abalone carpaccio, shark fin spring roll and pigeon cannelloni, and glutinous rice with Chinese sausage and compoy in lotus leaf. Open for dinner only from 6:00 to 10:30 P.M.; entrees are priced at about $20 to $30 each.

Celebrity chef and author Emeril Lagasse brings his blend of modern Creole/Cajun cooking with **Emeril's,** featuring his signature dish, New Orleans barbecue shrimp. Specialties include andouille-crusted redfish, garlic pork chop, and Creole boiled Maine lobster. Fresh fish is flown in daily; the restaurant is open for lunch from 11:30 A.M. to 2:30 P.M. and dinner from 5:30 to 10:00 P.M. Prices range from about $25 to $45. For reservations call (702) 891–7374.

The **Grand Wok and Sushi Bar** offers an array of Asian cuisine including Chinese, Japanese, Thai, Korean, and Vietnamese dishes. Before a floor-to-ceiling glass wall, a waterfall cascades down a 40-foot wall of polished rocks into a pond accented with moss and black rock; the illusion is that the restaurant floats on water. Special dishes include Pig Trotters Soup with egg noodles, sliced abalone with black mushrooms and seasonal greens, and Korean barbecued beef short ribs. Entrees range from about $8.00 to $12.00. The restaurant is open from 11:00 A.M. until 10:00 P.M. weekdays and until 1:00 A.M. on weekends.

In 2006, MGM Grand offered a set of dinner packages in combination with

Cirque du Soleil's *KÀ*. Available each evening Tuesday through Saturday, these packages feature special three- or four-course menus created exclusively for theatergoers by the chefs of Diego, Fiamma Trattoria & Bar, L'Atelier de Joël Robuchon, Nobhill, Pearl, Seablue, and Shibuya. The packages were priced at about $175 or $200 per person and included dinner, show tickets, gratuities, and taxes.

CBS Television City has a place along the resort's Studio Walk. The venue includes a research center for television pilots, an interactive experience for guests, as well as a full retail shop featuring VH-1, MTV, Nickelodeon, and CBS show merchandise. Some guests will be invited to participate in screenings and focus groups for new shows.

The hotel's Grand Oasis includes a swimming pool with beach. Nearby is the Grand Health Club & Spa, a fitness center that includes six Jacuzzis. Cristophe, renowned for his hair salons in Beverly Hills, Newport Beach, Washington, D.C., and New York City, opened **Cristophe Salon** in 2004. His team provides cut, color, styling, makeup and nail-care services, and portrait photography. If you wish to arrive in style, limousine service is available to the door.

In early 2005 Cirque du Soleil opened *KÀ*, which combines acrobatic performances, martial arts, puppetry, multimedia, and pyrotechnics. Created and directed by acclaimed theater and film director Robert Lepage, the show applies the visual vocabulary of cinema to a live spectacle, telling the story of separated twins, a boy and a girl, who embark on a perilous journey to fulfill their linked destinies.

The show's title is inspired by the ancient Egyptian belief in the *ka,* an invisible spiritual duplicate of the body that accompanies every human being throughout this life and into the next. A cast of seventy-two artists performs in the 1,951-seat **KÀ Theatre** nightly except Wednesday and Thursday; depending on the season, there are as many as two shows a night. Tickets in 2005 were $99, $125, or $150, including tax. For information on the show, consult www.ka.com.

The relatively cozy **Hollywood Theatre,** with 740 seats, is used for concerts and headliner acts.

The **La Femme Theatre,** just off the casino floor, is home to performances of *La Femme,* a show derived from the Crazy Horse Cabaret in Paris. The twelve members of the show are from the French troupe, which in some ways was the mother of many of the topless revues in Las Vegas. The dancers pose and strut and lip-synch to music in an "artistic" ninety-minute presentation. *La Femme* dancers are trained in ballet and perfectly integrate into sensuous choreography as their bodies are bathed in colored and textured lighting designs. Costumes, when there are any, couldn't cover a business card.

The small theater, seating 340 guests, is designed to re-create the Crazy Horse on Avenue George V in Paris, replicating the stage dimensions, interior design, and decor of the original, which debuted in 1951.

The sports book, to the left of the Grand Theatre, has a gigantic screen capable of displaying a single event like the Super Bowl or being divided into as many as twelve separate images for various sporting events.

We also mustn't overlook (as if we could) the **Grand Garden Arena** special-events center. This arena, modeled after New York's famed Madison Square Garden, offers seating for 15,200 for championship boxing. There's nothing very grand about the arena itself, except for its ability to change its configuration for events from ice shows, hockey games, and basketball games to prize fights and concerts.

The huge casino encompasses a total of 171,500 square feet and includes about 3,500 slot machines, 165 gaming tables, and a race and sports book. The casino is divided into four themed areas: Emerald City, Hollywood, Monte Carlo, and Sports.

MGM Grand Inc., controlled by billionaire Kirk Kerkorian, bought control of rival Mirage Resorts in early 2000. The company now owns fourteen casinos, including five of the most spectacular casinos on the Strip: the MGM Grand, New York–New York, Mirage, Bellagio, and Treasure Island.

MGM Grand. 3799 Las Vegas Boulevard South. 5,034 rooms. Standard room rates $109 to $499. (702) 891–7777, (800) 929–1111. www.mgmgrand.com or www.mgmmirage.com.

★★★★ THE MIRAGE

Every desert needs a mirage, although few are quite so unreal as this one: a volcano outside and the Beatles within.

Any description of the hotel has to start with the live volcano out front spewing smoke and fire 100 feet in the air from an artificial lagoon. When the hotel opened in 1989, locals were unsure which was more entertaining: the aerial show from the volcano or the stream of fender benders it caused on the Strip out front. The volcano is still there—more spectacular than ever—but now the resort also is home to one of the hottest tickets in town.

In mid-2006 the Mirage became home to a new show that combines the magic of the Beatles with the mystery of Cirque du Soleil. *The Beatles LOVE* marks the first time that the classic rock group's publishing company, Apple Corps Ltd., has agreed to a major theatrical partnership.

The tightly held resources of the Beatles was cracked when Cirque du Soleil founder Guy Laliberté struck up a friendship with George Harrison; they shared an enthusiasm for Formula 1 racing . . . and the music. After Harrison died in November 2001, Apple's surviving principals—Paul McCartney, Ringo Starr, and widows Yoko Ono and Olivia Harrison—agreed to make the project happen.

Sir George Martin, the original producer of the Beatles, and his son, Giles Martin, worked with the entire archive of Beatles recordings to create the musical component for *LOVE*. They used the master tapes of the group from Abbey Road Studios.

There are no new Beatles songs in the show, although the father-and-son team produced a ninety-minute soundtrack that remixes classic Beatles songs in surround sound, sometimes combining standard versions with outtakes and sometimes creating mash-ups in which pieces of one song are mixed into another. The Cirque tapes will be recast as a soundtrack album.

The production employs an international cast of sixty performers, and includes aerial performances, extreme sports, and freestyle dance.

The $150 million production is expected to run for at least ten years, bringing 2,000 people into the theater twice a night, five nights a week; if shows sell out, that will likely bring together more people than ever saw the Beatles perform live.

LOVE is presented in a custom-built theater at the Mirage featuring 360-degree seating and advanced high-definition video projections with 100-foot digital, moving images backed by a panoramic surround sound system. The space was formerly used for the Siegfried & Roy show. Ticket prices range from about $69 to $150. For information on show schedules, consult www.cirquedu soleil.com.

In 2007 the Mirage unveiled a bigger, more fiery update to its volcano, complete with explosions, more vivid "lava," and smoke. The volcano erupts every hour on the hour from 6:00 P.M. to midnight, weather permitting. The man-made, computer-controlled, 54-foot-tall volcano spits steam, gas-fed flames, and "lava" created with the aid of a sophisticated lighting scheme. During the show the pumping system moves 119,000 gallons of water per minute. As part of the construction, a thousand real palm trees were moved to the site; some of the trees nearest the flames are constructed of steel and concrete.

The Mirage was the first Strip property of what became the bizarre and successful empire of Steve Wynn; that all came to an end in March 2000 when the Mirage, along with sister resorts Treasure Island and Bellagio, were acquired in a takeover by MGM Grand. The resulting megacasino company is now called MGM Mirage.

The one-hundred-acre site has three thirty-story towers with 3,044 rooms, including one- and two-bedroom suites, eight villa apartments, and a cluster of lanai bungalows that have private gardens and pools. The top five floors of each tower are reserved for tower and penthouse suites.

The driveway delivers visitors to a white porte cochere that has full-length louvered shutters that suggest arrival at a colonial government house. Entering through the main doors, you walk into a 90-foot-high indoor atrium that has 60-foot-tall palm trees; a central forest includes tropical orchids and banana trees, an indoor waterfall, and lagoons.

Behind the hotel's registration desk stands a 20,000-gallon coral reef aquarium stocked with sharks, rays, and other sea life from the Caribbean, the Hawaiian Islands, Tonga, Fiji, the Marshall Islands, Australia, and the Red Sea. The 53-foot-long aquarium really is worth a look if you can find the check-in area in the complex maze of the casino.

Public areas are decorated in high-tone marble, teak, and rattan. In the atrium the bent palm trees are necessarily fake, but they are covered in real bark. Almost every other piece of greenery is real. The tropical theme is carried through in most of the rooms at the Mirage, featuring lush colors, rattan, and cane. The highest of the high rollers can claim one of six lanai bungalows, each with its own private garden and pool.

For nonbungalow dwellers, the Mirage has a pool—actually a set of wandering, interconnected lagoons linking two palm-tree–lined islands—where guests can swim, relax in cabanas, lunch at the Paradise Cafe, or enjoy drinks. A full-service spa and salon is also available.

The Mirage is one of just a few casinos in Las Vegas with $500 slot machines; there is a small nest of them in an alcove near the Caribe Cafe. The slots have a top payoff of $40,000 for a single coin. By the way, if you play the $500 machines for a while, you'll be offered a free catered meal. Of course they'll want you to eat it at the machines, feeding those expensive tokens all the while.

Nearby is the Salon Privé, a private gambling room for the highest rollers, where tens or even hundreds of thousands of dollars can hang on a single card in blackjack or baccarat, a roll of the dice in craps, or a spin of the roulette wheel. If you want to play, the casino will staff every table in the room in case you change your mind on which game to play.

The Mirage was the longtime home of Siegfried and Roy, their magic show, and their tigers. Alas, a tragic accident in 2003 stopped the show, but the guys are hardly forgotten. On the Strip in front of the Mirage are huge busts of Siegfried and Roy and one of their white tigers. Despite the size of the statues, they are not easy to spot from the hotel itself or from a car on the Strip. To pay proper homage you'll need to walk on the west side of the Strip between Treasure Island and the Mirage.

As part of their residency at the Mirage, Siegfried and Roy established their own Royal White Tiger breeding line. Their family has grown to a current total

The Mirage

of thirty-three tigers. Not all of them appeared in the show, and those that did were regularly given time off for good behavior. Unlike more common tigers that have black and gold markings, the white tiger is white with black stripes, pink paws, and ice-blue eyes. And the purest of the species have no stripes at all; there are only a few dozen white tigers in the world, making them among the rarest of species.

You can visit some of these beautiful creatures at the **White Tiger Habitat,** visible through the glass wall near the walkway entrance on the south side of the hotel. The re-creation of their native Himalayan world is open to the sky. And there is a hallway that runs from the exhibit area to their cages. I'd suggest you avoid opening unmarked doors in the casino. (Just kidding . . . I think.) Two or three tigers are usually on display in the habitat at the Mirage at all times, with new groups moved in several times each day.

Another interesting animal exhibit is the **Dolphin Habitat,** a 1.5-million-gallon tank for bottlenose dolphins located out back and open to the public for a nominal fee. Four connected pools, an artificial coral reef system, and a sandy bottom replicate a natural environment. The facility houses only dolphins that were either born at the habitat or relocated from other facilities. According to the Mirage, no animals are taken from the wild for the display.

And then there is the **Secret Garden,** a habitat for some of the white tigers, white lions, snow leopards, an Asian elephant, and other animals that used to appear—and disappear—with Siegfried and Roy on stage. Some of the stars of the exhibit include the white lions of Timbavati ("the river that never dries out"); Gildah, one of fewer than 50,000 Asian elephants left in the world; and offspring of Siegfried and Roy's conservation program, including the first male white lion cubs in the western hemisphere.

The Secret Garden is open for visits weekdays except Wednesday from 11:00 A.M. to 5:30 P.M. and on weekends and holidays from 10:00 A.M. to 5:30 P.M. The Dolphin Habitat is open every day on the same schedule.

The hotel includes the 1,260-seat **Danny Gans Theatre** to house the *Danny Gans Show,* which stars . . . Danny Gans. The singer and impressionist, a Las Vegas staple at Rio All-Suite for many years, has signed up for an eight-year run, performing forty-four weeks a year (dark Monday and Friday). General admission in 2006 was $100. When Gans is away from the place with his name on the door, other headliners fill in; regular substitutes include Jay Leno, Wayne Brady, and other comedians.

The Mirage also features some of the best and most attractive restaurants in Las Vegas. For reservations at any of the eateries, call (702) 791–7223.

Fine dining includes **Japonais,** the second branch of a Chicago favorite that opened in late 2006 merging European elegance and modern Japanese style and cuisine. The restaurant offers a menu of hot and cold Asian specialties prepared by executive chefs/partners Jun Ichikawa and Gene Kato. Japonais moved into the space formerly occupied by Mikado and the Ava Lounge. Offering seating for as many as 300 guests, Japonais includes the traditional Red Room, featuring formal tables and banquettes as well as a casual L-shaped sushi bar; the sophisticated Lounge, an enclosed tropical haven with cascading palm trees offering views of the casino; and an exclusive "island," created for private retreats and VIP lounging.

STACK is an intimate American bistro offering fine food in a casual atmosphere. Offerings range from a Kobe beef cheeseburger to a 44-ounce porterhouse steak for two. Other entrees include lamb shanks with lentils, lobster risotto, and spiced pumpkin ravioli.

Nearby is **Fin,** an edgy contemporary dining room with some extraordinary dishes you won't find at your neighborhood Chinese restaurant. Sample entrees include wok-fried lobster with spicy curry coconut sauce, braised whole fresh abalone, Cantonese barbecued duck, braised Mandarin-style tangy pork chops, and spicy oxtail in a clay pot. At the conclusion of the meal, guests are offered Fin's interpretation of a liquid fortune cookie. Combining fresh cream, Bailey's, and Amaretto Pistachio Cream, the libation is served cold in a shot glass and garnished with a handmade fortune cookie.

A recent addition is the only foreign branch of New York's **Carnegie Deli,** open daily from 7:00 A.M. to 2:00 A.M.; think pastrami, corned beef, blintzes, and cream pies in an Adam Tihany setting. The original Carnegie Deli has stood near Times Square since 1937.

The unusual **Samba Brazilian Steakhouse** is a riot of jungle colors, sounds, and food set in a small, faux rain forest just off the casino floor and open daily from 5:00 to 11:00 P.M. The highlight here is the All You Can Eat Rodizio Experience, and quite a happening it is: The Brazilian barbecue, priced at about $29 per person, includes sausage, turkey, churrasco beef, and salmon. Items are also available a la carte, ranging from about $18 to $37. Specialties include chili-crusted crab cakes, chicken skewers marinated in beer, and mahogany caramelized salmon fillet with red curry sauce.

Onda, a classy Mediterranean eatery, offers entrees by chef Todd English priced from about $20 to $35. Specialties include chicken Saltimbocca, veal scallopini over Parmesan risotto, traditional Italian neighborhood lasagna, and pan-roasted Chilean sea bass over shrimp and Swiss chard. Open for dinner from 5:30 to 11:00 P.M.

Kokomo's specializes in steaks and seafood in an "outdoor" setting within the atrium's tropical rain forest. Specialties include oven-roasted ginger soy marinated Chilean sea bass, blackened swordfish with spicy shrimp Cajun sauce, American Kobe steak, lobster, and crab. Open daily for dinner from 5:00 to 10:30 P.M. Entrees range from about $25 to $40.

An interesting alternative for lunch, or for dinner, is the **California Pizza Kitchen,** located near the sports bar. They use wood-fired ovens to create some of the strangest—and tastiest—pizzas in town: Jamaica jerk chicken, Peking duck, grilled garlic shrimp, and wild mushroom among them. Pies go for about $10 for individual size; also available are salads and pasta dishes. No reservations are accepted, and lines can build during busy times. Open Sunday to Thursday, 11:00 A.M. to midnight; Friday and Saturday, 11:00 to 2:00 A.M.

Cravings, the Mirage buffet (renamed following a major reconstruction in 2004) is located in an attractive, bright room just off the casino floor; it features new action stations and decor by Las Vegas favorite Adam Tihany.

The Mirage. 3400 Las Vegas Boulevard South. 3,044 rooms. Standard room rates $79 to $599. (702) 791–7111, (800) 627–6667. www.mirage.com.

★★★★ MONTE CARLO RESORT & CASINO

A tip of the hat to one of the classic gambling palaces of Europe—the famed Place du Casino in Monaco—the Monte Carlo Resort & Casino brings fanciful arches, chandeliered domes, marble floors, ornate fountains, and gaslit promenades to the Las Vegas desert.

The thirty-two-floor tower, with 3,002 rooms including 259 suites, is located on the west side of the Strip between Flamingo Road and Tropicana Avenue.

Within the Monte Carlo is an outpost of **Andre's French Restaurant,** a longtime insiders' favorite in its location near downtown Las Vegas. The two-story hotel restaurant, designed as a Renaissance chateau and outfitted with Versace china and Sambonnet silver, seats fifty-five downstairs and forty-two upstairs in three small dining rooms. Entrees range from about $26 to $38 and include homemade duck foie gras, tuna tartare, Provimi veal, venison, and Muscovy duck breast. Other specialties include baked poussin with dried fruit Madeira tarragon sauce, sautéed venison with sauce poivrade, and oven-roasted halibut in port wine.

Owner Andre Rochat's wine menu offers more than 1,000 selections. Open daily, 6.00 to 11.00 P.M. For more information consult www.andresfrenchrest .com.

Blackstone's Steak House offers hearty meals. Named for magician Harry Blackstone, this is an old-fashioned beefery with leaded-glass windows, giltframed posters, and mirrors. The menu features mesquite-grilled steaks and seafood entrees, with entrees starting at about $20.

The **Market City Caffé** offers Italian fare served in whopping portions at moderate prices, starting at about $14. A huge antipasto bar features a host of delicacies such as marinated fennel, grilled eggplant, and fresh mussels. The main menu includes pastas, pizzas, and grilled entrees.

The **Dragon Noodle Company** restaurant and tea shop offers quick Asian entrees. For more information consult www.dragonnoodleco.com.

The **Monte Carlo Pub & Brewery** features half a dozen specialty ales brewed on the premises that accompany fresh pizzas, sandwiches, and pasta; the setting is an old warehouse. Six styles of beer are produced regularly, including Las Vegas Lites, Winner's Wheat, High Roller Red, Silver State Stout, Jackpot Pale, and Brewmaster Special. You can buy a pint for $5.95, a sampler of all six brews for $7.95, or a gargantuan spigot jar of 166 ounces of beer for $24.95. Over the course of a year, the gleaming copper brewery produces about 108,000 gallons.

There's also a food court with Nathan's, McDonald's, Sbarro, and more.

Outside is an exotic pool area with waterfalls, a pool and spa, a wave pool, and an inner-tube ride. There's also a Surf Pond with twelve cannons that force strong currents of air into the water, creating surf up to 10 feet high.

Magician Lance Burton, a Las Vegas staple, performs in the 1,200-seat **Lance Burton Theatre.** In 2006 Burton celebrated his tenth year at the casino by unveiling a new illusion, *The Solid Gold Lady.* If everything goes right, Burton manages to make $10 million in real gold bricks disappear. According to the Monte Carlo management, the bricks are somehow returned to their vault each night and brought back on stage the next day by armed security guards. Tickets in 2006 ranged from about $67 to $73. The show is presented nightly except Sunday and Monday.

The $344 million resort was originally a joint venture between Mirage Resorts and Mandalay Resort Group. Today those two companies are subsumed within the huge MGM Mirage Company.

Monte Carlo Resort & Casino. 3770 Las Vegas Boulevard South. 3,002 rooms. Standard room rates $69 to $299. (702) 730–7777, (800) 311–8999. www.monte-carlo.com.

★★★★ NEW YORK–NEW YORK HOTEL & CASINO

At the northwest corner of Tropicana and the Strip, the Statue of Liberty faces the MGM Lion and holds her lamp high against the wretched excesses of the Excalibur castle.

In a town of superlatives, somehow the designers of New York–New York have managed to pull off a relative miracle: This casino and hotel is candy for the eyes and a whole lot of fun both inside and out. The Strip has been heading in this direction for some time: New York–New York is where Universal Studios meets Las Vegas. I kept looking for King Kong.

This place has added a metropolitan skyline to the south end of the Strip: a re-creation of Manhattan, complete with a dozen "skyscrapers" including replicas of the Empire State Building, the Chrysler Building, the AT&T Building, the 55 Water Tower, and other landmarks of Manhattan. Out front is a 150-foot-tall replica of the Statue of Liberty and a re-creation of the famed Brooklyn Bridge.

The $460 million project began as a joint venture of MGM Grand and Primadonna Resorts, which operated three successful casinos and resorts on the Nevada-California state line: Buffalo Bill's Resort & Casino, the Primadonna Resort & Casino, and Whiskey Pete's Hotel & Casino. In 1998 Primadonna was purchased by MGM Grand.

The twelve towers, which contain the hotel rooms, are built at about one-third scale with some clever touches that make them seem real. The tallest, of course, is the Empire State Building, which even in its reduced scale stands 529 feet tall, making it the tallest in Nevada.

Inside the eighteen-acre casino area are New York neighborhoods and landmarks including the Ellis Island Immigrant Receiving Station (the registration desk), a (plastic) tree-filled Central Park, Grand Central Station Terminal, and Wall Street. You can stroll the narrow lanes of a romanticized Greenwich Village.

There's also the Coney Island Emporium, an amusement area with carnival games, arcade machines, bumper cars, laser tag, and a fiber-optic fireworks show. Nearby is the entrance to the Manhattan Express, a wild roller coaster that twists, loops, and dives around the perimeter and through the center of the hotel like a subway train gone berserk. For more details see chapter 10.

If you fancy a royal flush, you might want to visit the **Rockefeller Restrooms** near the front entrance. The rooms are outfitted with ornate Murano crystal chandeliers and wall sconces, pedestal sinks with ornamental touchless faucets, gilded mirror frames, custom tile, and paintings of Mae West over marble and painted fireplaces. There's indoor plumbing, too, just like in New York.

New York–New York

Restaurants include **Il Fornaio,** where each month a different chef celebrates a particular region of Italy; entrees range from about $12 to $40. There's also an Il Fornaio Bakery, offering all manner of biscotti, cornettos, espresso, and cappuccino. Open daily for breakfast and dinner.

Nine Fine Irishmen is a pub named after an Irish ballad about unwanted citizens shipped from the United Kingdom to Australia in the 1800s; through various twists and turns, each of them went on to distinguished lives—as a prime minister of Australia, a governor of the state of Montana, a U.S. Army brigadier general, and members of parliament in Canada and the United Kingdom.

Located off the casino floor, it is still a loud and raucous place at dinnertime. The interesting but limited menu includes colcannon (an Irish potato soup), grilled oysters with champagne and caramelized onions, seared beef salad with horseradish, beer-battered fish and chips, and gourmet Irish sausage. Among the eatery's signature dishes is a grilled Irish goat cheese salad. Entrees range in price from $15 to $21, and there's a nice selection of Irish and other beers.

The interior replicates the style of many actual pubs in Ireland, with Victorian details. The pub is open daily from 8:00 A.M. to 11:00 P.M. for breakfast, lunch, and dinner. For more information about the pub and its offerings, consult www .ninefineirishmen.com.

Gallagher's Steakhouse brings a New York beef emporium that has served Gotham since 1927; outside its doors on the casino floor is a huge freezer with several steers' worth of aging beef. Specialties, beginning at about $20 and rising to $40 or more, include steaks, chops, and ribs with sauces including béarnaise, lemon-lime butter, brandied peppercorn, and caramelized shallot and Beaujolais. Open daily from 4:00 to 11:00 P.M. on weekdays and until midnight on weekends.

Chin Chin Café, a Los Angeles favorite, offers gourmet Chinese fare prepared in an exhibition kitchen, with entrees beginning at about $20. Specialties include shredded chicken salad, spicy seafood noodles, and dim sum. Open daily from 11:00 A.M. to 11:00 P.M. on weekdays and until midnight on weekends.

Gonzalez Y Gonzalez is a Mexican cafe with an outdoor courtyard, complete with lanterns, piñatas, and a tequila bar. Entrees, beginning at about $15, include enchiladas, tacos, chimichangas, and flautas to be washed down with imported beer, tequila, or frozen margaritas sold by the yard.

Coyote Ugly is a raucous bar inspired by the film of the same name that was based on a Manhattan bar . . . called Coyote Ugly. The Southern-style saloon, open nightly, is run by a squad of determinedly sassy female bartenders, who pour drinks and perform stunts ranging from flame shooting to dancing on top of the bar. There is also a "hall of fame" for various undergarments left behind by visitors. The cafe is open daily from 11:00 A.M. to 11:00 P.M. on weekdays and until midnight on weekends.

The **ESPN Zone** offers the Screening Room with tiered seating for broadcasts of live sporting events, the Sports Arena to challenge fans with interactive and competitive attractions, and the Studio Grill restaurant. More than 165 television monitors are spread throughout the sprawling two-story venue; it's all but impossible to miss a moment of a televised game, even in the restrooms. State-of-the-art production capabilities include facilities to broadcast radio and television programs from the site with links to ESPN Zones around the country and to ESPN Studios in Connecticut. The club is open daily from 11:00 or 11:30 A.M. until past midnight. For more information on the concept, you can check out www.espnzone.com.

America, a twenty-four-hour restaurant, offers a road trip around the country that includes menu items from across the nation, priced from about $12. You'll find buffalo wings, Philly cheesesteak, New England clam chowder, Texas barbecue baby back ribs, and more.

For casual dining, the most enticing part of New York–New York is at the back of the casino floor, a high-tone food court with streetscapes of New York City. Steam rises from manhole covers, tables are set on porches of brownstones, and overhead the roller coaster zooms by like a demented A-train. Along the cobblestone streets of Greenwich Village, Little Italy, and the Fulton Fish Market areas are some appropriate selections such as bagels, pizza, and hot dogs.

The Broadway Theatre is the home of *Zumanity,* an "adult" version of strangeness from Cirque du Soleil. A cast of fifty unusual and flirtatious performers—in suggestive clothing and acts—do their thing in a ninety-minute exotic and erotic show, with famed drag diva Joey Arias serving as the "Mistress of Seduction," an MC unlike most you may have run into before. Guests can buy cabaret stools, theater seats, love seats, and duo sofas. Tickets range in price from $65 to $95 for stools and seats to $125 for sofa seats. There's also a package deal that includes dinner at Nine Fine Irishmen and the show. For information call (866) 606–7111, or consult www.zumanity.com.

New York–New York Hotel & Casino. 3790 Las Vegas Boulevard South. 2,024 rooms. Standard room rates $89 to $129. (702) 740–6969, (800) 693–6763. www .nynyhotelcasino.com.

★★★★ PLANET HOLLYWOOD RESORT AND CASINO (Former Aladdin Casino and Resort)

Poof! Aladdin and Sinbad and even Jeannie of the magic lantern will all be faded from memory like the closing credits of a forgettable if not forgotten old movie by the end of 2007 when the Aladdin Casino and Resort completes its Arabian makeover to become Planet Hollywood in Las Vegas.

Midway through 2006 the sands of Arabia began to give way to the glitter of Tinseltown with massive renovation, retheming, and rearranging of the resort; the Aladdin stayed open throughout the makeover, demonstrating the sort of schizophrenia that probably works best only in two places: Las Vegas and Hollywood.

There was a lot of history tied up in the old place, which has one of the longest lineages on the Strip: It opened in 1959 as the Tally Ho; Elvis Presley married Priscilla Beaulieu there in 1967. The first version of the Aladdin vanished in a gala demolition in 1998, and a $1.4 billion makeover opened in 2000; but by 2004 it was back in financial distress once more and was sold to the owners of the Planet Hollywood empire.

Plans call for a new lobby, a revamped casino, and a new race and sports book.

The reworking of public rooms includes the import of some of Planet Hollywood's extensive movie memorabilia collection, the largest in the world. The fanciest of the suites will be themed to particular celebrities and the movies they made. Plans call for Starwood Hotels & Resorts to operate the hotel side of the business as a Sheraton Hotel.

A big part of the new design will be an emphasis on access to the Theater for the Performing Arts from the casino floor. Planet Hollywood announced an agreement with Clear Channel Entertainment to modernize the 7,000-seat Aladdin Theater for the Performing Arts (which may end up with a new name) and bring headliner entertainers to the resort. A new 1,450-seat theater is also planned.

An existing open rotunda between the casino and the large theater is due to receive a great deal of attention, with the installation of a new lounge and video screens that will link the entertainment venue and the casino floor.

The Desert Passage shops, one of the few obviously unsuccessful shopping districts in Las Vegas, will be remade into the Miracle Mile with $50 million in rework inside and out. The concept will make heavy use of massive video screens, fountains, and people movers: Vegas staples, with a Planet Hollywood edge.

One of the magnets of the reborn Miracle Mile will be a large outpost of the hip Urban Outfitters store, and a remodeled Sephora outlet. Also due are Quiksilver and the hipster Ben Sherman's first U.S. clothing store outside of New York. A new Trader Vic's restaurant will offer outdoor patio seating on two levels. When completed the mall will have nearly 160 outlets. Recent additions include United Colors of Benetton, Sisley, Crazy Shirts, BEBE Sport, and Indian River Southwest Gallery.

The new owners say the Miracle Mile will focus on stores with midrange price points. "Not everyone who comes to Las Vegas is out shopping for Prada, Gucci, and Louis Vuitton," an executive said.

Planet Hollywood and the Miracle Mile are also banking on more pedestrian traffic coming in from nearby megadevelopments that are under way, including Project CityCenter and the adjacent $1.8 billion Cosmopolitan resort.

At the southeast corner of the Miracle Mile, a new corridor will connect to the $400 million Planet Hollywood Towers, a fifty-two-story Westgate Resorts' time-share development also due to open sometime in 2007. Magician Steve Wyrick will open a theater in that area. The new blue-glass tower will include more than 800 two-bedroom premium suites; owners can also turn over their properties to the hotel for nightly rental, adding total capacity at Planet Hollywood to more than 4,000 rooms.

Planet Hollywood Resort and Casino. 3667 Las Vegas Boulevard South. Approximately 4,000 rooms. Standard room rates from about $125 to $500. (877) 933–9475. www.aladdincasino.com, www.planethollywood.com.

ECONOGUIDE ★★★ RESORTS

★★★ CIRCUS CIRCUS

From the sublime to the ridiculous, Circus Circus is unique, even in Las Vegas.

For many of us our expectations of Circus Circus were molded by the lurid account of Hunter S. Thompson in his gonzo classic, *Fear and Loathing in Las Vegas.* Just about everything Thompson wrote about in that book, including the acrobats tumbling overhead, the motorcyclists roaring around within a ball, and the general atmosphere of a Roman Circus, is true—although, alas, things are not quite as wild as his mind's eye saw them. (You might also recognize the place from the James Bond thriller, *Diamonds Are Forever.*)

In any case Circus Circus is one of the great grind-joint successes of Las Vegas. It has cheap rooms (including an RV park), cheap meals, and lots and lots of low rollers at the tables. The hotel obviously makes its money on the quantity of action, not the size of the bankrolls at play. (Some wags have called Circus Circus the Kmart of gambling establishments.)

Upstairs over the casino floor is an indoor carnival, midway, and video arcade that will entertain (and draw allowance money from) the kids while their parents drop the rent money downstairs. And then there is the famed circus up over the main casino; the acrobats, rope walkers, jugglers, and other acts perform about once an hour and then disappear so they don't distract too much from the gambling. Shows are presented daily from 11:00 A.M. to midnight.

Rooms at Circus Circus are located in four groups of towers.

The **Manor** is the budget area at the resort, comprising five three-story buildings. A moving walkway located near the front of the Manor area connects to the **Skyrise Tower,** a twenty-nine-story tower that includes a full-size casino facility and pool. The **Casino Tower** consists of two fifteen-story towers, two casinos, a circus arena, midway, a game arcade, multiple dining facilities, the sports book, and a wedding chapel.

The **West Tower,** the most recent construction, is located at the west end of the property. The thirty-five-story tower includes 1,000 rooms and houses the central registration lobby and shopping promenade. A walkway from the tower includes ten retail outlets, entrance to the Circus Circus theme park, and the Steak House.

Circus Circus often has the least expensive major hotel rooms in town; the rooms, especially in the main tower, are ordinary but quite acceptable.

At the back of the hotel is the **Adventuredome,** a five-acre entertainment park that presents a Las Vegas–eye view of the Grand Canyon, including 140-foot man-made peaks, a 90-foot re-creation of Havasupai Falls, and a river. The entire park is covered by a pink dome called the Adventuredome. The Fun House Express is an Imax thrill-ride simulator. See the description of the Adventuredome in chapter 10 of this book.

The **Steak House,** open only for dinner from 5:00 P.M. to midnight, has entrees in the range of $17 to $30 and is one of the better cuts of meat palaces in town. And even nicer, it's a dark, quiet, and private sanctuary from the circus. On Sunday there's a champagne brunch served from 10:00 A.M. to 2:00 P.M. that features steak, filet mignon, and seafood on ice, priced at $25. Reservations are suggested.

MexItalia X-Press, located on the Promenade, offers sauces and spices from two favorite cuisines for lunch and dinner. The **Circus Buffet** is served beneath a red-and-white circus tent ceiling, which is an assault on the eyes even by Las Vegas standards.

The **Pizzeria** features freshly baked pizzas, calzones, and salads and is open from 11:00 A.M. to midnight daily.

Circus Circus Hotel/Casino. 2880 Las Vegas Boulevard South. 3,770 rooms. Standard room rates $39 to $119. (702) 734–0410, (800) 634–3450. www.circus circus.com.

★★★ EXCALIBUR

To truly enjoy this place, you've got to buy into the concept: King Arthur's castle on the Strip.

Excalibur looks as if it were constructed out of a child's toy blocks. It's a place where the staff is drilled to finish conversations with "Have a royal day."

The best approach to the Excalibur is by night. The colors of the 265-foot-tall bell towers and the castle's fairy tale shape are amazing enough, but even weirder when looked at between the Egyptian pyramid of the Luxor and the tropical gardens of the Tropicana. What a city!

As only befitting a place like this, each evening a 51-foot-long fire-breathing dragon battles a robotic Merlin every hour on the hour from 6:00 P.M. until midnight in the moat at the front entrance. "The Glockenspiel Fairy Tale" is played out over the giant clock at the rear entrance, with shows at the top and the bottom of each hour from 10:00 A.M. until 10:00 P.M.

If anything, Excalibur is even more overwhelming inside. The designers seem to have collected all the missing high ceilings from the older casinos on the Strip and taken them to Nevada extremes. More so than at most other places in Vegas, the establishment's theme is carried through in almost every detail—decorations, costumes, restaurants.

In keeping with its orientation—or at least tolerance of families and other more casual visitors—the Excalibur is one of the few casinos in Las Vegas that welcomes cameras: still, movie, and video. (In keeping with state law, though, children younger than twenty-one must keep their distance from slot machines and gambling tables.)

There are no windows within the cavernous interior; one of the only ways to tell the time of day is to listen to the cocktail waitresses. As dawn breaks they add orange juice and coffee to their cocktail offers.

The Excalibur was holder of the title as the world's largest resort hotel for several years with 4,008 rooms in four twenty-eight-floor towers. Today it is certainly the world's largest resort hotel set inside a castle with a moat, a drawbridge, a jousting tournament, and a Western dance hall.

There are four levels to the hotel; you enter from the main parking lot or front entrance to Level I, which is, of course, the casino floor and registration desk. An escalator descends to the lower level Fantasy Faire, home of King Arthur's Arena, the Magic Motion Machines, and Fantasy Faire games. Or you can take an escalator up to Level II, the Medieval Village, home of the Round Table Buffet and other eateries. One more level up takes you to Level III, which includes the Canterbury Wedding Chapel.

The casino is a whopper, with nearly 3,000 slot machines and a hundred blackjack and craps tables, roulette wheels, and more spread out over three acres. The casino includes a central pavilion for high-rolling slot players. The poker room features eighteen regular tables and two Pai Gow poker tables.

The Excalibur's 900-seat showroom is unlike any other in Las Vegas. To begin with, the floor of the stage is dirt rather than polished wood and many of the stars have four legs.

For many years, the evening program has been the *Tournament of Kings,* an original musical production based on the legend of King Arthur. Presented once or twice each night, depending on the season, the show includes jousting, dragons, fire wizards . . . and dinner. Tickets are about $55 per person.

The story begins when Arthur gathers his fellow kings of Europe for a no-holds-barred competition to honor his son Christopher. The competitions, on horseback and on foot, grow increasingly intense. And then just when the party seems over, the evil fire wizard Mordred attacks, threatening to throw the land

The parapets of Excalibur

of Avalon into an age of fire and shadows. I don't want to spoil it for you, but I think you can guess who wins and who loses.

The best seats are in the center; in football terms, at the 50-yard line. Avoid the end zones and stay up high to avoid the dust from the horses. For reservations call (702) 597–7600.

Merlin's Theater has been invaded by the steamy Australia's All-Male Revue: *Thunder from Down Under.* The armor comes off at 7:30 P.M. nightly except Thursday, with tickets priced at about $39.95. Guests must be at least eighteen years of age.

The Medieval Village re-creates a vision of an ancient village, with shops, restaurants, strolling magicians, jugglers, and singers. Free ten-minute shows are presented every half hour on the Court Jester's Stage daily from 10:00 A.M. to 10:00 P.M. Many are a bit on the corny side but fun for the youngsters.

The Fantasy Faire level offers carnival games as well as a pair of "dynamic motion simulators" dubbed Merlin's Magic Motion Machines, which can take riders on a wild ride without ever leaving the room. There are six different "rides," changing during the course of a day, shown in a pair of identical forty-eight-seat theaters. The Fantasy Faire itself is an unusual mix of modern video arcade and pinball machines with medieval-theme carnival games. If you're into shooting galleries, be sure to check out the Electronic Crossbow with its animated, moving figures in the line of fire.

Each of the restaurants at Excalibur is a spectacular exercise in decoration and theme. Some of the food is decent, but overall it's a not-very-distinguished food factory; if you've got the time, cross the road to the Luxor or move on up a full step to the MGM Grand for nearby buffet fare.

The Steakhouse at Camelot offers gourmet dining in an intimate setting reminiscent of a royal chamber in a castle. There's a show kitchen, an impressive wine cellar, and a cigar room. Typical offerings include all the prime cuts of beef, as well as baby back ribs, free-range chicken, cioppino, sea bass, and lobster. With just 144 seats, reservations are necessary at busy times. Open for dinner from 6:00 to 10:00 P.M. Sunday through Thursday and from 5:00 to 11:00 P.M. on Friday, Saturday, and holidays. Entrees range in price from about $19 to $55. For reservations call (702) 597–7449.

Sir Galahad's Pub & Prime Rib House is open every night for dinner at 5:00 P.M. The specialties include prime rib, from the Traditional English cut to the whopping King Arthur cut, priced from about $18 to $26. Seafood and poultry dishes are also available, including pan-seared chicken breast, grilled salmon, and lobster. Reservations are recommended for the 234-seat eatery; call (702) 597–7448.

Regale Italian Eatery is open for lunch and light dinner from 11:00 A.M. to 2:30 P.M. daily and from 5:00 P.M. nightly. The fare is basic Italian, including antipasto, spaghetti, lasagna, and pizza in your basic trattoria setting. Entrees such as lasagna or ravioli and small pizzas are priced from about $11 to $24. Specialties include shrimp scampi and lobster fra diavolo. The "La Familia" special offers family-size portions for two or more; if it's not on the menu, ask for it. For reservations call (702) 597–7443.

The **Sherwood Forest Cafe** is a twenty-four-hour coffee shop with offerings that include Chinese dishes. Entrees range from about $12 to $22.

Some of the best free entertainment in town is beyond the glass wall at the large **Krispy Kreme** donut bakery. You can watch the pastries rise, march into an oil bath, and then shower under a stream of glaze; at the end of the assembly line is a retail counter, of course.

Nearby is the **Cold Stone Creamery,** whose slogan is "if you can dream it, we can ice cream it." They custom-fold nearly every conceivable flavor, fruit, candy, or cookie into your ice cream.

Excalibur is part of the MGM Grand resort group. Room rates start at about $47. The basic rooms are comfortable but a bit garish and inexpensive in appointments.

Excalibur Hotel & Casino. 3850 Las Vegas Boulevard South. 4,008 rooms. Standard room rates $47 to $171. (702) 597–7777, (800) 937–7777. www.excalibur casino.com.

Some Are More Equal than Others

Pay attention to the payoff rates promised on slots and video poker machines. Some machines in the same casino will have different payouts. One way to check this is to look at the payout for a full house in poker; one bank of machines offered a standard 40:1, while another set of machines promised 50:1.

★★★ LUXOR

The real and imagined treasures of another desert empire come to near life in the fabulous Luxor, a 4,408-room, thirty-story, pyramid-shaped complex. The interior of the hotel—a hollow pyramid—is about as spectacular a sight as you'll see on the Strip. The designers of the Luxor conceived of it as a simulation of a vast archaeological dig where the mysteries of ancient Egypt are revealed as though the interior was a vast excavation site. Replicas of Egyptian artifacts, including a full-size reproduction of King Tut's tomb, are on display.

As you approach, the hotel appears to be a huge sand-colored pyramid; the rooms of the hotel occupy the exterior steps of the structure. Out front is a huge replica of the Sphinx, the mythical Egyptian creature with a human head and the body of a lion. The figure was often meant to symbolize the pharaoh as an incarnation of the sun god, Ra. Blazing out of the top of the pyramid is a forty-billion-candlepower light that's claimed to be the most powerful beam of light in the world; orbiting Space Shuttle crewmembers fulfilled a PR person's dream when they reported seeing it from space. The light is actually forty-seven separate xenon units mounted in the top of the pyramid.

A computer-controlled light system makes the understated resort visible for Earthbound visitors as well; there are some 3,000 strobes in a special-effects display that send streaks of light up the sides of the pyramid.

To the pharaohs the pyramid was a symbol of eternal life, considered a "stairway to the stars." In the Las Vegas version, the Hanging Gardens of Babylon occupy the front entrance, while lagoonlike pools and a beach are at the rear entrance.

Since its opening the Luxor has gone upscale a bit, eliminating a few touristy gimmicks such as a river cruise and some of the less-than-extraordinary multimedia shows. The lobby and public areas have received handsome new appointments, and a semiprivate baccarat and high-limit gaming area has taken center stage in the casino.

Within the pyramid guests are transported to their floors on inclined elevators moving at a thirty-nine-degree angle up the sides or on more conventional vertical lifts.

The rooms themselves have an unusual feature that may be a bit disconcerting to some visitors; the outside window wall is slanted sharply because it is part of the exterior of the pyramid. Other visitors may find the view of the interior atrium a bit dizzying; interior balconies extend to the twenty-seventh floor, while the top three floors—mostly suites—have interior hallways. And residents of one of the first few floors of the hotel may find a great deal of pedestrian traffic right outside their doors. There are also two conventional hotel towers that do not have angled walls.

The 90,000-square-foot casino is decorated with reproductions of artifacts, columns, and tombs found in the temples of Luxor and Karnak.

Caffe Giorgio, based on the fare of Piero Selvaggio and Lucciano Pellegrini, features a northern Italian menu with specialties like lasagna a la Bolognese layered with veal ragu and a rich béchamel sauce; and pappa al pomodoro, a comforting thick Tuscan tomato soup made with day-old bread. Also featured are

Luxor

pizzas, gelati, desserts, assorted appetizers, and antipasti. The restaurant is open daily from 11:00 A.M. to 10:30 P.M.

For hearty appetites there's the **Luxor Steak House,** an elegant eatery on the casino level paneled in cherry wood. Steaks and chops are priced from about $25 to $40. Appetizers include cream of watercress soup. Dinner is served nightly from 5:00 to 11:00 P.M. For reservations call (702) 262–4778.

On the atrium level is **Fusia,** home to "new Chinese cuisine." Appetizers include blue crab rock shrimp rolls and spicy salt-and-pepper calamari. Specialties include white miso-lacquered sea bass with sambal aioli, Mongolian or Thai wok beef, "untraditional" sweet-and-sour chicken, and macadamia nut–glazed chicken. Open daily for dinner from 5:00 to 11:00 P.M., entrees range in price from about $16 to $40. Reservations are suggested at (702) 262–4774.

The menu at the **Pyramid Cafe** offers a wide range of salads plus entrees including burgers, grilled Pacific salmon, and fried chicken, starting at about $7.00.

Think of the **Backstage Deli,** located on the casino level near the Luxor Theater, as a New York Jewish delicatessen on the banks of the Nile. Large sandwiches, Philly cheesesteaks, Reubens, lox on a bagel, and other delicacies are priced from about $7.00 to $10.00.

La Salsa is a relatively inexpensive Mexican eatery.

The buffet at the Luxor is the awkwardly named **Pharaoh's Pheast,** which replaced the strangely named Manhattan Buffet beneath the apex of the pyramid.

There is, of course, an ancient shopping bazaar. The hotel features a 1,200-seat showroom for a nightly special-effects production show; the entrance to the arena resembles the ancient tombs of the pharaohs in the Valley of the Kings.

The third level offers the **Luxor Imax Theatre,** the **King Tut Museum,** and a set of multimedia attractions of varying appeal. For details see the section on Las Vegas attractions in chapter 10.

Two stepped, pyramid-shaped towers, located between Luxor and Excalibur, added 1,950 guest rooms in recent years. A moving walkway, located between the East and West Towers, transports guests to and from Excalibur.

Luxor's splashy lounge is **RA,** which features a spectacular light-and-sound system and nonstop dance music. The club includes a sushi and oyster bar, luxury VIP booths, and valet service. RA is open Wednesday through Saturday from 10:00 P.M. to 6:00 A.M. A semiformal dress code is enforced.

Luxor's Oasis Spa features sixteen treatment rooms, circuit training and weight rooms, a full range of body treatments, hydrotherapy, and the like.

Giza Galleria in the East Tower adds shops that include the Cairo Bazaar, offering Egyptian antiquities and artifacts; Treasure Chamber, selling what are billed as real treasures from royal tombs; and jewelry and clothing stores.

The Egyptian-themed Luxor Theater offers 1,200 theater-style seats. For several years this was the home of the unworldly Blue Man Group, until it moved north up the Strip. Next to visit was another extraterrestrial treat, a version of the Broadway show *Hairspray*, which was in turn based on the enchantingly strange movie of the same name by the unique author-director John Waters. The theater is located at the southwest corner of the pyramid and connects to the main casino by a dramatic foyer.

The smaller Atrium Showroom is used for headliner acts; in 2006 the comedian Carrot Top signed for a lengthy engagement.

And then there is **Fantasy,** your basic topless singing, dancing, and teasing Las Vegas show; and as befits this strange place, the midnight show takes place at 8:30 and 10:30 P.M. on Tuesday, Thursday, and Saturday; on Wednesday and Friday there is a single late show; and on Sunday there's a single early show. Tickets in 2006 were priced at about $45. For show information call (702) 262–4400.

The rooms are nicely appointed, from standard guest rooms (as low as $59 in off-season and more than twice that during conventions and at peak times) to the Jacuzzi Suites (starting at $150) and the spectacular upper level rooms that include the Presidential Suite, which rents for several thousand dollars per night.

Moving walkways transport you up from the casino at Luxor, across Tropicana Avenue, and down into the Excalibur, a journey from ancient Egypt to merry olde England. You can also cross over Tropicana Avenue to the New York–New York casino and from there across the Strip to the MGM Grand.

Luxor is part of the MGM Mirage group, which includes the MGM Grand, the Mirage, Circus Circus, Excalibur, Monte Carlo, and New York–New York.

Luxor Hotel/Casino. 3900 Las Vegas Boulevard South. 4,408 rooms. Standard room rates $59 to $399. (702) 262–4000, (800) 288–1000. www.luxor.com.

★★★ STRATOSPHERE CASINO HOTEL & TOWER

In modern-day Las Vegas every hotel and casino needs a "hook" to draw the crowds. The Stratosphere, which opened in the spring of 1996, offers the highest hook of them all: the nation's tallest freestanding observation tower at 1,149 feet.

In Las Vegas, where so much is simulated and re-created, the Stratosphere Tower is the real thing. Four high-speed, double-deck elevators travel at 1,400 feet per minute, zooming visitors to the top of the tower—three times taller than any other building in Las Vegas—in forty seconds.

Just to make things even more wild, there are three thrill rides bolted to the tower (we trust) more than a hundred stories in the air: the **Big Shot** zero-gravity ride and the **High Roller,** the world's highest roller coaster that starts at 909 feet aboveground and zooms around the Tower's pod. There's also **X-Scream,** which propels riders up to and over the edge. For details see chapter 10.

Oh, and there is a sprawling, colorful casino with a World's Fair theme at the base of the tower . . . and 2,444 suites and guest rooms.

Inside is Las Vegas's first Eiffel Tower, or at least a plywood cutout version of the lower legs. (The second set of legs is within the Paris Las Vegas casino, and the third, a scaled-down replica of the whole thing, rises outside Paris Las Vegas on the Strip.)

The place is huge, even stratospheric; at times, though, it may seem hollow within. Many rooms are booked by package tours or conventioneers. The 97,000-square-foot casino sports about 2,400 slot machines and sixty tables.

The casino has more than its share of penny and nickel slots and a McDonald's. But it's still a lively and attractive place and unusual on the Strip in offering some windows to the outside world at the casino level as well as the fantastic views from the top. In other words, there's a nod to the world out there. . . .

The tower began life as the creation of the wild and woolly Bob Stupak, the creator of the Vegas World Casino that previously stood on the site. Groundbreaking took place in 1991 with completion in April 1996—an unusually long time in speedy Las Vegas. The delays were caused by the escalating financial and operational problems faced by the freewheeling Stupak.

Las Vegas is subject to earthquakes, harsh desert winds, and the occasional nearby underground nuclear test. The designers assure us this has all been taken into account with computer simulations and wind tunnel testing.

The legacy of Stupak, and the casino's location in a spot midway between the Strip and downtown Las Vegas, contributed to financial difficulties for the Stratosphere, and the place entered into bankruptcy proceedings in late 1997.

The current majority owner is famed corporate raider Carl Icahn, who also operates Arizona Charlie's East and Arizona Charlie's in Las Vegas. An expansion added a twenty-four-story tower with 1,002 guest rooms in late 2001, taking the overall number of rooms to 2,444. On the sixth floor of the tower is a one-and-a-half-acre pool and recreation deck.

The Stratosphere Buffet includes cooking stations for pizza, Mexican, rotisserie meats, and eggs made to order.

The prime restaurant is **Top of the World.** At 833 feet in the air, you'll come for the view but stay to enjoy the meal. The revolving restaurant—one complete circuit per hour—features steaks and seafood, with entrees starting at $30. Along with the spectacular view of the Strip and the Las Vegas Valley, there is also an outdoor and a glassed-in observation platform and three wedding chapels. Open for dinner from 5:00 to 11:00 P.M. nightly, until midnight on Friday and Saturday. For reservations call (702) 380–7711.

The lounge, one floor above on Level 107, was improved in 2006 and re-named **Romance at the Top of the World.**

One of the jumpingest joints at the Stratosphere is the **Crazy Armadillo Tex-Mex Grill and Oyster Bar.** Set in a wild south-of-the-border cantina, Mexican dishes include hard- and soft-shell tacos, enchiladas, and fajitas. Specialties include *albóndigas* meatball soup and *camarones al mojo de ajo,* shrimp in garlic sauce. On the Tex-Mex and Southwest menu, selections include baby back ribs.

At the Tequila Sky Bar, bartenders juggle bottles of tequila, beer, and other fine spirits when they're not dancing on top of the bar with the Shooter Girls.

The Crazy Armadillo is adjacent to the Courtyard Buffet. It is open Thursday through Monday nights. The Oyster Bar opens at 4:00 P.M., seven days a week.

Fellini's Ristorante Italiano serves Italian food at moderate prices and is open for dinner nightly. For reservations call (702) 380–7711.

For a good-old American pie, sandwich, and a milkshake, you can visit **Roxy's Diner,** frozen in the rocking '50s and open twenty-four hours a day.

Naga is an Asian bistro and sushi bar, elaborately decorated in traditional art and colors; there is seating at the bar or on a patio with a view of the casino. Naga replaced the Hamada Asian Village. Open nightly except Monday and Tuesday.

The rooms in the World Tower rent for about $49 to $199; the rooms in the renovated Regency Tower start at about $69.

The observation deck atop the tower is open from 9:00 to 1:00 A.M. Sunday through Thursday, and until 2:00 A.M. on Friday, Saturday, and holidays. Admission is $9.95 for adults, $6.00 for children ages four to twelve and seniors ages fifty-five and older. Combination tickets with the thrill rides are also available and described in chapter 10. For information on the rides, call (702) 380–7777.

The entire history of the Stratosphere has been one of controversy and oddity, and there is no sign that it will come to an end. In late 2001 the Las Vegas City Council failed to approve a spectacular new thrill ride that would have taken visitors most of the way up one of the legs of the 1,149-foot tower and then dropped them on a track that would have crossed Las Vegas Boulevard at speeds of more than 120 miles per hour. Local residents somehow managed to convince politicians that this would have detracted from the value of their nearby homes. In response, Stratosphere executives said they might resurrect a plan to install a huge mechanical gorilla that would climb the tower—with passengers within. That project was actually approved by the city but was never built.

In 2005 **Insanity: The Ride** opened, spinning guests out from the top of the tower like prongs on an eggbeater. An arm reaches out 64 feet into space and then the spinning—at angles of as much as seventy degrees—begins.

Stratosphere Casino Hotel & Tower. 2000 Las Vegas Boulevard South. 2,444 rooms. Standard room rates $49 to $199. (702) 380–7777, (800) 998–6937. www.stratospherehotel.com.

★★★ TREASURE ISLAND

Who says there's no sense of irony in Las Vegas? How better to explain the creation of a casino with a pirate theme. At Treasure Island the pirates are out front as well as inside. (And just for the record, in recent years management has been trying to convince us all to call the place "TI" . . . which stands for . . .)

Of course in Vegas it's important to keep current with the latest (and the oldest) trends in town: The free show on the Strip was updated to emphasize that old favorite—damsels in distress, in short dresses. The twenty-minute show, *The Sirens of TI*, features a shipload of strong and sensual women who successfully battle it out with a band of renegade male pirates. The special effects are impressive and the songs bouncy; don't spend too much time trying to discern a deeper meaning, though. Well if you insist, here's a bit of a description: The sailing vessel *Song*, a ghostly ship crewed by an attractive cast of singing Sirens, is parked up against the left side of the entrance to the Mirage. In a mist of fog and the rumble of a growing storm, around the corner arrives the *Bull*, full of sailors.

A brave, or perhaps foolish, young man navigates his way across the choppy waters in a skiff, drawn by the haunting voices of the Sirens. Aboard ship the music swells as more Sirens seem to fall from the sky, closing in on the sailor, Eros, from all sides, challenging him in a teasing test of agility and strength. He fights and loses, dropping his sword and running up the spiral staircase only to be stopped by Sinnamon ("call me 'Sin'"), the Siren of Sirens.

As Sin begins to sing, she summons a tempest. Each crack of her whip sends electrical charges raining down on the *Bull*, a song of war. The panicked pirates struggle to save their ship. In a final blow, a massive lightning strike topples the bowsprit, blowing a hole; the pirates abandon ship and swim away into the darkness.

Eros, on his knees, asks Sin, "Why did it have to end this way?" She turns to the crowd. "You didn't really think it would end this way?"

With a barrage of rock 'n' roll lighting and pyrotechnics, the doors above the *Song* explode outward, revealing DJ Siren Sandy. The ship becomes the stage for a live concert as the Sirens summon the wet pirates to the deck of their ship from the cold waters below and revive them as only Sirens can.

Finally, the Sirens dance their way into TI, inviting all to join them inside to party the night away.

Admission to the show—presented nightly at 7:00, 8:30, 10:00, and 11:30 P.M.—is free, and there is standing-room space around the lagoon. For a better view you can purchase a ticket for a position on the Cove Deck; admission includes one drink.

As part of the update, the skull and crossed-swords marquee that had marked the hotel from the Strip is gone, replaced by a new high-tech video display and marked with a "TI" logo. And the hotel's walls were painted a darker, terra-cotta color.

At the heart of all the changes is a move away from all things family related and a rededication to the adult audience.

The **Tangerine Lounge & Nightclub** is run by a seductive staff of beautiful bartenders and burlesque dancers who bring back the speakeasy style of the

Treasure Island

1920s with costumes from evening attire down to barely-there garter belts. Tangerine features an indoor lounge and outdoor deck with a Las Vegas Strip view.

Treasure Island opened with a bang at the end of 1993 just north of its corporate cousin, the Mirage; the two hotels are connected by an automated tram. Both Treasure Island and the Mirage, along with Bellagio—all created by Stephen Wynn—were taken over by MGM Grand Inc., in early 2000.

Built at an original cost of $430 million, the Treasure Island resort includes 2,900 guest rooms with 212 suites in three thirty-six-floor towers. All rooms and suites have floor-to-ceiling windows.

Other facilities include Pirates Walk, a glittering main-street village lined with retail shops, two wedding chapels, and a lavish tropical pool with a slide, two cocktail bars, and a snack bar.

And a crossover bridge from Treasure Island, near the race and sports book, connects to the expanded Fashion Show Mall on the other side of Spring Mountain Road.

For reservations at most restaurants at Treasure Island, call (800) 944–3777 or (702) 894–7223.

Mist at Treasure Island, from the creators of Light at Bellagio, is a mix of a comfortable neighborhood bar with state-of-the-art technology and high-tech entertainment. Guests can relax and watch their favorite game or music video on one of the oversize plasma televisions. New in late 2006 was **Social House,** a sushi-sake-socialization scene. There is indoor seating as well as patio tables with a menu featuring a range of pan-Asian specialties such as orange peel miso-marinated cod and Snake River Farms Kobe beef served three ways: carpaccio, tataki, and tartare. There's also a live DJ, and technologies include hydraulic lifts that convert dining tables to cocktail tables later at night.

The **Steak House** is a very elegant and quiet hideaway with a setting of an educated pirate's booty-filled library. Entrees range from about $19 to $40, including cioppino, mesquite-grilled salmon, crackling pork shank, and steak with crabmeat and béarnaise sauce. Open daily 5:30 to 11:00 P.M. Children younger than five years old are not allowed.

Isla Mexican Kitchen and Tequila Bar is an upscale Mexican eatery from renowned restaurateur Richard Sandoval. Signature items include grilled spiced chicken breast with corn dumplings and pico de gallo; crispy red snapper with cactus salad and citrus epazote vinaigrette; and Isla sirloin with huitlacoche mashed potatoes and chimichurri sauce. Open daily from 4:00 to 11:00 P.M.

At **Canter's Deli,** a transplant of the Los Angeles favorite, the food is mahvelous and the staff is a lot less thrilled to see you than you are to see the menu. Canter's, in business in LA since 1931, claims to have sold more than ten million matzo balls, two million pounds of lox, and twenty-four million bowls of chicken soup . . . and that was before opening in Las Vegas.

Francesco's promises fine cooking like your momma probably never made, with entrees priced from about $18 to $58. Samples from the menu include fusilli pasta with duck prosciutto, tagliolini pasta with porcino mushrooms and black truffles, roasted whole dorade, and beef tenderloin with scamorza cheese. Open daily 5:30 to 11:00 P.M. Children younger than five are not allowed.

The **Kahunaville Tropical Restaurant and Bar,** located across from the Mystère Theatre, promises a taste of the tropics in an island paradise setting of purples, greens, and coral. The casual eatery is open daily for lunch and dinner, staying open for late dining until 4:00 A.M. on weekends. Specialties include lobster fritters, Jamaican jerk chicken satay, and coconut-crusted Thai shrimp.

The **Breeze Bar,** just off the casino, offers signature drinks including the Blue Goose, Breeze-Sling, and Perfect Ten.

The **Terrace Cafe** is a high-toned, twenty-four-hour coffee shop overlooking the swimming pool that offers dishes such as salmon, halibut, potpie, and burgers. Prices range from about $5.00 to $13.00.

The **Buffet at TI** is a flashy upscale smorgasbord with six live-action exhibition stations including barbecue, Asian, pasta sauté, a rustic pizza oven, a salad station, and a bakery. There's also a roving chili cart featuring two varieties of regional American chili. On Friday and Saturday nights, a selection of upgraded entree items, such as lobster ravioli, crab legs, peel-and-eat shrimp, and assorted soufflés, are offered at each station.

As for the casino: a sprawling 90,000-square-foot affair.

Entertainment at Treasure Island is built around a permanent 1,500-seat home for the Cirque du Soleil's **Mystère.** What we've got here is a one-ring human circus without animals, air cannons, motorcycles, or the other high-tech trappings of other shows. The emphasis is on strange and wonderful human performances. In 2006 tickets were priced from $60 to $95 for adults. Shows were presented Wednesday through Sunday nights at 7:30 and 10:30 P.M. To reserve tickets call (800) 392–1999 or (702) 796–9999.

Treasure Island at the Mirage. 3300 Las Vegas Boulevard South. 2,900 rooms. Standard room rates $79 to $599. (702) 894–7111, (800) 944–7444. www.treasure island.com.

CHAPTER SEVEN

THE REST OF THE STRIP

The Rest of the Strip

★★★ **Palms Casino Resort.** *A hot new local favorite off the Strip.*

★★★ **Sahara.** *A casbah with a coaster.*

★★★ **Westin Casuarina.** *A hotel with a casino, not the other way around.*

★★ **Bally's.** *Bally-who? Attractive but generic*

★★ **Flamingo Las Vegas.** *Bugsy sleeps with the fishes; the casino's tired, too.*

★★ **Harrah's Las Vegas.** *Old school, with some modern flash.*

★★ **Hooters Las Vegas.** *Surprisingly tame in a Las Vegas setting.*

★★ **Orleans.** *High-end for the low rollers.*

★★ **Tropicana.** *Squeezed out.*

★ **Barbary Coast.** *Shaky old San Francisco.*

★ **Gold Coast.** *Coasting along.*

★ **Imperial Palace.** *The parking garage is its best feature.*

★ **Palace Station.** *Lively locals.*

★ **Riviera.** *Old money.*

O'Shea's. *Low-roller mecca on the Strip.*

Terrible's. *Oil, lube, and slots.*

ECONOGUIDE ★★★ RESORTS

★★★ PALMS CASINO RESORT

Full of flash, locals, and the occasional celebrity, the Palms has been the latest unexpected surprise success in high-rolling Las Vegas. The relatively unspectacular casino resort, half a mile off the Strip on West Flamingo Road and without a connection to one of the major gaming companies, became a favorite of people who are famous for being famous. Clever marketing, including sponsorship of gaming, sports, and other tournaments, drew a great deal of attention . . . and money.

In late 2006 the resort opened a $300 million, forty-story Playboy tower, featuring the first Playboy Club in Las Vegas—in fact the first bunny club in more than two decades. The new tower, complete with the Playboy logo, includes a recording studio.

At the same time, a third tower, the forty-nine-story Palms Place luxury condo-hotel was under construction. When finished by early 2008, there will be about 600 units selling for as much as $1,500 per square foot. Palms Place will connect to the Palms hotel through the SkyTube, an enclosed moving walkway. The tower will include its own gated entry, a 60,000-square-foot pool and spa, valet parking, room service, a two-story conservatory, and business center.

The new trend toward condo-hotels includes the Residences at MGM, which is a resort under the Trump name, and the Platinum and Viera at Lake Las Vegas. Owners can allow the developer to rent out their units when they are not occupying them, sharing the revenue.

The Palms first opened at the end of 2001, built around a forty-two-story hotel tower with 455 supersize guest rooms, a fourteen-theater cinema multiplex, and a huge casino with 2,200 machines, a sprawling race and sports book, and a drive-up betting window.

The expansive casino has some exterior neon and art deco–like touches but within is hollow like a huge shopping mall. At the core is a food court with a McDonald's and a Panda Express and a multiplex movie theater.

Around the periphery of the casino are nickel slots and even a few machines that will eat pennies. Just off the floor is the Cosmic Corner, for emergency psychic readings.

Rain in the Desert is a multilevel nightclub and concert venue with a computer-programmed river of water and shooting flame from above. There are private booths and skyboxes available for high rollers and serious partygoers.

The elaborate **Spa at the Palms** offers some unusual indulgences: yoga classes by candlelight and Botox/collagen parties.

The **Skin Pool Lounge** offers officially sanctioned voyeurism. The lounge includes an elevated pool with portholes, the better to study the mermaids swimming within. By night the lounge includes a concert stage, fog machines, and dance platforms with aquatic go-go girls.

Featured restaurants at the Palms include Little Buddha Café from Paris and Nine from Chicago. The **Blue Agave Oyster and Chile Bar** offers more than 350 margaritas and 150 tequilas. Way up on the fifty-fifth floor, the **Ghost Bar** claims the title as the hippest joint at the Palms, an indoor-outdoor lounge with a spectacular view of the Las Vegas skyline. Decorated in cool silver, white, and gray within, doors open to an open-air sky deck.

The **Little Buddha Café** captures the eclectic atmosphere and style of the Buddha Bar, the cafe's sister restaurant in Paris. The menu for the high-tone Asian eatery is displayed on an attractive plasma screen display outside.

Appetizers, priced from about $6.00 to $8.00, include spring rolls, dumplings, and lettuce wraps. Entrees, priced from about $9.00 to $20.00, include Mongolian beef, seared sesame tuna, and spicy Szechuan shrimp.

Garduño's at the Palms is a Las Vegas favorite, installed in a new room at the Palms just off the casino floor. Specialties, priced from about $9.00 to $15.00, include tacos, enchiladas, fajitas, and chili dishes.

Steak House Nine is a Chicago import, serving prime aged steak and fresh seafood and offering a champagne and caviar bar.

Gourmet French chef André Rochat, operator of local favorite Andre's, oversees **Alizé**, on the top floor of the hotel-casino. Recent menus include entrees priced from about $30 to $40, including roasted stuffed saddle of Sonoma rabbit, rack of lamb, and fish and lobster dishes. Appetizers begin with Caspian Black Sea Caviar, priced from $60 to $95 per ounce.

The **Sunrise Café**, patterned after the successful Max's Cafés in San Francisco, is a casual Las Vegas version of an authentic New York deli.

The **Fantasy Market Buffet**, open for breakfast, lunch, and dinner, features six serving stations for international specialties, including a variety of Asian dishes. The Middle Eastern section includes a feta-and-olive bar and Lebanese dishes. A smoker prepares entrees in the delicatessen and barbecue area.

The **Brenden Theatres at the Palms** include fourteen auditoriums ranging in size from about 100 to 500 seats, with stadium seating, rocking chairs, and love seats. For those who spend the time to watch the film, the theaters offer digital sound and Lucasfilm THX audio. At the same time, the theaters hark back to the early days of cinema, with neon marquees, mirrored balls, and chrome pillars. Snack-bar items range from your basic popcorn and soda to cappuccino and gelato. Plans call for the addition of a large-format Imax theater in coming years.

The Palms Casino Resort was developed by the Maloof family. The Fiesta Casino was developed by the Maloofs in 1994 and later sold to Station Casinos. Family members own the Sacramento Kings of the NBA and the Sacramento Monarchs of the WNBA.

Palms Casino Resort. 4321 West Flamingo Road. 455 rooms. Standard room rates $89 to $329. (866) 942–7770. www.thepalmslasvegas.com.

★★★ SAHARA HOTEL & CASINO

In one of the more successful remakes of a Strip golden oldie, the Sahara completed in late 1997 a $100 million reconstruction program that included a spectacular tentlike porte cochere leading to the main entry; a new pool area with gazebo, spa, cabanas, and outdoor snack bar; and, of course, an expanded casino. The facade facing the Strip was redone with fountains and palm trees. It's still not an "A-list" casino, but it has risen to a solid spot in the middle.

The dowdy old plaster camels and bedouins that used to grace the front of the hotel have been touched up and moved to a small oasis along the road.

And apropos of nothing else, there is also a subtheme within the casino of auto racing with a high-tech simulator, a racing restaurant, and scattered road machines in the casino.

Atop it all is **Speed: The Ride,** a wild roller coaster that blasts through a hole in the front wall of the NASCAR racing simulator at the back of the hotel and through the sign out front on the Strip. The ends of the track run straight up to the sky; the cars then fall back to Earth and backward to the starting gate. Go figure. For more details see chapter 10.

The Sahara opened in 1952 and was an immediate sensation for the size and gaudiness of its outdoor sign. Actually it can draw its lineage back to the Club Bingo, which opened in 1947 and featured a 300-seat bingo parlor. It was sold, re-modeled, and opened as the Sahara five years later. At the time, it was the first casino visitors would come to as they left downtown. The hotel was sold in 1995 to William Bennett, the former

Sahara Hotel

chairman of Circus Circus, and he has turned on the money spigot to renew the place.

The **Sahara Theater** is used for large-scale magic shows and concerts, while the smaller **Congo Room** is home to traveling acts.

The **Las Vegas Cyber Speedway,** a $15 million virtual-reality attraction, uses twenty-four interactive, seven-eighths-scale Indy car simulators to give riders the look and feel of racing on a 1½-mile oval at the Las Vegas Motor Speedway or in a fantastic zoom up the Strip at 200 miles per hour. The virtual experience is provided by a 133-degree wraparound screen, realistic sound, and a moving car body.

The **NASCAR Cafe** includes giant projection television screens featuring auto racing and news; some twenty stock cars are on display in and around the restaurant. The Carzilla Bar features the world's largest stock car, a Pontiac Grand Prix that measures 34 feet in length. Mounted on a hydraulic platform, it regularly rises to the second level, fires up its engine, and blows smoke. The menu features steaks, ribs, chicken, and fast food named for or by some of the stars of the NASCAR world. For information consult www.nascarcafelasvegas.com.

I Wanna Hold Your Cash

The Beatles put on a pair of concerts in 1964 under the sponsorship of the Sahara, but they were held at the Las Vegas Convention Center. Tickets for the show averaged $4.00, and the Beatles were paid $25,000 for the appearance.

You'll find an interesting collection of photos of celebrities and stars of the '60s and '70s from Elvis to Jack Benny in drag. Look in the reception area, near the buffet over the NASCAR Cafe, and elsewhere.

The updated showplace restaurant is the **House of Lords** steak house. There are tables, chairs, an indoor waterfall, and a menu that features steak; lobster; double lamb chops served with rosemary mint glaze; medallion of veal prepared in picatta, franchaise, or marsala styles; and roast prime rib of beef au jus. Appetizer selections include escargot, lobster bisque, stuffed portobello mushrooms, and roasted crab cakes. Entree prices range from about $18.95 to $58.00.

Located just off the casino floor, House of Lords is open nightly from 5:00 until 10:00 P.M. For reservations call (702) 737–2111.

On the third floor is **Paco's Bar and Grille,** a Mexican eatery that offers entrees beginning at $7.95. Specialties include fish and shrimp, chicken, beef, and pork dinners, as well as traditional entrees and combination platters. The signature drink is the classic margarita.

The **Caravan Coffee Shop** offers nightly specials; a regular favorite is New York strip steak for about $7.95. The **Sahara Buffet,** which seats 1,120 close friends, is upstairs and away from the bustle. It includes three action stations for Asian, Italian, and traditional carving.

Sahara Hotel & Casino. 2535 Las Vegas Boulevard South. 1,720 rooms. Standard room rates $35 to $200. (702) 737–2111, (800) 634–6411. www.sahara vegas.com.

★★★ WESTIN CASUARINA

An upscale resort that puts the emphasis on the hotel side of the hotel-casino equation, the Westin Casuarina sprouted in late 2003 just off the Strip on East Flamingo Road. The hotel was constructed within the shell of the former Maxim Hotel-Casino, a former star of the 1970s that had fallen on very hard times.

A $75 million makeover took out Maxim's dark gangster-chic decor, replacing it with marble flooring, light wood, and luxury room appointments. The Westin Casuarina hopes to cater to business travelers, conventioneers, and leisure travelers looking for a handsome but relatively small hotel just a block away from the heart of the Strip near Paris Las Vegas, the Bellagio, and Caesars Palace.

The seventeen-story building includes 825 rooms and suites.

Among the special accoutrements at the hotel is the "Heavenly Bed," featuring a pillow-top mattress set, high-thread sheets, and extra-comfy pillows. Each of the rooms also promises the "Heavenly Bath," including a two-head shower and upscale amenities.

The Westin Casuarina

The **Silver Peak Grill** is a twenty-four-hour informal restaurant featuring steak, seafood, and Mediterranean cuisine for lunch and dinner; it is located just off the relatively quiet casino floor. Specialties include crisp ciabatta sandwiches, field-chopped salad with fennel bruschetta, yellowfin tuna tartare, and hazelnut-crusted sea bass. Menu items we saw included sesame-crusted yellowfin (ahi) tuna in wasabi soy vinaigrette and Asian greens for $24, and lobster risotto with white truffle oil, shitake mushrooms, and parmigiano reggiano shavings for $22.

A breakfast buffet is offered each morning. The hotel lobby includes a **Starbucks** coffee shop.

In addition to standard rooms and suites, the hotel also offers packages that include a helicopter ride along the Strip, nightclub hopping by limousine, golf green fees and carts, and other amenities.

There is a casino, of course, but its design echoes intimate European gaming houses rather than the typical sprawling, flashing Las Vegas pit. Sofas, tables, and love seats are interspersed with the gaming tables and slots.

Casuarina, by the way, draws its name from the Latin name for the Australian pine, a tree that was introduced to Florida in the 1800s and has flourished there. Westin uses the name for its upscale properties.

The hotel is owned by Columbia Sussex Corp., which also owns the Horizon Casino Resort in South Lake Tahoe and the River Palms in Laughlin.

Westin Casuarina. 160 East Flamingo Road. 825 rooms. Standard room rates $139 to $189. (702) 836–9775. www.westin.com/lasvegas.

ECONOGUIDE ★★ RESORTS

★★ BALLY'S LAS VEGAS

A quality joint that's well kept up but without much of an identity, Bally's includes a large convention facility often used for overflow exhibits from some of the larger trade conferences, so the place really jumps when a big show is in town. Attractive but generic, it now stands as a suburb of Paris, to which it is connected. The walk from Bally's to Paris Las Vegas is worth the effort just to see the spectacular stained-glass cupola at the place where the two hotels come together.

At the center of the casino is a twenty-four-hour poker room; if there's a wait for a seat, players are provided with beepers so they can move about the property until a table becomes available. And the casino was the first in town to offer a set of $1,000 slot machines; the maximum bet is a cool $5,000.

Bally's Steakhouse is in a simple, elegant, large room that's decorated in black and white and open for dinner nightly from 5:30 to 10:30 P.M. Entrees range in price from about $22 to $56. Specialties include herb-marinated chicken breast plus steaks and filet mignon. On Sunday from 9:30 A.M. to 2:30 P.M., the Steakhouse is the site of the **Sterling Brunch,** one of the more upscale buffets in town with tuxedoed servers offering caviar, sushi, oysters, beef tenderloin, lobster, and champagne. For reservations at the Steakhouse, call (702) 967–7999.

Chang's at Bally's is an Asian eatery featuring Hong Kong dishes with Taiwanese and Mandarin influences. They serve dinner from 6:00 to 11:00 P.M. For reservations call (702) 967–7999.

Specialties include wok-grilled minced chicken cake, Mongolian beef, Hai-Nan salmon, and braised whole fresh abalone; entrees are priced from about $16 to $29. Appetizers range from wonton and hot and sour soup to a house specialty of braised supreme shark fin soup, priced at $88 per bowl. The restaurant also includes a selection of imported Asian wines, beers, and spirits.

Al Dente offers light Italian specialties. Pizzas and pastas range from $11.00 to $14.00. We also saw grilled chicken with garlic, mushrooms, sausage, potatoes, and lemon for $17.00 and *pescespada salmorrigglio,* fresh swordfish lightly grilled with garlic, lemon, olive, and Italian parsley, for $22.50. Open Friday to Tuesday from 6:00 to 11:00 P.M., closed Wednesday and Thursday. For reservations call (702) 967–7999.

The **Big Kitchen Buffet** is an especially attractive buffet room. Well isolated from the casino, the only reminder of where you are lies in the keno boards and runners. If one of your measures of class is whether the shrimp are peeled and whether the orange juice served at breakfast is fresh, the Big Kitchen passes on both counts. By no means as impressive or large as the Rio, it is nevertheless one of the better buffets in town.

The buffet includes an Italian station specializing in made-to-order tossed pastas along with an antipasto bar. The Chinese station offers dim sum, barbecued spareribs, roast duck, and stir-fries. Chilled seafood hilled on ice includes crab legs, peeled shrimp, and cold mussels. A hot-seafood station features sautéed fresh fish along with paella and bouilla-baisse.

Bally's Las Vegas

The **Sidewalk Cafe** is open twenty-four hours and includes a wide range of sandwiches, appetizers, and finger foods. Offerings, priced from about $5.00 to $15.00, include chicken wings, Cobb salad, veal cutlet Parmesan, and the self-declared Bally's Famous Reuben.

The hotel's **Indigo Lounge,** on the casino floor, offers live jazz and swing music. The **Tequila Bar** dispenses something on the order of fifty types of its namesake liquor in a Mexican-style cantina on restaurant row bordering the casino. If you prefer, there are also margaritas including the Golden Cadillac, Tres Compadres, Bally's Raspberry Special, Fruit Infused Patron, the Million Dollar, the Horny, or Blue Sunset. A wide selection of Mexican and domestic beers are on tap as well. To complement the drinks, the Tequila Bar offers appetizers including Pasilla chili-dusted calamari and rock shrimp, spicy beef taquitos, lime-chipotle seared whitefish tacos, and sizzling carne asada tacos.

Jubilee! at the Jubilee Theater, one of the most expensive and elaborate stage shows ever produced, has been running since 1981. Here you'll see the sinking of the *Titanic* and the destruction of the temple by Samson. The 190-foot-wide stage is fifteen stories high from the bottom of the pit to the roof; it includes five separate areas to accommodate the massive set pieces. There are three main elevators and eight smaller ones to move scenery. Special effects include dry-ice fog, real flames, and a tank that drops 5,000 gallons of water in a Las Vegas salute to the final moments of the *Titanic.*

One way to get up close and personal with the sets of the show . . . and to a *Jubilee!* showgirl . . . is to take the Backstage Walking Tour. The one-hour excursion is Monday, Wednesday, and Saturday at 2:00 P.M. and is open to everyone over the age of thirteen. Tickets for the show (about $58 to $77) or the backstage tour ($10 with a show ticket or $15 without) are available at the Bally's box office or by calling (702) 946–4567.

Some of the function rooms and decorations still bear reminders of the former incarnation as the original MGM Grand, with names such as the Garland and Gable ballrooms. The original 2,100-room hotel opened in 1973 with all the hoopla of a Hollywood premiere; Cary Grant was master of ceremonies for the event, and the ribbon was cut by Fred MacMurray and Raquel Welch.

In 1980 the hotel was the scene of a horrific fire that killed eighty-four guests and employees and injured hundreds of others. After extensive renovations, including fire detection and fireproofing efforts, the hotel was sold to the Bally Corporation in 1985. Today Bally's may well be one of the safer hotels in Las Vegas, with fire detection devices, control systems, and alarm systems at every turn. There's even a safety lecture broadcast on the in-house video system. An additional 732-room tower was added in 1981.

A few years back the hotel underwent another major transformation with the construction of a $14 million dramatic moving walkway structure from the Strip to its front door and the installation of a mirrored-glass facade to the main building. Dramatically illuminated arches in changing colors beckon passersby into the hotel; of course there aren't that many pedestrians on this part of the Strip, but it's the principle of the thing, I guess.

The nearly 3,000 rooms at the hotel range from standard kings and doubles starting at about $59 per night to Hollywood Suites and the extravagant Royal Penthouse Suites, which rent for about $2,500 per night.

Bally's Las Vegas. 3645 Las Vegas Boulevard South. 2,814 rooms. Standard room rates $59 to $259. (702) 739–4111, (800) 634–3434. www.ballyslv.com.

★★ FLAMINGO LAS VEGAS

The Flamingo is one of the last Las Vegas hotels with a proven link to the gangster roots of the Strip. Recent owners have been hard at work to remove those links, but the name remains unchanged.

The Flamingo was the invention in 1946 of Benjamin "Bugsy" Siegel, who was among the first underworld figures to realize they could make money from legal gambling at least as easily as they could from illegal activities.

Siegel built his one-hundred-room pleasure palace in a spot that was at the time in the middle of nowhere, 6 miles south into the desert. He spent an astronomical $6 million and in the process began the world of Las Vegas glitz, a style that has not yet stopped escalating. He named the place after his pet nickname for his girlfriend, Virginia Hill.

The hotel closed in January 1947 after just fourteen days in business while construction was completed; behind-the-scenes power struggles grew. In June 1947 Siegel was assassinated at his Los Angeles home. The hotel reopened later that year under new management, including front man for a different leading light of the underworld, Meyer Lansky. Lansky held on to a hidden interest in the hotel until late in the 1960s.

Still standing at the Flamingo well into the 1990s was the Oregon Building, a rather unassuming low structure that included the fourth-floor penthouse

Like Mother

In 1957 Judy Garland brought her young daughter, Liza Minnelli, onstage with her in an appearance at the Flamingo. Eight years later Minnelli had her own act at the Sahara.

once occupied by Bugsy Siegel. Features of the apartment reportedly included a trap door exit to a basement tunnel that led to a neighboring building.

In the 1970s the Hilton Corporation became the first major hotel chain to "legitimize" the Las Vegas casino market. Over the years the hotel and casino have been all but rebuilt, including a series of huge towers with a total of nearly 4,000 rooms. Room rates range from about $70 to $290.

Today the resort is part of the Caesars Entertainment empire along with Bally's, Paris, Rio Suites, and Caesars Palace.

In back where Bugsy's suite once stood, there are now fifteen acres of tropical gardens and swimming pools, which include the **Flamingo Wildlife Habitat.** The habitat is home to African penguins, Chilean flamingos, mute swans, black-necked swans, Australian black swans, Gambel's quail, African crowned cranes, pheasants, helmeted guinea fowl, several varieties of ducks, Japanese koi fish, grass carp, sacred ibises, macaws, cockatoos, chub minnows, and albino channel catfish.

A contemporary form of craziness takes place six days a week in Bugsy's Celebrity Theatre when **Second City** takes the stage. A typical performance might include a spelling bee for fourth graders that takes on a whole new dimension when conducted by an admirer of the Marquis de Sade, or a driver's education instructor who teaches real-world driving skills, such as how to apply makeup and eat a Happy Meal while driving.

It's actually the fourth city for the famed comedy troupe, begun in Chicago in 1959 and now also performing in Toronto and Detroit. Alumni of Second City include Alan Arkin, Joan Rivers, Robert Klein, Fred Willard, John Belushi, Dan Aykroyd, Gilda Radner, Martin Short, John Candy, Betty Thomas, Bill Murray, George Wendt, Chris Farley, Mike Myers, Ryan Stiles, and others.

In 2006 Second City presented shows nightly except Wednesday with tickets about $40. For information call (702) 733–3333.

Long-running headliner acts at the Celebrity Theatre in recent years have included soul singer Gladys Knight, comedian George Wallace, and singer Toni Braxton.

The Flamingo Las Vegas also offers a variety of dining opportunities. **Pink Ginger** continues the pan-Asian trend, offering a mix of Japanese, Korean, Cantonese, and Thai cuisine. The entrance is reminiscent of a traditional Asian key,

Flamingo Las Vegas

Dino and the Kid

Dean Martin and Jerry Lewis made their Las Vegas debut at the Flamingo in October 1948; by 1952 their movies made them the top box-office draw in the country.

lit from the inside to create a transition into the dining area that is rich with red, tan, and gold accents. The menu includes sushi, sashimi, Pad Thai noodles, and Kalbi-marinated short ribs; many dishes, including the signature Pink Ginger Beef, use a pink ginger fusion. Appetizers include ginger wontons filled with crab, goat cheese, and fresh ginger essence or Peking duck sliders with shredded crisp roast duck, scallions, cilantro, and thin pancakes. As part of the Pink Ginger experience, a unique tea service is offered; connoisseurs may choose from a presentation of tea leaves; pairings are recommended by expert staff.

Pink Ginger is open for dinner nightly from 5:00 to 11:00 P.M. For reservations call (702) 733–3333.

Next door, near the resort's fifteen-acre wildlife habitat, **Ventuno Ristorante** offers modern Italian cuisine served in a warm and intimate setting. Ventuno (Italian for twenty-one) is an oval room decorated with Venetian touches, including patterned glass and plaster.

Signature dishes include Antipasto Misto, the chef's selections from the antipasto bar, and Salmon Ventuno with jumbo shrimp with sautéed leeks, mushrooms, roasted peppers, tomatoes, brandy, and a touch of cream tossed with fettuccini. Vitello di Parma is veal topped with prosciutto, eggplant, tomatoes, and fresh mozzarella.

Ventuno Ristorante is open nightly for dinner from 5:00 to 11:00 P.M. For reservations call (702) 733–3333.

For a more casual dining experience, **Ventuno Café** is open for breakfast, lunch, dinner, and late-night snacks daily from 6:00 to 2:00 A.M. The menu offers a variety of antipasto salads, wood-fired gourmet pizzas, light pasta dishes, and freshly prepared Italian pastries. The cafe is built around a large wood-burning oven and adjoins the promenade overlooking the resort's tropical gardens.

One of the coolest places in town is **Jimmy Buffett's Margaritaville,** located on the northern end of the Flamingo, across from O'Shea's and facing Caesars Palace across the Strip. Entrees, priced from about $10 to $14, include specialties such as fajitas, jerk salmon, crab cakes, jambalaya, and steaks. Sandwiches include Cuban meat loaf. Libations include beer and margaritas. And, of course, everything is served to a "Cheeseburger in Paradise" beat. Open daily from 11:00 A.M. to 2:00 A.M., and just a bit later on weekends.

Hamada of Japan is a Las Vegas favorite for authentic Japanese dining. The Flamingo version includes a sushi bar and a cocktail lounge offering deep-fried tempura, sushi, donburi, warm sake, and chilled Japanese beer. Entrees include beef sukiyaki, shabu-shabu, and seafood yosenabe, as well as teppanyaki dishes prepared on the hot table in front of diners. Hamada is open nightly from 5:00 to 11:00 P.M.

At **Conrad's Steakhouse** wood, brass, and mirrors encircle a show kitchen where specialties include poached veal tenderloin, baby suckling pig, ostrich Rossini, and garlic-crusted monkfish. You can start with appetizers such as seared diver scallop ceviche, roasted quail saltimbocca, scampi portabella, lobster bisque Citronelle, and warm plum-tomato gazpacho. Entrees range from about $30 to $40. Open nightly from 5:00 to 11:00 P.M.

The **Paradise Garden Buffet** basks in a tropical theme. And there is **Bugsy's Deli,** named after the hotel's gangster founder, serving fresh bagels and sandwiches.

Flamingo Las Vegas. 3555 Las Vegas Boulevard South. 3,565 rooms. Standard room rates $70 to $290. (702) 733–3111, (800) 732–2111. www.lv-flamingo.com or www.parkplace.com/flamingo/lasvegas.

★★ HARRAH'S LAS VEGAS

This place has been through changes, going from what was once the largest Holiday Inn in the world to one of the largest Mississippi riverboats on dry land to a new incarnation as a celebration of Carnaval around the world. It has become most famous through the ever-expanding reach of its parent company, which in 2006 was the second-largest casino company in town.

Harrah's has undergone a major renovation and expansion in recent years, including completion of the thirty-five-story Carnaval tower with 986 rooms and 74 suites and a new facade that sinks the former riverboat from sight. Other rooms are located in the twenty-three-story Mardi Gras North Tower and the fifteen-story Mardi Gras South Tower.

Among the highlights of the reworked casino is a ceiling mural with fiber-optic fireworks. At **Carnaval Court** outside on the plaza, the otherworldly *Carnaval Fantastique* show is presented a few times each night. There is live music on the plaza every day; bands play from 3:00 P.M. until midnight through the week, and from 1:00 P.M. on the weekend. Las Vegas lounge icon Cook E. Jarr appears regularly on weekends. And surprise: You'll even find several blackjack tables out under the stars on weekend evenings.

In late 2006 comedian **Rita Rudner** moved her act down the Strip from New York–New York where she had them rolling in the aisles for five years. She took over from singer Clint Holmes in the larger showroom at Harrah's with a contract due to run for at least a year and probably longer. In discussing the move Rudner told reporters she was thrilled to be moving closer to the shopping malls at the center of Las Vegas Boulevard South.

In 2006 the new adult revue was *Bareback,* which features scantily clad cowgirls and cowboys performing racy renditions of country music hits. The show is presented nightly except Thursday at 10:30 P.M.; Friday shows are at 10:00 P.M. and midnight; Sunday there is a covered version of the show at 7:30 P.M. with a return to toplessness at 10:30 P.M.

New in 2006 was **Penazzi,** serving classical Italian cuisine with a contemporary spin. Proprietor Gabriele Penazzi offers family recipes including *passatelli di nonna fiorna,* a beef soup with traditional passatelli noodles made from parmigiano cheese, eggs, and nutmeg. Another signature dish is *rollatini di sogliole alla Don,* a rolled fillet of sole stuffed with crabmeat poached in a tomato-caper sauce and garnished with wilted spinach. Dessert specialties include *ricotta mille* *fogile,* a whipped ricotta cheesecake layered between delicate puff pastry, served with sautéed strawberries and a honey-balsamic reduction.

Adjacent to the dining room is the **Oyster Bar at Penazzi,** where guests can sip cocktails and dine on fresh steamed clams, shrimp, lobster, crab, clam chowder, and calamari.

The Oyster Bar at Penazzi is open daily from 11:30 A.M. to 10:30 P.M., while Penazzi is open nightly from 5:30 to 10:30 P.M. Reservations can be made by calling (702) 369–5084.

Ming's Table offers a fusion of Chinese, Thai, and Szechwan cuisine, retaining some of the specialties of the former resident of the space, Asia. Entrees includes crispy roast duck with plum sauce, sizzling beef in a black-pepper sauce, and spicy kung pao shrimp and scallops. For the more adventurous palate, Ming's serves honey-glazed walnut shrimp, beef with satay sauce, and Dan Dan noodles. Several choices of live seafood may also be prepared to taste.

Ming's offers a selection of nine flavored iced teas, including mandarin orange, raspberry, kiwi, and desert pear. Tropical green tea, mountain spring jasmine green tea, and ginger twist herbal infusion hot teas are also offered.

Ming's Table is located down the escalator from the Harrah's Las Vegas monorail exit, on the casino floor next to the Cafe at Harrah's. The restaurant is open daily for lunch and dinner. Reservations are available by calling (702) 369–5084.

Country singer Toby Keith has lent his name to a new lounge eponymously named **Toby Keith's I Love This Bar & Grill.** The restaurant features downhome cooking drawn from Keith's Oklahoma and Texas roots, including fried bologna sandwiches, pulled pork with barbecue sauce, and sweet potato pecan pie with bourbon ice cream.

There's live music nightly, a dance floor, a private dining room, and twenty plasma television screens that broadcast major sporting events and other programming. The bar is shaped like a guitar, and picks line the walls. There also is a Toby Keith retail store.

The 262-seat restaurant, bar, and store are located at the interior promenade adjacent to the Harrah's Las Vegas monorail concourse. They are open from 11:30 A.M. to 2:00 A.M. Sunday to Thursday and until 3:00 A.M. Friday and Saturday. For more information or to make reservations in the private dining experience, call (702) 693–6111.

A private elevator leads to the **Range Steakhouse,** which offers a dramatic view of the Las Vegas Strip along with its upscale menu. They love chops here—veal, pork, lamb, and beef—with prices from about $22 to $55 and toppings like pistachio salsa butter. Open nightly from 5:00 to 10:30 P.M. For reservations call (702) 369–5000 or (800) 392–9002, extension 5084.

Within the Range is the **View,** a nightclub with a DJ. The club is open from midnight to 5:00 A.M. Thursday through Saturday.

The **Flavors Buffet** includes action stations for many entrees and a Sunday brunch. Specialty dishes include Brazilian churasco, pizza, steamed crab legs, and sushi. **Club Cappuccino** features all sorts of coffee (naturally) and is supervised by the hotel's very own certified roast master.

The **Winning Streaks** sports bar within the sports book is open daily from 11:00 A.M. to 11:00 P.M., offering casual fare like Texas League chicken tenders and burgers. Diners are surrounded by fourteen television monitors showing current sporting events and wager boards showing the latest odds.

Harrah's Las Vegas Casino Hotel. 3475 Las Vegas Boulevard South. 2,579 rooms. Standard room rates $65 to $300. (702) 369–5000, (800) 634–6765. www.harrahs.com.

★★ HOOTERS CASINO HOTEL LAS VEGAS

The restaurant chain whose tagline is "delightfully tacky yet unrefined" arrived in Las Vegas in 2006, transforming the once staid and dull San Rémo Casino & Resort into a lively but unremarkable attraction just off the Strip.

Hooters, in case you don't know, has nothing to do with owls; the company's image is based around young women in very tight white T-shirts, offering hot wings and sly flirting. The Las Vegas version adds slot machines, cocktails, and blackjack.

The resort is located about a block east of the Strip, within walking distance of the MGM Grand, New York–New York, Excalibur, Luxor, and Mandalay Bay casinos.

The makeover brought a **Hooters** cafe, a **Dan Marino's** steak house, **Pete & Shorty's Tavern and Sports Book,** and the **Nippers Pool Bar.**

The resort holds regular weekend parties, called the "Backyard Bash," around the small pool at the back of the property, with live music, lots of alcohol, and Hooters girls. The area includes a pair of heated pools, palm trees, a lagoon-style waterfall, and a twelve-person and sixty-person hot tub. The sixty-person hot tub features a swim-up bar, with Hooters girls available to serve beverages.

Hooters Casino Hotel Las Vegas. 115 East Tropicana Avenue. 711 rooms. Standard room rates range from about $79 to $109. (866) 584–6687. www .hooterscasinohotel.com.

Hooters

★★ ORLEANS HOTEL & CASINO

It's Mardi Gras all the time here, although it's impossible to visit this place without comparing it to the nearby Rio Casino, which celebrates the Carnaval atmosphere of Brazil with exuberance, extravagance, and eensy-weensy cocktail-waitress uniforms.

The Orleans, several blocks west of the Strip on Tropicana Avenue, is attractive and fun in its own way, including an above-average buffet, an interesting selection of restaurants, and skimpy cocktail-waitress uniforms, but the voltage level is much lower.

The hotel's facade combines French, Spanish, and Plantation Colonial influences in an interesting jumble. Guest rooms include 810 "Petite Suites" and thirty one- and two-bedroom suites in a twenty-two-story tower. The main casino sits beneath an attractive high ceiling, flanked by French Quarter–like verandas and ironwork.

The 9,000-seat **Orleans Arena** is used for a diverse range of events from concerts to ice shows, circuses, and sporting contests. It is the home of the Las Vegas Wranglers minor-league professional hockey team. For information and tickets call (702) 284–7777 or consult www.orleansarena.com. Ticket offices are also available at the Orleans, the Suncoast, the Gold Coast, the Boulevard Mall, Galleria Mall, and Meadows Mall.

Eateries include **Canal Street Grille,** an elegant steak-and-seafood restaurant with some attractive fireside booths; it is open nightly from 5:00 to 11:00 P.M. Entrees, priced from about $14 to $28, include Pacific salmon in lime ginger sauce and blackened gulf shrimp with pecan rice, classic slow-roasted prime rib, and steaks or chops served with a choice of seven sauces.

The **Prime Rib Loft** is a basic steakery, with moderate prices from about $8.00 to $16.00. Open from 5:00 to 11:00 P.M.

Big Al's Oyster Bar features oyster, shrimp, and crab pan roasts. Signature dishes include Voodoo Mussels (mussels simmered in beer, tomatoes, onions, garlic, and dill) and linguine with clams. Entrees are priced from about $12 to $16. Big Al's is open daily from 11:00 A.M. until midnight weekdays and until 10:30 P.M. on weekends.

Sazio is an informal Italian restaurant open daily from 11:00 A.M. to 10:00 P.M. weekdays and until 10:30 P.M. on weekends. Some of the items on the menu, including fresh pasta, are made in front of the diners in a show kitchen. Entrees range from about $12 to $18.

Koji offers Japanese fare and Chinese specialties. There's a nice selection of exotic and familiar sushi, plus udon soup and teriyaki. Entrees range from about $10 to $20, and the restaurant is open daily from 11:00 to 5:00 A.M.

Don Miguel's is a Mexican restaurant decorated in brass and mirrors. Specialties include chicken baldastano, fillet Colorado, and snapper cascabel, with tequila flan for the final touch.

The **Courtyard Cafe** is a twenty-four-hour coffee shop that serves New Orleans specialties including barbecue shrimp or a muffuletta, and Chinese dishes such as Singapore noodles, moo shu pork, Peking duck, and Szechuan salmon.

The **French Market Buffet** is set in a wrought-iron and redbrick re-creation of New Orleans. The menu features some unusual offerings including gumbo, jambalaya, crawfish, blackened turkey, and other Creole fare.

Brendan's Irish Pub features Irish music, Irish whiskey . . . and pizza. There's a regular schedule of live acoustic bands.

The 827-seat **Orleans Showroom** is used for headliner performances. The Bourbon Street Cabaret features classic jazz, blues, and zydeco.

The hotel also includes a seventy-lane bowling alley; a 500-seat food court; a New Orleans–themed restaurant, nightclub, and lounge with live entertainment; an assortment of bars and cafes; retail shopping areas; a 3,420-seat, twelve-screen stadium-seating movie theater; a child care center; and an arcade.

The Orleans is owned by Coast Hotels, which also owns the Gold Coast and the Barbary Coast in Las Vegas. A free shuttle bus travels between the three properties.

Orleans Hotel & Casino. 4500 West Tropicana Avenue. 840 rooms. Standard room rates $39 to $159. (702) 365–7111, (800) 675–3267. www.orleanscasino .com.

★★ TROPICANA

An interesting mix of colorful Miami schmaltz and flashy Las Vegas glitz, the Trop is among the favorite "old" hotels on the Strip. First built in 1957 it has had its share of mob intrigue and corruption through the years.

Once alone at the top of the Strip, now it is almost possible to miss the Trop in the flow of the flashy Excalibur, Luxor, and MGM Grand across the road. Recently, though, they added to the overdose at the corner with a tropical village facade, complete with huge Easter Island–like statues and a new main entrance; in case you still miss it, a nightly laser light show is presented. Overhead walkways connect the Tropicana and the MGM Grand, Excalibur, and New York–New York casinos.

Make a pilgrimage to see the leaded, stained-glass ceiling above the tables in the casino. Lovers of Miami staples such as dancing water fountains and chandeliers will not be disappointed. Slot machines sit under a blue sky in a forest of bamboo trees. Overall it's a very lively place.

Deep within the casino, sharing space with a coffee shop, is the **Legends of Gambling** museum, which is worth a visit; admission is about $7.00, but free tickets are often available from shills at the entrance to the casino. There's an interesting collection of chips from hundreds of casinos (many long gone), costumes, and contracts of the stars of Las Vegas; you'll also find a re-created showgirl's dressing room, decorated with a mannequin, alas.

Going with a tropical theme, there is an emphasis on watery decorations, including a five-acre water

Is That a Deed in Your Pocket?

Mae West was not only a successful entertainer, she also had a way with real estate, buying half a mile of undeveloped land on the Strip between the eventual site of the Dunes and Tropicana.

park that has lagoons, spas, waterfalls, and what is claimed to be the world's largest indoor/outdoor swimming pool. There are dozens of exotic birds and fish in surrounding cages and pools. There is even a swim-up blackjack table. The entire area is carefully lit at night and includes a laser light show.

Standard rooms are somewhat ordinary, jutting off long, boring hallways.

The long-playing show at the Trop is the **Folies Bergere,** which features $5 million in sets and costumes. The show is still based on the Paris original, including cancan dancing and splits and spectacular costumes . . . and some dancers who seem to have left parts of their outfits in the dressing room.

The Tropicana opened on the Las Vegas Strip in April 1957, and the *Folies* opened some two years later in December 1959. The current edition of the longest-running production show in Las Vegas history includes some of the best production numbers from past *Folies,* as well as new sequences. *Folies Bergere* plays at 7:30 P.M. for a mostly covered dinner or cocktails show with prices ranging from $65 to $76 and an adults-only show at 10:00 P.M. For information call (702) 739–2411.

Magician Dirk Arthur performs his *Xtreme Magic* show every afternoon except Friday; the act includes tigers, leopards, and a helicopter. In 2006 general admission tickets cost about $32 and reserved pit seating was about $34.

The **Savanna Steakhouse** offers the "Wild Side of Dining" starting with steaks and moving on from there. Well off the casino floor, entrees range in price from about $14 to $36. The menu recently included basil-pesto–crusted roasted rack of lamb, walnut-encrusted sea bass, and filet mignon Oscar. The casual eatery is open nightly from 5:00 to 11:00 P.M.

Pietro's is a casino outpost of a local favorite, a preserved bit of old-style Las Vegas located opposite the Savanna. Entrees range from about $21 to $52; typical items on the menu include chicken Kiev, veal Sorrentino, and steak Diane. Open for dinner Thursday to Sunday from 5:00 to 11:00 P.M.

Mizuno's Japanese Steak House offers teppanyaki dining nightly from 5:00 to 10:45 P.M. Complete dinners including salad, appetizer, and entree range from about $17 to $22 and include chicken teriyaki, mushroom steak teriyaki, and salmon teriyaki. A sumptuous Emperor's Dinner for two costs about $79. An Early Bird special, available nightly except Saturday, reduces the price of chicken teriyaki to about $12.

Tuscany Italian Café is a casual eatery specializing in Mediterranean fare. The menu includes chicken or veal in parmigiana, francese, or marsala styles; shrimp scampi; and pasta with marinara, Bolognese, or Alfredo sauces. Entrees range from about $9.95 to $19.95. Tuscany is open Friday through Tuesday from 5:00 to 11:00 P.M., closed Wednesday and Thursday.

Calypsos is a twenty-four-hour cafe offering burgers piled high with garnishes, garden-fresh salads, omelets, soups, and hearty dinner entrees. A regular promotion is a $15.95 steak and crab leg dinner.

The Trop offers the rather ordinary **Island Buffet** for breakfast and dinner.

There are plans afoot that call for the redevelopment of the Tropicana, perhaps resulting in construction of two new 3,000-room hotels on the site. In

2006 Columbia Entertainment—the gaming affiliate of Columbia Sussex, which owns more than eighty hotels, resorts, and casinos across the country—merged with Aztar Corp., owner of the Tropicana Resort and the Ramada Express casino hotel in Laughlin.

Tropicana Resort and Casino. 3801 Las Vegas Boulevard South. 1,878 rooms. Standard room rates $50 to $125. (702) 739–2222, (800) 634–4000. www .tropicanalv.com.

ECONOGUIDE ★ RESORTS

★ BARBARY COAST

Barbary Coast is a small place that's almost possible to overlook in the glare of its neighbors but is actually worth a look-see. The Barbary Coast is decorated in a turn-of-the-twentieth-century San Francisco motif with lots of wood, stained glass, and chandeliers. Dealers wear garters on their arms; cocktail waitresses wear adornments where they were meant to reside for all the world to admire.

The few rooms at the Barbary Coast are elegantly appointed; they are mostly kept for regular clientele. There is no pool, no showroom, and few other amenities except a pleasant ambience—which is not a bad thing for a hotel-casino. A warning, though: This property is almost too attractive to its meganeighbors; rumors arise regularly that it will be swallowed up.

Drai's on the Strip is a Hollywood and Beverly Hills favorite, served by its own elevator off the casino floor. On a recent visit entrees were priced from about $25 to $30 and included seven-hour leg of lamb, glazed Chilean sea bass, crispy duck confit, braised osso bucco, pepper steak filet mignon, and blackened ahi tuna. Open for dinner from 5:30 P.M. to midnight. For reservations call (702) 737–0555.

The menu at **Michael's** highlights Continental cooking and fine wines in a plush setting beneath a stained-glass cupola. Signature dishes include Dover sole, chateaubriand, scampi, and lamb, veal, and rib chops. Entrees start at about $35 for a boneless breast of chicken Vesuvio and rise to about $130 for a rack of lamb for two; a bowl of French onion soup goes for $15, and you've got to return the china when you're done eating. Open nightly from 6:00 P.M. to midnight. For reservations call (702) 737–7111.

The **Victorian Room** offers twenty-four-hour cafe fare and a Chinese menu, plus an $11.95 prime rib or sixteen-ounce T-bone steak special.

A free shuttle bus runs between the Barbary Coast and its corporate cousins, the Gold Coast and the Orleans.

Barbary Coast. 3595 Las Vegas Boulevard South. 200 rooms. Standard room rates $39 to $209. (702) 737–7111, (800) 634–6755. www.barbarycoastcasino .com.

★ GOLD COAST

A Kmart of a casino aimed at the low rollers, hidden behind a tremendous, blank stucco front wall, the Gold Coast features a sea of slot machines including what seems to be an unusually large number of video poker machines. The Gold Coast sits next door to the Rio, a mile west of the Strip. In 2002 the place went a bit upscale to compete with the neighbors—the Palms and the Rio All-Suite—adding a fancy new entrance, convenient parking garage, and a pedestrian walkway to the Rio.

The main point of distinction for this hotel is the second-floor, seventy-lane bowling alley (can you imagine the noise level when all the lanes are in use?). There are also two movie theaters and a bingo hall. At the back of the casino is a large dance hall featuring country-and-western high-kicking with free classes offered. A liquor store sits directly off the casino.

There has been some attempt at an old California theme with pressed-tin ceilings and chandeliers, though not anywhere near as successful as at the Barbary Coast on the Strip.

Ping Pang Pong serves a wide range of specialty dishes from the various provinces of China. Open nightly from 5:00 P.M. to 3:00 A.M. Specialties include double-braised scallop hot pot, julienne fresh abalone, tea-smoked duck, and black-pepper beef medallions. Entrees range in price from about $9.95 to $15.95.

Arriva offers all your basic Italian favorites, from chicken parmigiana to lasagna. Other specialties include trout, halibut, sea bass, orange roughy, salmon, or swordfish prepared in broiled, sautéed, blackened, or poached styles. The eatery is open Wednesday to Sunday from 5:00 to 11:00 P.M.

The **Cortez Room,** open daily from 4:00 to 11:00 P.M., offers chicken, steak, seafood, and a prime-rib special in the range of $8.00 to $25.00.

The **Monterey Room** is a twenty-four-hour coffee shop that includes Chinese dishes among its fare, priced from about $6.00 to $16.00.

The **Ports O'Call Buffet** has been upgraded a bit in recent years; it is still an unusually ordinary setting in one of the corners of the casino.

A free shuttle bus runs between the Gold Coast and its corporate cousins, the Barbary Coast and the Orleans.

Gold Coast Hotel & Casino. 4000 West Flamingo Road. 711 rooms. Standard room rates $39 to $129. (702) 367–7111, (800) 331–5334. www.goldcoastcasino.com.

★ IMPERIAL PALACE

An eclectic place, vaguely Oriental in style, this deceptively large hotel (2,700 rooms) sprawls up, down, left, and right at its location at the heart of the Strip across from the Mirage and Caesars Palace. After more than three decades as one of the only privately owned casinos on the Strip, it was sold to the Harrah's group in 2006 and its future could go in either of two ways: It could fall to the wrecker's ball as part of a new megaresort, or it could be rejuvenated in place. The smart betting: The Imperial Palace may be in its final years.

The Imperial Palace was begun in 1972 as the old Flamingo Capri Motel by Ralph Engelstad. Construction of the various towers of the complex began in 1974 with a mélange of Oriental themes. Subsequent renovations added an Oriental pagoda-like ceiling over the casino; the old crystal chandeliers still hang incongruously. The back half of the casino is pretty much untouched. Engelstad died at the end of 2002.

Among the interesting quirks of the Imperial Palace is the squad of celebrity impersonator dealers who work the floor most afternoons and evenings. Here's your chance to lose your paycheck to Elvis, Rod Stewart, Elton John, and Barbra Streisand, or at least people who sort of look like them.

It's actually a bit of fun, with musical accompaniment and a bit of acting by the dealers. One of the favorites is a Ray Charles impersonator, who uses a cane to find his way to his table. (You'd be advised not to try to pull any fancy tricks on him, though. Casino security is watching, and besides . . . he can see you perfectly well.)

By Las Vegas standards the hotel is on the ordinary side, although it has a distinction that is a secret to many visitors. Hidden on an upper floor of a parking garage in back is an amazing collection of antique and unusual cars; most of them are for sale, if you've got a few hundred thousand dollars or more for the down payment. Even if you are not the sort to gush over a classic 1928 Cadillac Dual Cowl Phaeton or an antique 1906 Ford Model K Touring Car restored to mint condition, there are other reasons to visit the museum. Concentrate instead on the history of vehicles used by world leaders and come close to the transportation of some of the greatest stars of the twentieth century. Look for more details on the car collection in chapter 10.

There's a nominal admission charge for the museum that almost no one pays; look for free passes at the entrance or ask a floor manager in the casino. The official rate is $6.95 for adults and $3.00 for children twelve and younger. The museum is open every day late into the night. Work your way all the way to the back and up an escalator and an elevator to the car museum.

The large casino is a busy place, and you may need to drop bread crumbs to find your way back to your room. The best rooms can be found in the newer tower; the hotel features an Olympic-size swimming pool and a health and fitness center.

The long-running show at the Imperial Theatre Showroom is **Legends in Concert,** which features re-creations of musical greats, including Elvis (surprise!), plus a changing cast that may include stand-ins for Garth Brooks, Faith Hill, Tim McGraw, Prince, Michael Jackson, the Beatles, Buddy Holly, Liberace, Roy Orbison, Nat King Cole, Marilyn Monroe, and Judy Garland. These look-alikes promise live performances—no lip-synching allowed.

The Imperial Palace features a double handful of restaurants. For information and reservations call (888) 777–7664.

Embers, tucked away on the fifth floor, offers steak, seafood, and Continental dishes in an intimate setting; it is open from 5:00 P.M. Wednesday through Sunday with reservations suggested. Menu offerings, priced from about $12 to

$25, may include items such as orange roughy sautéed with macadamia nuts and Alaskan king crab legs with lemon drawn butter.

Fireside offers home-style barbecue dishes including ribs, steaks, and chops as well as entrees like blackened and pan-seared jumbo sea scallops in a garlic-cilantro herb butter. Open for dinner nightly except Monday and Tuesday.

The newest eatery is the **Cockeyed Clam,** which specializes in New England–style seafood including clam chowder made with herbs and fresh cherrystone clams flown in from the East Coast. All fried fish selections are hand breaded with either batter made with Samuel Adams beer or a special panko and cornmeal breading. The restaurant replaced the Seahouse.

Ming features Mandarin and Cantonese cuisine and is open daily from 5:00 P.M. Among out-of-the-ordinary offerings are egg flower soup, black mushroom and sea cucumber stew, and sour cabbage with beef. Entrees range from about $9.00 to $29.00.

The **Teahouse** is a twenty-four-hour coffee shop.

The **Emperor's Buffet** is the basic buffet. There is also a slightly more upscale buffet, the **Imperial Buffet,** which is served in the Teahouse.

Other self-describing eateries include the **Pizza Palace** (daily from 11:00 A.M. to midnight) and **Burger Palace. Betty's Diner** features ice cream, sandwiches, hot dogs, and snacks.

From April to October adventurous sorts can visit the **Imperial Hawaiian Luau,** a poolside luau complete with a lavish buffet, unlimited mai tais and piña coladas, and a full-scale Polynesian show; it is presented Tuesday, Thursday, and Saturday nights. Tickets in 2006 ranged from about $34 for general admission to $54.95 for VIP seating.

The bars in the casino area include the Japanese-themed **Nomiya Lounge** and **Tequila Joe's,** a karaoke-daiquiri bar just off the Strip.

Imperial Palace Hotel & Casino. 3535 Las Vegas Boulevard South. 2,700 rooms. Standard room rates $79 to $159. (702) 731–3311, (800) 634–6441. www .imperialpalace.com.

★ PALACE STATION HOTEL & CASINO

The Palace is off the beaten track for most visitors, but it's a favorite of Las Vegas locals primarily because of its restaurants.

With more than 1,000 rooms and a large and lively casino with 2,200 slots and a 600-seat bingo parlor, the Palace is no small place. Out-of-towners can use the hotel's shuttle bus for free transport to the Strip, about a mile east.

The hotel suffered a catastrophic flood and roof collapse over the casino pit in mid-1998 after a record rainfall; no one was hurt, but think of all the gambling that was lost! The casino rebuilt the pit with an updated Victorian theme that includes polished wood columns and moldings, stained-glass accents, and vintage cast-iron chandeliers with the aura of an Old West dance hall.

The **Broiler** is a local favorite for seafood. Typical offerings include mesquite-broiled mahimahi, halibut, catfish, red snapper, and other fish for $11 to $15.

Landlubbers can also order steak and chicken dishes. Entrees are priced from about $17 to $35. Open daily from 11:00 A.M. to 11:00 P.M.

The **Gourmet Feast Buffet** is called an "action buffet" by the management because many of the dishes are prepared for guests as they wait. The Feast often wins "best" ratings from the locals, although on my visits it ranked in the second tier below spectacular offerings such as those of the Rio, Caesars Palace, and Bellagio.

The **Guadalajara Bar & Grille** offers authentic Mexican food along with Tex-Mex cuisine and Southwestern fare. Specialties are priced from as low as $10 all the way up to $40. The Guadalajara Bar & Grille is also known for its inexpensive margaritas. Open daily from 11:00 A.M. to 11:00 P.M.

For lighter fare there's the **Pasta Palace,** featuring pasta, scampi, veal, and pizza cooked in a wood-burning oven, with entrees priced from about $9.00 to $20.00. The casual Italian eatery, set inside a Las Vegas version of a Roman villa, is open daily for dinner from 4:30 to 11:00 P.M. Nightly specials include steak or lobster dinners.

The **Grand Café** is an expanded coffee shop with more than 120 menu items including waffles, pancakes, omelets, pasta, pizza, and seafood entrees.

Palace Station Hotel & Casino. 2411 West Sahara Avenue. 1,029 rooms. Standard room rates $59 to $169. (702) 367–2411, (800) 634–3101. www.palace station.com.

★ RIVIERA

A grand creation intended to bring a touch of the Côte d'Azur to the desert floor, the Riviera collapsed into bankruptcy almost immediately after its opening in 1955. (The opening headliner was Liberace, earning a then-spectacular $50,000 per week. In 1956 film and radio star Orson Welles appeared onstage with a magic act.) A series of subsequent owners, including the Chicago mob, took over with a tremendous spurt of new construction that culminated in another bankruptcy in 1983.

The Riviera includes one of the largest casinos in town. Although there is not much pedestrian traffic on the Strip, the casino does have an open front like some of the downtown joints. Inside is a riot of reds and golds, but otherwise there is nothing exceptional here.

The hotel is the longtime home of *Splash,* a water-theme topless production show. There's also the *Crazy Girls Sexiest Topless Revue,* which is one of the most explicit (in title and costume) adults-only shows. One or another version of *Crazy Girls* has been in place for more than a decade; a bronze statue of the cast's backsides stands at the hotel's entrance. More than a few rolls of film have also been exposed there.

Elvis Sighting Number Three/ Odd Couple Number One

Elvis Presley posed on stage in 1956 in a gold lamé jacket at the Riviera piano while Liberace, wearing Elvis's rocker duds, whipped at a guitar.

Riviera Hotel & Casino

Another longtime favorite—for some—is *An Evening at La Cage,* a cabaret of female impersonators, starring Frank Marino.

An overly simple name for a nice place is **Ristorante Italiano,** a classy Italian eatery decorated with brass, brick, and statuary with a fake skyline of Rome outside the painted "windows." It also has one of the more elaborate espresso machines in town. Tuscan and Milanese specialties, including all the usual pasta, veal, beef, and chicken preparations, are priced from about $12 to $30.

Within the restaurant's walls is **La Stanza Bella,** a private dining area for groups of as many as twenty-four people.

Kristofer's Steak House offers chicken, steak, filet mignon, and lobster tail from about $22 to $37. Signature dishes include baby pork ribs smoked over mesquite and roasted in honey-bourbon barbecue sauce or Cajun bourbon sauce, and Cabo Wabo crab cakes.

Kady's Coffee Shop is open twenty-four hours a day. Sandwiches, burgers, and entrees range from about $6.00 to $15.00, with overnight crab, steak, and lobster specials.

The Riviera buffet is called the **World's Fare Buffet.** Special themes include Mexican on Monday, Italian on Tuesday, Oriental on Wednesday, Hawaiian on Thursday, international on Friday and Saturday, and Western barbecue on Sunday. A steak buffet is offered after 10:00 P.M. nightly except Friday.

BB's Eatery serves up down-home smoked ribs, barbecued chicken, and prime rib along with all the essential side dishes: beer-battered onion rings, chicken wings, and soup-and-salad combos.

Riviera Hotel & Casino. 2901 Las Vegas Boulevard South. 2,100 rooms. Standard room rates $59 to $279. (702) 734–5110, (800) 634–6753, (800) 634–3420. www.theriviera.com.

★ SAM'S TOWN HOTEL & GAMBLING HALL

Catering mostly to locals, Sam's Town is your basic Old Western boomtown on the outside with a clanging and flashing casino within. But if you work your way deep inside to the registration desk, you'll find a spectacular glass-roofed atrium known as Mystic Falls Park that has trees and birds, sitting areas, bars, and restaurants. The Sunset Stampede, a laser-light–and-water show, is offered several times daily within the park.

> **Odd Couple Number Two**
>
> Marlene Dietrich and Louis Armstrong appeared together at the Riviera in 1962.

Sam's Town is located on the Boulder Highway south of Flamingo Road. One unusual feature is a Western dance hall on the second floor.

Restaurants include **Billy Bob's Steak House and Saloon,** rounding up all the usual suspects: steaks, ribs, chops, chicken, and fish, cooked over a mesquite grill and garnished with various sauces. The place is open for dinner only.

Willy and Jose's Cantina is a casual Mexican cafe, serving chips and salsa with margaritas. Closed Monday and Tuesday.

Fellini's Italian Dining is a casual pasta palace set in Mystic Falls Park.

The **Fresh Harvest Cafe** serves breakfast all day and a salad and soup bar, steaks, fish, and more the rest of the time.

The **Firelight Buffet** is in a flashy room where the lighting, thankfully, is adjusted through the day to more calming levels by night. A seafood buffet is served Friday.

Roxy's Lounge is home to a changing series of shows and events including karaoke nights, singers, and bands.

The hotel offers a free shuttle bus service to selected casinos on the Las Vegas Strip and downtown.

Sam's Town Hotel & Gambling Hall. 5111 Boulder Highway. 648 rooms. Standard room rates $40 to $150. (702) 456–7777, (800) 634–6371. www.sams townlv.com.

■ UNDER CONSTRUCTION: ECHELON PLACE

The **Stardust,** one of the last of the old Strip casinos, was scheduled to be razed by the spring of 2007 and replaced by the massive **Echelon Place** development, which is expected to be fully open by 2010.

Included as part of the $4 billion project will be the 3,300-room **Echelon Resort** hotel as well as three boutique hotels: the 400-room **Shangri-La,** the 600-room **Delano,** and the 1,000-room **Mondrian.** Developers also plan another huge shopping center, with 350,000 square feet of space; also on the property will be a million square feet of meeting and exhibition space.

Echelon Place is a project of Boyd Gaming, which has quickly become one of the major players in town, the third-largest gambling company in the world

(Harrah's is in first place, followed by MGM Mirage.) The sixty-three-acre development is by most estimates the second-largest single project in Las Vegas, surpassed only by MGM Mirage's $6 billion Project CityCenter.

The Echelon Resort, which will be owned and operated by Boyd, will consist of a 2,600-room tower and a 700-suite luxury tower, each containing its own spa. The two buildings will connect to a 140,000-square-foot casino, twenty-five restaurants and bars, and pool and garden areas. The resort will also include a 4,000-seat theater with stadium seating and a 1,500-seat theater for smaller shows and touring acts.

Shangri-La Hotels and Resorts, a leading luxury hotel group in Asia, will build a Shangri-La hotel, while the Morgans Hotel Group (which purchased the Hard Rock Casino in 2006) will build the Delano and Mondrian boutique hotels.

And then there will be the Las Vegas ExpoCenter at Echelon Place, with 650,000 square feet of exhibition space and 175,000 square feet of meeting and conference space.

As part of the Echelon Place announcement, Boyd Gaming said it also intends to redevelop its Barbary Coast property in coming years, although no details were given.

The Stardust was a venerable establishment if you were somehow able to overlook an extremely checkered history of involvement by various factions of organized crime. For many years the hotel was a semilegit operation of the Chicago mob, a connection that ended with the discovery of a massive "skimming" scandal—the raking off of profits from gaming operations before they were taxed.

The Stardust was famous for its reproduction of the *Lido de Paris* floor show, which saved millions on costume expenses for its showgirls, many of whom were dressed only in, err, stardust. The *Lido* finally departed a few years back after more than thirty years onstage. The next big man around the casino was singer Wayne Newton, who performed there from 1999 through 2005.

■ UNDER CONSTRUCTION: PROJECT CITYCENTER

The **Boardwalk Hotel and Casino,** which featured a phony roller coaster and Ferris wheel out front and an often-empty casino inside, also closed in 2006. Plans call for the development of MGM Mirage's $6 billion **Project CityCenter** on the property.

■ UNDER DEVELOPMENT: THE END OF THE FRONTIER

The long-promised (or threatened) demise of the **Frontier Casino** on the Strip may actually occur in 2007. Current plans call for the creation of a new resort based on Montreux, France, and possibly including elements of the famed Montreux Jazz Festival held there each year.

The Frontier would be closed and demolished to make way for the Montreux, which would have about 2,750 rooms, including about 750 suites, and cater to high-end customers. The new resort, which may open by 2010, may also have an "observation wheel" facing the Strip, tentatively called the Las Vegas Eye and modeled after the famed London Eye on the Thames. The Las Vegas version would rise about 450 feet above the Strip with slow-moving, temperature-controlled cabins.

OTHER LAS VEGAS STRIP RESORTS

■ O'SHEA'S CASINO

O'Shea's is a mecca for the low roller, albeit at a pretty tony location in the middle of the Strip. Now part of the Hilton family, it is located next to the Flamingo Las Vegas and across the road from Caesars Palace. The casino features nickel slots, offers cheap beer, and promises to cash out-of-state checks. There are no hotel rooms for rent.

This place is interesting for a glimpse of the old-style wood-and-mirror ceiling over the pit; if you look left and right, though, you're likely to spy a fast-food burger stand.

O'Shea's Casino. 3555 Las Vegas Boulevard South. (702) 697–2711.

■ TERRIBLE'S CASINO

In Nevada it's not unusual to find a slot machine in a convenience store or a gas station. I guess, then, that it was inevitable that a chain of convenience stores and gas stations would open its own casino. Terrible's Casino opened in late 2000 in the shell of the former Continental Casino on Paradise Road.

Inside is more like a downtown slot heaven than a palace on the Strip; after dark it is lively and crowded with locals and some of the less-flashy tourists. The front wall near the entrance has an interesting display of photos that chronicle the history of Terrible Herbst and his empire, which grew from a gas station to convenience stores to gambling casinos. Within the blockhouselike structure are 373 guest rooms and a courtyard pool.

Terrible's Buffet promises daily specials: a taste of Italy on Monday, a Far East feast on Tuesday, La Posada Mexicana on Wednesday, a seafood extravaganza on Thursday, Cajun on Friday, a cattleman's barbecue on Saturday, and prime rib and shrimp on Sunday.

The hotel's coffee shop, the **Bougainvillea Café,** features Tequila Chicken, a prestewed bird roasted in a rotisserie oven.

The Terrible's chain of eighty convenience stores, lubes, car washes, and gas stations are located in Nevada, California, and Arizona.

Terrible's Casino. 4100 Paradise Road. 373 rooms. Standard room rates $29 to $49. (702) 733–7000, (800) 640–9777. www.terribleherbst.com/casinos/lasvegas.

PRIMM: NEVADA'S BORDER TOWN

★★   **Buffalo Bill's.** *A casino within a coaster.*
★★   **Primm Valley Resort.** *Desert delight.*
★   **Whiskey Pete's.** *Sawdust in the desert.*

Thirty miles south of Las Vegas on Interstate 15 at the border with California lies the Primadonna empire. Basically a one-company town originally named Stateline, then known as Primadonna, and now officially renamed Primm (and thus avoiding confusion with the other Stateline at the south end of Lake Tahoe), it has grown from a two-pump, twelve-room truck stop to a resort destination with almost 2,700 hotel rooms.

  · Most of the visitors to Primm drive in from California; it's about a three-and-a-half-hour drive across the desert from Los Angeles. The hotels in Primm also include convention facilities and the top-rated Primm Valley Golf Club, making it a destination of its own. And the three hotels occasionally become a distant extension of Las Vegas when all of the big city's accommodations are taken by huge conventions.

For reservations at any of the three hotels, call (800) 386–7867 or consult the Web site at www.primmvalleyresorts.com.

Primm Valley Resort

Buffalo Bill's in Primm

★★ BUFFALO BILL'S RESORT

This Western theme hotel and casino features 1,242 rooms in two hotel towers. There's a waterslide, Jacuzzi, and a pool in the shape of a buffalo. Oh, and there's also the **Desperado,** which is claimed to be one of the world's tallest and fastest coasters—it is certainly the world's tallest and fastest roller coaster that passes through and circles a gambling casino. The first lift takes about one minute to climb and three and a half seconds to descend. During the nearly three-minute ride, cars reach speeds of close to 90 miles per hour and G-forces of close to 4.0. (By comparison, astronauts on the Space Shuttle feel a gravitational pull of 3.2 Gs.) One of only three "magnum-type" coasters in the world, Desperado is 5,843 feet long with a lift height of 209 feet and a drop of 225 feet. The lift goes through the roof of the casino and then drops through a tunnel at top speed. It also passes through the porte cochere arrival area. Three points on the ride deliver near-zero gravity.

Turbo Drop takes twelve riders ensconced in padded saddles and shoulder harnesses about 170 feet into the air, where they will have a spectacular view of the desert and distant mountains for a moment before they plunge back to the ground at 45 miles per hour, experiencing a negative-1-G feeling and then 4.5 Gs of force as they come to a stop via air brakes.

Near the Desperado is the Adventure Canyon Log Flume Ride, the Ghost Town Motion Simulator Theatres, and a video arcade. Boarding areas for both the coaster and flume ride are inside the hotel. In 2006 tickets for the coaster were priced at $7.00 and tickets for the flume ride cost $5.00. All-day, all-ride wristbands are also available with prices varying by season. The rides are open daily from 11:00 A.M. to 7:00 P.M. Also at Buffalo Bill's is the Star of the Desert Arena, a 6,500-seat venue for entertainment from major concerts to boxing matches and rodeos.

The Baja Bar & Grill offers Mexican and Southwestern fare; nearby is Miss Ashley's Buffet.

★★ PRIMM VALLEY RESORT AND CASINO

This Victorian-style playground has 624 rooms in a quartet of four-story buildings. The resort was originally called the Primadonna Casino. Visitors can cross over I–15 on a monorail that connects Primm Valley to Whiskey Pete's. A recent renovation and expansion includes a convention center and a retheming that emulates a private country club with a nod to the Primm Valley Golf Club, a pair of eighteen-hole championship courses 4 miles south across the border in California. The hotel surrounds an attractive pool, with a view of the McCullough Range of mountains.

The gourmet room at the resort is **GP's,** featuring what is described as classic American cuisine with an international flair. The all-you-can-eat establishment is the **Greens Buffet.**

Just off the casino is an outpost of the Fashion Outlet of Las Vegas.

★ WHISKEY PETE'S HOTEL & CASINO

In the mid-1950s when nothing more than a lonely two-lane highway crossed the desert to Las Vegas, travelers would stop at the California Nevada state line at a two-pump gas station run by a crusty old coot named "Whiskey Pete." He got his nickname because of a bootleg still he operated in a cave across the road from the station.

Today at his namesake hotel and casino, there are 777 rooms in an eighteen-story tower. The 700-seat showroom at the hotel regularly features headline acts. The signature restaurant at the hotel is the **Silver Spur Steak House.** There's also the Wagon Wheel Buffet.

CHAPTER EIGHT

DOWNTOWN LAS VEGAS

Econoguide Best Casino-Hotels in Downtown Las Vegas

★★★ **Golden Nugget.** *A gilded lady, the class of downtown.*
★★★ **Main Street Station.** *Uptown in a downtown kind of way.*
★★ **Vegas Club Casino.** *People come here to gamble.*

THE REST OF DOWNTOWN
★ **Binion's.** *Down and out . . . and back.*
★ **California.** *A smidgen of Hawaii in downtown Nevada.*
★ **Fitzgeralds.** *McCasino.*
★ **Four Queens.** *An unimpressive hand.*
★ **Fremont.** *Less than memorable.*
★ **Golden Gate.** *Recoup your losses at the shrimp cocktail bar.*
★ **Lady Luck.** *Not tonight . . . a facelift awaits.*
★ **Plaza.** *Flashy, by downtown standards.*

DOWNTOWN LAS VEGAS was where it all started, and though the flashiest and largest of the casinos can now be found south on the Strip, there's still more than a little life left in the old part of town and a glimpse of the real thing: sometimes gritty, sometimes tawdry, always interesting. It is the home of Vegas Vic and Sassy Sally and some of the other gaudy, flashy, and memorable neon signs that are part of the international mind's eye view of the place that became known as Glitter Gulch.

The lights of the various signs were so bright in the narrow man-made canyon that pedestrians enjoyed electric noon at midnight. The stretch was used as the

Visitor Resources

▶ **Las Vegas Chamber of Commerce.** 711 East Desert Inn Road, Las Vegas, NV 89109. (702) 735–1616.

▶ **Las Vegas Convention and Visitors Authority.** 3150 Paradise Road, Las Vegas, NV 89109. (702) 892–0711. www.lasvegas 24hours.com.

setting for many movies, including *Honey, I Blew Up the Baby, The Stand,* and *Diamonds Are Forever.*

But still downtown was losing ground against the big resorts to its south. Keep in mind that the Strip is not part of the city of Las Vegas; it is an unincorporated portion of Clark County—it is the tail that wags the dog called Las Vegas.

Old Las Vegas, born in and around Fremont Street, was in deep decline in the 1980s and 1990s as the Strip boomed with megaresorts: exploding volcanos, Egyptian pyramids, and what seemed to be a Cirque du Soleil show on every corner. The old sawdust joints were still doing business with serious gamblers—they offered (and still do) some of the best odds in town. But there was little to draw tourists downtown, and the historic core was in danger of becoming a distinctly unimpressive and nearly purposeless city.

But in 1995 the city and its principal business interests launched an aggressive and generally successful effort to revitalize downtown. The heart of the effort was the creation of the Fremont Street Experience—a space frame with lights, sound, . . . and casinos—put into place overhead in Glitter Gulch; several blocks were also closed off to vehicle traffic, creating a place for pedestrians to stroll and gawk.

Many of the casinos downtown put millions into impressive additions and renovations. There are at least ten major casinos within walking distance—and under a bit of cover. At the head of Fremont Street is a parking garage that has 1,500 parking spaces, plus the Plaza Shops, with 50,000 square feet of retail area, and the Promenade Shops at Fremont Street, a blend of patio cafes and marketplace shopping in kiosks, street carts, and pavilions.

The latest conception of the future of downtown, then, is as the "adult Las Vegas." Think of the Glitter Gulch Theme Park and Indoor Gambling Mall and you'll get the idea.

The payoffs on the slot machines near Fremont Street are just a bit better than up on the Strip, and the house rules for many table games are just a tad more liberal. And the characters are much more . . . interesting.

Although some of the side streets of downtown are a bit scary, even to the locals, a visitor who parks in one of the casino parking garages is unlikely to be exposed to the seedier side of town.

Downtown is also the home of some of the lower forms of entertainment and commerce, including strip clubs and pawnshops. You can just pass them by if that's not what you're looking for.

Most casinos offer free parking for several hours if you get your parking ticket validated inside; there is no requirement that you spend a dime at the tables or machines. Check the signs at the parking lots for details.

And you can easily stay on the Strip and commute to Fremont Street, or the other way around; it's a fifteen-minute drive by highway and a bit slower (but more interesting) to drive the length of Las Vegas Boulevard.

Station Casinos, which operates a string of casinos mostly aimed at locals, took down the Castaways Casino (formerly the Showboat) in 2006; no announcement has yet been made on what the company plans to do with the twenty-six-acre site on Fremont Street.

THE FREMONT STREET EXPERIENCE

The Fremont Street Experience consists of a one-of-a-kind Viva Vision canopy, which towers 90 feet above the street and stretches 1,400 feet long. The overhead entertainment uses twelve million LED lights and a 550,000-watt concert-quality sound system.

Among presentations in the library are:

- *Above and Beyond.* A tribute to anything and everything airborne.
- *Fahrenheit at Night.* An after-dark salute to another indoor Las Vegas sport, starring electronic dancing girls.
- *Downtown Divas.* A tribute to the ultimate girls' night out.
- *Lucky Vegas.* A salute to a hundred years of local history with images that date back to the birth of the city.
- *Speed, Smoke, and Spinning Wheels.* Race cars roar by overhead on a 5-block-long electronic track, accompanied by a thumping soundtrack.
- *Area 51.* From Fremont Street deep into outer space with a bit of a side trip to visit with the local aliens.
- *The Drop.* A psychedelic journey through an underwater paradise filled with beautiful creatures, inspired by nature and mythology.
- *American Freedom.* Rolling out the red, white, and blue, plus an electronic fighter jet flyby and fireworks.

The library of shows changes from season to season; shows are

A scene at the Fremont Street Experience

offered every hour on the hour from dusk to midnight. For information on shows and special events, call (800) 249–3559 or consult www.vegasexperience .com.

The Fremont Street Experience also features special events including a Holiday Festival that displays a 50-foot Christmas tree, an ice rink for public skating and special entertainment, and a New Year's Eve party.

DOWNTOWN LAS VEGAS

★★★ GOLDEN NUGGET HOTEL & CASINO

The Golden Nugget is the class of downtown. The lively casino is decorated with a San Francisco theme and is painted in white and gold with ornate chandeliers and ceiling fans. The most recent tower at the hotel is a local landmark with its brilliant gold reflective glass. There are a total of 1,907 rooms, including posh one- and two-bedroom suites, twenty-seven luxury apartments in the Spa Suite Tower, and six penthouse suites in the North Tower.

The Golden Nugget would be considered a fine hotel anywhere; it is possible to enter the hotel, register, and ride the elevator to your well-appointed room with barely a glance at a slot machine or a craps table. In 2006 it was well into a

The Golden Nugget

major remake using the funds—and brand names—of its new owner, Landry's Restaurants.

A remodel of the Spa Tower suites was completed in late 2005. Also redone was the North Tower lobby, the porte-cochere main entrance, and the pool area; high-limit and VIP areas were also brought up a few notches. At the same time, the new ownership told analysts that, although it sought to keep its place as the class joint in downtown, it would not attempt to compete with the Strip for the highest of the high rollers.

Vic & Anthony's Steakhouse is a world of mahogany and leather, featuring steaks, lamb, veal, and seafood. The restaurant, which replaced Zax, is one of Landry's many brands; the first steak house opened in 2003 in downtown Houston.

Another addition is **Lillie's Noodle House,** a traditional pan-Asian casual dining room, located near the Carson Street Cafe. **The Grotto,** an informal Italian trattoria-style restaurant specializing in fresh pasta as well as chicken, veal, and fish entrees, was installed just off the South Tower lobby in the former location of the sports book, with a patio area overlooking the redone pool.

The Buffet was enlarged and enhanced, moving into the former location of Stefano's and longtime favorite Lillie Langtry's. The offerings will draw on some of the specialties of the many restaurant brands of Landry's.

The Golden Nugget's new pool incorporates a glass wall that allows guests to swim inches away from sharks and other marine life in an adjacent aquarium. The Theatre Ballroom was also redone with new lighting and seats; the room, which now accommodates 600, will be used for headliners and special events.

The remake did not remove some of our favorite quirks, including a real golden nugget in a display case not far from the registration desk. The Hand of Faith Nugget is claimed to be the world's largest piece of unrefined gold. Weighing in at 875 troy ounces (almost sixty-two pounds), it was discovered with a metal detector in 1980 by a young man prospecting behind his trailer home near Wedderburn, in Victoria, Australia.

While you're in the area, check out the original painting by LeRoy Neiman near the lobby. Neiman has some celebrities worked in: Singers Kenny Rogers and Paul Anka are shown talking to former Golden Nugget owner Steve Wynn in the lower left corner; the artist himself is seated at the baccarat table.

As an aficionado of the brewing art, I am impressed with the **International Beer Bar,** which delivers more than forty varieties of familiar and exotic brews.

Carson Street Cafe, modeled after a European sidewalk cafe, serves breakfast, lunch, and dinner twenty-four hours.

Golden Nugget Las Vegas opened as a gambling hall in 1946, becoming the largest resort in downtown Las Vegas. The place has gone through at least four changes of ownership in recent years. In late 2003 MGM Grand, which had gained the resort as part of its buyout of Mirage (which owned it because founder Steve Wynn had begun his Las Vegas empire there), reached a deal to sell Golden Nugget Las Vegas and Golden Nugget Laughlin to Timothy Poster and Thomas Breitling, founders of the travel Web site Travelscape.com, now owned by Expedia. Tim and Tom made themselves semifamous in 2004 by starring in a reality television show about their takeover of the casino, and then turned around and sold the place in 2005 to Landry's Restaurants, the nation's second-largest casual, full-service seafood restaurant chain.

Among restaurants the company operates are Rainforest Café, Landry's Seafood House, and Joe's Crab Shack.

Golden Nugget Hotel & Casino. 129 East Fremont Street. 1,907 rooms. Room rates range from about $59 to $159. (702) 385–7111, (800) 634–3454. www.goldennugget.com.

★★★ MAIN STREET STATION

Main Street Station brings a touch of Victorian elegance, including historical treasures, opulent chandeliers, stained-glass windows, and four antique railroad sleeping cars. A walkway from the top of the Fremont Street Experience to the Main Street Station includes World War I–era street lamps from Brussels, Belgium. Overhead in the casino is a chandelier from the Figaro Opera House in Paris. The casino cashiers' cage windows feature the bronze grillwork of the teller windows from the Barclay Bank of London.

One of the railroad cars, now used as the Main Street Cigar Bar, was the personal coach of author Louisa May Alcott. Another of the cars was used by Buffalo Bill Cody and hosted Annie Oakley and Teddy Roosevelt.

When you're inside, look for the century-old apothecary cabinetry in the registration lobby. Another jewel is a stained-glass window that was given to actress Lillian Russell by "Diamond Jim" Brady in the 1880s.

The signature eatery at Main Street Station is the **Pullman Grille,** featuring steak and seafood for dinner every night of the week. The **Triple 7 Restaurant and Brewery** offers five microbrews produced on-site, wings, burgers, and sushi. The **Garden Court Buffet** follows the Las Vegas "action buffet" trend of individual stations with chefs cooking or carving to order, plus designer pizza and pasta, antipasto, and a barbecue.

Main Street Station. 200 North Main Street. 406 rooms. Room rates $45 to $100. (702) 387–1896, (800) 713–8933. www.mainstreetcasino.com.

★★ VEGAS CLUB CASINO

A lively, informal small club with a high mirrored ceiling, the Vegas Club Casino holds a special attraction for baseball and blackjack fans.

The casino claims the most liberal blackjack rules in the world; the somewhat complex rules do seem to reduce the house advantage, at least for experienced and knowledgeable players. Among the special rules are these: You can split and resplit aces and pairs as many times as you choose, and any hand of six cards totaling twenty-one or less is an automatic winner. The Vegas Club somewhat compensates for its loose rules by dealing cards from a multideck shoe, reducing the edge for card counters.

But back to the atmosphere: You'll notice things are a bit different when you see the uniforms worn by the dealers—instead of white shirts and string ties, they are each decked out in baseball jerseys. The cocktail waitresses wear cheerleader outfits.

Take the hint and head toward the back of the casino to examine the great collection of old sports photos and memorabilia—mostly baseball and boxing—near the Dugout Restaurant. Photos on the wall date back as far as the 1920s.

Among the favorite sports stars is speedster Maury Wills; you'll find his original 1950 minor-league contract to the Hornell Baseball Association in upstate New York. He was paid a whopping $150 a month with a $500 signing bonus. Also on display are Wills's shoes from 1962, the year he set a major-league record with 104 stolen bases.

Vegas Club Casino

(Wills, by the way, had a short career onstage in Vegas; among his appearances was a show at the Sahara in 1969 in which he played saxophone.)

The specialties at the **Great Moments Room,** priced about $13 to $20, include scalone, a combination of abalone and shrimp sautéed and finished with light white wine and garlic sauce, for about $14. Open Thursday through Monday from 5:00 to 10:00 P.M.

Mahalo Express offers Hawaiian Kine food with island specialties such as chicken katsu, Spam and eggs, beef curry, and fried mahimahi. Open daily from 11:00 A.M. to 1:00 A.M.

The casino originally opened in 1911, with the most recent hotel tower erected in 1961. The Vegas Club Hotel & Casino was purchased, along with the Plaza, Western, and Gold Spike hotel-casinos, by Barrick Gaming Corporation in mid-2004; plans call for redevelopment of the south end of downtown.

Vegas Club Hotel & Casino. 18 East Fremont Street. 410 rooms. Room rates $30 to $45. (702) 385–1664. www.vegasclubcasino.net.

THE REST OF DOWNTOWN

★ BINION'S GAMBLING HALL & HOTEL

If you want a sense of the freewheeling early days of gambling in Las Vegas, this is the place.

One of the eclectic oddities of Nevada, and worth a visit for that reason alone, Binion's is a rambling, dim place semidecorated in dark browns, black, and reds. Benny Binion was one of Las Vegas's old-time gambling men who ran a casino, which is quite a different thing from today's businesspeople who own gambling casinos. However, it is worth noting that Steve Wynn, the flamboyant developer of Bellagio, the Mirage, Treasure Island, and the new modestly named Wynn Las Vegas was in his early days a protégé of Binion.

Binion created the place he called the Horseshoe in the late 1940s out of two old downtown properties, the Apache Hotel and the Eldorado Casino. Today the casino occupies an entire city block, including the old Mint Hotel next door. After Benny's death in 1989, ownership of the hotel passed through several colorful levels of the Binion family. Binion's wild and woolly history caught up with the casino in early 2004. Binion's finally reached the end of the horseshoe in January of 2004, forced to close by state regulators because it did not have enough ready cash to pay bettors and staff. Riding to the rescue was Harrah's Entertainment, which purchased the company and its "World Series of Poker" competition. Between the purchase and the reopening of the casino, Harrah's turned around and sold the property to MTR Gaming Group, an operator of racetracks in Ohio, West Virginia, and Pennsylvania.

For many years the casino was considered a haven for the "serious" gambler with some of the highest limits in Las Vegas. Among the oddities on display was a display case that included a few notable firearms, including a .357 Magnum that belonged to Cleveland mobster Moe Dalitz, a former owner of the Desert Inn, and Benny Binion's Winchester with a gaming chip in the handle. The Poker Hall of Fame on the right wall of the casino displayed pictures of famous and infamous players.

Alas one of the place's quirky charms was sold in 2000: the framed million dollars in rare $10,000 bills went to a collector for a reported $6 million. Something like five million visitors went home with souvenir photos taken in front of the cash.

The new owners promise to spruce up **Binion's Ranch Steak House,** one of Las Vegas's grandest monuments to beef, way up on the twenty-fourth floor of the hotel with a great view of downtown. One of the more interesting hideaways of downtown, the steak house specializes in all things beef, lobster, and seafood including some unusual entries such as chicken-fried lobster. The steak house is open nightly

No Day of Rest

Sundays are surprisingly busy days at many casinos, bringing out the locals for brunches. It's also a common arrival day for big tour groups.

from 5:00 to 11:00 P.M., with entrees priced from about $25 to $50 (for that unusual lobster).

Binion's Original Coffee Shop is open twenty-four hours a day, offering breakfast and other basic Las Vegas fare.

Binion's Gambling Hall & Hotel. 128 East Fremont Street. 354 rooms. Room rates $35 to $65. (702) 382–1600, (800) 937–6537. www.binions.com.

Camp Las Vegas

Fremont Street is named after John Charles Frémont, a nineteenth-century American explorer who established a camp near Las Vegas Springs in 1844.

★ CALIFORNIA HOTEL AND CASINO

A hotel named California, located in Nevada, this old-style place draws some 70 percent of its visitors from Hawaii. There's an island motif in decor and dining, including the **Redwood Bar & Grille** and **Pasta Pirate.**

The hotel is connected by an enclosed pedestrian bridge to its corporate cousin in the Boyd Group, Main Street Station.

California Hotel and Casino. 12 Ogden Avenue. 781 rooms. Room rates begin at about $40 and reach to about $100. (702) 385–1222. www.thecal.com

★ FITZGERALDS CASINO HOTEL

If you have any doubt about whether this place intends to cater to the low rollers or the high rollers, a quick glance at the ubiquitous advertisements for the hotel should tell you: A regular come-on at Fitzgeralds is a free burger at the McDonald's within the casino.

In the core of the casino is a world of Irish green, including what is claimed to be a piece of the Blarney stone, a collection of four-leaf clovers, and a gaggle of leprechauns. In other words, lots of luck. The thirty-four-story tower is downtown's tallest casino-hotel.

The casino's second-floor balcony offers one of the best places to watch the Fremont Street Experience show; on busy nights, stake out a space at least fifteen minutes before the hourly display.

The prime eatery is **Limerick's Steakhouse,** open for dinner Thursday to Monday. The background is an Irish castle.

Fitzgeralds declared bankruptcy in 2000 and was purchased by Detroit businessman Don Barden, who became the first African American to wholly own a Las Vegas casino; today Fitzgerald's is a subsidiary of Barden's Majestic Star Casino company.

Fitzgeralds Casino Hotel. 301 East Fremont Street. 638 rooms. Room rates $18 to $120. (702) 388–2400, (800) 274–5825. www.fitzgeraldslasvegas.com.

★ FOUR QUEENS HOTEL & CASINO

By Las Vegas standards the Four Queens is a relatively understated hotel decorated in blue and beige with mirrored ceilings with a small but lively casino. The

Sky High

North Las Vegas, a few miles beyond downtown, is the home of Nellis Air Force Range. The North Las Vegas Air Show takes place each fall, usually near the end of October, drawing tens of thousands of visitors. Events include all sorts of aircraft, hot-air balloons, vintage autos, and various celebrations of Indian heritage.

hotel was first built in 1964 and supposedly drew its name from the fact that former owner Ben Goffstein had four daughters. Over the years the hotel has expanded to 690 rooms with twin nineteen-story towers, and it occupies the entire block at Fremont and Third Streets.

Hugo's Cellar is one of the better eateries in Las Vegas. The meal begins with a make-your-own salad from a tableside cart laden with offerings from bay shrimp to roasted pine nuts to hearts of palm. Entrees are priced from about $24 to $49.

At the more casual **Magnolia's Veranda,** you can try the Four Queens' Dip, a pair of French rolls filled with sliced beef and Swiss cheese, served au jus. Entrees are priced from about $5.00 to $15.00.

At the **Chicago Brewing Company and Cigar Lounge,** you can imbibe handcrafted microbrews along with appetizers, pizzas, and entrees.

The Four Queens claims the title for the world's largest slot machine, duly noted in the *Guinness Book of World Records.* The Queens Machine is 9 feet, 8 inches tall and 18 feet long. Six people can play the slot, for $1.00 to $5.00 per pull, at the same time.

Four Queens Hotel & Casino. 202 East Fremont Street. 690 rooms. Room rates start as low as $44 and reach to $144 for basic rooms, depending on the season and day of the week. (702) 385–4011, (800) 634–6045. www.fourqueens .com.

★ FREMONT HOTEL & CASINO

One of the first "carpet joints" in downtown, it also featured one of the first block-long neon signs in the neighborhood. The joint is always jumping. The Fremont and its sister, the California Hotel and Casino, cater to an Asian and Hawaiian clientele.

The hotel includes a branch of the **Tony Roma's** chain, open for dinner from 5:00 to 11:00 P.M. Specialties include prime rib, steak, and chicken, with prices ranging from about $15.00 to $25.00; early bird and late specials go for as little as $8.00. The **Second Street Grill** has for several years been a gourmet eatery in search of a good menu; it claims a Pacific Rim–contemporary mix; entrees range from about $17 to $35.

The **Paradise Cafe** offers American and Chinese cuisine for $15 or less. Open Monday to Thursday 7:00 to 2:00 A.M. and Friday to Sunday all day.

At the **Paradise Buffet** the weekend Champagne Brunch, served Sunday from 7:00 A.M. to 3:00 P.M., is one of the better deals in downtown. It includes breakfast omelets and eggs cooked to order, herring, sour cream, smoked salmon, New York strip loin, ham, turkey, and salads for $8.99.

The buffet's Seafood Fantasy is served Tuesday, Friday, and Sunday from 4:00

to 10:00 P.M. for $14.99. (The "regular" dinner is offered other nights for $9.95.)

Fremont Hotel & Casino. 200 East Fremont Street. 452 rooms. Room rates $40 to $80. (702) 385–3232, (800) 634–6182. www.fremontcasino.com.

★ GOLDEN GATE HOTEL & CASINO

Built in 1906 as the Hotel Nevada, the Golden Gate is the oldest hotel in Las Vegas. When the place first opened, it introduced such comforts as electric lighting, ventilation, and steam-heat radiators; some of the original rooms—upgraded slightly—are still in use. Except for the slot machines and the blackjack and roulette tables, it looks nothing at all like the pleasure palaces on the Strip.

The best thing here is the nondescript **San Francisco Shrimp Bar and Deli** way at the back. The 99-cent shrimp cocktails aren't half bad. Take two; they're small and they use tiny shrimp. The fake-crab cocktails are the same price and are even better. If you like larger crustaceans, you can buy a cup of Big Shrimp for $2.99.

Its restaurant, the **Bay City Diner,** is one of the more modern touches: it has a 1950s San Francisco setting. In recent years Golden Gate has worked to return the hotel's exterior to the look of that place and time, with window awnings and planter boxes and a hedge on the roof.

Inside the casino, near the shrimp bar, are photos from the filming of *Pay It Forward,* starring Helen Hunt and Kevin Spacey; some scenes took place inside the Golden Gate in 2000.

Golden Gate Hotel & Casino. 1 Fremont Street. 106 rooms. Room rates $38 to $75. (702) 382–6300. www.goldengatecasino.net.

Elvis Sighting Number Four

The King's first Las Vegas appearance took place at the original New Frontier in downtown in April 1956, and it wasn't a smashing success. At the time it seemed that the King of Rock 'n' Roll's appeal was to younger crowds than to those coming to Las Vegas. In 1969 he returned and made the first of a long series of appearances at the International Hotel (now the Las Vegas Hilton).

Alas one of the less-known Elvis sightings is no more: The tiny Normandie Hotel between the Strip and downtown was a rather jarring pink stucco motor court, one of the oldest motor courts in Las Vegas. In recent years the sign out front read ELVIS SLEPT HERE. (The other side of the sign read HIGHLY RECOMMENDED BY OWNER.)

★ LADY LUCK

You'll have to try your luck elsewhere, at least until deep into 2007; this old lady is taking a year off for a facelift. It's an unusual step: Most casinos keep their doors open even while the carpenters are at work.

There are no details on changes that may be made to the old place.

Lady Luck Casino Hotel. 206 North Third Street. 792 rooms. Room rates $25 to $99. (702) 477–3000, (800) 523–9582. www.ladylucklv.com.

Plaza Hotel

★ PLAZA HOTEL & CASINO

An attractive and well-kept hotel at the head of Fremont, it was for many years known as the Union Plaza as a reminder of the former railroad interests that once controlled Las Vegas and of the railroad station that formerly occupied the spot. The hotel today is still connected to the Amtrak station at one end and the Greyhound terminal at the other.

The hotel was opened in 1971 on the spot where the land auction of 1905 took place. At the time, it had the largest casino in Las Vegas, a distinction that has since been passed up the Strip many times.

The Plaza offers a wide range of gambling opportunities beginning with rarely seen penny slots and nickel progressive jackpot machines and moving upward from there.

The signature restaurant at the Plaza is **Center Stage,** on the second floor of the tower with a spectacular view up Glitter Gulch. The eatery is open from 5:30 to 10:30 P.M. most of the year, with later hours in peak times, with dinners priced from about $15 to $30 including basic steak-house fare such as prime rib, filet mignon, salmon, and chicken dishes.

In 2006 Center Stage added an Italian restaurant within the restaurant. The **Italian Chop House** expands the beefery's menu with saltimboca, linguine and clams, rigatonia alla Vodka, and other specialties.

The circular Center Stage was originally built in the 1970s as a swimming pool in the shape of a martini glass. The unusual design made it a natural for movies about Las Vegas, and it was used by Sharon Stone and Robert DeNiro for a tumultuous dinner in *Casino* and for the first date of Helen Hunt and Kevin Spacey in *Pay it Forward*.

And on the subject of elegant dining, the Plaza Hotel made a splash on the international competitive eating scene in early 2006 when it sponsored an event based around the nine-pound Big Daddy Burger; the basketball-size pile of meat came with a bun, ketchup, lettuce, and a big pickle. Other cultural events include arm wrestling competitions and televised poker championships.

The hotel was owned for many years by John "Jackie" Gaughan, also the proprietor of the El Cortez Hotel in downtown, the Vegas Club Casino, Western

Hotel & Bingo Parlor, and the Gold Spike. Current owner Barrick Gaming has disclosed plans to eventually replace the Plaza and some of its other downtown properties with new, more upscale hotel-casinos and condominiums.

Plaza Hotel & Casino. 1 Main Street. 1,037 rooms. Room rates $35 to $45. (702) 386–2110, (800) 634–6575. www.plazahotelcasino.com.

EL CORTEZ HOTEL

One corner of this now-sprawling downtown casino and hotel, at the corner of Fremont and Sixth Streets, constitutes the oldest continuously operating casino in Las Vegas. The El Cortez Hotel opened in 1941 with a Western theme and about eighty rooms; not much has changed other than the addition of a fourteen-story tower with 200 rooms opened in 1983.

The main restaurant is **Roberta's,** which offers steak-house fare, priced from about $11 to $20. Other specialties include lobster fra diavolo, roasted game hen, and baked sea bass. **Careful Kitty's Café** delivers moderately priced chicken, beef, and fish dishes plus a twenty-four-hour breakfast menu.

El Cortez Hotel. 600 East Fremont Street. 308 rooms. Room rates $25 to $40. (702) 385–5200, (800) 634–6703. www.elcortezhotelcasino.com.

STREET CASINOS

Not all of the casinos in Las Vegas are billion-dollar enterprises with thousands of slot machines and spectacular settings. Some are small, full of character, and populated with characters. Some are so tacky you'll want to take a shower immediately after you make a break for the exit.

The best of the little places can be found in downtown along Fremont Street, which on a busy night often becomes an outdoor block party with visitors strolling from one casino to the next.

Mermaids. A lively storefront sawdust casino, all slots, bouncy music, and special promotions. Care for a deep-fried Twinkie? In an earlier incarnation, this was Sassy Sally's Casino; in an even earlier

Mermaids

incarnation, as the Carousel, it had a bit part in a classic James Bond film, *Diamonds Are Forever*. 32 Fremont Street. (702) 382–5777.

La Bayou Casino. A vaguely New Orleans–style storefront, formerly known as the Coin Castle. 15 East Fremont Street. (702) 385–7474.

THE CLUBS

You cannot come to Las Vegas without being assaulted by ads for "topless entertainment." We're not trying to influence you, but if that's what you want, two examples can be found on Fremont Street under the skeletal protection of the space frame: the Golden Goose ("World Class Topless Girls") and Glitter Gulch ("Topless Girls of Glitter Gulch"). Both typically offer "free" admission with a two-drink minimum purchase; a pair of beers can set you back about $16 to $20.

CHAPTER NINE

LAS VEGAS SHOWROOMS AND NIGHTLIFE

—

Econoguide Best Production Shows

★★★★★	**The Beatles LOVE.** *Mirage*
★★★★★	**Cirque du Soleil's *KÀ.*** *MGM Grand*
★★★★★	**Cirque du Soleil Presents O.** *Bellagio*
★★★★	**Blue Man Group.** *Venetian*
★★★★	**Cirque du Soleil's *Mystère.*** *Treasure Island*
★★★★	**Cirque du Soleil's *Zumanity.*** *New York–New York*
★★★★	***La Femme.*** *MGM Grand*
★★★★	***La Rêve.*** *Wynn Las Vegas*
★★★★	**Celine Dion.** *Caesars Palace*
★★★★	**Danny Gans.** *Mirage*
★★★	***Jubilee!*** *Bally's*
★★★	**Lance Burton.** *Monte Carlo*
★★★	***Les Folies Bergere.*** *Tropicana*

WITH A FEW NOTABLE EXCEPTIONS, some of the best entertainment buys in America can be found in Las Vegas, with lavish stage shows, superstars, and fabulous music. Why are the prices generally so reasonable? In a word, gambling. Las Vegas, Inc., uses the shows and the buffets and anything else they can to try to lure you into the casino. You'll walk past every slot machine and gaming table they can possibly put in your way between the front door and the showroom; then you'll have to walk back past them on your way out.

The latest trend in Las Vegas is back to the basics: sex. Not that there hasn't been lots of sex over the years at the casinos and showrooms, but Las Vegas has

Showgirls at Harrah's Las Vegas

realized that its bread and butter lies not as a family attraction and that it also has been losing some business to more-blatant strip joints and adult entertainment clubs.

And so visitors now see things like **Shadows,** a bar at Caesars Palace that barely shields all-but-naked dancers behind a thin screen, and the **Skin Pool Lounge** at Palms Casino Resort officially sanctions the ogling of bathing beauties. *Ivan Kane's Forty Deuce* at Mandalay Bay is a classy girlie show, if such a thing can exist.

In the showrooms the skin quotient has increased with shows like *La Femme* at MGM Grand, which features a squad of a dozen young women clad in boots, hats, and smiles. The show is an import of the très risqué Crazy Horse cabaret in Paris. At New York–New York, Cirque du Soleil has an "adult" show called *Zumanity* that includes acrobats clad in nude bodysuits.

Other shows that make a clean breast of their entertainment include *Midnight Fantasy* at Luxor, *Skintight* at Harrah's, and *Showgirls* at Rio All-Suite.

Cirque du Soleil has at least five shows going on in Las Vegas: *O* at the Bellagio, *Mystère* at Treasure Island, *Zumanity* at New York–New York, and *KÀ* at MGM Grand. The newest is *The Beatles LOVE* at the Mirage.

They're all good, in a strange Cirque kind of way. My favorites are *KÀ* for the jaw-dropping production value, *O* for the whimsy, and *LOVE* for the music.

KÀ is a story of duality, bringing together acrobatic performances, martial arts from all over the world, plus astonishing innovations in puppetry, multimedia, and pyrotechnics to tell the epic story of a set of twins on a perilous journey to fulfill their shared destiny.

At the Mirage, **The Beatles LOVE** opened in mid-2006. See chapter 6 for details. To get in all you'll need is cash.

The longtime kings of the Strip, Siegfried and Roy, were forced to shut down their show in the fall of 2003 after magician Roy Horn was seriously injured when he was attacked by one of the tigers in the act.

And then there are the household names of Las Vegas: singers, magicians, and comedians who have signed up for long-term deals that often extend for years. Among the semipermanent residents are Penn & Teller, Rita Rudner, and Celine Dion.

Rudner is among my favorites, with her deadpan . . . and dark . . . take on Las Vegas. Of the town's odd appeals, she says: "This is a place where breasts are entertainment. I went to my doctor for a mammogram and there was a two-drink minimum."

French-Canadian singer Celine Dion returned from exile to headline a spectacular show at a new 4,000-seat Colosseum theater at Caesars Palace through 2007, with Elton John as her regular replacement act. Rumors abound that the next diva to occupy the stage at Caesars, sometime in 2008, will be Cher.

Before you buy your ticket for any show in town, be sure you understand what's included. A common deal includes two drinks, usually from a selection of house brands; both drinks are usually served before the show begins. Additional drinks and snacks are billed at lounge prices. Some shows offer dinner, again usually from a limited menu (and rarely worth writing home about). The final question is this: Does the ticket include gratuities for your servers?

Another important thing to know about Vegas shows: In the past most of the shows did not offer assigned seating and you were at the mercy of the maître d'. High rollers and those who slipped the guy at the door $10 or $20 or more got the best tables. Recently, though, many of the showrooms have gone over to assigned seats; high rollers still get the very best places. In any case there are very few really bad seats in the showrooms, which are most often designed to be wider than they are deep, with a lot of front-row tables across the very wide

The Colosseum at Caesars Palace, home to Celine Dion

stage. The worst seats put you at a long table perpendicular to the stage. You share your evening with ten or twelve strangers at the table. The best seats, although usually not the closest, are the first tier of couchlike booths.

SHOWS, COMEDY, AND CONCERTS

The major shows tend to settle in for long runs, but nothing is forever. Be sure to call beforehand; you'll need a reservation for most shows in any case.

Many of the Las Vegas revues include scantily clad or topless dancers and many comedy acts are R-rated; some showrooms have PG-rated early shows for families and those easily offended (what are you doing in Las Vegas in the first place?).

■ LONG-RUNNING LAS VEGAS SHOWS

Times are based on winter season; most shows add more performances in summer and holiday periods. For current listings and prices, we recommend you consult the Web sites of individual resorts; you'll find information about each in chapters 6 and 7 of this book.

Tickets to the most popular shows are often sold out days or weeks ahead of schedule, especially during major conventions or sporting events. You can, though, hope to get lucky. Casinos hold back some seats for their high rollers, and any unused seats are usually released a few hours before a performance. You can also enlist the assistance of a hotel concierge for tickets at full price, plus a premium.

You may also find tickets for the same day sold at half price (plus a service charge) at several ticket brokerages. One such company is Tickets 2Nite in the atrium of the World of Coke attraction at the Showcase Mall north of the MGM Grand. Participating producers start releasing unsold show tickets for half price as early as 2:00 P.M. on the day of performance. For more information call (888) 484–9264 or consult www.tickets2nite .com.

Another half-price ticket company is Tix4Tonight, with a booth at the Fashion Show Mall and other loca-

An inconspicuous statue of Siegfried and Roy outside the Mirage on the Strip

tions on the Strip, open daily from noon; for information call (877) 849–4868 or consult www.tix4tonight.com.

Here are the major shows that were running in 2006. Be sure to consult with the resorts for updated information.

Bally's. *Jubilee!*

Bellagio. *O* from Cirque du Soleil.

Caesars Palace. Celine Dion, Elton John, other headliners.

Excalibur. *Tournament of Kings,* Australia's All-Male Revue: *Thunder from Down Under.*

Hard Rock. Headliners.

Harrah's. Rita Rudner, *Bareback.*

Las Vegas Hilton. Barry Manilow.

Luxor. Large theatrical productions. In 2006 the Luxor Theatre presented *Hairspray.*

Mandalay Bay. House of Blues concerts, Mandalay Bay Theatre offered *Mamma Mia* in 2006.

MGM Grand. *KÀ, La Femme,* headliner acts.

Mirage. *The Beatles LOVE,* Danny Gans.

Monte Carlo. Lance Burton.

New York–New York. *Zumanity.*

Paris Las Vegas. Headliner acts.

Rio All-Suites. *Erocktica,* Chippendales, Penn & Teller.

Riviera. *Crazy Girls, Splash.*

Treasure Island. *Mystère.*

Tropicana. *Les Folies Bergere.*

Venetian. Blue Man Group, *Phantom of the Opera.*

Wynn Las Vegas. *Le Rêve.*

CASINO NIGHTCLUBS

Proper attire ranges from stylish casual to glitter and glam; if your wardrobe consists of an "I'm With Stupid" T-shirt and plaid shorts, you might want to check on the dress code ahead of time. Most clubs levy a cover charge; some are $25 or more per person.

Caramel. (Bellagio.) Cocktails and a light menu, with the emphasis on a lack of emphasis: low-key is in vogue. Open nightly from 5 P.M. to 4 A.M. (702) 693–8300. www.lightgroup.com.

Jet. (Mirage). Darkness and light, including a laser grid and cryogenic effects with three rooms (rock, hip-hop, and house mix) plus four bars. Opened in early 2006. (702) 792–7900. www.lightgroup.com.

Light. (Bellagio.) High-energy music and lighting with table seating (with reservations available) and bottle service; a DJ provides a changing mix of grooves. Open Thursday through Sunday from 10:30 P.M. to 4 A.M. (702) 693–8300. www.lightgroup.com.

Mist Bar and Lounge. (Treasure Island.) A cool and casual place, featuring rock and popular music with time and space for conversation as well. Open every night from 5 P.M. to 4 A.M. (702) 894–7330. www.lightgroup.com.

V Bar. (Venetian). The place that claimed to invent the term "ultra lounge" has kept up with the competition. Populated by stylish people sprawled in leather chaise lounges. (702) 414–3200.

LOUNGING AROUND OFF THE STRIP

The Beach. They claim it's spring break all year long, but some nights are wilder than any of my college memories. Sundays are Jekyll & Hyde nights, when women are encouraged to dress as their naughty or nice fantasy, from lingerie to lace. Local and national bands play Wednesday and other nights; on Friday and Saturday nights there's a VIP open bar for patrons who pay for the privilege. Located at 365 Convention Center Drive. (702) 731–1925. www.beachlv.com.

BURLESQUE, MODERN LAS VEGAS–STYLE

Ivan Kane's Forty Deuce. (Mandalay Bay.) A tacky burlesque joint in a classy Las Vegas kind of way. Based on the original Forty Deuce club in Hollywood, the Mandalay Bay's version includes bump-and-grind performances on stage; between the acts DJs help guests entertain themselves on the dance floor. The club is located on the casino level, behind the elevators to the Mandalay Place shopping district. Forty Deuce is open nightly except Tuesday and Wednesday, from 10:30 P.M. until dawn. (702) 632–9442. www.fortydeuce.com.

On the Rocks

The drinking age in Nevada is twenty-one, and in most of the state there are no closing hours for liquor sales or consumption. Visitors from states that have more restrictive laws will be surprised to see other laxities, including free drinks at casinos.

You don't suppose the casinos (and their partner the state) are happy to see customers a bit loosened, do you?

SOME NIGHTCLUBS OUTSIDE THE CASINOS

Gordon Biersch Brewpub. The lively brewpub is the flagship of the chain of restaurants. 3987 Paradise Road. (702) 312–2337 or (702) 312–5247. www.gordonbiersch.com/restaurants.

Tommy Rocker's Cantina & Grill. A misplaced beach bar, home of the Las Vegas Parrot Head Club. Open twenty-four hours. 4275 Dean Martin Drive (formerly South Industrial Road.) (702) 261–6688. www.tommyrocker.com.

CHAPTER TEN

Mama Don't Allow No Gambling 'Round Here: Area Attractions

Econoguide Best Attractions in and around Las Vegas

CASINO ATTRACTIONS

★★★★ Fountains at Bellagio. *Bellagio*

★★★★ Fremont Street Experience

★★★★ Imperial Palace Antique Auto Collection. *Imperial Palace*

★★★★ Masquerade Show in the Sky. *Rio All-Suite*

★★★★ Volcano Eruption. *The Mirage*

★★★ Shark Reef. *Mandalay Bay*

THRILL RIDES AND THEME PARKS

★★★★ Adventuredome. *Circus Circus*

★★★★ Manhattan Express. *New York–New York*

★★★★ Las Vegas Cyber Speedway. *Sahara*

★★★★ Speed: The Ride. *Sahara*

★★★★ Star Trek: The Experience. *Las Vegas Hilton*

★★★★ Stratosphere Tower Rides. *Stratosphere Tower*

★★ Flyaway Indoor Skydiving. *Convention Center Drive*

ALTHOUGH YOU SOMETIMES HAVE TO SQUINT through a forest of slot machines and neon lights to see it, there is life outside of the casinos. Hidden to most visitors to Las Vegas is a wide variety of cultural and outdoor activities.

They are not quite high culture, but the biggest attractions in Las Vegas—other than tens of acres of slot machines and table games, dozens of magicians, divas and divos, and squadrons of nearly nude showgirls—include theme parks based on speed, height, and fear. Among the leaders: the **Adventuredome** at Circus Circus, **Star Trek: The Experience** at the Las Vegas Hilton, the heights of thrill atop the **Stratosphere Tower,** and roller coasters at New York–New York and the Sahara.

At the start of the 1990s, Las Vegas proposed to lure new business to town by claiming to be a "family" destination. The pitch: Bring the kids to town and let them play at our theme parks while Mom and Dad go out and gamble. Then the casino owners woke up. Although more families came to Las Vegas, visitors were spending time at the new attractions instead of at the slots and gaming tables. Suddenly the lure of family entertainment lost its appeal, at least to the casino operators.

In 2001, after several years as the incredible shrinking theme park, MGM Grand Adventure was closed; a year later Caesars Magical Empire disappeared to clear the way for the new diva in town. Longtime favorite Wet 'n Wild, right on the Strip, did not open for the 2005 season and will eventually be replaced . . . by a casino and condo project.

Downtown, the Fremont Street Experience continues to amaze; you can read about it in chapter 8.

LAS VEGAS HILTON

★★★★ STAR TREK: THE EXPERIENCE

For decades visitors to Las Vegas have been boldly going where no one has gone before. But all that is prologue to extraterrestrial thrills at the Las Vegas Hilton, a one-of-a-kind collaboration with Paramount Parks that includes a pair of separate Star Trek adventures.

Borg Invasion 4D combines live actors and special effects in one of the most advanced entertainment attractions on the planet—at least until the twenty-fourth century arrives for real. A Borg, in case you are not up-to-date on your alien taxonomy, is a collective cybernetic life-form much advanced beyond the state of Federation knowledge. The Borg seems to have only two principal goals: the consumption of technology and the "assimilation" of other species, including humans, into their collective consciousness.

It's not really Las Vegas and you're not a tourist with a pocketful of chips, you see; you're at Copernicus Station and you're a willing volunteer to save the peaceable universe. It's been found that you have a rare base pair DNA that makes you capable to fend off alien viruses. Lucky you; this means you just might be resistant to nanoprobe used by the Borg.

The Borg arrive, of course, and attempt to hijack your rescue effort. "Resistance is futile," we're told . . . but the human spirit manages to overwhelm the aliens.

The show begins with a tour of a research facility of the twenty-fourth century. Greeted by the creepy Borg, you'll be escorted to seats in a specially built theater. The digitally projected 3-D film includes an extraordinary number of special effects, including atmospheric and hydraulic effects, physical probes, pneumatic actuators, and an array of audio transducers. That means you'll be pushed, prodded, sprinkled upon, and moved in your seat.

The research facility and the film use actual or re-created props from *Star Trek* television episodes and movies such as *Star Trek Nemesis* and *Star Trek: First Contact*. The film features Robert Picardo (the Doctor), Alice Krige (Borg Queen), and Kate Mulgrew (Admiral Janeway).

The Borg Invasion can accommodate 300 guests per hour; the attraction itself takes about twenty-two minutes, including a movie of about seven minutes.

The original attraction, **Star Trek: The Experience,** begins with a visit to the **History of the Future Museum**—a collection of "real" artifacts, uniforms, and weapons from the *Star Trek* universe—where you're escorted into a shuttlecraft. Everything seems to go well until your travel is interrupted by a transport beam. When the beam stops, you find yourself on the bridge of the Federation Starship *Enterprise;* what's more, you have passed through a temporal rift in the space-time continuum and have arrived in the year 2371.

According to Commander Will Riker, bad things are afoot: Captain Picard has been kidnapped, and the Klingons have hatched a plan to eliminate one of Picard's ancestors so that Picard will never be born. Apparently someone in your group is that ancestor. So you'd better hightail your way out of there.

And so you're off to take a Turbolift (you might call it a futuristic elevator) to the transport vehicle. That sounds like a good idea until the Klingons somehow manage to latch on to your cab and send it into a free fall. (Your helpful elevator operator may inquire whether any of his passengers suffered "protein spills" on the way down.)

Finally you're at the Shuttlecraft *Goddard.* Sit in one of the first three rows for the best view of your return voyage. The screens in front and overhead show a spectacular view of a deep space battle that extends all the way down to a high-speed run through the Strip from the Excalibur Hotel to the Las Vegas Hilton.

The attraction is reminiscent of the groundbreaking *Back to the Future* attractions at Universal Studios in Orlando and Hollywood, adding actors and special effects to a whiz-bang multimedia motion platform. The simulator uses a six-axis platform similar to those used to train military jet pilots and NASA astronauts. The cast of a few dozen actors does a good job of staying in character throughout the experience, which takes about twenty-two minutes.

To experience the shuttlecraft ride/motion simulator, you must be at least 42 inches tall. Pregnant women and people with heart or back conditions are advised not to visit. Photography is not allowed during the Voyage through Space. Alas visitors cannot sit in the captain's chair on the bridge.

The casino and the promenade are open to visitors without charge. An all-in-one ticket for the Star Trek Experience, Borg Invasion 4D, and the History of the Future Museum was priced at $33.99 in 2006. Individual missions, including the museum, were priced at about $20 each. Open daily from 11:00 A.M. to 11:00 P.M.

At **Quark's Bar and Restaurant,** you can be the first from your corner of the galaxy to sample Romulan Ale, a specially brewed blue beer. Other unusual concoctions include a Ferengi Freeze, Vulcan Volcano, and the Harry Mudd Martini. The Warp Core Breach blends several rums; vodka; blue Curaçao; cranberry, pineapple, grapefruit, guava, and orange juices; grenadine; and more, served on a platform of dry ice. Specialty drinks range from about $5.00 to $14.00, higher when served in souvenir glasses.

At the 180-seat restaurant, specialties include the Talaxian Turkey Wrap, Dr. Bashir's Roasted Veggie Pizza, and Romulan Warbird, which looks very much like a charbroiled chicken breast in lemon, lime, and orange-zest vinaigrette. There are also a few contemporary dishes from Sisko's Restaurant in New Orleans including Bayou Linguini. Entrees range in price from about $8.00 to $18.00. For reservations and information call (702) 697–8725.

At the exit is the **SpaceQuest Casino,** a half-acre home to more than 400 slots and video games. Some slots have no handles; players pass their hand through a beam of light to spin the reels. Note that kids are not permitted to loiter at the casino, which is located at the show's exit.

You enter into the casino traveling through space. Overhead, a set of three huge "windows" displays scenes of the galaxies, rendered in high-resolution by computer. Earth appears outside the windows, about 1,500 miles away: dawn over North America, noon over the Mediterranean Sea, sunset over Asia, and night over the South Pacific. If you watch carefully, you'll see intergalactic trucks delivering Pepsi (one of the more unusual commercials you're likely to see anywhere) as well as space limousines and taxis depositing visitors.

There are, of course, slot machines and blackjack tables . . . but these are put forth as twenty-fourth-century money grabbers with fiber-optic lighting and multimedia effects. The spectacular roulette tables include fiber-optic elements, and computers read the drop of the ball and display winning combos; table games use hologram-like chips with an exploding SpaceQuest logo.

By the way, the SpaceQuest Casino is not the first Hilton in space: A Hilton hotel was featured on Space Station One in the film *2001: A Space Odyssey* in 1968 and on Mars in *Total Recall* in 1990.

Star Trek: The Experience at the Las Vegas Hilton. For information call (888) 462–6535 or (702) 697–8717, or consult www.startrekexp.com.

SAHARA

★★★★ SPEED: THE RIDE
★★★★ LAS VEGAS CYBER SPEEDWAY

At Las Vegas Cyber Speedway at the Sahara is your chance to experience most of the thrills and none of the risk of driving at 220 mph around a Grand Prix racetrack: The Cyber Speedway is a high-tech hoot. Or you can strap yourself into a slingshot roller coaster and cruise along the Las Vegas Strip at speeding-ticket velocity.

Speed: The Ride bursts through the front wall of the **NASCAR Café** and through the sign at the front of the casino. The unusual roller coaster sends riders up the starting hill with linear induction motors that propel the cars without old-fashioned chains; a second set of motors is out front of the casino along the Strip. The coaster reaches a top speed of 70 mph as it moves through the Sahara's huge marquee sign. After an inverted loop the cars climb up a nearly vertical incline and then fall backward through the entire track, returning to the NASCAR Café after their two-minute trip. Tickets in 2006 were $10 for one ride; an all-day attractions (cars and coaster) unlimited pass was $20. Riders must be at least 54 inches tall. Open Monday through Thursday noon to 10:00 P.M., Friday and Saturday from 11:00 A.M. to midnight, and Sunday from 11:00 A.M. to 10:00 P.M.

The other fast attraction at the Sahara is the **Las Vegas Cyber Speedway** (Speedworld when it first opened), created by a company that has manufactured flight and tank simulators for the military. This $15 million installation at the back of the Sahara casino puts you within the cockpit of an Indy-class race car on a six-axis motion base with a 133-degree wraparound projection screen.

You can't flip the car, and crashes into the wall or another car register as a shudder; other than that, though, the feel of the simulator is said to be very close to the real thing. After my uncertain and somewhat dizzying trip around the track, I'm willing to take that on faith.

Strapped into place in a seven-eighths-scale Indy car, you feel the wind in your face and the tilt of the track. You can choose an automatic transmission or shift for yourself with a semiautomatic clutchless system with six forward speeds. (The semiautomatic yields about a 10 percent boost in speed, but new drivers will have more than enough to worry about just staying on the track and probably should opt for the auto transmission.)

There are twenty-four cars split into groups of eight. The groups can race separately, or all cars can be on the track. There are two eight-minute courses, one a simulation of the Las Vegas Motor Speedway and the other a somewhat unusual road course up the Las Vegas Strip (most major hotels and landmarks are recognizable along the way, but they don't exactly match their locations on the map). The course on the Strip is more interesting, but the Speedway is more challenging and realistic.

The attraction is open daily from 10:00 A.M. until 11:00 P.M. on Friday and Saturday and until 10:00 P.M. other nights. Tickets for a single race were $10 in 2006; an unlimited all-day attractions pass (cars and coaster) was $20. Drivers must be at least 48 inches tall, and there is a weight restriction of 300 pounds for entry into the very tight confines of the simulator cockpit.

Even if you don't take a drive, it's worth the time to stand along the rail and watch the contestants; in Las Vegas, where almost anything goes, you might want to place a bet among friends about the results of any particular race. Car fans can also gawk at some real NASCAR, CART, and Indy cars parked in the aisles near the simulators.

Las Vegas Cyber Speedway. For information call (702) 737–2111 or consult www.saharavegas.com.

BELLAGIO

★★★★ FOUNTAINS AT BELLAGIO

At the **Fountains at Bellagio,** water from more than a thousand fountains flies high into the air in the artificial lake at the front of the resort, accompanied by music and a changing palette of colors. The shows are presented every half hour during the week from 3:00 to 7:00 P.M. and every fifteen minutes from 7:00 P.M. to midnight. On weekends the shows begin at noon. For information call (702) 693–7111.

The **Bellagio Gallery of Fine Art** offers a changing collection of work by Old Masters, modern artists, and great photographers. Admission is $15 for adults; students and seniors $12. Open daily 9:00 A.M. to 10:00 P.M. Reservations available and recommended for popular shows and prime time slots. For information call (702) 693–7871 or consult www.bellagio.com/pages/attrac_gallery.asp.

CIRCUS CIRCUS

★★★★ THE ADVENTUREDOME

This is the largest indoor amusement park in the country and a strange place even by Las Vegas standards. There are about two dozen rides and simulators of various sorts within the dome, located behind the hotel, ranging from a small but intense looping, corkscrewing roller coaster to kiddie rides.

Only in Las Vegas could they come up with something like this: a five-acre indoor entertainment park that presents a Las Vegas–eye view of the Grand Canyon, including 140-foot man-made peaks, a 90-foot re-creation of Havasupai Falls, and a river. The entire park, attached to the Circus Circus Hotel and Casino, is covered by a sparkling pink space-frame dome known as the **Adventuredome.**

According to industry sources, Adventuredome is the most popular indoor theme park in the country, attracting about 4.5 million visitors in 2005, making it number eleven among theme parks in the United States. (The Magic Kingdom at Walt Disney World in Orlando was the leading attraction, with 16.1 million admissions.)

Among the stars here is **Chaos.** Eighteen two-passenger seats whirl riders into many dimensions of motion, and no two rides are ever the same. The spinning riders come very close to one of the supports of the dome on one side, and then are whisked away from riders on the Canyon Blaster roller coaster.

Frog Hopper allows children who are at least 36 inches tall to "hop" straight up nearly 19 feet.

The **Fun House Express** multimedia experience is a computer simulation of a roller coaster ride that uses 3-D Imax images in three pitching and bucking fifteen-seat theaters. Guests must be 42 inches or taller for the four-minute ride. There's a story, too: It seems that Jimmy the clown is mad at his boss, so he sends visitors to his rickety old fun-house ride on a drop into . . . Clown Chaos.

The Canyon Blaster speeds by a dino at the Adventuredome

The park includes **Canyon Blaster,** billed as the world's only indoor double-looping roller coaster. If you're not already dizzy from the gambling, the neon, the all-you-can-eat buffets . . . then you are ready for the Canyon Blaster. You'll know this is a serious ride as you walk nearby: The floor shakes beneath your feet as the cars rumble by. The Canyon Blaster emphasizes speed and twists and turns over height; its track circles in and around much of the sphere. There are two loops, two corkscrews, and some interesting views of the Strip if you keep your eyes open.

The **Rim Runner** is a three-and-a-half-minute indoor water flume ride, mostly in the dark. THIS IS A WET RIDE. YOU WILL GET SOAKED, warn the signs. Disposable ponchos are sold at the gift shop.

The Adventuredome is open every day and into the night; call for current hours. Admission is free, and individual tickets cost $4.00 to $6.00, depending on the ride. An unlimited-rides pass in 2006 sold for $22.95 for those 48 inches and over, $14.95 for those 33 to 48 inches, and free to the littlest visitors. Circus Circus has changed its admission policy numerous times in recent years and sometimes makes seasonal adjustments.

The busiest times at the park come weekends and holidays, with nighttime crowds larger than in the morning and afternoon.

The Adventuredome. For information call (702) 794–3939 or consult www.adventuredome.com.

LUXOR

The hollow interior of the Luxor pyramid was originally conceived as an ancient Egyptian playground, featuring attractions created by special-effects designer Douglass Trumbull (responsible for the spectacular *Back to the Future* ride at Universal Studios in Orlando, Florida). The attractions, alas, proved to be somewhat of an ancient dud.

The IMAX Theatre offers a changing roster of spectacular films projected on a seven-story-high screen; some films are shown in 3-D. Tickets in 2006 were about $12.

The Tomb and Museum of King Tutankhamen showcases a replica of the gold-filled tomb discovered by archaeologist Howard Carter in 1922. Admission includes an audio-guided tour. Individual tickets for the museum were priced at about $10 in 2006.

A changing series of high-octane simulations are offered at the **Motion Simulator** daily from 9:00 A.M. to 11:00 P.M.

Former matinee idol turned comic actor turned swashbuckler Leslie Neilsen stars in a "multisensory" film adventure not quite like any other pirate movie in town. Tickets for *Pirates 4D* in 2006 were about $8.00, and the theater was open from 9:00 A.M. daily, closing between 6:00 and 11:00 P.M. depending on day of the week and season.

In addition to individual tickets, various combination packages of attractions within the pyramid at the Luxor are also available

Luxor. For information and hours call (702) 262–4400 or consult www.luxor .com.

PARIS LAS VEGAS

★ EIFFEL TOWER

It's not Paris, and it's not the real Eiffel Tower, but this is the nearest thing to one of the symbols of France's City of Lights in Las Vegas (the other extravagantly lit metropolis.) The elevator ride to the top of the fifty-story downsized replica of the tower delivers a spectacular view of the Strip. In 2006 tickets were $9.00 to $12.00 for adults and $7.00 for children and seniors; a family pass was also available for about $28.00. The elevator is open daily from 10:00 A.M. to midnight.

Paris Las Vegas. For information call (702) 946–7000 or consult www.caesars .com/paris/lasvegas.

★★ FLYAWAY INDOOR SKYDIVING

Only in Las Vegas would this sound only slightly out of the ordinary: a vertical wind tunnel powered by an airplane propeller where you can skydive without an airplane.

Lucky participants fly in a column of air 12 feet across and 22 feet high, moving at airspeeds of up to 115 mph. They wear flight suits and helmets, but no parachutes are necessary. And yes, there is a heavy-duty screen between divers and the engine's propeller.

Classes are scheduled every half hour and the whole experience takes about an hour, including a fifteen-minute flight session shared by five flyers. In 2006 prices for a first flight were about $60; subsequent dives cost a bit less. Check with Flyaway for height, weight, and age restrictions. Located at 200 Convention Center Drive, it's open Monday to Saturday from 10:00 A.M. to 7:00 P.M. and until 5:00 P.M. on Sunday.

Flyaway Indoor Skydiving. For information call (702) 731–4768 or (877) 545–8093 or consult www .flyawayindoorskydiving.com.

IMPERIAL PALACE

★★★★ IMPERIAL PALACE ANTIQUE AUTO COLLECTION

With more than 200 antique and classic cars, the **Imperial Palace Antique Auto Collection** is the most impressive used-car dealership you will ever see.

In recent years one corner of the museum was a room full of Deusenbergs worth more than $50 million.

Among the cars I saw on a recent visit were a 1930 Deusenberg town car priced at $1.1 million; a 1933 Deusie touring car like the ones owned by Clark Gable, Mae West, and other stars and priced at $1.95 million; and a bulletproof 1988 Mercedes-Benz 500 SEL purchased by Imelda Marcos and used by her husband Ferdinand Marcos in exile.

This Explains a Lot, Doesn't It?

As if Las Vegas wasn't already one weird place, consider the fact that 50 or so miles north and west of town is the neighborhood nuclear test site.

From its start in the depths of the cold war in 1951 through today, there have been nearly 700 tests of nuclear bombs. At first the explosions were conducted in the atmosphere, and it was not an unusual sight to see a mushroom cloud cresting over downtown Las Vegas. Since the 1960s the explosions have taken place underground. Nuclear testing was suspended in 1992, but some fear it may be resumed.

The Nevada Test Site at Yucca Flat is part of the huge Nellis Air Force Range. The test site is 1,350 square miles, about the size of the entire state of Rhode Island.

The museum is open every day from 9:30 A.M. to 11:30 P.M. Admission for adults is $6.95; children (five to twelve) and seniors pay $3.00. Free ticket coupons are usually available in the casino and at www.autocollections.com.

Want to watch Michael Jackson (or someone who looks weirdly like him) deal blackjack? How about a hunka-hunka burning love from an Elvis clone, or a bit of coolness from a version of the Blues Brothers? These and a cast of other changing look-alikes (regulars also include doubles for Barbra Streisand, Gwen Stefani, and even Ray Charles—although the clone does keep a close eye on the chips) work the **Dealertainers Pit** at the Imperial Palace daily from noon until near dawn.

Remember, though, that this attraction is free only if you can resist buying some chips and making a bet; there is no charge to watch from a discrete distance.

Imperial Palace Hotel & Casino. For information call (702) 731–3311 or consult www.imperialpalace.com.

MANDALAY BAY

★★★ SHARK REEF

Safely behind a huge glass wall, gawk at some 2,000 dangerous and unusual creatures of the sea, including fifteen species of shark, at the **Shark Reef.** Open daily from 10:00 A.M. to 11:00 P.M. Admission in 2006 was about $16 for adults and $10 for children ages five to twelve.

Mandalay Bay Resort & Casino. For information call (702) 632–4555 or consult www.mandaybay.com.

NEW YORK–NEW YORK

★★★★ MANHATTAN EXPRESS AT NEW YORK–NEW YORK

People actually pay for this: The **Manhattan Express** is the world's first roller coaster to feature a "heartline" twist-and-dive maneuver. A heartline roll is similar to the sensation a pilot feels during a barrel roll when the center of rotation is the same as the passenger's center of gravity. In the twist-and-dive portion of the ride, the train rolls 180 degrees, suspending riders 86 feet above the casino roof before diving directly under itself.

The portion of the ride visible from the Strip is only a small piece of the fun; most of the track runs out back over the parking lot. A good view of the track is from the sidewalk on Tropicana Avenue or from across the road at Excalibur.

Riders board sixteen-passenger trains from within the New York–New York casino and then ascend a 203-foot lift. The first drop of 75 feet is just a warm-up for the fifty-five-degree, 144-foot second drop that passes within a few feet of the hotel's valet entrance at 67 mph. The ride is also unusually long, lasting just short of four minutes; it will probably seem a lot longer to you.

There are lockers near the entrance for personal possessions—you don't want to carry anything droppable from the coaster.

New York–New York also includes one of the largest arcades and carnival game rooms in town.

Tickets for the coaster are about $12.50, with rerides for $6.00 and an all-day Scream Pass for $25.00. You can also purchase a Family Fun Flight for Four for $49.99, which includes four ride tickets and two souvenir photographs. Riders must be at least 54 inches tall. The ride is open Sunday through Thursday from 10:30 A.M. to 11:00 P.M. and until midnight on Friday and Saturday.

The Manhattan Express crosses in front of New York–New York.

Manhattan Express at New York–New York. For information call (702) 740–6969 or consult www.nynyhotelcasino.com.

THE MIRAGE

★★★★ VOLCANO ERUPTION

Only in Las Vegas can you set your watch by the scheduled eruptions of a 54-foot volcano in a lagoon, called **Volcano Eruption.** The show includes smoke, fire, and water and takes place daily on the hour between 6:00 P.M. and midnight.

The **Siegfried and Roy Secret Garden and Dolphin Habitat** is a very special zoo and aquarium that was set up by the magicians who once headlined at the Mirage. Residents include white lions, Bengal tigers, and Atlantic bottlenose dolphins. Open daily from 10:00 A.M. to 7:00 P.M. In 2006 admission was about $15 for adults and $10 for children ages four to twelve.

Note that you can see one or two of the white tigers in their free habitat near one of the entrances to the casino.

Banjo, a dolphin at Siegfried and Roy's Secret Garden at the Mirage

At the **Royal White Tiger Habitat,** a floor-to-ceiling glass window stands between visitors and several of Siegfried and Roy's white tigers in an environment near the Strip entrance to the Mirage. Sometimes the animals pace and prowl, and sometimes they act like house kittens—fast asleep and oblivious to the gawkers.

The Mirage. For information call (702) 791–7111 or visit www.themirage.com.

RIO ALL-SUITE HOTEL & CASINO

★★★★ MASQUERADE SHOW IN THE SKY

The *Masquerade Show in the Sky* is a floating, mechanical carnival. Floats follow tracks hung from the ceiling; aboard are some of the dancers and performers from the various Rio shows plus a few ringers from the audience. There's no charge to watch, but you can pay about $13 to ride along. Note that children younger than eighteen must watch from one of the shopping balconies and cannot stand on the floor near the slot machines. The show schedule, subject to change during peak seasons, usually begins at 3:00 and continues until 9:00 or 9:30 P.M.

The **Bevertainers** at the Rio All-Suite give you two choices: You can watch cocktail waitresses jump up onto platforms among the slot machines and sing, dance, or gyrate, or you can have singers and dancers step down from their small stages to bring you drinks. Performances break out regularly, twenty-four hours a day. There's no charge to watch.

Rio All-Suite Hotel & Casino. For more information call (702) 252–7777 or visit www.harrahs.com.

STRATOSPHERE LAS VEGAS

★★★★ THE STRATOSPHERE TOWER

The Stratosphere Tower, the nation's tallest free-standing observation tower at 1,149 feet, is topped off by four of the highest thrill rides in the world: X-Scream, the Big Shot zero-gravity simulator, and the Let It Ride High Roller, the world's highest roller coaster starting at 909 feet aboveground and zooming around the Tower's pod.

Insanity: The Ride is an insane ride consisting of an arm that extends out 64 feet over the edge of the tower holding cars filled with paying customers. Once it begins to spin, riders feel the equivalent of up to three Gs. The arm tilts as much as seventy degrees, pushing strapped-in riders over the edge and downward toward the Strip.

X-Scream is like a giant teeter-totter, not quite child's play, though; the open vehicle propels riders head-first 27 feet over the edge of the Stratosphere Tower at 30 mph and then dangles them weightlessly above the Strip.

The **Let It Ride High Roller** travels around on the top of the tower on 1,865 feet of track. The nine four-passenger cars make three clockwise rotations around the tower, banking at thirty-two-degree angles. The High Roller may be removed in 2006 to make room for a new ride.

The **Big Shot** ride was designed by a major bungee-jumping company and offers the same sort of a straight up-and-down terror ride by thrusting sixteen passengers 160 feet in the air along a 228-foot mast extending like a needle from the top of the tower. Traveling at speeds of up to 45 mph, the ride shoots passengers from the 921-foot level of the tower to the 1,081-foot level and then lets them free fall back to the launching pad. Riders experience up to four Gs as they near the top and negative Gs on the way down.

In 2006 tickets for the elevator to the top of the tower were $9.95 for adults and $6.00 for children ages four to twelve and seniors. Tickets for Insanity, Big Shot, or X-Scream were $8.00 each, and High Roller tickets cost $4.00. Various all-in-one and combination tickets are also available.

The Stratosphere Tower. For information call (702) 380–7777 or consult www .stratospherehotel.com.

VENETIAN RESORT

★ GONDOLA RIDES

The **Gondola Rides** are the next best thing to the real thing, in a Las Vegas sort of way: The gondoliers at the Venetian steer replica gondolas along a ¼-mile-long indoor canal and a shorter outdoor lagoon. They'll sing to you, too. In 2006 a ride cost $12.50 for adults on the lagoon and $15.00 under the painted ceiling within; a couple can also rent a private gondola for $50.00 outside and $60.00

inside. Open daily from 10:30 A.M. to 10:30 P.M. or later. For information call (702) 414–4500.

A selection of some of the masterpieces of the Hermitage Museum in St. Petersburg, Russia and other museums can be found at the **Guggenheim Hermitage Museum**. Admission is $19.50 for adults, $15 for seniors, and $9.50 for students and children ages six to twelve. Free audio guide provided; guided tours offered afternoons and evenings. Open daily from 9:30 A.M. to 8:30 P.M. For information call (702) 414–2440 or consult www.guggenheimlasvegas.org.

It sounds like a contradiction, but they call **Madame Tussaud's Celebrity Encounter** an interactive wax museum. The simulated celebrities, historical figures, and sports stars are still rather stiff and unresponsive, but at this outpost of the famous wax museum company, visitors are encouraged to "interact" with their favorites: Bring your camera.

The attraction is located near the Strip on the right side of the broad entrance to the Venetian. Ticket prices in 2006 were about $22.95, and the museum opened daily at 10:00 A.M., with closing hours varying by season.

For information see chapter 6, call (702) 367–1847, or consult www.madame-tussauds.com.

OTHER ATTRACTIONS

▪ Elvis Presley Enterprises, which owns just about everything connected with the King's name, likeness, and possessions, purchased and shut down the collection of jumpsuits, sweaty handkerchiefs, and other relics that made up the **Elvis-a-Rama** museum on Industrial Road in late 2005.

The company plans to bring a "world class Elvis-themed attraction" to the Strip in coming years.

▪ **Bonnie Springs Ranch/Old Nevada.** Located off Highway 159, 23 miles west of Las Vegas. A re-creation of an 1860s Western mining town, complete with gunfights, hangings, a museum . . . and gift shops. Also on the premises is the Red Rock Riding Stables. The attraction is open seven days a week from 10:30 A.M. to 5:00 P.M. and until 6:00 P.M. in the summer. Admission in 2006 was $10.00 per car (up to six passengers). Shuttle service from Las Vegas is available. For information call (702) 875–4191 or consult www.bonniesprings.com. Also see the section on Red Rock Canyon in chapter 14.

▪ **Desperado.** Buffalo Bill's, Primm. A major-league coaster, with a 225-foot first drop, out in the middle of the desert in the minicasino settlement of Primm, about 30 miles west of Las Vegas near the California line. Single-ride, multiple-ride, and all-day passes are available for prices ranging from $10 to $20 during the week, and $12 to $30 on weekends. Open Thursday through Sunday; hours vary depending on the season. For information call (702) 382–1212.

▪ **Ethel M Chocolates.** One Sunset Way, Henderson. (702) 458–8864. You don't have to be from Mars to sniff out this local attraction: a free self-guided tour of a gourmet chocolate factory surrounded by a carefully tended cactus garden that has more than 350 species of the desert plant and succulents from around the world. There's also a smaller version of M&M's World. Ethel M was the matriarch of the Mars candy family (as in Mars Bars and M&Ms); the chocolates here are a cut above.

You'll be offered a small sample and the opportunity to open your wallet to bring home more. Open daily from 8:30 A.M. to 7:00 P.M.

■ **Forum Shows.** The Forum Shops at Caesars.

The statues at the Festival Fountain come to audio-animatronic life once an hour in a strange mix of theater, special effects, and a wink and a nod at Roman history.

At the Atlantis show, stand back for fire, smoke, and an electronic aquarium.

Shows are presented every hour on the hour from 10:00 A.M. to 11:00 P.M. For information call (702) 893–4800.

■ **Fremont Street Experience.** Downtown Las Vegas. A one-of-a-kind light show presented on a huge overhead screen above the historic Las Vegas downtown district. A changing series of shows is offered on the hour from 6:00 P.M. to midnight. Free concerts and special events, including New Year's and other holiday celebrations, are also offered. For information call (702) 678–5600.

■ **Gameworks.** Showcase Mall, 3785 Las Vegas Boulevard South. More than 200 video games and other coin-eating devices and a huge indoor rock-climbing wall; there's also a snack bar. Next door is M&M's World. For information call (702) 432–4263.

■ **Lion Habitat.** MGM Grand. Walk through a glass hallway into the domain of Goldie and Metro and a few of their other leonine friends. Open daily from 11:00 A.M. to 10:00 P.M. For information call (702) 891 7777.

■ **M&M's World.** Showcase Mall, 3785 Las Vegas Boulevard South. All things M&M's: candy (including some unusual colors), clothing, toys, and other souvenirs to prove your affinity for chocolate and Las Vegas. Admission is free to the store and a short 3-D movie . . . starring Red and Yellow candies. Open Sunday to Thursday 9:00 A.M. to 11:00 P.M. and Friday and Saturday until midnight. For information call (702) 736–7611.

■ **Magic Motion Film Ride.** Excalibur. A rotating series of simulator experiences located at the Fantasy Faire midway. In 2006 tickets were about $5.00 per experience, and

Hard Rock Cafe

the ride was open daily from 11:00 A.M. to 10:45 P.M., until midnight or later on Friday and Saturday nights. For information see chapter 6, call (702) 597–7777, or consult www.excaliburlasvegas.com.

■ **Sirens of TI.** Treasure Island. A ship full of pirates is beckoned—and ultimately captured—by a crew of sexy sirens in the pond between Treasure Island and the Strip; the choreographed show includes cannon fire, explosions, aerial acts, and music. Presented nightly at 5:30, 7:00, 8:30, and 10:00 P.M. The best free standing places fill up as much as thirty minutes before each show; you can buy a drink at one of the outdoor bars for a closeup view. For information call (702) 894–7111.

MUSEUMS

■ **Atomic Testing Museum.** 755 East Flamingo Road. From the 1940s through the early 1990s, the desert north of Las Vegas was one of the nation's primary atomic testing sites. Admission is $10, with discounts for seniors, students, and military personnel. Open Monday to Saturday from 9:00 A.M. to 5:00 P.M. and Sunday from 1:00 to 5:00 P.M. For information call (702) 794–5151 or consult the Web site at www.atomictestingmuseum.org.

■ **Boulder City Hoover Dam Museum.** 1305 Arizona Street in Boulder City. Historic artifacts of the construction of Hoover Dam. Open Monday to Saturday from 10:00 A.M. to 5:00 P.M. and Sunday noon to 5:00 P.M. Admission: adults $2.00, children and seniors $1.00. For information call (702) 294–1988 or consult www.bcmha.org.

■ **Clark County Heritage Museum.** 1830 South Boulder Highway in Henderson. A collection of area history including railroad rolling stock and memorabilia; Heritage Street, a collection of historic homes in a park; and a time line from prehistoric to current. Open daily except holidays, 9:00 A.M. to 4:30 P.M. Admission: adults $1.50, children and seniors $1.00. For information call (702) 455–7955 or consult www.co.clark.nv.us/Parks/Clark_County_Museum.htm.

■ **Las Vegas Art Museum.** 9600 West Sahara Avenue. Three galleries that offer displays of local and national artists; the displays change monthly. The original building was constructed in the 1930s from wooden railroad ties; the museum moved into its current architectural swoop of a building in 1997. Some of its national exhibits come through an affiliation with Smithsonian Museum. Open Tuesday through Saturday from 10:00 A.M. to 5:00 P.M. and Sunday 1:00 to 5:00 P.M. Admission: adults $6.00, students with ID $3.00, seniors $5.00. For information call (702) 360–8000 or consult www.lasvegasartmuseum.org.

■ **Las Vegas Historic Museum.** Tropicana Resort. A peek into the not-so-secret and not-so-glamorous early history of Las Vegas, including information about the pioneers of all the things that made the place what it is today: gambling, brothels, mobsters, and entertainers. More of a wink and a nudge than a real pulling back of the covers, but visitors must be at least eighteen years old or accompanied by an adult. Admission in 2006 was about $7.00 for adults and $6.00 for seniors; open daily from 9:00 A.M. to 9:00 P.M. For information call (702) 739–2222.

- **Las Vegas Natural History Museum.** 900 Las Vegas Boulevard North. Wildlife, an educational gift shop, and a nice collection of dinosaurs, including the skull of a T-rex. Open daily from 9:00 A.M. to 4:00 P.M. Admission: adults $7.00, students and seniors $6.00, and children (three to eleven) $3.00. For information call (702) 384–3466 or consult www.lvnhm.org.

- **Liberace Museum.** 1775 East Tropicana Avenue. "Mr. Showmanship" is gone but the glitter remains. Much of his collection of costumes, pianos, candelabras, and cars stands vigil in this museum, operated by the Liberace Foundation for the Performing and Creative Arts, which provides educational grants to schools and colleges.

Some of his outfits were wilder than those worn by showgirls on the Strip, including a suit made of ostrich feathers. There are some eighteen Liberace-special pianos; five Liberacemobiles, including a Rolls Royce covered with mirror tiles; and jewelry including a piano-shaped ring containing 260 diamonds in a gold setting with ivory and black jade keys.

The main museum includes the Piano, Car, and Celebrity Galleries; the annex includes the Costume and Jewelry Galleries and a re-creation of Liberace's office and bedroom from his Palm Springs home. The library includes personal mementos including a lifetime's worth of press clippings and photographs.

The museum is five minutes east of the Strip on Tropicana Avenue, in a strip mall. The collection is spread among three sites: A collection of pianos and cars is found in a freestanding building near Tropicana; and two storefronts in the plaza display some of Liberace's fabulous outfits, furniture, and personal effects, including photos. There is, of course, a gift shop; it's one of the only places I know where you can buy fake rhinestone vests and all manner of piano-themed neckties, scarves, and costume jewelry.

Treasures of the museum's collection include the following:

- An Empress chinchilla and blue silk brocade outfit valued at $600,000.
- A $1 million Rolls Royce Phantom V Landau Limousine, one of only seven made, covered with rhinestones and mirror tiles and formerly used to drive Liberace onstage for grand entrances.
- Red, white, and blue jeweled hot pants worn at a Radio City Music Hall celebration of the hundredth birthday of the Statue of Liberty.
- A fabulous antique desk reputed to be among the possessions of Czar Nicholas II taken from the Imperial Palace in St. Petersburg and sold after the Russian Revolution. Almost Alice in Wonderland–like, with loopy curves and filigrees, Liberace used it in the office of his Tivoli Gardens Restaurant.

Open Tuesday to Saturday from 10:00 A.M. to 5:00 P.M., Sunday 1:00 to 5:00 P.M. Admission in 2006 was $12.50 for adults, $8.50 for seniors and students. Children younger than twelve are admitted free. For information call (702) 798–5595 or consult www.liberace.org.

- **Lied Discovery Children's Museum.** Across from Cashman Field at 833 Las Vegas Boulevard North. A hands-on place for kids, including Toddler Towers, a model of the Space Shuttle, a radio station, a collection of computer toys, and more. Open Tuesday to Sunday from 10:00 A.M. to 5:00 P.M.; closed Monday except most school holidays. Admission: adults $7.00, juniors (two to seventeen) and seniors $6.00. For information call (702) 382–5437 or consult www.ldcm.org.

▪ **Lost City Museum of Archeology.** Located in Overton, 60 miles northeast of Las Vegas via Interstate 15, at 721 South Highway 169. Artifacts and interpretations of Pueblo Grande de Nevada, the so-called Lost City of the Anasazi, who occupied the area for about 1,200 years until the year 1150. Open daily from 8:30 A.M. to 4:30 P.M. Admission: $3.00. For information call (702) 397–2193 or consult http://dmla.clan.lib.nv.us/docs/museums/lost/lostcity.htm.

▪ **Marjorie Barrick Museum of Natural History.** Located on the campus of UNLV at 4505 South Maryland Parkway. This is the University of Nevada at Las Vegas's collection, which includes a selection of lizards, snakes, and spiders guaranteed to make your skin crawl; there's also an impressive display of arrowheads. The museum features exhibits on Mojave Desert wildlife, traditional baskets of southern Paiutes, Navajo textiles, Hopi kachina dolls, and early Las Vegas life, as well as Mexican dance masks, Guatemalan Huipils, and pre-Columbian pottery.

Open Monday through Friday from 8:00 A.M. to 4:45 P.M., Saturday 10:00 A.M. to 2:00 P.M. Admission free. For information call (702) 895–3381 or consult http://hrcweb.nevada.edu/museum.

▪ **Nevada State Museum & Historical Society.** 700 Twin Lakes Drive in Lorenzi Park (take Interstate 95 to Valley View). The history of southern Nevada from the dawn of native culture some 13,000 years ago to the present, including the Hoover Dam, Nevada's role as a nuclear test site, and its mining industry. Open daily from 9:00 A.M. to 5:00 P.M. Admission: $4.00 for adults, $3.00 for seniors; free for children younger than eighteen. For information call (702) 486–5205 or consult http://dmla.clan.lib.nv.us/docs/museums/lv/vegas.htm.

▪ **Searchlight Museum.** Located in the Searchlight Community Center, 60 miles south of Las Vegas. An outpost of the Clark County Heritage Museum at 200 Michael Wendell Way, it chronicles the history of the former mining town of Searchlight and the story of famed Hollywood fashion designer Edith Head and screen stars Clara Bow and Rex Bell, all of whom lived there. Open weekdays from 1:00 to 5:00 P.M. and Saturday from 9:00 A.M. to 1:00 P.M. Admission free. For information call (702) 297–1055 or consult www.co.clark.nv.us/parks/clark_county_museum.htm#Searchlight.

▪ **Southern Nevada Zoological-Botanical Park (Las Vegas Zoo).** 1775 North Rancho. Nevada's only public zoo, with a small collection including endangered cats, the last family of Barbary apes in the United States, a chimpanzee, eagles, ostriches, emus, talking parrots, wallabies, flamingos, large exotic reptiles, and every species of venomous reptile native to southern Nevada. The zoo also features exhibits by the Las Vegas Gem Club and botanical displays of endangered cycads and rare bamboos. Open daily from 9:00 A.M. to 5:00 P.M. Admission: adults $7.00, children (two to twelve) $5.00. For information call (702) 647–4685 or consult www.lasvegaszoo.org.

CHAPTER ELEVEN

LOCAL PROTOCOL

SEX, MARRIAGE, SHOPPING, COMPS, AND TIPPING

SEX, SEX, SEX

There, I got your attention, didn't I? That is the philosophy of Nevada, too, and especially Las Vegas. The casinos and hotels and just about everything else in town are tied to sex, from the costumes on the cocktail waitresses, the togas on the greeters at Caesars Palace, and the production shows to the more-directly-to-the-point topless bars.

Getting past the idea of sex as tease, there is also a small but apparently thriving industry in prostitution in much of the state.

Prostitution is perhaps no more common in Nevada than it is in most other parts of the country and certainly on a par with most convention and entertainment centers. It is, however, legal in several parts of the state, and there are about thirty-six legalized houses or "ranches" in the state. The industry is centered just outside of Reno and up or down the road from Las Vegas. For the record, the Nevada Supreme Court upheld the rights of the counties to legalize and regulate brothels; Clark County, which includes Las Vegas, and Washoe County, home of Reno, are among the few that do not permit brothels.

In Las Vegas, though, the streets are littered with brochures from "escort" services that offer what they describe as "in-room entertainment" and other such euphemisms. And Reno is ringed by special-service companies.

Many of the companies masquerade as massage services, entertainment bureaus, or escort services.

Among the brothels outside of Las Vegas is the Cherry Patch in Crystal, about 80 miles northwest; the Chicken Ranch in Pahrump; and Sheri's Ranch in

Pahrump. In the Reno area there are the Old Bridge Ranch outside of Sparks and the Wild Horse Canyon Resort in Patrick.

Although the licensed brothels make claims to carefully follow health regulations, I would be remiss not to warn that using the services of a prostitute—legal or illegal—is a highly dangerous activity. There is the chance of exposure to disease, including AIDS, and there is the possibility of being robbed on the street or in your hotel room. A much safer diversion is to read the entertainment section of the Yellow Pages in your hotel room for a few dirty laughs.

GETTING HITCHED

Speaking of more socially acceptable forms of bonding, the idea of Las Vegas as a wedding—and divorce—mecca dates back to the same "anything goes" mentality that gave birth to the gambling industry and other adventures. Today Las Vegas and Reno continue to have thriving wedding industries with the added lure of the grand hotels and casinos. In 2005 Clark County issued 122,259 marriage licenses, a slight decline from the record reached the year before, but that's still an awful lot of white lace and promises.

If you're the type to be impressed by celebrity name-dropping, check out some of the ads or billboards for the wedding chapels. According to the proprietors those who have done the deed at their establishments include Joan Collins, Mia Farrow, Eddie Fisher, Michael Jordan, Jon Bon Jovi, Demi Moore, Dudley Moore, Mickey Rooney, Frank Sinatra, Elizabeth Taylor, and Bruce Willis. And then there were quickie (and short) marriages for Britney Spears and Nicky Hilton.

Now let's get Elvis out of the way (please) first: The Graceland Chapel (named after EP's modest bungalow in Memphis) claims to be the first to bring out the King . . . or a simulacrum thereof . . . to entertain at the wedding of a pair of strangers (to him). Other Elvis-theme weddings include a package at the Silver Bell Wedding Chapel with a private performance and a souvenir replica scarf.

At Treasure Island a bride and groom can tie the knot aboard the *Song,* one of the battleships tied up in the harbor along the Strip. At the Venetian visitors can get hitched on a romantic bridge over the canal and be serenaded by a gondolier on a celebratory cruise.

You can get married dressed as King Arthur and Guinevere at the Excalibur, in a toga at Caesars Palace, or as just about anything else at any of a number of chapels. And there are dozens of small establishments that do nothing else but service the needs of the betrothed.

The busier chapels require advance reservations, but many of the chapels in Las Vegas can also deal with walk-in customers. For those in a hurry, there is a drive-up window at the Little White Chapel, where the bride and groom can exchange rings and a kiss and then get back into traffic. At the other end of the spectrum, you can spend thousands on Elvis, knights in shining armor, and a rented maid of honor and best man.

But let's back up for a moment; once the wining and dining and proposing are out of the way, the first step is to obtain a marriage license. If you are planning to get married in Las Vegas, check with the county clerk's office for the current legalities about obtaining a license. For recorded information on marriages in Clark County, call (702) 671–0600. The Clark County Marriage License Bureau is located in the Regional Justice Center at 201 Clark Avenue. Bureau hours are 8:00 A.M. to midnight Monday through Thursday. On weekends it is open around the clock from 8:00 A.M. Friday to midnight Sunday. On legal holidays the bureau is open twenty-four hours.

In 2006 the license fee in Clark County was $55 in cash. You can also obtain information about the process on a Web page at www .co.clark.nv.us/clerk/marriage_ information.htm.

There is no requirement for a blood test or a waiting period for a marriage between a man and a woman age eighteen or older in Las Vegas.

A wedding party sets sail at the Venetian

If you want to take your new license around the corner for an immediate civil ceremony conducted by a county clerk, the Office of Civil Marriages is located at 309 South Third Street. Ceremonies are conducted daily from 8:00 A.M. to 10 P.M., including weekends and holidays; no appointment is necessary—just get in line. The fee is $50 cash, exact change please. One witness is required; if you don't bring your own, you may be able to borrow one from bystanders or the next couple in line.

There are branches of the Clark County office in Laughlin, (702) 298–4622, and Mesquite, (702) 346–5262.

■ CHAPEL CEREMONIES

For many visitors, though, a civil ceremony at the commissioner's office is not what it is all about. Instead they want to do it up in grand (by Las Vegas standards) style at one of the dozens of wedding chapels. You can get just about anything you want, from a choir of Elvis impersonators to a chapel on wheels to a ceremony in King Arthur's Court. Rates vary and reservations are necessary at some—but not all—of the chapels.

Here is a listing of some:

Candlelight Wedding Chapel. 2855 Las Vegas Boulevard South. (702) 735–4179, (800) 962–1818. www.candlelightchapel.com.

Chapel of the Bells. 2233 Las Vegas Boulevard South. (702) 735–6803, (800) 233–2391. www.chapelofthebellslasvegas.com.

Chapels of Love. 1431 Las Vegas Boulevard South. (702) 387–0155, (800) 922–5683. www.chapelsoflove.com.

Cupid's Wedding Chapel. 827 Las Vegas Boulevard South. (702) 598–4444, (800) 543–2733. www.cupidswedding.com.

Double Happiness Wedding Chapel. Chinatown Plaza, 4215 Spring Mountain Road. (702) 252–0400, (800) 599–8228.

Graceland Wedding Chapel. 619 Las Vegas Boulevard North. (702) 382–0091, (800) 824–5732. www.gracelandchapel.com.

A Hollywood Wedding Chapel. 2207 Las Vegas Boulevard South. (702) 731–0678, (800) 704–0478. www.ahollywoodweddingchapel.com.

Little Chapel of the Flowers. 1717 Las Vegas Boulevard South. (702) 735–4331, (800) 843–2410. www.littlechapel.com.

Little Church of the West. 4617 Las Vegas Boulevard South. (702) 739–7971, (800) 821–2452. www.littlechurchlv.com.

A Little White Chapel. Drive-through weddings (The Tunnel of Vows) as well as hot-air balloon ceremonies. 1301 Las Vegas Boulevard South. (702) 382–5943, (800) 545–8111. www.alittlewhitechapel.com.

Shalimar Wedding Chapel. 1401 Las Vegas Boulevard South. (702) 382–7372, (800) 255–9633. www.shalimarweddingchapel.com.

Victoria's Wedding Chapel. 2800 West Sahara Avenue. (702) 252–4564, (800) 344–5683. www.avictorias.com.

Viva Las Vegas Wedding Chapel. 1205 Las Vegas Boulevard South. (702) 384–0771, (800) 574–4450. www.vivalasvegasweddings.com.

Wee Kirk o' the Heather. 231 Las Vegas Boulevard South. (702) 382–9830, (800) 843–5266. www.weekirk.com.

Here are some of the hotel chapels in Las Vegas:

Bally's Celebration Wedding Chapel. 3645 Las Vegas Boulevard South. (702) 894–5222, (800) 872–1211.

Caesars Palace Wedding Chapel. 3570 Las Vegas Boulevard South. (702) 731–7110, (800) 634–6661. www.caesars.com.

Canterbury Wedding Chapel & Gardens. Excalibur Hotel and Casino, 3850 Las Vegas Boulevard South. (702) 597–7777, (800) 937–7777. www.excalibur casino.com.

The Chapel at Monte Carlo Resort. 3770 Las Vegas Boulevard South. (702) 730–7575, (800) 822–8651. www.monte-carlo.com.

Chapel at the Plaza. Plaza Hotel & Casino, 1 Main Street. (702) 386–2110, (800) 634–6575. www.plazahotelcasino.com.

Chapel by the Bay—Mandalay Bay Hotel. 3950 Las Vegas Boulevard South. (702) 632–7490, (877) 632–7701. www.mandalaybay.com.

Chapel of the Fountain. Circus Circus, 2880 Las Vegas Boulevard South. (702) 794–3777, (800) 634–6717. www.circuscircus.com/weddings.

Flamingo Las Vegas Garden Chapel. Flamingo Hotel, 3555 Las Vegas Boulevard South. (702) 733–3232, (800) 732–2111. www.flamingolasvegas.com.

Forever Grand Wedding Chapel at the MGM Grand Hotel. 3799 Las Vegas Boulevard South. (702) 891–7984, (800) 646–5530.

Island Wedding Chapel. Tropicana Resort and Casino. 3801 Las Vegas Boulevard South. (702) 739–2222, (800) 634–4000. www.tropicanachapel.com.

Mystic Falls Park Wedding Services. Sam's Town Hotel and Gambling Hall, 5111 Boulder Highway. (702) 456–7777, (888) 634–6371. www.samstown.com.

Paris Wedding Chapel. 3655 Las Vegas Boulevard South. (877) 650–5021. www.caesars.com/Paris/LasVegas/Weddings.

Riviera Royale Wedding Chapel. Riviera Hotel and Casino, 2901 Las Vegas Boulevard South. (702) 734–5110, (800) 634–6753. www.las-vegas-wedding .com.

The Wedding Chapels at Bellagio. Bellagio, 3600 Las Vegas Boulevard South. (702) 693–7111, (888) 987–6667. www.bellagio.com.

The Wedding Chapels at Treasure Island. Treasure Island at the Mirage, 3300 Las Vegas Boulevard South. (702) 894–7111, (800) 944–7444. www.treasure island.com.

We've Only Just Begun Wedding Chapel, Imperial Palace. 3535 Las Vegas Boulevard South. (702) 733–0011, (800) 346–3373.

Wynn Las Vegas. 3131 Las Vegas Boulevard South. (866) 770–7107. www .wynnlasvegas.com.

MONEY, MONEY, MONEY

Arriving with foreign currency? No problem. Every major casino will be glad to exchange your marks, yen, bucks, pounds, or whatever into cash or gambling chips. They'll extract a fee in the form of a discount from the official exchange rate; you will probably get the best deal at a commercial bank.

Traveler's checks are no problem at hotels, casinos, restaurants, or stores in Las Vegas; some places may require a photo ID card.

Need to cash a check? This is no problem for guests at a major hotel, although some establishments may enforce a limit on the amount they will release each day. At the casinos the cashier will often cash checks for clients known to the casino or who are in some way guaranteed by a credit card.

Need a loan? Most casinos will extend "markers" (credit vouchers) to gamblers who apply for such a loan in advance of their visit. Unsecured loans on the spot are more difficult to obtain.

Need a cash advance? Most major casinos have automated teller machines that permit withdrawal of cash from bank accounts or as cash advances against credit cards. Bank machines generally work with one of the national syndicates such as Cirrus, NYCE, or Plus. If you ask for a cash advance, be sure to read the notices on the machine carefully; some systems apply a hefty service charge to the amount of money you are withdrawing, over and above any interest the holder of your credit card will charge.

A notch down on the pecking order are check-cashing agencies that special-ize in out-of-state personal checks, money orders, and even savings account passbooks. You'll need personal identification, and you can expect to pay a fee that will increase with the complexity of the verification and transfer of funds.

You may also find one of my least favorite come-ons: an instant tax refund stand. Even assuming you come to the desk with a professionally prepared tax return, what you are essentially doing is taking out a short-term loan at a very high interest rate; by some calculations, the cost of the loan can be the equiva-lent of as much as 100 percent in interest. If you are that hard up that you seek an instant return of your tax refund, you might want to consider whether you really should be spending the money in a casino once you obtain it.

And then there are the pawnshops of downtown Las Vegas, filled with jewelry, cameras, furs, and other items left behind to raise cash. There are more than four pages of listings in the local phone book. If you are that desperate for cash, per-haps you should seek counseling of a different sort than is available in these pages.

Your best bet: Carefully use a credit or debit card and limit the amount of cash you carry.

COMPREHENDING COMPS

Let's get one thing out of the way: There is no such thing as a free lunch, not even in Las Vegas.

There are, however, "comp" lunches, breakfasts, dinners, drinks, hotel rooms, shows, airline tickets, and more. That's comp as in complimentary, but as we say, they're not quite free.

The distinction is this: Almost all of the casinos in Nevada offer all sorts of freebies to gamblers. They do so because they know that, over the long haul, they will win and you will lose.

The system starts with free drinks for players, which is actually one of the more insidious come-ons in marketing. Not only does it encourage players to sit at the slot machine or at the gaming table, but alcohol dulls the senses, reduces inhibitions, and otherwise aids in the removal of cash from your wallet. If you sit at a slot machine or at one of the tables, a waitress will sidle up to you and offer a drink; at most casinos, house brands of liquor and domestic beer are free. It is customary to tip the waitress.

The next step up is the provision of free meals. At a smaller casino the process might be as simple as this: The pit boss, perhaps alerted by the dealer to your consistent gambling, will drop by and hand you a card good for dinner. It might be a free pass to the coffee shop or the buffet, or you may be "comped" into the gourmet restaurant. Either way it's a reward for playing at the casino, and it also keeps you on the premises before and after the meal.

At larger casinos the process has become a bit more complicated. Ask the floor manager or the pit boss to "evaluate" your play; he or she may actually chart your bets or may consult with the dealer. Generally a comp rating will be given based on several hours of play at a consistent level.

Many casinos now use electronic means to track the play of visitors at slot and video poker machines; they will issue a magnetically coded card that is placed in readers attached to the slots to record the amount of action. The cards can be cashed in for free meals or shows after a certain amount of play. You can also be monitored while you are playing by casino hosts watching the results of your play on a computer monitor. A tip: You can increase your "action" by having both halves of a couple play on the same account.

Some casinos have a less sophisticated means of tracking slot players: relying on records kept by change booths or strolling change attendants. There is, of course, more of an opportunity to cheat here; one scheme would be to change a few hundred dollars in bills into coins but play only a small portion of the silver.

It doesn't hurt to ask one of the supervisors about how you can be evaluated. If you don't like the answer, you can always take your business elsewhere.

It all comes down to the amount of "action" you will provide the casino. Action is the amount of money you will put at risk over a particular period of time. For example, if you bet $25 per hand in blackjack for four hours a day over a three-day weekend, you are giving the casino something like $7,500 in action; at most middle-of-the-road casinos, that should be worth a free hotel room for the length of your stay.

There is no official rulebook to the distribution of comps. Smaller casinos more desperate to attract action may be more generous than the bigger places. However, the most spectacular casinos—places such as Caesars Palace and the Mirage—offer the most spectacular comps to the highest of rollers. The suites, many of which are larger than a typical private home, are described by the casinos as "priceless" because they cannot be rented by guests. They are offered as comps, along with free meals, room service, shows, limousine service, and other amenities to people for whom money must truly hold no meaning.

According to insiders, the serious freebies start at about the $25-per-hand level for free rooms. "RFB" players (recipients of free rooms, food, and beverages) generally are $75- to $125-per-hand gamblers. The penthouses, limousines, and other perks are usually offered at about the $150-per-hand level.

Some hotels are more up front about their comp programs than others. Players can earn free meals, shows, and reductions in room rates, up to and including an RFB rating. If you're playing the slots, you'll earn points based on "coin-in," which is the number of coins you put in the slot, no matter if you win or lose. At table games members alert pit supervisors to their presence to earn points based on their level of play.

Playing time is calculated based on six handle pulls per minute (once every ten seconds) using the maximum number of coins for each machine. In other words if you are playing at a $1.00 machine, the club payoffs are based on betting the maximum number of tokens—usually five—for that machine. Fewer coins bet or fewer handle pulls per minute will require more playing time.

The quickest way to freebies is to play a $5.00 machine where you can obtain a dinner buffet, coffee shop, or food court pass for two for one hour of play. Does that sound like a good deal? Consider that at $25 per pull, six times a minute, this means you are risking $9,000 in hopes of obtaining $20 worth of food.

Of course unless you are completely luckless, you should be able to avoid losing all of your money. Slot machines generally pay back between 90 and 99 percent of money bet. Remember, though, that this percentage applies over the very long haul and includes the very rare huge jackpot payoffs.

If you want to earn comps, keep in mind a few pointers. It is against your own interests to move from casino to casino because by doing so you are diluting your influence. (And don't think that casinos don't know this. That's why they have those "clubs" for loyal patrons.) And if you change from one area of the casino to another, be sure that whoever is evaluating you is aware of where you are going and can transfer supervision.

Note that I have not talked about winning versus losing here. At any particular moment the casino doesn't really care whether a player is ahead or behind. They know which way the dollars will eventually flow; in fact, if you're ahead of the game, they very much want you to stick around at their casino until the odds start to run the other way.

And one more piece of advice: If you have spent a few days at a hotel and have paid for your own room and meals, you might want to make a visit to the casino host before you check out. Tell him or her how much you have enjoyed staying at the hotel and gambling there and ask—politely—for a discount on your bill. You may receive a credit, or you may be invited to call the casino host before your next visit to receive prearranged comps or a casino rate discount on the hotel room.

A GUIDE TO TIPPING

Las Vegas, Reno, and Lake Tahoe are very much dependent on the tourist and conventioneer, and tipping is an essential element of the economy. In fact it has its own name in the casino: "toking."

You will have an extraordinary opportunity to grease the palms of dozens of strangers on your visit, but it's not necessary to pay everyone you meet.

Here's a guided tour to outstretched hands:

Transportation. The standard tip for taxi drivers is in the range of 15 percent to 20 percent of the fare; you might want to give more for a driver who helps with the bags or one who puts out his or her cigarette at your request. Limousine drivers expect a tip of 15 percent to 20 percent of the bill.

Tour Guides. Bus drivers and trip leaders expect a few dollars per person; if you are on a private tour, the tip should be larger.

Valet Parking. A tip of about $1.00 to $2.00 is standard.

Bartenders and Cocktail Waitresses. Most casinos offer free drinks to players at the tables, and some extend the privilege to slot players; a tip of 50 cents per drink or $1.00 per round is standard.

Restaurant Servers and Room Service. A tip in the range of 15 percent to 20 percent is standard. A sore point among some waiters and waitresses are visitors to buffets who don't leave money for the people who clear away your dishes and bring your drinks.

If you have received a free meal, check to see if your comp includes a gratuity for the staff; if it does not, you should leave a tip equal to 15 percent to 20 percent of what the bill would have been.

Bell Captains and Bellmen. The usual rate is about $1.00 to $2.00 per bag; give $1.00 or $2.00 to a bellman who summons a cab for you.

Bingo and Keno Runners. A dollar or two every few cards, and a larger tip with a winning card.

Dealers. A small tip in the form of cash or a chip a few times an hour is standard. Some dealers might prefer that you place a small bet for them every once in a while, especially if you are winning; ask them how they'd like to be toked. In theory this will not give you any special advantage at the table, but it might earn you more friendly treatment.

Maids. About $1.00 per day per person is standard; more if you have created an unusual amount of work or if extra services have been provided.

Showroom Maître d'Hotel. In the past nearly every casino showroom had a maître d' out front who determined where each guest was seated. Ignore him and you might end up in the back corner behind the coffeepot; make him happy and you could end up down front and center. The current trend, though, is toward reserved seats at most shows, especially the more expensive ones. Therefore tipping the maître d'—if there is one—is optional.

SHOP UNTIL YOU DROP IN LAS VEGAS

If you've got any money left in your wallet—or if you are traveling with a spouse who prefers to gamble on clothing or accessories instead of the roll of the dice— Las Vegas offers several major shopping areas.

▇ THE FORUM SHOPS AT CAESARS

The Forum Shops at Caesars is one of the wonders of the world: One of the largest and most successful shopping malls in the world, it is without doubt among the most visually stunning places in Las Vegas, more than 16 acres (about 675,000 square feet) under an ever-changing ceiling that moves from dawn to cerulean noon to dusk to darkness and back again over the course of two hours—the sun rises in the east and sets in the west.

The storefront facades and common areas are made to appear like an ancient Roman streetscape, with huge columns and arches, central piazzas, ornate fountains, and classic statuary.

There are now 160 shops and eateries; the third expansion of the shops, which opened in 2005, brings the shops right out to the Strip, with a formal Roman entryway that's all but impossible to miss. In case you think it's a mere casino, there are three stories of glass windows advertising the shopping within. A unique spiral escalator climbs toward a skylight in the new section.

Recent additions include Bruno Magli, Modafino Italian Design, Harry Winston, Casa Fuente, Roberto Cavalli, Chopard, Dolce & Gabbana, D & G Sport, Furla, MAC Cosmetics, Donald Pliner, Tod's, Tourneau, and Valentino. In addition, two existing stores, Louis Vuitton and Christian Dior, expanded into larger spaces.

According to its owners, foot traffic at the Forum Shops draws some twenty million visitors per year. Compare that to about fourteen million visitors per year at the Magic Kingdom at Walt Disney World, and you get some idea of the scale of this place.

Amazingly there are no casinos within the Forum Shops area itself, although there are a few banks of slot machines right by the entranceway just to ease the transition.

The Forum Shops are attached to the north side of Caesars Palace, and the main entrance connects to the main casino. An entrance and exit at the far end of the Forum Shops allows visitors to come into the shops without having to meander through the casino and saves the need to doubleback at the end of a tour; the door may not be open in the evening, though.

The Forum Shops are open daily from 10:00 A.M. to 11:00 P.M., until midnight Friday and Saturday; some restaurants and shops are also open earlier and later For information call (702) 893–4800 or consult the Las Vegas page on www.shop simon.com.

At the casino entrance to the mall is the *Quadriga* statue, four gold-leafed horses, a charioteer, and five heroic arches, an ancient symbol of great achievement. (*Quadriga* is a Latin word for a team of four and is pronounced Kwod-*reye*-ja.) As you look at the fountain, Jupiter is perched up top. Mars faces Gucci. Diana the Huntress checks out Louis Vuitton, and Venus and Plutus keep an eye on the casino. A 150-foot-high re-creation of the Pantheon—one of the greatest architectural masterpieces in Roman history—stands at the entrance at the northeast corner of Caesars Palace.

The mall includes a huge FAO Schwarz store with a giant hobbyhorse parked like a Trojan Horse at its entrance; a spectacular two-floor Virgin Megastore selling music, books, and software; Gap and Gap Kids; Abercrombie & Fitch; Emporio Armani; Lacoste; the Polo Store/Ralph Lauren; and Niketown.

A gathering place is the *Atlantis* statue at the back of the addition. Animatronic statues appear at least as lifelike as some slot machine players at three in the morning. Atlas, Gadrius, and Alia struggle to rule Atlantis, while projected images on walls simulate a descent to the ocean floor and smoke, fire, fog, and fountains fill the air. The whole thing is surrounded by a 50,000-gallon saltwater aquarium.

At the far end of the U-shaped mall is the spectacular Festival Fountain. It may look like marble, but it is not; every hour on the hour, starting at 10:00 A.M.,

The entrance to the Forum Shops at Caesars

the statuary comes to life. A seven-minute animated show stars Bacchus, god of merriment and wine, who has already had more than a few sips from his goblet. He enlists the power of Apollo (god of music), Venus (goddess of love), and Plutus (god of wealth) in preparing a party for all the guests gathered around his fountain. When the party is over, the statues return to marblelike silence. The statues are on a rotating platter and make a complete circle.

The best seats are probably on the floor about 10 or 15 feet back from the statues. Young kids may become fidgety after a minute or two, and most adults will not want to see the show a second time. Like most free entertainment in Las Vegas, it's worth every penny you pay for it.

■ **Antiquities.** Not to be missed, this unusual store is proof of the theory that one man's garbage is another's collectible investment. Where else can you buy a beautifully restored Coke machine, a classic jukebox, or a fortune-telling machine?

The owners of the store include among their treasure mines the backyards of the deep South and the cellars of Brooklyn; recovered items are repaired, repainted, and in some cases improved. Everything works just as it did when the item was new.

On one visit we found a 1942 Wurlitzer Model 950 Gazelle jukebox, the one with colored liquid bubbles and neon. Only 3,400 were made, and the unit on display required more than 300 hours of restoration. It was a bargain at $47,000.

Nearby was a 1940s coin-operated photo booth in working order for $9,800.

The Gucci store at the Forum Shops

Other unusual offerings included a restored 1937 Dodg'em bumper car and a Gypsy Grandma Fortune Teller from the 1940s. We saw a bleacher seat from the dear-departed Comiskey Park in Chicago; there are lots of autographed pictures and movie memorabilia, some more impressive than others. For information consult www.antiquitieslv.com.

■ **Foto-Forum.** Here's your chance to put your face on the body you've always dreamed of: a biker babe, a bikini beauty, or Southern belle for the ladies, or perhaps a hockey star, beefcake stud, or Hollywood leading man. The shop uses computer and video wizardry to merge your face with images on file; the result can be a poster, a small portrait, a personalized coffee cup, or just about anything else.

According to the operators, the most popular image for men is (what else could it be in Las Vegas?) Elvis; for women it's the chance to sit atop a pair of D cups barely contained in a string bikini.

Women's Fashions: Ann Taylor, bebe, Escada, St. John.

Specialty Apparel: A/X Armani Exchange, Gianni Versace, Gucci, Victoria's Secret.

Specialty Shops: Antiquities, Brookstone, Christian Dior, Davante, Endangered Species, Field of Dreams, Kids Kastle, Louis Vuitton, Magnet Maximus, Sports Logo, West of Santa Fe.

Men's Apparel: Bernini, Cuzzens, Lacoste, Polo by Ralph Lauren, Vasari.

Jewelry: Bulgari, Roman Times.

Shoes: Avventura, Shoooz at the Forum, Stuart Weitzman.

Art Gallery: Galerie Lassen.

■ FORUM SHOPS DINING

The Forum Shops also helped introduce the celebrity restaurant to Las Vegas with an interesting collection of eateries.

■ **Bertolini's.** The most spectacular setting in the Forum, this "sidewalk cafe" Italian eatery faces the Fountain of the Gods. Specialties include unusual pizzas for about $9.00 and pasta dishes from about $10.00 to $20.00, including *tagliolini al frutti di mare.* Other specialties include a sausage/polenta grill and salmon piccata. It's the place at which to see and to be seen, although the noise of the water in the fountain can become a bit overbearing. The restaurant is the flagship of a developing national chain. (702) 735–4663.

■ **Chinois.** Wolfgang Puck's bistro offers a wide-ranging Asian menu; small entrees are priced at about $15 to $20. Items on a recent visit included Thai basil shrimp, stir-fried Hoisin pork, and spicy Shanghai noodles. (702) 737–9700.

■ **Palm Restaurant.** An elegant extension of the famed New York eatery, with "outdoor" seating under the faux sky. Among its offerings is a $12 prix fixe lunch menu that includes petite filet mignon, prime rib, or pasta. Dinner offerings include seafood crab cakes for $26, a New York strip steak for $27, and a 36-ounce double steak for two for $57; a variety of salads are also available. (702) 732–7256.

■ **Planet Hollywood.** Don't count on meeting the Hollywood film stars of your dreams; they're busy counting their money earned from this successful chain of fancified burger joints decorated with cinema stuff. You can contribute, though: Hamburgers cost $6.50, vegetable burgers $6.75, barbecued pizza goes for $9.95, and a Mexican shrimp salad for $10.00. Dinner platters include St. Louis ribs for $12.95 and grilled ranch chicken for $10.95. There is also a sales counter out front of the restaurant where you can purchase Planet Hollywood merchandise, if you must. (702) 791–7827.

■ **Spago.** Not your average pizzeria. Specialties at the open-air cafe, which sits under the beautiful artificial Roman sky, include spicy chicken pizza with caramelized red onions and chili pesto for $12, Mediterranean fish soup with lobster and couscous for $24, and grilled tuna with tomato-fennel salsa and crisp smoked salmon ravioli for $23. (702) 369–0300.

■ **The Stage Deli.** A New York–style delicatessen with sandwiches and entrees from about $5.00 to $17.00. (702) 893–4045.

■ THE VENETIAN'S GRAND CANAL SHOPPES AND THE SHOPPES AT THE PALAZZO

The opulent Venetian Resort brought an indoor version of the Grand Canal of Venice to the Strip, an opulent competitor to the Forum Shops at Caesars Palace.

And in late 2007, the Shoppes at the Palazzo will open in the new Palazzo Resort Hotel Casino that is being added onto the Venetian on the Strip. The anchor for the new mall will be a branch of Barneys New York.

At the Grand Canal you can stroll down stone walkways along nearly a quarter mile of canal-side shops and restaurants; many of the shops are the only ones of their kind outside of Europe.

The shopping district culminates at St. Mark's Square, beneath a 70-foot ceiling filled with the ever-changing Venetian sky.

The mall is open Sunday to Thursday from 10:00 A.M. to 11:00 P.M. and until midnight on Friday and Saturday. For information call (702) 414–4500. A directory of stores can be found at www.venetian.com/shoppe/directory.cfm.

Women's Apparel: Amore, Ann Taylor, Banana Republic, BCBG Max Azria, bebe, Burberry, Caché, Gandini, Kenneth Cole, Lido Beach Shop, Lior, Marshall Rousso, Privilege, St. John Sport, Wolford.

Men's Apparel: Banana Republic, Burberry, Gandini, Kenneth Cole, Lior, Pal Zileri.

Specialty Shops: Acca Kappa, Ancient Creations, Brighton, Brookstone, Canyon Ranch Living Essentials, Davidoff, Diamond Resorts International, Dolcé due, Dooney and Bourke, Houdini's Magic, Il Prato, In Celebration of Golf, Lior, Lladro, Ripa de Monti, Sephora, Tolstoy's.

Shoes: Banana Republic, Brighton, Jimmy Choo, Kenneth Cole, Privilege, Rockport, The Walking Company.

Jewelry: Agatha, Ancient Creations, Bernard K. Passman Gallery, Ca' d'Oro, Erwin Pearl, Gal, Horologio, Landau, Mikimoto, Movado, Simayof Jewelers, Venetzia.

Children's Apparel and Toys: Burberry, David & Goliath, Kids Karnivale.

Gifts: Brookstone, Buon Giorno, Ciao, Godiva.

Restaurants: Canaletto, Canyon Ranch Café, Postrio, Tao, Taqueria Canonita, Tintoretto, Tsunami Asian Grill, Zefferino.

■ THE MIRACLE MILE AT PLANET HOLLYWOOD (DESERT PASSAGE)

The 500,000-square-foot shopping and dining place at Planet Hollywood (formerly Aladdin Resort and Casino) includes more than 130 shops with a few unusual international offerings and a dozen or so restaurants in what was originally envisioned as a Las Vegas version of Spain, North Africa, the Arabian Sea, and old India.

By the end of 2007, new owners plan to unveil an upgraded and updated shopping mecca; after $50 million worth of renovations, the former Desert Passage is due to be reborn as the Miracle Mile. The interior of the mall will be reworked to remove its winding "souk" design and dim lighting and replace them with more modern and energetic settings. Goodbye Middle East, hello Planet Hollywood.

A new facade, flanked with massive television screens, fountains and waterfalls, and three people movers, will lure shoppers from the Strip. A 12,000-square-foot Urban Outfitters and remodeled Sephora store will stand at the entrance; a 15,000-square-foot Trader Vic's will be nearby; and a Polynesian-themed restaurant will offer outdoor patio seating on two levels.

According to the owners new tenants will include Quiksilver and an outpost of New York retailer Ben Sherman. A new corridor will connect the mall to the $750 million Planet Hollywood Towers, a fifty-story Westgate Resorts' time-share development that should be completed by 2008. Magician Steve Wyrick will open a theater near that corridor.

For information call (702) 785–5555 or consult www.desertpassage.com.

Footwear: Aldo, Alpaca Pete's, Brighton Collectibles, David Z NYC Footwear, Footworks, Napoleon, Parallel, Steve Madden, Two Lips Shoes, The Walking Company, Wild Pair.

Health and Beauty: Aveda, Clinique, GapBody, H2O+, L'Occitane, Origins, Sephora.

Home Furnishings: Crystal Galleria, Metropolitan Museum of Art Store, Sur la Table, Swarovski, Thomas Barbey, Z Gallerie.

Jewelry: Ancient Creations, Boccia Titanium, Gioia, Landau, Modern Watch Co., Occhiali Da Sole, Shermoni, Silver City, TeNo, World of Charms.

Men's and Women's Fashions: Ann Taylor Loft, BCBG Max Azria, bebe, Ben Sherman, Betsey Johnson, Bikini Bay, Caché, Chico's, Eddie Bauer, Fitelle, French Connection, Gap, Georgiou, Herve Leger, Hugo/Hugo Boss, Lucky Brand Jeans, Max Studio, Metropark, Mimi Mango, Napoleon, Parallel, Quiksilver, Santiki, Sisley, Stash, Tommy Bahama, United Colors of Benetton, Urban Leather, Urban Outfitters, Victoria's Secret.

Specialty: ABC Stores, Asian Gifts, Bikini Bay, Corona Zona, Department 56, The Discovery Channel Store, Eclectic Collections, Havana Republic, Just a Second, NASCAR, Olde China, Sharper Image, Super Steam, Tahiti Village.

Restaurants: Aromi D'Italia, Blondies Sports Bar & Grill, Cheeseburger Las Vegas, Commander's Palace, Fashionistas, Fat Tuesday, Krave, La Salsa Cantina, Lombardi's Romagna Mia, Max's Cafe, Oyster Bay Seafoord & Wine Bar, Pampas Churrascaria, Tacone Global Grill, Taverna Opa, Todai Japanese Seafood Buffet, Trader Vic's.

■ FASHION SHOW MALL

Calling the Fashion Show Mall a shopping center is kind of like calling Radio City Music Hall a movie theater: The description is technically accurate, but this place is on a whole other plane. Think of it as a cathedral to shopping and you get the idea.

Following a 2003 remodeling that more than doubled its size, the mall is now one of the nation's largest shopping malls with more than 250 specialty shops and restaurants as well as seven high-end flagship department stores including Bloomingdale's Home Furniture Store, Dillard's, Macy's, Neiman Marcus, Nordstrom, Robinsons-May, and Saks Fifth Avenue.

In 2006 a new pedestrian bridge linked TI, the resort formerly known as Treasure Island, to the Fashion Show Mall.

The centerpiece of the shopping mecca is a massive hall with a fashion show runway; in addition to fashion, the room can be used for the introduction of other types of products and as a show area for exhibitors at conventions. Images from the show can be broadcast to television monitors throughout the mall and to a huge outdoor video screen facing the Strip.

About that outdoor screen: It's the ceiling of a 480-foot-long, 160-foot-wide "cloud" along Las Vegas Boulevard South. By day it provides shade from the bright sun, and by night four huge full-motion video screens are visible to pedestrians and drivers on the Strip. It's used for special events, concerts, premieres, and press conferences.

Department Stores: Bloomingdale's Home, Dillard's, Macy's, Neiman Marcus, Nordstrom, Robinsons-May, Saks Fifth Avenue.

Women's Fashions: Abercrombie & Fitch, Adrienne Vittadini, Ann Taylor, Ann Taylor Loft, Aqua, Arden B, Bally of Switzerland, Banana Republic, BCBG

Max Azria, bebe, Betsey Johnson, Caché, Carolee, Chico's, Claire's Boutique, Coldwater Creek, Cole Haan, Deetour, Diesel, Express, Fitelle, Fossil, Fredericks of Hollywood, French Connection, Fresh Produce, Gap, Guess, Hollister, Hot Cats, Hot Topic, J. Crew, J. Jill, Jessica McClintock, Lacoste, Leather by Michael Lawrence, Levi's, Lillie Rubin, The Limited, Louis Vuitton, Marciano, Metropark, No Fear, Nurielle, PacSun, Paul Frank, Quiksilver, Rampage, Soho Collections, Soma, Still, Talbots, Taluhah G, Tommy Bahama, Victoria's Secret, Villa Moda, Wet Seal, Whie House/Black Market, Zara.

Shoes: Adrienne Vittadini, Aerosoles, Aldo, Arteffects, Baker Shoes, Bally of Switzerland, BCBG Max Azria, Brighton Collectibles, Champs Sports, Clarks England/Bostonian, Cole Haan, Diesel, Easy Spirit, Foot Locker, Johnston & Murphy, Journeys, Louis Vuitton, Marmi, Nine West, Nurielle, Payless, Puma, Shiekh, Skechers, Steve Madden, The Walkin Company, Timberland.

Men's and Family Apparel: Brats, Gap, Gymboree, Harris & Frank, J. Crew, Johnston & Murphy, Uomo.

Jewelry: Bailey Banks & Biddle, Ben Bridge Jeweler, Berger & Son Fine Jewelers, Brendan Diamonds, Brighton Collectibles, Carolee, Claire's Boutique, Fossil, Fred Meyer, Kay Jewelers, Michael Minden, Whitehall Co. Jewelers, Zales.

Specialty: ABC Stores, Brookstones, Coach Store, NASCAR, Sanrio, Swarovski.

Technology: Apple, Bang & Olufsen, EB Games, Futuretronics, Nokia, Sharper Image.

The Fashion Show Mall is located directly on the Strip at 3200 Las Vegas Boulevard South at the head of Convention Center Drive and next to the Mirage and across from Wynn Las Vegas. It is within walking distance of most center-Strip motels and the Las Vegas Convention Center. Valet parking is available. Hours are Monday to Friday from 10:00 A.M. to 9:00 P.M., Saturday 10:00 A.M. to 8:00 P.M., and Sunday 11:00 A.M. to 6:00 P.M. For information call (702) 369–8382 or consult www.thefashionshow.com.

■ MANDALAY PLACE

The handsome Mandalay Place shopping district is a welcome break from the many painted skies elsewhere in town. The high ceiling above the wide halls is topped with a handsome, ornate skylight. The 100,000-square-foot mall is within a 310-foot-long bridge that crosses the road from Mandalay Bay to Luxor.

The forty-one stores within are an eclectic mix of trendy clothing and accessory shops including Urban Outfitters, the world's first Nike Golf store, Samantha Chang, Davidoff, Pearl Moon, Italy's Fornarina, Dutch children's and women's clothier Oilily, and Sauvage, a women's swimwear boutique. The Reading Room is a small but lively independent bookstore.

■ WYNN ESPLANADE

There is nothing understated about Wynn Las Vegas, a rippling wall of glass that nearly overwhelms not just the nearby competitors on the Strip but the mountains to the west. When it comes to the shops on the Wynn Esplanade, well, there's nothing in the way of subtlety . . . or discount pricing.

Founder Stephen Wynn and his wife Elaine participated in groundbreaking ceremonies in the spring of 2006 for a second huge tower, the Wynn Encore. Mrs. Wynn told reporters she was sympathetic to the tourist with a limited budget: Anyone can come and gawk for free, she said. And she recommended as a souvenir a $28 T-shirt that advertises the hotel and the family name.

Stores at the Esplanade include a Penske Ferrari/Maserati dealership; if you're there to buy one of the vehicles (the budget line is priced about $100,000, with the zippiest Ferraris tagged at $250,000 or more), they'll refund the $10 admission charge to enter the showroom. Other high-tone shops, where admission is free, include Manolo Blahnik, Dior, Louis Vuitton, Cartier, Oscar de la Renta, Jo Malone, Graff, Judith Leiber, Brioni, and Chanel.

Wynn Esplanade is located at 3131 Las Vegas Boulevard South. Hours are 10:00 A.M. to 11:00 P.M. Sunday through Thursday and 10:00 A.M. to midnight on Friday and Saturday. For more information call (702) 770–7000 or consult www .wynnlasvegas.com.

■ THE BOULEVARD MALL

The Boulevard Mall, Nevada's largest traditional shopping center, is a typical group of shops decorated with plants under an atrium. There's an open, bright feeling—sort of like being outdoors. It is located at 3528 South Maryland Parkway at the intersection with Desert Inn Road, about five minutes east of the Strip. Hours are 10:00 A.M. to 9:00 P.M. weekdays, 10:00 A.M. to 8:00 P.M. on Saturday, and 11:00 A.M. to 6:00 P.M. on Sunday. For information call (702) 735–8268 or consult www.blvdmall.com.

Department Stores: Dillard's, JCPenney, Macy's, Marshall's, Sears.

Accessories: Claire's Boutique, Farrah's Sunwear, Front Row Sports, Icing, Leather Zone, Lids, Michael Lawrence Leather, Sporting Eyes, Sunglass Designs.

Men's Apparel: Anchor Blue, B'Koz, d.e.m.o., Express, Gap, Hot Topic, Pac Sun, Workmen's, Zumiez.

Women's Apparel: Agaci Too, Anchor Blue, B'Koz, Basic, Charlotte Russe, d.e.m.o., Express, Forever 21, Frederick's of Hollywood, Gap, Hot Topic, Jada Nicole, Lane Bryant, Marianne, New York & Co., Roland's of Las Vegas, Victoria's Secret.

Specialty: Bath & Body Works, Body Shop, Brookstone, Things Remembered.

Shoes: Bakers, Champs Sports, Famous Footwear, FinishLine, Foot Action, Foot Locker, Lady Foot Locker, Payless, Robert Wayne Footwear, Shiekh Shoes, Two Lips Shoes, Underground Station, Wild Pair.

Jewelry: Body Jewelry, The Chainery, Crescent, Designer, Fred Meyer Jewelers, Gordon's Jewelers, Hawaiian Jewel Gallery, Intrigue, Kay, Lundstrom Jewelry, Morgan, Silver Safari, Whitehall Jewelers, Zales.

■ MEADOWS MALL

North of downtown near U.S. Highway 95 at Valley View Boulevard, the 144-store, two-level mall includes Dillard's, JCPenney, Macy's, and Sears. The mall provides its own Downtown Trolley that shuttles back and forth to the Downtown Transportation Center. Open weekdays from 10:00 A.M. to 9:00 P.M., Saturday from 10:00 A.M. to 7:00 P.M., and Sunday from 10:00 A.M. to 6:00 P.M. For information call (702) 878–4849 or consult www.themeadowsmall.com.

■ SHOWCASE MALL

Showcase Mall, just north of the MGM Grand, features four floors of unusual offerings including M&M's World and Ethel M Chocolates (both offshoots of the Mars candy family). Another strange attraction, the World of Coca-Cola, closed in 2000, although the big Coke bottle still stands outside and a soda-theme gift shop continues in operation.

The mall, located at 3785 Las Vegas Boulevard South, is open daily from 10:00 A.M. to midnight and until 1:00 A.M. on Friday and Saturday. For information about the Showcase Mall, call (702) 597–3122.

■ CHINA IN LAS VEGAS

There's a little bit of Asia about a mile west of the Strip, in the 4000 block of Spring Mountain Road. The Las Vegas Chinatown Plaza includes Chinese and Vietnamese restaurants, an Asian supermarket, and jewelry and gift shops. For information call (702) 221–8448 or consult www.lvchinatown.com.

■ LAS VEGAS OUTLET CENTER

The Las Vegas Outlet Center (formerly the Belz Factory Outlet World) has 130 stores, including Adidas, Bass Shoes, Bon Worth, Burlington Brands, Calvin Klein, Carter's Childrensware, Chez Magnifique, Corning-Revere, Danskin, Designer Labels for Less, Hush Puppies, Kitchen Collection, Kitchen Place, Leathermode, L'egg's/Hanes/Bali, Levi's, Music 4 Less, Naturalizer, Nike, Oneida, Osh Kosh b'Gosh, Perfumania, Pfaltzgraff, Ritz Camera Outlet, Stride Rite, and Van Heusen.

The center is located at 7400 Las Vegas Boulevard South, Interstate 15 at Blue Diamond, south of Las Vegas. Hours are 10:00 A.M. to 9:00 P.M. Monday through Saturday and 10:00 A.M. to 6:00 P.M. on Sunday. Call (702) 896–5599 or consult www.lasvegasoutletcenter.com.

■ OTHER STORES

Here are a few of our favorite unusual stores located outside of shopping malls.
■ **Bare Essentials.** 4029 West Sahara. (702) 247–4711. www.bareessentialsvegas .com. Leather, lace, and lingerie—the stuff of life for women and men.
■ **Bass Pro Shops Outdoor World.** 8200 Dean Martin Drive, next to the Silverton Casino. Most everything you want, and a lot you never knew you needed, for hunting, fishing, camping, golfing, and water sports at this theme park of a store with its own trout stream. Open daily 9:00 A.M. to 10:00 P.M., Sunday from 10:00 A.M. to 7:00 P.M. (702) 730–5200.
■ **Bell, Book & Candle.** 1725 East Charleston Boulevard. (702) 386–2950. www .lasvegasbbc.com. Crystal balls, magic potions, and classes in witchcraft.
■ **Cowtown Boots.** 2989 South Paradise Road. (702) 737–8469. www.cowtown

boots.com. A factory outlet for handmade leather boots from cowhide to snakeskin to Teju lizard.

■ **Desert Indian Shop.** 108 North Third Street. (702) 384–4977. Art and artifacts of the West.

If you're determined to bring a bit of Las Vegas home with you (and if you've left a bit of money in your wallet or on your credit card), you may want to visit one of several stores that sells gambling equipment. Be sure you investigate state and local laws before you bring back machines.

■ **Gamblers Book Club.** 630 South Eleventh Street. (702) 382–7555, (800) 634–6243. www.gamblersbook.com. They take their games seriously here, offering the biggest collection of gambling arcana we know of as well as a fine collection of local history, travel, and fiction.

■ **Gamblers General Store.** 800 South Main Street. (702) 382–9903, (800) 322–2447. www.gamblersgeneralstore.com. Open to the public for slot machines, poker machines, personalized poker chips, and craps tables.

■ OTHER PEOPLE'S MISFORTUNE: PAWNSHOPS

Earlier in this chapter I mentioned the sad fact that some visitors to Las Vegas end up leaving more than merely their money behind; pawnshops are well stocked with rings, necklaces, musical instruments, cameras, and just about anything else that can be carried in for quick cash at a deep discount.

If you are a particularly adventurous shopper and you are able to tell the difference between a dud and a diamond, an Instamatic and a Nikon, and a Gibson and garbage, you may want to go to a pawnshop. There are more than a dozen pawnshops in Las Vegas and many more throughout the state.

Be aware that most of these operations are not in the nicest parts of town, and few spend any money at all on decorations. Most are located on the side streets of downtown, not far from the original casinos of Las Vegas, the criminal and bankruptcy courts, and the bail bondsmen. Get the picture?

CHAPTER TWELVE

EATING YOUR WAY ACROSS LAS VEGAS

Econoguide Best Buffets

LAS VEGAS STRIP

★★★★   Carnival World Buffet. *Rio*

★★★★   The Buffet at Bellagio. *Bellagio*

★★★★   Cravings. *Mirage*

★★★★   Dishes. *Treasure Island*

★★★★   Masquerade Village Seafood Buffet. *Rio*

★★★★   The Buffet. *Wynn Las Vegas*

★★★   Bayside Buffet. *Mandalay Bay*

★★★   The Buffet. *Las Vegas Hilton*

★★★   Le Village Buffet. *Paris Las Vegas*

★★   Flavors. *Harrah's*

★★   Grand Buffet. *MGM Grand*

DOWNTOWN LAS VEGAS

★★★   The Buffet. *Golden Nugget*

★★★   Garden Court Buffet. *Main Street Station*

FOOD AS A COME-ON

Like most everything else inside and outside a casino, restaurants are part of the come-on. You'll find some of the best deals, the best food, and the wildest settings in Las Vegas. You can dine inside a Roman catacomb, a Russian vodka bar,

Econoguide Best Restaurants

CASINO RESTAURANTS

★★★★★   Picasso. *Bellagio*

★★★★   Ah Sin. *Paris Las Vegas*

★★★★   Andre's French Restaurant. *Monte Carlo*

★★★★   Bradley Ogden Fine American Cuisine. *Caesars Palace*

★★★★   Commander's Palace. *Planet Hollywood/Aladdin (Miracle Mile)*

★★★★   Craftsteak. *MGM Grand*

★★★★   Emeril's. *MGM Grand*

★★★★   Empress Court. *Caesars Palace*

★★★★   Fiamma Trattoria. *MGM Grand*

★★★★   Fin. *Mirage*

★★★★   Fleur de Lys. *Mandalay Bay*

★★★★   Guy Savoy. *Caesars Palace*

★★★★   Le Cirque. *Bellagio*

★★★★   Lutèce. *Venetian*

★★★★   Piero Selvaggio's Valentino. *Venetian*

★★★★   Prime Steakhouse. *Bellagio*

★★★★   Red Square. *Mandalay Bay*

★★★★   Royal Star. *Venetian*

★★★★   Rumjungle. *Mandalay Bay*

★★★★   Stack. *Mirage*

★★★★   Star Canyon. *Venetian*

★★★★   Tao Asian Bistro. *Venetian*

★★★★   Top of the World. *Stratosphere*

★★★★   Zeffirino. *Venetian*

OUTSIDE THE CASINOS

★★★★   Andre's French Restaurant

★★★★   Le Pamplemousse

★★★★   P. F. Chang's China Bistro

★★★★   Rosemary's

an Irish pub, or a rain forest. You can find $5.00 steaks, $50.00 chickens, $60.00 burgers, and $500.00 wines.

Like I've said, it's all a come-on. The goal is to get you to stroll by the slot machines and the tables on your way to and from dinner. But that doesn't mean you have to gamble on anything more than the quality of the menu.

In the listings in this chapter, I've included some of the best and most interesting places to eat in Las Vegas. You won't find fast-food outlets (although they do exist in Las Vegas and even within some of the casino-hotels) or ordinary coffee shops. But we do deal with that special Las Vegas creature, the fabulous buffet.

LAS VEGAS'S FAVORITE FOOD: BUFFETS

Comedian Garry Shandling offered the best reason I've ever heard for the popularity of buffets in Las Vegas. He told us of an unlucky visitor who dropped $800 at the tables and moved on to an all-you-can-eat buffet at the casino. "By God," the man said, "I am going to eat $800 worth of food if it kills me!"

Buffets in Las Vegas may go back to the town's origins as a provisioning center for miners and railroad workers. Bars would compete for business by offering the proverbial "free lunch" to customers who kept their glasses full.

Today's casinos view the buffet in somewhat the same way. They figure if they can lure you into their doors with the offer of an inexpensive meal, you are quite likely to stop to play the tables or the slot machines on your way in or out. The casinos try to encourage this as much as they can by placing the buffets at the back of the casinos. The casinos also try to find ways to encourage all-night gamblers to stick around for breakfast.

Whatever the reason for the buffets, it is true that some of the offerings represent the best values for food anywhere I know of. The best of the buffets offer top-quality meals in attractive settings for a mere fraction of the price of a sit-down restaurant. (The worst of the buffets are spectacularly ordinary and unattractive but still represent better values than McDonald's or the neighborhood greasy spoon.)

In general the best meals are the dinner buffets and the weekend brunches; a few casinos offer spectacular breakfasts. As you might expect, the more popular buffets can build lengthy lines; the best strategy is to eat a bit early—before 8:00 A.M. for breakfast and before 6:00 P.M. for dinner.

Remember that prices, hours, and offerings are subject to change—sometimes from day to day. At most buffets breakfast is offered from about 7:00 to 11:00 A.M., lunch from about 11:00 A.M. to 3:30 P.M., and dinner from about 4:30 to 10:00 P.M. Brunches are typically offered from about 8:00 A.M. to 3:00 P.M. Some buffets close, or at least stop admitting new patrons, between breakfast and lunch and lunch and dinner. Call to check hours.

At buffets that operate without interruption, one way to save a few dollars on lunch or dinner is to arrive half an hour before the changeover from breakfast or dinner.

Most buffets offer lower rates for children. Soft drinks, coffee, and tea are included with most meals; alcoholic drinks are extra.

Prices and hours at buffets change regularly. Call ahead to check on rates at the time of your visit. We have ranked prices in three ranges:

$ Economy. About $10 to $12 for dinner, less for breakfast and lunch.
$$ Moderate. About $12 to $20 for dinner, less for breakfast and lunch.
$$$ Expensive. More than $20 for dinner, less for breakfast and lunch.

■ LAS VEGAS BUFFETS

Arizona Charlie's Boulder. *The Wild West Buffet.* **$**. Breakfast, lunch, dinner. Weekend brunch. (702) 258–5200.

Bally's. *Big Kitchen Buffet.* **$$**. Brunch daily, dinner. *Sterling Brunch* (in Bally's Steakhouse). **$$$**. Sunday. (702) 739–4111.

Bellagio. *The Buffet at Bellagio.* **$$$**. Breakfast, lunch, dinner. Gourmet dinner Friday and Saturday nights. Champagne brunch weekends. (702) 693–7111.

Boulder Station. *The Feast Gourmet Buffet.* **$**. Breakfast, lunch, dinner. Brunch Saturday and Sunday. *Broiler Champagne Brunch.* **$$**. Sunday. (702) 432–7777.

Buffalo Bill's. *Miss Ashley's Buffet.* **$**. Breakfast, lunch, dinner. (702) 679–5160.

Cannery. *Cannery Row Buffet.* **$$**. Lunch Monday to Saturday; dinner. Champagne brunch Sunday. (702) 507–5700.

Circus Circus. *Circus Buffet.* **$**. Breakfast, lunch, dinner. Weekend brunch. (702) 734–0410.

Excalibur. *The Round Table Buffet.* **$$**. Breakfast, lunch, dinner. Sunday champagne brunch. (702) 597–7777.

Fiesta Henderson. *Festival Buffet.* **$–$$**. Lunch, dinner. Weekend brunch and dinner. (702) 631–7000.

Flamingo. *Paradise Garden Buffet.* **$$**. Brunch daily. (702) 733–3111.

Fremont. *Paradise Buffet.* **$**. Breakfast, lunch weekdays; dinner Monday and Thursday. Seafood Fantasy Tuesday, Friday, and Sunday; steak dinner Wednesday and Saturday. **$$**. Champagne brunch weekends. (702) 385–3232.

Gold Coast. *Ports O' Call Buffet.* **$**. Breakfast, lunch, dinner. Seafood night Thursday; Sunday steak dinner; Sunday brunch **$$**. (702) 367–7111.

Golden Nugget. *The Buffet.* **$$**. Breakfast, lunch, dinner. Seafood dinner Friday; champagne brunch Sunday **$$**. (702) 385–7111.

Harrah's. *Flavors.* **$$**. Breakfast, lunch weekdays; dinner nightly. Champagne brunch weekends. (702) 369–5000.

Imperial Palace. *Emperor's Buffet.* **$**. Breakfast, lunch, dinner. *Imperial Buffet.* Champagne brunch daily; dinner. (702) 731–3311.

Las Vegas Hilton. *The Buffet.* **$$**. Breakfast, lunch, dinner with beer and wine. Champagne brunch weekends. (702) 732–5111.

Luxor. *Pharaoh's Pheast.* **$$**. Breakfast, lunch, dinner. (702) 262–4000.

Main Street Station. *Garden Court Buffet.* **$$**. Breakfast, lunch weekdays; dinner. Steak night Tuesday. Steak and scampi buffet Thursday. Seafood Friday. Champagne brunch weekends. (702) 387–1896.

Mandalay Bay. *Bayside Buffet.* **$$$**. Breakfast, lunch, dinner. Sunday champagne brunch. (702) 632–7777.

House of Blues at Mandalay Bay. *Gospel Brunch.* **$$$**. Sunday, including gospel show. (702) 632–7600.

MGM Grand. *Grand Buffet.* **$$$**. Breakfast, lunch, dinner. Champagne brunch weekends. (702) 891–1111.

Mirage. *Cravings.* **$$$**. Breakfast, lunch, dinner. Weekend champagne brunch. (702) 791–7111.

Monte Carlo. *Monte Carlo Buffet.* **$$**. Breakfast, lunch, dinner. Champagne brunch Sunday. (702) 730–7777.

Orleans. *French Market Buffet.* **$**. Breakfast, lunch Monday to Saturday; dinner Tuesday and Thursday to Sunday. Seafood dinner Monday. Steak dinner Wednesday. Sunday brunch. (702) 365–7111.

Palace Station. *The Gourmet Feast Buffet.* **$**. Breakfast, lunch weekdays; dinner Sunday to Wednesday. Weekend brunch. (702) 367–2411.

Palms Casino Resort. *Fantasy Market Buffet.* **$$**. Breakfast, lunch, dinner Saturday to Tuesday and Thursday. Italian dinner Wednesday. Crab legs and prime rib dinner buffet Friday. Sunday champagne brunch. (702) 942–7777.

Paris Las Vegas. *Le Village Buffet.* **$$$**. Breakfast, lunch, dinner. Champagne brunch Sunday. (702) 967–4401.

Planet Hollywood/Aladdin. *Spice Market Buffet.* **$$$**. Breakfast, lunch, dinner. Champagne brunch Saturday and Sunday. (702) 785–5555.

Primm Valley. *The Greens Buffet.* **$**. Breakfast, lunch, dinner. Sunday champagne brunch. (702) 679–5160.

Rio. *Carnival World Buffet.* **$$$**. Breakfast, lunch weekdays; dinner. Brunch weekends. *Masquerade Village Seafood Buffet.* **$$$**. Dinner. (702) 777–7777.

Riviera. *World's Fare Buffet.* **$$**. Breakfast, lunch weekdays; dinner. Champagne brunch weekends. Late-night steak dinner Saturday to Thursday. (702) 734–5110.

Sahara. *The Sahara Buffet.* **$**. Brunch weekdays; dinner. Prime rib night Saturday. Champagne brunch weekends. (702) 737–2111.

Sam's Town. *Firelight Buffet.* Lunch weekdays. Mexican night Monday. Italian night Tuesday. Steak night Wednesday. All-American Thursday. Seafood night Friday. Prime rib Saturday. Barbecue night Sunday. Champagne brunch weekends. (702) 456–7777.

Silverton. *All American Buffet.* **$$**. Brunch, dinner, and speciality dinner items. Weekend champagne brunch. (702) 263–7777.

Stratosphere. *Courtyard Buffet.* **$$**. Brunch, dinner. Seafood buffet Friday and Saturday. Champagne brunch Sunday. (702) 380–7700.

Suncoast. *St. Tropez International Buffet.* **$$**. Breakfast, lunch, dinner. Tuesday steak with beer. Friday seafood. Sunday brunch. (877) 677–7111.

Sunset Station. *Feast Buffet.* **$–$$**. Breakfast weekdays, lunch, dinner. Thursday through Saturday steak nights. Brunch weekends. (702) 547–7777.

Terrible's Hotel and Casino. *Terrible's Buffet.* **$–$$**. Breakfast, lunch weekdays; dinner Friday to Wednesday. Thursday seafood. Champagne brunch weekends. (702) 691–2413.

Texas Station. *Feast Around the World.* **$**. Breakfast, lunch weekdays; dinner. Champagne brunch weekends. (702) 631–1000.

Treasure Island. *Dishes.* **$$$**. Breakfast, lunch Sunday to Thursday; dinner. (702) 894–7111.

Tropicana. *Island Buffet.* **$$**. Breakfast, lunch, dinner. Champagne brunch weekends. (702) 739–2222.

Wynn Las Vegas. *The Buffet.* **$$$**. Breakfast, lunch, dinner. (702) 248–3463.

LAS VEGAS RESTAURANTS

You can get just about anything you want at a Las Vegas restaurant. Most are open for lunch and dinner; weekend hours may vary. Be sure to call to confirm hours and check to see if a reservation is necessary; some restaurants have direct phone lines, while others can be reached through the casino's main number. Most casino restaurants are open weekends; some eateries outside of the hotels are closed on Sunday.

The price ranges listed here are for entrees served at dinner. Luncheon prices are usually a bit less.

■ CASINO RESTAURANTS

Many of the better restaurants in Las Vegas can be found within the casinos. You'll find details about many of them in chapter 6. Here are some of the best in town; not included here are casino coffee shops and fast-food restaurants.

Bally's Las Vegas

(702) 967–7999. www.ballyslv.com.

Al Dente. Pasta, pasta everywhere. (702) 967–7999. $10–$20.

Bally's Steakhouse. Steaks, chops, and seafood served in a New York club atmosphere. (702) 967–7999. $20 and up.

Chang's at Bally's. Hong Kong, Mandarin, and Taiwanese cuisine. (702) 967–7999. $10–$20.

Barbary Coast

(702) 737–7111. www.barbarycoastcasino.com.

Drai's on the Strip. French, with a touch of California and the Pacific Rim. (702) 737–0555. $15–$20.

Michael's. Gourmet steak and seafood in a Victorian setting. (702) 737–7111. $20 and up.

Victorian Room. American and Continental seafood, beef, and chicken. (702) 737–7111. $20 and up.

Bellagio

(702) 693–7111. www.bellagio.com.

Circo. Tuscan specialties. (702) 693–8150. $20 and up.

Le Cirque. ★★★★ Classic Continental. (702) 693–7223. $20 and up.

Fix. American fare. $20 and up.

Jasmine. Gourmet Chinese fare. (702) 693–7223. $20 and up.

Michael Mina Bellagio. Fine seafood. (702) 693–7223. $29 and up.

Noodles. Regional noodle dishes of Asia. (702) 693–7111. $15–$20.

Todd English's Olives. Mediterranean sidewalk cafe. (702) 693–8181. $15–$20.

Picasso. ★★★★★ Mediterranean works of art. (702) 693–7223. $20 and up.

Prime Steakhouse. ★★★★ Chicago speakeasy and chophouse. (702) 693–7223. $20 and up.

Sensi. Asian fusion. (702) 693–7223. $25 and up.

Shintaro. Pacific Rim haute cuisine. (702) 693–7223. $20 and up.

Binion's Gambling Hall & Hotel

(702) 382–1600. www.binions.com.

Binion's Ranch Steak House. Victorian-style decor with a panoramic view from the twenty-fourth floor, specializing in huge steaks and prime rib. $20 and up.

Boulder Station

(702) 432–7777. www.boulderstation.com.

Boulder Cafe. American/Continental. $10.

The Broiler. Steak and seafood. $15–$20.

Guadalajara Bar and Grill. Mexican specialties in a lively setting. $10–$15.

Pasta Palace. The name says it all. $10–$15.

Buffalo Bill's

(702) 679–7692. www.primmvalleyresorts.com.

Tony Roma's. Franchised ribbery. (702) 382–1212. $10–$15.

Caesars Palace

(702) 731–7731. www.caesars.com/Caesars/LasVegas.

Bradley Ogden Fine American Cuisine. ★★★★ Bay-area chef's "fresh American" fare. $15–$20.

808. European-Hawaiian-Asian fusion. (702) 731 7731. $20 and up.

Empress Court. ★★★★ A most elegant Hong Kong–style Cantonese restaurant, with meals including abalone, jellyfish, shark's fin, and bird's nest soup using rare spices from the Orient. (702) 731–7731. $20 and up.

Guy Savoy. ★★★★ French finery. (702) 731–7731. $25 and up.

Hyakumi. An elaborate sushi bar with expansive (and expensive) Japanese menu. (702) 731–7731. $15–$20.

Mesa Grill. Bobby Flay's kicky Southwestern fare. (702) 731–7731. $20 and up.

Nero's Steak & Seafood. High-tone Continental fare in an elegant room just off the casino floor. (702) 731–7731. $20 and up.

Rao's. Classic Italian, all the way from East Harlem. (702) 731–7731. www.raos .com.

Terrazza. An elegant spot by the Garden of the Gods pool. (702) 731–7731. $10–$15.

Forum Shops at Caesars Palace:

Bertolini's Authentic Trattoria. Wood-oven pizza, pasta, and gelato. (702) 735–4663. $15–$20.

The Palm. The Vegas branch of the venerable New York steak-and-seafood house; casual and fun. (702) 732–7256. $20 and up.

Planet Hollywood. Although the glitz of Hollywood doesn't seem quite so wild set against the backdrop of Las Vegas, this is still an entertaining eatery. (702) 791–7827. $10–$15.

Spago. Trendy yuppie fare for trendy yuppies; includes an "outdoor" cafe on the streets of ancient Rome. (702) 369–6300. $20 and up.

California Hotel

(702) 385–1222. www.thecal.com

Market Street Cafe. American and Asian specialties. $10–$15.

Pasta Pirate. Basic Italian. $10–$15.

Redwood Bar & Grill. Chops, seafood, and poultry. $10–$15.

Circus Circus

(702) 734–0410. www.circuscircus.com.

Blue Iguana. Mexican specialties and thirty varieties of tequila. (702) 836–6526. $10.

The Steak House. A class act in a funky joint. (702) 794–3767. $15–$20.

Excalibur

(702) 597–7777. www.excalibur-casino.com.

Regale Italian Eatery. Pasta, pizza, and more. (702) 597–7443. $10–$15.

Sherwood Forest Cafe. American. (702) 597–7777. $10.

Sir Galahad's Pub and Prime Rib House. A prime ribbery. (702) 597–7448. $10–$15.

The Steakhouse at Camelot. High-tone beefery. (702) 597–7449. $20 and up.

Fiesta Rancho

(702) 631–7000. www.fiestacasino.com.

Blue Agave Steakhouse. Casual steakery. $15–$20.

Garduno's Mexican Food. Mexican specialties. $10–$15.

Fitzgeralds

(702) 388–2400. www.fitzgeraldslasvegas.com.

Limerick's Steakhouse. Steaks, ribs, and an Irish castle. (702) 388–2411. $10–$15.

Flamingo

(702) 733–3111. www.lv-flamingo.com.

Hamada of Japan. Traditional steak house and sushi bar. (702) 733–3455. $20 and up.

Jimmy Buffett's Margaritaville. Cheeseburgers (and more) in Vegas. (702) 733–3111. $10 and up.

Steakhouse46. Classic casino steak house, reborn. (702) 733–3333. $20 and up.

Ventuno Ristorante. Casual Italian. (702) 733–3111. $15 and up.

Four Queens

(702) 385–4011. www.fourqueens.com.

Hugo's Cellar. A local institution; fine steaks, seafood, and fowl. $20 and up.

Magnolia's Veranda. Casual fare, including juicy dips. $10 and up.

Fremont

(702) 385–3232. www.fremontcasino.com.

Lanai Express. Chinese and American fare. $10–$15.

Second Street Grill. American and Pacific Rim specialties. $20 and up.

Tony Roma's. Familiar ribs, chicken. $15–$20.

Gold Coast

(702) 367–7111. www.goldcoastcasino.com.

Arriva. Elegant Italian. $15–$20.

Cortez Room. Steak and seafood, and lots of it. $10–$15.

Monterey Room. Casino fare, American to Chinese. $10–$15.

Ping Pang Pong. Gourmet Asian. $15–$20.

Golden Nugget

(702) 385–7111. www.goldennugget.com.

Grotto. Seafood. $20 and up.

Lillie's. Above-the-ordinary Cantonese cuisine. $15–$25.

Vic & Anthony's. Seafood and pasta. $20 and up.

Hard Rock

(702) 693–5000. www.hardrock.com.

AJ's Steakhouse. Classic Vegas steak house, reborn. (702) 693–5500. $20 and up.

Mr. Lucky's. American/Continental coffee shop. (702) 693–5000. $10–$15.

Nobu. Classic Asian. (702) 693–5090. $20 and up.

Pink Taco. Country Mexican fare. (702) 693–5525. $10.

Simon Kitchen. Chef Kerry Simon's showcase. (702) 693–4440. $15–$20.

Harrah's

(702) 369–5084. www.harrahs.com/our_casinos/las.

Ming's Table. Asian. $20 and up.

Penazzi Italian Ristorante. Classical Italian. $40 and up.

The Range Steakhouse. High above the Strip. $15–$20.

Toby Keith's I Love This Bar & Grill. $15 to $20.

Hooter's Casino Hotel

(702) 739–9000.

Dan Marino's Fine Food & Spirits. Steak house. $20 and up.

Imperial Palace

(702) 794–3261. www.imperialpalace.com/vegas.

Cockeyed Clam. Cape Cod on the Strip. $15–$20.

Embers. Intimate steak house setting. $10–$15.

Ming Terrace. Mandarin and Cantonese specialties. $10–$20.

Las Vegas Hilton

(702) 732–5755. www.lv-hilton.com.

Andiamo. Northern Italian. $15–$20.

Benihana Village. Hibachi grill in a Japanese village. $15–$20.

Garden of the Dragon. Upscale Chinese. $15–$20.

Hilton Steakhouse. One of the classiest casino steak houses. $20 and up.

Quark's Bar and Restaurant. Your basic twenty-fourth-century diner at the Star Trek Experience. $10–$15.

888 Noodle Bar. Asian noodles of almost every variety. $15 and up.

Luxor

(702) 262–4000. www.luxor.com.

Fusia. "New Chinese cuisine." (702) 262–4774. $20 and up.

Luxor Steak House. Elegant beefery. (702) 262–4778. $15–$20.

Nile Deli. A New York kosher-style deli on the banks of the Vegas Nile. $10–$15.

Main Street Station

(702) 387–1896. www.mainstreetcasino.com.

Pullman Grille. A steak house so intimate it bears the name of the family farm in Illinois where the corn-fed Black Angus beef is raised. $15–$20.

Triple 7 Restaurant and Brewery. Pub food with four signature brews and a changing specialty brew. $10–$15.

Mandalay Bay

(702) 632–7777. www.mandalaybay.com.

Aureole. Seasonal American dishes. (702) 632–7401. $20 and up.

Border Grill. Upscale Southwestern taqueria. (702) 632–7403. $10–$15.

Charlie Palmer Steak Restaurant. Clublike beefery at Four Seasons Hotel within Mandalay Bay. (702) 632–5120. $20–$35.

China Grill. Chinese brasserie. (702) 632–7405. $15–$20.

Fleur de Lys. ★★★★ Hubert Keller's fine French fare. (702) 632–7777. $20 and up.

Giorgio Caffe. Casual Italian at Mandalay Place. $25–$50.

Noodle Shop. Hong Kong fast food. $10–$15.

Raffle's Cafe. American/Continental. (702) 632–7406. $15–$20.

Red Square. ★★★★ Pre-Marxist menu. (702) 632–7407. $20 and up.

Red, White, and Blue. American comfort food and seafood specialties. (702) 632–7405. $15 and up.

restaurant rm. Seafood bistro. $25 and up.

Rumjungle. ★★★★ Brazilian liveliness. (702) 632–7408. $15–$20.

Shanghai Lilly. Upscale Chinese. (702) 632–7409. $15–$20.

Wolfgang Puck's Trattoria del Lupo. Northern and southern Italian specialties. (702) 632–7410. $15–$20.

MGM Grand

(702) 891–7777. www.mgmgrand.com.

Craftsteak. ★★★★ The elements of steak house style. (702) 891–7318. $40 and up.

Diego. Traditional Mexican. $20 and up.

Emeril Lagasse's New Orleans Fish House. ★★★★ Creole and Cajun specialties and a seafood bar. (702) 891–7374. $30 and up.

Fiamma Trattoria. ★★★★ Regional Italian specialties. (702) 891–7600. $30 and up.

Grand Wok and Sushi Bar. Chinese, Japanese, Thai, Korean, and Vietnamese dishes. (702) 891–1111. $10–$15.

Nobhill. San Francisco's finest. (702) 891–3110. $30 and up.

Pearl. Modern high-end Cantonese and Shanghai fare. (702) 891–3110. $30 and up.

Rainforest Cafe. The great outdoors, indoors. (702) 891–8580. $10–$15.

Seablue. Jet-fresh seafood. (702) 891–3485. $30 and up.

Shibuya. Modern Asian. $20 and up.

Studio Café. High-tone coffee shop. $10–$15.

Wolfgang Puck Café. Trendy pizzas and other dishes at a lively restaurant on the casino floor. (702) 895–9653. $10–$15.

The Mirage
(702) 791–7223. www.themirage.com.

California Pizza Kitchen. Quirky pizzas. $10 and up.

Carnegie Deli. New York's finest. $10 and up.

Fin. ★★★★ Contemporary Chinese in an elegant setting. $15 and up.

Japonais. High-tone Japanese. $20 and up.

Kokomo's A Continental restaurant with seafood specialties in a rain forest within a Las Vegas casino; we're not sure what it all has to do with a city in Indiana of the same name. $20 and up.

Onda. Classic Mediterranean fare. $15–$20.

Samba Brazilian Steakhouse. Saucy *rodizio*. $20 and up.

Stack. ★★★★ A minimalist steak house, to the max. $20 and up.

Monte Carlo Resort
(702) 730–7777. www.monte-carlo.com.

Andre's French Restaurant. ★★★★ Haute cuisine in the casino version of a Las Vegas favorite. (702) 730–7955. $20 and up.

Blackstone's Steak House. Casino steak house fare, well done. (702) 730–7405. $15–$20.

Dragon Noodle Co. A casual Asian food and tea emporium. (702) 730–7965. $10–$20.

Market City Caffe. A southern Italian trattoria. (702) 739–7966. $10–$15.

Monte Carlo Pub & Brewery. Pizza, pasta, sandwiches, and half a dozen microbrews. $10.

New York–New York
(702) 740–6969. www.nynyhotelcasino.com.

America. All-American food, wine, and beer. (702) 740–6451. $10–$15.

Chin Chin Café. Asian and Pacific Rim specialties. (702) 740–6300. $15–$20.
ESPN Zone. Fast food and sports. (702) 933–3776. $10–$15.
Gallagher's Steakhouse. A Vegas version of the Big Apple original. (702) 740–6450. $20 and up.
Gonzalez Y Gonzalez. Mexican cafe. (702) 740–6455. $10–$15.
Il Fornaio. A little bit of Little Italy. $15–$20.
Nine Fine Irishmen. A bit of the old sod, a transplanted Irish pub. (702) 740–6350. www.ninefineirishmen.com. $15–$20.

Orleans

(702) 365–7111. www.orleanscasino.com.
Big Al's Oyster Bar. Mussels, clams, and lobster, too. $10–$15.
Brendan's Irish Pub. Where nobody knows your name. $10.
Canal Street Grille. Use your clout to reserve a fireside table and enjoy fine steaks and seafood. $20 and up.
Don Miguel's. Watch tortillas being made while you wait. $10–$15.
Koji. Family-style sushi, sashimi, and Chinese fare. $10 and up.
Prime Rib Loft. Beef and poultry. $10–$15.
Sazio. Italian specialties. $10–$15.

Palace Station

(702) 367–2411. www.palacestation.com.
The Broiler. Seafood and steak in an old California setting. $15–$20.
Guadalajara Bar & Grill. Tex-Mex specialties. $10–$15.
Pasta Palace. Pasta, pasta, pasta. $10–$15.

Palms Casino

(702) 942–7777. www.palms.com.
Alizé. Gourmet French fare, way up high with a view of the Strip, and 6,000 bottles of wine, port, Armagnac, and cognac. (702) 951–7000. $20 and up.
Garduño's. An outpost of a New Mexico favorite; the Sunday margarita brunch is promising. (702) 942–7777. $10–$15.
Little Buddha. Asian specialties with a French accent, in the first American version of a Paris favorite. (702) 942–7778. $10–$15.
Steak House Nine. A classic Chicago steak house, also with some worthy seafood and shellfish offerings. (702) 933–9900. $20 and up.

Paris Las Vegas

(702) 946–7000. www.paris-lv.com.
Ah Sin. ★★★★ Fancy Asian food with a tinge of French. (702) 946–7000. $20 and up.
Eiffel Tower Restaurant. Gourmet fare, eleven stories above the Strip. (702) 948–6937. $20 and up.
JJ's Boulangerie. Soup, sandwiches, and pastries. (702) 946–7147. $10–$15.
Les Artistes Steakhouse. French show kitchen. (702) 967–7999. $20 and up.

Le Provençal. French-Italian cuisine of Provence. (702) 967–7999. $15–$20.
Mon Ami Gabi. Parisian street cafe. (702) 944–4224. $10–$15.
Ortanique. Cuban/Caribbean by way of Florida. (702) 946–4346. $15–$20.

Planet Hollywood/Aladdin

(702) 785–5555. www.aladdincasino.com. The lineup of restaurants will change as Planet Hollywood puts its stamp on the former Aladdin, and as the Desert Passage shopping area becomes the Miracle Mile. Be sure to call first to obtain current information.

Commander's Palace. ★★★★ Creole and New Orleans specialties. (702) 892–8272. www.commanderspalace.com/las_vegas. $20 and up.

Elements. Gourmet steak and seafood, with a sushi bar. (702) 785–9003. $20 and up.

Lombardi's Romagna Mia. Italian trattoria. (702) 731–1755. $15–$20.

Todai Japanese Seafood Buffet. Flashy Japanese fare in the Desert Passage. (702) 892–0021. www.todai.com. $20 and up.

Tremezzo. Italian with patio seating on the Strip. (702) 785–9013. $20 and up.

Plaza

(702) 386–2110. www.plazahotelcasino.com.

Center Stage. Steak house with a view. $10 and up.

Rio All-Suite

(702) 252–7777. www.playrio.com.

All American Bar and Grille. Loud and boisterous, just off the casino floor. (702) 247–7923. $10–$15.

Antonio's Ristorante. Traditional Italian. (702) 247–7923. $15–$20.

Bamboleo Mexican Restaurant. Mexican and Tex-Mex. (702) 252–7777.

Buzio's Seafood Restaurant. Pan roasts and steamed shellfish. (702) 247–7923. $10–$15.

Fiore Steak House. The elegance of the Rio, in a hideaway off the casino floor. (702) 247–7923. $20 and up.

Gaylord Indian Restaurant. Northern Indian cuisine. (702) 247–7923. $15–$20.

Hamada's Asiana Restaurant. Teppanyaki, sushi, tempura, steaks, and Chinese dishes. (702) 252–7777. $15 and up.

Mah Jong Chinese Kitchen. Casual noodlery. (702) 252–7777. $15–$25.

Sao Paulo Café. American, Chinese, and Italian. (702) 252–7777. $10 and up.

Tilted Kilt. Quirky and kinky Irish pub. (702) 252–7777. $10 and up.

VooDoo Café. Best of the Bayou with an unbeatable view from the top. (702) 247–7923. $15–$20.

Riviera

(702) 734–5110. www.theriviera.com.

BB's Prime Rib & Barbecue. As described. (702) 734–5110. $$.

Kristofer's Steak House. Prix fixe gourmet fare. (702) 794–9233. $15–$20.

Ristorante Italiano. Fancy Italian. (702) 794–9363. $10–$15.

Sahara

(702) 737–2111. www.saharavegas.com.

House of Lords. Steak house. (702) 737–2111. $15–$20.

NASCAR Cafe. Fast fast food. (702) 734–7223. $10.

Paco's Bar and Grill. Mexican fare. (702) 737–2111. $10.

Sam's Town

(702) 456–7777. www.samstownlv.com.

Billy Bob's Steak House and Saloon. Just like it sounds. (702) 454–8031. $15–$20.

Fellini's Italian Dining. Casual Italian dining. (702) 454–8041. $10–$15.

Willy and Jose's Cantina. Mexican and Western specialties. (702) 454–8044. $10–$15.

Stratosphere

(702) 380–7777. www.stratlv.com.

The Crazy Armadillo. Tex-Mex and oysters. (702) 383–5230. $10–$15.

Fellini's Ristorante Italiano. Family Italian. (702) 383–4859. $10–$15.

Lucky's Cafe. American/Continental/Asian. (702) 383–7711. $15–$20.

Roxy's Diner. American fare. (702) 380–7711. $10.

Top of the World. ★★★★ Steaks, seafood, and more, served on a revolving platform 833 feet above the Strip. $20 and up. (702) 380–7711.

Suncoast Casino

(877) 677–7111. www.suncoastcasino.com.

Primo's. English-style cafe. $15–$20.

Señor Miguel's. Mexican fare. (702) 636–7111. $10–$15.

Via Veneto. Italian trattoria. (702) 636–7111. $10–$15.

Sunset Station

(702) 547–7777. www.sunsetstation.com.

The Capri. Italian specialties. (702) 658–4900. $15–$20.

Costa del Sol. Seafood from around the world. (702) 547–7777. $15–$20.

Guadalajara Bar & Grille. Casual Mexican and Southwestern. (702) 547–7777. $10–$15.

Sonoma Cellar Steakhouse. Gourmet beefery. (702) 547–7777. $20 and up.

Viva Salsa. Tacos, quesadillas, burritos. (702) 547–4444. $10 and up.

Terrible's Hotel and Casino

(702) 733–7000. www.terribleherbst.com.

Bougainvillea Café. American and Chinese specialties and rotisserie. $10–$15.

Texas Station

(702) 631–1000. www.texasstation.com.

Austins Steakhouse. Steak, seafood, and rib platters. (702) 631–1033. $15–$20.

San Lorenzo Italian Restaurant. Wide-ranging Italian menu. $10–$15.

The Steakhouse. Surf and turf. $20 and up.

Texas Star Oyster Bar. Etouffée, bouillabaisse, and oysters. $15–$20.

Treasure Island

(702) 894–7111. www.treasureisland.com.

Canter's Deli. Direct from LA. $15 and up.

Francesco's Cucina Italiana. Family-style. (702) 894–7223. $20 and up.

Isla Mexican Kitchen and Tequilla Bar. Upscale Mexican. (702) 894–7111. $15 and up.

Kahunaville. American/Continental with a Polynesian flair. (702) 894–7390. $15–$20.

Social House. Sushi and sake. $15 to $20.

The Steak House. Like the sign says. (702) 894–7223. $20 and up.

Tropicana

(702) 739–2222. www.tropicanalv.com.

Mizuno's Japanese Steak House. Teppanyaki dining nightly. (702) 739–2713. $15–$20.

Pietro's. Mediterranean specialties. (702) 739–2783. $20 and up.

Savanna Steakhouse. Exotic fare. (702) 739–2376. $15–$20.

Tuscany Italian Café. (702) 739–2655. $15–$20.

Venetian Resort Hotel Casino

(702) 414–1000. www.venetian.com.

Aquaknox. Fresh and fancy seafood. (702) 414–3772. $25 and up.

Bouchon at Venezia Tower. Fancy French. (702) 414–1000.

Canaletto High-tone Italian. (702) 733–0070. $20 and up.

Delmonico Steakhouse. Old-school steak house. (702) 414–3737. $20 and up.

Grand Lux Café. From the creators of the Cheesecake Factory. (702) 414–1000. $10–$15.

Lutèce. ★★★★ Modern French and oh-so-tony. (702) 414–2220. $20 and up.

Piero Selvaggio's Valentino. ★★★★ Mediterranean and Adriatic fare. (702) 414–3000. $15–$20.

Pinot Brasserie. Elegant steak, game, and seafood. (702) 414–8888. $20 and up.

P.S. Italian Grill. Grilled pizza and entrees from Piero Selvaggio. (702) 414–3000. $15–$20.

Royal Star. ★★★★ Upscale Asian. (702) 414–1888. $20 and up.

Star Canyon. ★★★★ High-concept chuckwagon. (702) 414–3772. $20 and up.

Tao Asian Bistro. ★★★★ One of the hottest Asian restaurants in New York makes its local appearance. (702) 414–1000. $20 and up.

Taqueria Canonita. High-tone Mexican. (702) 414–3773. $15–$20.

Tsunami Asian Grill. Unusual Asian specialties. (702) 414–1000. $25 and up.

Zeffirino. ★★★★ Fancy Italian. (702) 414–3500. $20 and up.

Westin Casuarina

(702) 836–9775. www.westin.com/lasvegas.

Silver Peak Grill. Casual Mediterranean and Asian fare.

Wynn Las Vegas

(702) 248–3463. www.wynnlasvegas.com.

Alex. French. $25 and up.

Bartolotta Ristorante di Mare. Italian, seafood. $20 and up.

Corsa Cucina. High-tone Italian. $25 and up.

The Country Club. A new American steak house. $25 and up.

Daniel Boulud Brasserie. American, French. $20 and up.

Okada. Japanese. $20 and up.

Red 8 Asian Bistro. Asian. $20 and up.

SW Steakhouse. SW as in Steve W. $20 and up.

Wing Lei. Chinese, Asian. $20 and up.

THEME RESTAURANTS

The rest of the world has already discovered Planet Hollywood and the Hard Rock Cafe, but the local versions of those quiet establishments are presented Las Vegas–style.

The Hard Rock Cafe has its own theme casino and restaurant on Paradise Road equipped with a giant guitar outside and a collection of the guitars of the giants within. You'll find details about the casino in chapter 6.

The other big franchise in town is Planet Hollywood, with a restaurant along the ancient streets of Rome in the Forum Shops at Caesars Palace and at its own casino, the former Aladdin.

Along the streets of New York at the spectacular New York–New York casino is a lively sports bar, the ESPN Zone.

Other entrants include the Harley-Davidson Cafe at Harmon Avenue on the Strip and the Gordon Biersch Brewery Restaurant on Paradise Road, serving German and American food and beer.

■ A SELECTION OF THEME RESTAURANTS

ESPN Zone. New York–New York, 3790 Las Vegas Boulevard South. (702) 740–6969. $10–$15.

Harley-Davidson Cafe. 3725 Las Vegas Boulevard South. (702) 740–4555. www.harley-davidsoncafe.com. $10–$15.

House of Blues. Mandalay Bay, 3250 Las Vegas Boulevard South. (702) 632–7600. $10–$15.

Jimmy Buffett's Margaritaville. Flamingo. (800) 732–2111. www.flamingo lasvegas.com or margaritaville.com/lasvegas.htm. $15–$20.

NASCAR Cafe. Sahara, 2535 Las Vegas Boulevard South. (702) 734–7223. $10.

Planet Hollywood. Forum Shops at Caesars Palace, 3570 Las Vegas Boulevard South. (702) 791–7827. $10–$15.

Quark's Bar and Restaurant. Hilton Las Vegas at the Star Trek Experience, 3000 Paradise Road. (702) 697–8725. $10–$15.

Rainforest Cafe. MGM Grand. (702) 891–8580. $10–$15.

MICROBREWERIES

Have a thirst for some locally produced suds? If you think about it, microbreweries in Las Vegas are among the only places in town where something is actually manufactured, with the exception, I suppose, of myths.

Here's a selection of some interesting breweries inside and outside of casinos; the local brews are accompanied by sandwiches, pizza, ribs, and other thirst inducing fare.

Barley's Casino & Brewing Co. 4500 East Sunset Road. (702) 458–2739. $10–$15.

Chicago Brewing Company. 2201 South Apache Road. (702) 254–3333. $10–$15.

Gordon Biersch Brewery Restaurant. 3987 Paradise Road. (702) 312–5247. www.gordonbiersch.com. $10–$15.

Monte Carlo Pub & Brewery. Monte Carlo Hotel, 3770 South Las Vegas Boulevard. (702) 730–7777, (800) 311–8999. www.monte-carlo.com. $10–$15.

Tenaya Creek Restaurant & Brewery. 3101 North Tenaya Way. (702) 362–7335. $15–$20.

Triple 7 Brew Pub. Main Street Station, 200 North Main Street. (702) 387–1896. www.mainstreetcasino.com/restaurants/index.cfm. $10–$15.

Big Dog Hospitality Group:

Big Dog's Bar and Grill. 1311 North Nellis Boulevard. (702) 459–1099 $10–$15.

Big Dog's Cafe and Casino. 6390 West Sahara Avenue. (702) 876–3647. $10–$15.

The Draft House. 4543 North Rancho Drive at Craig Road. (702) 645–1404. $10–$15.

RESTAURANTS OUTSIDE THE CASINOS

■ AMERICAN/THEME

Big Mama's Rib Shack. 2230 West Bonanza Road. (702) 597–1616. $10–$15.

Bix's Supper Club. 4495 South Buffalo Road. (702) 889–0800. $20 and up.

Black Mountain Grill. 11021 South Eastern Avenue. (702) 990–0990. $10–$15.

Bob Stewart's Soul Kitchen. 89106 Martin Luther King. (702) 647–8228. $10–$15.

Brat Works. 4755 South Maryland Parkway. (702) 891–0008. $10–$15.

Brooklyn Queens Expressway. 613 West Sahara Avenue at Jones Boulevard. (702) 365–9900. Deli fare. $10–$15.

Canyon Dining Room. Mount Charleston Hotel, 2 Kyle Canyon Road. (702) 872–5500. $15–$20.

Rosemary's. ★★★★ 8125 West Sahara Avenue. (702) 869–2251. Rapidly expanding beyond a local favorite to a national attraction. $15–$25.

Tenaya Creek Restaurant & Brewery. 3101 North Tenaya Way. (702) 362–7335. $15–$20.

Tommy Rocker's Cantina & Grill. 4275 South Industrial Road. (702) 261–6688. www.tommyrocker.com. The food is mild, but the atmosphere is wild. $10–$15.

■ ASIAN

Amlee Gourmet. 3827 East Sunset Road. (702) 898–3358. $15–$20.

Asia Palace Restaurant. 5485 West Sahara Avenue. (702) 364–5559. $10–$15.

Bamboo Garden. 4850 West Flamingo Road. (702) 871–3262. $15–$20.

Bangkok Boom. 3111 South Valley View Boulevard. (702) 252–0329. $10–$15.

Bangkok 9. 663 Stephanie Street. (702) 898–6881. $10–$15.

Bangkok Orchid. 4662 East Sunset Road, Henderson. (702) 458–4945. $15–$20.

Beijing Restaurant. 3900 Paradise Road. (702) 737–9618. $15–$20.

B-Won. 953 East Sahara Avenue. (702) 791–3992. Asian and Korean specialties. $10–$15.

Cafe Noodle & Chinese Barbecue. 4355 Spring Mountain Road. (702) 220–3399. $10–$20.

Canton Chinese Cuisine. 3740 East Flamingo Road. (702) 458–2920. $10–$15.

Cathay House. 5300 Spring Mountain Road. (702) 876–3838. Dim sum carts overlooking the Strip. $10–$15.

Chang of Las Vegas. 3055 Las Vegas Boulevard South. (702) 731–3388. $20 and up.

China Garden Restaurant. 5485 West Sahara Avenue. (702) 312–1717. $10–$15.

China King. 3175 North Rainbow Boulevard. (702) 656–2200. $10–$15.

China Queen. 4825 South Rainbow Road. (702) 873–3288. $10–$15.

China Star. 2590 South Maryland Parkway. (702) 731–6822. $10–$15.

Chung King. 2710 East Desert Inn Road. (702) 693–6886. $10–$15.

Classic Buffet House. 3331 East Tropicana Avenue. (702) 435–1881. $10–$15.

Com Tam Ninh Kieu. 4725 Spring Mountain Road. (702) 889–2906. Japanese specialties. $10–$15.

Diamond China. 2239 North Rampart Boulevard. (702) 363–8262. $10–$15.

Diamond China. 3909 West Sahara Avenue. (702) 873–6977. $10–$15.

Dynasty Restaurant. 2750 North Green Valley Parkway. (702) 454–6882. $10–$15.

Fong's Garden. 2021 East Charleston Boulevard. (702) 382–1644. $10–$15.

Fuji Japanese Restaurant. 3430 East Tropicana Avenue. (702) 435–8838. $15–$20.

Genki. 4001 South Decatur Boulevard. (702) 938–1448. $10–$15.

Ginza. 1000 East Sahara Avenue. (702) 732–3080. $10–$15.

Golden Flower. 3315 East Russell Road. (702) 454–1177. $10–$15.

Ho-Ho-Ho. 2550 South Rainbow Boulevard. (702) 876–6856. Szechuan, Mandarin, and vegetarian cuisine. $10.

Joyful House. 4601 Spring Mountain Road. (702) 889–8881. $10–$15.

Kabuki Japanese Restaurant. 1150 Twain Avenue. (702) 733–0066. $15–$25.

Koreana BBQ. 2447 East Tropicana Avenue. (702) 458–6869. $10–$15.

Kyoto Japanese Restaurant. 2680 South Maryland Parkway. (702) 731–3330. $20 and up.

Lotus of Siam. 953 East Sahara Avenue. (702) 735–3033. $15–$25.

Ocean Forest. 1000 East Sahara Road. (702) 732–3080. $10–$15.

168 Shanghai. 4215 Spring Mountain Road. (702) 365–9168. $10–$15.

Osaka Japanese Restaurant. 4205 West Sahara Avenue. (702) 876–4988. www .lasvegas-sushi.com. $15–$20.

Pad Thai Restaurant. 850 South Rancho Drive. (702) 870–2899. $10–$20.

P. F. Chang's China Bistro. ★★★★ 4165 Paradise Road. (702) 792–2207. $15–$25.

Saigon Restaurant. 4251 West Sahara Avenue. (702) 362–9978. A very ordinary storefront restaurant with extraordinary Vietnamese cooking. $10–$20.

Sam Woo BBQ. 4215 Spring Mountain Road. (702) 386–7628. $10–$15.

Shiba of Tokyo. 4130 South Decatur Road. (702) 227–0342. $20 and up.

Sushi House Manda. 230 West Sahara Avenue. (702) 382–6006. $10–$15.

Sushi on Tropicana. 2625 East Tropicana Avenue. (702) 898–8835. $10.

Thai Garden. 5600 West Spring Mountain Road. (702) 873–9798. $10.

Thai Spice. 4433 West Flamingo Road. (702) 362–5308. $10–$20.

Tokyo Japanese Restaurant. 953 East Sahara Avenue. (702) 735–7070. $10–$15.

Xinh Xinh Restaurant. 220 West Sahara Avenue. (702) 471–1572. Vietnamese specialties. $10–$15.

Yama Sushi. 1350 East Flamingo Road. (702) 696–0072. $10–$15.

Chinatown Plaza. A mile west of the Las Vegas Strip at 4215 Spring Mountain Road, Chinatown Plaza is a collection of twenty-eight shops and restaurants including some unusual offerings. For information call (702) 221–8448. Among the eateries:

Chinatown Express. Mandarin. (702) 364–1122. $10–$15.

Dragon Sushi. (702) 368–4336. $10–$20.

Emperor's Garden. Mandarin and Szechuan. (702) 889–6777. $10–$20.

Harbor Palace Seafood Restaurant. Dim sum and Cantonese. (702) 253–1688. $10–$20.

Kapit Bahay Filipino Fast Food. Philippine specialties. (702) 889–4922. $10–$20.

Kim Tar Seafood Restaurant. Southern Chinese. (702) 227–3588. $10–$20.

168 Shanghai Restaurant. Shanghai cuisine and dumplings. (702) 365–9168. $10–$20.

Pho Vietnam Restaurant. Vietnamese cuisines and noodles. (702) 227–8618. $10–$20.

Sam Woo BBQ. Hong Kong barbecue. (702) 368–7628. $10–$20.

■ BRAZILIAN

Yolie's. 3900 Paradise Road. (702) 794–0700. $15–$20.

CONTINENTAL

Cafe Trattoria Magia. 4650 East Sunset Road. (702) 436–2522. Romanian specialties. $10–$15.

Eliseevsky. 4825 West Flamingo Road. (702) 247–8766. Russian specialties. $10–$15.

Green's Supper Club. 2241 North Green Valley Parkway, Henderson. (702) 454–4211. $15–$25.

Renata's Supper Club. 4451 East Sunset Road, Henderson. (702) 435–4000. $15–$25.

FRENCH

Andre's French Restaurant. ★★★★ 401 South Sixth Street. (702) 385–5016. www.andresfrenchrest.com. A Las Vegas favorite in a re-created French country house near downtown. $20 and up.

Bonjour. 8878 South Eastern Avenue. (702) 270–2102. $15–$20.

Le Pamplemousse. ★★★★ 400 East Sahara Avenue. (702) 733–2066. www.pamplemousserestaurant.com. A changing menu of French country specialties. $20 and up.

GERMAN

Cafe Heidelberg. 610 East Sahara Avenue. (702) 731–5310. $10–$15.

Danube Cafe & Market. 4865 South Pecos. (702) 454–5535. $10–$15.

Gordon Biersch Brewery Restaurant. 3987 Paradise Road. (702) 312–5247. www.gordonbiersch.com. $10–$15.

GREEK

Grape Street Cafe. 7501 West Lake Mead Boulevard. (702) 228–9463. $20 and up.

INDIAN

Dosa Den. 3430 East Tropicana Avenue. (702) 456–4920. $10–$15.

Gandhi. 4080 Paradise Road. (702) 734–0094. $10–$15.

House of Kabob. 4110 South Maryland Avenue. (702) 732–2285. $10–$15.

India Oven. 226 West Sahara Road. (702) 366–0222. $10–$15.

India Palace. 505 East Twain Avenue. (702) 796–4177. $10–$15.

Priya's Fine Indian Cuisine. 2605 South Decatur Boulevard. (702) 257–6833. $10–$15.

ITALIAN

Anthony's Fine Dining. 1550 East Tropicana Avenue. (702) 795–6000. $15–$20.

Bacio Organico. 1020 East Desert Inn Road. (702) 699–9980. $15–$20.

Battista's Hole in the Wall. 4041 Audrie Way. (702) 732–1424. A classic, comfortable family Italian restaurant. $15–$20.

Bella Luna. 7905 West Sahara Avenue. (702) 227–7900. $10–$15.

Bertolini's. 9500 West Sahara Avenue. (702) 869–1540. $15–$20.

Bootlegger Ristorante. 7700 Las Vegas Boulevard South. (702) 736–4939. $10–$15.

Buca Di Beppo East. 412 East Flamingo Road. (702) 866–2863. www.bucadibeppo.com. $15–$20.

Carluccio's Tivoli Gardens. 1775 East Tropicana Avenue. (702) 795–3236. $15–$25.

Carraba's Italian Grill. 10160 South Eastern Avenue, Henderson. (702) 990–0650. $10–$15.

Cipriani Restaurant. 2790 East Flamingo Road. (702) 369–6711. $15–$25.

DiMartino's. 100 North Green Valley Parkway. (702) 269–7144. $10–$15.

Ferraro's. 5900 West Flamingo Road. (702) 354–5300. $15–$20.

La Scala Ristorante Italiano. 1020 East Desert Inn Road. (702) 699–9980. $15–$20.

Manhattan of Las Vegas. 2600 East Flamingo Road. (702) 737–5000. $15–$20.

Montesano's Italian Deli. 3441 West Sahara Avenue. (702) 876–0348. $10–$15.

Nana B's Trattoria. 5795 West Tropicana Avenue. (702) 220–6900. $10–$15.

Old Spaghetti Factory. 721 Mall Ring Circle. (702) 458–0845. $10–$15.

Panini. 3460 East Sunset Road. (702) 436–3100. $15–$25.

Pasta Mia West. 4455 West Flamingo Road. (702) 251–8871. $10–$15.

Piero's Italian Cuisine. 355 Convention Center Drive. (702) 369–2305. Quality Italian pasta, seafood, and meat across the street from the convention center. $20 and up.

■ MEXICAN, CARIBBEAN, SOUTH AMERICAN

Alberto's Mexican Food. 3025 Las Vegas Boulevard South. (702) 732–8226. $10–$15.

Bahama Breeze. 375 Hughes Center Drive. (702) 731–3252. $15–$20.

Bonito Michoacan. 4485 South Jones Boulevard. (702) 257–6810. $10–$15.

Caribbean Cabana. 3190 West Sahara Avenue. (702) 873–3345. $10–$15.

Casa Don Juan. 1202 South Main Street. (702) 384–8070. $10–$15.

Casa Mercado. 4500 East Sunset Road. (702) 435–6200. $15–$20.

Chapalas. 2101 South Decatur Boulevard. (702) 871–7805. $10–$15.

Chapalas. 3335 East Tropicana Avenue. (702) 451–8141. $10–$15.

Chico's Tecate Grill. 2341 North Rainbow Boulevard. (702) 646–4636. $10–$15.

Chico's Tecate Grill. 8410 West Cheyenne Avenue. (702) 645–5656. $10–$15.

Cordobes Mexican Restaurant. 235 North Eastern Avenue. (702) 382–3803. $10–$15.

Cozymel's Coastal Mexican Grill. 355 Hughes Center Drive. (702) 732–4833. $15–$20.

Cuba Cafeteria. 552 North Eastern Avenue. (702) 382–6688. $10–$15.

Cuba Mia Café. 3035 East Tropicana Avenue. (702) 435–6797. $10–$15.

El Alacran. 3711 South Valley View Boulevard. (702) 871–0794. $10–$15.

El Ausente. 2536 Fremont Street. (702) 384–0484. $10–$15.

El Jalisco. 3400 South Jones Boulevard. (702) 251–4742. $10–$15.

El Rincon Salvadoreno. 1106 South Third Street. (702) 384–7673. $10–$15.

El Sombrero Café. 807 South Main Street. (702) 382–9234. $10–$15.

Lindo Michoacan. 2655 East Desert Inn Road. (702) 735–6828. $10–$15.

Ricardo's of Las Vegas. 4930 West Flamingo Road. (702) 871–7119. $10–$20.

Rubio's Baja Grill. 1500 North Green Valley Parkway, Henderson. (702) 270–6097. $10–$15.

■ MIDDLE EASTERN

Al Basha. 3969 South Maryland Parkway. (702) 699–7155. $10–$15.

Anita's House of Kabob. 4110 South Maryland Parkway. (702) 732–2285. $10–$15.

Byblos Cafe. 4825 West Flamingo Road. (702) 222–1801. $10–$15.

Daily Chicken. 4632 South Maryland Parkway. (702) 795–8444. Lebanese, Middle Eastern. $10–$15.

■ SEAFOOD

Bullshrimp. Green Valley Ranch, 2300 Paseo Verde Parkway. (702) 221–6560. $20 and up.

Joe's Crab Shack. 1991 North Rainbow Boulevard. (702) 646–3996. $15–$20.

Landry's Seafood House. 2610 West Sahara Avenue. (702) 251–0101. $15–$20.

Lobster House. 3763 Las Vegas Boulevard South. (702) 740–4431. $15–$20.

McCormick & Schmick's Seafood Restaurant. 335 Hughes Center Drive. (702) 836–9000. www.mccormickandschmicks.com. As fresh as you could hope for, at least out here in the desert. $15–$20.

Tillerman Restaurant. 2245 East Flamingo Road. (702) 731–4036. www .tillerman.com. $20 and up.

■ SOUTHWESTERN

Border Grill. Green Valley Ranch, 2300 Paseo Verde Parkway. (702) 221–6560. $15–$20.

Z'tejas Grill. 3824 South Paradise Road. (702) 732–1660. www.ztejas.com. $15–$20.

Museum of Mixology

There's a museum for just about everything, and in Las Vegas it seems perfectly apt to note the Museum of the American Cocktail, located inside Commander's Palace restaurant at the Miracle Mile at Planet Hollywood (formerly the Desert Passage shops at the Aladdin Casino and Resort). The collection traces the history of the cocktail through the past 200 years and includes vintage cocktail paraphernalia ranging from shakers, advertisements, and barware to music and Prohibition-era literature. For information call (702) 892–8272 or consult www.museumofthe americancocktail.org.

■ STEAK HOUSE

Del Frisco's Double Eagle Steakhouse. 3925 Paradise Road. (702) 796–0063. $20 and up.

Kiefer's. 105 East Harmon Avenue. (702) 739–8000. Veal, steak, and seafood specialties with a penthouse view of the Strip. $15–$25.

Lawry's the Prime Rib. 4043 Howard Hughes Parkway. (702) 893–2223. $20 and up.

Memphis Championship Barbecue. 4379 Las Vegas Boulevard North. (702) 869–9112. $10–$15.

Ruth's Chris Steak House. 3900 Paradise Road. (702) 791–5940. www.ruths chrislasvegas.com. $20 and up.

Ruth's Chris Steak House. 4561 West Flamingo Road. (702) 248–7011. www .ruthschrislasvegas.com. $20 and up.

Smith & Wollensky. 3767 Las Vegas Boulevard South. (702) 862–4100. $20 and up.

VEGETARIAN

Sweet Tomatoes. 2080 North Rainbow at Lake Mead. (702) 648–1957. A salad lover's dream. $10–$15.

Wild Sage Café. 600 East Warm Springs Road. (702) 944–7243. $10–$15.

CHAPTER THIRTEEN

SPORTS AND RECREATION

SPECTATOR SPORTS

■ LAS VEGAS 51s BASEBALL

The AAA farm club of the Los Angeles Dodgers in the Pacific Coast League, one step below the majors, plays a 144-game season from April through September. Home games are at Cashman Field, which has 9,334 permanent seats and 3,000 bleachers in the outfield. Fans can also have dinner at the Club Level Restaurant and watch the game from there.

About that unusual name: It's a reference to the not-officially-there government base at Area 51, about 50 miles from Cashman Field (or maybe not).

In its first eighteen seasons, the team was called the Las Vegas Stars and was an affiliate of the San Diego Padres. A name change came with a switch to the Los Angeles Dodgers organization in 2001; the team's uniforms are Dodger blue with the addition of an alien or two.

Among major-league stars who played for the minor-league team in Las Vegas are Roberto and Sandy Alomar, Carlos Baerga, Joey Cora, Ozzie Guillen, John Kruk, Tony Gwynn, Benito Santiago, Kevin McReynolds, and Shane Mack.

The sixteen teams in the Pacific Coast League are divided into two divisions; for information on the league, consult www.pclbaseball.com. The Pacific Division includes the Las Vegas 51s as well as the Fresno Grizzlies, Sacramento River Cats, Tucson Sidewinders, Colorado Springs Sky Sox, Portland Beavers, Salt Lake Bees, and Tacoma Rainiers.

In the American Division are the Albuquerque Isotopes, Iowa Cubs, Memphis Redbirds, Nashville Sounds, New Orleans Zephyrs, Oklahoma Redhawks, Omaha Royals, and the Round Rock Express.

In typical minor-league fashion, there are many special promotions at games, including fireworks nights. In recent years major-league teams have played at least one spring training game against other major-league teams; in 2005 the Chicago Cubs and Seattle Mariners played a pair of games in early April.

To get to Cashman Field, take U.S. Highway 93/95 to the Cashman Field/Las Vegas Boulevard exit. At the light on Las Vegas Boulevard, turn left; at the third light you will see Cashman Field. For ticket information call (702) 386–7200 or consult www.lv51.com. Tickets are available through Ticketmaster at (702) 474–4000. Prices range from about $7.00 to $12.00.

■ LAS VEGAS MOTOR SPEEDWAY

If the traffic on the Las Vegas Strip isn't thrilling enough for you, you can head to the city's newest major sporting attraction, the Las Vegas Motor Speedway. On a 1,600-acre plot north of the city, the $200 million speedway includes a 1½-mile NASCAR race course, a 2½-mile infield FIA road course, a half-mile dirt oval, and a drag strip.

There are 117,000 grandstand seats; a one-hundred-space RV camp overlooks the speedway. Organizers expect several major national races each year as well as a regular schedule of regional and local competitions. Among major events in 2005 were various NASCAR contests as well as drag strip, truck, and other races. Even with the huge capacity of the track, most major events sell out ahead of time.

The speedway is located at 7000 Las Vegas Boulevard North, off Interstate 15. CAT buses serve the facility, with increased service for major events. For information call (800) 644–4444 or consult www.lvms.com.

■ UNLV RUNNIN' REBELS

The nationally ranked college basketball team plays home games at the Thomas and Mack Center in a season that runs from mid-November through the beginning of March. Tickets are scarce for some matchups. Other sports teams include baseball, swimming, and golf. For information call (702) 739–3267 or consult www.unlvrebels.com.

■ UNLV LADY REBELS

The women's basketball team, also a national power, plays at the South Gym of UNLV. For information call (702) 739–3267 or consult www.unlvrebels.com.

■ RODEO

For two weeks in December, Las Vegas becomes a wild cow town, home to the National Finals Rodeo. The event has been held in the city for nearly two decades. Events are held at the Thomas and Mack Center and other venues; tickets for some of the events can be very difficult to obtain. For information call (702) 260–8605 or consult www.prorodeo.com.

RECREATION

■ BOWLING

Gold Coast Hotel & Casino. 4000 West Flamingo Road. Seventy lanes. Open twenty-four hours. (702) 367–4700. www.goldcoastcasino.com.

Orleans Hotel & Casino. 4500 West Tropicana Avenue. Seventy lanes. (702) 365–7111. www.orleanscasino.com/bowling.

Sam's Town Hotel & Gambling Hall & Bowling Center. 5111 Boulder Highway. Fifty-six lanes. Open twenty-four hours. (702) 454–8023. www.sams townlv.com/bowling.

Santa Fe Station Hotel and Casino Bowling Center. 4949 North Rancho Drive. Sixty lanes. (702) 658–4995. http://santafe.stationcasinos.com.

Silver Nugget Casino. 2140 Las Vegas Boulevard North, North Las Vegas. Twenty-four lanes. (702) 399–1111. www.silvernuggetcasino.net/bowling.htm.

Suncoast Hotel & Casino. 909 Alta Drive. Sixty-four lanes. (702) 636–7111. www.suncoastcasino.com/bowling.

Texas Station Gambling Hall & Hotel. 2101 Texas Star Lane, North Las Vegas. Sixty lanes complete with fog machines, laser lights, go-go dancers, and late-night disco Cosmic Bowling on Friday and Saturday. (800) 654–8888. www .texasstation.com.

■ HORSEBACK RIDING

Bonnie Springs Old Nevada. Highway 159 west of Las Vegas. Seven days a week through Red Canyon. (702) 875–4191. www.bonniesprings.com/horseback .html.

■ ICE-SKATING

Sobe Ice Arena at Fiesta Ranch Hotel & Casino. 2400 North Rancho Drive. (702) 647–7465 or (702) 631–7000. www.lvskating.com/rink_information.htm.

■ ROLLER-SKATING

Crystal Palace Boulder. 4680 Boulder Highway. (702) 458–7107. www.skate vegas.com.

Crystal Palace Rancho. 3901 North Rancho Drive. (702) 645–4892. www .skatevegas.com.

■ SKIING AND SLEDDING

Las Vegas Ski and Snowboard Resort. Route 156, Mount Charleston. Snow and road conditions: (702) 593–9500 or (702) 646–0008. www.skilasvegas.com.

Vertical	Elevation	Lifts
1,000	9,510	three double chairs

Base: 8,510 feet. Summit: 9,510 feet.

Rates
Adults about $40 (afternoon about $30), children about $30 (afternoon about $20).

A secret to many winter visitors to Las Vegas is that there is a ski hill less than an hour north of the Strip, only 47 miles away. Las Vegas Ski and Snowboard Resort, which used to be called Lee Canyon, is not to be confused with one of the

Sierra Nevada monsters in and around Lake Tahoe, but it does offer decent skiing from about December through April. The resort typically receives about 120 inches of snow; snowmaking helps out where Mother Nature fails. The resort offers shuttle bus service from Las Vegas, and you can rent ski equipment and clothing.

Lift tickets at the area are a relative bargain. Visitors can rent skis, boots, snowboards, and even winter clothing.

This is predominately an intermediate hill with about 20 percent beginner slopes and 20 percent expert terrain. Chairs 1 and 2 are each 3,000 feet long, rising 1,000 feet to intermediate and advanced runs; chair 3 serves Rabbit Peak for novice skiers. The Mount Charleston Hotel is on Kyle Canyon Road. Call (702) 872–5500 for directions, or consult www.skilasvegas.com.

Foxtail Snow Play Area. Lee Canyon Road, Mount Charleston. Bring your own sled, inner tube, or cafeteria tray. The area is owned and maintained by the USDA Forest Service and is opened when there is sufficient natural snow. Call (702) 515–5400, or check with Las Vegas Ski and Snowboard Resort, for local snow conditions first.

Cross-Country Skiing. The USDA Forest Service, 4701 North Torrey Pines Boulevard, (702) 515–5400, has maps of Mount Charleston available for sale.

Brian Head Ski Resort. Off I–15 in Brian Head, Utah, about 240 miles northeast of Las Vegas. For information and lodging reservations, call (800) 272–7426 or consult www.brianhead.com.

Vertical	Elevation	Lifts
1,320	11,307	8

Rates
Adults about $42 (afternoon about $35), children about $27 (afternoon about $24).
Rates about $6.00 to $7.00 higher during holiday periods.

It's a bit of a haul, more than four hours from Las Vegas into Utah on I–15, but the reward is a serious ski area. Brian Head has Utah's highest base elevation at 9,600 feet, drawing an average of more than 450 inches of snow per year. The resort typically opens in early November.

The ski resort is spread over two mountains and includes fifty trails. Brian Head Peak reaches to 11,307 feet; across the valley is the strictly beginner and intermediate Navajo Peak. Brian Head offers lodging packages in the Brian Head Hotel or surrounding condominiums; there are also hotels and inns near the resort, and packages that include both Brian Head and Las Vegas are also offered.

■ THRILLS AND SPILLS

Flyaway Indoor Skydiving. 200 Convention Center Drive. An indoor skydiving simulator using an airplane engine for lift. (702) 736–4768, (877) 545–8093. www.flyawayindoorskydiving.com. See chapter 10.

Skydive Las Vegas. Boulder City. (702) 759–3483. www.skydivelasvegas.com.

■ GOLF COURSES

The Nevada Commission on Tourism maintains a special Web site with information about golf courses throughout the state. Consult www.golf.travelnevada .com.

Aliante Golf Club. 3100 West Elkhorn, North Las Vegas. Public. (702) 399–4888. www.aliantegolf.com.

Angel Park Golf Club. 100 South Rampart Boulevard. Thirty-six holes on Cloud Nine, Mountain, and Palm courses. Public. (702) 254–4653. www.angel park.com.

Arroyo Golf Club at Red Rock. 2250 C Springs Drive. Public. (702) 258–2300. www.arroyogolfclubatredrock.com.

Badlands Golf Club. 9119 Alta Drive. Twenty-seven-hole Johnny Miller course with view of Red Rock Canyon. Public. (702) 242–4653. www.badlands gc.com.

Bali Hai Golf Course. Las Vegas Boulevard and Russell Road. At the southern end of the Strip. Public. (702) 597–2400, (888) 297–2499. www.balihaigolf club.com.

Bear's Best Golf Club. 11111 West Flamingo Road. Semiprivate. (702) 804–8500. www.bearsbest.com.

Black Mountain Golf and Country Club. 500 Greenway Road, Henderson. Public. (702) 565–7933. www.golfblackmountain.com.

Boulder City Municipal Golf Course. 1 Clubhouse Drive, Boulder City. Eighteen holes. Municipal. (702) 293–9236.

Callaway Golf Center. Las Vegas Boulevard at Sunset Road. Public. (702) 896–4100.

Craig Ranch Golf Course. 628 West Craig Road. Municipal. (702) 642–9700. www.tpcatcraigranch.com.

Desert Rose Golf Course. 5843 Club House Drive. Municipal. (702) 431–4653. www.desert-rose-golf-course.com.

Durango Hills Golf Club. 3501 North Durango Drive. Public. (702) 229–4653. www.durangohillsgolf.com.

Eagle Crest Golf Club/Sun City. 10201 Sun City Boulevard. Semiprivate. (702) 254–7010. www.golfsummerlin.com.

Highland Falls Golf Club/Sun City. 10201 Sun City Boulevard. Resort. (702) 254–7010. www.golfsummerlin.com.

Las Vegas Golf Club. 4300 West Washington. Municipal. (702) 646–3003. www.americangolf.com.

Las Vegas National Country Club. Las Vegas Hilton Country Club. 1911 East Desert Inn Road. Semiprivate. (702) 796–0016. www.lasvegasnational.com.

Las Vegas Paiute Resort. 10325 Nu-Wav Kaiv Boulevard. Public. (702) 658–1400. www.lvpauitegolf.com.

Los Prados Golf and Country Club. 5150 Los Prados Circle. Public. (702) 645–5696. www.losprados-golf.com.

North Las Vegas Golf Course. 324 East Brooks Avenue, North Las Vegas. Public. (702) 633–1833. www.cityofnorthlasvegas.com.

The Las Vegas National Country Club

Painted Desert Country Club. 5555 Painted Mirage Way. Public. (702) 645–2880, (888) 367–3386. www.golfpainteddesert.com.

Palm Valley Golf Club/Sun City. 9201 Del Webb Boulevard. Semiprivate. (702) 363–4373. www.golfsummerlin.com.

Red Rock Country Club Arroyo Course. 2250 Red Springs Drive #B, Summerlin. Views of the Spring Mountain Range and the Red Rock Canyon National Conservation area. Public. (702) 258–2300. www.redrockcountryclub.com.

Rhodes Ranch Golf Club. 20 Rhodes Ranch Parkway. Public. (702) 740–4114. www.rhodesranch.com.

Rio Secco Golf Club. 2851 Grand Hills Drive, Henderson. Semiprivate. (702) 889–2400. www.harrahs.com/our_casinos/rlv/rio_secco.

Royal Links. 5995 East Vegas Valley Drive. Course by Perry and Pete Dye. Public. (702) 450–8000, (888) 427–6682. www.waltersgolf.com.

Shadow Creek. MGM-Mirage's course. Semiprivate. (702) 791–7111, (866) 260–0069. www.shadowcreek.com.

Siena Golf Club. 10575 Siena Monte Avenue. Public. (702) 341–9200. www.sienagolfclub.com.

Silverstone Golf Club. 8600 Cupp Drive. Resort. (702) 562–3770. www.silverstonegolfclub.com.

Tournament Players Club at the Canyons. 9851 Canyon Run Drive, Summerlin. Semiprivate. (702) 256–2000. www.tpccanyons.com.

Wynn Las Vegas. 3145 Las Vegas Boulevard South. Resort. (702) 770–7800. www.wynnlasvegas.com.

■ PARKS AND SCENIC AREAS

Floyd Lamb State Park. 9200 Tule Springs Road. (702) 486–5413. www.parks .nv.gov/fl.htm.

Hoover Dam. (702) 293–8367. www.usbr.gov/lc/hooverdam.

Lake Mead Recreation Area. Alan Bible Visitor Center. (702) 293–8990. www .nps.gov/lame.

- Boulder Beach: (702) 293–8990
- Callville Bay: (702) 297–1464
- Cottonwood: (800) 255–5561
- Las Vegas Bay Marina: (702) 565–911
- National Park Service: (702) 293–8907

Lee Canyon. Mount Charleston in Toiyabe National Forest, northwest of Las Vegas on U.S. Highway 95 to Highway 156. (775) 331–6444.

Spring Mountain Ranch. Blue Diamond. (702) 875–4141. www.parks.nv .gov/smr.htm.

Valley of Fire. Overton. (702) 397–2088. www.parks.nv.gov/vf.htm.

CHAPTER FOURTEEN

JOURNEYS NORTH OF LAS VEGAS

AREA 51, RED ROCK CANYON, MOUNT CHARLESTON, LEE CANYON, AND VALLEY OF FIRE

BY THIS TIME IT SHOULD BE EVIDENT that Las Vegas is a lot more than just green felt, computer-controlled volcanic eruptions, and mock Egyptian pyramids. Few things make that point more clearly than a journey north of town along U.S. Highway 95.

Just past downtown the trappings of Las Vegas fall away quickly, yielding to the near-barren Mojave Desert. On the plateau to the right is the huge Nellis Air Force Base, and beyond that are two of the area's less well-known attractions: the **Nellis Air Force Range** that runs for almost 125 miles from Las Vegas to near Tonopah and the **Nevada Test Site,** a nuclear weapons testing area included within the range.

NELLIS AIR FORCE RANGE

Nellis is generally off-limits to civilians except for occasional open houses, and visits have been curtailed because of the current security environment. From time to time visitors are permitted onto the base to tour the home of the famed Thunderbirds aerial demonstration team. For information call (702) 652–1110 or consult www.nellis.af.mil.

Aviation Nation is a two-day air show held at Nellis Air Force Base each autumn, usually in mid-November. Participants include the Thunderbirds and the U.S. Aerobatic Team. For more information on this annual event, consult aviation nation.org.

The top-secret status of the Nellis base and the vast size of the area have regularly spawned all sorts of interesting rumors about goings-on in the area, including reports ranging from testing of strange military aircraft (including the Stealth bomber) to detailed reports of military experiments on captured UFOs and their alien crews. I got that last tidbit, by the way, from Elvis, who has his hideaway on the range.

NEVADA TEST SITE

In the aftermath of World War II, the federal government used a big chunk of Nevada—an area larger than the state of Rhode Island—to conduct nuclear detonations and other tests of atomic weaponry; many of the explosions were visible from downtown Las Vegas, 65 miles to the southeast. If this is the sort of thing that lights you up with desire, you can take a tightly supervised tour of the site.

Among the points of interest on the tour is Frenchman Flat, where on January 27, 1951, the first atmospheric nuclear test on the Nevada Test Site took place. Thirteen subsequent atmospheric nuclear tests were conducted at the site between 1951 and 1962. If that's not electrifying enough for you, the tour also visits the Hazardous Material Spill Center, used by the chemical and petroleum industry and government agencies to test spill dispersion and cleanup procedures, and the Low Level Radioactive Waste Management Site for the disposal of radioactive waste from the dismantlement and cleanup of the weapons-production complex.

And then there is Sedan Crater, part of the "Plowshare" program that explored nonmilitary uses of nuclear explosives. A 104 kiloton nuclear explosion at the site displaced about twelve million tons of earth, creating a crater 1,280 feet in diameter and 320 feet deep. Testing continued into the 1970s.

The Department of Energy promises that the levels of atomic radiation have dropped to safe levels for a quick tour; visitors are prohibited from bringing home any samples of dirt, rocks, or anything else. Even cameras and cell phones are prohibited.

The tour usually takes place aboard a chartered bus equipped with a restroom, covering about 250 miles. There are no lunch stops, but participants can bring their own food and drinks. Visitors to the test site must be at least fourteen years old. Pregnant women are discouraged from participating in tours because of the long bus ride and uneven terrain.

Free public tours are offered about eight times a year; the bus departs once a month except for the hot summertime months of July and August and the quiet winter months of December and January. Tours depart at about 7:00 A.M. and return about 4:00 P.M. They leave from the Atomic Testing Museum at 755 East Flamingo Road in Las Vegas.

To sign up for one of the tours, you'll need to apply well in advance for a place and provide full identification. For information call the Office of Public Affairs and Information at (702) 295–0944 or consult www.nv.doe.gov/nts/tours.htm.

GOING TO DREAMLAND: AREA 51

And then things get even weirder. About 120 miles northwest of Las Vegas is a huge government military installation that officially doesn't exist. There are several very long runways and dozens of hangars and buildings, but according to FAA pilot charts and U.S. Geological Survey topographic maps, it just ain't there.

The military facility, located at Groom Lake, is known to some as Dreamland; old government maps call it Area 51. When officialdom is pushed, they will acknowledge the existence of something called a "remote test facility."

According to published accounts, every weekday ten to twelve Boeing 737 jets depart from special terminals operated by a defense contractor at McCarran Airport in Las Vegas or in Palmdale, California. The planes, painted white with a broad red stripe down their lengths, make low-level thirty-minute flights to Groom Lake carrying an estimated 1,500 to 2,000 employees per day. The carrier is sometimes identified as "Janet Airways." It's not a huge secret; you can see the terminal and the planes from some of the hotel rooms of the Luxor, which sits directly across Las Vegas Boulevard South from its location.

What goes on there? According to unofficial observers, the base has been used for projects from testing of the ultrasecret SR-71 spy plane in the 1960s to flight tests of Soviet Sukhoi Su–22 and MiG-23 fighters somehow obtained by the military to training with F-117A Stealth attack planes. And there are those who maintain that the U.S. government has captured UFOs and keep them at the base.

There is not much chance of taking a sightseeing trip to Dreamland, though. About as close as you can get is up in the hills near the tiny town of Rachel (population about a hundred). The Bureau of Land Management property outside the base is patrolled by sheriff's deputies and private security forces nicknamed "Cammo Dudes"; closer in is the boundary of the base itself, which is guarded with detection devices, video cameras, and signs warning USE OF DEADLY FORCE AUTHORIZED.

By the way, if you go to the trouble of making the two-and-a-half-hour drive to Rachel (Interstate 15 north to U.S. Highway 93 north, picking up Highway 375 westbound near Ash Springs), you'll find the Little A'Le'Inn (pronounced "alien"), its walls covered with UFO memorabilia and a large photo of the base that doesn't exist. You can consult a Web site about the place at www.aleinn.com and another page about the town of Rachel at www.rachel-nevada.com.

The famous "black mailbox" view spot, said to be a great place for a close encounter of some kind or another, is at mile marker LN 29.5 on Route 375.

With a wink and a nudge to tourism, Route 375 is known as the Extraterrestrial Highway.

For years locals and interested visitors used to hike or drive to a remote area they called "Freedom Ridge" along Groom Lake Road that offered a distant view of the sprawling air base. In April 1995, though, the government succeeded in taking the land and closing off access. In 1996 Area 51 fans devoted their attention to hikes to the top of Tikapoo Peak within the Pahranagat National Wildlife

Refuge; there, a difficult ninety-minute hike leads to an even more distant view of the area.

According to those who seem to make this their life's work, the government agencies that run Area 51 halt any secret operations anytime they detect unauthorized eyes, and that is why you won't see any UFOs or unusual military operations if you bother to make the climb. Turn your back, though, and they're there. (Sort of like the unanswerable question of whether the refrigerator light really does go off when the door is closed.)

NATURAL WONDERS

On the left side of I–15 and the Strip, heading out of Las Vegas, are three expeditions worth taking. Fill up the gas tank in your car before heading out on a tour; gas stations are few and far between in this area.

■ RED ROCK CANYON

Here is an extraordinary world of rusty red cliffs, Joshua trees, yucca plants, and sagebrush; just as otherworldly as and much more real than the nearby man-made canyons of Las Vegas. It's heaven for hikers, perfect for picnickers, and a delightful drive, even if you never leave your car.

Take I–15 to the West Charleston exit and drive west on Charleston Avenue toward the hills. About 10 miles out of town, Las Vegas is a garish memory and Red Rock Canyon is a garish reality. The sandstone cliffs, towering 2,000 feet above the desert floor, are an artist's palette of red, orange, yellow, pink, purple, and brown.

For much of the past 600 million years, the land that is now Red Rock Canyon was the bottom of a deep ocean basin; the western coast of North America was in present-day western Utah. A rich variety of marine life in the waters left behind deposits of shells and skeletons more than 9,000 feet thick, which were eventually compressed into limestone and other carbonate rocks. Large bodies of salt water became cut off from the sea and eventually evaporated, leaving behind salt and gypsum. The exposure of the sediments to the atmosphere caused some of the minerals to oxidize, changing their colors to red and orange.

Another stage in the geologic history of Red Rock Canyon occurred about 180 million years ago when the area became an arid desert. A giant dune field stretched eastward to Colorado with sand more than half a mile deep in some areas. The shifting sands left behind curved and angled lines known as "crossbeds" that were eventually cemented into sandstone in combination with calcium carbonate and iron oxide; this is the source of some of the red rock cliffs.

Over thousands of years at least four and possibly several other Native American cultures occupied the Red Rock area. They were drawn to the relative abundance of water in the canyon, which includes more than forty springs and catchment basins. Archaeologists have found roasting pits and a historic sandstone quarry.

Roll of the Dice

In 1942 actress Carole Lombard was killed when her DC-3 airplane slammed into Mount Potosi southwest of Las Vegas in the Spring Mountains. She was returning from a war bonds rally in the Midwest to Los Angeles and husband Clark Gable.

In remembrance of the popular Miss Lombard, an orange butterfly with black spots peculiar to the local hills was named "Carole's fritillary."

The name holds Las Vegas significance: "Fritillary" comes from the Latin *fritillus,* meaning "dice box."

In more recent times the canyon has served as the backdrop for many Hollywood westerns, television shows, commercials, and . . . cartoons. Beep, beep! One of the most famous residents of Red Rock Canyon is the roadrunner. And yes, this chicken-size bird really does streak across the desert on foot. (And though there are coyotes, too, we are not aware of a local franchise for the Acme Dynamite Company.)

Check at the Bureau of Land Management visitor center on Red Rock Road to pick up hiking, bicycling, climbing, or nature brochures. Marked hiking trails range from about 2 miles to a 14-mile tour to the top of the escarpment. There's also a 13-mile, one-way driving loop with pull-offs at some of the more spectacular views, with even more "oohs" per mile than on the Las Vegas Strip. The Sandstone Quarry area offers a climbing trail with access to some ancient Indian petroglyphs in Brownstone Canyon. Visitors by car now must pay $5.00 to drive through the loop; the fee was imposed by the Bureau of Land Management to maintain and finance roads, buildings, trails, signs, exhibits, and historic structures. For information consult www.redrockcanyonlv.org.

Bonnie Springs Old Nevada. Long before there were sequined showgirls, $500 slot machines, or even a serious settlement at Las Vegas, there were isolated ranches like this one, which originally dates back to about 1840. Today, though, the Bonnie Springs Old Nevada is a somewhat tired Western theme park in a very pretty setting at the southern edge of Red Rock Canyon. The park includes a petting zoo, a small railroad, a Western street with shops, demonstrations, and the occasional shootout. Guided horseback tours of the area are also available. Alongside, the **Bonnie Springs Ranch** offers horseback riding and other adventures.

Located on Highway 159, the park is south of the exit from Red Rock Canyon in Blue Diamond. It is open seven days a week. Tickets in 2006 were priced at about $10 per car (up to six occupants). For information call (702) 875–4191 or visit www.bonniesprings.com.

Spring Mountain Ranch State Park. An isolated 520-acre ranch owned at one time (along with hundreds of other Nevada properties) by Howard Hughes and used as a business retreat, it was originally the home of Lum of the *Lum 'n Abner* radio show of the 1930s and then the home of Vera Krupp, widow of the German weapons maker.

The first-known settlement on the property was a mid-1830s campsite along the wash that runs through the ranch, an oasis for travelers on a branch of the Spanish Trail through Cottonwood Valley. Some of those who used the trail were outlaws involved in Indian slave trading and raids on passing caravans. Travelers by pack and wagon train continued to come through until the trail was replaced by a railroad in 1905.

Spring Mountain is now operated by the state park system; tours of the home are available. There is a $6.00 entrance fee per vehicle. For hours and information call (702) 875–4141 or consult http://parks.nv.gov/smr.htm.

■ MOUNT CHARLESTON

About 20 miles north of town on US 95 after a long jaunt along a flat desert floor, look for the Kyle Canyon exit (Nevada Route 157) branching off to the left. From here you will begin a long, steady climb. The road is one of the more dramatic ones we know of. For much of the early part of the climb, you are able to look straight into the face of the mountain ahead of you.

Mount Charleston is a serious hill, reaching to 11,919 feet, the highest peak of the Spring Mountain Range and nearly 2 miles above the floor of the Las Vegas valley. Much of the surrounding area is part of the Toiyabe National Forest.

The trip is an interesting exploration of the effect of elevation on climate and plant and animal life. The yucca, Joshua trees, and creosote bushes are able to survive the intense heat and lack of rain at the desert floor. Somewhere around the 5,000-foot level, you'll find junipers, scrub pine, and sagebrush. Higher up the mountain the vegetation gives way to bristlecone pines that are adapted to the extremes of cold and wind on the mountain. Bristlecones are among the longest-living things on Earth, with some plants believed to be nearly 5,000 years old.

About 10 miles up the road, you'll come to the Mount Charleston Hotel, an old-timey mountain lodge (OK, so it's about thirty years old; it still feels like an antique) with beam ceilings and a large open fireplace. Some suites have their own fireplaces. The Canyon Dining Room is a pretty place to eat, especially on a moonlit night. The hotel underwent a major renovation that was completed in 2006. For information call (702) 872–5500 or consult www.mtcharlestonhotel.com.

At the very end of Kyle Canyon Road is a stunning resort area first developed by the Civilian Conservation Corps during the Depression and now offering vacation homes, campgrounds, and picnic areas.

At the top of the road, the mountain continues to rise; there are a number of trails, including a short walk to Mary Jane Falls or a more strenuous 15-mile hike to the Charleston Peak, where on a clear day, you can see into four states: Nevada, California, Utah, and distant Arizona. Forest Service Road 22, a branch road off Route 157, leads to near Robbers' Roost Caves, a gathering of limestone caverns used as hideouts in the mid-nineteenth century by Mexican bandits who preyed on settlers and travelers in the area.

Route 158 branches off to the right, just before the Mount Charleston Hotel. This is a stunning, twisty mountain road that traverses a ridge over to Lee Canyon Road (Route 156). At the T, turn left into the mountain and climb for another 4 miles to reach the Las Vegas Ski and Snowboard Resort in Lee Canyon.

An alternate route to Mount Charleston is to go past Route 157 and continue on US 95 for about 14 miles to Route 156. This road goes directly to the ski area; from there you can also cross over the upper trail (Route 158) and descend on Route 157.

▉ VALLEY OF FIRE STATE PARK

A bit farther away than Red Rock Canyon and a bit wilder, this park includes spectacularly colored desert sandstone that has been sculpted by the wind and rain into fantastic shapes. The geology dates as far back as the Jurassic period. You'll also find petroglyphs (prehistoric rock drawings) on canyon walls; they are believed to date back more than 2,000 years to the time of the Anasazi.

Trails lead to isolated parts of the park including Mouse's Tank, a shallow natural bowl that collects the scarce rainfall in the area. It was the hiding place of Mouse, a Paiute Indian who terrorized some of the area settlers a century ago.

The Valley of Fire is about 50 miles northeast of Las Vegas, off I–15 in Overton; you can make a loop that connects to the top of Lake Mead and down to Boulder and the Hoover Dam for a nice day trip. Be forewarned that temperatures in the valley can become downright brutal in the summer; the best time to visit is from September through May. Bring water and supplies with you, even for a single day of travel.

The visitor fee in 2006 was $6.00 per vehicle or $14.00 for entrance and camping. Stop at the visitor station for maps and information, or call (702) 397–2088. You can also consult http://parks.nv.gov/vf.htm.

GHOST TOWNS AND ANCIENT CULTURES

Nevada is littered with ghost towns—mostly the leftovers of the boom-and-bust cycles of mining operations. Deeper in the past are the ghosts of ancient native cultures.

▉ OVERTON

The small town of Overton on Route 169 was once the commercial center for the early Mormon settlements in the Moapa Valley in the nineteenth century. Before then the area was populated by Anasazi tribes who developed farms, including irrigation canals branching off the Virgin and Muddy Rivers more than a thousand years ago. The largest of their buildings, the fabled Lost City at the confluence of the Virgin and Muddy Rivers, included ninety-four rooms; that area is now below the waters of Lake Mead.

The **Lost City Museum,** outside of Overton, includes one of the most complete collections of ancient Pueblo Indian relics dating back thousands of years. It continues through the ancient Basket Maker cultures and through the Paiutes, who arrived about the year 1000 and whose descendants still live in southern Nevada. Outside the museum is a replica of a Pueblo home built as a Civilian Conservation Corps project during the Depression era. Also displayed are artifacts of the Mormon settlement of the region. The museum is open daily, with a $3.00 admission fee for visitors eighteen and older. For information call (702) 397–2193 or consult http://dmla.clan.lib.nv.us/docs/museums/lost/lostcity.htm.

South of Overton within the Valley of Fire State Park is **Overton Beach,** a recreational area on upper Lake Mead. Beneath the waters east of the area is the former location of Saint Thomas, a Mormon farming community; when the water level is low, parts of some of the buildings can be seen offshore.

■ RHYOLITE

Rhyolite, a real live dead ghost town, is just off US 95 to the west of the Nellis Air Force Range, about 115 miles from Las Vegas. The town is named for the most common type of rock in the area. At its peak around the turn of the twentieth century, Rhyolite was a booming gold-mining community, complete with opera house, symphony, red-light district, more than fifty saloons, six barber shops, eight physicians, and two undertakers, all to serve a population of nearly 10,000. The town's rapid decline began with the San Francisco earthquake of 1907. By the early 1920s the population was down to one.

Today Rhyolite's ruins include a two-story school building from 1909, a train depot, an old jail, and the stone skeleton of the Cook Bank Building. Each March the Rhyolite Resurrection Festival brings the ghost town back to life through vignettes and a reunion of Rhyolite descendants.

Rhyolite is 35 miles from the Furnace Creek Visitor Center on the way to Beatty, Nevada. A paved road heading north from Highway 374 leads to the heart of the town.

For information on Rhyolite consult www.nps.gov/deva/rhyolite.htm. You can also contact the Nevada Commission on Tourism for more information at (702) 486–2424 or online at www.travelnevada.com.

CHAPTER FIFTEEN

JOURNEYS SOUTH OF LAS VEGAS

HENDERSON, HOOVER DAM, BOULDER CITY, LAKE MEAD, AND LAKE MOHAVE

HENDERSON

Henderson, south of Las Vegas toward Boulder City, is Nevada's third-most populous city (after Las Vegas and Reno), with more than 80,000 residents.

The town sprouted during World War II because of the Basic Magnesium plant, a huge facility that processed the mineral for use in munitions. The plant closed in 1944, but unlike the dozens of other ghost towns in Nevada, the residents of Henderson managed to find other industries. Henderson also serves as a bedroom community for workers in tourism and government installations. Downtown Henderson (like Boulder City) is somewhat frozen in time.

The Boulder Highway (Route 582) has been supplanted by superhighways that link Las Vegas to Boulder City and on to Los Angeles, but if you're looking for a glimpse of the past, this is still the best route to Henderson.

The Southern Nevada Museum on Boulder Highway includes Heritage Street, a collection of buildings from old southern Nevada; some are houses built for the magnesium workers, early Las Vegas residences, and mining villages. An Indian village celebrates the Native American culture of the area.

With an eye north to Las Vegas, Henderson has embarked on an ambitious series of developments in recent years, including the creation of **Lake Las Vegas,** one of the largest civil-engineering projects in the country. A $100 million earthen dam has created a 2-mile lake that is already circled by several thousand homes, several golf courses, and (of course) half a dozen hotel-casinos. For information consult www.lakelasvegas.com.

■ HENDERSON FACTORY TOURS

Ethel M Chocolate Factory. Cactus Garden Drive off Sunset Road at the Boulder Highway. Free factory tour and botanical garden and cactus display. And, yes, there are samples. Ethel was the mother of candy-bar magnate Forrest Mars, the family behind the Mars Bar, M&M's, Milky Way, and other sweets. The kitchens and manufacturing areas can be seen behind large glass windows on the tour; for most of the year, though, the lines are open only on weekdays.

The first room is the kitchen, where fillings are prepared; specialized equipment includes cream beaters for butter creams and a nut-sorting table. The second area includes two "enrobing lines" where nut clusters, butter creams, and caramels are drenched with chocolate. In front is the molding line where solid pieces, truffles, and cream liqueur chocolates are created. The last room is the packing area where candies are wrapped and boxed.

There's a large shop on the property, and you can expect a few fresh samples. The cactus garden showcases more than 300 varieties of prickly plants; if that's the sort of thing you're looking for, here's a fine example. Open daily from 8:30 A.M. to 7:00 P.M. For information call (702) 435–2641 or (888) 627–0990 or consult www.ethelm.com and click on "Tours."

Ron Lee's World of Clowns. 7665 Commercial Way. Sculptor Ron Lee has made a career out of clowning around and has a devoted following of collectors to show for it. His factory, where as many as one hundred employees cast and decorate his art pieces, is open to the public, and Lee is often there to sign his work and meet collectors. There's a small carousel, a gallery . . . and a gift shop. Open Monday through Friday from 9:00 A.M. to 4:00 P.M. For information call (702) 434–1700 or consult www.ronlee.com.

Visitor Resources

▶ **Boulder City Chamber of Commerce.** 1305 Arizona Street, Boulder City, NV 89005. (702) 293–2034.

▶ **Boulder City Visitor Center.** 100 Nevada Highway, Boulder City, NV 89005. (702) 294–1220.

▶ **Henderson Chamber of Commerce.** 590 South Boulder Highway, Henderson, NV 89015. (702) 565–8951. www .hendersonchamber.com.

HOOVER DAM

If they had a casino within Hoover Dam, it would be a building that would rival Luxor, Excalibur, Caesars Palace, and MGM Grand combined. They don't, of course, and though nearly one million visitors a year come to visit this incredible monument to the attempts of our species to exercise control over our environment, this means that nearly thirty-four million other visitors to Las Vegas don't make the 40-mile trip south. There ought to be a law. . . .

The Colorado River, which flows 1,400 miles from the Rocky Mountains in Colorado to the Gulf of California, is one of the great geological forces in the West that has created spectacular natural wonders, including the Grand Canyon.

In the early days of settlement, the Colorado was the source of great respect and fear. Early settlers attempted to divert water for irrigation purposes. They were defeated by the tremendous seasonal changes from steady flow to summertime trickle to wild flooding in the spring as mountain snows melted.

Steam-powered riverboats navigated the Colorado River upstream from its mouth in the late 1800s and were able to reach as far north as the Mormon settlement of Callville during certain parts of the year. One of the most difficult parts of the 600-mile trip was passage through the Black Canyon rapids. Crews had to use a system of winches and cables strung through ring bolts anchored in the canyon walls.

It took a disastrous flood in California's Imperial Valley in 1905 to begin the move to finally tame the river. In that year early-spring flash floods washed away small earthen dams that had been created to divert water from the river to the Imperial Canal. The heavy water flow changed the course of the river and caused it to flow for the next two years into the Imperial Valley and the large Salton Sea east of San Diego, increasing the size of that body of water from 22 to 500 square miles; to this date the Salton Sea has not fully retreated to its early-twentieth-century size, still covering about 300 square miles today.

The first step in harnessing the Colorado was agreement among the governments of the seven states through which it flows. In 1922 a commission headed by Herbert Hoover, then Secretary of Commerce, produced the Colorado River Compact, which divided use of the water between Upper and Lower Colorado River Basins. In 1928 Congress passed the Boulder Canyon Project Act; construction of the dam was begun in 1931.

The first task for the construction crews in April 1931 was to deal with the water already passing through the canyon. Four huge diversion tunnels, each nearly 60 feet in diameter, were dug out of the canyon walls to the left and right of the dam's eventual location. A year and a half later, they were ready to send the Colorado River through the tunnels and leave dry the dam's base.

More than 5,000 men worked day and night in a continuous pour of concrete that took two years—a total of 4.4 million cubic yards of concrete for the dam and supporting structures. Although there is a common belief that some of the ninety-six workers who died during the dangerous construction project are entombed within the concrete, dam tour guides will tell you otherwise.

The dam itself is described as an arch-gravity structure. Still the highest concrete dam in the Western Hemisphere, it rises 726 feet above the bedrock of Black Canyon. It is 660 feet thick at its base and 45 feet thick at the top, with a span of 1,244 feet across the canyon.

The dam was completed in 1935, two years ahead of schedule, which has to be a record for a government project. The diversion tunnels were closed in February 1935, and Lake Mead began to form behind the dam. The first power generator began operation in 1936; the seventeenth and final generator went on line in 1961.

The dam cost about $175 million to build at the time, and the cost has been repaid through revenues from the generation of power and the supply of water. The dam sends about 19 percent of generated power to Arizona, 25 percent to

Nevada, 28 percent to the Metropolitan Water District of Southern California, and the remainder to various municipalities in California, including Los Angeles.

The two-lane highway atop the Hoover Dam connects Nevada and Arizona. If you plan to stay on one side or the other, you may want to adjust your watch. Nevada is in the Pacific time zone, while Arizona is one hour later in the mountain time zone.

The Lake Mead reservoir, pent up behind the dam, extends for 110 miles and usually stores about two years of average Colorado River flow, which is released as needed for irrigation and power generation. Water stored in the lake irrigates more than one million acres of land in the United States and half a million acres in Mexico.

The generators can produce about four billion kilowatt-hours of energy per year, enough for 500,000 homes. The gravity-fed generators are nonpolluting, and, of course, water flow is a renewable resource.

Another effect of the dam is to clear the once-muddy waters of the Colorado for much of its downstream run and within Lake Mead itself.

In recent years historically low annual rainfall has lowered the level of the lake, forcing the closure or relocation of a number of recreational facilities.

■ THE ART OF THE HOOVER DAM

The exterior and interior of the dam include sculptures by Oskar J. W. Hansen, a Norwegian-born naturalized American. Hansen told historians that to him, Hoover Dam represented the genius of America, comparable to the great pyramids of Egypt.

Hansen's major work is the dedication monument on the Nevada side of the dam. Rising from a polished black base is a 142-foot-tall flagpole flanked by the two Winged Figures of the Republic. The four-ton sculptures were placed on the base on blocks of ice and guided into place as the ice melted.

Around the base is a terrazzo floor inlaid with a star chart that freezes in time September 30, 1935, the date President Franklin D. Roosevelt dedicated the dam.

Hansen also created a plaque to memorialize the ninety-six men who died during the construction of the dam and a set of bas-relief artworks on the Nevada and Arizona elevator towers. The Nevada art shows the intended benefits of Hoover Dam: flood control, navigation, irrigation, water storage, and power. On the Arizona side the art celebrates Native American tribes of the region.

■ HOOVER DAM TOURS

Visitors can tour the exterior of the dam and view part of the generating facilities. New security measures in place after the terrorist attacks of 2001 mean that tourists can no longer prowl the immense interior of the dam itself.

You can park in one of the designated lots and walk across the dam, during daylight hours only. Cars can no longer stop on the top of the dam, and both pedestrians and vehicles are subject to search.

The impressive visitor center, cantilevered out from the rock wall of the canyon on the Nevada side, was completed in 1995. Critics pointed out that the price tag for the center was higher than the cost of the dam itself.

Some of the most spectacular and unusual sights in the United States are within a day trip from Las Vegas; you can make a trek by yourself with a rental car and a good map, or you can enlist the assistance of professionals.

Touring companies based in the Las Vegas area use small four-wheel-drive vehicles, minivans, large buses, helicopters, and airplanes. Some concentrate on hiking and adventuring, while others are strictly sightseeing tours.

One interesting operation is **Adventure Photo Tours,** which maintains a small fleet of SUVs for guided trips to the west rim of the Grand Canyon as well as expeditions north of Las Vegas to ghost towns, mining sites, Red Rock Canyon, the Valley of Fire, and a distant peek at Area 51.

I took an Adventure Photo Tours trip south from Las Vegas across the Hoover Dam and into the Mojave Desert to the west rim of the Grand Canyon, about a three-hour drive including stops at the dam and at a frozen-in-time gas station and souvenir shop on old Route 66 in Arizona.

This section of the canyon, near its western outlet, is a bit less spectacular than the more popular north and south rims, but also much more intimate. There are no gift shops, souvenir stands . . . and very few tourists. There are also no guardrails.

The vehicle drives down a wash alongside Diamond Creek from the small town of Peach Springs to the Colorado River for a view from the river of the last few miles of the canyon; entry to the area requires purchase of a permit from the Hualapai Reservation. The unpaved, rough road descends gradually from an elevation of 4,950 feet at the town to 1,550 feet at the river. The road ends at a sandy beach where Diamond Creek meets the Colorado River. The surrounding rocks of Lower Granite Gorge are among the oldest in the canyon, dating from the pre-Cambrian era, more than 700 million years ago.

The trip later visits another section at the top of the canyon, at a small settlement called Grand Canyon West near the Grand Wash Cliffs that mark the edge of the Colorado Plateau and the end of the Grand Canyon.

Here are some tour operators; call for information and advance reservations. Some offer discounts for advance bookings or groups.

▶ **Adventure Photo Tours.** (702) 889–8687 or (888) 363–8687. www.adventurephototours.com.

▶ **All American Adventure Tours.** (702) 631–3091. Bus, plane, and helicopter tours.

▶ **Las Vegas Tour and Travel.** (702) 739–8975. Bus, Hummer, and helicopter tours.

▶ **Magic Tours.** (702) 380–1106. Bus, helicopter tours.

▶ **Sightseeing Tours Unlimited.** (702) 471–7155. Bus, plane, and helicopter tours.

The visitor center at the dam is open every day except Thanksgiving and Christmas, from 9:00 A.M. to 5:00 P.M. The center includes a three-compartment rotating turntable that seats 145 people in each compartment. The audience sees a trio of historical films.

The Discovery Tour includes a twenty-five-minute film that features original footage of the construction of the dam and a second film about the Bureau of Reclamation's works to tame the rivers of the West and provide water and power to the region. An elevator takes visitors 500 feet down through the wall of Black Canyon to a 250-foot tunnel drilled out of the rock and a viewing platform for the eight huge generators in the Nevada wing of the power plant. There's also an overlook alongside the visitor center with views of the dam, Lake Mead, and the Colorado River. Across the top of the dam is a self-paced walking tour to six locations.

Fees for the Discovery Tour in 2006 were adults $11.00, juniors (seven to sixteen) $6.00, seniors (sixty-two and older) $9.00. Parking was $7.00. For information call (702) 293–8321 or consult www.usbr.gov/lc/hooverdam. Note that there are restrictions against closed trucks crossing the dam, and recreational vehicles and buses are likely to be searched. A lengthy detour for such vehicles passes through Laughlin on U.S. Highway 95.

Work has begun on the construction of a new bridge about 1,600 feet south of the dam to reduce truck and car traffic across the top; the $240 million crossing is expected to be open by the end of 2008. The second phase of the project will add a detour around Boulder City, avoiding the slowdown there.

Davis Dam in Pyramid Canyon, 67 miles downstream from Hoover Dam and about 2 miles upstream from Laughlin, was finished in 1953. That rock-and-earth wall controls the flow of water from Lake Mohave.

BOULDER CITY

Boulder City is a planned community created by the U.S. Bureau of Reclamation as housing for some of the construction workers for Hoover Dam and for administrative offices. The construction of the town coincided with a period of architectural design and government master planning. The result was a designed town with a great deal of un-Nevada–like greenery and parks.

The U.S. Bureau of Reclamation continued to own and operate Boulder City, controlling almost every detail, until 1960 when it gave up dominion and the town was incorporated. Only then were alcohol sales permitted; today Boulder City continues as the only city in Nevada that bans public gambling.

The Boulder City/Hoover Dam Museum is worth a visit to ogle the impressive collection of construction photos. The museum is located within the historic Boulder Dam Hotel at 1305 Arizona Street, erected for the use of government VIPs during the time the dam was under construction. The museum is open daily from 10:00 A.M. to 5:00 P.M. and Sunday from noon to 5:00 P.M.; admission is $2.00 for adults and $1.00 for seniors and children. For information call (702) 294–1988 or consult www.bcmha.org.

LAKE MEAD

It seems odd to speak of a fabulous outdoor wonderland such as Lake Mead as a creation of man, but so it is.

Before Lake Mead was formed in 1935, this area was almost untouched by humans. Indian tribes once inhabited some of the canyons. Explorers like John Wesley Powell went deep into the Grand Canyon and other areas and passed through the region; the first foreign settlers included fur trappers, Mormon settlers, and hardy prospectors.

Anson Call established Callville, a Mormon colony, in 1864 with a trading post to service emigrants on their westward passage along the Colorado River. Callville was abandoned five years later, although the walls of part of the settlement were still visible when the entire region—including many ancient Indian sites—was flooded by the waters of the developing lake. It is an interesting question to ask whether Hoover Dam could have been built under today's historic preservation and environmental impact laws.

In any case Lake Mead today is an incredible contrast of desert and water, mountain and canyon, magnificent wilderness and the triumph of man-made technology.

Lake Mead National Recreation Area includes the 110-mile-long Lake Mead; the 67-mile-long Lake Mohave, which backs up behind the smaller Davis Dam at Laughlin; the surrounding desert; and the isolated Shivwits Plateau in Arizona, which connects into the Grand Canyon National Park. Together the two huge (274-square-mile) lakes sparkle in one of the driest, hottest places known to man.

In summer daytime temperatures regularly rise above one hundred degrees. From October to May, temperatures range from the thirties to the fifties.

Plan to include a stop at the Alan Bible Visitor Center, 4 miles northeast of Boulder City on Route 166, just past the junction with U.S. Highway 93. Travel south from Las Vegas on US 93/95 and stay on US 93 at the split. The visitor center offers maps and information on services in the park. You can also go to the park headquarters at the intersection of Nevada Highway and Wyoming Street in Boulder City or visit one of the many park ranger stations.

Reservations may be necessary for most lodging and many services in the summer. Campsites are available, for a fee, on a first-come, first-served basis; some have time limits for stays. Each camp area includes picnic tables, grills, water, restrooms, and a trailer sewage dump; no utility hookups are provided. Backcountry camping is permitted along the shore on both lakes and in designated sites along unpaved backcountry roads.

You Can't Get There from Here

The Shivwits Plateau can be reached only by unpaved roads from the north; check with park rangers for information on access (702–293–8906).

Outside of the parks you can find hotels, restaurants, and services in Las Vegas, Boulder City, Henderson, Laughlin, Searchlight, and Overton in Nevada; Bullhead City and Kingman in Arizona; and Needles in California.

LAKE MEAD CRUISES

Several companies offer cruises all year long on Lake Mead near Hoover Dam.

The *Desert Princess* paddle wheeler sails daily from the Lake Mead Cruises Landing. The *Desert Princess,* sister ship to the MS *Dixie II* on Lake Tahoe, has breakfast, sightseeing, and dinner/dance cruises priced from about $20 to $54. There are several sailings daily, year-round. For information and reservations call (702) 293–6180 or consult www.lakemeadcruises.com.

ANIMAL LIFE IN THE LAKE MEAD AREA

Living things have to be very hardy to survive the temperature extremes of the desert and an annual rainfall of less than 6 inches.

The creation of Lake Mead dramatically changed the ecology of the region, bringing waterbirds, fish, and aquatic plants. In the surrounding desert more than a thousand bighorn sheep live along the mountain ridges; they are among the few desert animals active in the heat of the day. Other creatures include lizards, squirrels, rabbits, insects, and spiders.

The desert blooms year-round, but some of the flowers are so tiny that it is easy to miss them. A winter rain can cause a brief but glorious overnight bloom of wildflowers on the desert.

FISHING

The lake is a year-round bonanza for anglers. The most sought-after fish is striped bass, which can reach fifty pounds or more. In Lake Mohave, especially in the upper reaches in Black Canyon, rainbow trout is the most popular. Other species include largemouth bass, channel catfish, black crappie, and bluegill.

Nevada and Arizona share jurisdiction over the two lakes. You must have a state fishing license to fish from shore. To fish from a boat, you must have a license from one state and a special-use stamp from the other. Licenses and stamps are available at most marinas.

SWIMMING AND BOATING

Both lakes are clear and clean for swimming. Water temperatures across most of the two lakes average about seventy-eight degrees in spring, summer, and fall. The coldest water is usually found in the northern portion of Lake Mohave. Lifeguards are on duty in summer at Boulder Beach on Lake Mead and Katherine Beach on Lake Mohave.

Boaters can reach some spots inaccessible to cars and roam the 274 square miles of Lake Mead, including the steep gorge of Iceberg Canyon. Around the lake many secluded coves are formed by fingers of the desert jutting into the water; these are among the most popular campsites. Sailboarding is increasingly

Down the Drain

Nearly all the state's streams and rivers drain internally into lakes or dry lake beds known as playas, or sinks. The major exception is the Colorado River.

The Humboldt rises in the northeast and flows west to disappear into the Humboldt Sink; and the Walker, Carson, and Truckee Rivers rise in the Sierra Nevada and flow east to the Walker, Carson, and Pyramid Lakes. Many other streams are dry for most of the year, filling their banks only in the spring with snowmelt or after the rare summer rainfall.

popular on the lake. Participants generally prefer near-shore areas that have stronger breezes.

There are six privately operated marinas along Lake Mead and three on Lake Mohave, each offering services and supplies year-round. Free public launching ramps and parking areas (parking limited to seven days) are found at each site. Several companies offer boat tours, including a paddle-wheel boat departing daily from the Lake Mead Marina. In the summer a boat tour through Boulder Canyon departs from Callville Bay every day. On Lake Mohave one-day raft trips are offered through the slow-moving waters of Black Canyon from Hoover Dam to Willow Beach.

■ HIKING

The best hiking months are October through May. Temperatures the rest of the year make for furnace-like conditions. You can explore on your own or join an escorted tour led by naturalists. Always carry one gallon of water per person per day and let someone know where you are going and when you expect to return.

■ HEALTH CONSIDERATIONS

The desert includes several species of dangerous animals, including rattlesnakes, scorpions, and Gila monster lizards. All of these will likely leave you alone if you do not disturb them. Wear sturdy boots to protect your feet.

A microscopic amoeba common to some hot springs can cause a rare and sometimes fatal infection; do not dive or submerse your head in springs and streams. Oleander, a toxic plant, is common in nonwilderness areas, and hikers are advised not to eat unknown plants or drink water from ditches.

■ LAKE MEAD RESORTS AND RECREATIONAL FACILITIES

Callville Bay Resort. Callville Bay. Snacks, marina, houseboat rentals, small boat rentals, trailer village, RV sites, showers, laundry, fuel, boat storage, store. (702) 565–4813. www.callvillebay.com.

Echo Bay Resort. Overton. Marina, restaurant/lounge, boat rentals, houseboat rentals, trailer village, RV sites, hotel, showers/laundry, fuel, store, dry boat storage. (702) 394–4000 or (800) 752–9669. www.sevencrown.com.

Lake Mead Resort. 322 Lakeshore Road, Boulder City. Restaurant, marina, boat rentals, store, dry boat storage, fuel, and motel. (702) 293–3484. Call (702) 293–2074 for lodging reservations only, (800) 752–9669 for other reservations, or consult www.sevencrown.com.

Lake Mead RV Village. 268 Lakeshore Road, Boulder. Trailer village with RV sites, showers, and laundry. (702) 293–2540. www.riverlakes.com/lakeshorerv .htm.

Overton Beach Resort. Overton. Snack bar, boat rentals, moorings, fuel dock, auto and boat gas, store, showers, laundry, trailer village, RV sites, dry boat storage, summer Jet Ski rental. (702) 394–4040. www.nps.gov/lame/overtonarm .html.

Temple Bar Resort. Temple Bar, Arizona. Restaurant/lounge, motel, trailer village, dry boat storage, store, marina, boat rentals, showers, laundry, auto and boat gas, RV sites. For reservations call (800) 752–9669. www.sevencrown.com.

■ CANOE/RAFT SERVICES

Down River Outfitters. Boulder City. Canoe/raft delivery and retrieval. (702) 293–1190. www.downriveroutfitters.com.

Jerkwater Canoe Company. Topock, Arizona. Canoe delivery and retrieval. (928) 768–7753. www.jerkwater.com.

■ SCUBA INSTRUCTION

Lake Mead is a popular dive site because of its warm and clear waters. Special attractions include several wrecks as well as the remains of Callville and other submerged communities.

American Cactus Divers. Las Vegas. (702) 433–3483. www.diving.net/amcactus .html.

Blue Seas Scuba Center. Las Vegas. (702) 367–2822.

Colorado River Divers. Boulder City. (702) 293–6648. www.diving.net/gr8divn .html.

LAKE MOHAVE RESORTS AND RECREATION

Cottonwood Cove Resort. Cottonwood Cove. Cafe, marina, boat rentals, houseboat rentals, fuel, dry boat storage, store, showers, laundry, motel, RV sites. (702) 297–1464. www.riverlakes.com/cottonwood_cove.htm.

Lake Mohave Resort. Bullhead City, Arizona. Restaurant/lounge, store, motel, auto and boat gas, marina, boat rentals, houseboat rentals, trailer village, RV sites, showers, laundry, dry boat storage. For reservations call (800) 752–9669.

Willow Beach Store. Willow Beach, Arizona. Boat rentals, auto and boat gas, store. (520) 767–4747. For Black Canyon/Willow Beach River Adventures, call (800) 455–3490 or consult www.blackcanyonadventures.com.

CHAPTER SIXTEEN

LAUGHLIN

Econoguide Best Casino-Hotels in Laughlin

★★★ **Flamingo Laughlin.** *A flashy joint.*
★★★ **Golden Nugget.** *A bit of Glitter Gulch all the way south.*
★★★ **Harrah's Laughlin.** *Rollin' on the river, in style.*
★★ **Colorado Belle.** *A landlocked riverboat.*
★★ **Don Laughlin's Riverside.** *The start of it all, now a bit of a relic.*

THE REST OF LAUGHLIN

★ **Edgewater.** *The low-water mark.*
★ **Ramada Express.** *Circled by a train that goes nowhere.*
★ **River Palms.** *Less than memorable.*
★ **Pioneer.** *Not-very-wild Western theme.*

THE BURGEONING COMMUNITY OF LAUGHLIN is unique in Nevada in at least two respects. First, it is among the few major settlements that have no real history of their own other than as a camp for the construction of the Davis Dam. There wasn't even a rest stop there! Second, the place was named by and for its founder, who still operates a major casino there.

Laughlin is the most important settlement of the tristate area, where Clark County, Nevada; Mohave County, Arizona; and San Bernardino County, California, come together. If something seems even stranger than usual for a Nevada gambling town, consider that almost nothing in Laughlin dates back more than about thirty years; everything you see has grown up around the Riverside Casino. Most construction only dates as far back as the mid-1980s.

Today there are about 11,000 rooms at nine hotels and two motels in Laughlin;

LAUGHLIN AND NEARBY CALIFORNIA AND ARIZONA

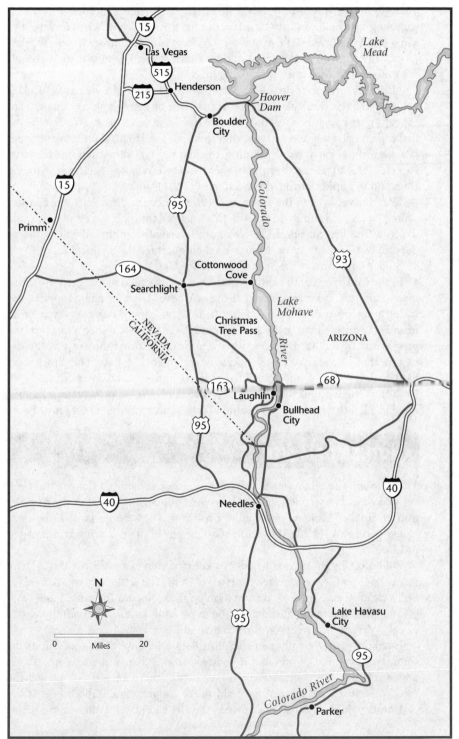

a nearby Indian reservation has a hotel with 302 rooms. Across the river in gambling-free Bullhead City, Arizona, twenty-five small hotels and motels offer some 1,500 rooms. About five million travelers visit Laughlin each year; the majority drive in from Arizona and other western states. For information consult the tourism Web site at www.visitlaughlin.com.

Although some scientists believe that humans lived in the area as far back as 10,000 years ago, available evidence in the form of petroglyphs on the walls of canyons near Laughlin dates only some 4,000 or so years back. The first identified Indian tribe was the Patayan, who split into the Hualpai and Mojave tribes (*Patayan* is a Hualpai word meaning "ancient ones"). More than one hundred Patayan campsites have been identified between Willow Beach near Hoover Dam and Pyramid Canyon, the location of Davis Dam.

The Mojaves lived in the area for centuries and were there when the Spanish claimed their land and when the Americans passed through and eventually came to settle. The first Europeans arrived in the sixteenth century when conquistadors led by Coronado came through on their quest for the mythical Seven Cities of Gold. Along the way the Spanish found the Grand Canyon.

In the mid-nineteenth century stern-wheeler steamboats chugged upstream from California as far as the present site of Hoover Dam, bringing supplies and taking away minerals and other booty. In 1857 Lt. Edward Beale surveyed a trail from Fort Smith, Arkansas, to the Colorado River and established a fort near the present site of Bullhead. Beale's other significant accomplishment was the deployment of a caravan of camels operating out of Fort Mohave. The camels were used to carry freight and mail in the desert and were taken as far north in Nevada as the foothills of the Sierra Nevada. Today the camels are commemorated in a lighthearted way in the annual camel races in Virginia City near Reno.

ANOTHER DAM SITE

The possibility of a dam across the Colorado River at Pyramid Canyon had been considered as far back as 1902, but work was not begun until after the completion of Hoover Dam some 67 miles upstream. Work began in 1942 but was halted during World War II because of a shortage of materials; it was completed in 1953.

Bullhead City in Arizona began as a construction camp for the Davis Dam, just as Boulder City was created for Hoover Dam. The settlement was named for Bull's Head Rock, a geological formation on the Colorado River used as a navigation point by steamboat captains. Today the landmark lies beneath the waters of Lake Mohave, the reservoir formed behind Davis Dam.

Laughlin was originally named South Pointe because of its location at the southernmost point of Nevada. It boasted a motel, bar, and a few other businesses to serve the construction workers. After the dam was completed, the motel was closed and most of the residents of Laughlin and Bullhead City left.

Don Laughlin, who had once owned the 101 Club casino in Las Vegas, came to the area in 1964. He purchased the shuttered motel along the river and rebuilt it as the Riverside Resort; he and his family lived in four of the motel rooms and rented out the other four. He added a small casino and restaurant.

According to local lore the postal service gave Laughlin its name; others say the promoter volunteered it. Either way, from this very humble beginning, a new city was born. Today Laughlin ranks third among Nevada resorts in gaming revenue, behind Las Vegas and Reno and ahead of Lake Tahoe. From 450 rooms in 1983, Laughlin now offers nearly 11,000 rooms and boasts near-sellout conditions in the summer. In the winter off-season the resort offers some of the best room rates anywhere; I have seen rates as low as $15 per night, and one resort gave the second night free.

Laughlin is different from Reno and Las Vegas in another way in that it has a real connection to the natural surroundings of the area. Among other things, most of its casinos are designed with windows that let in sunlight and views of the Colorado River flowing in front of the buildings.

If you're driving from Las Vegas, as you descend into Laughlin from Highway 163, the first major landmark is the smokestack of the Mohave Power Project above town. The plant has a total capacity of 1,580 megawatts from its two coal-fired steam turbine generators—about one-third the capacity of the massive Hoover Dam up the river. The generators receive their fuel from an underground river of their own: an 18-inch pipeline that brings a slurry of coal and water 275 miles from a mine on the Navaho-Hopi Indian Reservation in Kayenta, Arizona. The plant was forced to close at the end of 2005 as the result of lawsuits by environmentalists over its operations, including emissions and water pollution; the options appear to be either a $1 billion upgrade or the permanent shutdown of the plant.

The Laughlin airport, located across the river in Bullhead City, opened in 1991 with a 7,500-foot runway. Sun Country Airline's southwestern hub is located in Bullhead City. For information call (800) 359–6786 or consult www.sun country.com. Western Express Air provides service to Bullhead City from Deer Valley and Mesa, Arizona, and Riverside, California. For information call (866) 887–5969 or consult www.westernexpressair.com. Several of the casinos at Laughlin also arrange for charter flights.

For information about the Bullhead City/Laughlin Airport, call (928) 754–2134 or consult www.bullheadcity.com/tourism/airport.asp.

TRAIN AND BUS SERVICE TO LAUGHLIN

Greyhound Bus Lines provides service to a terminal in Bullhead City, just across the river from Laughlin; most casinos offer free shuttle bus service from the terminal for guests and visitors. For information about Greyhound call (800) 231–2222 or consult www.greyhound.com.

The nearest **Amtrak** stations are in Needles, California (about 32 miles south of Laughlin) or Kingman, Arizona (about 45 miles east).

You can also travel by bus from McCarran International Airport in Las Vegas. Companies offering scheduled service or tours include the following:

Aloha Arizona Tours. (800) 442–5642

Mills Tours. (877) 454–7433

Tri-State Super Shuttle. (800) 801–8687

CAR RENTAL COMPANIES IN LAUGHLIN

Avis Rent A Car. Laughlin/Bullhead City Airport. (928) 754–4686, (800) 331–1212. www.avis.com.

Enterprise Rent-a-Car. Laughlin/Bullhead City Airport. (928) 754–2700, (800) 261–7331. www.enterprise.com.

Hertz Rent A Car. Laughlin/Bullhead City Airport. (928) 754–4111, (800) 654–3131. www.hertz.com.

RIVER TAXIS

Americana River Ride. Cruises along the Colorado River and taxi service to all casino docks except the Pioneer. (928) 754–3555.

River Express Water Taxi Service. Taxi service on the river. (928) 754–4391.

DRIVING FROM LAS VEGAS TO LAUGHLIN

Driving from Las Vegas to Laughlin is a bit like taking a trip from Disneyland to Walt Disney World. What you leave and what you come to are pretty much the same; the interesting part is what you see along the way. It's an interesting tour and worth a day trip when you are ready to take a break from Las Vegas. Be sure to fill your gas tank and check your car's condition before heading out into the desert.

Take U.S. Highway 93/95 south from Las Vegas through Henderson to the point where the roads split. US 93 heads to Boulder City and across the Hoover Dam and then south through Arizona; the direct route to Laughlin follows US 95, and we'll take that road.

Soon after the split the barren desert is broken by electrical power lines that march across the landscape toward Las Vegas from Hoover Dam. You'll get a very real appreciation for the wildness of the desert that had to be crossed by the early settlers. On the broad, open desert between Nelson and Searchlight, there are no houses or settlements at all. It is almost impossible to gauge the distance to the mountains that frame the desert because the land is so flat and there are no structures to give you a sense of perspective.

About 4 or 5 miles before Searchlight, you'll come to some modern-day Wild West mining operations, made up mostly of ramshackle sheds and trailers. The signs say GUARD ON DUTY, DON'T TRESPASS. YOU WILL BE SHOT.

At Searchlight you'll come to the first major crossroad since you left Boulder City some 36 miles back. Route 164 eastbound is a one-way path to Cottonwood Cove, a recreational area 14 miles away on Lake Mohave in the Lake Mead National Recreation Area. Westbound Route 164 connects to Interstate 15, which eventually makes its way to Los Angeles. We'll stay on US 95.

Searchlight is a town of one gas station, a small general store, a liquor store, and (of course) a small gambling parlor, the **Searchlight Nugget Casino.** There is some additional development including a museum a mile east on Route 164 toward Cottonwood Cove.

The **Searchlight Heritage Museum** chronicles the story of the mining boom-town, which once surpassed Las Vegas in population. The story of Searchlight's mining and railroad heritage and its many colorful pioneer citizens is told through photos, artifacts, and an outdoor mining park. Located at 200 Michael Wendell Way, the museum is open weekdays from 1:00 to 5:00 P.M. and Saturday from 9:00 A.M. to 1:00 P.M. Admission is free. For information call (702) 297–1055 or consult www.co.clark.nv.us/parks/Clark_County_Museum.htm#Search light/.

Searchlight received its name from a mining claim in the area, which was in turn named after a popular brand of matches. American composer Scott Joplin took note of the lively town with the "Searchlight Rag." Costume designer Edith Head grew up in Searchlight, and movie stars Rex Bell and Clara Bow had a ranch there in the 1930s before moving north and helping to launch the age of glamour in Las Vegas.

The next settlement is CalNevAri, named after the three nearby state borders. Even smaller than Searchlight, it nevertheless has a market, a part-time gas station . . . and a casino.

A bit farther along you'll come to Highway 163, which leads into Laughlin. A direct trip from Las Vegas to Laughlin on US 95 to Highway 163 is about 101 miles and just under two hours in time.

A good place to stop as soon as you enter Laughlin is the Laughlin Visitor Information Center at 1555 Casino Drive, just before the Riverside Casino. The office has a healthy supply of brochures, newspapers, and magazines. For information call (702) 298–3321 or consult www.visitlaughlin.com.

A WONDROUS DETOUR

Just after Searchlight is a shortcut that adds about an hour to the trip; by that I mean that there is a road that cuts the corner into Laughlin, although I use the term *road* very loosely.

Christmas Tree Pass separates the men from the boys, the women from the girls, and the intrepid explorer from the white-knuckle driver. The unpaved switchback road branches off to the left about 2 miles past CalNevAri, heading up and over to Grapevine Canyon just above Laughlin. In dry, clear weather the road should be passable in a passenger car; in wet conditions or snow, I'd recommend a four-wheel-drive vehicle or a resolution to come back another day.

And if your personal vehicle or your rental car is in less than great shape, I'd suggest you stay on the main highway.

The winding hard-packed dirt road gets narrower and narrower the farther along you travel, becoming about a lane and a half wide as you reach the top of the pass. Not that you are likely to meet any other cars on your expedition; I didn't pass another soul on my hour-long 17-mile trip. (I also saw no gas stations or emergency services.)

The road is marked by tiny white signs on the sides of the road that say DES-IGNATED ROUTE; resist the urge to follow the side roads off this side road unless you have a topographical map and an off-road vehicle.

At the very top of the pass—about 9 miles along—the road suddenly turns into a one-lane switchback; go slowly, and honk your horn before you make the blind turn just in case there is another almost-lost soul ascending the pass.

Somewhere near the top you are likely to find a few forlorn desert bushes festooned from time to time with windblown Christmas ornaments; the pass got its name from an old tradition apparently started by travelers through the pass. In more recent times, Native Americans in the area have removed most of the trinkets to return the canyon closer to nature. On the down side of the pass, you enter into the Lake Mead Recreation Area, leading up to Lake Mohave. The roads in the park are even worse than the first half of the trip, although not quite as winding. You'll pass some spectacular rock-slide areas, including several mountains that seem to be made entirely of balanced boulders.

And then finally you are in a valley and on a paved road. On your right is Grapevine Canyon with its ancient petroglyphs. Just ahead is Route 163, at this point a four-lane highway zooming down to the Colorado River and Laughlin.

CASINOS AND HOTELS IN LAUGHLIN

★★ DON LAUGHLIN'S RIVERSIDE RESORT HOTEL & CASINO
The start of it all, today offering 1,401 rooms, 740 RV spaces, a six-screen movie theater, five restaurants, and a casino.

Restaurants include the **Gourmet Room,** featuring Continental and American dishes from chateaubriand to rack of lamb to lobster specials; open for dinner only. The **Prime Rib Room** offers beef carved at your table and an all-you-can-eat salad, potato, and dessert bar. The **Riverview Restaurant** is a twenty-four-hour coffee shop. A recent addition is the **Rice Garden Chinese Cookery,** a casual Asian cafe. The **Riverside Buffet** offers basic and uninspired breakfast, lunch, and dinner; on Friday night, seafood is the special, and Saturday and Sunday feature champagne brunches.

At the front entrance to the hotel is a showroom for part of Don Laughlin's **Classic Car Collection;** admission is free. Upstairs is **Riverside Lanes** with thirty-four bowling alleys, and nearby are six high-tech movie theaters. Across the street is a 740-space multilevel RV park, connected to the casino by an enclosed walkway.

The Riverside even has its own "luxury" cruise ship, a spiffed-up houseboat

LAUGHLIN CASINOS

Lake Mohave

Davis Dam

Colorado River

To Las Vegas (163)

(68)

MCCORMICK BLVD.

CASINO DR.

LAUGHLIN

Laughlin/Bullhead
Intl. Airport

LOCUST BLVD.

Laughlin

Laughlin
Visitor Center

CIVIC DR.

BIG BEND DR.

Horizon
Outlet
Center

Riverside

Flamingo
Laughlin

(95)

Edgewater

BULLHEAD PKWY.

Ramada
Express

Colorado Belle

Pioneer

Golden Nugget

DESERT RD.

EDISON WAY

River Palms

Harrah's

To Bay
Shore Inn

NEVADA

Bullhead City

CASINO DR.

Colorado River

ARIZONA

(95)

N

0   Mile   1

grandly dubbed the USS *Riverside,* that sails daily on short cruises along the Colorado River to the Davis Dam.

Starring acts are featured at Don's **Celebrity Theatre.** For information call (800) 227–3849, extension 616. Live country music is presented in the **Western Ballroom.** And there is the aptly named **Losers' Lounge,** comforting visitors with Top-40 bands.

Don Laughlin's Riverside Resort Hotel & Casino. 1650 Casino Drive. 1,401 rooms. Standard room rates $35 to $59, but can be as low as $19 in winter. (702) 298–2535, (800) 227–3849. www.riversideresort.com.

★★ COLORADO BELLE HOTEL/CASINO

Here's your basic 608-foot-long, six-deck Mississippi River gambling boat, only it's on the Colorado and never has gone and never will go anywhere. The "boat" features four huge environmentally safe (they don't work) smokestacks; at night strobe lights make the faux paddle wheels appear to turn.

Within the boat the decorations are those of a turn-of-the-twentieth-century New Orleans gambling (and probably more) house with excesses of red and bright brass. The high-ceilinged interior is made to look like the inside of a riverboat with lots of red and gold furnishings. There are 206 rooms in the "boat" and another 1,082 in a more conventional structure nearby.

Restaurants include the **Orleans Room,** the hotel's gourmet eatery, offering seafood, steaks, and pasta with a price range from about $15 to $40. The room, encased in wrought iron, offers a river view. Specialties include paneed breast of chicken with New Orleans bordelaise sauce for $13, shrimp scampi for $19, and

The Colorado Belle in Laughlin

a porterhouse steak for $37. Open nightly except Monday and Tuesday.

Mark Twain's Chicken, Ribs & Steaks features barbecued guess what, with entrees priced from about $8.00 to $15.00; also available are fried chicken and fish dishes.

Nearby is the **Mississippi Lounge,** offering appetizers and specialty cocktails in a French Quarter setting from noon until late night. The **Captain's Buffet** offers a breakfast, lunch, and dinner buffet.

The **Boiler Room Brew Pub,** Laughlin's only microbrewery, offers half a dozen beers brewed on-site in a set of copper tanks. Specialties include Golden Ale, Red Lager, Amber Ale, and a sweet stout that includes chocolate as one of its ingredients. The kitchen features mesquite grilling as well as wood-fired pizza ovens. Specialties include Drunkard Rib Eye Steak, herb-seasoned salmon, sandwiches, and desserts. You can try a platter of five-ounce samplers of five beers, which would nicely complement the Brewer's Platter of bratwurst and Cajun hot links braised in ale. Prices range from about $10 to $20 for food.

The Colorado Belle is owned by the MGM Mirage group, which puts it in the same company as the MGM Grand, Mandalay Bay, Excalibur, Luxor, and Circus Circus in Las Vegas, as well as the Edgewater in Laughlin.

Colorado Belle Hotel/Casino. 2100 South Casino Drive. 1,288 rooms. Standard room rates about $40 to $100, but can be as low as $19 in winter. (702) 298–4000, (866) 352–3553. www.coloradobelle.com.

★ EDGEWATER HOTEL/CASINO

Next door to the Colorado Belle is its corporate cousin in the MGM Mirage group, a 1,475-room budget behemoth. The Edgewater is at the low-water mark of casinos in Laughlin.

A blue neon waterfall cascades down the exterior face of the Edgewater; inside hand-painted Native American designs decorate many of the walls.

Restaurants include the **Hickory Pit Steakhouse,** open for dinner and serving steaks, seafood, chops, barbecued ribs, and chicken. The basic steak house offers a twenty-four-ounce porterhouse steak for $24.00, a mixed grill for $14.00, and shrimp scampi for $17.00. An early-bird special delivers chicken or beef for $8.00 to $9.00. Specialty appetizers include a "colossal onion flower" and stuffed mushrooms.

The **Garden Room,** a twenty-four-hour coffee shop, features specials including all-day steak and eggs for $6.89 or ham and eggs for $3.89. The **Black Angus Grand Buffet** is said to be Laughlin's largest buffet with a trio of 90-foot serving lines. If those are too high-tone for you, there's a McDonald's, a Krispy Kreme, a Pizza Hut, a Dairy Queen, and a few other fast fooderies.

Kokopelli's Lounge in the south casino area is named for a mythical Southwestern Indian flute player, an ancient bearer of good luck and health.

Edgewater Hotel/Casino. 2020 South Casino Drive. 1,475 rooms. Room rates generally range from about $19 to $40; in the winter, rates are as low as $16 per night. (702) 298–2453, (800) 677–4837. www.edgewater-casino.com.

A water taxi connects casinos on the Colorado River in Laughlin.

★★★ FLAMINGO LAUGHLIN

A flashy Las Vegas–like resort with mirrors on the ceilings and lots of chrome in the casino, the Flamingo Laughlin contains 2,000 rooms in twin eighteen-story towers.

Restaurants include **Alta Villa,** open evenings for fine Italian dining with prices ranging from about $13 to $50; closed Wednesday and Thursday. Located a bit off the floor, this casual eatery includes specialties such as pepper-crusted filet mignon for $22, pine nut–crusted chicken for $17, and a variety of pastas.

Beef Barron is an informal Old West–theme steak house open for dinner; fare includes prime rib from $14 to $18. Casual eateries include the **Flamingo Diner,** a twenty-four-hour '50s-style diner. The **Paradise Garden Buffet,** with an attractive window wall along the river, is open for breakfast, lunch, and dinner.

There are also fast-food outlets including Burger King, Panda Express, Subway, and Dreyers Ice Cream.

The Club Flamingo Showroom presents cabaret and lounge acts. An outdoor amphitheater on the river is used for major acts. And at the hotel's dock is *Celebration,* the largest tour boat in the area, with daily cruises for guests.

The **Nevada Gold Museum** on the first floor of the California Tower is home to what may be the world's largest collection of rare gaming memorabilia valued at more than $2 million. The hotel is owned by American Casino & Entertainment, which also owns the Stratosphere Tower in Las Vegas and Arizona Charlie's in Boulder.

Flamingo Laughlin. 1900 Casino Drive. 2,000 rooms. Standard room rates $19 to $199; can be as low as $17 midweek in the off-season. (702) 298–5111, (800) 352–6464. www.flamingolaughlin.com.

★★★GOLDEN NUGGET–LAUGHLIN HOTEL AND CASINO

This opulent tropical–theme resort encompasses an indoor rain forest and more ferns than a Los Angeles singles bar.

The hotel is partially hidden by a large parking garage on Casino Drive. Visitors enter through an arcade adorned with animatronic singing birds into a tropical atrium, a miniature tribute to the greenery of the Mirage in Las Vegas. The hotel has 300 rooms.

Under the new ownership of Landry's Restaurants (which also purchased the original Golden Nugget in downtown Las Vegas), the Laughlin resort is set to undergo a major transformation that will focus on its dining offerings and a complete renovation of the hotel's guest rooms.

The new restaurants will be drawn from among the many brands owned and managed by Landry's around the nation.

Harlow's, just off the casino floor, is the resort's twenty-four-hour eatery. It replaced Jane's Grill. Offerings include salads, pizza, chicken wings, pot roast, and other comfort foods.

Joe's Crab Shack takes over the resort's riverfront, the former location of the Deck. The restaurant is decorated with the best of fish camp decor, and the menu features crab (barbecued, steamed, and otherwise) as well as grilled and broiled fish, chicken, and steak.

Saltgrass Steakhouse, designed to give diners the feel and flavor of an open campfire with chargrilled steak, chicken, and seafood, replaced the River Cafe. The theme is "Texas to the bone," featuring beef and country and western music.

The **Buffet** is open for breakfast, lunch, and dinner.

The Golden Nugget is the successor to the second casino opened in Laughlin. The Bobcat Club opened in 1967 as a bar and sold in 1970 to be renamed the Nevada Club and run as a hotel and casino.

Golden Nugget–Laughlin Hotel and Casino. 2300 South Casino Drive. 300 rooms. Standard room rates $21 to $95. (702) 298–7111, (800) 950–7700. www .gnlaughlin.com.

★ RIVER PALMS RESORT HOTEL AND CASINO

The former Gold River Resort was reincarnated as the River Palms Resort in 1999. Built as a 1,003-room riverside box near the Emerald River Golf Course, it was designed to feel like being inside a mining camp. It has been recast with a vaguely South Atlantic/Bermuda theme that includes a few palms here and there; in places, though, there's no theme at all.

Restaurants include the **Lodge** for steaks and seafood. For some reason the design here is centered around wooden beams and mounted moose heads; it's been a while since moose and palms have coexisted. Specialties include steak Madagascar, a version of steak au poivre, for $25.

Pasta Cucina is a very basic, Italian

River Palms in Laughlin

family restaurant with red-checkered tablecloths. **River Palms Cafe** is a garden spot for breakfast, lunch, and dinner. The **No Ka Oi Buffet** also serves breakfast, lunch, and dinner.

The hotel was purchased in late 2003 by Columbia Sussex Corp., which also owns the Westin Casuarina in Las Vegas and the Horizon Casino Resort in South Lake Tahoe.

River Palms Resort Hotel and Casino. 2700 South Casino Drive. 1,003 rooms. Standard room rates $21 to $40. (702) 298–2242, (800) 835–7904. www.rvrpalm .com.

★★★ HARRAH'S LAUGHLIN

A little bit of Mexico along the river, this 1,571-room outpost of the Harrah's chain is set a bit apart from the rest of the casinos in a small canyon and features a small sandy beach along the river.

Restaurants include the **Range Steakhouse** for Continental cuisine, seafood, and steaks in a Southwestern setting; open for dinner only. Steaks are priced from about $16 to $20; other offerings include veal, seafood, and broiled ahi. Specialties include halibut in Malibu rum sauce, porterhouse steak, and seared duck breast with sun-dried cherries in port wine. The very attractive room is decorated in white-and-gold painted wood, with a window view of the river.

Baja Blue Restaurant & Cantina, just off the casino floor, offers fine Mexican and American dishes for dinner. Fajitas, tacos, and such fare are priced from about $6.00 to $12.00. The restaurant also features "flair" bartenders who put on performances with bottles, glasses, and most anything else within reach. Late after sunset the restaurant becomes **Baja Blue After Dark,** a rocking nightclub.

The **Fresh Market Square Buffet** serves breakfast, lunch, and dinner; it is one of the more attractive and ambitious buffets in town. Nightly specials include barbecues on Monday and Thursday, seafood on Friday, and steak on Saturday and Sunday. **Cabo Cafe** offers twenty-four-hour dining.

The **Del Rio Beach Club** rents one- and two-passenger Jet Skis in season. Harrah's runs a free shuttle from Harrah's up to the **Regency Casino,** which is at the far end of the strip next to Laughlin's Riverside.

A popular local entertainment spot is the 3,156-seat Rio Vista Outdoor Amphitheater, where the likes of Jeff Foxworthy and the Beach Boys have performed. Shows take place only in the fall and spring.

Harrah's Laughlin. 2900 South Casino Drive. 1,571 rooms. Standard room rates $21 to $69; can be as low as $19 in winter. (702) 298–4600, (800) 447–8700. www.harrahs.com.

Visitor Resources

▶ **Laughlin Chamber of Commerce.** Box 2280, Laughlin, NV 89029. (702) 298–2214, (800) 227–5245. www.laughlin chamber.com.

▶ **Laughlin Visitor Center.** 1555 South Casino Drive, Laughlin, NV 89029. (702) 298–3321. www.visit laughlin.com.

★ PIONEER HOTEL AND GAMBLING HALL

This Wild West–theme hotel with 414 rooms and riverfront suites has a swinging-door entrance. The river facade features a huge neon cowboy known as River Rick, a paean to its old neon cousin Vegas Vic in downtown Glitter Gulch.

Eateries include **Granny's Gourmet Room** for fine dining; located upstairs from the main casino, offerings include a buffalo T-bone steak, broiled lobster tail, sea bass Kiev, and veal picatta priced from about $20 to $50.

The **Boarding House Restaurant** is at the low end of the spectrum, offering menu items or buffet.

The casino has a smoky, dark Western feel; the cocktail waitresses wear costumes that are out of "Li'l Abner."

Pioneer Hotel and Gambling Hall. 2200 South Casino Drive. 414 rooms. Standard room rates $25 to $75. (702) 298–2442, (800) 634–3469. www.pioneer laughlin.com.

★ RAMADA EXPRESS HOTEL-CASINO

The 1,500-room railroad-theme hotel sits on a hillside a block up from the river. The main gambling hall is set up like an old train barn with an arched roof. Replicas of railroad signs and some old railroading equipment decorate the walls, from lines including the Tonopah Goldfield Railroad and the Goldfield Bullfrog Railroad Company. A train that circles the hotel is an unrealistic replica.

Eateries include the **Steakhouse,** dark and quiet and isolated from the casino. Specialties include a New York strip steak for $33, pecan chicken for $23, and seafood Zarzuela, described as a "light opera" of a dish, for $46.

The Ramada Express in Laughlin

Passaggio Italian Gardens offers pizza, pasta, and checkered tablecloths. Carnegie's is a twenty-four-hour dining car, named after the nineteenth-century railroad man and industrialist. **Tularosa Cantina** is a casual Southwestern eatery under red-chili lightbulbs; enchiladas, burritos, tacos, and other dishes are priced from about $7.00 to $10.00.

The showcase at the Ramada is the **Pavilion Theater.** For show information call (800) 243–6846. A free multimedia show, *The American Spirit,* is presented once an hour from 10:00 A.M. to 3:00 P.M., saluting American heroes from World War II to the present day. After dark the theater is used for headliners and production shows.

In 2006 Columbia Entertainment—the gaming affiliate of Columbia Sussex, which owns more than eighty hotels, resorts, and casinos across the country—merged with Aztar Corp., owner of the Tropicana Resort in Las Vegas and the Ramada Express Hotel-Casino in Laughlin.

The Ramada Express Hotel-Casino. 2121 Casino Drive. 1,500 rooms. Standard room rates about $21 to $149; can be as low as $15. (702) 298–4200, (800) 243–6846. www.ramadaexpress.com.

OUTSIDE OF LAUGHLIN

AVI HOTEL/CASINO

A 302-room hotel and casino on the Fort Mohave Indian Reservation, 15 miles south of Laughlin, the Avi (which means "loose change" in the Mojave language) includes a beach and marina on the river; a bridge connects the two sides of the reservation in Arizona and Nevada. The casino includes the **MoonShadow Grille,** the **Feathers Café,** and the **Native Harvest Buffet,** as well as several fast-food eateries. There's also the largest bingo hall in town.

Avi Hotel/Casino. 10000 AHA Macav Parkway, Laughlin. 302 rooms. Standard room rates about $35. (702) 535–5555, (800) 430–0721. www.avicasino.com.

LAUGHLIN AREA ATTRACTIONS

■ **Davis Dam.** The second leg in man's reworking of the Colorado River for water control and power generation, the Davis Dam stops the Colorado's water and fills out Lake Mohave, a narrow 67-mile-long waterway that reaches upstream to Hoover Dam. The third dam on this portion of the Colorado is the Parker Dam, 80 miles downstream; Lake Havasu backs up behind it.

The earth-filled Davis Dam is 200 feet tall, 151 feet above the streambed, and not as large, nor as visually impressive, as the Hoover Dam up the river. But it does have its own peculiar appeal.

Lake Mohave is an after bay to regulate water releases from Hoover Dam. The main purpose of the Davis Dam is to regulate the water to be delivered to

Mexico under the Mexican Water Treaty. Power production is a secondary benefit. The plant has an installed capacity of 240,000 kilowatts produced by five vertical shaft generators.

Lake Mohave, built up behind the wall of Davis Dam, has 200 miles of shoreline reaching back upstream to the Hoover Dam at Boulder City. The waters are active with rainbow trout and bass.

Tours are no longer offered at the dam.

■ **Grapevine Canyon.** To see the petroglyphs at Grapevine Canyon, take Christmas Tree Pass road (see A Wondrous Detour earlier in this chapter), off Highway 163 about 6 miles west of Davis Dam. The gravel road runs into a flat valley dominated by sharp peaks, including Spirit Mountain, the most dominant hill. About 2 miles into the valley, you will come to a spur road to the left, the entrance to the parking area for Grapevine Canyon. The walking trail leads several hundred feet to the mouth of the canyon.

Archaeologists believe there are three eras of art represented on the walls of the canyon, with the oldest about 600 to 800 years old and the most recent dating from about 150 to 200 years ago. Some of the oldest carvings may be below the present level of earth in the area, and others may have been eroded by water. The drawings seem to have some religious significance.

■ **Colorado River Historical Museum.** An interesting and eclectic small collection of historical and household objects. The museum is located on the Arizona side of the river, toward Davis Dam; cross the Laughlin Bridge and make a left turn onto Highway 68 and get into the left lane to cross the road a half mile east.

Outside the museum is a small model of Don Laughlin's first casino, which opened in 1966 and brought South Pointe and Bullhead City back to life. Inside you'll find photographs of some of the old mines, including Oatman and the Tom Reed Gold Mine, a fabulous find that produced $13 million worth of gold between 1906 and 1931. Another display shows barbed wire from the 1880s.

Nearby is a steamboat anchor found in the Colorado River near Hardyville. When a steamboat approached a sandbar, it would turn stern-to and send a small boat ahead with the anchor; the anchor would be sunk in the sand and then as the paddle wheeler dug its way through the sand, the anchor chain would be winched in to pull the boat over the sandbar.

Admission is free, although donations are welcome. The museum is closed in July and August. For more information consult www.bullheadcity.com/tourism/hismuseum.asp.

■ **Katherine's Landing.** A rich gold and silver strike was made here in 1900 on the Arizona side of the river, 3 miles north of the present site of Davis Dam. The mine produced $12 million worth of gold in four decades until it was closed down in 1942. Today Katherine's Landing is a resort community and marina on Lake Mohave with boat slips, boat rentals, a launch ramp, and sandy beaches with barbecues and picnic areas. For information call (928) 754–3245.

■ **Oatman.** The town was born in 1906 as a gold-mining tent camp; after tens of millions of dollars were extracted from the area, the town went bust in 1942 after Congress declared gold mining was no longer essential to the war effort.

At its height the town had a population of more than 12,000 and featured its own local stock exchange. The scenery around Oatman has been used for a number of movies, including *How the West Was Won.*

The ghost town and historic gold-mining area include museums, shops, and eateries. Gunfighters stage weekend showdowns on the town's main street, on historic Route 66, approximately 30 miles southeast of Laughlin. For information call (928) 768–6222 or consult www.oatmangoldroad.com.

■ **London Bridge, English Village, and Lake Havasu.** London Bridge did not fall down; it was taken apart stone by stone and shipped to Arizona, where it is the centerpiece of a small British theme park and a retirement town. Make sure you know which bridge it is you are looking for; this is *not* the famous lift bridge that still spans the Thames in London; the bridge that was brought to Arizona is old and is from London, but it is not the one many people picture in their minds.

Depending on whether you take backcountry roads or interstates, the distance is 67 or 97 miles, respectively; either way it's about a two-hour drive. (Highway route: east on Highway 68 to Kingman, Interstate 40 west 40 miles to Needles, south on US 95 to Lake Havasu City.) For information call (928) 453–3444 or consult www.lakehavasucity.com.

■ **Grand Canyon Caverns.** About a hundred miles east of Laughlin on Highway 66 between Kingman and Seligman, Arizona, the extensive caverns are made up of limestone formed in prehistoric times by an inland sea. Explorers have found fossils and the bones of long-extinct animals within. An elevator takes visitors 210 feet underground for forty-five-minute tours every half hour. Admission: adults $12.95, children (four to twelve) $9.95; also available is a flashlight tour for $14.95/$9.95 and an explorers' tour that goes off the regular route for $44.95 per person. For information call (928) 422–3223 or consult www.gccaverns.com.

■ **Grand Canyon Railway.** Steam engines from Williams, Arizona, run from Memorial Day through September; vintage diesels work the line for the rest of the year. Trains depart at 10:00 A.M. and arrive at 12:15 P.M., heading back at 3:30 P.M. for a 5:45 P.M. arrival. Tickets range from about $60 to $158 for adults and $35 to $130 for children, depending on class. Packages including tours of the Grand Canyon and overnight accommodations are also available. For information call (800) 843–8724 or consult www.thetrain.com.

OUTDOOR RECREATION NEAR LAUGHLIN

■ GOLF

Chaparral Country Club. 1260 Mohave Drive, Bullhead City, Arizona. Nine holes. Semiprivate. (928) 758–3939.

Desert Lakes Golf Course. 5835 South Desert Lakes Drive, Fort Mohave, Arizona. Eighteen holes. Public. (928) 768–1000.

Emerald River Golf Course. 1155 West Casino Drive, Laughlin. Eighteen holes. Semiprivate. (702) 298–0061.

■ COLORADO RIVERBOAT TOURS

London Bridge Jet Boat. Daily six-hour round-trips from the Pioneer dock to the London Bridge English Village at Lake Havasu. Adults $52, children (three to twelve) $32. (702) 298–5494, (866) 505–3545. www.jetboattour.com.

River Jet Tours. Daily six-hour round-trips from Golden Nugget and Flamingo Laughlin to London Bridge English Village at Lake Havasu. Adults $52, children (three to twelve) $32. (702) 298–8363, (800) 327–2386.

USS *Riverside*. Daily trips on the Colorado River from the Riverside Casino to the face of Davis Dam. Adults $10.00, children $6.00. (702) 298–2535. www.riversideresort.com/Html/Uss_tours.htm.

RETURNING TO LAS VEGAS VIA ARIZONA

We'll return to Las Vegas with a slightly longer tour that will head east toward Kingman, Arizona, and then northwest in the valley alongside the Cerbat Mountains and then across the Hoover Dam and back into Nevada. The trip totals about 140 miles and should take just under three hours.

Cross the Laughlin Bridge toward Bullhead City and make an immediate left turn onto Highway 68 toward Kingman, Arizona. About 10 miles past the Colorado River, you will come to Katherine Mine Road on your left, which will take you down to the shores of Lake Mohave, the ruins of the once-fabulous gold mine there, and the town that grew up around it.

Gold and silver mining began in the area in the mid-1860s, reaching a peak between 1900 and 1907. The mines reopened in 1933 when the value of gold rose, but the facilities were severely damaged by fire in 1934. Sporadic mining continued until 1943. All that remains of the mine is a group of concrete pillars; the deep labyrinth of passages is now mostly flooded by Lake Mohave.

You'll cut through the first set of mountains on Union Pass at about 3,600 feet. The panorama of sharply peaked mountains on the Arizona side are much more spectacular than the ones you drove through coming down. After you are over the mountain pass, you are into a mostly flat, high desert plateau within a ring of mountains known as Golden Valley.

Kingman is where Highway 66, US 93, and Highway 68 all come together. Just short of Kingman the road comes to a T at US 93; head left to go north.

In the Cerbat Mountains to your right are dozens of small mining camps, some of which grew large enough to qualify as towns at their peak. The first you'll pass is Cerbat, which came into existence in the 1860s as a mining camp and had a mill, a smelter, a post office, a school, stores, and saloons.

A few miles north on US 93 brings you to a road to Mineral Park, located 5 miles northeast into the mountains. Now abandoned, it was the county seat from 1873 to 1887 and included a courthouse and jail, hotel, saloons, assay offices, and two stagecoach stations. I drove up Route 255 to Mineral Park. It had been raining in the valley, but as I climbed, it began to turn into snow and up above, the mountains were blanketed. The road ends in a box canyon and a mineral-processing plant within barbed wire. On both sides of the road are capped pipes that sit over the top of former mine shafts. In the valleys are a few gigantic piles of tailings as tall as some of the mountains.

The next town of interest is Chloride, another mining boomtown. A road leads directly to Chloride from US 93, but I chose to explore a very rough dirt road that led from Route 255 near Mineral Park; I almost did not make it. The back road is made of soft earth, and the rain had turned the path into mud. Just to make things worse, the rough road is marked at several points with warnings about the possibility of flash flood areas. As with Christmas Tree Pass, I'd recommend against taking the back road in less-than-perfect weather.

Chloride sits 4 miles east of Grasshopper Junction, off US 93. It began in about 1863 with the discovery of the first silver mines in the area. By 1900 it had a population of 2,000 with more than seventy-five mines in operation, including the Tennessee Schuykill, a large producer of gold, silver, copper, lead, and zinc. The post office is the oldest continuously operated station in Arizona, dating from 1871. A coach line known as the Butterfield Stage served Chloride from 1868 until 1919; the Santa Fe Railroad had a spur to Chloride from 1898 until 1935. The last of the mines was shuttered in 1944.

Today, though, some 350 hardy souls live on the hill. Each summer they cater to tourists who come to see the somewhat-preserved boomtown. There are a couple of lean-to shacks, and a few shops, three cafes, two saloons, and the old post office to visit. The town celebrates Old Miners Day on the last Saturday of June with a parade (at high noon, of course), music, melodramas, and gunfights. Vaudeville shows are performed on the first and third Saturday of the month in the summer. For information call the Chloride Chamber of Commerce and Visitor Center at (928) 565–2204 or consult www.chloridearizona.com.

Back on US 93 there's a small community and gas station near Willow Beach, and then the road climbs up into the mountains again, then drops down through a series of spectacular switchback turns that eventually lead to the Hoover Dam. The road passes right over the top of the dam and into Boulder City.

PART III

RENO, VIRGINIA CITY, AND LAKE TAHOE

CHAPTER SEVENTEEN

THE BIGGEST LITTLE CHAPTER IN THIS BOOK: RENO

Econoguide Best Casino-Hotels in Reno-Sparks

★★★★★ **Harrah's.** *Reborn as the class of downtown.*
★★★★★ **Peppermill.** *The liveliest (and gaudiest) place in town.*
★★★★ **Atlantis.** *Not undiscovered anymore.*
★★★★ **Eldorado.** *A classic fable of riches.*
★★★★ **John Ascuaga's Nugget, Sparks.** *A quirky gem.*
★★★★ **Reno Hilton.** *A city within the city.*
★★★★ **Silver Legacy.** *A theme park with slot machines.*
★★ **Circus Circus.** *Best-named casino in town.*
★★ **Siena Hotel Spa & Casino.** *Mediterranean on the Truckee.*
★ **Sands Regency.** *Nothing to write home about.*

WELCOME TO RENO, semifamously known as the "Biggest Little City in the World."

The odd title comes from the slogan on the famous arch that crosses Virginia Street in downtown Reno. Historians point to an early advertising campaign used to promote the Jeffries-Johnson heavyweight fight of 1910: the "Biggest Little City on the Map." The original arch was erected in 1927 honoring an exposition to mark the completion of the transcontinental highway system, which passed through Reno. The most recent update to the arch, a not-at-all understated art deco design with 800 linear feet of neon and 1,600 lightbulbs, was completed in 1987.

Reno sign

The train tracks still run right through the center of town, rumbling the casinos and stopping traffic regularly. Local politicos have been trying for years to fund a major "big dig" plan to relocate the tracks in a trench.

Reno has fought mightily against the decline of the downtown area with projects such as the Silver Legacy Resorts, improvements at Harrah's, a city-financed multiplex movie theater a block from South Virginia Street, and the closure of most of its downtown sawdust joints. It is still much more of a working-class place than Las Vegas, home of bowling competitions rather than computer expositions.

The city's Events Center opened downtown at East Fourth and Lake Streets in 2005 to host small conventions, sporting events, trade shows, and concerts. Four hotel-casinos, the Silver Legacy, Harrah's Reno, Circus Circus, and the Eldorado, were partners in the $29 million project, funded by the hotel room tax and a special assessment.

Other additions include the year-round Truckee River Whitewater Park and kayak racing course and a public plaza on the site of the former Mapes Hotel.

The glittery Peppermill has been growing by leaps and bounds, and Harrah's bought up a whole chunk of downtown for an outdoor stage and expansion.

Winter is value season in Reno, which means rates at world-class hotel-casinos and motel lodgings are at their rock-bottom lowest except for the Christmas to New Year's period. And dining, whether it be a full-out breakfast buffet or a midnight snack, is more accessible and less expensive than at other winter resort destinations.

I love Reno most as a gateway to two of my favorite places: Lake Tahoe and Virginia City. I can stay in a city hotel, eat at casino restaurants, and be within ninety minutes of some of the best winter and summer activities in the country.

RENO AND LAKE TAHOE CLIMATE

The climate in the Reno-Tahoe area can vary greatly by elevation and location. The overall climate is very arid; the Reno area receives very little precipitation with an average of about 7.5 inches per year. Snowfall can vary greatly from about 6 inches per month from December to February to measurements by the yard in some mountainous areas.

Although highways and major roads are plowed and sanded, many mountain passes may be closed due to poor visibility, ice, or blowing and drifting snow. Drivers are generally advised to carry tire chains when crossing mountain passes in winter. At times the use of snow tires and/or chains is mandatory. Driving in the Sierra Nevada can be very dangerous during the winter, and motorists should use extreme caution, especially when heading down steep grades.

For road and weather information, contact the following:

California Department of Transportation Road Reporting Service. (916) 445-7623. www.dot.ca.gov/hq/roadinfo.

Nevada Department of Transportation Road Reporting Service. Winter Road Conditions. (775) 793–1313. www.nevadadot.com/traveler/roads/winter.

National Weather Service. (775) 673–8100. www.wrh.noaa.gov/rev.

Reno-Sparks Convention and Visitors Authority. (800) 367–7366. www.rscva .com.

The area enjoys warm and dry days in spring, summer, and early fall, turning crisp though sunny for much of the winter. Nights turn cool year-round, and sweaters or light jackets are usually appropriate even in summer. Sweaters and coats are needed in the winter. In ski season ski clothing is acceptable in most casual restaurants and all casinos.

Reno-Sparks Average Temperatures

	Jan	Feb	Mar	Apr	May	Jun	Jul	Aug	Sep	Oct	Nov	Dec
High	45	50	54	63	70	79	89	87	81	70	56	48
Low	19	24	27	32	39	45	50	47	41	33	24	21

Mileage to Reno

Carson City	30
Elko	289
Fallon	60
Genoa	40
Heavenly Ski Resort	55
Incline Village	35
Jackpot	406
Las Vegas	440
Los Angeles	469
New York City	2,711
Pyramid Lake	33
Sacramento	125
Salt Lake City	526
San Francisco	229
South Lake Tahoe	59
Sparks	3
Squaw Valley USA	50
Truckee	30
Virginia City	24
Yosemite National Park	137

ABOUT RENO

The site of present-day Reno was settled around 1858 and was first known as Lake's Crossing. The town grew with the discovery of the Comstock Lode in nearby Virginia City. The railroad arrived in 1868, and the city was renamed for General Jesse Lee Reno. A native of Virginia, Reno was a popular military leader in the U.S. Civil War and before that in the Mexican War. He was killed as he led the Union Army's 9th Corps at South Mountain in 1862.

The city straddles the Truckee River, and civic leaders celebrate the revitalized downtown's Truckee River Walk with a festival in early June to begin the summer season and with a Christmas gala on the river in early December.

The early history of Reno, like Las Vegas, Carson City, and Genoa, was as a rest stop for travelers heading elsewhere. Many of the westward-bound settlers who chose a northern crossing of the Sierra Nevada followed the Humboldt-Carson trail; various branches of the trail crossed over at Carson Pass (north of Lake Tahoe) or a pathway through Truckee Meadows and over Donner Summit, named after the ill-fated 1846 winter expedition.

The wagon trains needed to find a place to cross the Truckee River, especially in the spring when the waters ran high, and several private entrepreneurs built toll bridges in the area. A young New Yorker named Myron Lake bought one of the bridges and opened an inn for travelers; his bridge crossed the Truckee at the spot that is today the heart of Reno: First and Virginia Streets. Lake expanded his operations when he obtained the franchise to collect tolls on the Sierra Valley Road (now Virginia Street) and made his fortune with the boom that came with the discovery of the Comstock Lode in Virginia City.

Lake's Crossing, as the enterprise was known, came to control much of what would become Reno. In 1868 Lake made a deal with the Central Pacific (CP) Railroad, giving the company sixty acres of land; the CP agreed to use the town site as a freight-and-passenger depot. Very much like what would take place thirty-seven years later in Las Vegas, the railroad auctioned off 400 lots in May 1868, and a town was born.

With its roots as a rough-and-tumble railroad city and trading post for the even-rougher mining men of Virginia City, Reno fulfilled the urgent demands of many of its clients. The red-light district was on Lake Street, and the gambling halls were semihidden on Douglas Alley.

RENO

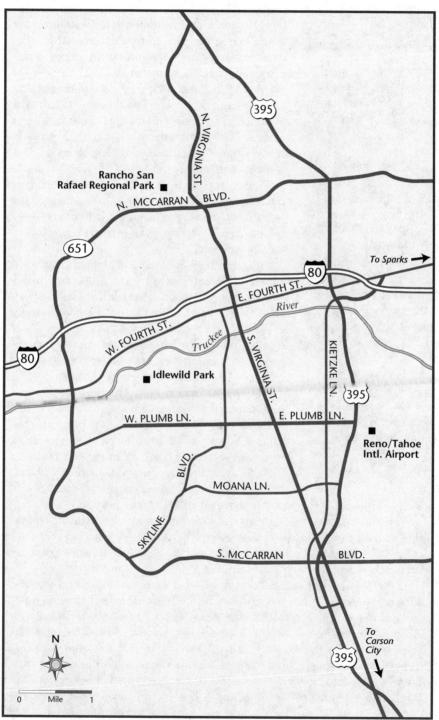

Point of Reference

The Truckee River, which runs from Lake Tahoe to Pyramid Lake, travels from west to east as it passes through downtown Reno. Where the river and Virginia Street intersect is the zero point for the street numbering of the city. Fourth Street, for example, is called West Fourth Street west of Virginia and (you figured this out, right?) East Fourth Street east of Virginia.

The north-south roads are similarly split: The main drag of Virginia Street is called North Virginia on the north side of the river and South Virginia on the south side. The higher the number, the farther away from the heart of downtown at the river.

Just as in Las Vegas, a power struggle over gambling, liquor, and prostitution took place just after World War I; the push to tone down what had become known as the "biggest little city in the world" eventually came to a vote in the 1923 election for mayor. E. E. Roberts, backed by some of the political and economic forces who had the most to gain, ran for office on a platform promising to do away with or ignore all laws that affected "personal choice." He won easily and kept his word to close his eyes.

Reno, with its proximity to California, began to pick up a large trade in quickie divorces and marriages because of the liberal laws in Nevada. And the fact that there were other diversions in the town helped make it a very popular place with residents of the Golden State.

Of course the Wild West had always been a place where social mores were a bit . . . looser. So it was with legalities like divorce. Nevada had a law allowing almost immediate divorce for any citizen for a variety of reasons. And because Nevada had such a history of massive influxes for its various mining and railroad booms, citizenship was available to anyone living within its boundaries for at least six months.

The wealthy industrial class of the early twentieth century realized that this combination offered a relatively easy way out of marriages; the procedure became a national affair when former showgirl Laura Corey moved to Reno for six months to initiate a "quickie" divorce from her philandering husband, William Corey, the multimillionaire president of U.S. Steel in Pittsburgh. The publicity launched an industry in Reno.

The conservative establishment tried to reel in Nevada's freewheeling reputation with a ban on gambling in 1909—widely ignored—and a 1913 change in citizenship rules to twelve months. But an obvious decline in Reno's economy led to a 1915 repeal of the citizenship rule.

In 1931, faced with competition from other states including Arkansas and Arizona, Nevada dropped the residency period to six weeks and threw in legalized gambling for good measure. Thus Reno's divorce industry was reborn, with about 5,000 cases—about twenty a day—in 1931. (Some Reno hotels had "divorce specials" for the six-week stays.) It was said that newly happy divorcees would kiss the white columns of the Washoe County Courthouse and then throw their wedding bands into the Truckee River from the Virginia City Bridge—called by many "Wedding Ring Bridge" or, with a nod to old Venice, the "Bridge of Sighs." Hundreds of hotels, motor courts, and boarding houses were devoted to the divorce trade in Reno; there were also "divorce ranches" where women putting in their waiting time were entertained by very-available ranch hands. All told, about 32,000 marriages were ended in the period from 1929 through 1939.

Reno's casinos, though they were now legal, seemed stuck in the mold of the hidden, illegal enterprises they had once been. This began to change with the arrival of Raymond "Pappy" Smith and his sons Raymond Jr. and Harold; their Harolds Club on Virginia Street was the first "carpet joint" in Reno, an attempt to swap sin for fun as an image. The Smith family sold the casino in 1970 to Howard Hughes. It changed hands several times in the following years; in 1999 the property was purchased by Harrah's, which demolished the structure.

And there is life outside the casinos, including the giant National Bowling Stadium with seventy-eight lanes and 1,200 seats. See chapter 19 for more details.

RENO CASINOS AND HOTELS

★★★★★ HARRAH'S CASINO/HOTEL RENO

Harrah's has been rebuilt and redesigned and recast more times than a Hollywood starlet, and it still is one of the classiest joints of downtown Reno with handsome public spaces and eateries and a well-run hotel side.

The highlight of today's South Virginia Street is the **Plaza at Harrah's,** a football-field–size open concert-and-special-events center, lit up each night by a music-and-laser-light show. A covered walkway begins at the base of the famous Reno Arch and leads into a rotunda entrance attached to the original casino. Strolling entertainers and gourmet food carts mix among the guests. The plaza occupies the former site of two venerable casinos, Harolds Club and the Nevada Club.

About the Sierra Nevada

The Sierra Nevada range lies mostly in California, reaching into Nevada near Lake Tahoe. Bounded on the north by a gap south of Lassen Peak and by the Cascades, and on the south by Tehachapi Pass, the range runs from northwest to southeast for about 400 miles.

The tallest peak in the Sierra Nevada is Mount Whitney, which at 14,494 feet is also the tallest peak in the lower forty-eight states.

According to geologists, the Sierra Nevada is made up of a single block of the Earth's crust tilted upward toward the east. The predominant rocks of the range are granite, other igneous rocks, and metamorphic slate. Great quantities of gold have been found embedded in quartz, while silver has been mined on the eastern slope.

The history of Harrah's reaches back to 1946 when it was the first major casino of William Harrah and one of the classiest joints in town; he had previously run several tiny operations around Reno.

Entertainment is presented in **Sammy's Showroom,** named after Sammy Davis Jr., who made more than 400 appearances there over twenty-two years.

Harrah's Steak House is a well-respected restaurant, decorated in muted reds and hidden a floor below and a world away from the jingle-jangle of the casino. Favorites include rack of lamb with pine-nut–pinot-noir sauce and steak Diane.

Visitor Centers in Reno-Sparks

For information and reservations call the Reno-Sparks Convention & Visitors Center at (800) 367-7366.

Visitor centers are located at Reno Cannon International Airport; Reno Downtown Visitors Center, 300 North Center Street in the National Bowling Stadium; Reno-Sparks Convention Center, 4590 South Virginia Street; and Sparks Downtown Visitors Center, Pyramid Way and Victorian Avenue, Sparks.

Lunch is served from 11:00 A.M. to 2:30 P.M. weekdays, and dinner starts at 5:00 P.M. every day. Luncheon offerings are priced from about $9.00 to $14.00. The extensive dinner menu includes oyster, shrimp, and salmon appetizers and entrees priced from about $18 to $35. Call (775) 788–3232 for reservations.

The **Ichiban Japanese Steakhouse and Sushi Bar** offers teppanyaki dishes prepared at the table as well as an all-you-can-eat sushi and tempura bar. Open nightly for dinner.

Andreotti is open for dinner at 5:00 P.M. Thursday through Monday nights. The kitchen is open to view and is worth a peek. For an appetizer you can create your own pasta misto. Pastas include spaghetti, linguine, cheese tortellini, and cheese ravioli, and sauces include tomato basil, white wine, and red or white clam. Entrees are priced from about $8.00 to $15.00. There are also nightly dinner specials that include a sampling of dishes plus salad and dessert for $20.00. Call (775) 788–2908 for reservations.

Carvings Buffet features international service stations with offerings that include Chinese, Italian, vegetarian, American, and other fare. Brunch is served daily from 8:00 A.M. to 2:00 P.M.; dinner is served nightly.

The Lucky Noodle Bar, open for lunch and dinner near the East Tower elevators, offers one-dish specials such as shrimp and noodle tom yum koong. There are also Western pasta specialties such as spaghetti marinara.

Cafe Napa, a twenty-four-hour coffee shop on the Skyway level of the hotel, offers California-themed entrees such as crab cakes with pesto hollandaise sauce; the Seafood Golden Gate, a bread bowl filled with smoked salmon, crabmeat, bay shrimp, avocado, and tomatoes; and Thai chicken or pork chops. Also within the restaurant is the **Chinese Kitchen,** offering Asian fare including lunch specials.

Harrah's Entertainment owns and operates casinos under the Harrah's, Showboat, and Rio brands, including the sprawling Rio All-Suite in Las Vegas.

Harrah's Casino/Hotel Reno. 206 North Virginia Street. 928 rooms. Room rates $59 to $169. (775) 786–3232, (800) 648–3773. www.harrahs.com.

★★★★★ PEPPERMILL HOTEL/CASINO

The Peppermill is a thoroughly modern assault on the senses with a riot of purple, green, and pink neon and electronic signboards like a sports stadium. A few miles south of downtown, the Peppermill is one of the more lively casinos in the area. The now-sprawling complex had its beginnings in 1971 as a relatively humble coffee shop and restaurant built by two young contractors.

In 1999 the Peppermill completed the first phase of an ambitious expansion plan. The hotel/casino bought out a movie theater, restaurant, and motel along Virginia Street to expand its property to forty acres overall. The former movie theater was converted into a high-tech concert hall with 1,560 reclining seats.

And in the fall of 2007, the Peppermill is due to open a $270 million expansion that will bring the total number of rooms to 1,631. The new seventeen-story curved-glass tower will add 600 suites, ranging from 550-square-foot Tuscany suites to a number of house-size 2,800-square-foot Palace suites. Cabana Level rooms will open to the pool deck and gardens.

Each suite features private foyers off the main hallways, rich mahogany furnishings, luxurious bedding, elegant marble bathrooms with steam showers and spa tubs, two high-definition plasma screen televisions, and wireless broadband Internet access.

Seven-up

Founder Bill Harrah had a gambler's view of the world. According to lore he drank exactly seven cups of coffee each day and opened his first casino in 1937; he even managed to marry seven times. At one time the Harrah's logo sported seven stars atop the seven letters of the company name.

Also part of the expansion is a new grand entrance and a Tuscan-themed hotel lobby. A 1,600-space parking plaza will offer speed ramps, digital space-availability readouts, and a skywalk to the casino.

Two restaurants are also part of the addition. **Café Giardinio** offers *alfresco* dining in the midst of the poolside gardens. **Baciami,** a two-story nightclub, is nearby. And the expanded casino area includes a new lounge.

The Peppermill also gained an additional 65,000 square feet of convention space, bringing the total to 105,000 square feet, the third-largest such space in Reno.

The Peppermill's perennial local favorite is **Romanza Ristorante Italiano,** an Italian showplace under a sky dome that changes from sunrise to sunset to starry sky, featuring imported Italian marble and fabrics and a surround-sound system with individual speakers recessed into each booth.

Specialties include *bistecca alla Fiorentina* (olive oil and herb-marinated T-bone steak); *branzino al cartoccio* (Chilean sea bass sealed in parchment with fennel); *osso bucco alla Romanza* (veal shank braised in Barolo); and *salmone affumicato* (pan-smoked salmon fillet served on black fettuccine). Entrees are priced from about $15 to $36.

At the center of the restaurant is a statue of the Roman emperor Antinous surrounded by a pair of young maidens; the revolving statue is at the center of a special-effects show for diners. Circling the restaurant are Corinthian columns topped with real flames. For reservations call (775) 689–7474.

Just off the hotel lobby is **White Orchid,** open for dinner nightly. Entrees range in price from about $30 to $40 and include medallions of elk with lobster, abalone in tomato basil sauce, and pan-roasted chicken stuffed with wild-mushroom mousse. For reservations call (775) 689–7300.

The **Steak House** offers a menu of specialties including herb-crusted rack of lamb and pan-seared medallions of veal. Entrees range from about $19 to $42. The restaurant is open nightly from 5:30 P.M., and reservations are recommended. Call (775) 689–7111.

Oceano, designed as if diners were underwater, serves a wide range of seafood, including lobster, mesquite-grilled fish, pan roasts, and chowders. The eatery, at the Peppermill's north parking lot, is open daily for lunch and dinner.

The expansive **Island Buffet** is set within a rain forest with four 20-foot-wide waterfalls that are used as projection screens. Overhead the rumble of thunder and the flashes of a lightning storm mix with a liquid-nitrogen fog. The buffet includes a daily seafood and Asian wok station, a Southwestern section, an omelet and frittatas station, and a steak and carving table.

The **Flamingo Food Court** includes several serving sections, offering Italian, American, Chinese, and Mexican specialties, ranging from 99-cent tacos to shrimp scampi and Chinese offerings for about $5.00.

Peppermill Hotel/Casino. 2707 South Virginia Street. 1,631 rooms. Room rates $49 to $399. (775) 826–2121, (800) 648–6992. www.peppermillreno.com.

★★★★ ELDORADO HOTEL/CASINO

The Eldorado is an attractive modern casino worth a visit. Among its lures is a collection of some of the better hotel restaurants in town.

The hotel was expanded and refurbished in 1995 to make the most of its second-floor skyway connection to its corporate half-cousin, the Silver Legacy Casino, with a microbrewery and a buffet that earned the *Econoguide* ranking as the best feed-your-face eatery in town. Other enhancements included a snazzy upper lobby, a new tower with thirty-six supersuites for high rollers, and a new showroom.

The Grand Plaza on the mezzanine level includes a fanciful 50-foot marble and bronze *Fountain of Fortune,* a trompe l'oeil sky dome, and a splashy restaurant called Project Bistro 21. The lively casino includes what is billed as the world's largest roulette table, seating as many as forty people.

Golden Fortune offers more than ninety Hong Kong and other Asian specialties in a classic Chinese setting. Specialties include prawns with honey-glazed walnuts, braised oysters with ginger and green onions, Singapore-style rice noodles, and Mongolian beef. Entrees range from $10 to $28.

La Strada is a more formal room, serving dinner nightly from 5:00 P.M. Pizzas are prepared in a wood-fired brick oven. In addition to the basics, toppings include *pescatore* (fresh tomato, shrimp, scallops, clams, and calamari with garlic and basil). Entrees range in price from about $15 to $25.

The nearby **Prime Rib Grill** has entrees ranging from about $10 to $25. Specialties include honey-bourbon barbecue pork ribs, chicken fettuccine, and, of course, prime rib.

And the attractions go on: Be sure to stop at **Tivoli Gardens,** a high-scale coffee shop decorated with overhead arbors and lots of brass with offerings from around the world including Asia, Mexico, Italy, and America. You'll know things are a bit different when you come to the elaborate coffee roaster at the entrance. The selection of beans is made by the restaurant's executive chef, who chooses premium arabica green coffee beans from the high altitudes of Central America, Africa, Indonesia, and Hawaii.

Depending on your age, sex, and degree of sweet tooth, you may find the dessert carousel at Tivoli Gardens even more attractive than the cocktail waitresses at the casino who, just for the record, wear some of the skimpiest outfits in town.

Tivoli Gardens serves breakfast all day. International specials, priced from about $5.00 to $12.00, are served from 11:00 to 3:00 A.M. The **Chefs' Buffet**—an *Econoguide* best—features American, Chinese, Italian, Mongolian, and Hispanic cuisine prepared on grills and woks at the center of the dining area. On Friday night lines form early for the All-You-Can-Eat Lobster, Shrimp & Crab Buffet.

The **Brew Brothers** microbrewery is located on the south end of the skywalk linking the Eldorado to the Silver Legacy. Food items, priced from about $6.00 to $15.00, include hot wings, onion rings, club sandwiches, pizzas, sausage, and baby back ribs. Brews we found on a research trip included Eldorado Extra Pale Honey Ale, Big Dog Ale, Wild Card Wheat Ale, Gold Dollar Pale Ale, Redhead Amber Ale, Double Down Stout, and Brewmaster's Special.

The food is one of the best deals in town outside of the buffets and the greasy-spoon specials at coffee shops. There's a happy hour most days from 3:00 to 6:00 P.M. with home brews selling for about $2.00 a glass. They also produce a root beer.

Roxy's is a Paris-style bistro with American influences; there are seven settings including an ancient wine cellar, a turret to an old city wall, a European sidewalk cafe, a Parisian-style bistro, an old-fashioned exhibition bakery, and a Toulouse-Lautrec–inspired atrium bar. The wine list includes 450 selections, and the bar claims knowledge of 150 different martini recipes. Specialties include spit-roasted pork loin and chicken, pan-seared Chilean sea bass, and fresh quail. Entrees range in price from about $20 to $30. The restaurant is open daily from 5:00 P.M.

Eldorado Hotel/Casino. 345 North Virginia Street. 800 rooms. Room rates $59 to $89. (775) 786–5700, (800) 648–5966. www.eldoradoreno.com.

★★★★ RENO HILTON

A city within a city with 2,001 rooms, bowling alley, movie theater, golf driving range, video arcade, shopping mall . . . and a casino.

Downstairs is a pair of high-tech movie theaters showing first-run and art features. (The back sections of the theaters include love seats for those who are amorously inclined or who are generally more used to watching movies in the comfort of their living rooms or beds.)

Out front is the **Ultimate Rush Thrill Ride,** a sky tower where up to three riders are suspended from a 185-foot tower and then launched out into space on a cable. And they get to pay for the privilege, about $25 per person. For information call (775) 786–7005.

The shopping arcade includes a broad selection of stylish shops and tourist magnets, as well as the large Fun Quest Arcade and fast-food offerings. Outside is the **Hilton Bay Aqua Golf on Lake Hilton,** an artificial pond created during the excavation for the hotel. Using floating golf balls, players can test their swings on 100-, 150-, and 200-yard holes and hope to win prizes. Club rental is free with the purchase of two buckets; the unusual course is open from 7:00 to 2:00 A.M. For more information call (775) 789–2122. There is also one of the largest hotel health clubs I have seen, along with five indoor and three outdoor tennis courts. There are fifty lanes for bowling, too.

The expanded sports and race book includes state-of-the-art electronics in an attractive corner of the casino. There are small TV screens at each table as well as larger ones up on the wall. Hanging from the ceiling are some experimental and acrobatic airplanes, including a Rutan canard-wing plane. At **Johnny Rockets,** on the floor of the sprawling casino, the waiters and waitresses sing along with the oldies issuing forth from the jukebox. The food, of course, is good ol' American burgers, fries, and malts.

Most of the hotel's restaurants are located on Restaurant Row, a semiprivate alcove off the casino floor. The premier Italian restaurant at the Hilton is **Andiamo,** an elegant place with lots of space between the tables. Appealing appetizers include *scampi alla livornese* (jumbo shrimp sautéed in olive oil with garlic, shallots, white wine butter sauce, and diced peppers) for $6.95. Entrees, priced from about $8.00 to $24.00, include *ravioli di gamberi* (raviolis filled with bay shrimp, fresh salmon mousse, and zucchini served in a light creamy tomato sauce) and *tournedos al bardolino* (two petite filets mignons sautéed with mushrooms, rosemary, and garlic in bardolino red sauce). You can finish off the meal with dessert and espresso or cappuccino, available plain or spiked with anisette or brandy.

The **Steak House** features an English Tudor manor house setting. Specialties include steak Diane, roasted duck with brandied orange sauce, and broiled Chilean sea bass, with prices from about $22 to $59.

Asiana is a high-tone noodle shop and restaurant fusing Asian ingredients and California cuisine; it is open for dinner only. Specialties include Philippine pork adobo, garlic soy braised pork with red pepper and potato; wok-tossed calamari with *sichimi* pepper in citrus red onion *noac cham*; Mongolian-style spareribs with sesame cabbage and bell peppers; and Thai lemongrass crispy prawns with stir-fried cabbage and Bangkok curry sauce.

The Hilton redesigned its **Lodge Buffet** to feature action stations with carved meats, Mexican specialties, a pizza oven, and crab, shrimp, and prime rib nightly. It is open for breakfast, lunch, and dinner. There's also **Chevy's Fresh Mex,** a twenty-four-hour Mexican food outlet.

Entertainment at the Reno Hilton centers on the **Hilton Theater,** the hotel's premier showroom with 2,000 seats. Production shows have included *Cats,* the Moscow Circus, and *Spellbound;* entertainers including Frank Sinatra, Liza Minnelli, and Randy Travis have appeared here in addition to—would you believe it?—Dr. Ruth Westheimer. (I can only imagine the floor show.) The theater has one of the biggest showroom stages in the world. An interesting sidelight is the fact that when the showroom was constructed along with the hotel in 1978, the stage was built around a large mock-up of a jet plane that was used in the original long-running musical show at the hotel. The prop is so big—and the stage area so huge—that the plane was still there years later and pops up in various shows from time to time.

An outdoor amphitheater, seating 8,500 guests, is used for the hotel's "100 Days of Summer" concert series as well as other special events.

The Reno Hilton has an attractive wedding chapel for those who feel the urge or need for nuptials. Among the most unusual ceremonies performed there was the marriage of a pair of llamas who were in town for a rather sizable convention of llama lovers. For humans, emergency wedding cakes, gowns, and suits are available at stores in the shopping arcade.

> ## Hot Tickets
>
> The mahogany ticket booth located on the Silver Legacy casino's mezzanine level—transformed into a cappuccino stand—was brought to Reno from its former location at a classic theater in Saint Louis.

Reno Hilton. 2500 East Second Street. 2,001 rooms. Room rates $69 to $179. (775) 789–2000, (800) 648–5080. www.renohilton.com.

★★★★ SILVER LEGACY RESORT CASINO

The class of downtown Reno is the Silver Legacy, which is the first Vegas-like theme-park gambling mall in northern Nevada. The project occupies 2 city blocks in downtown Reno with a skywalk linking it to its corporate partners, Circus Circus Hotel/Casino on the north and the Eldorado Hotel/Casino on the south.

The hotel's exterior facade of storefronts re-creates Reno of the 1890s and early 1900s. Three hotel towers in a Y shape add 1,720 guest rooms. One of the buildings is Reno's tallest hotel and casino tower at thirty-seven stories.

The 85,000-square-foot casino, with 2,300 slot machines and ninety table games, lies beneath a 180-foot-diameter dome. Rising from the gaming floor is a huge automated mining machine of steel and brass with a special-effects light-and-sound show including thunder and lightning; the show occurs every hour on the hour between 9:00 and 1:00 A.M. The machine appears to produce coins that cascade into a giant bucket at its base.

An expanded Legend of the Legacy Laser Show is presented several times during the day; it tells the fable of the Silver Legacy with strobes, lights, smoke, fog, and Tchaikovsky's "1812 Overture."

The whole place is supposed to be the legacy of the mythical silver baron Sam Fairchild. According to the modern myth, "Old Silver" Sam discovered a deep vein of blue quartz ore beneath what is now the Silver Legacy casino. The story goes on: He searched for a famous European engineer to design an automated mining machine. He commissioned the steam-driven mining machine now seen under the dome of the casino, constructed from gleaming steel and iodized brass and continuously in motion with ore wagons and pumping bellows.

To support the story the hotel is decorated with antique treasures including an authentic Wells Fargo stagecoach on the mezzanine level, antique cash registers, and a collection of antique model planes, trains, and automobiles.

On display at the hotel in recent years is a collection of artifacts unearthed from the Old Corner Bar at Piper's Opera House in Virginia City. A two-year project of the Comstock Archaeology Center in Nevada, the centerpiece of the collection is an ornate carbon water filter imported to Virginia City from London and used to purify water served at the Old Corner Bar. The archaeology team spent two summers in 1997 and 1998 excavating, cleaning, and cataloging an estimated 100,000 artifacts, which were buried under ash from devastating fires in 1875 and 1883. Preserved by time and soot, these remnants were carefully restored by a team of volunteers. Items on display include a wine bottle with cork and wine intact, bottled water containers from Germany, a cribbage board, ornate hygiene sets from the Opera House's dressing room, and spittoons and vases.

The signature restaurant is **Sterling's Seafood Steakhouse,** where a recent menu featured spicy roast chicken for about $15, red-pepper linguine for $10.00, and medallions of filet mignon for $21.00.

In addition to a fresh shellfish bar, **Fairchild's Oyster Bar** offers seafood pan roasts based on crab, scallops, oysters, or shrimp priced from about $15.00 to $25.00. The **Sweetwater Cafe** twenty-four-hour coffee shop has Chinese and American specialties, with entrees from about $6.00 to $12.00.

The **Victorian Buffet** is an attractive, open room with a view of the upper level of the mining works and good-quality but uninspired food.

A Harley-Davidson/Buell retail store, an extension of a Reno motorcycle dealership, opened in 2006.

Silver Legacy Resort Casino. 407 North Virginia Street. 1,720 rooms. Room rates $40 to $150. (775) 325–7401, (800) 687–8733. www.silverlegacy.com.

★★★★ ATLANTIS CASINO RESORT

In the 1980s there was only a small motel on the corner. Today the motel is still there, all but surrounded by one of Reno's largest and liveliest casinos, a place that seems to be constantly expanding.

Recent expansions include a twenty-seven-story tower with Jacuzzi suites. There's also a full-service health club with indoor and outdoor pools, and the city's only concierge tower. Expansion projects have changed the shape and configuration of the property every few years, including the Sky Terrace, a glass walkway across South Virginia Street from the casino to the parking lot across the street.

The casino floor has a tropics theme with a waterfall and lots of greenery. Among the more attractive casinos in town, it's popular with locals who come for gambling and dining.

Monte Vigna Italian Ristorante offers fresh pasta, wood-fired Tuscan-style meats, and a 4,000-bottle wine cellar. Specialties include *ravioli di vitello,* Tuscany-style ravioli stuffed with veal and simmered in marinara sauce; cioppino; and *anatra al balsamico,* slow-roasted Sonoma duck in a balsamic peppercorn sauce. Open for dinner only; for reservations call (775) 825–4700.

The **Atlantis Seafood Steakhouse** includes a 1,100-gallon saltwater aquarium for decoration and a menu with specialties including veal scallopini, seafood pan roast, porterhouse steaks, and a "duet" of any two surf or turf items on the menu.

Café Alfresco serves wood-fired pizza, pasta, salads, soups, and fresh-baked garlic breadsticks for lunch and dinner.

Toucan Charlie's Buffet and Grille is open for breakfast, lunch, dinner, and an elegant Sunday champagne brunch. On the Sky Terrace spanning South Virginia Street, the **Oyster Bar** and the **Sushi Bar** serve their namesake delicacies. Oyster Bar items, priced from about $5.00 to $24.00, include oysters, lobster, and pan roasts.

Atlantis Casino Resort. 3800 South Virginia Street. 1,000 rooms. Room rates $59 to $199. (775) 825–4700, (800) 723–6500. www.atlantiscasino.com.

★★ CIRCUS CIRCUS HOTEL/CASINO

Yowzah, yowzah! It's Circus Circus, a smaller cousin of the Las Vegas original, but definitely a Reno must-see.

With 1,572 rooms, Circus Circus lost its title as downtown Reno's largest resort with the opening of the Silver Legacy next door. But in typical Nevada fashion, its owners have it their way anyhow: Circus Circus is partners with the Eldorado in ownership of the Silver Legacy and is connected to the flashy showplace by a second-floor walkway. And the place has been spiffed up a bit in recognition of its tony neighbor.

In any case Circus Circus Reno is indisputably the world's second-largest hotel and casino with a circus and midway, a few notches behind Circus Circus in Las Vegas. It's a lively low-roller haven that draws a lot of families to its mix of slots, video games, circus acts, and blackjack tables.

In recent years the hotel's cheesy pink exterior was redone in whites with cheesy gold and green trim. Inside, the public areas have been upgraded a bit with an early 1900s European circus theme. Circus acts—including high-wire bicyclists, aerialists, gymnasts, and clowns—start at about 11:15 A.M. and continue until nearly midnight. The circus acts are introduced by a ringmaster and sometimes accompanied by a somewhat bored two-piece band. Each act is about eight to ten minutes long—the management doesn't want people to stay away from the tables too long. The performers change regularly but usually include trapeze artists, high-wire walkers, teeterboard acts, unicycle and trick bicycle performers, jugglers, and clown acts.

The midway is a lure for children of all ages, offering coin toss, ring toss, a shooting gallery, a video arcade, face painting, and other such carnival entertainment. Concession stands offer food, drinks, and balloons. Check out the shooting gallery that uses beams of light from the rifles; it's much better than your average mechanical ducks. I especially like the poor little canary atop the piano who will dance for you; hit the piano player in the behind and he'll provide the music.

And, of course, there is a casino, which is a pretty lively place at all hours. As you might expect, there seem to be a few families with the youngsters dispatched upstairs to the circus and carnival while mom and dad are downstairs gambling the dinner money.

The circus performers, according to the hotel, constitute a minor league for the major shows including Ringling Brothers and Barnum & Bailey Circus, the Moscow Circus, the Romanian State Circus, and other troupes.

The **Steakhouse at Circus** features all the usual steak house fare including charbroiled steak, prime rib, chicken dishes, and seafood selections. It is open Friday through Tuesday.

The pizza joint is **Bonici Brothers,** with an open kitchen for pies, sandwiches, wings, and salads. Pitchers of beer and margaritas are available from the popular **Gecko's Bar.** Inside Gecko's, **Kokopelli's Sushi** serves seafood delicacies including nigiri, long rolls, and hand rolls as well as signature Kokopelli's rolls for lunch and dinner.

The **Courtyard Buffet** is an improvement over the former chowline that was served beneath a red and white striped circus big top. The buffet includes an omelet station and a Chinese exhibition kitchen.

Circus Circus Hotel/Casino. 500 North Sierra Street. 1,572 rooms. Room rates $40 to $129. (775) 329–0711, (800) 648–5010. www.circusreno.com.

★★ SIENA HOTEL SPA & CASINO

Another bit of Tuscany arrived in downtown in 2001 with the opening of the upscale Siena Hotel. Decked out in Mediterranean decor and colors, the lower level features restaurants and bars overlooking the Truckee River, including an outdoor terrace. The hotel is a remaking of the former Holiday Hotel Casino that stood on the same site for decades. It's an attractive, modern design with brick and stone walls outside and a cathedral-like interior—a bit monastic for a casino and very empty on a midweek afternoon.

The showplace restaurant at the hotel is **Enoteca,** a wine bar and lounge serving more than 200 fine wines by the glass with a special appetizer menu that includes more than a hundred European cheeses to complement an 18,000-bottle wine cellar. Wednesdays feature memorable Food & Wine Pairings, teaming gourmet appetizers with splendid wines, while Liquid Lessons, the Wine Book You Drink, are available Tuesday through Saturday from 4:30 P.M. on.

Lexie's on the River, a contemporary Italian restaurant and bar, overlooks the Truckee River. The menu includes seasonal seafood and beef dishes such as Black Angus steak topped with cremini mushrooms, mustard herb-crusted salmon with pinot grigio buerre blanc, and sautéed garlic shrimp with a light parmigiano reggiano sauce.

Contrada Café is a twenty-four-hour coffee shop with an open kitchen displaying preparation of rotisserie meats and poultry, homemade sausage, daily fresh-baked breads, and desserts. In the summer there's a barbecue spare rib, chicken, or beef brisket special.

Siena Hotel Spa & Casino. 1 South Lake Street. 214 rooms. Room rates $89 to $149. (775) 337–6260, 877-SIENA-33. www.sienareno.com.

★ SANDS REGENCY HOTEL/CASINO

An older hotel casino a few blocks off Virginia Street, the Sands is a strange jumble of slot machines, gaming tables, hotel desks, and donut counters.

The matriarch of the founding Cladianos family is honored with **Antonia's Italian Buffet.** There's a branch of the **Tony Roma's** chain, offering ribs for about $8.00 to $14.00 and boneless chicken. Appetizers include potato skins and chicken wings. Special offers include a ribs-and–barbecued-chicken combo and an all-you-can-eat Cajun or Carolina honey ribs dinner served Tuesday nights. **Mel's** is a twenty-four-hour coffee shop.

Sands Regency Hotel/Casino. 345 North Arlington Avenue. 1,000 rooms. Room rates $29 to $179. (775) 348–2200, (800) 648–3553. www.sandsregency .com.

OTHER HOTELS AND CASINOS IN RENO

CLUB CAL–NEVA VIRGINIAN CASINO

Earplugs are optional at this adult playroom, which brings together two of Reno's older gambling spots. Some of the slots are built into not-all-that-realistic mock-ups of trains and Western buildings. There's a somewhat interesting collection of old railway signs scattered about.

A recent addition is **Muy Sabroso,** a Mexican restaurant on the mezzanine open for lunch and dinner and serving *muy sabroso* (very tasty) fajitas, burritos, and specialty margaritas.

The **Copper Ledge Restaurant** is a more casual steak-and-seafood place. There's also the **Top Deck** coffee shop, featuring a twenty-four-hour prime rib special at $4.95 or ham and eggs for 99 cents.

Club Cal-Neva Virginian Casino. East Second and North Virginia Streets. 422 rooms. Room rates $29 to $89. (775) 323–1046. (877) 777–7303. www.clubcal neva.com.

FITZGERALDS CASINO-HOTEL

The wearing of the green can become a bit wearing in this little piece of Ireland in Reno. The mirrored ceilings add to the visual overload.

But for a touch of the blarney, if not the bizarre, be sure to visit the Lucky Forest on the second floor. There has got to be something here that will improve your luck at the tables: four-leaf clovers, rabbits' feet, a horseshoe from Triple Crown winner Secretariat, a wishing well made of stones from Blarney Castle, a lucky waterfall, Asian gods—all your basic good-luck charms in one place.

Fitzgeralds, located in the heart of downtown in the shadow of the Virginia Street arch, is named after Lincoln Fitzgerald, another of the early casino developers of Reno.

Limericks Pub & Grille celebrates Ireland with hand-painted wall murals of the Irish countryside. The menu features a decent collection of imported beers and ales. Specialties include roasted lamb shank, Killarney chicken breast, and steaks and ribs. **Molly's Garden** on the second floor of the casino is a casual all-day diner; specialties include potato leek soup in a bread bowl and "killer" burgers. On the third floor is **Lord Fitzgeralds Feast and Merriment,** the casino's buffet.

Fitzgeralds Casino-Hotel. 255 North Virginia Street. 351 rooms. Room rates $28 to $100. (775) 785–3300. www.fitzgeraldsreno.com.

STILL MORE RENO CASINOS, HOTELS, AND MOTELS

You'll find motels from most of the major chains in and around downtown Reno, including Best Western, Econolodge, Holiday Inn, LaQuinta, Motel 6, Residence Inn, Rodeway Inn, and Travelodge. Among prime locations are South Virginia Street and near the airport.

Consult Web sites for the individual chains, or use a travel gateway such as:

- www.expedia.com
- www.orbitz.com
- www.travelocity.com

ABOUT SPARKS

Sparks was Nevada's "Instant City," going from zero to 1,500 residents in 1904 when it was created out of swampland by the Southern Pacific Railroad.

The Golden Spike that united the westward and eastward tracks across the continent had been driven in 1870. Just thirty years later railroad engineers decided to straighten out some of the railroad lines in northern Nevada to eliminate treacherous curves and steep grades. As part of that effort, the Southern Pacific decided to abandon its former division point in Wadsworth near Pyramid Lake and move its operations south about 30 miles to a new site in the Truckee Meadows.

The previous owner of the railroad, the Central Pacific, had bypassed the area below Reno because of the swamplands. But the Southern Pacific decided to make its own dry land; it used its trains to haul in thousands of carloads of rock and dirt for four years to build a base for track and a huge roundhouse that could hold forty-one engines.

The summer of 1904 saw the massive migration of workers, families, houses, and belongings from Wadsworth to the new town; all of the railroad equipment was also moved. By the fall Wadsworth was all but empty and the new town—complete with a library, hotel, store, and boarding houses—was open for business.

In 1905 the settlement was officially named the city of Sparks in honor of Governor John Sparks. In 1907 Sparks became the home of the Mallet, the largest steam engine ever built; it was used to haul long trains over the Sierra Nevada into the Sacramento Valley of California.

Until deep into the twentieth century, Sparks was a railroad company town. The old roundhouse and most of the other trappings of the railroad are gone, but the history of Sparks lives on in Victorian Square downtown, a restored early-twentieth-century center.

History and railroad buffs should make a stop at the **Sparks Heritage Foundation & Museum,** located at 820 Victorian Avenue in Victorian Square. The two unpretentious, connected buildings include a fascinating but helter-skelter collection of railroad and community memorabilia. How about a mechanical device from about 1900 used to punch initials in hat bands to help owners keep track of their chapeaus?

You'll find a complete turn-of-the-twentieth-century barber shop, railroad uniforms and equipment, and household furnishings. There is also a collection of very old front pages—would you believe a New York paper's report of the death of George Washington on January 4, 1800?

A section of the museum features some of the fixtures from the Perry's Grocery Store as they appeared in 1918. In the back room is a collection of items from an old railroad station master's office, including a telegraph key. One of the photos on the wall shows an incredible snow scene on Donner Summit with a Central Pacific Railroad locomotive up against a wall of snow in 1889.

The free museum is open from 11:00 A.M. to 4:00 P.M. Tuesday to Friday and from 1:00 to 4:00 P.M. on Saturday. Closed Sunday and Monday; call (775) 355–1144 for information.

Across the square from the museum is the Sparks Visitor Center set within a replica of the original Southern Pacific Depot in Sparks. Pulled up at the station is a 1907 Southern Pacific ten-wheeler Baldwin Steam Locomotive, which had been used in and around Reno on branch lines. You can walk into the driver's compartment, an old-style affair where the engineer had to lean out the side of the cab to the left or the right to see around the big boiler.

Next in line is a Houston Club Car, constructed by the Pullman Company in 1911 and converted to an executive car in 1929 for the private use of a division superintendent of the Southern Pacific; it includes a parlor, several bedrooms, and a small kitchen. The end of the small train is a period caboose, complete with a cupola for observation and a stove for cooking.

The Sparks Tourist Information Office near the railroad museum is open Monday through Friday from 8:00 A.M. to 5:00 P.M.

The revival of the 8-block Victorian Square area includes a fourteen-screen, 3,200-seat theater complex and a 702-space parking garage.

The **Wild Island** entertainment complex is open daily from May to October and includes a water park with water slides, a tide pool, and rafting. A recent addition was a recreation center including the sixteen-lane Coconut Bowl alley, a billiards area, a children's play zone with slides and tunnels, and the **Water Dogs** snack bar. Call (775) 359–2927 or consult www.wildisland.com for information. Tickets in early 2006 were $22.95 for visitors 48 inches and taller and $17.99 for those beneath the barrier.

Sparks is home to the **Sparks Indian Rodeo** in September.

A valued addition to Sparks is a microbrewery and restaurant known as the

Great Basin Brewing Co., located on Victorian Square. The pleasant little pub, home to jazz and other music from time to time, offers a range of beers including Nevada Hold, Wild Horse Ale, Ichthyosaur Pale Ale, and Jackpot Porter. There are also seasonal brews that in the past have included Kringle Cranberry, Outlaw Oatmeal Stout, McClary's Irish Red, Chilebeso Jalapeño Ale, and Ruby Mountain Red. You can buy them by the pint or get a row of four-ounce samplers to try them all. The pub also offers burgers, sausages, sandwiches, and other nibbling food. For information call (775) 355–7711 or consult www.greatbasin brewingco.com.

SPARKS'S HOTEL-CASINO

★★★★ JOHN ASCUAGA'S NUGGET

By now you should have guessed that my favorite hotels and casinos are those with a bit of quirkiness and individuality. By those criteria John Ascuaga's Nugget qualifies as a must-see in the Reno Valley.

The large hotel and casino complex definitely caters to large bus tours, but it is certainly a step up from most of the downtown houses. A major addition to the casino was completed in 1997 with a second tower that added 802 rooms and a new restaurant. The hotel's large parking garage is among the more attractive homes for autos I have visited and includes a huge video arcade at its skywalk entrance to the hotel.

The dear departed Liberace used to make his stage entrance at the Nugget riding on the back of Bertha the elephant; the animal made her own stage debut, appearing on *The Steve Allen Show* in 1963 and *Hollywood Palace*. Bertha, alas, died in 1999, and her coworker Angel was packed off to a zoo.

Then there is the Golden Rooster, which may be the only member of its species ever to serve time in a federal lockup. The story is this: In 1958 the Nugget was preparing to open a new restaurant called the Golden Rooster, and it was decided the place would be decorated with an unusual work of art—a solid gold statue of a rooster.

Seven months after it went on display inside a fortified glass case, officials of the U.S. Treasury Department charged the Nugget with violation of the Gold Reserve Act, which made it unlawful for a private individual to possess more than fifty ounces of gold. Legal skirmishes continued until 1960 when the hotel was formally presented with a complaint titled "United States of America vs. One Solid Gold Object in the Form of a Rooster." The statue was confiscated; the Nugget's offer to put up bail was denied.

Two years of captivity for the golden bird followed until a jury trial was held in 1962; the government was unable to counter the arguments of the Nugget and art critics that the statue was a work of art, so the rooster was sprung and returned to its perch at the restaurant. In 1987 the Golden Rooster Room closed, but the bird was given a new place of honor behind the registration desk. The 18-karat solid gold statue weighs 206.3 troy ounces (14.1 pounds).

Also within the casino are the gold scales used at the U.S. Mint in Carson City from about 1875 until it closed in 1893. Millions in gold and silver crossed its plates; it is claimed that the scale is accurate enough to weigh a postage stamp.

An interesting eatery is **Restaurante Orozko,** named for the Pyrenees mountain hamlet in northern Spain where the Ascuaga family originated. Specialties include Basque dishes, paella, mesquite-broiled steaks, pasta, and pizza. The **Rotisserie Buffet** has a vaguely French flavor and a glassed-in chicken rotisserie near the entryway.

Trader Dick's, a dark, lush tropical garden setting with palm fronds and grass thatching, sits just off the main casino floor and serves South Sea and Polynesian lunches Monday through Friday and dinner every night. A prix fixe dinner is available for $22.00 to $27.50; specialties range from about $13.00 to $25.00. At the center of the room is a large Chinese smoke oven used to prepare spareribs, chicken, and pork menu items.

The Steak House Grill serves steaks—lots of them. A sign outside its entrance tracks steaks served since 1956. In 2007 the counter was approaching the four-million marker. Steak, seafood, and Italian entrees are priced from $20 to $30.

Rosie's Cafe is a twenty-four-hour cafe offering American family-kitchen menus, with weekly specials priced at $5.95. **Gabe's Pub & Deli,** located near the race and sports book, serves a quick deli menu. The **Noodle Hut,** near Trader Dick's, dispenses quick Asian dishes including won ton soup and pad thai as well as Italian pasta dishes.

Nearby is **John's Oyster Bar,** which carries a bit of a nautical theme that includes a ship's mast and yardarm overhead. Specialties include Lobster Surprise Salad (topped with a remoulade sauce of mayonnaise, mustard, gherkins, chervil, tarragon, and capers with a touch of chablis).

John Ascuaga's Nugget. 1100 Nugget Avenue. 1,500 rooms. Room rates $79 to $135. (775) 356–3300, (800) 648–1177. www.janugget.com.

SMALLER CASINOS IN SPARKS

A smaller, unusual joint worth checking out is **Baldini's Sports Casino.** This is not a place for the claustrophobic; in fact it feels as if you have descended directly into the innards of a slot machine.

Baldini's is located at 865 South Rock Boulevard. (775) 358–0116. www .baldinissportscasino.com.

The **Silver Club Hotel & Casino** is an attractive, high-ceilinged place, quieter and smaller than the Nugget but with some amenities of its own. **The Town Square Restaurant,** which is open 24 hours, offers late-night specials and all-day steak and eggs. **Victoria's Steak Buffet** is available Thursday through Sunday nights.

The Silver Club is located at 1040 Victorian Avenue. (775) 358–4771 or (800) 905–7774. www.silverclub.com.

TRANSPORTATION

Reno and Sparks are served by a local bus system, RTC/Citifare, as well as private minibuses to the airport plus shuttles and buses to Lake Tahoe and Mammoth Lakes.

■ BUS SERVICE

Airport Mini Bus. Airport, Reno, and Tahoe. (775) 786–3700.
Greyhound Lines West. Reno. (775) 322–2970, (800) 231–2222. www.grey hound.com.
Mammoth Shuttle. Serving Mammoth Lakes. (760) 934–3030.
RTC/Citifare. For information on bus service, call (775) 348–7433. www.citi fare.com.

■ LIMO AND PRIVATE CAR SERVICES

Bell Luxury Limousine. Reno and Tahoe. (775) 786–3700.
Executive Limousine. (775) 333–3300.
Sierra West Limousine. (775) 329–4310.
Squaw Creek Transportation. (800) 327–3353.

■ CAR RENTALS IN RENO

Advantage Rent A Car. (800) 777–5500. www.arac.com.
Alamo Rent A Car. (775) 323–8306, (800) 327–9633. www.goalamo.com.
Avis Rent A Car. (775) 785–2727, (800) 331–1212. www.avis.com.
Budget Car & Truck Rental. (775) 785–2690, (800) 527–0700. www.budget .com.
Enterprise Rent-a-Car. (800) 736–8222. www.enterprise.com.
Hertz Rent A Car. (775) 785–2554, (800) 654–3131. www.hertz.com.
National Car Rental. (775) 785–2756, (800) 227–7368. www.nationalcar.com.
Thrifty Car Rental. (775) 329–0096, (800) 873–0377. www.thrifty.com.

■ RENO/TAHOE INTERNATIONAL AIRPORT

www.renoairport.com.
Alaska Airlines. (800) 426–0333. www.alaska-air.com.
Aloha Airlines. (800) 367–5250. www.alohaairlines.com.
American Airlines. (800) 433–7300. www.aa.com.
Continental Airlines. (800) 525–0280. www.continental.com.
Delta. (800) 221–1212. www.delta.com.
Frontier Airlines. (800) 432–1359. www.flyfrontier.com.
Horizon Air. (800) 547–9308. www.horizonair.com.
Skywest (Delta Connection). (800) 439–9417. www.skywest.com
Southwest Airlines. (800) 435–9792. www.southwest.com.
United Airlines. (800) 241–6522. www.united.com.
U.S. Airways/America West. (800) 428–4322. www.usairways.com.

CHAPTER EIGHTEEN

EATING YOUR WAY THROUGH RENO-SPARKS

Econoguide Best Casino Buffets in Reno-Sparks

- ★★★★★ **Toucan Charlie's.** *Atlantis*
- ★★★★ **Chefs' Buffet.** *Eldorado*
- ★★★★ **Carvings Buffet.** *Harrah's Reno*
- ★★★★ **Island Buffet.** *Peppermill*
- ★★★★ **Rotisserie Buffet.** *John Ascuaga's Nugget*
- ★★★★ **Victorian Buffet.** *Silver Legacy*

Econoguide Best Casino Restaurants in Reno-Sparks

- ★★★★ **Andreotti.** *Harrah's Reno*
- ★★★★ **Harrah's Steak House.** *Harrah's Reno*
- ★★★★ **Restaurante Orozko.** *John Ascuaga's Nugget*
- ★★★★ **Peppermill Steak House.** *Peppermill*
- ★★★★ **La Strada.** *Eldorado*

RENO-SPARKS BUFFETS

Atlantis. ★★★★★ *Toucan Charlie's.* Eight specialty stations, including wood-fired meats, Mongolian barbecue grill, Chinese wok, and Asian exhibition kitchen. Prices range from $8.99 for weekday breakfast to $25.99 for Friday night dinner. (775) 824–4433. www.atlantiscasino.com.

Bonanza. *Branding Iron Cafe.* Lunch, dinner daily. Saturday and Sunday brunch. Seafood buffet Friday and Saturday nights. Prices range from $6.95 to $12.95. (775) 323–2724. www.bonanzacasino.com.

Boomtown. *Silver Screen Buffet.* Entrees and an especially ambitious dessert counter. Weekday breakfast, weekend brunches, daily lunch, and international dinner buffets, with a lobster special on Sunday. Prices range from about $6.99 to $11.99 during the week, higher on weekends, including lobster, steak, and seafood buffets on Friday, Saturday, and Sunday for about $20.00. (775) 345–6000. www.boomtownreno.com.

Circus Circus. *Courtyard Buffet.* Includes Chinese exhibition kitchen and omelet station. Breakfast, lunch, dinner, weekend brunch. Prices range from about $5.49 to $12.99. (775) 329–0711. www.circusreno.com.

Eldorado. ★★★★ *Chefs' Buffet.* Among the best in town. Breakfast, lunch, dinner. Friday seafood buffet. Saturday steak, shrimp, and crab brunch. Sunday champagne brunch. Prices range from $7.99 to $18.99. (775) 786–5700. www.eldoradoreno.com/dining.

Fitzgeralds. *Lord Fitzgeralds Feast and Merriment.* Breakfast, lunch, dinner. Prices range from about $6.00 to $10.00. (775) 785–3300. www.fitzgeraldsreno.com.

Harrah's Reno. ★★★★ *Carvings Buffet.* Weekday brunch and dinner, weekend brunch, and Friday and Saturday steak and seafood dinner. Prices range from $10.99 to $18.99. (775) 786–3232. www.harrahs.com/our_casinos/ren/dining.

John Ascuaga's Nugget ★★★★ *Rotisserie Buffet.* Among the best. Lunch Monday through Saturday, dinner daily, Sunday brunch. Prices range from about $7.50 to $16.95. (775) 356–3300. www.janugget.com.

Peppermill. ★★★★ *Island Buffet.* Attractive setting and tempting fare. Breakfast, lunch, dinner, Saturday and Sunday brunch, Friday seafood dinner. Prices range from $8.99 to $26.99. (775) 826–2121. www.peppermillreno.com/restaurants/restaurants.html.

Sands Regency. *Antonia's Italian Buffet.* Open for dinner Wednesday to Sunday and breakfast on weekends, with prices ranging from $8.99 to $11.99. (775) 348–2200. www.sandsregency.com.

Silver Legacy. ★★★★ *Victorian Buffet.* Attractive and lively. Breakfast, lunch, and prime rib dinner Sunday through Friday. Friday seafood dinner buffet, international Saturday dinner, Sunday brunch. Prices range from about $10 to $15. (775) 329–4777. www.silverlegacyreno.com.

RENO'S BEST NON-CASINO RESTAURANTS

(Be sure to also see restaurant descriptions in the hotel listings in chapter 17.)

■ AMERICAN, BARBECUE, AND STEAK HOUSES

Adele's Restaurant. 1112 North Carson, Carson City. A local gourmet tradition. Lunch and dinner. Reservations suggested. (775) 882–3353.

Famous Murphy's Restaurant Grill and Oyster Bar. 3127 South Virginia

Street. The Grill serves sandwiches, burgers, salads, scampi, pan roasts, pasta, steamers, oysters, chowder, hot rocks, and more for lunch and dinner. The dining room serves steak, pasta, chicken, and seafood specialties. Lunch and dinner daily. Reservations suggested. (775) 827–4111. www.famousmurphys.com.

Jeremiah's Steakhouse. 880 East Plumb Lane. A local favorite for a quarter of a century, specializing in your basic steak house fare: beef, poultry, seafood, pasta, and a large salad bar. (775) 827–2080.

P.J. & Co. Restaurant and Saloon. 1590 South Wells Avenue. A local hangout for huevos rancheros, fajitas, burgers, and other hearty fare. (775) 323–6366.

Silver Peak Restaurant and Brewery. 124 Wonder Street. Pizza, beer, seafood, beer, chops, and beer. South of downtown. (775) 324–1864. www.silverpeak brewery.com.

■ ASIAN

Bangkok Cuisine. 55 Mount Rose Street. A wide range of Thai fare for lunch and dinner. (775) 322–0299.

Café de Thai. 3314 South McCarran and Mira Loma. (775) 829–8424.

Dynasty China Bistro. 1185 California Avenue. Mandarin, Szechuan, and Cantonese Chinese fare and some Thai specialties. (775) 786–5768.

Ichiban Japanese Steak House. 210 North Sierra Street. Teppanyaki cooking in a garden setting; Chopstix Restaurant at same location offers Japanese, Chinese, and Korean fare. Lunch weekdays, dinner nightly. (775) 323–5550.

King Buffet. 3650 Kietzke Lane. A king-size Chinese buffet. (775) 828–7978.

Soochow Chinese Restaurant. 656 East Prater Way, Sparks. A highly rated local favorite. (775) 359–3344.

■ CONTINENTAL/FRENCH

The Crown Point. Main Street (Highway 342), Gold Hill. Built in 1859 within the Gold Hill Hotel. The stone structure is Nevada's oldest hotel. Lavish accommodations with period antiques. (775) 847–0111. www.goldhillhotel.net/rest.htm.

■ GERMAN

Bavarian World. 595 Valley Road at East Sixth Street. Pork roast, sauerbraten, Alpine cuisine from schnitzel to schweinebraten, and famous rye bread. Open daily for breakfast, lunch, *und* dinner. (775) 323–7646.

■ ITALIAN

Casale's Half-Way Club. 2501 East Fourth Street. A local favorite for more than sixty years, much better within than it appears from outside. (775) 323–3979.

La Vecchia. 3501 South Virginia Street. Northern Italian chefs prepare traditional favorites plus house specials like duck salad with radicchio and white truffle salad. (775) 825–1113.

Viaggio Italian Cuisine. 2309 Kietzke Lane. Family-style favorites and a huge selection of wine. (775) 828–2708. www.viaggio.net.

■ MEXICAN

Buenos Grill. 3892 Mayberry Drive. Tacos and other specialties; in the Mayberry Landing shopping center. (775) 787–8226.

La Fuente Mexican Restaurant. 790 Baring Boulevard, Sparks. Authentic and unusual Mexican fare including *parrilladas, tamiquena, quezo fundido, lomo relleno,* and more-familiar dishes. (775) 331–1483.

■ NATURAL AND VEGETARIAN FOOD

Anthony's Dandelion Deli. 1170 South Wells Avenue. Natural food, vegetarian, and gourmet specialties for lunch. (775) 322–6100.

Meadowood Wild Oats Marketplace. 5695 South Virginia Street. (775) 829–8666. www.wildoats.com.

■ SOUTHWESTERN

Café Soleil. 4796 Caughlin Parkway. Contemporary American food. (775) 827–3111.

THE BASQUE INFLUENCE

The Basques, an adventuresome people with origins in the Pyrenees mountains of France and Spain, came to Nevada in a circuitous route that began with migration to Argentina, where they worked as shepherds. Many thousands, lured by the California gold rush, moved north in the 1850s, and some then came over the Sierra Nevada eastward to work in the mines of the Comstock and elsewhere in Nevada.

There are still remnants of the once-thriving Basque culture in and around Reno, including festivals and restaurants. Most Basque eateries are decidedly informal, serving dishes family-style. You will likely be served at a large table with strangers in a boisterous atmosphere. Basque restaurants are not the place for a romantic getaway, but they are a lot of fun and offer a lot of food for a reasonable price—usually in the range of $10 to $20 for a complete dinner.

A local favorite is the **Santa Fe Basque Restaurant** in the Santa Fe Hotel, at 235 Lake Street, next to Harrah's. The restaurant, closed for several years, reopened in early 2000, although the hotel's future is uncertain. Open daily except Monday. (775) 323–1891.

Louis' Basque Corner, at 301 East Fourth Street, features Basque cuisine such as *tripas callos,* chicken, oxtails, shrimp, and *tonque à la basquaise,* paella, *lapin chasseur* (hunter's rabbit), and *veau panne* (breaded veal) served family-style. A local institution; the quality of the food is sometimes inconsistent. Lunch Tuesday through Saturday from 11:30 A.M. to 2:30 P.M. Dinner nightly from 5:00 to 9:30 P.M. (775) 323–7203.

A high-tone Basque eatery is **Restaurante Orozko** within John Ascuaga's Nugget, at 1100 Nugget Avenue in Sparks. (775) 356–3300. www.janugget.com/restaurants/orozko.cfm.

CHAPTER NINETEEN

RENO-SPARKS AREA ATTRACTIONS

LIKE LAS VEGAS, Reno is a lot more than casinos, showrooms, and restaurants. Here is a listing of the more interesting museums and entertainment areas, as well as sports and outdoor activities.

Be sure to also check listings in this book for Carson City, Virginia City, and Lake Tahoe. Information about ski areas at Mount Rose, Incline Village, South Lake Tahoe, and North Lake Tahoe, as well as other winter sports including sledding, skating, and snowmobiling, can be found in the section about Lake Tahoe.

NATIONAL BOWLING STADIUM

The National Bowling Stadium is the visual counterpoint to the dome on the Silver Legacy in downtown Reno; instead of the beeps and whirls of slot machines and the cheers and groans of the craps tables, beneath the stadium's silver dome is the rumble and crash of a whole lot of bowling.

This is one heck of an alley: a high-tech palace of pins with seventy-eight tournament-level lanes.

The American Bowling Congress (ABC) championship is due to return to Reno in 2007 and again in 2010, drawing some 80,000 participants over a six-month period in the first half of the year. The Women's International Bowling Congress (WIBC) is scheduled for 2009, drawing another 85,000 or so keglers to town.

The stadium offers permanent seating capacity for 1,200. The video scoring system at the stadium includes the longest rear-projection, high-definition video display in the world, measuring 450 feet in length. The Bowlervision II scoring system in the spectator section does more than keep score; visitors can order drinks and food from the monitor.

The bowling lanes are not available for public use; they are reserved for tournaments. Admission is free to many tourneys, but some events may sell tickets.

National Bowling Stadium

The stadium has been used in several movies, most notably in 1997 for the final scenes of the bowling comedy *Kingpin*, starring Woody Harrelson, Bill Murray, and Randy Quaid.

The stadium pro shop includes a fully functioning bowling lane so that shoppers can try out equipment before they buy. An instant-replay video system allows you to watch yourself in action with new equipment.

The focal point of the stadium is its giant silver ball, decorated on the outside with 15,000 feet of fiber-optic lights that wash it with color at night. Within the ball is a 177-seat movie theater with an Iwerks 70mm projection system and a 12-foot-wide by 31-foot-tall wraparound screen. Kicks, a dance club with a small restaurant, is also located within.

For information about the bowling mecca, consult www.renolaketahoe.com/bowl.

MUSEUMS

◼ WILBUR MAY CENTER

Located in Washoe County's Rancho San Rafael Park, 1502 Washington Street in Reno, this is a museum, arboretum, botanical garden, and a fabulous assortment of animal trophies and other items from the personal collection of Wilbur May, the son of the founder of the department store chain that bears his name. May was a traveler of great renown in the 1920s and 1930s, making some forty trips around the world.

The Living Room section of the museum includes some of May's own paintings, collections, and a recording of May's greatest hit, "Pass a Piece of Pizza Please," a song he wrote together with comic Jerry Colona. Artifacts he collected include an elephant's ear, a shrunken head, and other trophies. An indoor arboretum includes a three-story waterfall and a hands-on science room dubbed the Sensorium.

Admission and operating hours vary with the changing exhibits. Call (775) 785–5961 for information about the museum and (775) 785–4153 for arboretum schedules, or consult www.maycenter.com.

Next door to the May Museum is the **Great Basin Adventure** theme park designed for children ages two to twelve. Included are mining exhibits, gold panning, a petting zoo, a dinosaur park, and more. Open weekends from Memorial Day to the end of the school year from 10:00 A.M. to 5:00 P.M. on Saturday and noon to 5:00 P.M. on Sunday. Open daily except Monday in summer through Labor Day from 10:00 A.M. to 5:00 P.M., Sunday from noon to 5:00 P.M. Admission: adults $5.00, seniors and children (three to twelve) $3.50; combination tickets with the May Museum or special exhibits are as much at $10.00. For information call (775) 785–4319 or consult www.maycenter.com.

■ NEVADA MUSEUM OF ART

An eclectic collection of modern and fine art, the museum reopened in mid-2003 with impressive new facilities at 160 West Liberty Street. The design of the new museum is inspired by the stark Black Rock Desert of Nevada.

The collection of the E. L. Wiegand Gallery focuses on the art of the Great Basin region and nineteenth- and twentieth-century American art. The new facility includes expanded exhibition space, a theater, and the Café Musée. The museum is open Tuesday through Sunday 10:00 A.M. to 5:00 P.M., and it's open late Thursday until 8:00 P.M. Admission: adults $10.00, students and seniors $8.00, children (six to twelve) $1.00. For information call (775) 329–3333 or consult www.nevadaart.org.

■ NEVADA HISTORICAL SOCIETY MUSEUM

A well-stocked and attractively presented collection of Indian artifacts, mining devices, and other elements of the Silver State's history, from prehistoric times to the Wild West to modern days. A research library includes many priceless manuscripts, records, maps, and other historical data. The small gift shop is the answer to a history buff's prayer.

Located on the University of Nevada at Reno (UNR) campus at 1650 North Virginia Street near U.S. Highway 395 on the north side of the UNR campus, just up the street from Lawlor Events Center and adjoining the Fleischmann Planetarium.

Open Monday through Saturday from 10:00 A.M. to 5:00 P.M. Admission: adults $3.00, seniors $2.00, and children (younger than eighteen) free. For information call (775) 688–1190 or consult http://dmla.clan.lib.nv.us/docs/museums/reno/his-soc.htm.

Area Codes

Nevada is split into two telephone area codes. Most of the state outside of the Las Vegas, Boulder City, and Laughlin area is in the (775) area code. Here is the split:

► (702): Las Vegas, North Las Vegas, Henderson, Boulder City, Laughlin, most of Clark County.

► (775): Reno, Sparks, Carson City, remainder of state.

The areas north, west, and south of Reno and Lake Tahoe are in California's (530) area code; farther south of South Lake Tahoe is (209) in California.

Visitor Resources

► **Reno-Sparks Convention and Visitors Authority.** 4590 South Virginia Street, Reno, NV 89502. (775) 827–7600, (775) 827–7366, (800) 367–7366. www.rscva.com.

► **Reno-Sparks Indian Colony Tribal Council.** 98 Colony Road, Reno, NV 89502. (775) 329–2936. www.rsic.org.

► **Sparks Chamber of Commerce.** 831 Victorian Avenue, Sparks, NV 89431. (775) 358–1976. www.sparkschamber.org.

► **Virginia City Chamber of Commerce.** V&T Railroad Car, C Street, Virginia City, NV 89440. (775) 847–0311. www.virginiacity-nv.com.

► **Nevada Department of Wildlife.** Box 10678, Reno, NV 89520. (775) 688–1500. www.ndow.org.

► **Pyramid Lake Fisheries.** Star Route, Sutcliffe, NV 89510. (775) 476–0500. www.pyramidlakefisheries.org.

► **Bureau of Land Management.** Box 12000, Reno, NV 89520. (775) 785–6402. www.nv.blm.gov.

■ FLEISCHMANN PLANETARIUM

Next to the Historical Society Museum on the University of Nevada at Reno campus, this is a stargazer's fantasy: a fascinating planetarium show, films, a display of meteorites, and scheduled use of telescopes. The planetarium presents a number of theme shows, including a Halloween special and coverage of planetary events that includes the passage of comets and planets.

The SkyDome 8/70 uses extralarge film and special audio effects to present spectacular movies including *Seasons* and *Africa the Serengeti*. Planetarium show admission: adults $7.00, children (younger than thirteen) and seniors (older than sixty) $5.00. For information and hours call (775) 784–4811 or consult www.planetarium.unr.nevada.edu.

The building, which features a stellar swoop of a roof, was constructed in 1963; the structure included an early experimental solar heating and cooling system.

■ W. M. KECK MUSEUM, MACKAY SCHOOL OF MINES

If a mining museum is what you're looking for, here is a fine example: an incredible collection of mineral wealth from Nevada, including gold and silver from the Comstock as well as copper, lead, and other rocks that shaped the state. The collection was originally endowed by John Mackay, one of the men who made a fabulous fortune in the early days of Virginia City.

In addition to mining equipment and samples of minerals, you can also see some of the products produced with Comstock silver. The Mackay Silver Collection includes some of the most impressive pieces created for mine owner John Mackay. As a gift for his wife, Mackay sent more than 1,000 pounds of silver to Tiffany and Company in New York, and there 200 silversmiths created 1,350 pieces. The silver was displayed at the 1878 Paris Exposition.

At the time of his death in 1902, Mackay's estate was estimated to be worth at least $30 million.

The museum is on the UNR campus, within the Mackay Mining School. Admission is free. Call the school for hours and information at (775) 784–4700 or consult www.mines.unr.edu/museum. For information about the building that houses the museum, a structure designed by the famed New York architectural firm of McKim, Mead, and White, consult www.cr.nps.gov/nr/travel/nevada/mac.htm.

■ NATIONAL AUTOMOBILE MUSEUM

A spectacular collection of just some of the more than 1,000 vintage vehicles owned by casino developer William Harrah. Most of the cars were auctioned off after Harrah's death (some were bought for the equally spectacular and quirky collection at the Imperial Palace in Las Vegas); about 200 were given to a foundation set up by his heirs. The collection is housed in an attractive modern downtown structure; the architecture of the building is reminiscent of some of the chrome boats within.

A tour begins with a twenty-minute multimedia presentation that includes some of the actual cars from the exhibit; visitors then enter the museum through a re-created antique gas station.

Located at 10 Lake Street South, at Mill Street. Open daily except Christmas, Monday through Saturday from 9:30 A.M. to 5:30 P.M. and Sunday from 10:00 A.M. to 4:00 P.M. Admission: adults $8.00, seniors $7.00, children (six to eighteen) $3.00. For information call (775) 333–9300 or consult www.automuseum.org.

AMUSEMENT PARKS

■ WILD ISLAND FAMILY ADVENTURE

The park offers a wave pool, water slides, and other wet entertainment in warm weather.

Located at 250 Wild Island Court (head north from Sparks Boulevard exit off Interstate 80). Admission to the water park in 2006 was about $23 for visitors 48 inches and taller and $18 for those beneath that height. There's an additional charge for tubes and lockers. Free for children three and younger. Open Memorial Day through Labor Day weekends. Call (775) 331–9453 for operating days. www.wildisland.com.

A thirty-six-hole miniature golf course called Adventure Golf is open year-round, weather permitting. Also at the park are three go-kart raceways, a bowling alley, a roller coaster, and the Tut's Tomb video game arcade.

PERFORMING ARTS AND THEATER GROUPS

Nevada Festival Ballet. (775) 785–7915. www.aci.net/nfb.
Nevada Opera Association. (775) 786–4046. www.nevadaopera.com.
Reno Philharmonic Association. (775) 323–6393. www.renophilharmonic.com.
Sierra Arts Foundation. (775) 329–2787. www.sierra-arts.org.
UNR Performing Arts Series. (775) 784–4444. www.unr.edu/artscalendar.

NIGHTCLUBS

Baldini's. 865 South Rock Boulevard, Sparks. (775) 358–0116.

Cantina Los Tres Hombres. 7111 South Virginia Street. (775) 852–0202. www
.cantinalth.com.

The Garage in the Reno Hilton. 2500 East Second Street. (775) 789–2000. www
.parkplace.com/hilton/reno.

Reno Live Dance Club Complex. 210 North Sienna Street. (775) 329–1952.

ZOOS AND ANIMAL PRESERVES

Animal Ark. 1265 Deer Lodge Road, Red Rock. Animal Ark is a wildlife sanctuary that shelters animals that do not have the skills to survive in the wild. Open
April 1 to October 31, with limited programs in winter. Admission: adults $6.00,
seniors $5.00, children (three to twelve) $4.00. (775) 969–3111. www.animalark
.org.

Sierra Safari Zoo. 10200 North Virginia Street, Reno. A small private zoo
about 10 miles north of Reno on US 395 at Red Rock. More than 200 animals
representing forty species. Admission: adults $6.00, children (two to twelve)
$5.00. Open 10:00 A.M. to 5:00 P.M. daily, April 1 to October 31. (775) 677–1101.
www.sierrasafarizoo.com.

CHAPTER TWENTY

THE GREAT OUTDOORS IN RENO-SPARKS

GOLF COURSES

Most Reno-area courses are open year-round or close to it; courses north and south may be closed in the winter. Call for hours and fees.

Brookside Municipal Golf Course. 700 South Rock Boulevard, Sparks. Nine holes. Public. Year-round. (775) 856–6009.

Lake Ridge Golf Course. 1200 Razorback Drive, Reno. Eighteen holes. Championship course designed by Robert Trent Jones Jr. (with consultation by Trent Jones Sr.). Public. Year-round. (775) 825–2200. www.lakeridgegolf.com.

Northgate Golf Club. 111 Clubhouse Drive, Reno. Eighteen holes. Public. Year-round except December 15 through January 31. (775) 747–7577. www.reno laketahoe.com/golf/northgate.

Rosewood Lakes. 6800 Pembroke Drive, Reno. Eighteen holes. Public. Year-round. (775) 857–2892. www.cityofreno.com/res/com_service/golf/rosewood/.

Sierra Sage Golf Course. 6355 Silver Lake Road, Reno. Public. Year-round. (775) 972–1564.

Washoe Golf Course. 2601 South Arlington Avenue, Reno. Built by the government's Works Progress Administration (WPA) in the 1930s. Eighteen holes. Public. Year-round. (775) 828–6640.

Wildcreek Golf Course. 3500 Sullivan Lane, Sparks. Eighteen holes. Public. Year-round. (775) 673–3100. www.renolaketahoe.com/golf/wildcreek.

HUNTING INFORMATION

Contact the Nevada Department of Wildlife, P.O. Box 10678, Reno, NV 89520, or call (775) 688–1500. www.ndow.org. Information is also available at most sporting goods stores.

TENNIS COURTS

City of Sparks Parks and Recreation Department. (775) 353–2376. www.ci
.sparks.nv.us/departments/parks.

Lakeridge Tennis Club. (775) 827–3300. www.ltcreno.com.

Reno Parks & Recreation Department. (775) 334–2260. www.cityofreno
.com/com_service.

Washoe County Parks Department. (775) 828–6642. www.washoecounty
parks.com/parks/pk_sea.asp.

YMCA of the Sierra. (775) 323–9622. www.ymcasierra.org.

PARKS AND RECREATION

City of Sparks Parks and Recreation. (775) 353–2376. www.ci.sparks.nv.us/
departments/parks.

Nevada State Parks Division. (775) 687–4384. www.state.nv.us/stparks.

Reno Parks & Recreation Department. (775) 334–2260. www.cityofreno
.com/com_service.

USDA Forest Service/Toiyabe National Forest. (775) 331–6441. www.fs.fed
.us/htnf.

Washoe County Parks and Recreation. (775) 828–6642. www.washoecounty
parks.com.

YMCA of the Sierra. (775) 323–9622. www.ymcasierra.org

CHAPTER TWENTY-ONE

SHOPPING AND GETTING MARRIED

SHOPPING MALLS

■ MEADOWOOD MALL

Located off South Virginia Street near the intersection with South McCarran Boulevard, past the Reno-Tahoe International Airport and the Reno-Sparks Convention Center. Open Monday through Friday from 10:00 A.M. to 9:00 P.M., Saturday 10:00 A.M. to 7:00 P.M., and Sunday 11:00 A.M. to 6:00 P.M. (775) 827–8450. www.shopmeadowood.com.

Citifare buses are available to Meadowood from downtown (Fourth and Center Streets), City Station in Sparks on C Street between Ninth and Tenth, the Atlantis Casino on Virginia Street, and the Peppermill on Virginia Street.

Meadowood Mall has more than a hundred stores, including Macy's Reno, one of the largest single department stores in the state. Other major draws include JCPenney, Sears, Ann Taylor, Express, Bath & Body Works, Body Shop, Caché, The Disney Store, Gap, Hot Topic, Sephora, and Zales.

■ PARK LANE MALL

At the southeast corner of South Virginia Street and Plumb Lane. Open weekdays from 10:00 A.M. to 8:00 P.M., Saturday from 10:00 A.M. to 7:00 P.M., and Sunday from 11:00 A.M. to 6:00 P.M. (775) 825–9452.

More than ninety stores including Gottschalk's.

■ MORE SHOPPING

In recent years malls have proliferated north, south, and west of South Virginia Street near Meadowood Mall. Here you'll find national discount stores as well as upscale shops, bookstores including Barnes & Noble and Borders, and small restaurants.

SHOPPING IN SOUTH LAKE TAHOE AND STATELINE

A few miles over the border into California is a stretch of factory outlet stores offering clothing, accessories, and household items.

■ FACTORY STORES AT THE Y

Intersection of Highways 50 and 89, South Lake Tahoe (at the point where Highway 50 continues on toward the California coast and Highway 89 heads up along the western shore of Lake Tahoe). The California number is (530) 541–8314. Stores include Bass Shoes, Geoffrey Beene, Great Outdoor Clothing Outlet, Home Again, Izod, Sierra Shirts, and Van Heusen.

■ MIKASA FACTORY STORE

2011 Lake Tahoe Boulevard, South Lake Tahoe. (916) 541–7412.

■ ONEIDA FACTORY STORE

2016 Lake Tahoe Boulevard, South Lake Tahoe. (916) 541–0826.

SHOPPING IN TRUCKEE

Tahoe-Truckee Factory Stores. Interstate 80 to 12047 Donner Pass Road. Bass Shoes, Big Dogs, Dansk, Geoffrey Beane, Home Again, Izod, L'egg's/Hanes/Bali, Van Heusen. www.tahoetruckeefactorystores.com.

GETTING HITCHED RENO-STYLE

Marriage licenses are issued to males and females eighteen or older. Both must appear before the County Clerk. The marriage license fee is $55 and may be obtained at the Marriage Bureau in the courthouse. Legal identification with proof of birth date is required, such as a certified copy of the birth certificate, a valid driver's license, identification from the Department of Motor Vehicles, or a passport. No witness is necessary to obtain a license.

Courthouse Location: Washoe County Clerk's Office, at the corner of South Virginia and Court Streets, P.O. Box 11130, Reno, NV 89520. Hours: 8:00 A.M. to midnight daily. (775) 328–3274.

Civil Marriages: Civil marriages in Reno and Sparks are performed by the Commissioner of Civil Marriages at 350 South Center Street, Suite 100, Reno. Fee: $50. No appointment is necessary. (775) 337–4575. www.co.washoe.nv.us/clerks.

In Incline Village/Crystal Bay, civil marriages are performed by the Incline Village Justice of the Peace, 865 Tahoe Boulevard. Open 8:00 A.M. to 5:00 P.M. Tuesday through Saturday; the office closes from noon to 1:00 P.M. Fee: $50. www.co.washoe.nv.us/clerks.

All Nevada license fees must be paid with cash or credit card.

■ WEDDING CHAPELS IN RENO, SPARKS, AND NEARBY

Adventure Inn. (775) 828–9000, (800) 937–1436. www.adventureinn.com.

Chapel of the Bells. (775) 323–1375. www.renochapel.com.

Heart of Reno Chapel. (775) 786–6882. www.heartofrenochapel.com.

Nugget Hotel Wedding Chapel. (775) 356–3300, extension 3480; (800) 843–2427. www.janugget.com/hotel/wedding.cfm.

Park Wedding Chapel. (775) 323–1770.

Reno Hilton Wedding Chapel. (775) 789–2472, (800) 255–1771. www.park place.com/hilton/reno.

Silver Bells Wedding Chapel. (775) 322–0420, (800) 221–9336. www.silver bellsweddingchap.com.

Starlite Wedding Chapel. (775) 786–4949.

White Lace & Promises Wedding Chapel. (775) 786–7020, (800) 613–0348. www.whitelacereno.com.

CHAPTER TWENTY-TWO

Drive, He Said: Eight Trips from Reno and Lake Tahoe

Econoguide Best Driving Trips from Reno and Lake Tahoe

★★★★ Pyramid Lake
★★★★ Lake Tahoe
★★★★ Virginia City
Emerald Bay
Heavenly
Incline Village
Squaw Valley

A MIRAGE IN THE DESERT: NORTH TO PYRAMID LAKE

TRIP 1: PYRAMID LAKE

Reno ▶ Pyramid Lake

A spectacular sea in the desert, **Pyramid Lake** is unlike any body of water in the world. Named for the distinctive rock formation that rises from its waters, Pyramid Lake is the largest remnant of a giant inland sea that once covered more than 8,000 square miles. Ancient petroglyphs depicting Paiute Indian life line the hills surrounding the lake, and its Anahoe Island (closed to the public) is a sanctuary for beautiful pelicans.

RENO, VIRGINIA CITY, AND LAKE TAHOE

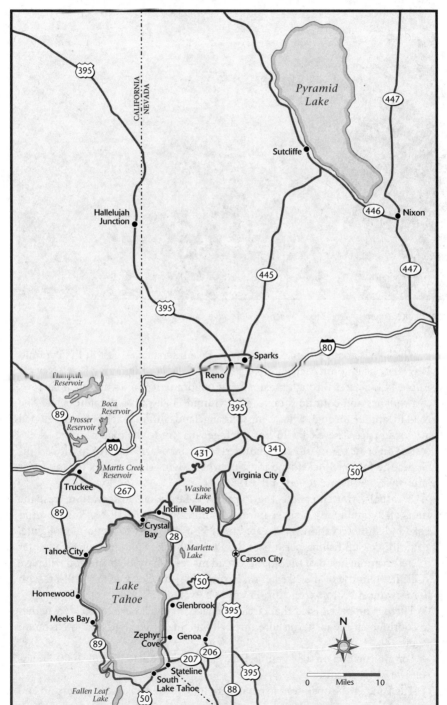

Pyramid Lake. *Courtesy Reno-Tahoe, America's Adventure Place*

The lake is about 25 miles from Reno. Take Interstate 80 east to the Pyramid Way exit, near John Ascuaga's Nugget. The four-lane Pyramid Way (Nevada Route 445) crosses through the northeast quadrant of Sparks, and then narrows to two lanes and continues on as the Pyramid Highway to Pyramid Lake. The road meanders through what is mostly rangeland, although it's being developed at a rapid pace. There's a wild-horse refuge adjacent to the road near the lake.

As you cross the mostly barren desert toward the lake, the area to the east includes the former Rocketdyne test site, where the rocket engines for the lunar lander were built and tested in the 1960s.

Eventually you enter into the **Pyramid Lake Indian Reservation,** past the ruins of Pyramid City, a silver-mining boom camp of the 1870s. The Pyramid Lake Indian Reservation was created in 1859 in an effort to contain the Paiute. You can pick up fishing permits at the Pyramid Lake Store just after you enter the reservation; just past the store the road makes a sharp turn and you will have your first glimpse of the lake below. Eventually you will come to a pull-off with the view most visitors come for: **Frémont's Pyramid.**

There is no paved road that circles the lake, so you'll have to decide whether to continue up the western shore through Sutcliffe or go southeast to Nixon on Route 446.

For information on the Pyramid Lake Paiute Tribe, call (775) 574–1000 or consult www.plpt.nsn.us.

The Paiute tribe operates a fish hatchery for Pyramid Lake cutthroat trout and cui-ui at Sutcliffe; informal tours are usually available. Call (775) 476–0500 for information or consult www.pyramidlakefisheries.org.

The road to Nixon meets up with Route 447 north, which follows the eastern shore of the lake from a distance. You will be rewarded with some starkly beautiful scenery, but you'll have to double back unless you want to go the very, very long way around; there's hardly a settlement for hours in any direction.

Pyramid Lake is a remnant of ancient Lake Lahontan, which covered some 8,450 square miles in western Nevada at the time of the Ice Age. In caves and rock shelters along the shores of the lake, explorers have found evidence of a prehistoric people who had a well-developed community life.

John C. Frémont came upon the lake on January 10, 1844, and named it for the pyramid-shaped island just off the east shore. Just south of the pyramid is **Anahoe Island,** which was established as a national wildlife refuge in 1913; today it is one of the largest white-pelican nesting grounds in North America.

The road comes to a T near the shoreline of the lake, with Highway 445 continuing north a short distance to Sutcliffe and 446 turning south along the shoreline of the lake toward Nixon. You might want to go north for a short distance to get a good view of the pyramid across the lake before turning back and descending to the lake on 446.

The shoreline features all kinds of strange rock formations. The first big formation you come to as you head toward Nixon is **Indian Head.** It looks more like a stone castle as you approach it, but as you look back over your shoulder while heading away, you can see a small outcropping of rock near the top and figure out where the rock gets its name.

If you take Route 447 south from Nixon toward Wadsworth along the Truckee River, you can pick up I–80 west back to Sparks and Reno. As you drop down on Route 447, you will be driving through the area of the **Pyramid Lake War of 1860.**

Although early relations between explorer John Frémont and the Paiutes at Pyramid Lake were peaceful, the increasing influx of whites created by the Comstock bonanza brought problems. In May 1860 several whites were found killed near Williams Station on the Carson River east of Carson City. The circumstances of their deaths were never fully explained, and historians say the attack may have been made in retribution for the kidnapping and rape of several Indian women just before.

Nevertheless, an "army" of more than a hundred volunteers was gathered. The men arrived at Wadsworth, about 15 miles south of Pyramid Lake, on May 12, 1860, and marched into a trap set by the Paiutes. More than half of the men were killed. The battle began with an ambush north of Nixon and continued along the plateau almost to the present site of Wadsworth. More white men died than in any prior white-Indian engagement in the far West.

A second, larger army of nearly 1,000 came back to the lake on June 2 and this time prevailed over the natives, killing 160 of them. Several hundred braves fought long enough to allow their women, children, and elders to escape. A forced peace treaty was negotiated, ending the "war."

About a half mile farther down past the historic marker for the Pyramid Lake War, you will come to the **Numana Hatchery Visitors Center,** operated by the Pyramid Lake Fisheries and the Pyramid Lake Paiute Tribe. The center is open daily from 9:00 to 11:00 A.M. and 1:00 to 3:00 P.M.

If you're up for a full day of exploring, you can continue on Route 447 past I–80 to Silver Springs and pick up U.S. Highway 50 west, which enters into the south end of the Comstock silver-mining area and into Carson City. At Carson City you can head back north to Reno on U.S. Highway 395 or cross the front range of the Sierra Nevada on US 50 to Lake Tahoe.

THE JEWEL IN THE MOUNTAINS: SOUTH TO LAKE TAHOE

From Reno and Carson City there are three passages through the front range of the Sierra Nevada to Lake Tahoe. All are spectacular, and each has its own appeal. Any road will be fine in summer and early fall; winter conditions can make driving treacherous, as can spring melts and refreezes.

TRIP 2: THE EASY WAY TO SOUTH LAKE TAHOE

Reno ▶ Spooner Summit ▶ Glenbrook ▶ Cave Rock ▶
Zephyr Cove ▶ Edgewood ▶ Stateline

The easiest and almost weatherproof route from Reno to Lake Tahoe is across Spooner Summit at midlake. Take US 395 south out of Reno past Carson City for 35 miles then turn right onto US 50 toward the face of the mountains. From there it's 10 miles up and over Spooner Summit at 7,146 feet and down to the lake; continue 25 miles farther south through the Cave Rock Tunnel, Zephyr Cove, and Edgewood to Stateline.

Except in the worst of weather, these roads are kept clear of snow and ice and are well patrolled. The trip is about 62 miles and takes about seventy-five minutes in good weather.

The first climb from Carson City on US 50 is a 6 percent grade for 5 or 6 miles, one of the most sustained climbs on a major road in this country. On one of my trips on a stormy January day, each twist and turn in the road revealed a new winter sight. There was a blizzard under way at the top of distant peaks, light snow on the pass, huge snowbanks in the canyons, and even a few blue holes in the clouds overhead.

There's not much of a descent after **Spooner Summit** before you come to the alpine level of Lake Tahoe. On one stormy day I could see wind-whipped waves on the lake.

At the bottom of the grade, where US 50 meets the lake and turns south toward Stateline, is **Glenbrook,** once the center of the logging industry that all but denuded the hills for miles around to serve the needs of the Comstock Mines and Virginia City. It was also the location of the first large, fancy hotel on the lake, the Glenbrook House.

Lumbering and logging operations in Glenbrook began in 1861. By 1872 consolidation of flume systems in and around Clear Creek Canyon made it possible to float lumber and logs from Spooner Summit to Carson City and to eliminate wagon hauling over the narrow and treacherous mountain roads. A small rail line ran from Glenbrook to Spooner Summit and the top of the flume.

Logging began first on the east shore of the lake and later moved across to the west shore, where the trees were logged and dropped by flumes into the lake and then towed across by a tugboat to the mill at Glenbrook.

Depletion of the timber at Lake Tahoe and the slowdown of mining in the Comstock ended lumbering in the area in 1898, after the Glenbrook operation had taken 750 million board feet of lumber and 500,000 cords of wood from the Tahoe Basin forest.

The highway takes a short detour at **Cave Rock** and passes through a pair of tunnels through a gigantic volcanic rock. Cave Rock had been a place of religious significance to the native Washoes, who believed that the cave at the site was the home of an avenging Giant of the Sierra Nevada. Much of the cave was destroyed with the construction of the road at the turn of the twentieth century.

Tahoe Tessie, the mysterious monster of the deep, is said to live in an underwater cavern beneath the cave; that is, when she is not on vacation at Loch Ness.

By the way, there have been enough reported sightings of an unusual creature in the waters of Lake Tahoe to have drawn some scientific interest; some scientists believe the "monster" may be a large lake sturgeon, a particularly ugly fish known to have existed in area waters. In 1888 a 7-foot sturgeon was caught at Pyramid Lake above Reno; Pyramid Lake is connected to Lake Tahoe by the Truckee River.

Put aside your preconceptions of the aesthetic merits of California versus Nevada and consider the fact that while there are many communities and developments on the western side of the lake, the east shore in Nevada from Glenbrook north to Incline Village is mostly untouched.

The 10-mile gap was preserved mostly as the result of the acquisitive career of a most eccentric millionaire, Captain George Whittell Jr. Today Whittell's **Thunderbird Lodge** near Sand Harbor sits on 143 acres of land, the last vestige of what once was a sprawling empire that covered more than 32,000 acres and more than 14 miles of Lake Tahoe's East Shore.

At one time Whittell owned one-sixth of the entire Tahoe Basin. Most of his property today is within Nevada's **Lake Tahoe State Park** and the latter-day planned community of **Incline Village.**

Whittell, born into a wealthy San Francisco family that built a fortune during the gold rush, blazed the path that was followed later by strange characters Howard Hughes and Michael Jackson. His sprawling estate included a menagerie of exotic animals; some of the creatures made appearances at wild parties he put on for Hollywood stars and other celebrities.

According to newspaper reports of the time,

Reno-Sparks Information

Reno-Sparks Convention & Visitors Authority Information Center.
(800) 367–7366.
www.renolaketahoe.com.

Forewarned

Pay attention to weather forecasts in the winter and spring, especially if you must cross one of the mountain passes. Rain at the "lower" elevations of Lake Tahoe or Reno may be heavy snow in the passes. Highway 431 and Highway 207 are regularly shut down because of winter storms. And Route 89 on the west shore of the lake is closed so often that there are barriers that can be swung across the road to stop traffic at Emerald Bay.

Much of Route 89 on the California side and Highway 207 and Highway 431 in Nevada have no guardrails to block the spectacular view—or the tremendous drop to the rocks below.

Whittell was once seen leading a pack of dogs in a chase of naked guests. And he was sued several times by guests who claimed injuries from his pet tigers and lions.

The landscaping around the rustic stone house was intricate and included an artificial waterfall and a pair of private lighthouses. Along the lake was a 150-foot-long boathouse blasted out of the bedrock; it was home to his 56-foot-long chrome-and-mahogany speedboat, the *Thunderbird*, powered by four 400-horsepower engines.

Beneath it all is a 500-foot-long rock-lined tunnel from Thunderbird Lodge to the boathouse and the outlying Card House; the entrance to the tunnel from the Card House was hidden behind the wall of a shower. Other oddities include large speakers he used to broadcast warnings to uninvited boaters and microphones installed in the guest and servant rooms to eavesdrop on conversations.

Near the end of his life, Whittell fought a losing battle against tax claims, and in the late 1960s the state of Nevada purchased 5,300 acres of his Tahoe estate for $3 million. He also made donations of much of his land to the University of Nevada, a local hospital, and a South Shore high school. Whittell died in 1969 at the age of eighty-seven, leaving most of his estate to animal welfare groups. His last words were reportedly, "I shall come back as a lion."

The lodge is open for ninety-minute guided tours in the summer, including trips that come in by boat or by shuttle bus. In 2006 tickets were $25 for adults and $10 for children (through high school age) plus boat tour tickets if used. For information call the Incline Village/Crystal Bay Visitor Center at (800) 468–2463 or consult www.thunderbirdlodge.org.

Zephyr Cove draws its name from the winds that often sweep across the lake. In summertime the beach, marina, and stables are popular attractions; the glass-bottom MS *Dixie* paddle wheeler is based there. In the winter it is a takeoff point for snowmobile tours, sleigh rides, and cross-country ski trails.

Pull in at the **Visitor Center** and the **Tahoe Douglas Chamber of Commerce**, just past Zephyr Cove on the mountain side of the road, to mine a treasure load of brochures, coupons, and maps.

Things have changed greatly in **Edgewood**, a residential community just outside of Stateline. In the 1860s it was the site of **Friday's Station**, a way station on the Pony Express route established by Friday Burke and Big Jim Small. It was the home station of "Pony Bob" Haslam, one of the most famous of the Express riders. The tollbooth in front of Friday's Station was one of the most profitable such franchises at the height of the reverse migration from California to the Comstock, bringing in as much as $1,500 per day.

The Pony Express was a privately owned and operated courier service, sort of the FedEx of its day. The service, which charged $5.00 per ounce for letters, stretched from Saint Joseph, Missouri, to Sacramento, California. There were about seventy-five way stations where horses were swapped. As famous as the Pony Express was, it is interesting to note that it lasted less than two years, put out of business by the transcontinental railroad and the telegraph.

The restored Friday's Station Inn—now a private residence—still stands across the highway from today's watering hole, the **Edgewood Golf Course**. The golf resort is considered one of the top public courses in the country.

Next stop is Stateline.

TRIP 3: TO THE TOP OF THE LAKE AND DOWN THE EASTERN SHORE

Reno ▶ *Mount Rose* ▶ *Incline Village* ▶ *Crystal Bay* ▶
Sand Harbor Beach ▶ *Stateline*

The views keep getting better and better as you follow the switchbacks on **Mount Rose Highway.** This is the most direct route to the north end of Lake Tahoe and a slower, scenic route to the eastern shore and the south end of the lake.

Take US 395 south from Reno about 11 miles to the intersection with Highways 431 and 341. If you turn left onto Highway 341, you will climb Geiger Grade into Virginia City; see Trip 6 for details on that must-see tour. Instead turn right onto Highway 431 toward the imposing face of the mountains.

At the intersection of US 395 and the Mount Rose Highway and a bit farther up the approach road to the mountains, you will find several places where you can buy snow chains for your car if necessary. You can also rent ski equipment, tubes, and snowboards before you get to the ski areas. Ski reports can be heard on several radio stations in the area, including 590 AM.

The Mount Rose Highway presents a 25-mile, twist-and-turn climb up **Mount Rose.** The road reaches an altitude of 8,911 feet; Mount Rose itself continues to a summit elevation of 10,338 feet.

The road includes several switchbacks hanging out into space and very few guardrails. If you have a little bit of nerve and a decent car with a good set of tires, and most important, dry pavement, the Mount Rose Highway is quite an exciting approach to the north end of the lake.

Near the top of the highway, just before you get to the **Mount Rose–Ski Tahoe** ski area, sneak a peek back to your left for a view that extends all the way north to Reno and south toward Carson City. Now try to put yourself back in the days before there were cars and a paved road. Imagine what it was like to lay out this trail through the tall trees and along the mountain ridges. And then think about what it was like to go up the trail by foot, by horse, or by wagon.

Galena Creek Park, on the slopes of the mountain, includes picnic areas, hiking trails, and other facilities for summer and winter recreation. The park is run by the Washoe County Department of Parks & Recreation; call (775) 828–6642 for information, or contact the park ranger at (775) 828–6612. You may also visit www.washoecountyparks.com.

Mount Rose is named after Jacob Rose, who exploited diggings in Gold Canyon and brought a large crew of Chinese workers to the area in 1856 to build a water ditch.

A bit farther on is the Mount Rose ski area itself, which has the region's highest base elevation at 8,250 feet, a pretty good guarantor of dependable snow. There is a 1,450-foot vertical drop with twenty-seven trails served by a half-dozen lifts. For information call (775) 849–0704 or consult www.skirose.com.

At the highest point on the road is a turnoff to the left to **Mount Rose Campground.** The road begins a gradual descent, and about 6 miles later you will enter Incline Village at the northeast corner of Lake Tahoe.

At **Incline Village,** bear left onto Highway 28 south for 14 miles to where it joins with US 50 south into Stateline. Incline Village was wilderness until the mid-1800s, when loggers began using timber to shore up the silver mines of Virginia City some 20 miles away on the other side of the eastern mountain range. The mountainsides were stripped of nearly all hardwood, and the sawdust and debris from sawmills choked many of the creeks, all but destroying the trout population of Lake Tahoe for decades.

On the mountain at Incline Village, behind the Ponderosa Ranch, lie the remains of the **Great Incline of the Sierra Nevada.** Completed in 1880, this 4,000-foot-long lift was constructed by the Sierra Nevada Wood and Lumber Company. A steam powered cable railway pulled wood up the double tracks to the top on canted cars. At the top the wood was automatically dumped into a V-flume and tumbled down to the Washoe Valley where it was loaded onto wagons for use in the mines of the Comstock. At the height of the enterprise, 300 cords of wood per day were moved from the mill at what is now Mill Creek.

Just a few years after it was completed, the railway pulled free of its moorings and fell down the mountain, leaving scars on trees and rocks that can still be seen. The bull wheels of the railway can be seen near the **Diamond Peak Ski Area.**

A small settlement was established in 1884, but the area did not gain much attention until 1927 when the first casino was built in **Crystal Bay.**

The **Cal-Neva Resort Hotel Spa Casino** at Crystal Bay is famous for its swimming pool, which sits atop the state border, allowing swimmers to start in California and end up in Nevada where there is, of course, a casino. The hotel, which claims lake views from each of its 200 rooms, also includes the **Frank Sinatra Celebrity Showroom.** Sinatra was at one time a part owner of the hotel, a regular gathering place for the Rat Pack.

The wood-paneled Indian Room, on the noncasino California side of the resort, is like a time capsule of the 1940s. A stone hearth that has a roaring fire sits on the state line, surrounded by a collection of old photographs and Indian artifacts, including a pair of life-size Hopi kachina dolls.

Room rates range from $89 to $200, higher for chalets and suites, depending on season and day of week. Winter packages with ski tickets are also available. The resort is located at 2 Stateline Road, Crystal Bay, Nevada. For information call (775) 832–4000 or (800) 225–6382 or consult www.calnevaresort.com.

Nearby off Reservoir Drive is the **Crystal Bay Fire Lookout,** which offers a spectacular view of the lake from the north shore. To drive to the lookout tower, follow Reservoir Road, which lies between the **Tahoe Biltmore Casino** and the former **Tahoe Mariner Casino;** turn right at the firehouse and climb the hill to the USDA Forest Service road and proceed to the parking lot.

The development of the area for condominiums and homes also began in the 1960s and included a spectacular eighteen-hole championship golf course designed by Robert Trent Jones Sr. and the development of Ski Incline. The ski area, greatly expanded, is now known as **Diamond Peak.**

Other major construction included the **Hyatt Regency Lake Tahoe Resort and Casino,** a second golf course, beach facilities, and the **Lakeside Tennis Resort.**

By the way, Crystal Bay was not named after the clear waters of Lake Tahoe, but rather after lumberman George Iweis Crystal, who owned much of the area in the 1860s.

In the summer, special events at Incline Village include the **Shakespeare at Sand Harbor** festival, with plays presented from the end of July through August. Call (775) 832–1616 or consult www.tahoebard.com for information.

The **Ponderosa Ranch,** a theme park that was the mythical setting of the Cartwright family made famous in the *Bonanza* television series, closed in 2004.

Sand Harbor Beach State Recreational Area, about 5 miles south of Incline Village, offers a small but pretty sand beach on an inlet of Lake Tahoe. Rocks are piled on top of each other reaching out into the lake like little jetties. The beach sits at the base of an almost sheer-cliff mountainside. In summer there is an entrance fee of $2.00.

Follow the outlines of the lake toward **Spooner Lake,** where you will meet up with US 50. Swimming is not recommended in Spooner Lake because of harmless but annoying leeches. Continue on US 50 south through the Cave Rock Tunnel to Zephyr Cove and into Stateline.

The regular traffic to and from the Mount Rose ski area and the top of the lake and other points in California to Reno will keep the roads clear except in the worst weather, but the mountain crossing here is twice as long as the one at Spooner Summit at midlake. The trip is about 66 miles and takes about ninety minutes in good weather.

TRIP 4: DRIVING THE ROUTE OF THE PONY EXPRESS

Reno ▶ Genoa ▶ Kingsbury Grade ▶ Stateline

My favorite approach to South Lake Tahoe is a piece of cake in good weather, a white-knuckle trip in ordinary winter weather, and all-but-impossible in a storm. But what a ride!

Take US 395 out of Reno past Carson City for 46 miles (11 miles past the point where US 50 branches off). Just past the tiny Douglas County Airport, look for the signs to the historic settlement of Genoa; turn right toward the wall of mountains.

Genoa, pronounced Jen-*oh*-uh, was the first permanent settlement in what would become the state of Nevada. It was established by one of Brigham Young's traders in 1849 and was originally called **Mormon Station.** It was located at the base of the front range of the Sierra Nevada in a meadow fed by a small creek that came down from the mountains. At the station the trader sold supplies—brought all the way from Salt Lake City—to travelers who were preparing to go up and over the mountains westward to California.

For a short time the little outpost was the most important point between Salt Lake City and Placerville on the road to San Francisco. In 1854 Mormon Station was renamed Genoa and became the seat of government of Carson County of the Utah Territory. In 1857 most of the Mormons were recalled to Salt Lake City to bolster Brigham Young in a confrontation against federal troops over local government; they mostly abandoned their settlement in place.

In 1857 the history of the area changed dramatically with the discovery of gold in a placer deposit—in the runout of a stream—on what was to become known as **Gold Creek,** a tributary of the Carson River near the village now known as **Gold Hill.** Significant amounts of gold in rock outcroppings were found in January 1859 a bit to the north on Sun Mountain, sparking a gold rush. The boom took off when miners realized that the "blue mud" that stood in the way of the gold and was treated as a nuisance actually contained significant amounts of silver.

The result was a reverse migration, with many miners returning across the Sierra Nevada from California, through Genoa, and on to the Gold Creek area. For a while the **Johnson Cutoff Trail** (now known as the Pioneer Trail above the present location of Stateline, at the southern end of Lake Tahoe) became the most heavily traveled highway in the West. That same year the first territorial legislature met in Genoa in 1859 and drafted a demand to separate the region from the Utah Territory.

Most of the town, including the original Mormon fort, was destroyed by fire in 1910. There's a small display in the **Genoa Courthouse Museum** on Main Street. The building served as the justice center from 1865 to 1916 and as a school from 1916 through 1956. It is open daily from mid-May to mid-October; call (775) 782–4325 for information.

Displays at the Courthouse include the Buckaroo Room, with ranching and farming items from the early nineteenth century, including snowshoes for a horse. A blacksmith shop, located in the former jail, includes tools and a bellows that once belonged to Colonel John Reese, the founder of Genoa. A period classroom includes old maps, textbooks, and furniture.

Late each September Genoa presents the **Candy Dance,** a fund-raising weekend that dates back to 1919 when a group of local women raised funds for gas streetlights with a "social." Today the Candy Dance Ball, held in the Town Hall, raises money to pay the town's expenses—including some of those old lights. For information on events call the Genoa Town Board at (775) 782–8696.

There are nearly thirty buildings on the National Register of Historic Places in the tiny settlement, including the **Genoa Saloon,** said to be Nevada's oldest bar.

On nearby Highway 206 (Foothill Road) is **Mormon Station Historic State**

Park. A museum and restored trading post is open from about May 1 to October 15. For information call (775) 782–2590 or consult www.parks.nv.gov/ms.htm.

At Genoa turn left and follow the base of the mountains on Foothill Road until you come to Route 207, known as **Kingsbury Grade.** The road was built around 1860 as the route of the Pony Express; it was also the principal path for the Bonanza traffic from the west to Virginia City.

Head west up and over **Daggett Pass** (elevation 7,334 feet) and descend into Stateline through Haines Canyon, dropping about 3,000 feet over 6 miles. This path should take a bit less than two hours.

The Kingsbury Grade is a shorter but somewhat more treacherous pass over the front range than US 50 over the Spooner Summit.

You'll proceed up an incredible set of switchbacks on a two-lane highway with what looks like a dangerously frail guardrail between you and the abyss. At some points you can see three or four stepped levels of the road above or below.

TRIP 5: INTO THE OLYMPIC VALLEY AND DONNER LAKE

Reno ▶ Kings Beach ▶ Tahoe Vista ▶ Carnelian Bay ▶ Tahoe City ▶ Alpine Meadows ▶ Squaw Valley ▶ Truckee ▶ Donner Lake ▶ Verdi Boomtown

Take US 395 south from Reno about 11 miles to the intersection with Highways 431 and 341. Turn right onto Highway 431 toward the imposing face of the mountains and go up and over the summit.

Kings Beach, across the border into California, sits at the absolute "top" of the lake and affords a spectacular view down its length. On a clear day—and there are many—you will be able to see the **Heavenly** ski resort 22 miles away, towering over the casinos of Stateline. Kings Beach, which includes some lovely beaches and marinas for boating and other water sports, was given its name by Joe King, a gambler who supposedly won the property in a poker game in 1925.

Just past Kings Beach, Route 267 branches off toward Truckee. At that intersection is a popular snowmobiling course on the nine-hole **Old Brockway Golf Course.**

Skiers and tourists can take a 6-mile side trip on Route 267 to explore **Northstar-at-Tahoe,** a resort complex that includes a ski area, golf course, stables, and more. Northstar is a serious ski hill with a 2,200-foot vertical drop.

The next settlement westward around the lake is **Tahoe Vista,** which overlooks Agate Bay. It was named after a spectacular hotel of the early 1900s, which sat up on a hill overlooking the lake. Tahoe Vista was also one of the first subdivisions on the lake in 1911, a period when speculators almost succeeded in ruining the pristine wilderness forever. In a strange turn of fate, Tahoe Vista's subdivision may have failed because of the notoriety attached to one of its first land buyers, Miss Cherry de St. Maurice, an infamous Sacramento madam.

Although much land was sold in small lots, the region's wilderness was preserved in part by the stock market crash and the Great Depression, which caused many of the purchase contracts to go unpaid in the 1930s.

Carnelian Bay takes its name from the reddish semiprecious stones known as carnelian that were found on its beach by the Whitney Survey party in the 1860s. An early establishment there was Dr. Bourne's **Hygenic Establishment,** a health resort later renamed as the **Carnelian Springs Sanatoria.** Dr. Bourne also tried to rename Lake Tahoe as Lake Sanatoria, an attempt that thankfully failed.

Tahoe City was established as a lumbering camp and as a port for freight traffic on the lake. Today it sits at the northern end of man's intrusion on the lake's beauty.

A small city of about 5,000 year-round, Tahoe City is built at the site of a dam first built across the mouth of the Truckee River, the only outlet from Lake Tahoe. The passage over the river is known as the **Fanny Bridge;** it supposedly draws its name from the outstretched posteriors of those leaning over the railing to gawk at cutthroat trout below.

Alongside the bridge is the **Gatekeeper's Cabin and Museum,** which includes artifacts of the early days of Lake Tahoe development, items from ancient Indian history, and items from the 1960 Winter Olympics held at nearby Squaw Valley. The cabin was used from about 1909 until it was destroyed by fire in 1978; the museum occupies an exact replica built by the **North Lake Tahoe Historical Society.** Call (530) 583–1762 for information.

The dam was first built in 1870 as part of a plan to drain some of the lake's waters to San Francisco through a tunnel to be bored through the Sierra Nevada. This was before environmental concerns, of course, but the tunnel was never built. One result of the damming of the outlet, though, was that the level of the lake rose by several feet, changing its outlines in many places.

There were actually several efforts to drain the lake for the use of San Francisco, including a proposal in 1900 to construct a system that would divert from thirty million to one hundred million gallons of Tahoe water per day. A second plan in 1903 called for a tunnel under the Sierra Nevada to send the water into the Rubicon branch of the American River, which leads into San Francisco. The final—and almost successful—effort was supported by the U.S. Reclamation Service and would have sent the water into the dry Nevada desert for irrigation and power needs. Luckily bureaucracy stalled the plan when the chief forester for the Department of Agriculture held up the project for years on something close to environmental objections.

In 1871 the **Grand Central Hotel** was opened at Tahoe City, setting a new level of luxury at the lake. The completion of a narrow-gauge spur railroad in 1900 from Tahoe City to Truckee, where the transcontinental main line passed, established the area as an important gateway to Lake Tahoe.

The **Big Tree** in the center of town is a big tree, celebrated as a landmark and town Christmas tree for more than a century. The **Watson Cabin Living Museum** is within a small, authentic Lake Tahoe cabin. Nearby are several small shopping areas: the **Boatworks Mall,** the **Roundhouse Mall,** and the **Lighthouse Shopping Center.** To go to Alpine Meadows and Squaw Valley USA, turn right (north) onto Highway 89 at Tahoe City and enter the **Olympic Valley.**

On your left about 6 miles up the road, you will come to the **Alpine Meadows** ski area. Though not as well known or anywhere near as large as Heavenly to the south or Squaw Valley USA just north over the mountain range, Alpine Meadows is still one big hill full of snow that has about a hundred runs.

A few miles farther along on Route 89 is the approach road to **Squaw Valley USA** with its Tower of Nations and the Olympic rings, a remnant of the Winter Olympic Games VIII held here in 1960.

The ski resort, with thirty-three lifts, including a 150-passenger gondola and more than a hundred runs, is set in a bowl of mountains that include KT-22 at 8,200 feet, Emigrant Peak at 8,700 feet, Squaw Peak at 8,900 feet, and Granite Chief at 9,050 feet. Summer activities include arts and writers conferences and a world-class golf course.

After it leaves Squaw Valley, Route 89 meets up with I–80, just west of Truckee. **Truckee** presents an interesting freeze-frame of the old Wild West in its historic downtown. Like much of Nevada, it grew as a rest stop—first as a point on the Emigrant Trail westward, then when the Transcontinental Railway passed through in 1868, and then in the early twentieth century when the Lincoln Highway opened up the pass to transcontinental cars and trucks.

More than a hundred of the structures in and around Commercial Row date from the nineteenth century, and at least one—the **Truckee Hotel**—dates from Truckee's lumber and railroading boom in 1871. The thirty-six-room Truckee Hotel was completely restored a few years back, with its Victorian parlor and marble fireplace as a centerpiece. Most of the rooms are "European," which means the bathroom is down the hall; the eight with private bathrooms sport claw-foot tubs. Another important industry was ice harvesting. Cakes of ice were cut from rivers and lakes and stored in warehouses; Truckee ice was shipped east and west for hundreds of miles by railroad until the 1920s. Truckee ice was considered a delicacy in San Francisco.

Canopied wooden walkways are maintained in some of the sections of town. **Jibboom Street,** one street in from Commercial, was the active red-light district of Truckee and also houses the Truckee Jail, in use from 1875 until 1964. The streets are not quite as redolent of history as Virginia City, but worth a visit if you're on the north end of the lake.

The town received its name in honor of a Paiute Indian guide who helped a party migrating west across the Sierra Nevada; Truckee was a chief and father of Winnemucca. The westward party named the lake they found Mountain Lake; it was named Truckee's Lake in 1846 when the ill-fated Donner Party was stranded there for the winter.

Sites to see in downtown Truckee include the famed **Rocking Stone,** a seventeen-ton boulder that was balanced atop a larger rock and was used by ancient Indians as many as 15,000 years ago as a place to grind meal and by later generations as a ceremonial location. Though first thought to be a natural occurrence, more recent studies have concluded that the upper stone may have been chiseled to serve the purpose of a grinding place thousands of years ago. The stone was enclosed within a tower in 1893 and again in the 1950s; it has been cemented into a fixed position for safety's sake.

A plaque on Front Street records the actions of the **601,** a vigilante group

Someone Has to Do It

Yes, that really is a U.S. Coast Guard station just north of Tahoe City at Lake Forest Park. Because of its size and the fact that it is an interstate-navigable waterway, the entire lake falls under the supervision of the federal Coast Guard in what must be one of the most desirable assignments in the service.

from the Wild West days. Across Commercial Row is the **Southern Pacific Depot,** which dates to 1896.

From Truckee you can head east back to Reno or take a short jog about 4 miles west on Donner Pass Road to **Donner Lake** and the **Donner Memorial State Park.** The story of the Donner Party is one of the most famous tragedies of the American cultural consciousness. The Donners and the Reeds made up the largest family groups among the eighty-seven emigrants who left Sangamon County, Illinois, in 1846 for California.

Under the leadership of George Donner, they made a series of bad decisions and mistakes in choosing trails across the Great Salt Lake in Utah and then the Sierra Nevada. They were trapped by unusually heavy snows in the mountains above Reno in October and were forced to camp for the winter at a small lake about 13 miles northwest of Lake Tahoe. They ran out of food and other supplies, and some of the members of the group finally resorted to cannibalism to survive—those few who would talk about their experience afterward claimed they ate only those who had died naturally from the harsh conditions.

When spring finally arrived, forty-seven of the eighty-seven emigrants were eventually brought to California by rescue parties, traveling over what is now known as **Donner Pass.**

A memorial and museum about the ill-fated Donner Party expedition is located at Donner Memorial State Park. At the site is the Emigrant Monument with a statue representing the Donner Party at the top of a 22-foot-high pedestal; the marker represents the depth of snow recorded in and around the lake in the terrible winter of 1846–1847.

The park is a strange mix of pleasant surroundings and awful memories, a sense of history and a connection to the present in the form of I–80, which passes by a few hundred feet away with a steady stream of trucks.

But if you walk down the little trail that leads from the museum, you enter into a much quieter place, an area that hints at the terrifying loneliness of this place in 1846. You'll come to a large house-size rock bearing a plaque that reads: THE FACE OF THIS ROCK FORMED THE NORTH END AND THE FIREPLACE OF THE MURPHY CABIN. GENERAL STEPHEN W. KEARNY ON JUNE 22, 1847, BURIED UNDER THE MIDDLE OF THE CABIN THE BODIES FOUND IN THE VICINITY. There is a listing of several dozen names, including seven Donners. Kearny, by the way, went on to become commander of the Army of the West in the Mexican War and served as military commander of California.

The small **Emigrant Trail Museum** at the park is open year-round and includes a selection of books about the Donner Party and the area; the campgrounds are open from Memorial Day into October. Admission to the museum is $2.00 for adults and $1.00 for children ages six to seventeen. For information call (530) 582–7892 or consult www.parks.ca.gov/default.asp?page_id=503. You can also call the Truckee-Donner Chamber of Commerce at (530) 587–2757 for more information.

As you head east back into Nevada toward Reno, you will pass through the former logging boomtown of **Verdi.** The town grew in the early 1860s around a logging mill that cut wood for railroad ties for the Central Pacific Railroad and a bridge across the Truckee. The settlement was named in honor of Italian opera composer Giuseppe Verdi, who was at his peak of fame at the time.

Verdi is claimed to be the site of the first train robbery in the West. Bandits held up a CP train in 1870, making off with some $40,000 in payroll money for the Yellow Jacket mine. The robbers were eventually collared in mine shafts on **Peavine Peak** above the town; all but $3,000 of the cash was recovered.

The town was kept alive as a rest stop on U.S. Highway 40 and later moved a bit east to serve I–80. The area is now known as **Boomtown.**

The **Boomtown Hotel Casino,** just off the interstate, is a Kmart of a casino that includes an indoor miniature carousel and an arcade with one hundred games and a truck stop that lures long-distance drivers into the casino. There are 522 basic rooms and a buffet. Other features at Boomtown include a **Dynamic Motion Theater,** a Ferris wheel, an indoor eighteen-hole miniature golf course, and an indoor swimming pool. The Laughing Lady animatronic greeter at the casino entrance cracks Western jokes and puns for visitors. For information call (775) 345–6000 or (800) 648–3790 or consult www.boomtownreno.com.

A round-trip from Reno over Mount Rose to Crystal Bay and on through the Olympic Valley should take about three hours.

THE MINES OF THE BONANZA

TRIP 6: FROZEN IN TIME

Reno ▶ Virginia City ▶ Gold Hill ▶ Silver City ▶ Carson City

Follow US 395 south out of Reno and drive to its intersection with Highways 431 and 341, about 11 miles from downtown Reno. Turn left onto Highway 341 and begin the slow but steady climb up **Geiger Grade** into Virginia City.

When you finally make it up the hill, you will find yourself in **Virginia City** itself; there is no mistaking where you are, either. Every Western movie ever made included a Hollywood version of this place. See chapter 23 for more details about Virginia City.

After you've visited the wonders of Virginia City, continue on Highway 341 to the point where it splits: Take the right fork, marked as Route 342, to see the ruins of **Gold Hill** and **Silver City,** two of the mining outposts of the time. The road will soon join up with Highway 341 again, which will eventually come to a T at US 50. Make a right turn, heading west.

US 50 will come to another T, at US 395. Head south for a short jog to explore **Carson City** or head north for the rapid return to Reno.

On your way back to Reno, you may want to branch off the highway at Route 429 to visit the historic **Bowers Mansion,** built by one of the discoverers of the Comstock Lode, Lemuel Sanford Bowers.

Bowers's new wife, Eilley Orrum, spent what was at the time a fortune—at least $200,000 and perhaps $400,000—on building and furnishing the house in 1864. Her husband, though, did not live to enjoy the house much, dying of miner's lung disease in 1868. By that time, too, the Gold Hill mine had gone bust, and there was not much money left for Mrs. Bowers—she tried running the mansion as a hotel and resort but eventually saw it sold at public auction. The home is closed from November through April. Admission is $3.00 for adults and $2.00 for children twelve and younger. For information on the mansion, call (775) 849–0201 or consult www.cr.nps.gov/nr/travel/nevada/bow.htm.

The trip from Reno to Virginia City takes about forty-five minutes. To make the full tour from Reno to Virginia City, continuing on to Gold Hill and to US 395 at Carson City before returning to Reno, allow about two hours. Add extra time to visit Virginia City, Carson City, and the Bowers Mansion.

NORTH FROM STATELINE

The western side of the lake offers some of the most spectacular waterside views and the older, more historic communities. Much of the development of the west shore came from California money with San Francisco's high society setting up camp along the lake.

TRIP 7: NORTH ALONG THE WESTERN SHORE

Stateline ▶ Bijou ▶ Camp Richardson ▶ Tallac Historic Site ▶ Fallen Leaf Lake ▶ Emerald Bay ▶ Meeks Bay ▶ Rubicon Bay ▶ Sugar Pine Point State Park ▶ Homewood ▶ Idlewild ▶ Tahoe City

West of Stateline on the California side is the little community of **Bijou.** It draws its name from a lovely little beach along the lake; don't look for the strand, though: It's gone. In 1910 the lake's level was raised by the construction of a dam at its outlet near Tahoe City, and the beach was drowned.

Bijou now hosts two marinas, including the home of the *Tahoe Queen* paddle wheeler, which makes cruises year-round.

The **Osgood Toll House** near Rufus Allen Boulevard is the oldest building in the Lake Tahoe area. Dating to 1859, it once served as a tollhouse on the Bonanza Route near Meyers; it was moved to the city for preservation.

Along the mountain side of US 50 is a park that includes the **Lake Tahoe Arts Center** and the **North Lake Tahoe Historical Society Museum.** The museum includes old photographs of the valley; for information call (530) 541–5458.

Back on US 50 at the very base of the lake is **Al Tahoe,** a turn-of-the-twentieth-century subdivision of cottages and campgrounds. It draws its unusual name from developer Al Sprague, who named his hotel and the land around it after himself and the lake. A small beach meets the water.

Continue on US 50 to the Y where US 50 continues westward toward Sacramento and Route 89 heads in a northerly direction around the lake as far as Tahoe City and from there to Truckee and Donner Pass. Bear right onto Route 89 and the trappings of the tourist zone fall away quickly.

Camp Richardson, the first settlement you'll come across as you head north on Emerald Bay Road, was established in the 1880s as a logging camp; a narrow-gauge steam railroad line ran from the site. It later became an early resort along the shores of Lake Tahoe. Today it offers a large campground, marina, and horse stables.

Heaven's Gate

The state controls a gate across the road just short of Emerald Bay that closes off Route 89 when the danger of snow avalanches or rock slides is high or when the road is actually blocked. If the road is closed, there is no real alternative other than to backtrack and take US 50 around the eastern side of the lake.

Just past the camp is the **Tallac Historic Site,** a USDA Forest Service preserve that includes the sites of nearly a dozen former grand residences and the location of the fabled Tallac Hotel. The Tallac, opulent for its late-nineteenth-century time, was known as the "Saratoga of the Pacific." The Tallac Point House was built in the 1870s. In 1880 it was taken over by Elias "Lucky" Baldwin, who expanded it into a luxurious resort that included a ballroom with a spring-mounted dance floor and croquet and tennis courts; guests could also take steamer excursions from the hotel. The hotel was torn down in 1916.

Among the estates open to the public at Tallac are the **Baldwin, Pope,** and **Valhalla** estates. The Pope estate dates from 1894. It was expanded in 1899 to become one of the most spectacular in the area; it now serves as the visitor center for Tallac. The Baldwin home was built in 1921 by Dextra Baldwin, granddaughter of Lucky Baldwin. The Valhalla estate dates from 1924; it is used for community events. Special events held at the site include a Renaissance Festival each June and a Native American Festival in August. For information call the Tallac Historic Site at (530) 541–4975 or (888) 632–5859.

The **Kiva Beach Recreation Area** offers one of the nicest beaches on the lake, set in a nearly untouched pine grove. The USDA Forest Service Visitor Center on Kiva Beach Road offers trail guides and an interesting display about the geology and wildlife of the region. Nearby is an outdoor amphitheater where slide shows and other presentations are made in summer.

Several short interpretive trails branch off from the visitor center at Kiva. They include the **Rainbow Trail** that leads through a mountain meadow to the **Stream Profile Chamber** where you can look through an underwater window into a salmon-spawning pool. The **Lake of the Sky Trail** descends to the lakeshore, while the **Trail of the Washoe** climbs a small section of the hill across the road from the visitor center.

Across the road is **Mount Tallac,** at 9,735 feet, the tallest mountain directly on the lake itself. On the northeast face of the mountain is a cross-shaped indentation that is known as the "Snowcross" when filled with the snows of winter.

If it weren't for the overshadowing glories of Lake Tahoe, **Fallen Leaf Lake** might be world famous as a spectacular alpine lake in the Sierra Nevada. As it is this is a side trip well worth taking on a tour of the California side.

Fallen Leaf Lake is 3 miles long and a mile wide, with depths up to 418 feet. The **Fallen Leaf Lodge** and surrounding cabins, dating back to the 1910s, are now privately owned. A boathouse and marina are opposite the lodge, and the lake is a prime fishing area. Hiking trails—some of them quite isolated—lead into some even more remote and smaller lakes, including **Azure** and **Heather.**

There are two resorts and marinas and several campgrounds at the lake, as well as the trailheads of several hiking trails that lead into the Desolation Wilderness. One of the private homes along the lake was used in the film *The Bodyguard.*

The lake, at 6,377 feet, is about 100 feet higher than Lake Tahoe. The waters are fairly cold for swimming most of the year, warming up to a tolerable level by the end of summer. The lake is open to fishing year-round.

To reach the lake, turn left onto Fallen Leaf Lake Road. The lake lies at the end of the road, about 5 miles in; it may not be accessible in winter.

There's an even more remote set of lakes on the mountainside above: **Upper Angora Lake** and **Lower Angora Lake.** They draw their names from a flock of Angora goats tended by a man named Nathan Gilmore around the turn of the nineteenth century. Today you will find the **Angora Lake Resort.** There are a few cabins for rent; call (530) 541–2092 for information.

To reach Angora Lakes, start on Fallen Leaf Lake Road and take the first left and then the first right. You will come to the **Angora Fire Lookout** at 7,290 feet; continue on the dirt road until you come to a parking lot. A half-mile trail continues to the resort.

Information about trails in the Fallen Leaf Lake area can be found at the visitor center on Highway 89 near Fallen Leaf Lake Road.

North of Tallac the road begins to twist and climb, finally revealing the spectacular **Cascade Lake** and even more spectacular **Emerald Bay.**

Cascade Lake, on the mountain side of the road, was the setting for several well-loved motion pictures, including *Rose Marie* with Nelson Eddy and Jeanette McDonald. The lake is named for **White Cloud Falls** at its southwest corner; mountain streams plunge 100 feet into the lake. The falls are usually at their fullest in the spring as the snow melts; in winter the stream and the lake itself are often frozen. Visitors to the lake have included writers Mark Twain, John Muir, and John Steinbeck.

You'll know you've reached Emerald Bay when you hear a collective "Wow" from everyone in your car; it's an automatic reaction to one of the most spectacular sights in the West. The road approaches the southern edge of the bay and then circles 180 degrees around it. There are several spots where you can stop to take a picture.

In the mouth of the bay is tiny **Fannette Island,** the only island in the lake. It holds a tiny one-room "teahouse" built in the 1930s by the owner of the Vikingsholm estate during another of the periodic tourist booms around the lake.

If you can take your eyes away from the view of the bay to the right, look to the left to see the foothills of **Desolation Wilderness,** some 60,000 acres of, well, desolate wilderness. Several rough roads and hiking trails lead off into the hills. They are not for amateurs and often inaccessible in winter; check with park rangers for conditions.

At the north end of the bay is a parking lot at the head of a steep mile-long trail that descends to the shoreline of the lake and **Vikingsholm,** another treasure of the Tahoe Valley. The thirty-eight-room stone structure, built in 1929 by Lora Josephine Moore Knight, a wealthy socialite, is a replica of a 1,200-year-old Viking castle. Actually Mrs. Knight had planned to bring back fabulous antiquities from Norway and Sweden, but the Scandinavian governments declined to allow them to be removed, and instead expensive replicas were made.

Some 200 workmen were brought to Lake Tahoe in the spring of 1929, and the house was completed by summer's end. The estimated cost of Vikingsholm, in 1929 dollars, was $500,000.

There are two towers with turrets; part of the building is topped, in Viking style, with sod roofs that bloom with wildflowers in the spring. Inside, the castle is filled with antique and reproduction furnishings from Norway and other Scandinavian countries. The beams in the ceiling of the living room are intricately carved with dragon heads.

Vikingsholm is now managed by the state of California, and tours are conducted in summer months, generally from July 1 to Labor Day. There is a $5.00 admission fee for adults and $3.00 for children. For information call (530) 525–7277 or consult www.vikingsholm.com.

The **Rubicon Trail,** a 4-mile hiking path, connects to **D. L. Bliss State Park** at the north end of the lake in **Meeks Bay.** Some tour boats pull up at a dock near the castle; private boats can also come in from the lake.

The state park includes 1,237 acres of forests and a sand beach at **Rubicon Bay.** Naturalist programs are offered in the summer; the park is open from mid-June through mid-September. There is a daily use fee. In the summer parking is extremely limited at Bliss Park, with only twenty-five $5.00 day passes sold per day; the parking lot is usually filled by 10:00 A.M. For information call (530) 525–7277 or consult an unofficial fancier's page at www.rubicon-trail.com/Rubicon.

A hiking trail within Bliss Park leads to **Balancing Rock,** a 130-ton boulder resting on a small pedestal.

The 2,000-acre **Sugar Pine Point State Park** runs from Sugar Pine Point on the lake across the highway and up **General Creek** into Desolation Wilderness and the **Tahoe National Forest.** The park includes many majestic sugar pines, some as tall as 200 feet. Down near the lake is the **Ehrman Mansion,** a 1903 estate that was one of the social centers of the west shore in the Roaring Twenties.

The rock-and-wood estate was the summer cottage of Isaias Hellman, a businessman who was to become president of Wells Fargo Nevada National Bank. It was sold to the California State Park System in 1965, which today conducts tours in the summer. For information call (530) 525–7982 or consult www.parks.ca.gov/default.asp?page_id=510.

Summer hiking trails, including the **Dolder Nature Trail,** become Nordic ski trails in the winter.

The **Homewood Ski Area** extends to within feet of the highway at Homewood, with a marina on the lake side of the road. North of the ski area is a seaplane base for tourist flights and charters.

Idlewild, just below Tahoe City, was developed in the 1890s as a colony of the well-to-do from San Francisco.

Just south of Idlewild, you'll pass the imposing stone walls of **Fleur du Lac** (Flower of the Lake), built in 1939 for wealthy industrialist Henry Kaiser. There was a fabulous stone mansion surrounded by six cottages intended for the heads of Kaiser's six companies. Kaiser got his start with a road-paving business and went on to participate in the construction of the Boulder (now Hoover) Dam, the Grand Coulee Dam, and the San Francisco–Oakland Bridge. His Kaiser Industries included steelmaking, construction, and auto making.

Fleur du Lac was used for much of the location filming for *Godfather II* in the 1970s. Many of the original buildings are now gone, replaced by privately owned condominiums.

We're now at **Tahoe City.** From here you can continue across the top of the lake and back to Reno on the Mount Rose Highway, or go northwest to Truckee and Donner Lake and then east to Reno.

THE GREAT BONANZA ROAD FROM CALIFORNIA

TRIP 8: EASTWARD HO!

Meyers ▶ Stateline ▶ Pioneer Trail

Although our modern movie-shaped perceptions put the emphasis on the great westward rush of settlers personified by the Donner Party tragedy of 1846–1847, the process reversed for a while in the 1860s with the discovery of silver in and around Virginia City.

The present US 50 brought back thousands of miners and merchants from Sacramento and Placerville, California. The road follows the south fork of the American River for part of its route and then descends from the mountains into **Meyers.** From there it heads north to near the present site of South Lake Tahoe and adjoining Stateline, Nevada. Also from Meyers, though, is the Pioneer Trail, also known as the **Placerville-Carson Road,** which stays above the shoreline of the lake and heads for the front range of the Sierra Nevada.

We'll start our short tour from Meyers and head toward South Lake Tahoe and Stateline. If you're coming from Stateline, you can follow US 50 along the lake west to Meyers and then double back.

Meyers was settled in 1851 and included the **Yank's Station** trading post, named for owner Ephraim "Yank" Clement. About a decade later Yank's Station became an important remount point for Pony Express riders.

Today Meyers is a popular winter sports area with cross-country ski trails in and around **Echo Lake;** several companies run snowmobile tours to the mountain meadows.

Coming from California, the **Pioneer Trail** bears off to the right at Yank's Station, about 6 miles before the Y where Route 89 heads north around the lake and US 50 turns toward Stateline. At the peak of the eastward return from California to Virginia City around 1864, this section of the trail was said to be the busiest road in the West. Thousands of would-be miners and workers crossed above Lake Tahoe on foot, by stagecoach, or by horse. Each day some 300 tons of cargo were pulled along the narrow dirt or corduroy-wood roads. There were many inns and other way stations; the locations of many of them are marked with wooden pegs or signs.

Among the inns along the road, near where Cold Creek crosses the road, was the **Sierra House.** This inn was supposedly frequented by the infamous highway robbers Black Bart and Jack Bell, among others.

The completion in 1869 of the transcontinental railroad farther to the north through Truckee and across Donner Summit ended most of the slow traffic on the Pioneer Trail.

CHAPTER TWENTY-THREE

VIRGINIA CITY:
A SIDE TRIP BACK IN TIME

A CENTURY AGO VIRGINIA CITY went from desolation to the richest place in the country and then back to desolation in the course of a few decades.

Today it is a living ghost town, a museum in place, and one of my favorite places to visit and dream, wander and time travel. There are few places on Earth that, by their mere existence, speak so eloquently of their history.

As you stand on C Street in Virginia City and feel the mass of Mount Davidson over your shoulder, you may think you are on solid ground, but in fact you are perched atop a near-hollow shell. Millions of tons of rock have been removed from beneath your feet, and the hills around you are honeycombed with 750 miles of tunnel.

THE CARSON VALLEY REST STOP

Like many of the settlements described in this book, Carson Valley began as a rest stop. Thousands of emigrants seeking their riches in the 1840s gold rush in California passed through northern Nevada, and many of them stopped for provisions or spent the winter in the valley before making the treacherous crossing of the Sierra Nevada.

While they were in the area, some of the California gold-seekers explored a bit on the eastern side of the mountains. In July 1849 Abner Blackburn and the members of a Mormon wagon train spent some time on the banks of the Carson River; Blackburn found a few specks of gold in his pan near the present-day town of Dayton, but it was not enough to make the travelers stay.

In the coming few years, there were small discoveries among wagon trains waiting for the snows to melt in the mountain passes. One group panned its way up a small stream that flowed into the Carson River; they optimistically named the waterway **Gold Creek.** On June 1, 1850, one of the men discovered a gold nugget at an isolated rock formation now known as **Devil's Gate.**

During the following decade many small finds were made, including, according to the legend, a major discovery in **Gold Canyon** by brothers Allen and Hosea Grosh. Unfortunately both brothers died—one from blood poisoning caused by an accident and the other as the result of severe frostbite suffered on a crossing of the Sierra Nevada on a trip to California to raise money for a new mine.

This brings us, then, to scrappy miners Pat McLaughlin, Peter O'Reilly, and their grabby neighbor Henry Comstock. They began to mine the area at the head of **Six-Mile Canyon** in 1859, grinding the rock in search of gold and casting aside the black rock that got in the way.

Early gold miners complained about the sticky blue gray mud that fouled their picks, clothing, and shovels. It wasn't gold; some thought it was low-value lead. McLaughlin, O'Reilly, and the other miners, who had been earning about $876 per ton for gold-bearing ore, stopped complaining when the mud was assayed and discovered to be silver ore, worth $2,000 to $3,000 per ton. The Comstock Lode had been discovered.

Virginia City got its name from one of the first miners, James Finney, nicknamed "Old Virginny" after the state of his birth. Returning from a revelry, he supposedly dropped and broke a bottle of booze. Instead of crying over spilt whiskey, he christened the tent city on the slopes of Mount Davidson "Old Virginny Town" in his own honor.

GETTING TO VIRGINIA CITY

U.S. Highway 395 South ends about 10 miles south of Reno and becomes a two-lane highway; continue until you come to a traffic light at the intersection of two of the most interesting roads most drivers will ever experience: Highways 341 and 431. If you head left, you'll climb a mountain to Virginia City on 341; if you go right, you'll ascend 431 to Lake Tahoe.

Virginia City sits at 6,200 feet; Route 341 follows the **Geiger Grade,** which twists back and forth for 13 miles to its highest point of 6,799 feet before descending slightly as you reach the town. The trip is a total of 33 miles from Reno.

Insert Peg A into Slot B

Several years into the boom, a German engineer named Philip Deidesheimer invented the square-set method of timbering that supported the crumbling rock and enabled shafts to be dug to depths of more than 3,000 feet.

The timbering of the mine had another effect: the near denuding of the forests for miles around. In fact the search for more wood to timber the mines of Virginia City and Gold Hill extended over the Sierra Nevada.

One of the more ambitious engineering schemes of the day took place in what is now known as Incline Village, at the north end of Lake Tahoe. There, a lumber company built a primitive tramway that lifted logs up the side of a mountain to a flume where they were tumbled back down to waiting wagons that transported them to Virginia City.

Remnants of the tram can be seen near today's Incline Village.

Dying to Get In

Just below town is the Virginia City Cemetery. According to legend, there were eighty-eight violent deaths before someone spoiled the story by dying of natural causes.

As you drive up the serpentine Geiger Grade to Virginia City, think about how the miners and the suppliers brought their equipment and logs up the grade and how they brought their silver and gold ore back down. Take advantage of some of the turnoffs on the drive up; from some of the higher points, you can see the remains of the original **Geiger Trail,** which was even steeper and more twisty than the road you are negotiating in the relative comfort of your car.

The **Old Geiger Grade** was constructed by Davison M. Geiger and John H. Tilton in 1862 and served as the most direct connection between the Comstock Lode and **Truckee Meadows** until it was replaced by the present paved highway in 1936. Concord stages, mud wagons, and ten-mule "freighters" carried thousands of passengers and millions of dollars in precious cargo across this section of the Virginia Range.

In addition to the unpredictable winds, snow, and landslides, this area was also popular with highwaymen. A marker near the top of the grade points out the location of the descriptively named **Dead Man's Point** and **Robbers Roost.**

Just after you cross the summit of Geiger Peak, you will find a marker on your left for Louse Town. Near its location was a station established in 1860 on Geiger and Tilton's new toll road from Truckee Meadows.

Around Louse Town—what a picture that name paints—was a large population of teamsters, stock, and sheep men. The steep hillside included a racetrack, a trap-shooting range, and the first railroad surveys.

As you drive up the Geiger Grade, you will be assaulted by signs proclaiming your approach to something known as the "Suicide Table" at the **Delta Saloon.** It sounds a lot more sinister than it really is: The Suicide Table is an 1860 faro table that apparently was the source of lost fortunes for three of its owners, each of whom killed himself.

When you reach the town itself, find a parking space—a lot easier in the winter than the summer, when you may have to use an outlying lot—and walk to C Street. One good place to start is the privately run visitor center, which, in addition to selling knickknacks, continuously shows an interesting video about Virginia City.

A CITY ABOVE AND A WORLD BELOW

Mark Twain, under his real name of Samuel Clemens, worked for a while as a reporter for the *Territorial Enterprise.* Years later he wrote: "Virginia was a busy city of streets and houses above ground. Under it was another busy city, down in the bowels of the earth, where a great population of men thronged in and out among an intricate maze of tunnels and drifts, flitting hither and thither under

Virginia City

a winking sparkle of lights, and over their heads towered a vast web of inter-locking timbers that held the walls of the gutted Comstock apart."

The moneymaking engine for Virginia City was the fabled Comstock Lode, a 2½-mile deposit that paid out some $500 million in silver and $700 million in gold. About twenty million tons of ore were brought out of the 750 miles of workings.

Discovered in 1859 the **Comstock Lode** led to a wild twenty-year boom that helped bring Nevada into statehood in 1864, contributed funds to the Union Army, and helped build San Francisco. There were seven major mines, several of which can be seen from C Street.

At its peak Virginia City was home to an estimated 40,000 people, six brew-eries, one hundred saloons, four banks, five newspapers, and fifty dry-goods stores. The local payroll was about $500,000 a month. Restaurants imported lob-sters, raw oysters, champagne, caviar, and other fineries from San Francisco; the wives of the mine owners furnished their homes with European crystal and wore Parisian gowns.

According to one of many versions of the discovery of the riches in the hills and valleys south of Reno, miners Pat McLaughlin and Peter O'Reilly discovered a small quantity of gold-bearing rock at the head of **Six-Mile Canyon** in 1859. Henry Comstock, another prospector, made a loud but dubious claim that the men were trespassing on his property, and the lucky-then-unlucky miners set-tled the dispute by giving Comstock a neighboring piece of land. It was there

Low Finance

In 1869 John Mackay and James Fair bought an interest in the failing Hale and Norcross Mines. Joined by James Flood and William O'Brien, a pair of San Francisco saloon keepers turned stockbrokers, they bought the barren Consolidated Virginia Mine in 1872 for about $50,000.

They sunk an even deeper shaft and eventually struck the "Big Bonanza" 1,167 feet down. That one lode brought out $135 million in ore; in today's money that is worth more than $2 billion.

Mackay went on to lay the first Trans-Atlantic and Pacific telegraphic cable for a company competing against Western Union. Fair became a U.S. senator from the new state of Nevada. O'Brien and Flood spent their money.

that the gigantic lode was first found, and its riches were named after him and not its unfortunate previous owners.

By the 1880s, though, most of the riches had been extracted, with the profits taken to San Francisco, New York, or overseas. In fact between 1880 and 1890, the population of all of Nevada declined by 25 percent, and between 1890 and 1900 it declined still further. Nevada's mining boom reignited around 1900 with the discovery of gold and silver in the center of the state at Tonopah and Goldfield; those fields led in great part to the development of Las Vegas as a railroad town.

The decline of the boomtowns on the western and northwestern sides of the state continued, though. Virginia City probably would have completely disappeared were it not for the birth of the tourist industry in the second half of the twentieth century.

■ ALMOST EVERYTHING YOU WANTED TO KNOW ABOUT MINING

Dan DeQuille, whose real name was William Wright, headed west from Ohio with the news of the silver discoveries in the Comstock Lode. Failing as a miner, he became a journalist and in 1862 joined the staff of the *Territorial Enterprise* in Virginia City. In that same year the newspaper also hired Sam Clemens (later to gain fame as Mark Twain) for a brief stint. In 1875 Clemens persuaded Wright to publish his remembrances of the wild times in Virginia City. Wright's book was called *The Big Bonanza,* and it paints a vivid picture of the difficulties and rewards of the time.

As rich as the Comstock Lode was, the Hollywood myth of miners carving out huge chunks of gold or silver rarely actually happened. Instead there were tiny flakes of precious metal embedded in quartz or other rocks. There was much hard work involved in extracting the wealth. The first test of the worth of a piece of ore was usually done on the spot.

The results of the test in a vessel known as a "horn" were generally enough to tell the miner whether to load up a larger sample and bring it into town to an assayer's office. There a determination would be made of the value of the ore by the ton.

Wright reported:

If a specimen of ore was supposed to contain silver, it was pulverized in the same way as gold-bearing quartz, then was placed in the horn, and the lighter matter it contained washed out. . . . The heavy residuum was then washed from the horn into a matrass (a flask of annealed glass, with a narrow neck and a broad bottom). Nitric acid was then poured into the matrass until the matter to be tested was covered, when the flask was suspended over the flame of a candle or lamp and boiled until the fumes escaping (which are for a time red) came off white.

When the contents of the matrass had been allowed to cool and settle, the liquid portion was poured off into a vial of clear, thin glass, called a test-tube. A few drops of a strong solution of common salt was now poured into the test-tube. If the ore . . . contained silver, the contents of the test-tube would at once assume a milky hue.

Anyone who has worked in a darkroom has worked with the same basic set of chemicals, by the way. What the test produced was a silver salt, which is the basis of photographic film and paper. In fact some miners would take the test tube out into the desert sun for a few minutes and observe the effect of strong light on the solution: If there was silver in the salt solution, the liquid would turn purplish black.

VIRGINIA CITY: HISTORY UNDERFOOT

Stop for a moment in Virginia City and absorb the history that surrounds you. The old buildings with their wooden walkways on C Street mostly date from about 1875, the year when fire nearly wiped out the town, destroying more than 2,000 structures. After the Great Fire the entire town was rebuilt within six months, so strong was the faith that the underground riches would continue forever. Of course this did not happen, but there was just enough activity in the mines to keep the town alive.

In 1875 30,000 people lived in town. The **Fourth Ward School,** built in 1876 and still standing, was one of the first commercial buildings west of the Mississippi that had indoor plumbing. The six-story **International Hotel** had the West's first elevator, which they named a "rising room."

As befits a wild place with a lot of money, Virginia City quickly became home to celebrities, Shakespearean plays, opium dens, newspapers, competing fire companies, police precincts, and a red-light district.

The **Combination Mine** was the deepest mine in the region, going down 3,262 feet—half the way to sea level. These deep mines did suffer from a significant problem, that of flooding from underground springs. To make things even more difficult, the water was often hot and sulphurous. Mine owners were forced to install huge devices such as the Cornish pump at the **Union Mine,** which had a 45-foot flywheel and a pump rod that extended 2,500 feet down the shaft and could lift more than one million gallons of water to the surface each day.

The grandest scheme for removing the water from the mines, though, was that of businessman Adolph Sutro who came from Prussia in 1850 in search of wealth in California. He amassed his first fortune in retail and real estate ventures in San Francisco, but he was drawn to Virginia City in 1860. He ran a successful reduction mill at Dayton.

Citizen Hearst

George Hearst, the father of newspaper magnate William Randolph Hearst, started the family fortune as a stockbroker in Virginia City. He claimed that his fortune was built entirely on commissions from the sale of stock and that he never had any direct involvement in Comstock shares.

Sutro saw the problems of ventilation and removal of water from the deep mines and came up with the idea of a deep tunnel that would run from 3 miles east of Dayton near the Carson River under the base of the mountains to link up with the mines of Virginia City. Mine operators would only have to drain their operations to the Sutro Tunnel and not to the surface. He expanded his concept to include the use of the tunnel as an emergency evacuation route for miners and as an underground transportation system that would bring the ore from the various mines to mills at the mouth of the tunnel.

It took more than eight years to secure financing, permits, and permissions. He even had to obtain a special act of Congress, the Sutro Tunnel Act of 1866, which granted him the land and the right to charge royalties to companies using the tunnel. Investors came from as far away as England and Germany.

Construction of the 3.8-mile tunnel began on October 19, 1869; it was July 8, 1878, when the tunnel connected with the **Savage Mine** at the 1,640-foot level. However, by the time the tunnel was completed, most of the major mines had gone far deeper than that. The tunnel did serve its original purpose as a means of getting some of the water out of the tunnels, but little more. Sutro eventually returned to California, where he made more money in real estate and even served a term as mayor of San Francisco, from 1895 to 1897.

The **Ponderosa Saloon,** established in 1873, has some of its walls lined with old flume boards from the Virginia and Gold Hill Water Company. Iron pipes brought water from the High Sierra down across the Washoe Valley and up to a reservoir 5 miles from town. From there wooden flumes brought water to Virginia City. The original system was used until 1957.

The Ponderosa Saloon is located in the former site of the Bank of California, established in 1864. Within the saloon you can walk into the old bank vault; the Bank of California provided much of the capital for the early growth of the Comstock mines. Much of the billion dollars in earnings passed through the doors to be stored in the vault, which is lined from ceiling to floor with half-inch steel plate; the outside walls are 2 feet thick.

On October 25, 1927, the Bank of California was robbed of $32,000. The robbers were eventually caught, but much of the loot was never recovered and is supposedly hidden in the hills around Six-Mile Canyon.

At the back of the Ponderosa is a hoisting cage salvaged from one of the many mines in the area. There are some rather unique safety features in the upper frame. The weight of the cage hanging on the flat woven steel cable would turn the safety to the flat side; if the cable should break, the theory was that the safety would roll outward, sinking the gear teeth into the wooden guide beams on the side of the shaft and stopping the cage from plunging to the bottom.

One of the greatest dangers of the mines was the extremely fast ascent and descent of the cages. The waist-high fencing on the cage was installed to protect miners from being injured or killed by banging into the sharp rock on the sides of the shaft.

You can visit a portion of the **Ponderosa Mine** from the back of the Ponderosa Saloon on South C Street. The mine tour at the Ponderosa is a walking tour that goes about 300 feet through a modern shaft that reaches a portion of the 1869 **Best and Belcher Mine.** Admission to the twenty-five-minute tour is about $4.00 for adults, $1.50 for children, or $8.50 for a family of two adults and all children younger than twelve. Tours are available year-round from 10:00 A.M. to 4:30 P.M.; in winter open weekends only. For information call (775) 847–0757.

A few steps past the back room of the Ponderosa puts you into the access shaft to the abandoned Best and Belcher Mine. The mine closed for the first time in 1863 during the Civil War; the Bank of California built its office at the location, and around 1874 the mine was reopened when a higher grade of ore was found. In 1917 the owners closed the mine and walked away, leaving tools, dynamite, and rail cars in place.

The tour heads 377 feet straight back into the mountainside, in year-round temperatures of fifty to sixty degrees; off to the sides of the horizontal stope (working area of the mine) are several 200-foot-deep shafts. A single miner would be lowered to the bottom of the shaft in a bucket; he would fill the same bucket with ore, which would be lifted back up.

At the end of his shift, he would use the same bucket to ride back up—as our guide pointed out, the miner at the bottom would work hard to make sure he remained good friends with the man at the top.

Among major problems for miners was the lack of oxygen or the pressure of methane gas. The mines were lit by candlelight, and the fixtures also included hooks to hold caged canaries to serve as early warning devices. Mules were commonly used in the mines. Some of the animals spent their entire lives underground; they were bred and born without ever seeing the sun. In fact they were not allowed to come up to daylight for fear that they would be blinded.

Stamping Mill

About twenty-five men worked in the mine at a time, making about 12 feet of progress per day.

Deep into the tour, at a point where the stope ends at a wooden platform covering a 500-foot-deep shaft, the guide may turn out the electric lights to show you the scene by candlelight . . . and then blow out the candle to plunge you into the darkest darkness you are ever likely to experience. Because pumping is no longer performed in the tunnels, water has risen about halfway up the shaft.

The **Chollar Mine** at South F Street and D Street is open for walking tours from mid-May through late October from 10:00 A.M. to 4:00 P.M. Visitors can also pan for gold. Admission is about $4.00 for adults and $1.00 for children ages five to fourteen. Panning costs an extra $5.00. For information call (775) 847–0155.

On my most recent trip, I went with a group about 400 feet into the side of the mountain through a narrow, low-ceilinged access tunnel. At the face of the mine it feels very lonely.

The front window of the **Red Garter Saloon** celebrates the gift made by "Barbara," one of the most sought-after ladies of the night, to her new husband. The inscription reads, "To Judge Orville Hardison from his loving wife Barbara on the occasion of her retirement and our marriage, July 23, 1893." The gift came from Barbara's personal collection of business tools: a dagger with a bone handle, a .41-caliber ivory-handle Colt Derringer, and her red garter.

You're not likely to be able to resist the insistent come-ons to see the Suicide Table at the **Delta Saloon.** While you are there, check out the old nickelodeon at the back of the saloon, which features "Grandpa's Pin-Up Girls in 3D." The Delta also includes a collection of old coin-operated devices, including a gypsy fortune teller and an Electric Traveling Crane that can scoop up candy and trinkets.

The Delta was the first saloon rebuilt after the disastrous fire of 1875.

Of the one hundred saloons—that's no mistake, one hundred—in Virginia City, the Delta was the most famous because of its gaming room where a significant part of the riches of the Bonanza was gambled away in games of Rocky Mountain (a variation of blackjack) or another card game known as faro. Today the game of choice is a collection of more than a hundred slot machines. For information call (775) 847–0789 or (888) 429–8635.

Directly opposite the Delta Saloon on C Street is a small monument constructed from pieces of ore from every Nevada county. It was erected in 1958 commemorating the one-hundredth anniversary of the discovery of silver.

The *Territorial Enterprise* **Museum** on C Street commemorates the famous newspaper, as well as some of its best-known employees, including Samuel Clemens (Mark Twain) and Dan DeQuille. The *Enterprise* was Nevada's first newspaper and most celebrated in the Old West. Founded at Genoa in 1858, it was moved to Virginia City in 1859. The paper suspended publication in 1916 but was revived in 1952. For information consult www.territorial-enterprise.com or www.cr.nps.gov/nr/travel/nevada/ter.htm.

The **Crystal Bar** on C Street first opened in 1871; it has remained in one family since 1909. The original crystal chandeliers and mirrors arrived at San Francisco by ship from France and were sent by railroad to Virginia City. During

Prohibition the Crystal Bar was officially converted to an ice cream parlor; unofficially it continued as a speakeasy.

At the top end of C Street is the **Fourth Ward School,** built in 1875. The cut stone foundation is anchored in solid granite from Mount Davidson. The four-story structure was built to accommodate 1,025 students in fourteen classrooms and two study halls. The last grammar and high school students to use the school were members of the Class of 1936. After sitting dormant for many years, it was restored by the Nevada State Museum and includes a fascinating exhibit about the history of the Comstock, including models of the mines and their works. The museum, at the end of C Street on the way out of town toward Gold Hill, is open from May to November. For information call (775) 847–0975 or consult www.cr.nps.gov/nr/travel/nevada/fou.htm.

The modern-day Virginia City High School, home of the "Muckers" football team, is down in the valley below the town.

For a decidedly offbeat view of old Virginia City, you might want to check out the **Julia Bulette Red Light Museum** at 5 C Street. (The sign out front warns that the exhibit is not for the "faint of heart.") We didn't see anyone being carried out on stretchers, but we did see an exhibit not often seen in museums: Opium pipes and other drug paraphernalia, slightly risqué (by today's standards) French postcards, and leftovers from the local brothels were among the items on display. Open daily from 10:00 A.M. to 7:00 P.M. or later. Admission: $1.00. For information call (775) 847–9394.

The **Virginia & Truckee Railroad** was built to serve the needs of the mines in 1869. The first track linked Virginia City to Carson City; in 1872 the line was connected to Reno, 30 miles north, directly linking Virginia City to the transcontinental line from the East to San Francisco on the West Coast. At its height as many as forty-five trains a day arrived and departed from Virginia City. Think about that number: That's several an hour, day and night.

Work began in April 1868 with more than 1,000 mostly Chinese workmen working on parts of the line spread from Virginia City to Carson City; the rails were tied together and the first train ran on November 12 of that year. The line had an almost immediate effect, dropping the cost of supplies brought into the mining area and reducing the freight for the ore moving out; the lowered cost made some of the marginal mines more profitable and extended the boom.

The trip to Carson City was only 21 miles long, but it was a very difficult distance to traverse. Tracks dropped about 1,600 feet over 13 miles, making twenty complete circles and crossing a huge wooden trestle at Crown Point.

By 1938 traffic had diminished so much that the link to the state capital was discontinued, and in 1950 the last train was run to Reno. Parts of the line were rebuilt and restored in 1976 for the tourist trade, and the railroad takes visitors on an interesting circuit through the mining areas in the summer months, pulled by a real steam engine.

The half-hour trips go from the V & T depot on F Street past the Chollar Mine and through Tunnel Number 4 to Gold Hill and back; passengers can get off the train at Gold Hill and catch a later trip back to Virginia City. Trains run from the

Pool's Gold

The Brunswick Ledge, a rich ore body about a mile east of the Comstock Lode, probably received its name in honor of the billiard tables in the back rooms of several of the bars in Virginia City.

end of May through late October, weather permitting. Fares are about $5.50 for adults and $2.75 for children; an all-day pass is $10.00. For information call (775) 847–0380 or consult www.steamtrain.org.

Work is under way on a resurrection of at least some of the former glory of the railroad, with hopes of more to come. In 2006 track was restored 2 miles past Gold Hill, in the direction of Carson City. One of the V & T's original steam engines, the Dayton, has been housed at the Nevada State Railroad Museum and is now on display in Virginia City. The engine was used in several movies, including *Union Pacific* with Barbara Stanwyck, *The Lady from Cheyenne* with Loretta Young, and *Nevada City* with the original Hollywood cowboy, Roy Rogers.

In 1952 the *Territorial Enterprise* was bought by former New York society columnist Lucius Beebe and his associate Charles Clegg. They came to town in great Eastern style, running the paper until 1961. Among the changes they brought to Virginia City were their ornately decorated railroad cars.

The Virginia & Truckee Railroad train ticket window is located within a bright yellow rail car on C Street. V & T Car No. 13 is said to be the only railroad car ever designed expressly for transportation of precious metals, built in 1874 for the Virginia & Truckee and used until 1939 to transport millions of dollars in silver and gold from Virginia City to the mint at Carson City and to the Southern Pacific Railroad at Reno. Like much of Virginia City, there's not much to see or do on the train, except to soak in the history that is all around and below you. And that's a good thing.

The **Nevada Gambling Museum** is a small display of slot machines—some of them playable for free and one of the few chances for children to lay hands on a slot machine, even though they can't win any money—as well as guns, knives, cheating devices, rare photos, and gambling artifacts. The museum is at 50 South C Street. Open year-round from 10:00 A.M. to 5:00 P.M. For information call (775) 847–9022.

And now we come to one of the stranger elements of today's Virginia City: the **International Camel Races.** It all began with the little-known fact that camels were used in some parts of the Wild West as pack animals; there was even a U.S. Army Camel Corps. They were brought to the Comstock to carry salt and general supplies in the early, disorganized days of mining. After the major mines were functioning and the Virginia & Truckee Railroad was the main freight carrier, the camels—not known as particularly affectionate pets—were turned loose in the hills and eventually disappeared.

In the 1950s, though, in the tradition of Mark Twain, Dan DeQuille, and other tongue-in-cheek writers for the paper, the *Territorial Enterprise* published a totally fabricated account of the result of a great camel race. In 1960 a race was held for real in a challenge that reached to San Francisco, with movie director

John Huston winning the first race on a camel borrowed from the San Francisco Zoo. Quite logically, ostrich races were added in 1962.

Traditionally the camel races are held on the weekend after Labor Day in Virginia City in an arena east of F Street and in mid-May in Alice Springs, Australia, sister city to Virginia City. For more information consult www.all camels.com/storefront/vccr.

Other unusual events in Virginia City include the **Ferrari Club of America Hill Climb** and apparently unrelated **World Championship Outhouse Races and Privy Parade,** all held in October of each year. In November and December Virginia City celebrates **Christmas on the Comstock.** And in March there is the **World Championship Mountain Oyster Fry.** (If you don't know what a mountain oyster is, be sure to ask before you take a bite. Or ask the emasculated bull cowering in the brush.)

For information on events contact the chamber at (775) 847–0311.

A recent convenience for visitors is the **Silver Line Express** ticket, which offers all-in-one admission to a number of Virginia City's attractions. Included are the Ponderosa Mine Tour, Mackay Mansion, Saint Mary's Art Center, and Piper's Opera House. For more information consult www.virginiacity-nv.org.

OFF THE BEATEN TRACK IN VIRGINIA CITY

Virginia City is laid out in an aboveground mirror of the square-set timbering that holds up the mines below ground. The main streets run north and south and are labeled from A Street (highest up on Mount Davidson) to F Street down in the valley. Cross streets run east and west and carry names, many drawn from those of the founders or wealthy landowners of early days.

The main commercial district, described above, runs along C Street; many of the once-grand mansions were built on Millionaire's Row on B Street up the mountain, while some of the workers lived down below. Some of the upper homes managed to escape the 1875 fire.

Start your tour at the south end of town on B Street at the **Castle.** This local must-see is a snapshot of how the world came to Virginia City when it was at its peak. Built from 1863 to 1868 for Robert Graves, the superintendent of the Empire Mine, the sixteen-room mansion was designed to look like a castle in Normandy and was furnished with the best money could buy. Furnishings include a 600-year-old Heidelberg sideboard, crystal chandeliers from Czechoslovakia, and elegant wallpaper from France. It is even more amazing when you consider that virtually everything in the Castle was sent by boat from Europe around the Horn to San Francisco and then overland through the Sierra Nevada and into Virginia City.

The Castle was above the fire, and most of the original furnishings are still intact; it is open for tours from May to November. Admission: adults $4.50, children ages thirteen to seventeen $2.00, children ages six to twelve 50 cents. For information call (775) 847–0275.

At 158 South B is the **A. M. Cole Mansion,** a classic Victorian built in 1887 for a successful pharmacist. Nearby at 130 South B is the **Water Company Building,** constructed in 1875 for the offices of the Virginia City and Gold Hill Water Company.

Providing drinking water to the burgeoning city at the top of the mountain was a difficult matter; what little groundwater there was available quickly became fouled by runoff from the mines, and in any case there was nowhere near enough for 40,000 residents.

The solution was yet another gargantuan project for Virginia City, a system that imported water nearly 20 miles from Hobart Creek near Lake Tahoe, 8 miles across Washoe Valley, and back up a 1,500-foot climb over the mountains to Virginia City. Almost immediately the water supply was insufficient, and so the wooden pipes and sluiceways were extended another 8 miles to Marlette Lake, high up in the Sierra Nevada.

Our tour continues on to the **Storey County Courthouse,** built in 1877 to replace an earlier building destroyed by the fire. The Victorian-style courthouse is still open and used for government offices. Take a close look at the statue of Justice. What's wrong with the picture? Justice is not blindfolded, and the scales are in balance. It could be sloppy work; then again, it may be a message from the past. The working building is open to the public during business hours.

The next building of note is **Piper's Opera House.** Every decent Western boomtown had to have an opera house; in fact the miners and upper class of Virginia City probably received a richer diet of culture than do modern Americans. John Piper's wooden structure—the third in a succession of theaters he built on the Comstock—was completed in 1885 and featured carpeted floors, hanging balconies, and a spring-mounted dance floor. Performances ranged from Shakespearean plays to Italian operas to dog fights. Great actors and performers seen at Piper's included Edwin Booth, Harry Houdini, Lillie Langtry, John Philip Sousa, and Buffalo Bill Cody. Inside are the raked stage and elegant proscenium boxes along with some of the original scenery.

In recent years the opera house was renovated and reopened for live performances, lectures, and music in the Victorian Grand Ballroom. And the **Nevada Shakespeare Festival** has conducted a summer season of plays by Shakespeare and others.

The opera house is open for tours afternoons in the spring and summer on an irregular schedule at an admission price of $3.00; for information call (775) 847–0433 or consult www.pipersoperahouse.org or www.cr.nps.gov/nr/travel/nevada/pip.htm.

Three different **International Hotels** once stood on a single spot just below Piper's Opera House. The first hotel, a fourteen-room wood structure, was built in 1860 and dismantled in 1863. The second, a one-hundred-room, four-story brick building, was destroyed by the Great Fire of 1875. The third and grandest International Hotel opened its doors in March 1877 with 160 rooms on six floors, complete with hot and cold running water, steam heat, gas lighting, and the first hydraulic elevator in Nevada. The hotel was destroyed by fire in 1914 and was not rebuilt because of the Comstock's decline.

Past the courthouse is the **Knights of Pythias Hall,** built in 1876. Next door is the **Miners Union Hall,** organized in 1863 as the first such protective association for miners; among its accomplishments was the negotiation of a munificent minimum daily wage of $4.00; the Union Hall offered the rough and tough miners a ballroom, library, and chess room.

As you face the Union Hall, look up the mountain and to the right to see the **Orphir Pit,** the site of the original gold strike.

Climb up to A Street; from here we will head back to the south. At 6 South A Street is the Victorian home built for George Hanning, a prosperous Virginia City merchant.

Here you'll find a marker near where the Great Fire began early in the morning of October 26, 1875, when a coal oil lamp was knocked over in Crazy Kate's boardinghouse. Strong winds spread the flames, and supplies of blasting powder in and around the mines made the blaze much worse. In all, 33 blocks of structures were leveled. Losses included Saint Mary's in the Mountains Catholic Church, the Storey County Court House, Piper's Opera House, the International Hotel, and city offices of most of Virginia City's business district. The offices and hoisting works of nearby mines were also destroyed. The marker is near a small hose house that was part of a hydrant system put into place after the fire. The system is still in use today.

There are two short streets above A Street with a commanding view of the valley. At 66 Howard Street is the **King Mansion,** a castlelike structure built in 1861 for George King, secretary of the Virginia & Truckee Railroad.

Now we drop down below the C Street commercial district. The former red-light district is located on D Street, just below the **Silver Dollar Hotel** between Union and Sutton Streets.

According to legend the queen of lower Virginia City was Julia Bulette. Some of the grand stories about her—which may or may not be true—said that she was at the center of Virginia City's cultural establishment with her own box at the opera and drove around town in a formal horse-drawn brougham with her own crest on the door. The tourist guides will tell you she also sold her charms for as much as $1,000 per night. They'll say she was a favorite of the miners and had a mine named after her; the railroaders put her name on a V & T car, and she was named an honorary member of Fire Engine Company No. 1. Perhaps.

An undisputed fact is that on the morning of January 20, 1867, Bulette was found brutally murdered in her bed; a chest full of valuable jewelry and other possessions may have been missing. Many of the men of the town, including the firemen, showed up for her funeral and again for the trial and eventual hanging of the accused murderer, a Frenchman named Jean Millain.

Bulette's house was located on D Street at Union directly above the V & T depot and freight yards. Look above the row of slot machines in the Ponderosa Saloon for a rosy painting of Ms. Bulette.

Moving southward, you will come to the **Mackay Mansion** at 129 South D

Street, originally built as the office for the Gould & Curry Mine, which had its shaft across the street. The first occupant was mining superintendent George Hearst, the originator of the Hearst family fortune; after the Great Fire of 1875, mining millionaire John Mackay took over the building as his home. Now open year-round as a museum, its treasures include old mining equipment, original furnishings, and Tiffany silverware. Admission: about $3.00. For information call (775) 847–0173 or consult www.mackaymansion.com.

Continue south to the **Savage Mansion** at 146 D Street; this building had a similar history with the offices of the Savage Mine on the ground floor and the residence of the mine manager on the upper two levels.

Near the south end of D Street, below the Fourth Ward School, is the **Chollar Mansion,** built in 1883 as an office and residence for the Chollar-Potosi Mining Company. For information consult www.cr.nps.gov/nr/travel/nevada/cho.htm.

Drop down one more row to E Street to **Saint Mary's in the Mountains** church. The Victorian Gothic structure was rebuilt after the Great Fire; according to legend, silver king John Mackay paid for the reconstruction after he had convinced the priest to send his parishioners to help save the mine buildings and let the church burn. Within the church is a display of history. A railroad tunnel for the V & T once ran in front of the church to the depot at the end of the line.

On F Street at Union at the bottom of town is **Saint Mary's Hospital,** built in 1875 with much of the funding from Mackay; the former Chinatown, a community of almost 2,000 people, was located in front of the hospital. Saint Mary's is now an arts center.

SURROUNDING TOWNS

As you drive out of Virginia City toward Carson City, you will come to **Gold Hill,** site of other major discoveries. There are remains of former mines on the left and right as you traverse the switchbacks, including one of the sharpest S-turns you will ever experience, alongside a mountainside that has been completely dug away in modern-day pit mining.

Gold Hill, just outside Virginia City, was the actual location where the Comstock Lode was first found. By 1865, just six years after the first strike, Gold Hill had three foundries, two banks, two newspapers, and several thousand residents; the population peaked at 9,000. The mines, though, petered out in the 1870s, and Gold Hill became a ghost town in the first half of the twentieth century. Since then there have been sporadic attempts to bring out ore using modern methods, the most recent ending in 1983.

You'll see some old workings and hoisting wheels in and around the **Gold Hill Hotel and Saloon.** The 1859 stone-and-brick building was the first hotel in the Comstock and the oldest hostelry in the state. Restored to something approaching its boomtown finest, it is once again open for guests.

A nearby marker is on the site of the first recorded claim in the Comstock Lode. Across from the saloon is the site of the **Gold Hill Brewery.**

The former terminal for the Virginia & Truckee Railroad is at the north end of town, about a mile south of Virginia City on Highway 342. Completed in 1869 it was in use until 1938. For information consult www.cr.nps.gov/nr/travel/nevada/gol.htm.

▥ SILVER CITY

Silver City was another mining town on the Comstock and the location of the tollbooth for the locally famed **Devil's Gate Toll Road** that led up the winding canyon from Dayton and Carson City to Virginia City.

But for an accident of history, the story of the Comstock Lode might have centered on Silver City instead of Virginia City up the road. The brothers Allen and Hosea Grosh discovered silver here in 1856, but both died in 1857 before their ore was assayed.

Below Silver City is the former location of **McCone's Foundries,** first established in 1862 at John Town, 2 miles southeast in Gold Canyon. After two years the operation was moved to Silver City. A fire on May 15, 1872, left nothing standing but the walls. McCone then bought the Fulton Foundry in Virginia City and made it the largest in the state, employing 110 men at its peak. All the early castings of the Virginia & Truckee Railroad were manufactured at Fulton's.

Henry Comstock, who horned his way into history with a cut of the fabulous lode that now bears his name, operated a store in Silver City for a short while after he sold his claim (for a paltry $10,000); he went broke when the mines petered out, and he left for new boomtowns in Montana, eventually committing suicide in 1870.

▥ DAYTON

Dayton, at the location where the Gold Canyon empties into the Carson River, was a rest stop for travelers on their way to California and a Pony Express station. A permanent settlement and a tent trading post were established around 1851, just after Genoa was founded; the area was at first named Chinatown because of the Chinese railroad workers who populated the area. After the gold discoveries on the other side of the range, the community was renamed Dayton and, with a population of about 2,500, was considered as a site for the state capital before it ended up a few miles west in Carson City.

Adolph Sutro lived in Dayton and operated a stamp mill there to serve mining interests. It was in Dayton where Sutro located the exit for his fantastic tunnel into the Comstock Lode to drain water and remove the ore; there were great hopes when the **Sutro Tunnel** was being planned and constructed, but the boom never came.

Dayton has the oldest cemetery in the state, with tombstones recording the names of many of the pioneers mentioned in this book, including James "Old Virginny" Finney, who gave Virginia City its name.

The **Dayton Historic Society Museum** features memorabilia and photographs from Dayton's history depicting pioneers, woodcutters, Native Americans, Chinese immigrants, ranching, railroading, the Sutro Tunnel, and early Lyon County history. The museum, located in Nevada's second-oldest schoolhouse, on Shady Lane, is open Saturday from 10:00 A.M. to 4:00 P.M. and

Sunday from 1:00 to 4:00 P.M. from Memorial Day through Labor Day, and by special appointment. Admission is free. For information call (775) 246–3256 or consult www.daytonnvhistory.org.

After a hundred years of decline, Dayton was once again a glittering boom-town for a short time in 1960 when Hollywood came to town to film *The Misfits* with stars including Marilyn Monroe and Clark Gable.

ACCOMMODATIONS IN THE VIRGINIA CITY AREA

Remember: You're looking for historical ambience and realism, right? You are not going to find the opulence of a Harrah's or the big-city hotel amenities of a Reno Hilton here in the hills. You will, though, find old-time bed-and-breakfasts, inns, and an antique hotel or two. (If you must have more modern facilities, continue on down the hill to Carson City.)

For general information about Virginia City, call (775) 847–0311.

Chollar Mansion. 565 South D Street, Virginia City. A bed-and-breakfast within the former mansion and office built in 1861 for a mine superintendent. The hotel includes rooms decorated with Victorian-era furnishings, an arched vault that once stored millions of dollars' worth of silver and gold bullion, and the paymaster's booth. The guest library includes a large collection of books on Virginia City and the surrounding area. Rooms range from about $75 to $110 for a double; there is also a guest cottage available for $125. (775) 847–9777.

Comstock Lodge. 875 South C Street, Virginia City. A motel-like lodge just outside of downtown with room rates of about $48 to $65 for a double. (775) 847–0233.

The Crooked House B&B. 8 South F Street, Virginia City. Room rates about $65 to $125. (800) 340–6353 or (775) 847–4447.

Gold Hill Hotel and Crown Point Restaurant. 1540 Main Street, Gold Hill. Nevada's oldest operating hotel, this Victorian country inn—very ordinary from the outside—was built in 1859, less than a mile down the canyon from Virginia City in Gold Hill. There are fifteen refurbished guest rooms, four with private fireplaces; a separate building offers three kitchen suites. The hotel's great room features a massive open-hearth stone fireplace. Room rates range from about $40 to $200. (775) 847–0111.

Silver Queen Hotel. 28 North C Street. The only original hotel in the heart of Virginia City, more than one hundred years old. Twenty-nine rooms, with rates ranging from about $45 to $95. (775) 847–0468.

Sugar Loaf Mountain Motel. 416 South C Street. Parts of the building date from 1878. Rates from $40 to $58. (775) 847–0551.

Tyson's Canyon Ranch. Seven-Mile Canyon, Virginia City. A civilized dude ranch about a mile north of Virginia City, with furnished homes and horses for rent. Rooms range from about $125 to $135. (775) 847–7223. www.nevadadude ranch.com.

CHAPTER TWENTY-FOUR

CARSON CITY: A CAPITAL BEFORE THERE WAS A STATE

LIKE THE STATE FOR WHICH IT SERVES as capital, Carson City is a bit unusual. To begin with, it is one of the smallest capitals in the nation with just 53,000 or so residents.

The site of Carson City lay in the Eagle Valley on the Overland Trail, over which stages and the Pony Express crossed the Sierra Nevada on the south side of Lake Tahoe on route to Sacramento, California. Once again here is the story of a city—a state capital, even—that grew from a rest stop.

The commercial founder of Carson City was Abraham Curry, a businessman from Ithaca, New York, who arrived in Eagle Valley in 1858 just a year before the discovery of the Comstock Lode. Curry sought his riches as a merchant, buying an existing ranch and trading post to serve both the emigrants heading to California and, as it turned out, the gold seekers coming the other direction to the Comstock.

Though the idea of Nevada as a state was still a rather remote dream, Curry started out developing the site as a future capital, even calling the "downtown" of his hardscrabble sand empire Capitol Square.

He named the developing town Carson City after the famed guide Kit Carson, who was still alive at the time.

In addition to his skill as a merchant, Curry proved to be an able politician. He promoted his town site at every opportunity and also struck an alliance with the territorial governor, James Nye, who was another refugee from New York. The first territorial government was centered in Carson City, and in 1864 when statehood was granted, it became the capital.

Among his other activities Curry served as the warden of the first territorial prison—inmates constructed many of the early sandstone buildings that make up the core of the city today. In 1865 the federal government ordered the construction of a branch of the U.S. Mint in Carson City to convert some of the gold and silver into the coinage of the realm, and Curry built the structure to house it and served as its first superintendent.

Carson City, along with much of the western part of the state, went into decline around 1880 as the Comstock Lode petered out. The population did not recover to its 1880 level of about 7,500 until about 1960.

TOURING CARSON CITY

Stop at the Carson City Convention and Visitors Bureau at 1900 South Carson Street to pick up a touring map for the capital. At more than twenty "talking houses," small transmitters broadcast to car radios and portable radios on the AM band. Among the "celebrity" broadcasters are actors portraying Mark Twain, Carson City founder Abe Curry, and Hannah Clapp, the town's original feminist. For information about the broadcasts, you can call the bureau at (775) 687–7410 or consult www.carson-city.org.

The **Nevada State Museum** is a small but rich collection of artifacts and displays that tell the story of Nevada from prehistoric times to the current day. The museum is located within the old Carson City Mint Building, which operated from 1870 to 1893, producing nearly sixty million coins, including the famous Carson City silver dollar. According to official records, the Carson City mint struck a total of $49,274,434.30 in coinage.

The sandstone blocks for the building were quarried at a nearby prison. Installed out front is a time capsule put in place on October 31, 1964, for the centennial of Nevada, to remain sealed until the year 2064. On display just inside the doors of the museum is the original coin press, a massive six-ton apparatus manufactured by a Philadelphia company. The big press struck its first coin, a silver dollar, in 1870.

Up to 175 tons of pressure was required to strike a gold double eagle. The intense strain soon caused a crack to develop in the arch of the press; the foundry at the shops of the Virginia & Truckee Railroad in Carson City cast a new three-ton iron arch in 1878 to repair the press. In 1899 the press was dismantled and shipped to the Philadelphia mint. It was rebuilt in 1930 to work with an electric motor and was transferred to the San Francisco mint in 1945, where it operated for ten more years. When that mint closed, the press was saved from the scrap heap and

Carson City Area Information

▶ **Carson City Chamber of Commerce.** 1900 South Carson Street, Suite 100, Carson City, NV 89701. (775) 882–1565. www .carsoncitychamber.com.

▶ **Carson City Convention and Visitors Bureau.** 1900 South Carson Street, Suite 200, Carson City, NV 89701. (775) 687–7410, (800) 638–2321. www .carson-city.org.

▶ **Carson Valley Chamber of Commerce and Visitors Authority.** 1512 Highway 395, No. 1, Gardnerville, NV 89410–7814. (775) 782–8144, (800) 727– 7677. www.carsonvalleynv .org.

▶ **Reno-Sparks Chamber of Commerce.** 133 North Sierra Street, Reno, NV 89503. (775) 686–3030. www.reno-sparkschamber .org.

returned to its first home as part of the Nevada State Museum. In 1964 the coin press was loaned to the Denver mint for three years to help alleviate a national coin shortage. The old press is still used occasionally to make commemorative bronze and silver coins sold at the museum's gift shop.

Another exhibit displays the exquisite silver dinner service from the USS *Nevada*, commissioned in 1916. The plates and serving pieces, fashioned from 5,000 ounces of silver, were a gift from the state of Nevada to its battleship namesake. In World War II the *Nevada* served in the Aleutians and then stood off the coast of France during the Normandy landing of D-day, its 14-inch guns pounding the shore.

The *Nevada* ended its life a bit ignominiously, serving as a target ship for an atomic bomb test at Bikini Atoll in the Pacific. According to observers, even the atomic bomb could not sink her, and the U.S. Navy was forced to scuttle the ship. The silver service was taken off first.

An exhibit on the geology of Nevada includes the skeleton of an *Imperial mammuthus* (a North American woolly mammoth) that perished about 17,000 years ago in Nevada's Black Rock Desert; it is the largest mammoth skeleton on exhibit in America. Nearby is the skeleton of an *Equus pacificus,* a large Ice Age horse about 25,500 years old recovered from near Pyramid Lake.

The well-stocked book section in the gift shop is worth some serious browsing. On a recent visit the nearby rotating exhibit was devoted to the Chinese influence on Nevada, including some beautiful clothing and artifacts brought to America by Asian railroad and mine workers.

Little Big Man

The famed mountain guide and trapper Kit Carson was born in 1809 in Missouri. He was a little guy, never topping 5 feet, 6 inches in height. Carson's father was killed by a falling tree limb when the boy was just nine, and when he was fifteen, his mother apprenticed him to a saddler and harness maker. There he met some of the early adventurers heading west; he talked his way into one of the lowliest jobs on the wagon train—that of cavy boy, the driver of the spare mules and oxen.

He went on to demonstrate his prowess as a frontiersman, and he was hired by John C. Frémont as a guide for expeditions in 1842 and 1843, including a midwinter crossing of the High Sierra. He went on to great fame during the Mexican War.

The Environmental Gallery teaches about the animal and plant life of the state from dinosaurs to today; the Earth Science Gallery explains the complex geology that formed not only the gold and silver deposits of Nevada but also the dramatic mountain ranges and deserts. Also on display is an impressive collection of artifacts of ancient Native American cultures.

The last exhibit is a re-creation of one of the mines of the Comstock, so well done that some visitors may suffer from claustrophobia. Along the low-ceilinged path, you will step into a "Dillon Box," a mine cage used to lower men into the deep shafts. The floors of the "mine" include pieces of old rails, which were actually wood covered with metal straps; displays include mine faces made up of actual ore.

The Nevada State Museum is located at 600 North Carson Street and is open

Safer That Way

In Nevada the legislature is very much a part-time job, in session (except for emergencies) only for a few months at the beginning of odd-numbered years. There are only sixty-three legislators—twenty-one senators and forty-two members of assembly, the fourth-smallest state legislature in the nation. (Representatives are paid just $130 per day for a sixty-day session, too.) We might all be better off if the U.S. Congress was to adopt such semiretirement.

every day from 8:30 A.M. to 4:30 P.M. Admission is $5.00 for adults and $3.00 for seniors; children eighteen and younger are admitted free. For information call (775) 687–4810 or consult http://dmla.clan.lib .nv.us/docs/museums/cc/carson.htm. You can also learn more about the Mint Building at www.cr.nps .gov/nr/travel/nevada/usm.htm.

Another essential stop on the tour of Carson City is the **State Capitol** on Carson Street between Second and Musser Streets. The stone building, first erected in 1871 and expanded in 1915, is distinctive for its huge log rafters within. It is set in a 4-block, elm-shaded park—Abraham Curry's **Capitol Square.** The governor maintains his office in the building, but the original legislative and Supreme Court chambers are used for exhibits, including an amazing museum of official and unofficial state items on the second floor.

There is a strange mix of buildings as you move on to the **Legislative Building,** home of the Assembly and Senate. Visitors can see many of the government rooms by themselves; for information on guided tours, call in advance to (775) 687–5030. For information on the capitol, consult www.cr.nps.gov/nr/travel/nevada/nev.html.

The legislative mall includes heroic statues of Kit Carson, Adolph Sutro, and Abraham Curry.

The **Nevada Supreme Court** is located at 201 South Carson Street and is jarringly modern in this old city. Completed in 1992 the building is sometimes used to house exhibits on state history. Oral arguments are open to the public during the session from September to June; for information call (775) 684–1600. The Supreme Court also meets in Las Vegas, on the other side of the state, for part of its schedule.

Not a trace remains to be seen today, but at one time Carson City had the state's largest Chinese population behind and to the east of the capitol. The state bought the remains of Chinatown in the 1950s and razed the last of its buildings in the 1960s. You can see some artifacts from Carson City's Chinatown at the Nevada State Museum.

Just outside Carson City and before the point where U.S. Highways 50 and 395 split is the office of the **Carson Ranger District** of the USDA Forest Service. You can stop in for a wilderness permit or obtain information on hiking trails in the area. It is also a good place to check on road conditions and weather forecasts. The ranger station is open weekdays from 8:00 A.M. to 4:30 P.M.

Railroad buffs and children of all ages are not going to want to miss the **Nevada State Railroad Museum,** which mostly commemorates the Virginia &

Truckee Railroad. The V & T rail line running from Virginia City to Carson City was completed in 1869, and the tracks were extended north to Reno in 1872, where they met the transcontinental lines.

At the museum there are engines, passenger cars, railroad construction equipment, and a display of model railroad cars that is definitely a cut above the old Lionel set you had as a kid. Among locomotives on display are the Dayton and Inyo, both of which served on the V & T between the 1870s and the 1930s. The locomotives were sold to Paramount Pictures Corp. in 1937 and were used in films and promotional activities before returning to near their former home. The National Park Service recently added the McKeen Car No. 70, currently housed at the museum, to the National Register of Historic Places. The car is a self-propelled gasoline-engine railway motorcar built by the McKeen Motor Car Company and bought by the Virginia & Truckee Railroad in 1909 for $22,000. The car's sleek design, including its aerodynamic wedge-shaped nose, rounded tail, and self-supporting tensed steel body, was a cutting-edge innovation at the time and eventually became the standard long after the McKeen Motor Company had ceased production.

> ### Map Your Course
>
> Stop at the cartographic mother lode in the State Department of Transportation at 1263 South Stewart (Room 206), where you can purchase a full range of official maps of almost every description. For information call (775) 888–7000.

In the summer season you can take a short ride around the museum property on an old engine. The museum, located south of Carson City at 2180 South Carson Street (US 395 at Fairview Drive), is open daily from 8:30 A.M. to 4:30 P.M. Admission is $4.00 for adults and $3.00 for seniors; free for children younger than eighteen. Train rides cost $5.00 for adults and $4.00 for children ages six to eleven. For information call (775) 687–6953 or consult www.nsrm-friends.org. You can also find more information about the railroad at www.cr.nps.gov/nr/travel/Nevada/vtr.htm.

Next door to the railroad museum is the **Carson City Visitor Center** and the chamber of commerce. An old covered wagon—a real prairie schooner—sits outside.

The **Brewery Arts Center** celebrates the arts, not beer, although it is located within the former site of the Carson Brewing Company at King and Division Streets. The building was constructed in 1864 and was operated as a brewery more or less continually until 1948; it then became the printing plant for the *Nevada Appeal*, the state's oldest continuously published daily newspaper. It became the center of Carson City's cultural arts in 1975, offering art exhibits and sponsoring performances in the area. For information call (775) 883–1976 or consult www.breweryarts.org. For information on the building, consult www.cr.nps.gov/nr/travel/nevada/bre.htm.

Mills Park, located on US 50 East at Saliman Street, features a miniature train ride, the Pony Express Pavilion, swimming, tennis, and the like.

YES, THERE ARE CASINOS

You cannot compare the gambling establishments of Carson City with those of Las Vegas or Reno or even with the historically interesting slot palaces of Virginia City. But you can make a bet of almost any description.

The **Carson Nugget** is definitely a casino for the hard core. How else would you describe a place that was nearly packed with locals at noon on a drizzly Friday? At the time of our visit, the Nugget offered an eminently forgettable buffet that offered several varieties of indeterminate meat, poultry, and fishlike substances, tired salads, and scary Jell-O. A display in the casino shows gold nuggets estimated at more than $1 million in value. The casino is located at 507 North Carson Street. For information call (775) 882–1626 or (800) 426–5239 or consult www.ccnugget.com.

■ CARSON CITY CASINOS, HOTELS, AND MOTELS

Drivers headed to Lake Tahoe and Reno can now bypass downtown Carson City on a highway at the north end of town, which will alleviate congestion in the city but probably contribute to its local recession. A pair of hotels, a Hampton Inn and a Holiday Inn Express, opened near the bypass.

In downtown you'll find most of the major motel chains including Best Western, Days Inn, Motel 6, Super 8, and others. You can also check travel portals such as www.expedia.com or www.travelocity.com.

CHAPTER TWENTY-FIVE

LAKE TAHOE:
MOUNTAIN SHANGRI-LA

Econoguide Best Lake Tahoe Area Casinos and Hotels

★★★★ **Harrah's.** *Lake Tahoe*
★★★★ **Harvey's Resort.** *Lake Tahoe*
★★★★ **Hyatt Regency Lake Tahoe.** *Incline Village*
★★★★ **MontBleu Resort**
★★★★ **Resort at Squaw Creek.** *Squaw Valley USA*
★★★ **Embassy Suites.** *South Lake Tahoe*
★★★ **Ridge Tahoe.** *Stateline*
★★ **Cal-Neva Resort.** *Crystal Bay*

Econoguide Best Restaurants around Lake Tahoe

★★★★ **Friday's Station.** *Harrah's Lake Tahoe*
★★★★ **19 Kitchen~Bar.** *Harvey's Lake Tahoe*
★★★★ **Scusa!** *South Lake Tahoe*
★★★★ **Summit Restaurant.** *Harrah's Lake Tahoe*

Econoguide Best Casino Buffet in Lake Tahoe

★★★ **Forest Buffet.** *Harrah's Lake Tahoe*

LAKE TAHOE

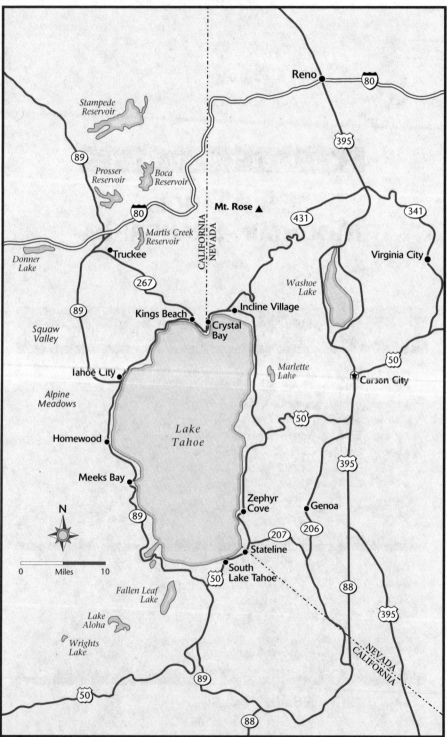

A HEAVENLY EMERALD

As a travel writer and journalist, I have been to many spectacular places around the world, but on a stressful day at the keyboard, my mind regularly drifts back to a view of Lake Tahoe from Emerald Bay with the Heavenly ski area towering over the casinos of Stateline.

Lake Tahoe is, without argument, one of the most breathtaking places on Earth, and its natural beauty is complemented, for the most part, by resorts and developments to suit most tastes.

The lake was formed by the rise and fall of faults about five million to ten million years ago, which created a deep valley; then about two million years ago, lava flowing from the Mount Pluto volcano on the north shore blocked the northeastern outlet of the basin. Geologists say the initial height of Lake Tahoe was 600 feet higher than its present level.

Today the lake itself covers the border between Nevada and California, 59 miles southwest of Reno and 100 miles northeast of Sacramento. Lake Tahoe has a circumference of 72 miles, a surface area of about 192 square miles, and contains some 39.75 trillion gallons of water.

At 12 miles wide and 22 miles long, it is the largest alpine lake, the third-deepest lake in North America, and the tenth-deepest in the world with an average depth of 989 feet and 1,645 feet at its lowest point; at its bottom the lake is 92 feet below the level of Carson City on the other side of the Sierra Nevada range in Nevada.

The lake is fed by sixty-three streams, but only one waterway—the Truckee River—flows out; it goes through Reno and on to Pyramid Lake. As such Lake Tahoe is one of the few major bodies of water in North America that does not eventually empty into the ocean.

The surface of Lake Tahoe, at 6,227 feet, is more than a mile above sea level. During times of drought the surface of the lake can drop below the outlet to the Truckee and become a self-contained lake. In late 2003 the lake dropped below its natural level for the first time in years.

Over and Under

The U.S. Bureau of Reclamation controls the top 6.1 feet of Lake Tahoe as a reservoir. The water is claimed to be 99.9 percent pure. The lake contains an estimated 39.75 trillion gallons of water, enough to cover the entire state of California to a depth of 14 inches.

Lake Tahoe Average Temperatures

	Jan	Feb	Mar	Apr	May	Jun	Jul	Aug	Sep	Oct	Nov	Dec
High	36	39	44	50	60	69	79	80	70	51	47	40
Low	16	18	21	26	32	37	43	42	37	31	24	20

Mileage to South Lake Tahoe

Las Vegas	468
Reno	59
Sacramento	100
San Francisco	198
Virginia City	50

In the summer the top 12 feet of the lake warms to as much as sixty-eight degrees. In winter months, and in the lower depths of the lake, the temperature remains at a constant—and life-threatening—thirty-nine degrees. However, the lake is not known to have ever frozen over because of the constant turnover of water from the bottom to the surface; Emerald Bay has frozen, though, in especially cold winters, most recently in 1989.

The highest peak rising directly from the shoreline is Mount Tallac at 9,735 feet. The highest point in the basin is Freel Peak at 10,881 feet.

The exact source of the name "Tahoe" is a bit obscure. In any case the spectacular body of water has held many names during the years. When explorer John C. Frémont, accompanied by famed guide Kit Carson, came to the lake on February 14, 1844, he named it Lake Bonpland after a French botanist who had been with him on earlier explorations. But mapmaker Charles Preuss wrote it down as Mountain Lake.

Despite all this it was commonly referred to as Frémont Lake until 1852, when California governor John Bigler led a party to the area to rescue some snowbound travelers; the lake was renamed Lake Bigler at the time.

But again other names were applied to the still-remote area, including Truckee Lake and Maheon Lake. When the Civil War broke out, the politically correct on the Union side sought to strike Bigler's name from the lake because of his supposed Southern sympathies. It was at this time that the word *Tahoe* was proposed, supposedly meaning "high water." There was little historical support for the meaning of the word, but it nevertheless stuck; some suggest the word is actually a corruption of the Spanish word *tajo*, pronounced *ta*-ho and meaning a "cut."

Just to make things difficult, the state of California went ahead and entered into its laws an official designation of the waterway as Lake Bigler, a name that was not officially withdrawn until 1945.

LIKE NO OTHER NEVADA CASINOS

If you are going to Nevada to gamble, there is not a lot of difference between the major resorts of Stateline, Reno, or Las Vegas. They all have slot machines and blackjack tables and myriad other ways to lose your money. Several of the major resorts offer stage shows and headliner acts—admittedly, the stars are bigger and production shows more lavish in Las Vegas. The best of the restaurants in Stateline, Reno, and Las Vegas are all satisfying.

But what you get in Lake Tahoe that you get nowhere else is the combination of the excitement of the casinos and all they offer with the tremendous range of outdoor activities available in the Tahoe Basin. Here are just a few: downhill skiing, cross-country skiing, ice-skating, sleigh rides, sledding, dogsled rides, snowmobiling, horseback riding, indoor and heated outdoor pool swimming in the winter; waterskiing, lake and pool swimming, hiking, camping, horseback riding, hot-air ballooning, boating, and cruises in the summer, spring, and fall. And oh, the view.

MontBleu Resort Casino is the most showily opulent Las Vegas–like casino in town; Harrah's displays the most understated class; and Harvey's is usually the liveliest place in town. The Horizon and Bill's Casino make up the low-rent district.

GETTING TO LAKE TAHOE FROM RENO

Lake Tahoe is an easy drive from Reno, less than an hour to Crystal Bay, and about ninety minutes to South Lake Tahoe. See chapter 22 for guides to tours from Reno to the lake.

South Tahoe Express offers bus service from Reno-Tahoe International Airport to South Lake Tahoe resorts with fourteen daily departures. In 2006 tickets were $21 one way and $38 round-trip. Scheduled stops include MontBleu, Embassy Suites, Harrah's, Harvey's, Horizon, and the Lakeside Inn. For information call (775) 325–8944 or consult www.southtahoeexpress.com.

Coming from Sacramento the primary road to South Lake Tahoe is U.S. Highway 50, and to the north end of the lake, Interstate 80. Massive snows followed by rainstorms in January 1997 resulted in closure of US 50 west of Stateline for several weeks in the heart of the season, forcing drivers to take more northern or southern routes.

For information on road conditions in California, call (800) 427–7623 in the state or (916) 445–7623 from other states; for Nevada conditions call (775) 785–2260 or (775) 782–9900.

■ AIR TRAVEL

More than two million passengers pass through the Reno-Tahoe International Airport each year; in winter months about 25 percent of all travelers are destined for Lake Tahoe.

The small Lake Tahoe Airport near South Lake Tahoe is primarily used for private planes, although there has been sporadic commercial and charter service there in recent years. For information consult www.laketahoeairport.com.

HOTELS AND CASINOS IN SOUTH LAKE TAHOE

The state border runs through Lake Tahoe, dividing it so that about one-third is in Nevada and the remainder is in California, demarking the line between two rather different cultures.

The Nevada communities of Crystal Bay, Incline Village, and Stateline feature small-scale versions of Reno or Las Vegas casino resorts with all that entails: gambling, glitzy shows, buffets, and fine dining. The largest collection of casinos can be found in Stateline along both sides of a half-mile stretch of US

50. The very last casinos sit just short of the border between California and Nevada.

On the other side of the border, the hotels in California offer different lures. They generally go for high luxury or low price; either way, they do not have casinos to subsidize the room rates.

Tahoe resorts are generally more expensive than their equivalents in Reno and some Las Vegas resorts, partly because of the additional appeal of winter and summer recreation.

High season in Lake Tahoe is generally from mid-June into September. Low season is April through May and November into early December. New Year's and Christmas are busy times. The "shoulder" or middle season is February and March, when ski and winter sports enthusiasts sell out the hotels on weekends.

BILL'S LAKE TAHOE CASINO

This is a high-fun, low-roller joint, the self-proclaimed "Quarter Capital of Nevada." Bill's, which is part of the same company that owns the next-door Harrah's Casino and is named after Bill Harrah, has gone out of its way to encourage its young staff of dealers and attendants to be friendly to its crowd of skiers, summer vacationers, and partygoers. The serious gamblers are elsewhere.

You can buy a dog and a brew for a few bucks, one of the better deals in town for those who don't qualify for a free ride. The lively restaurant in the casino is appropriately named the **Road House.** They even encourage the taking of photographs on the casino floor.

Bill's Lake Tahoe Casino. U.S. Highway 50, Stateline. (775) 588–2455. www .harrahs.com/our_casinos/tah/bills_casino.

★★★ EMBASSY SUITES RESORT

An all-suites hotel with 400 rooms, just across the state line into California, the Embassy Suites Resort shares some of its facilities with its corporate and physical neighbor, Harrah's.

The resort offers an indoor pool, whirlpool spa, and workout room. Entertainment is presented at the **Turtles Sports Bar & Dance Emporium.** Other restaurants include Zackary's, Pasquale's, and Julie's Deli.

And guess what? No casino. That is unless you want to walk a few feet into Nevada. Room rates run from about $149 to $359 across the seasons; lower-priced packages are offered at slow times.

Embassy Suites Resort. 4130 Lake Tahoe Boulevard, South Lake Tahoe, California. 400 rooms. Room rates $149 to $359. (530) 544–5400, (800) 362–2779. www.embassysuites.com.

★★★★ HARRAH'S CASINO HOTEL LAKE TAHOE

Harrah's is one of the class acts of South Lake Tahoe. The eighteen-story, 525-room hotel begins with some of the most beautiful views of the mountains and the lake and also includes a domed swimming pool and an indoor family fun center. By Nevada standards Harrah's is one of the more understated and elegant hotels in town.

The lobby is decorated like an alpine lodge with slate tile floors and Persian rugs, wood and brass, a natural stone fireplace, and a waterfall. Not far from the registration desks is a small Warner Brothers Studio Store.

A large L-shaped casino, it is relatively muted compared to some of the other casinos in town. Harrah's draws a lively mix of skiers, lake visitors, and gamblers. It offers a set of nice restaurants, most of them away from the casino floor.

Guests staying in the nicely appointed rooms have access to a dome-covered swimming pool and spa and health clubs. The hotel runs a number of special promotions throughout the year, including midweek and weekend packages. Also available are ski packages in conjunction with Heavenly, Kirkwood, Sierra-at-Tahoe, or Northstar ski resorts, and golfing packages with the Dayton Valley Golf Course.

Value season runs from January 1 to mid-June and from mid-September through mid-December with room rates starting at about $119 (higher on weekends). The summer season occupies the middle of the year with rooms starting at about $179 in midweek.

Harrah's Family Fun Center, located on the lower level of the hotel, is a smoke- and alcohol-free indoor playground that includes two levels of slides, ball pools, climbing areas, and games of skill, including video games, skee-ball, and air hockey. The play area is open to midnight or later. The PlayPal indoor playground includes a two-story obstacle course with tunnels, ball bins, ladders, slides, and moonwalks. There is also an extensive program for youngsters called Kids Camp that allows parents to ski or gamble or just be alone. For information call (775) 267–6399 or (866) 454–3386, or visit www.tahoekids.com.

The exquisite ★★★★ **Summit Restaurant** is on the sixteenth and seventeenth floors, not quite the summit of the High Sierra, but still a highly recommended gourmet experience for dinner; reservations are necessary. The two-story windows offer spectacular views. The restaurant is located in the former site of the Star Suite, one of Harrah's private luxury suites for high rollers.

Among entrees at the Summit on one of my visits were grilled ono with soba noodles and tamarind-ginger glaze, individual prime Wellington with truffle-Madeira sauce, and sautéed veal loin with Apple Hill–Calvados confit. Desserts include a sinful Grand Marnier soufflé, individual baked Alaskas, and a chocolate "piano" with white chocolate mousse.

Kid Stuff

Hotel guests in South Lake Tahoe can leave the kids for the day at Kids Camp. Open to youngsters ages six to thirteen with day and evening sessions available, the camp offers a range of activities including hiking, swimming, movies, bowling, and trips to the arcade. In 2006 the day session was priced at $90 per child, and the evening at $60 per child. The camp is limited to fifteen children per session, and reservations are suggested. For more information call (775) 267–6399 or consult www.tahoekids.com.

Entrees range from about $22 to $65. The chef's selection dinner is about $60 per person without wine, $90 with wine. The Summit is closed Monday and Tuesday.

Another fine restaurant is ★★★★ **Friday's Station Steak & Seafood Grill** on the eighteenth floor. Named after a famous stop on the Pony Express near Stateline, it offers views of Lake Tahoe and the Sierra Nevada matched only by the food.

A favorite appetizer at Friday's Station is blackened shrimp; I'm also partial to the roasted elephant garlic and the grilled artichoke. Entrees range from about $8.50 to $50.00. On one visit entrees included aged steaks and chops with choice of sauces, including Jack Daniel's whiskey, teriyaki, béarnaise, salsa fresca, and green peppercorn with grappa. Salmon dishes are offered poached in chardonnay, pistachio-crusted with lemon-wine butter, or blackened with fried ginger. Prime rib is offered in big, bigger, and gigantic servings. And you can also order a steak house combination with chicken, salmon, shrimp, and other dishes. If you have room for dessert, consider roasted banana decadence or white chocolate cheesecake with dark chocolate chunks.

A budget-priced showplace is the **American River Cafe** on the lower level. The attractive eatery is set among redwood trees and a babbling brook. Specialties include maple-glazed barbecued baby back ribs, Hangtown fried oyster omelet, and forty-niner chili. You'd hardly know about the mayhem going on next door in the Family Fun Center or upstairs on the casino floor.

The **Forest Buffet** is one of the most attractive buffets in any of Nevada's casinos, located on the eighteenth floor of the hotel with spectacular views of the lake and surrounding Sierra Nevada. The room was extensively renovated a few years back, adding an exhibition-style kitchen. Specialties include brick-oven pizza, an Italian pasta bar, an Asian Wok station, a French rotisserie, and a seriously tempting dessert station.

Casual eateries include **Manchu Wok**, a branch of Fatburger, and **LA Italian Kitchen.**

The 800-seat **South Shore Room** has been the home of regular headline entertainment including Hollywood and Broadway-theme productions. In the summer season the stage is held by big-name performers. The **Altitude Nightclub** takes over the South Shore Room when shows are not scheduled there.

Visitors can also partake of a bit of luxury with a cruise aboard Bill Harrah's former yacht, the 54-foot-long *Tahoe Star.* Daily cruises are offered from about May 1 through the end of October; capacity is limited to thirty-six guests. There are two tours offered, each about eighty minutes; tickets in 2006 were $40 for adults and $28 for children (younger than twelve). The Historic East Shore tour passes by some of the most spectacular lakefront homes and visits Glenbrook Bay, final resting place of the one-hundred-year-old steamship SS *Tahoe.* The Emerald Bay tour enters the fjordlike bay and passes near historic Vikingsholm Castle and the teahouse on Fannette Island.

Harrah's Casino Hotel Lake Tahoe. U.S. Highway 50, Stateline. 525 rooms. Room rates $179 to $209. (775) 588–6611, (800) 427–7247. www.harrahs.com/our_casinos/tah.

★★★★ HARVEY'S RESORT HOTEL/CASINO

It pretty much all started here. Harvey Gross moved to South Lake Tahoe around 1940 to operate a meat company. In 1944 he opened Harvey's Wagon Wheel Saloon & Gambling Hall in Stateline on US 50. It was a one-room log cabin with a six-stool lunch counter and the only twenty-four-hour gas pump between Placerville, California, and Carson City on the other side of the Sierra Nevada. Oh, and it also included three slot machines and a pair of blackjack tables.

From that humble beginning, Harvey and his wife Llewellyn helped build Stateline into a year-round resort; one early winter they joined with Tahoe residents in shoveling out Echo Summit before the state of California committed heavy equipment to the task.

Harvey's has undergone several stages of expansion with its two main towers rising in the 1960s and 1980. (In 1980 an extortionist's bomb blew a five-story hole in the hotel tower.)

In late 2001 Harvey's was sold to Harrah's Entertainment, which operates hotels and casinos under the Harrah's, Rio Suite, and Showboat names.

Today Harvey's occupies the catbird seat in Stateline with some of the best views of the lake from its towers and restaurants. The attractive lobby is a floor away from the casino and nicely insulated; it is possible to forget there is a world of blinking lights, bouncing coins, and shuffling cards.

Rest assured, though, there is a full-featured casino at Harvey's, including the Land of the Giants, five 7-foot-tall slot machines against the wall between the California Bar and Sage Room. Harvey's has a Vegas-size casino at 88,000 square feet, offering 2,300 slot machines; 121 table games that include blackjack, red dog, fast action hold 'em, poker, Pai Gow, baccarat, craps, and roulette; plus a race and sports book. The cocktail waitresses glide by in (skimpy) black velvet.

The 740 rooms and suites are among the nicest in Lake Tahoe. The prime Lake Suites include a Jacuzzi, private lake-view balcony, two color TVs, and a marble bath and dressing area. Hotel facilities include a heated outdoor swimming pool, health club, wedding chapel, and four tennis courts.

On the lower level is a lively dungeon of an arcade where snow bunnies can try out electronic alpine ski racing, Daytona cars, and wrestling. At the heart of the arcade is the Orbitron, a motion simulator that includes jet-fighter chases, roller coasters, and bobsleds. The arcade is open daily until 10:00 P.M. and later on the weekends.

Lake Tahoe Area Information

▶ **Lake Tahoe Visitors Authority.** 1156 Ski Run Boulevard, South Lake Tahoe, CA 96151. (530) 544–5050 or (800) 288–2463.

▶ **Incline Village/ Crystal Bay Visitor and Convention Bureau.** 969 Tahoe Boulevard, Incline Village, NV 89451. (800) 468–2463. www.gotahoe.com.

▶ **North Lake Tahoe Chamber of Commerce.** 950 North Lake Boulevard, Suite 3, Tahoe City, CA 96145. (530) 581–6900, (800) 024–6348. www.tahoe-4-u.com.

▶ **North Lake Tahoe Resort Association.** Box 5578, Tahoe City, CA 95730. (530) 583–3494, (800) 824–6348. www.tahoefun.org

At the heart of the casino is a branch of the **Hard Rock Cafe** chain, serving hamburgers, barbecued ribs, soups, salads, and souvenirs in an Alpine ski lodge decor. For those who need to stay in the action, the triangular bar in the restaurant's center features a bank of video poker machines.

The small **Pacifica Seafood Buffet** is near the casino entrance, open for dinner only, from Thursday through Sunday.

At the top of the tower, on the nineteenth floor, is ★★★★ **19 Kitchen~Bar.** The fine dining restaurant offers stunning views of Lake Tahoe. Specialties include dry- or wet-aged ribeye, New York, or filet mignon steak; Kobe steak in red wine, shallot, and peppercorn sauce; "drunken" lobster; and sea bass with risotto. Entrees range from about $28 to $85. 19 Kitchen replaced the longtime signature restaurant Llewellyn's.

The **Sage Room Steak House,** open for dinner from 6:00 P.M., features entrees including peppercorn steak filet mignon with béarnaise sauce and roast duckling *bigarrade* (Long Island duckling topped with an orange sauce and flambéed with Grand Marnier). Other unusual offerings include honey rabbit sausage lasagna and venison *grand veneur* with melted Brie cheese. The old-style Nevada eatery is decorated with works by Western artists Remington and Russell. Entrees range from about $22 to $36.

The **Carriage House** is an attractive twenty-four-hour coffee shop that features a variety of standard offerings as well as breakfast and lunch on-the-run deals for skiers and travelers: You get an egg or pancake breakfast and leave the restaurant with a box lunch of fried chicken or a ham-and-cheese sandwich, plus fresh fruit, a cookie, and a granola bar.

The **Cabo Wabo Cantina** is a high-energy south-of-the-border bistro offering Machacha beef empenadas, grilled pork achiote sugar cane skewers, and spicy shrimp with tequila marinade. Other entrees include chile relleno lobster burritos and fajitas. And there is an entire menu of specialty drinks based on Cabo Wabo tequila.

A pedestrian underpass connects Harvey's to its corporate cousin, Harrah's, across the road.

Harvey's Resort Hotel/Casino. U.S. Highway 50, Stateline. 740 rooms. Room rates $120 to $700. (775) 588–2411, (800) 427–8397. www.harrahs.com/our_casinos/.

HORIZON CASINO RESORT

A very lively and busy casino with a big collection of nickel slots; I recommend dark glasses. The mirrored ceiling makes you feel like you're inside a huge powder room turned sideways.

Payment Due

Some casinos advertise "overdue" jackpots on progressive machines, implying that your chances of winning are higher if you play on one of them. Actually—assuming as you must that the machines are honest—the chances of winning on a machine are the same if it has been ten years since it has paid off or if the machine paid off five minutes ago.

Think of it this way: If you flip an honest quarter forty-nine times and it comes up heads every time, the odds of it coming up tails on the next toss are still fifty-fifty.

Back in the '60s, when the place was the Sahara Tahoe, the King played and stayed here. The Presley Suite is available for rent for special functions.

There are 539 rooms and suites, many with lake-view balconies. Facilities include a large outdoor pool and hot tubs.

Entertainment featuring headline acts is presented in the 1,200-seat Grande Lake Theatre. Shows and revues are offered in the 200-seat Golden Cabaret, and there is live music nightly in the Aspen Lounge.

Josh's restaurant, a rather ordinary setting, offers Nevada steak house fare. Specialties include grilled Alaskan salmon with lump crabmeat, shrimp, and grilled asparagus; sesame-crusted yellowfin ahi tuna with wasabi soy vinaigrette; and twenty-four-ounce porterhouse steak; entrees range from about $26 to $40.

The Four Seasons Restaurant is a twenty-four-hour cafe with a prime rib special. The **Town Square Buffet** lives up to its name: It is one of Lake Tahoe's largest buffets. Specialties include Mexican and Chinese stations.

Horizon Casino Resort. U.S. Highway 50, Stateline. 539 rooms. Room rates $89 to $179. (775) 588–6211, (800) 648–3322. www.horizoncasino.com.

LAKESIDE INN & CASINO

This is a small casino and hotel with 124 motel units, located a bit off the main drag at the base of Kingsbury Grade.

The **Timber House Restaurant and Bar** features casual fare under an attractive vaulted ceiling, featuring an $8.00 prime rib dinner, shrimp scampi for $16.95, and seared filet mignon with a Roquefort crust for $19.95.

The **Taberna Mexican** is a casual taqueria with a broad and inexpensive menu.

Lakeside Inn & Casino. 168 US 50, Stateline. 124 rooms. Room rates $59 to $99. (775) 588–7777, (800) 624–7980. www.lakesideinn.com.

★★★★ MONTBLEU RESORT CASINO & SPA

Caesar has left the building, replaced by a reborn upscale resort with an unusual (forgettable?) name: MontBleu, as in "blue mountain."

Many of the 440 suites and rooms offer circular bathtubs for those who like to bathe in the round. Other facilities include an indoor pool, health spa, and racquetball and tennis courts. The complete fall of Rome will include a renovated casino, theming, and new restaurants.

Ciera Steak and Chophouse offers meat, seafood, and other specialties complemented by a wine cellar with 300 selections. Ciera is open nightly for dinner.

Del Soul takes northern Nevada south of the border with a picante menu of "Nuevo Mexicano" dishes, for dinner only.

The **Opal** ultralounge will include a Eurasian tapas and sushi menu for dinner. The **20-Four** round-the-clock diner is just off the casino floor.

And then there is the **unbuffet,** which is . . . a buffet with claims to be different from others you have seen and experienced.

The resort makes use of the 1,600-seat showroom, as well as the **Blu Nightclub,** formerly Club Nero.

MontBleu Resort Casino & Spa. U.S. Highway 50, Stateline. 440 rooms. Standard room rates $80 to $150. (775) 588–3515, (800) 648–3353. www.montbleu resort.com.

★★★ THE RIDGE TAHOE RESORT

Tucked away on the Kingsbury Grade and just above the Stagecoach Lodge of Heavenly ski resort, the Ridge offers guests private ten-passenger gondolas to take them to the lodge for a day of skiing. Other amenities include a health club, indoor/outdoor pool, and tennis and racquetball courts.

The Ridge Tahoe Resort. Stateline. 300 rooms. Room rates $115 to $165. (775) 588–3553, (800) 334–1600. www.ridgetahoeresort.com.

RESTAURANTS IN SOUTH LAKE TAHOE AND STATELINE

As befits a year-round vacation playground, the south end of Lake Tahoe is well supplied with a wide variety of restaurants. Following are some of the more interesting eateries outside of the casinos.

■ **The Beacon.** 1900 Jamison Beach Road, Camp Richardson. Lunch and dinner. Burgers and sandwiches for lunch on the beach. Dinner entrees include rosemary chicken, bourbon New York steak, and macadamia nut prawns priced from about $15 to $25. (530) 541–0630.

■ **Cafe Fiore.** 1169 Ski Run Boulevard. Breakfast, lunch, and dinner. (530) 541–2908. www.cafefiore.com.

■ **The Dory's Oar.** 1041 Fremont Avenue. A little bit of Cape Cod on the lake, featuring Maine lobster, Chesapeake Bay crabs, and fish from both coasts. (530) 541–6603. www.dorysoar.com.

■ **The Eagles' Nest.** 472 Needle Peak Road. Lunch and dinner. Restaurant and jazz club with live performances most weekends. A lively eatery with entrees in the range of about $13 to $22 that include steak, lamb chops, and venison. (775) 588–3245.

■ **Fresh Ketch.** 2433 Venice, Tahoe Keys Marina. Lunch and dinner. Oysters to smoked salmon, sashimi to burgers, chowder to filet mignon. Entrees priced from about $7.00 to $23.00. (530) 541–5683. www.thefreshketch.com.

■ **Nepheles.** 1169 Ski Run Boulevard. Lunch and dinner. "Creative California Cuisine." Appetizers include seafood cheesecake and swordfish egg rolls. Entrees, priced from about $10 to $25, include baked fresh ahi in Asian peanut sauce, wild boar in prunes and cabbage topped with orange apricot brandy sauce, and chicken teriyaki. (530) 544–8130. www.nepheles.com.

■ **Samurai.** 2588 US 50. Dinner. Sushi, teriyaki, tempura, and *nabemono* grilled beef or seafood, priced from about $11 to $25. (530) 542–0300. www.sushitahoe .com.

■ **Sato.** 3436 US 50. Dinner. Japanese fare from a full range of sushi dishes to tempura and teriyaki entrees priced from about $8.00 to $14.00. Sato's Love Boat is a special sampler dinner that includes California roll, sushi, tempura, teriyaki, and soup, priced at about $18 per person. (530) 541–3769.

■ **Scusa!** ★★★★ 1142 Ski Run Boulevard. Dinner. From unusual pizzas such as smoked chicken, andouille sausage, cilantro, and mozzarella to stuffed eggplant, seared sea scallops Mediterranean, and chicken piccata, priced from about $10 to $20. (530) 542–0100.

■ **Tep's Villa Roma.** 3450 US 50. Dinner. Serious Italian fare, including all the usual suspects such as various pasta dishes; a full range of shrimp, veal, steak, and chicken offerings; and more. Entrees, priced from about $9.00 to $17.00, include a salad bar. (530) 541–8227. www.tepsvillaroma.com.

SOUTH LAKE TAHOE CASINO BUFFETS

Harrah's. ★★★ Forest Buffet. (775) 588–6611.
Harvey's. Pacifica Seafood Buffet. (775) 588–2411.
Horizon. LeGrande Buffet. (775) 588–6211.
MontBleu. Unbuffet. (775) 588–3515.

HOTELS AND CASINOS IN NORTH LAKE TAHOE

⋀ ⋀ CAL-NEVA RESORT HOTEL SPA CASINO, CRYSTAL BAY

Cal-Neva Resort is famous for its swimming pool, which sits atop the state border. Swimmers can start in California and end up in Nevada, where there is, of course, a casino.

There are 220 rooms, including lake-view rooms and suites, chalets with fireplaces, and celebrity cabins that include rooms where Marilyn Monroe or Frank Sinatra slept. In the winter standard rooms start at about $109; the same room in the summer goes for $139. A VIP chalet in the winter starts at $239 for the weekend, rising to as much as $289 in prime summer weeks.

Early guests included mobster Pretty Boy Floyd. During Prohibition the Cal-Neva was one of the most famous speakeasies in the country. Later on the hotel was owned by Frank Sinatra and was one of the gathering places for the "Rat Pack" Hollywood crowd during the 1960s.

The hotel's main room is the impressive Indian Room, featuring a vaulted ceiling and huge beams and a rock fireplace split by the state line. The room includes a display on the Washoe tribe as well as antique hunting trophies from the lake region. As befits a casino, the room is open twenty-four hours a day.

Cal-Neva Resort Hotel Spa Casino. 2 Stateline Road, Crystal Bay. 220 rooms. Room rates $109 to $219. (775) 832–4000, (800) 225–6382. www.calnevaresort .com.

White Stuff

Snowfall at alpine skiing elevations averages 300 to 500 inches per year. At the lake level the average is about 125 inches. At high elevations it has been known to snow in any month of the year. On December 28, 1992, snow began to fall at South Lake Tahoe, eventually reaching rates of up to 6 inches per hour. During the next forty-eight hours, the ski resort received more than 9 feet of snow, one of the largest recorded snowfalls ever.

★★★★ HYATT REGENCY LAKE TAHOE RESORT & CASINO, INCLINE VILLAGE

A 436-room, four-star resort with mountain- and lake-view rooms and suites as well as twenty-four lakeside cottages on the hotel's private beach. You'll also find a health club, outdoor heated pool, and jet spa. Camp Hyatt is for kids ages three to twelve. The resort's design echoes the rustic design of the grand Tahoe homes of the 1900s.

Restaurants include the **Lone Eagle Grill,** with breakfast, lunch, and dinner buffets as well as coffee-shop service.

Room rates start at about $185, with lakeside cottages going for about $1,200; winter specials drop well below those levels.

Hyatt Regency Lake Tahoe Resort & Casino. 111 Country Club Drive, Incline Village. 436 rooms. Room rates $185 to $1,200; lower in winter. (775) 832–1234, (888) 899–5019. www.laketahoehyatt.com.

★★★★ RESORT AT SQUAW CREEK, SQUAW VALLEY USA

With a spectacular setting in and among the trails at Squaw Creek, the Resort offers ski-in/out access, cross-country trails, a golf course, three swimming pools, four spas, a tennis center, horseback riding, and more. There are 405 rooms, including 204 suites.

Restaurants at the resort include the **Six Peaks Grille** with salad, seafood, and steak all day; **Sandy's Pub** for burgers and microbrews in a sports bar setting; **Ristorante Montagna,** with Italian pasta and other specialties; the **Bullwhackers Pub;** the **Sun Plaza Deck** barbecue wagon for lunch; and the **Sweet Potatoes Deli.**

Resort at Squaw Creek. 400 Squaw Creek Road, Squaw Valley. 405 rooms. Room rates $179 to $1,900. (530) 583–6300, (800) 403–4434. www.squawcreek .com.

TAHOE BILTMORE LODGE & CASINO

This is a big old-style hotel with a group of small wooden motel units along the lake. The place was recently renovated to bring back more of the ambience of classic Tahoe lodges, implementing river-rock fireplaces, wrought-iron railings, and a stone facade. The lobby is lined with historic pictures of the area and celebrities who have visited the hotel.

Tahoe Biltmore Lodge & Casino. 5 Highway 28, Incline Village. Ninety-two rooms. Room rates $49 to $149. (775) 831–0660, (800) 245–8667. www.tahoe biltmore.com.

NORTH LAKE TAHOE RESTAURANTS

- **Bacchi's Inn.** Lake Forest, northeast of Tahoe City. Italian and seafood specialties priced from about $11 to $40, including fettuccine a la Romana, spaghetti Caruso with chicken livers and mushrooms, veal piccante tenderloin, Italian barbecued spareribs, and beef a la Stroganoff. Dinners include hors d'oeuvres, minestrone soup, salad, and pasta. (530) 583–3324.
- **Boulevard Cafe & Trattoria.** 6731 North Lake Boulevard, Tahoe Vista. Classic northern Italian fare, including *osso bucco di vitello con Gremolada* (braised veal shanks with vegetables, garlic, and herbs), *anatra al Forno all Ciliege* (roast duck with balsamic vinegar and sun-dried-cherry glaze), and *conchiglie con spinaci e salsicce* (pasta shells stuffed with spinach, sausage, and ricotta cheese). Prices range from about $14 to $26. (530) 546–7213.
- **Captain Jon's Seafood.** 7220 North Lake Boulevard, Tahoe Vista. Entrees include oysters Florentine (baked Malpeque oysters on a bed of spinach topped with Brie cheese); filet mignon Roquefort broiled and served in a cognac, demiglace, and Roquefort sauce; and angel-hair pasta in white cream sauce with scallops and prawns. Open for lunch and dinner in summer and dinner only in winter; prices range from about $18 to $23. (530) 546–4819.
- **Jason's Saloon & Grille.** 8338 North Lake Boulevard, Kings Beach. An interesting mix of seafood, chicken, steak, and burgers, including Bayou shrimp, Louisiana chicken, baby back ribs, and a Russian burger (with horseradish cream sauce and bacon). Entrees range from about $12 to $18. (530) 546–3315.
- **Lakehouse Pizza.** 120 Grove Street, Tahoe City. Not just pizza, they say: Polish *pirushki* stuffed with peppers, mushrooms, olives, tomatoes, onions, and sauce; Italian calzone; American salad . . . and pizza. (530) 583–2222.
- **Las Panchitas.** North Lake Boulevard, Kings Beach. A full range of Mexican specialties that include tacos, enchiladas, burritos, chili, and tostadas. Dinners, priced from about $9.00 to $15.00, include steak Ranchero and *achiote* halibut served on black beans. (530) 546–4539.
- **Mofo's Pizza.** Christmas Tree Village, Incline Village. New York–style pizza from basic to unusual—such as clam and garlic, spinach, and vegetarian. Also offered are sandwiches, calzones, lasagna, and a salad bar. (775) 831–4999.
- **Soule Domain Restaurant.** Stateline Road, Crystal Bay. Gourmet dining in a log cabin across from the Tahoe Biltmore Casino. Start with garlic raviolis, wild shiitake mushrooms, and soft-shell crabs. Entrees, priced from about $16 to $23, include sea scallops poached in champagne with kiwi and papaya cream sauce; fresh pasta with lobster, prawns, and scallops in lemon garlic butter; and curried cashew chicken. (530) 546–7529. www.souledomain.com.
- **Yama Sushi & Robata Grill.** 950 North Lake Boulevard, Tahoe City. A wide range of the real thing from more than two dozen types of sushi to *gyoza* dumplings to *robatayaki* skewers of asparagus, eggplant, quail eggs, beef tongue, salmon, and a dozen more. Entrees, priced from about $10 to $25, include tempura, sashimi, and udon soups. (530) 583–9262.

LAKE TAHOE REGION ACCOMMODATIONS

Here are some resorts and hotels beyond the casinos. Rates vary by season and are likely to be higher during holiday periods and major events and lower in slow periods.

■ NORTHERN LAKE TAHOE RESORTS AND MOTELS

Brockway Springs Resort. 101 Chipmunk Street, Kings Beach. (530) 546–4201. www.brockway-tahoe.com. Seventy-eight rooms.

Chinquapin. Tahoe City. (530) 583–6991. www.chinquapin.com. Sixty rooms.

Franciscan Lakeside Lodge. 6944 North Lake Boulevard, Tahoe Vista. (530) 546–6300. www.franciscanlodge.com. Sixty rooms.

Granlibakken. Granlibakken Road, Tahoe City. (530) 583–4242. www.granli bakken.com. 160 rooms.

PlumpJack Squaw Valley Inn. 1920 Squaw Valley Road, Olympic Valley. (530) 583–1576. www.plumpjack.com. Sixty rooms.

Resort at Squaw Creek. 400 Squaw Creek Road, Squaw Valley. (530) 583–6300, (800) 403–4434. www.squawcreek.com. 405 rooms.

Squaw Tahoe Resort. 2000 Squaw Loop Road, Squaw Valley. (530) 583–7226. Fifty-eight rooms.

Squaw Valley Lodge. Olympic Valley. (530) 583–5500. www.squawvalley lodge.com. 220 rooms.

Squaw Valley-Olympic Village Inn. Olympic Village. (530) 581–6000. Ninety rooms.

Travelodge Lake Tahoe City. Tahoe City. (530) 583–3766. www.travelodge .com. Forty-seven rooms.

Vacation Station. 110 Country Club Drive, Incline Village. (775) 831–3664, (800) 841–7443. www.vacationstation.com. 130 rooms.

The Village at Squaw Valley USA. 1735 Squaw Valley Road, Squaw Valley. (530) 584–1000. www.thevillageatsquaw.com. 139 rooms.

■ NORTH LAKE TAHOE CONDOMINIUM BROKERS

Coldwell Banker/Incline Village Realty. Incline Village. (775) 831–4800, (800) 572–5009. www.2ctahoe.com/incline. Ninety rooms.

Incline at Tahoe Realty. Incline Village. (775) 831–9000, (800) 843–9399. www.inclineattahoe.com. Seventy-five rooms.

Lake Tahoe Accommodations. Incline Village. (775) 832–4475. www.tahoe accommodations.com.

■ SOUTH LAKE TAHOE HOTELS AND MOTELS

Bavarian Village. 1140-B Herbert Avenue, South Lake Tahoe. (530) 541–8191. www.bavarianrentals.com. Forty rooms.

Best Tahoe West Inn. 4107 Pine Boulevard, South Lake Tahoe. (530) 544–6455. www.bestwestern.com. Seventy-two rooms.

Indian Reservations and Councils

Western Nevada is home to many Native American councils; many operate businesses and cultural exhibits. For a listing of many of the councils, consult www.itcn.org/tribes.

▶ **Battle Mountain Band Council.** 35 Mountainview Drive, #138–13, Battle Mountain, NV 89820. (775) 635–2004.

▶ **Carson Colony Community Council/Dresslerville Community Council/ Washoe Tribal Council/Woodfords Community Council.** 919 Highway 395 South, Gardnerville, NV 89410. (775) 265–4191.

▶ **Carson Indian Community Council.** 2900 South Curry Street, Carson City, NV 89701. (775) 833–6459.

▶ **Duck Valley Shoshone-Paiute Tribes.** P.O. Box 219, Owyhee, NV 89832. (775) 757–3211.

▶ **Duckwater Shoshone Tribe.** P.O. Box 140068, Duckwater, NV 89314. (775) 863–0227.

▶ **Elko Band Council.** 511 Sunset Street, Elko, NV 89801. (775) 738–8889.

▶ **Ely Shoshone Tribe.** 16 Shoshone Circle, Ely, NV 89301. (775) 289–3013.

▶ **Fallon Paiute Shoshone Tribe.** 8955 Mission Road, P.O. Box 1650, Fallon, NV 89406. (775) 423–6075.

▶ **Fort McDermitt Indian Reservation.** P.O. Box 457, McDermitt, NV 89421. (775) 532–8259.

▶ **Moapa Tribal Store.** P.O. Box 340, Moapa, NV 89025. (775) 865–2787.

▶ **Pyramid Lake Paiute Tribe.** P.O. Box 256, Nixon, NV 89424. (775) 574–1000.

▶ **Reno-Sparks Indian Colony.** 98 Colony Road, Reno, NV 89502. (775) 329–2936.

▶ **Shoshone Paiute Business Council.** Owyhee, NV 89832. (775) 757–3161.

▶ **Stewart Indian Museum.** 5366 Snyder Avenue, Carson City, NV 89701. (775) 882–1808.

▶ **Tribal Council of the Te-Moak Western Tribe.** 525 Sunset Street, Elko, NV 89801. (775) 738–9251.

Best Western Lake Tahoe Inn. 4110 US 50, South Lake Tahoe. (530) 541–2010. www.bestwestern.com. 400 rooms.

Best Western Station House Inn. 901 Park Avenue, South Lake Tahoe. (530) 542–1101. www.bestwestern.com. One hundred rooms.

Best Western Timber Cove Lodge. 3411 Lake Tahoe Boulevard, South Lake Tahoe. (530) 541–6722. www.bestwestern.com. 262 rooms.

Days Inn. 3530 US 50, South Lake Tahoe. (530) 544–3445. www.daysinn.com. Forty-two rooms.

Embassy Vacation Resort. 901 Ski Run Boulevard, South Lake Tahoe. (530) 541–6122. 264 rooms.

Fantasy Inn & Wedding Chapel. 3696 Lake Tahoe Boulevard, South Lake Tahoe. (530) 541–4200. www.fantasy-inn.com. Fifty-three rooms.

Forest Suites Resort. 1 Lake Parkway, South Lake Tahoe. (530) 541–6655. www.forestsuites.com. 116 rooms.

Holiday Inn Express. 3961 Lake Tahoe Boulevard, South Lake Tahoe. (530) 544–5900. www.holiday-inn.com. Eighty-nine rooms.

Holiday Lodge. 4095 Laurel Avenue, South Lake Tahoe. (530) 544–4101. www.holidaylodge.com. 165 rooms.

Inn by the Lake. 3300 Lake Tahoe Boulevard, South Lake Tahoe. (530) 542–0330. www.innbythelake.com. One hundred rooms.

Lakeland Village Beach & Mountain Resort. 3535 Lake Tahoe Boulevard, South Lake Tahoe. (530) 544–1685. www.lakeland-village.com. 212 rooms.

Quality Inn & Suites. 3838 Lake Tahoe Boulevard, South Lake Tahoe. (530) 541–5400. www.choice.com. 112 rooms.

The Ridge Tahoe Resort. 400 Ridge Club Drive, Stateline. (775) 588–3553, (800) 334–1600. www.ridge-tahoe.com. 300 rooms.

Rodeway Inn. 4082 Lake Tahoe Boulevard, South Lake Tahoe. (530) 541–7900. www.rodeway.com. 102 rooms.

Stardust Tahoe. 4061 South Lake Tahoe Boulevard, South Lake Tahoe. (530) 544–5211. www.stardust-tahoe.com. Eighty rooms.

Super 8 Motel. 3600 South Lake Tahoe Boulevard, South Lake Tahoe. (530) 544–3476. www.super8.com. 108 rooms.

Tahoe Chalet Inn. 3860 South Lake Tahoe Boulevard, South Lake Tahoe. (530) 544–3311. www.tahoechaletinn.com. Sixty-six rooms.

Tahoe Keys Resort. 599 Tahoe Keys Boulevard, South Lake Tahoe. (530) 544–5397. 200 rooms.

Tahoe Marina Inn. 930 Bal Bijou Road, South Lake Tahoe. (530) 541–2180. Seventy-nine rooms.

Tahoe Seasons Resort. 3901 Saddle Road, South Lake Tahoe. (530) 541–6700. www.tahoeseasons.com. 157 rooms.

Travelodge. 4003 US 50, South Lake Tahoe. (530) 541–5000. www.travelodge.com. Sixty-six rooms.

Travelodge South Lake Tahoe. 3489 US 50, South Lake Tahoe. (530) 544–5266. www.travelodge.com. Fifty-nine rooms.

Zephyr Cove Resort. 760 US 50, Zephyr Cove. (775) 588–6644. www.tahoedixie2.com. Thirty-three rooms.

■ SOUTH LAKE TAHOE CONDOMINIUM BROKERS

1st Choice Vacation Properties. Zephyr Cove. (800) 343–2891, (208) 578–0921. www.choice1.com.

Lake Village Vacation Condos. Zephyr Cove. (775) 588–2481, (800) 242–5387. www.tahoe-estates.com.

Tahoe Management Company. South Lake Tahoe. (775) 588–4504, (888) 624–3887. www.tahoevacations.com.

Tahoe Rental Connection. South Lake Tahoe. (530) 542–2777, (800) 542–2100.

CABINS AND CAMPGROUNDS

Carson Valley Inn RV Park. Minden. (775) 782–9711. www.cvinn.com.

Echo Creek Ranch. (530) 544–5397, (800) 462–5397.

Inn at Heavenly Reservation Bureau. (916) 544–4244, (800) 692–2246. www.innatheavenly.com.

Lake Tahoe South Shore KOA Campground. (530) 577–3693. www.koakampgrounds.com.

Richardson's Resort. (530) 541–1801. www.camprich.com.

Sorensen's Resort. (530) 694–2203. www.sorensensresort.com.

Tahoe Keys Resort. (530) 544–5397, (800) 698–2463.

Walley's Hot Springs Resort. (800) 628–7831.

Zephyr Cove Lodge and Campground. (775) 588–6644. www.zephyrcove.com.

CRUISES AROUND THE LAKE

■ **MS *Dixie II*.** A modern version of a Lake Tahoe classic that makes one- to four-hour cruises to Emerald Bay (about $27.00 to $31.00 for adults and $9.00 to $12.00 for children) and summer sunset dinner and dance cruises (about $56.00, including dinner). The ship is based at the Zephyr Cove Marina, 4 miles north of Stateline on US 50. The glass-bottom stern-wheeler can accommodate 350 passengers.

Passengers on the *Dixie* can also watch *The Sunken Treasures of Lake Tahoe,* a video presented on each cruise; cameras show underwater canyons, ancient petrified forests hidden by the lake, the sheer vertical cliffs of Rubicon Bay, and the scuttled steamer *Tahoe,* 500 feet below the surface of Glenbrook Bay.

The boat runs year-round, weather permitting. Free shuttle service is available from South Lake Tahoe, Carson City, Reno, or the north shore of the lake. Call (775) 588–3508 or (775) 882–0786 or consult www.tahoedixie2.com.

■ ***Woodwind II.*** A large trimaran sailing vessel, it makes day cruises (for about $28 for adults and $12 for children) and sunset champagne cruises (about $36 for adults) from May to October. Call (775) 588–3000 or consult www.sailwoodwind.com for information.

GETTING AROUND IN LAKE TAHOE

■ AIRPORTS

Carson Airport. Carson City, Nevada. (775) 884–1163. Private aviation.

Lake Tahoe Airport. South Lake Tahoe, California. (530) 541–4082. www
.laketahoeairport.com. Private aviation.

Minden-Tahoe Douglas County Airport. Minden, Nevada. (775) 782–8277.
www.mindentahoeairport.com. Private aviation.

Tahoe Valley Airport. South Lake Tahoe, California. (530) 543–1259. Private
aviation.

Truckee-Tahoe Airport. Truckee, California. (530) 587–4119. www.truckee
tahoeairport.com. Private aviation.

■ CAR RENTAL

Avis Rent A Car. Montbleu Resort, Stateline: (775) 588–4450. South Lake
Tahoe: (530) 542–5710. Nationwide: (800) 331–1212. www.avis.com.

Enterprise Rent-a-Car. Horizon Casino Resort, Stateline. (775) 586–1077.
www.enterprise.com.

Hertz Rent A Car. 1875 Lake Tahoe Boulevard, South Lake Tahoe. Also other
nearby locations. (530) 542–4804. Nationwide: (800) 654–3131. www.hertz.com.

Tahoe Rent-a-Car. Tahoe Valley Motel, South Lake Tahoe. (530) 544–4500.

■ ROAD AND WEATHER INFORMATION

California Highway Conditions. (916) 445–7623, (800) 427–7623.

California Highway Patrol. (916) 657–7261.

Nevada Highway Patrol. (775) 793–1313.

■ BUS SERVICE

Greyhound Lines West. South Lake Tahoe: (530) 544–2351. Truckee: (916)
587–3822. www.greyhound.com.

STAGE (South Lake Tahoe Area Ground Express). South Lake Tahoe area.
(530) 573–2080.

■ SKI-AREA SHUTTLE BUSES

Many of the Lake Tahoe area ski areas provide shuttle services; call for schedules
and pickup locations.

Alpine Meadows. (530) 583–4232.

Diamond Peak. (775) 832–1177.

Mount Rose. (775) 849–0704.

Northstar-at-Tahoe. (530) 562–2248.

Squaw Valley. (530) 583–6985, extension 7182.

Sugar Bowl. (530) 426–3651.

LAKE TAHOE HEALTH

Altitude sickness. Feeling a bit faint, tired, nauseated, headachy, or short of breath? Having trouble sleeping or does the fabulous spread of a casino buffet hold no particular appeal? You may be suffering from altitude sickness. Lake Tahoe sits at about 6,235 feet above sea level; if you have come from an East or West Coast city, you are living more than a mile higher than ordinary.

The cure is to avoid overexertion, get plenty of rest, and drink plenty of fluids. You also should eat lightly and cut down on alcohol consumption. The ultimate cure is time: Your body should adjust within two or three days.

If your symptoms are especially severe or if they don't seem to pass, you should see a doctor. Persons with heart conditions or high blood pressure should check with their doctors at home before heading for the mountains.

Frostbite. It gets very cold up in the hills. Wear warm, layered, dry clothing, including hats and gloves; avoid alcohol and take indoor breaks.

Frostbite occurs when the water in your body cells literally freezes. Superficial frostbite usually involves the fingertips, ears, nose, toes, and cheeks; symptoms include a burning sensation, tingling, or numbness and a whitish discoloration of the skin. Deep frostbite is a more serious condition and can result in the death of the cells and open wounds susceptible to infection.

If you develop frostbite, find warm shelter immediately. Do not rub frostbitten skin; instead, immerse the affected parts of the body in lukewarm (not hot) water. If the skin does not return to its normal color, or if blistering, swelling, pain, or numbness develops, seek medical attention.

Hypothermia. This serious condition results when the body's core (internal) temperature drops below the normal range of about 98.6 degrees. Untreated hypothermia can lead to organ malfunction, damage, and eventual death. Symptoms include fatigue, mood changes, and impaired motor skills.

Sunburn. Ultraviolet rays in the mountains are about five times as strong as at sea level. Use a sunscreen with an SBF rating of at least 20 that includes PABA; lip balms with PABA or zinc oxide are also suggested. Wear UV-blocking sunglasses.

If you get a sunburn, apply cool compresses; if your doctor approves, take aspirin for pain and Benadryl to relieve itching. Blisters are a sign of a second-degree burn. Don't pop blisters, and stay out of the sun to avoid more damage. See a doctor for any facial blisters, blisters with cloudy fluid, or for severe pain.

CHAPTER TWENTY-SIX

WINTER SPORTS IN THE LAKE TAHOE REGION

The Best Ski Areas in the Lake Tahoe Region

★★★★★   Heavenly
★★★★★   Squaw Valley USA
★★★★   Alpine Meadows
★★★★   Kirkwood Ski Resort
★★★★   Northstar-at-Tahoe
★★★★   Royal Gorge Cross-Country Ski Area
★★★★   Sierra-at-Tahoe

I DON'T KNOW OF MANY PLACES more breathtaking than Lake Tahoe, especially when seen from the top of a spectacular snowpacked peak.

And there aren't many places in the world where you can find a dozen or so world-class ski resorts within a one- to two-hour drive from a major city. Then consider the lure of the casinos, restaurants, and showrooms of Reno and Lake Tahoe, and you've got a wintertime bet worth making.

If you're in Reno for a casino visit or a business stop, it is a very simple matter to rent a car or take a shuttle bus down to Lake Tahoe and take in a day's skiing; if you are staying at Lake Tahoe, it is equally easy to take a break from the slopes to drive north to Reno to see the big city.

DOWNHILL SKI AREAS

The Lake Tahoe ski season typically runs from about November through mid-April. Many of the major areas now have snowmaking capability.

Combined, the six largest Lake Tahoe resorts—Alpine Meadows, Heavenly, Kirkwood, Northstar-at-Tahoe, Sierra-at-Tahoe, and Squaw Valley USA—offer more than 17,000 acres of terrain serviced by more than one hundred chairlifts, including more wide-open bowls and high-speed chairlifts than any other ski destination in North America.

The queen of South Lake Tahoe ski areas is Heavenly, a massive resort whose lower slopes can be seen from Stateline/South Lake Tahoe and from much of the lake itself. Ruling over the north end of the lake area is Squaw Valley USA, site of the 1960 Winter Olympics.

For information about resorts around the lake, consult www.skilaketahoe .com. For information about other areas, go directly to their Web pages listed later in this chapter.

FACTS AND FIGURES ON LAKE TAHOE SKIING

★★★★★ HEAVENLY

Vertical	Summit	Lifts	Novice–Intermediate–Advanced
3,500	10,010	30	20%–47%–33%

Number of trails: ninety-one. *Longest trail:* 5.5 miles. *Base:* 6,540 feet in California, 7,200 feet in Nevada. *Lifts:* one eight-passenger gondola, one tram, two high-speed six-seaters, seven high-speed quads, five triples, four doubles, and ten surface tows. Complimentary shuttle throughout South Lake Tahoe. *Location:* South Lake Tahoe, on the California/Nevada border, 55 miles southwest of Reno and 180 miles east of San Francisco.

Skiers get to see sights that many of the flatlanders miss. Though I have been to many of the most spectacular ski areas of the world, Heavenly took my breath away.

Heavenly opened in 1955 with one chairlift and a small hut on USDA Forest Service land. Today it includes thirty lifts, six day lodges, 4,800 acres of terrain, 700 acres of snowmaking, and parts of two states—fifteen of the lifts are in California and fifteen in Nevada. The resort is part of Vail Resorts.

In late 2000 Heavenly inaugurated a 138-car gondola system that whisks skiers from the resort-casinos in Stateline, Nevada, to the mountaintop. Skiers and snowboarders can walk to the gondola attraction and ride 2½ miles to the 9,100-foot summit on the California side in less than twelve minutes.

Lake Tahoe Area Ski Resorts

SKI RESORT	DISTANCE FROM RENO (MILES)	VERTICAL DROP (FEET)
Alpine Meadows	50	1,800
Boreal Mountain Resort	42	1,500
Diamond Peak	35	1,840
Donner Ski Ranch	46	1,750
Heavenly	55	3,500
Kirkwood	90	2,000
Mount Rose	22	1,440
Northstar-at-Tahoe	40	2,280
Sierra-at-Tahoe	75	2,212
Ski Homewood	50	1,650
Squaw Valley USA	45	2,850
Sugar Bowl	44	1,500
Tahoe Donner	38	1,600

The gondola is part of a major remaking of the area that includes new hotels and resorts just across the border in South Lake Tahoe, California; more shopping; an ice-skating rink; and environmental improvements aimed at preserving the lake.

The area redevelopment project focuses on a 2-mile stretch of U.S. Highway 50, which comprises what is now considered downtown South Lake Tahoe and the Stateline commercial-core area. The completed area is the focus of visitor activity on the South Shore, featuring shopping, improved access to the lake and watercraft activities, and direct access to the Heavenly ski resort. Heavenly has other dreams and plans, including half a dozen new lifts, two new on-mountain lodges, new trails on the Nevada side of the mountain, and an extensive remodeling of base facilities.

Today the view from the road in South Lake Tahoe is perhaps one-third of just one face of the mountain. The hill, impressive as it is, is a decidedly intermediate area. There are eighty-six runs—20 percent novice, 47 percent intermediate, and 33 percent advanced/expert. That's not to say there aren't challenges for experts: Among the skiable areas is the Mott Canyon Trail, one of the steepest in America.

The vertical drop is 3,500 feet with the top elevation at 10,040 feet. The longest mountain descent is 5½ miles.

Heavenly receives an average annual snowfall of 340 inches, and in recent years it has put down an additional 120 inches of machine-made snow. The season usually runs from mid-November through early May. Area hotels usually offer packages based on three seasons, running from least crowded to busiest.

Value season runs from after Thanksgiving to just before Christmas, approximately November 29 to December 17. Regular season includes Thanksgiving and January through the end of March, except for Presidents' Week. Holiday season runs from Christmas through New Year's, plus Presidents' Week in mid-February.

The **Lakeview Lodge** is located at the top of the Heavenly tram, 2,000 feet above Lake Tahoe. It's an unusually sophisticated (tablecloths and silverware!) restaurant for a ski resort, especially for one where many of the visitors are wearing boots. The restaurant serves an interesting mix of Italian and Asian cuisine, salads and sandwiches, and spectacular vistas.

Most South Shore and Stateline lodging properties are on Heavenly's ski shuttle route with buses running from hotels and lodges to the California Base Lodge and the Boulder and Stagecoach Lodges in Nevada.

2005–2006 rates: about $55 to $70 adults, with a reduction of a few dollars per day on multiday passes. The lowest rates are charged at the beginning and end of the season, with the highest rates charged during the Christmas and New Year's holiday periods. Also available were tickets for young adults (thirteen to eighteen) priced about $10 less per day, and juniors (five to twelve) about $25 less per day. Scenic gondola rides: adults about $25, children (twelve and younger) about $15.

Heavenly. P.O. Box 2180, Stateline, NV 89449. Information: (775) 586–7000. Reservations: (800) 243–2836. www.skiheavenly.com.

★★★★ ALPINE MEADOWS

Vertical	Summit	Lifts	Novice–Intermediate–Advanced
1,800	8,637	14	25%–40%–35%

Number of trails: one hundred. *Longest trail:* 2.5 miles. *Base:* 6,840 feet. *Lifts:* one high-speed six-seater, two high-speed quads, three triples, five double chairs, and two surface lifts. Call for information on multiple-day tickets and interchangeable multiple-day tickets for other North and South Lake Tahoe areas. Complimentary shuttle bus from South Lake Tahoe/Stateline and from North Shore of Lake Tahoe. *Location:* 6 miles northwest of Tahoe City on State Route 89.

Right outside the base lodge are high-speed lifts that access two mountain peaks and six open bowls. Alpine Meadows claims the longest season in the Tahoe region, usually from mid-November through the end of May, and sometimes even later.

2005–2006, depending on date: $41 to $49 adults, $39 teens, $15 children (seven to twelve), $15 seniors (seventy and older), free six and younger.

Alpine Meadows. P.O. Box 5279, Tahoe City, CA 96145. Information: (530) 583–4232, (800) 441–4423. Snowphone: (530) 581–8374. www.skialpine.com.

★★ BOREAL MOUNTAIN RESORT

Vertical	Summit	Lifts	Novice–Intermediate–Advanced
500	7,700	12	30%–55%–15%

Number of trails: forty-one. *Longest trail:* 1 mile. *Base:* 7,200 feet. *Lifts:* two high-speed quads, three triples, four doubles, and three surface lifts. *Location:* at the top of Donner Summit, 10 miles west of Truckee, 90 miles east of Sacramento.

Boreal is part of the POWDR Corporation, which also owns Alpine Meadows Ski Area near Lake Tahoe and Park City Ski Area near Salt Lake City. The resort offers night skiing and allows parents of a young skier to share a single adult lift ticket.

2005–2006 rates: $38 adults, $10 juniors, $25 seniors. Parent's shared ticket, $38. Night tickets: $22 adults, $10 juniors, $18 seniors.

Boreal Mountain Resort. P.O. Box 39, Truckee, CA 96160. (530) 426–3666. www.borealski.com.

★★★ DIAMOND PEAK

Vertical	Summit	Lifts	Novice–Intermediate–Advanced
1,840	8,540	6	18%–46%–36%

Number of trails: thirty. *Longest trail:* 2.5 miles. *Base:* 6,700 feet. *Lifts:* one high-speed quad, two quads, three doubles. Free shuttle service within Incline Village. Pickup by reservation for groups of ten or more from Reno or South Lake Tahoe. *Location:* northeast shore of Lake Tahoe in Incline Village. Diamond Peak is directly above Incline Village.

2005–2006 rates: $46 adults, $36 youths (thirteen to seventeen), $17 children, $17 seniors (sixty to seventy-nine); younger than four and older than eighty, free.

Diamond Peak. 1210 Ski Way, Incline Village, NV 89451. Information: (775) 832–1177. Snowphone: (775) 831–3211. www.diamondpeak.com.

★★ HOMEWOOD MOUNTAIN RESORT

Vertical	Summit	Lifts	Novice–Intermediate–Advanced
1,650	7,880	8	15%–50%–35%

Number of trails: fifty-nine. *Longest trail:* 2 miles. *Base:* 6,230 feet. *Lifts:* one quad, two triples, one double chair, four surface lifts. *Location:* Highway 89 on the west shore of Lake Tahoe, 19 miles north of South Lake Tahoe.

Homewood has added new and improved snowmaking equipment that will enable it to blow more snow on the Face so it can be groomed top to bottom more often, even in early- and late-season conditions.

2005–2006, depending on date: $27 to $45 adults, $27 to $33 juniors (eleven to eighteen), $15 to $22 seniors. Half-day: $27 to $40 adults, $27 to $30 juniors.

Homewood Mountain Resort. Box 165, Homewood, CA 96141. (530) 525–2992. www.skihomewood.com.

★★★★ KIRKWOOD SKI RESORT

Vertical	Summit	Lifts	Novice–Intermediate–Advanced
2,000	9,800	12	15%–50%–35%

Number of trails: sixty-five. *Longest trail:* 2.5 miles. *Base:* 7,800 feet. *Lifts:* two high-speed quads, one quad, six triples, one double, and two surface lifts. Shuttle from major South Lake Tahoe resorts. *Location:* 35 miles south of South Lake Tahoe, Highway 88 at Carson Pass. Take Highway 89 south to 88 west.

Kirkwood sits in a spectacular alpine meadow valley. The views from the summit extend into the central valley of California. The 2,300 acres of skiable terrain include sixty-five runs, wide trails, steep chutes, and open bowls. The base elevation of 7,800 feet is the highest in northern California, and the natural snow magnet attracts an average of 450 inches each year, allowing Kirkwood to sometimes stay open as late as July 4.

The Cornice Express, a high-speed quad from the base of the mountain directly to the top, cuts the trip time in half to about four minutes. For 2003 Kirkwood introduced a superpipe just off the Plaza, right on the lower face of Chair 5, in plain view of all.

2005–2006 rates: $62 adults, $50 juniors, $34 seniors sixty-five to sixty-nine, and $13 for seniors seventy years and older. Afternoon tickets are also sold. Rates are highest during holiday periods and decline near the end of the season.

Kirkwood Ski Resort. P.O. Box 1, Kirkwood, CA 95646. Information: (209) 258–6000. Snowphone: (209) 258–3000. Reservations: (209) 258–7000, (800) 967–7500. www.kirkwood.com.

★★★ MOUNT ROSE–SKI TAHOE

Vertical	Summit	Lifts	Novice–Intermediate–Advanced
1,440	9,700	8	20%–30%–50%

Number of trails: sixty. *Longest trail:* 2.5 miles. *Base:* 8,260 feet. *Lifts:* two high-speed six-seaters, two quads, two triples, two surface tows. *Location:* 22 miles southwest of Reno, on State Route 431, 11 miles from Incline Village.

The nearest of the Lake Tahoe ski areas to Reno, the high base elevation makes good conditions likely even into the spring. The area offers a morning half-day ticket, which might allow a bit of skiing on your departure day, and discount skiing on nonholiday Mondays and Tuesdays.

In 2004 the resort opened extreme chutes at the peak of the mountain, with three expert and five superexpert plunges.

2005–2006 rates: $54 adults, $38 teens, $12 children. Seniors sixty to seventy-four ski for $34, and seniors over the age of seventy ski free. Half-day passes are also available.

Mount Rose–Ski Tahoe. 22222 Mount Rose Highway, Reno, NV 89511. (775) 849–0704. www.skirose.com.

★★★★ NORTHSTAR-AT-TAHOE

Vertical	Summit	Lifts	Novice–Intermediate–Advanced
2,280	8,610	16	25%–50%–25%

Number of trails: seventy-three. *Longest trail:* 2.9 miles. *Base:* 6,330 feet. *Lifts:* one six-person gondola, six high-speed quads, two triples, two doubles, five surface tows, one tubing lift. Interchangeable tickets with other Lake Tahoe resorts available. Complimentary shuttle bus between Incline Village/Kings Beach and Northstar. Reno airport pickup for groups. Shuttle to South Lake Tahoe runs twice weekly. *Location:* 40 miles southwest of Reno on California Highway 267 and 196 miles northeast of San Francisco.

New development on the "backside" of Mount Pluto opened up 200 more acres, including tree skiing. Also added was a high-speed quad chairlift that provides access to 200 acres of expert terrain on Lookout Mountain, a 1,200-foot vertical drop. The trails include five black diamond runs and a significant amount of tree skiing.

2005–2006 rates, depending on date: $63 to $66 adults, $53 to $56 young adults (thirteen to twenty-two), $22 to $25 children (five to twelve), $43 to $46 seniors sixty-five to sixty-nine, $17 to $20 seniors seventy and older.

Northstar-at-Tahoe. P.O. Box 129, Truckee, CA 96160. Information: (530) 562–1010. Snowphone: (530) 562–1330. Reservations: (800) 466–6784. www.skinorthstar.com.

★★★★ SIERRA-AT-TAHOE

Vertical	Summit	Lifts	Novice–Intermediate–Advanced
2,212	8,852	12	25%–50%–25%

Number of trails: forty-six. *Longest trail:* 2.5 miles. *Base:* 6,640 feet. *Lifts:* three high-speed quads, one triple, five doubles, three surface tows. Complimentary shuttle bus from South Lake Tahoe/Stateline casino area. *Location:* 12 miles west of South Lake Tahoe on US 50, 72 miles west of Reno.

The 2,000 acres of terrain feature forty-six trails including heart-stopping fall line plunges on the West Bowl. In 2003 Sierra-at-Tahoe built a new access road to the resort and enhanced its snowmaking capabilities.

2005–2006 rates: adults $59 to $62 depending on time of year, children $14 to $17, young adults $49 to $52, seniors (sixty-five to sixty-nine) $34 to $36, and super seniors (seventy and older) $17 to $23. Half-day afternoon tickets are also available.

Sierra-at-Tahoe. 1111 Sierra-at-Tahoe Road, Twin Bridges, CA 95735. Information: (530) 659–7453. Snowphone: (530) 659–7475. www.sierratahoe.com.

★★★★★ SQUAW VALLEY USA

Vertical	Summit	Lifts	Novice–Intermediate–Advanced
2,850	9,050	34	25%–45%–30%

Number of trails: one hundred. *Longest trail:* 3.5 miles. *Base:* 6,200 feet. *Lifts:* one 150-passenger tram, one twenty-eight-person funitel, one six-person pulse lift, three six-passenger chairs, four high-speed quads, one quad, eight triples, ten doubles, five surface tows. *Location:* 50 miles west of Reno, 200 miles east of San Francisco.

Squaw Valley USA is one of only three places in America where you can point your skis down a slope once zoomed by the Olympians. (The others are Whiteface Mountain near Lake Placid, New York, and several ski areas near Salt Lake City.) Founded in 1949 amid 8,000 acres of wilderness preserve in the California High Sierra, Squaw Valley was the site of the VIII Olympic Winter Games in 1960—the first Winter Games to be televised.

The Olympics propelled Squaw Valley onto the world stage and helped fuel the growth of skiing in America. In 1960 the resort had four double chairs and a rope tow; today there are thirty-four lifts, including a 150-passenger cable car and a high-tech funitel tram, and an automated "pulse lift" that connects the two midmountain lodges.

You're in for a bit of a shock—a pleasant one for most of us—when you look at the trail map for Squaw Valley USA. Because most of the area consists of expansive open bowls, there aren't really "trails," especially in the sense that Eastern skiers are used to. Pay attention to the rating that is assigned to the chairlifts to see what kind of terrain they serve; then head down the hill on a bowl that seems appropriate to your skiing style. In some parts of the resort, you'll find the easiest way down the hill marked with signs.

For most visitors the wide-open bowls and the consistent snow here generally make it possible to ski one notch above normal—accomplished novices will be able to cruise intermediate bowls, and dedicated intermediates should be able to try out some of the black diamond terrain. If you get in over your head, there is plenty of room to traverse the fall line.

Shuttle services run from various North Lake Tahoe and South Lake Tahoe locations. The *Tahoe Queen* Ski Shuttle connects one end of Lake Tahoe to the other. A bus runs from the south shore (Stateline) to Squaw Valley in the morning, with a return trip by paddle wheeler at the end of the day; the price includes transportation, a lift ticket, dinner, and entertainment. For information call (530) 577–4676.

2005–2006 rates depending on date: adults about $48 to $64 all day and night, about $46 afternoon and night, about $22 night; juniors (thirteen to fifteen) about $32; seniors sixty-five to seventy-five about $32; seniors seventy-six and older, free.

Squaw Valley USA. P.O. Box 2007, Olympic Valley, CA 96146. Information: (530) 583–6985. Snowphone: (530) 583–6955. Reservations: (800) 545–4350. www.squaw.com.

★★ SUGAR BOWL

Vertical	Summit	Lifts	Novice–Intermediate–Advanced
1,500	8,383	12	17%–45%–38%

Number of trails: eighty-four. *Longest trail:* 2 miles. *Base:* 6,883 feet. *Lifts:* one four-person gondola, four high-speed quads, three quads, three doubles, one surface tow. *Location:* Donner Summit near Soda Springs, 44 miles from Reno.

2005–2006 rates, depending on date: $46.00 to $59.00 adults, $40.00 young adults (thirteen to twenty-one), $15.00 children (six to twelve), $44.00 seniors, $5.00 seniors seventy and older.

Sugar Bowl. 629 Sugar Bowl Road, Norden, CA 95724. (530) 426–3651. www.skisugarbowl.com.

TAHOE DONNER

Vertical	Summit	Lifts	Novice–Intermediate–Advanced
600	7,350	3	40%–60%–0%

Number of trails: fourteen. *Longest trail:* 1 mile. *Base:* 6,750 feet. *Lifts:* one quad, one double, one surface tow. *Location:* west of Truckee.

2005–2006 rates: $34 adults, $13 juniors, $13 seniors.

Tahoe Donner. 11509 Northwoods Boulevard, Truckee, CA 96161. (530) 587–9444. www.tahoedonner.com.

MULTIAREA SKI PASSES

The North Lake Tahoe Resort Association offers the Ski Tahoe North interchangeable lift ticket. The pass, valid all season with no blackout dates, allows guests to ski or snowboard at resorts at the northern end of the lake including Alpine Meadows, Diamond Peak, Homewood Mountain Resort, Mount Rose/Ski Tahoe, Northstar-at-Tahoe, Squaw Valley USA, or Sugar Bowl. In 2006 the pass was priced at $54 per day for three or more day tickets. The pass is good as two for one at lower-priced Homewood and Diamond Creek. For information call (888) 434–1262 or consult www.PureTahoeNorth.com.

Lake Tahoe Region Cross-Country Ski Areas

CROSS-COUNTRY SKI AREA	DISTANCE FROM RENO (MILES)	TRAIL NETWORK (KILOMETERS)
Kirkwood	90	180
Lakeview	45	165
Northstar-at-Tahoe	40	165
Royal Gorge	45	328
Spooner Lake	40	101
Squaw Creek Nordic	45	130
Tahoe Donner	38	194

CROSS-COUNTRY SKI RESORTS

There are some great Nordic tracks in the high meadows of the Tahoe Valley. Some are accessible by road and others use uphill lifts from alpine ski resorts.

For information on many of the resorts at the north end of the lake, call the North Lake Tahoe Resort Association at (888) 434–1262 or consult www.Pure TahoeNorth.com. In years past the association has offered an interchangeable trail pass for six cross-country resorts.

★★★★ **Royal Gorge Cross-Country Ski Area** offers the largest private trail system in North America. Located at the Soda Springs/Norden exit off Interstate 80 near Donner Summit in Soda Springs, California; the Van Norden Trailhead is 1 mile east on Highway 40 near the Sugar Bowl Ski Resort. The resort can make snow on some trails.

Eighty-eight trails, 328 kilometers of track. That's not a typographical error: Royal Gorge claims it is North America's largest cross-country ski resort and the world's largest groomed track system with eighty-eight trails spread across 9,000 acres, with two hotels, four cafes, a day lodge, and ten warming huts. There are even four surface tows in steep areas. In a typical season the area at 7,000 feet in the Sierra Nevada receives about 600 inches of snow; just to be on the safe side, though, snowmaking covers 15 kilometers.

The Wilderness Lodge is tucked into the track system, offering meals, food, and lodging. The smaller Rainbow Lodge dates to the 1920s and is set along a bend in the Yuba River.

Royal Gorge typically operates from mid-November to mid-April.

In 2005–2006, trail tickets for weekends and holidays/midweek were $28/$24 for adults and $15/$14 for teens (thirteen to sixteen). For information call (530) 426–3871 or (800) 500–3871 or consult www.royalgorge.com.

Kirkwood, off Route 88 at Kirkwood Meadows, 30 miles south of Lake Tahoe, offers 80 kilometers of groomed trails. 2005–2006 rates: adults $18.00, juniors (thirteen to eighteen) $15.00, children $8.00. Half-day: adults $18.00, juniors

$12.00, children $6.00. Rentals: adults $20.00, children $10.00. For information call (209) 258–7248 or consult www.kirkwood.com/xcountry.html.

Northstar-at-Tahoe Cross-Country & Telemark Center has 65 kilometers of groomed trails for cross-country skiing and snowshoers. Located 8 miles south of Truckee off Route 267 on Northstar Drive, near the day lodge and downhill slopes. 2005–2006 rates: adults $27, children $15. Half-day: $21/$10. Rentals: $27/$15. For information call (530) 562–2475 or consult www.skinorthstar.com.

Spooner Lake Cross-Country Ski Area, north of the junction of US 50 and Route 28 at the parking lot for Lake Tahoe–Nevada State Park, has 101 kilometers of groomed trails, including a 19-kilometer backcountry trail. A backcountry cabin is available for rent. 2005–2006 rates: adults $16.50 midweek and Sunday, $21.00 Saturday and holidays; juniors (thirteen to eighteen) $9.00. Tuesday adult passes $10.00, daily twilight passes $9.00. For information call (775) 749–5349 or (775) 887–8844 for snow conditions, or consult www.spooner lake.com.

Squaw Creek Cross-Country Ski Center is a small area at the Resort at Squaw Creek that has rentals and lessons. Trails cover 18 kilometers. 2005–2006 rates: adults $18.00, children $5.00. For information call (530) 308–0375 or consult www.squaw.com/winter/crosscountry.html.

Tahoe Cross-Country Ski Area, 2 miles east of Tahoe City, offers 65 kilometers of groomed skating lanes and tracks. 2005–2006 rates: adults $20, juniors (ten to seventeen) $15, seniors (sixty to sixty-nine) $15. For information call (530) 583–5475 or consult www.tahoexc.org.

The **Tahoe Donner Cross-Country Area** has 100 kilometers of trails, including California's only lighted night tracks. Take the Donner State Park exit from I–80, ½ mile east on Donner Pass Road to a left turn on Northwoods Boulevard. 2005–2006 rates: adults $21, juniors (twelve and under) free, seniors (sixty to sixty-nine) $16, and super seniors (seventy and older) free. For information call (530) 587–9484 or consult www.tahoedonner.com.

■ SMALLER CROSS-COUNTRY AREAS

Bijou. South Lake Tahoe. (530) 542–6056. 4 kilometers open terrain, all beginner, in Bijou Community Park.

Camp Richardson. Route 89, South Lake Tahoe. (530) 541–1801. 35 kilometers of groomed trails.

Clair Tappaan Lodge. Norden, California. (530) 426–3632. www.sierra club.org. Rustic mountain lodge at the top of Donner Pass, owned and operated by the Sierra Club.

Eagle Mountain Nordic. Nevada City, California. (530) 389–2254. 75 kilometers marked and groomed trails.

Granlibakken. Route 89, Tahoe City. (530) 583–8464. www.granlibakken .com. 7.5 kilometers to Page Meadow.

Hope Valley Cross-Country at Sorensen's Resort. Highway 88 in Hope Valley. (530) 694–2266, (800) 423–9949. 51 kilometers marked trails, 10 kilometers groomed.

J & M Winter Sports. US 50 at Meyers, California. (530) 577–1813.

Lake Tahoe Basin. (530) 573–2600. Various trails maintained by the USDA Forest Service.

USDA Forest Service Trails. For Sno-Park and wilderness permits, snow conditions, and trail safety information, call (530) 543–2600.

SKI SHUTTLES

Ski shuttle services allow you to sample more than one mountain without the need to check in to a new hotel or rent a car.

The **Tahoe Area Regional Transit (TART)** operates from 6:10 A.M. to 6:30 P.M., seven days a week, on State Routes 28 and 89 along the northern and western shores of Lake Tahoe, from Incline Village, Nevada, on the northeast to Sugar Pine Point State Park in El Dorado County on the southwest, and to Truckee via Route 89. The base fare is about $1.25 and buses are about an hour apart. For more information or schedules, contact TART at (530) 581–6365 or (800) 736–6365.

The town of **Truckee** operates a transit service between downtown Truckee and Donner Lake year-round. During the winter additional routes serve the Route 267 corridor between Truckee, Northstar, and Kings Beach as well as to Donner Summit ski areas. For information or schedules call Aztec Transportation at (530) 587–7457.

The **Blue Go System** serves the south shore of Lake Tahoe, operating seven days a week, twenty-four hours a day. Six routes are operated. Between September and May an additional single van (previously called DART) operates in Douglas County serving the lower Kingsbury area between Zephyr Cove/Round Hill and the South Shore Stateline area along US 50. The base fare for service is about $1.25. Call South Shore Area Transit Management at (530) 542–6077 for more information.

Heavenly, Sierra-at-Tahoe, Alpine Meadows, Squaw Valley, Ski Incline, and Northstar are among ski areas offering shuttle service on their own or in conjunction with one of the established companies. Contact the ski area for information.

Several of the major South Lake Tahoe casinos are cooperating to operate the Tahoe Casino Express between the South Shore Stateline area and Reno/Tahoe International Airport. A number of smaller resorts also provide shuttle service from their locations to the casinos. Contact the hotels for information.

SNOWMOBILING

There are few places where snowmobiling has a more spectacular perch than high up in the mountain meadows above Lake Tahoe. There are quite a few companies renting machines and offering trail rides. No experience is necessary; outfits offer training and will even rent out cold-weather boots, jumpers, and parkas. Some of the companies offer two-person machines.

Rates for two-hour tours range from about $80 for a single rider to about $100 for a two-person sled. Here are some of the best companies:

■ **Eagle Ridge Snowmobile Outfitters.** Incline Village, Nevada. Tours on some 200 miles of groomed trails in the Tahoe National Forest north of Truckee. Riders get to visit some extremely remote areas including Treasure Mountain, the Sierra Buttes, and Lakes Basin. The company also offers two- and three-day overnight tours. (530) 546–8667. www.tahoesnowmobiling.com.

■ **J & M Winter Sports.** US 50 at Meyers, California (3 miles south of Lake Tahoe Airport). (530) 577–1813.

■ **Lake Tahoe Snowmobile Tours.** South Lake Tahoe, California. Tours to Mount Watson, the highest point on the North Shore. (530) 546–4280. www.lake tahoesnowmobile.com.

■ **Northstar-at-Tahoe.** Truckee, California. Two-hour tours around the edges of the downhill and cross-country ski trail system. Moonlight tours to the lookout atop Mount Watson are also offered. (530) 562–1010. www.skinorthstar.com.

■ **USDA Forest Service.** Snowmobiling is open in most national forest lands within the Lake Tahoe Basin, provided there is at least 6 inches of snow on the ground. Recommended areas include Spooner Summit, Hell Hole, and Blue Lakes Road in Hope Valley. Contact the USDA Forest Service for maps. (530) 543–2600.

■ **Zephyr Cove Snowmobile Center.** 760 US 50, Zephyr Cove, Nevada. A range of tours including two-hour guided trips running from Thanksgiving through mid-April that reach the ridgeline on the Nevada side of the lake, some 9,000 feet above sea level. Experienced riders can book three-hour tours. Parkas, bibs, gloves, and boots are available for rental; required helmets are free. (775) 588–3833.

SNOW PLAY AREAS

The California Department of Parks requires purchase and display of a permit to use Sno-Park parking areas during the season. Permits may be obtained at many sporting goods stores, ski rental and snowmobile shops, automobile clubs, and the South Lake Tahoe Chamber of Commerce. For information call the **Sno Park Hotline** (916) 324–1222; many are listed on a Web page at http://ohv.parks .ca.gov/default.asp?page_id=1233.

If you go sledding in an "unofficial" area, be aware of avalanche warnings, never sled alone, and don't sled onto bodies of water or across roads or trails.

Here are some designated sledding spots in and around the Lake Tahoe region:

Blackwood Canyon Sno-Park. Off Highway 89, 3 miles south of Tahoe City. Bring your own equipment; there is a $3.00 day fee. (530) 541–5255.

Boreal Ski Area. Ten miles west of Truckee, off I–80 in Donner Pass. Snow play area with two groomed slopes; plastic disk use only. $10 fee includes rental. Open weekends and holidays. (530) 426–3666. www.borealski.com.

Echo Lake. Off US 50, 1 mile west of Echo Summit on Echo Lake Road. Popular cross-country ski area, no snowmobiles. USDA Forest Service, (530) 644–6048.

Echo Summit. US 50, on south side at Echo Summit. Popular snow play area; extensive sledding hill. USDA Forest Service, (530) 644–6048.

Emigrant Gap. Laing Road, off I–80, 10 miles west of Soda Springs on the south side of the freeway. Bring your own equipment.

Granlibakken Ski Area. Off Highway 89 in Tahoe City. Hill for saucers only; $4.00 day-use fee. Saucers available for rent for $3.00. (530) 581–7333. www .granlibakken.com.

Hansen's Resort. 1360 Ski Run Boulevard, South Lake Tahoe, California. $6.00 per hour per person, including sled or tube. The area includes some bob-sledlike banked runs. (530) 544–3361. www.hansensresort.com.

Heavenly. There are several toboggan and sled hills where you can rent equipment and use the hills off Ski Run Boulevard leading to Heavenly.

Hope Valley. Highway 88, 5 miles east of Carson Pass. Snow play, groomed snowmobile trails, cross-country skiing. USDA Forest Service, (775) 884–8101.

Incline Village. On the driving range next to the Chateau. Bring your own equipment.

Meiss Meadow. Highway 88, quarter mile west of Carson Pass. Very popular cross-country ski area; no snowmobiles. USDA Forest Service, (209) 295–4251.

Mount Rose. Undeveloped and very steep area 8 miles up Mount Rose Highway (Highway 431). Bring your own equipment. www.skirose.com.

Northstar-at-Tahoe. Northstar Drive off Highway 267. Tubing hill with lift and groomed slope. Must use equipment provided. $13 for unlimited runs. (530) 562–1010. www.skinorthstar.com.

North Tahoe Regional Park. At the end of National Avenue in Tahoe Vista, California. Snow hill for toboggans, saucers, and inner tubes. No charge for play area; equipment rentals available for about $3.00. (530) 546–4212.

Sierra-at-Tahoe. East of Echo Summit on US 50. (530) 659–7453.

Sorenson's Resort. Hope Valley off Highway 88, just east of junction with Route 89. (530) 694–2203.

Spooner Summit. Highway 28, off US 50. West side of Highway 28, about 9 miles south of Incline Village where two roads come together. Steep hill; bring your own equipment.

Tahoe City. Off Highway 89, south of Fanny Bridge. Bring your own equipment.

Tahoe Vista. North Tahoe Regional Park snow play area. Turn left at top of National Avenue, off Highway 28. $3.00 parking.

Taylor Creek. West side of Highway 89 near Camp Richardson. Cross-country skiing to Fallen Leaf Lake. Limited snowmobile use. Small sledding hill. USDA Forest Service, (530) 543–2600.

Truckee. Donner Pass Road, central Truckee. Bring your own equipment.

SLEIGH RIDES/HORSEBACK RIDING

Borges Sleigh Ride. US 50 at Lake Parkway, South Lake Tahoe. Thirty-five-minute rides daily when snow conditions permit. Call for prices. (775) 588–2953, (800) 726–7433. www.sleighride.com.

Rancho Red Rock. 15670 Red Rock Road, Reno. Thirty-minute rides daily when conditions permit. Call for prices. (775) 969–3315. www.ranchoredrock .com.

ICE-SKATING

Resort at Squaw Creek. Ice-Skating Pavilion and Sports Activity Center at Squaw Valley. Rental shop. Open Thanksgiving to spring. (800) 327–3353. www .squawcreek.com.

South Lake Tahoe Ice Arena. An NHL-size indoor ice rink for skating and competitions. 1180 Rufus Allen Boulevard, South Lake Tahoe. (530) 542–6056.

Squaw Valley USA. Olympic-size outdoor ice rink at the High Camp Bath and Tennis Club. Rental shop and lessons. Open year-round. (530) 581–7246. www.squaw.com.

CHAPTER TWENTY-SEVEN

WARM-WEATHER AND YEAR-ROUND ACTIVITIES IN THE LAKE TAHOE REGION

MORE PEOPLE COME TO LAKE TAHOE in the summer than in the winter to enjoy the spectacular setting of the lake, forests, and mountains. You can play on the water or take a gondola to the summit for hiking and views beyond comparison.

HEAVENLY TRAM AND GONDOLA

You don't have to be a skier to ascend to the summit of Heavenly and enjoy the spectacular views. The ski resort's 2.4-mile-long gondola is available for rides to an observation point high above Lake Tahoe for most of the summer, except during scheduled maintenance periods. The gondola is open for the Memorial Day holiday and then again from mid-June through mid-October. Be sure to call for schedules.

Access to marked trails is included with sightseeing tickets. The East Peak Trail wanders through the forest for about 1.6 miles with views of Lake Tahoe and the Carson Valley. The 2.2-mile-round-trip Sky Meadows Trail gives the chance to enjoy the alpine wildflowers that grow at Heavenly. The most adventurous of routes is the East Peak Lake Trail, with a three-hour meander along the ridgeline to East Peak Lake.

In 2006 summer trips on the gondola ran daily from 10:00 A.M. to sunset midweek and 9:00 A.M. to sunset weekends and holidays. Round-trip tickets were $24 for adults (thirteen to sixty-four), $22 for seniors (sixty-five plus), and $15 for children (six to twelve). Children five and under ride free.

Heavenly, South Lake Tahoe, California. Summer information: (916) 544–6263; winter: (775) 586–7000. www.skiheavenly.com/summer/gondola_heavenly. Dinner reservations: (775) 586–7000, extension 6347.

PARKS AND MUSEUMS

■ **D. L. Bliss State Park.** Highway 89, South Lake Tahoe, California. From Rubicon Point in the park, you can see more than 100 feet into the depths of Lake Tahoe. (530) 525–7277. www.parks.ca.gov/default.asp?page_id=505.

■ **Donner Memorial State Park.** Highway 40, Truckee, California. A simple but affecting memorial to the ill-fated Donner Party of 1846. There's also the small **Emigrant Trail Museum** on-site. Open Memorial Day to mid-October, weather permitting. (530) 582–7892. www.parks.ca.gov/default.asp?page_id =503.

■ **Emerald Bay State Park.** Highway 89, South Lake Tahoe, California. If you've got a camera, this is the place to take it for breathtaking views of Lake Tahoe; if you didn't bring a camera, buy one and bring it here. (530) 541–3030. www .parks.ca.gov/default.asp?page_id=506.

Within the park is **Vikingsholm Castle** at the head of the bay near Eagle Falls and Creek. Tours are offered June through September from 10:00 A.M. to 4:00 P.M. Emerald Bay State Park, Highway 89, Emerald Bay, California. (530) 525–7277. www.vikingsholm.com.

■ **Gatekeeper's Log Cabin Museum** 130 West Lake Boulevard, Tahoe City, California. A reconstructed hand-carved log cabin standing on the same foundation as the original Gatekeeper's Cabin, which was destroyed by fire in 1978. The gatekeeper's duties included the measuring and regulation of Lake Tahoe's water level. A small museum tells the story of various water control and diversion plans for the lake.

The facility also includes the **Marion Steinbach Indian Basket Museum.** Open Wednesday to Sunday in the spring and fall and daily in the summer. Admission: $3.00 adults, $2.00 seniors, and $1.00 children.(530) 583–1762. www .northtahoemuseums.org.

■ **Hellman-Ehrman Mansion (Pine Lodge).** Sugar Pine Point State Park, Highway 89, Tahoma, California. Tours of the mansion, a 1903 summer home of a wealthy family, are conducted from 11:00 A.M. to 4:00 P.M. July through September. (530) 525–7982. www.parks.ca.gov/default.asp?page_id=991.

■ **Washoe Tribe of Nevada and California Archive & Cultural Center.** 861 Crescent Drive, Carson City. (775) 888–0936.

WATER SPORTS AND CRUISES

■ SOUTH SHORE BOAT RENTALS AND MARINAS

Action Watersports of Tahoe. Boating and parasailing. (530) 544–5387. www .action-watersports.com.

Camp Richardson Marina. Highway 89, South Lake Tahoe, California. (530) 542–6570. www.camprich.com.

Kayak Tahoe. (530) 544–2011. www.kayaktahoe.com.

Lakeside Marina. End of Park Avenue, South Lake Tahoe, California. (530) 541–6626.

Ski Run Marina. 900 Ski Run Boulevard, South Lake Tahoe, California. (530) 544–0200. www.skirunmarina.com.

Tahoe Keys Boat Rental. Tahoe Keys Marina, South Lake Tahoe, California. (530) 544–8888.

Tahoe Whitewater Tours. Tahoe City, California. Guided kayak tours of Emerald Bay, Sand Harbor, and other spots. Raft tours on American, Carson, and Truckee Rivers. (530) 581–2441.

Tributary Whitewater Tours. 20480 Woodbury Drive, Grass Valley, California. Guided white-water trips. (530) 346–6812, (800) 672–3846. www.whitewatertours.com.

Truckee River Raft Rentals. (530) 583–0123. www.truckeeriverraft.com.

Whitewater Connection. (530) 622–6446, (800) 336–7238. www.whitewaterconnection.com.

Zephyr Cove Resort & Marina. 760 US 50, Zephyr Cove, Nevada. Boating and snowmobiling. (775) 588–3833. www.zephyrcove.com.

■ NORTH SHORE BOAT RENTALS AND MARINAS

Homewood High & Dry. Homewood, California. (530) 525–5966.

North Tahoe Marina. Tahoe Vista. Boat rentals and fishing charters. (530) 546–8248. www.northtahoemarina.com.

Sand Harbor. Sand Harbor. (775) 831–0494.

Tahoe Paddle & Oar. Kings Beach. Canoe and kayak rentals. (530) 581–3029. www.tahoepaddle.com.

Tahoe Whitewater Tours. Tahoe City. Guided tours of Emerald Bay and area rivers. (530) 581–2441, (800) 442–7238. www.gowhitewater.com.

■ CRUISES

■ *Tahoe Queen* and **MS *Dixie II*.** Re-created stern-wheelers depart from the Ski Run Marina in South Lake Tahoe. Various cruises, including sightseeing, theme cruises, and dinner trips were priced in 2006 from $31.00 to $59.00 for adults, $28.00 to $56.00 for seniors, and $9.00 to $31.00 for children. For information call (775) 589–4906 or (800) 238–2463 or consult www.zephyrcove.com.

■ *Tahoe Star.* Casino and hotel mogul Bill Harrah's 54-foot-long former yacht offers daily cruises from about May 1 through the end of October; capacity is limited to thirty-six guests. You can read details in chapter 25 in the section about Harrah's Casino Hotel Lake Tahoe in Stateline.

■ **Woodwind Sailing Cruises.** Departs from Zephyr Cove, Nevada. Five departures a day, including a sunset champagne cruise each night on a 41-foot glass-bottom catamaran. You'll find more details on the cruise schedule in chapter 25. (775) 588–3000. www.sailwoodwind.com.

▪ FISHING

All of Lake Tahoe and most of the hundreds of smaller backcountry lakes are open for fishing year-round. Certain exceptions apply to tributaries of Lake Tahoe on both the California and Nevada sides—obtain a copy of fishing regulations from sporting goods stores in the area.

Federal and state authorities regulate fishing activities in Lake Tahoe, surrounding lakes, and tributaries. For a full set of rules, contact the **California Department of Fish & Game** at (916) 227–2245 or www.dfg.ca.gov, or the **Nevada Division of Wildlife** at (775) 688–1500 or www.ndow.org.

I hope you fancy trout: There are at least six variants of that fish in the rivers and lakes of the Tahoe Basin: brook, brown, cutthroat, golden, Mackinaw, and rainbow. Golden trout are scarce and likely to be found only in the most remote, high mountain lakes. Lake Tahoe also has kokanee salmon.

Fishing in Lake Tahoe is allowed from one hour before sunrise until two hours after sunset; hours for other bodies of water are similar. Most areas impose a limit of five trout, with stricter limits on scarce Mackinaw and golden trout.

▪ **Lake Tahoe.** Locals advise getting out into the deep water on a boat; if you do fish from the shore, the best spots are where the bottom falls off sharply, including Cave Rock on the east shore and Rubicon Point on the west.

▪ **Fallen Leaf Lake.** Deep waters offer the most promise; fishing within 250 feet of the dam at the northwest corner of the lake is forbidden.

▪ **Echo Lakes.** Shore fishing from the dam is a good bet.

▪ **Blue Lakes.** High mountain lakes at more than 0,000 feet, about 12 miles south of the Tahoe Basin, off Highway 88. Locals recommend fishing from the dams.

▪ **Carson River, West Fork.** A popular fishing area, south of Lake Tahoe along Highway 88 and Blue Lakes Road. Carson River, East Fork is closed to fishing above Carson Falls. There are size limits on catches from Hangman's Bridge south of Markleeville to the Nevada line.

▪ **Truckee River.** Fishing is prohibited in and around the dam at Lake Tahoe, with other restrictions applied at various times of the year.

Here are some fishing services and resorts catering to anglers:

Caples Lake Resort. Highway 88, Kirkwood, California. (209) 258–8888. www.capleslakeresort.com.

First Strike Sportfishing. (530) 577–5065.

Mac-a-Tac Charters. Tahoe Vista. (530) 546–2331.

Tahoe Sportfishing Company. Ski Run Marina, South Lake Tahoe, California. (530) 541–5448, (800) 696–7797.

Truckee River Outfitters. Truckee. (530) 582–0900.

CAMPGROUNDS AND BEACHES

Camp Richardson. Highway 89, South Lake Tahoe, California. (530) 541–1801. www.camprich.com.

Davis Creek Park. U.S. Highway 395 to Bowers Mansion exit. Twenty miles south of Reno. Sites for tents and trailers. Fishing. Open all year. (775) 849–0684.

D. L. Bliss State Park. Highway 89, north of Emerald Bay. (916) 525–7277. www.parks.ca.gov/default.asp?page_id=505.

Echo Lakes. Echo Chalet, a privately leased USDA Forest Service resort open in summer only. Echo Summit Road off U.S. Highway 50. (916) 659–7207. www .echochalet.com.

Emerald Bay State Park. Highway 89, Emerald Bay. (530) 541–3030. www .parks.ca.gov/default.asp?page_id=506.

Grover Hot Springs State Park. Highway 89 South, 3 miles west of Markleeville, California. (530) 694–2248. www.parks.ca.gov/default.asp?page_id=508.

Lake Tahoe Nevada State Parks. (775) 831–0494. www.parks.nv.gov/lt.htm.

Mount Rose Campground. Route 431. Twenty miles southwest of Reno on the slopes of Mount Rose. Twenty-four sites for tents and trailers up to 16 feet. Elevation 8,900 feet. Open July to mid-September. (877) 444–6777.

South Lake Tahoe Parks & Recreation Department. (530) 542–6055.

Sugar Pine Point State Park. Highway 89. (530) 525–7982. www.parks.ca.gov /default.asp?page_id=510.

USDA Forest Service, Lake Tahoe Basin. (530) 543–2600. www.r5.fs.fed.us/ ltbmu.

Warrior Point Beach. Route 445, past Sutcliffe 9 miles to the end of the pavement. Forty miles north of Reno. Permits for fishing and camping available. (775) 476–1155.

Washoe Lake State Park. US 395, Washoe Lake State Park exit. Twenty-five miles south of Reno. Twenty-five sites for tents and trailers up to 30 feet. Equestrian area, swimming, fishing, boat launch. (775) 607–4319. www.parks.nv .gov/wl.htm.

HIKING TRAILS

The star among stars in hiking trails along Lake Tahoe is the **Tahoe Rim Trail,** a hiking and horseback-riding trail through national forest lands at the north end. Built with donations and volunteer labor, the last 12 miles of a 150-mile circle were added in 2000, ending a seventeen-year-long project.

The trail passes through two states, three national forests, high mountain lakes, streams, and meadows and offers views from as high as 10,000 feet at Freel Peak and Alpine Meadows. The trail does not exceed a 10 percent grade and is suitable for beginner through advanced hiking. Camping is allowed along the trail.

In the summer and early fall, some 3,000 hikers trek along portions of the beautiful mountain trail each week.

TAHOE VISTA TRAILS AT HEAVENLY

The Heavenly ski resort offers guided tours and marked trails that lead off from the top of its tram, which operates year-round. It's a good way to take the easy way up to the 8,250-foot mark, and the three main trails offer a moderate challenge with spectacular rewards.

The Tahoe Vista Trail traverses a ridgeline high above the lake. The longest trail is a 2.1-mile hike to the Fremont Camp, up a series of switchbacks to the 9,000-foot level. The camp was established by Kit Carson and Colonel John C. Frémont in February 1844 when they became the first nonnatives to see the lake.

A second trail leads to Snowshoe Ridge, named after John A. "Snowshoe" Thompson, Tahoe's earliest known skier. Thompson became a legend in the Sierra by carrying mail in the 1860s on a route that led from Placerville, California, to Genoa, Nevada, on the east side of the Sierra Nevada.

Neumann Point is named in remembrance of Terry Neumann, a Heavenly ski instructor who was killed in a huge avalanche at this location in 1974.

■ EAST SHORE TRAILS

Rim Trail South. Take the hint from the name: This is a southerly walk along the top of the Lake Tahoe world, a strenuous jaunt of about 21 miles that reaches up to 10,778 feet at its highest point.

The trail begins behind the Nevada Department of Transport building at the Spooner Summit Rest Area on US 50. If the views of Lake Tahoe to the west and the Carson Valley to the east from the Rim Trail aren't enough for you, branches of the trail head off to even more isolated peaks, including Duane Bliss Peak, South Camp Peak, and Genoa Peak.

Rim Trail North. A slightly less challenging 18-mile hike that begins about half a mile up US 50 from the junction with Route 28. There's a small parking area at the trailhead. This wooded trail reaches to about 8,000 feet as it heads north. Just before Snow Peak, the trail comes to a fork. The left fork switchbacks down a steep slope to Marlette Lake, while the right fork leads to Tunnel Creek Road.

Lake Tahoe Nevada State Park. On the East Shore, off Highway 28. Trail to Sand Harbor, Marlette Lake, and the upper elevations of the Carson Range. Access from Spooner Lake at the intersection of US 50 and Highway 28. For information call (775) 831–0494.

Marlette Lake. A 5-mile uphill jaunt of moderate challenge through North Canyon to Marlette Lake. To get to the trail, park at the Spooner Lake Trailhead in Lake Tahoe Nevada State Park, northwest of the junction of US 50 and Highway 28; a parking fee is charged in season.

■ NORTH SHORE/MOUNT ROSE TRAILS

Mount Rose Trail. A view to the north of Reno and to the southwest of the Tahoe Basin from the 10,778-foot summit. A 5-mile hike of moderate difficulty, the trail begins 1 mile south of the summit on Highway 431 (Mount Rose Highway). The trail crosses a high mountain meadow before making a final 2-mile switchback ascent to the ridge.

Mount Rose Wilderness. This recent addition to the protected wilderness around Lake Tahoe includes the land at the northeast corner of Lake Tahoe above Incline Village. For information and maps contact the Carson Ranger District in Carson City at (775) 882–2766.

■ SOUTH SHORE/MOUNT ROSE TRAILS

Echo Lakes Trail. A moderate trail that reaches deep into the wilderness to Lower and Upper Echo Lakes and several other alpine waterways, including Tamarack, Lucille, Margery, and Aloha. In the summer a water taxi offers a shortcut across Upper Echo Lake. The trail is reached from Echo Lakes Road, off US 50 at Echo Summit. Bear left on Echo Lakes Road to a parking area. Upper Echo lies about 2½ miles up the trail with other lakes farther on, several miles apart.

Glen Alpine Trailhead. Several hikes of moderate to strenuous challenge depart from this trailhead off Fallen Leaf Lake Road, which itself branches off Highway 89 3 miles north of South Lake Tahoe. This is a slightly less strenuous 6-mile path to the top of Mount Tallac.

Half Moon and Alta Morris Lakes. A moderate trail of about 5 miles.

Kirkwood. Highway 88 at Carson Pass. Along the south shore, 8,000 acres with trails for all abilities. Passes high country lakes and streams with access to Pacific Crest and Mormon Emigrant Trails. (209) 258–6000.

Lake Aloha. A 6-mile hike that includes a high mountain meadow, three alpine lakes, and a small waterfall.

Meiss Lake Country. USDA Forest Service land south of South Lake Tahoe, California. The trails encompass 10,000 acres at intermediate and advanced levels and pass several high country lakes. Access off Highway 89, 5 miles south of US 50 in Meyers, California. (530) 543–2600.

Mount Tallac Trail. The Big Kahuna of the southern end of the Tahoe Basin, a difficult 9-mile ascent to a view worth 10,000 words of description. The trail begins on a fairly easy level, heading for Floating Island Lake and Cathedral Lake. The trail turns steep and difficult past Cathedral Lake for the final 5 miles to the top of Tallac at 9,735 feet. The trailhead can be found on Highway 89, about 3½ miles north of South Lake Tahoe. The road to the parking area is across the road from the entrance to Baldwin Beach.

Pope-Baldwin Recreation Area. The Fallen Leaf Trail System leads to the south shore of Fallen Leaf Lake. Access from the USDA Forest Service Lake Tahoe Visitor Center on Highway 89. (530) 543–2600.

Tallac Historic Site. An easy half-mile walk through the area of the former Tallac mansions. Accessible from the Kiva Picnic Area or the Lake of the Sky Trail from the Lake Tahoe Visitor Center.

■ WEST SHORE TRAILS

Bayview Trail. A difficult trail up Maggie's Peak 1 mile to Granite Lake; from there it continues on to Dicks Lake, intersecting the Eagle Falls Trail along the way.

Cascade Creek Fall Trail. An easy, nearly flat, 1-mile hike to the 200-foot Cascade Falls at Cascade Lake. The falls are at their most spectacular in the spring as winter snows melt on the slopes above.

Cascade Creek Trailhead. Several spectacular trails lead off from this trailhead, including an easy jaunt to Cascade Falls and a difficult climb to three hidden high lakes. Located about 8 miles north of South Lake Tahoe on Highway 89 at the Bayview Campground across the road from Inspiration Point.

Desolation Wilderness. Permits are required to enter the 63,475 acres of woods and lakes, and travel is by foot or horseback only. Open campfires are prohibited and overnight camping permits are strictly limited in the heart of the season, from June 15 to Labor Day.

Half of each day's permits can be reserved up to ninety days in advance, with the remainder available only on the day of entrance. Permits are available year-round at the Forest Service office in South Lake Tahoe and in summer at the Forest Service visitor center off Highway 89 and at some of the trailheads.

Among the most spectacular trails in all the Lake Tahoe region is the path up Mount Tallac, which leads from near the northwestern end of Fallen Leaf Lake some 6 miles along and 3,400 feet up to a spectacular vista overlooking Lake Tahoe. For information on wilderness areas, contact the Lake Tahoe Basin Management Unit in South Lake Tahoe at (530) 543–2600.

Eagle Falls Trail. A steep and difficult 10-mile plunge deep into the Desolation Wilderness, passing Eagle Lake and then Velma, Middle Velma, and Upper Velma Lakes and ending at Fontanillis Lake. The trailhead is at the Eagle Falls Picnic Area off Highway 89, 8 miles north of South Lake Tahoe.

Granite Chief. A hiking area on the back sides of the Alpine Meadows and Squaw Valley USA ski areas, south toward Twin Peaks and Barker Pass.

Rubicon Trail. A moderately difficult 7.5-mile trail along the shoreline of Lake Tahoe, passing through a number of secluded coves and beaches and reaching 3 miles to Emerald Point and ending at Vikingsholm Castle. The trail is reached from D. L. Bliss State Park, about 10 miles north of South Lake Tahoe on Highway 89.

Vikingsholm Trail. An easy 1-mile descent to Lower Eagle Falls and Vikingsholm Castle with views of Emerald Bay and Fannette Island. The trail leaves from a parking lot off Highway 89, about 9 miles north of South Lake Tahoe.

GOLF COURSES

■ SOUTH SHORE GOLF COURSES

Bijou Municipal Golf Course. 1180 Rufus Allen Boulevard, South Lake Tahoe, California. Nine holes. (530) 542–6097.

Edgewood Tahoe Golf Course. Lake Parkway, Stateline. Adjacent to the Horizon Casino Resort. Eighteen holes. Rated as one of the top courses in the country. Open May through October. Public. (775) 588–3566. www.edgewood-tahoe.com.

Lake Tahoe Golf Course. US 50, Meyers, California. Eighteen holes. (530) 577–0788.

Tahoe Paradise Golf Course. US 50, Meyers, California. Eighteen holes. Nine-hole executive course. Public. (530) 577–2121. www.paradisegc.com.

◾ NORTH SHORE GOLF COURSES

Carson Valley Golf Course. Gardnerville, Nevada. Eighteen holes. (775) 265–3181. www.carsonvalleygolf.com.

Incline Village Championship Golf Course. Incline Village, Nevada. Eighteen holes. Public. Designed by Robert Trent Jones Jr. Open May 1 to October 15. (775) 832–1146. www.golfincline.com.

Incline Village Mountain Golf Course. Incline Village, Nevada. Eighteen holes. May to September 30. (530) 832–1150. www.golfincline.com.

Northstar-at-Tahoe Resort Golf Course. Highway 267 between Truckee and North Lake Tahoe. Eighteen holes. Public. May through October. (530) 562–2490. www.skinorthstar.com.

Old Brockway Golf Course. 7900 North Lake Boulevard, Kings Beach. Rated as one of the top nine-hole courses in northern California and home of the first Crosby Tournament in 1934. (530) 546–9909.

Ponderosa Golf Course. 10040 Reynold Way, Truckee. Nine holes. (530) 587–3501. www.ponderosagolfclub.com.

Resort at Squaw Creek Golf Course. 400 Squaw Creek Road, Squaw Valley. Deisgned by Robert Trent Jones Jr. Eighteen holes. Public. (530) 583–6300, extension 6637 or (800) 327–3353.

Tahoe Donner Golf Course. 12850 Northwoods Boulevard, Truckee. Eighteen holes. Mid-May through mid-October. (530) 587–9443. www.tahoedonner.com.

BICYCLING

Bike trails in and around Reno and Lake Tahoe range from nearly flat tours around lakes and across valleys to steep hill climbs on the Geiger Grade, the Mount Rose Highway, and across the top of the Sierra Nevada ridgeline. And there's the spectacular and sometimes challenging 72-mile coastline around Lake Tahoe, North America's largest alpine lake.

Kaspian Beach and Campground is Lake Tahoe's only bicycle campground. Located on Highway 89 between Sunnyside and Homewood, the site is 2½ miles from scenic Blackwood Canyon and Creek. There are only ten campsites available, though.

The **Pope-Baldwin Beach Trail** runs through several historical and educational sites along the south shore of Lake Tahoe; the 3½-mile path passes through the Tallac Historic Site, Lake Tahoe Visitor Center, stream profile chamber, Fallen Leaf Lake, and Pope and Baldwin Beaches.

The **Tahoe City to River Ranch Path** runs approximately 5 miles alongside the Truckee River. Contact the USDA Forest Service at (775) 882–2766 or (530) 265–4531 to check the status of trails, or consult www.r5.fs.fed.us/tahoe.

Mountain bikers are prohibited from riding in wilderness areas, developed recreation sites, and self-guided nature trails. The Forest Service recommends several area trails for mountain bike usage: Meiss/Big Meadow, Angora Ridge Road, McKinney-Rubicon OHV Trail, Mount Watson, Brockway Summit to Martis Peak, Genoa Peak, and Marlette Lake.

Like the Lake Tahoe paths, Reno's trails also border bodies of water. Here is a selection of some of the more interesting routes:

■ The 6½-mile **Truckee River Trail** begins at Broadhead Park, near Wells Avenue and Kuenzi Lane, and continues along the river ending near the Vista Boulevard exit on Interstate 80. The **Idlewild Route** also follows the Truckee River from Riverside and First Streets and continues 3½ miles through Idlewild Park to Caughlin Ranch.

■ **Bowers Mansion to Franktown** is a scenic, sparsely traveled country road. This 4-mile stretch starts at Bowers Mansion about 15 miles south of Reno and makes a right turn on Franktown Road, winding its way past farmlands, meadows, towering pines, and large estates.

■ BICYCLING TO EXTREMES

The **Markleeville Death Ride** attracts 1,500 avid cyclists in a tour over mountain passes, pedaling as many as 128 miles each July. Markleeville is about 80 miles south of Reno. For information call (530) 694–2475 or consult www.death ride.com.

■ BICYCLE RENTAL AGENCIES

South Lake Tahoe Area

Anderson's Bicycle and Skate Rentals. 645 Emerald Bay Road, South Lake Tahoe, California. (530) 541–0500.

Mountain Sports Center. Camp Richardson Resort, Highway 89, South Lake Tahoe, California. (530) 542–6584. www.camprich.com.

Cyclepaths. 1785 Westlake Boulevard, South Lake Tahoe, California. (530) 581–1171. www.cyclepaths.com.

Lakeview Sports. 3131 US 50, South Lake Tahoe, California. (530) 544–0183.

Shoreline Ski & Sports. 259 Kingsbury Grade, Stateline, Nevada. (888) 877–7669. www.shorelinesnowboards.com.

Sierra Cycle Works. 3430 US 50, South Lake Tahoe, California. (530) 541–7505. www.sierraskiandcycleworks.com.

Tahoe Cyclery. 3552 Lake Tahoe Boulevard, South Lake Tahoe, California. (530) 541–2726.

A Village Mountain Surf & Sports. 3552 Lake Tahoe Boulevard, US 50, South Lake Tahoe, California. (530) 541–4444.

North Lake Tahoe Area

The Backcountry. Tahoe City, California. (530) 581–5861.

Northstar-at-Tahoe. Truckee, California. (530) 562–2248. Ride chairlifts to midmountain trails.

Olympic Bike Shop. 620 North Lake Boulevard, Tahoe City, California. (530) 581–2500.

Paco's Truckee River Bicycle. 11400 Donner Pass Road, Truckee, California. (530) 587–5561.

Porter's Ski & Sport. 501 North Lake Boulevard, Tahoe City, California. (530) 583–2314. Crossroads Center, Truckee, California. (530) 587–1500. 885 Tahoe Boulevard, Incline Village, California. (775) 831–3500.

Squaw Valley USA Olympic Valley. California. (530) 583–6985. Ride the cable car with your bicycle to mountain trails.

BOWLING

Bowl Incline. 920 Southwood Boulevard, Incline Village, Nevada. (775) 831–1900.

Tahoe Bowl. 1030 Fremont Avenue, South Lake Tahoe, California. (530) 544–3700.

HORSEBACK RIDING THE RANGE

Make like a real cowboy on the wide-open ranges around the Reno–Lake Tahoe area. Here are some stables that rent horses and offer sleigh rides in winter:

■ NORTH SHORE

Alpine Meadows Stables. Tahoe City, California. Open daily June through October. (530) 583–3905.

Rancho Red Rock. 15670 Red Rock Road, Reno. Trail rides through beautiful, forested areas all year, weather permitting. (775) 969–3315.

Squaw Valley Stables. Squaw Valley, California. Ride the site of the 1960 Winter Olympics. Guided rides, rentals, pony rides. (530) 583–7433.

Tahoe Donner Equestrian Center. Five miles west of Truckee, California, the center is open May through October for trail rides; overnight pack trips are offered in the summer. (530) 587–9470.

Verdi Trails West. Verdi, Nevada. Trail rides and hayrides. (775) 345–7600. www.verditrailsranch.com.

Winters Creek Ranch. Located at 1201 US 395 North in Washoe Valley, Nevada, offering winding mountain trails through tall pines, over creeks, and through meadows. Open year-round, weather permitting. (775) 849–3500.

Wolf Creek Pack Station. Ten miles south of Markleeville, California, offering guided day rides or fully outfitted camping trips in the Carson Iceberg and Mokelumne Wilderness Area. Open from May 15 through the end of October. (916) 345–0333. www.r5.fs.fed.us/stanislaus/visitor/mokelumne.

■ SOUTH SHORE

Borges Carriage & Sleigh Rides. US 50 and Lake Parkway. South Lake Tahoe, California. (775) 588–2953. www.sleighride.com.

Camp Richardson Corral. Emerald Bay at Fallen Leaf Road, South Lake Tahoe, California. Trail rides, wagon rides, sleigh rides in winter. Overnight and extended pack trips. (530) 541–3113. www.camprichardson.com.

Sunset Ranch. US 50, South Lake Tahoe, California. Ride through the open meadows of the Upper Truckee River, with or without a guide. Children's pony rides and petting zoo. Hayrides and sleigh rides in season. Open year-round. (530) 541–9001.

Zephyr Cove Stables. Zephyr Cove Resort, US 50, Zephyr Cove, Nevada. (775) 588–5664. www.zephyrcovestables.com.

BALLOON RIDES

If you've got the nerve, I can't think of very many more thrilling ways to explore Lake Tahoe or Carson Valley than from a hot-air balloon at 5,000 feet. The rides are generally offered from spring through fall.

There are several companies offering tours; most offer a one- to two-hour trip and charge between $100 and $200 per person. The trips leave early in the morning, before the air heats up and makes things even more unpredictable. The balloon pilots, by the way, have only a limited ability to steer their bags of air, and they are chased by ground crews who will retrieve the equipment and passengers and bring them back to the base.

Lake Tahoe Balloons. P.O. Box 19215, South Lake Tahoe, CA 96151. (530) 544–1221, (800) 872–9294. www.laketahoeballoons.com.

Mountain High Balloons. Truckee, California. (530) 587–6922, (888) 462–2683.

SOARING

Graceful, engineless gliders soar over the mountains and meadows of the Lake Tahoe region year-round in good weather, offering a spectacular view.

Soar Minden. Nevada. (775) 782–7627, (800) 345–7627. www.soarminden.com.

Soar Truckee. California. (530) 587–6702. www.soartruckee.com.

HOT SPRINGS

Carson Hot Springs. Carson City, Nevada. (775) 885–8844. www.carsonhotspringsresort.com.

Steamboat Villa Hot Springs Spa. Steamboat, Nevada. (775) 853–6600. www.steamboatsprings.org.

Wally's Hot Springs. Genoa, Nevada. (775) 782–8155.

PART IV

ABOUT GAMBLING

CHAPTER TWENTY-EIGHT

GAMBLING IS NOT A SPORT: A CAUTIOUS VIEW

A QUARTER HERE, A DOLLAR THERE, a hundred-dollar chip on the craps table, a $500 token in a video poker machine, or a nickel in the slot machine at a downtown sawdust joint: Sooner or later, we're talking about real money— billions of dollars.

Let's start with two very important points: The fabulous resorts of Las Vegas, Reno, Lake Tahoe, Laughlin, and everywhere in between were not built as exotic gifts by eccentric multimillionaires. Exotic they are, and eccentric were their developers, but each and every one was built as a business.

Point number two: The business of the fabulous resorts of Nevada is based on the fact that nearly every visitor can be counted upon to *lose* money at gambling tables and slot machines. Some will lose more than others, and a few will come away with an occasional small or large or huge win, but always remember that the streets of Nevada are paved by the losers.

Before you even *think* about making money gambling, take a good look around you. Do you see those huge casino buildings with their spectacular come-ons outside and opulent decorations within? Do you see those cheap-to-free meals and drinks? Do you see the hundreds of dealers, supervisors, cocktail waitresses, change clerks, keno runners, glad-handers, and assorted others in the cast?

Someone has to pay for all of this. Guess who?

PLAYING SMART

It is not the purpose of this book to teach you to become a professional gambler. There are any number of detailed tomes that purport to do just that. And I'm not going to attempt to preach at you about the evils of risking your family's rent money at the tables. If that is a problem, you should seek the help of a professional counselor or a twelve-step program. (In fact Nevada has quite a collection of counseling services and organizations, which says something about something.)

Instead I'm going to explain some of the more popular games played at the casinos and help you have a bit of fun as you lose the money you brought with you. If you win, perhaps you'd like to send an offering to the author.

Econoguide Rule Number One of Gambling: Do not bet more than you can afford to lose.

Corollary to Econoguide Rule Number One of Gambling: Do not bring with you to the table (or with you to the hotel) more money than you can afford to lose.

Second Corollary to Econoguide Rule Number One of Gambling: Don't beg, borrow, or steal more money than you can afford to lose. The casinos will make it very easy for you to tap into credit cards or savings accounts and may even offer unsecured loans. Whatever the source, it will still be a debt.

THE HOUSE ALWAYS HAS AN ADVANTAGE

Let's start with a very basic concept, that of the **house advantage.**

The simplest form of gambling might be a bet between two individuals over whether the next flip of a coin will come up heads or tails. If the coin and the person doing the flipping are both honest, the odds of the coin coming up heads or tails are exactly even. This means that the true odds are 1:1, also called even money. If you bet $5.00 on the flip of the coin and won, you would receive your $5.00 back plus $5.00 in winnings.

If a casino (the house, in gambling parlance) was to pay off at those odds, over the course of time, both the player and the casino would break even. (Which, in the case of the casino, means it would lose a lot of money, since it costs a great deal for the fancy building, the exploding volcano or the bubbling fountain, the dealers, the free drinks . . . you get the idea.)

The way the casino makes its money is to charge a commission on winning bets. The house will try to take as much as it can get. However, as in any pricing scheme, there comes a point at which the consumer refuses to buy. The typical range of commission on betting is between 2 and 10 percent.

For example, if the house were to charge a 5 percent commission, a $100 winning bet on a coin toss would receive $195 back instead of $200. (The wager of $100 is returned untouched, and the commission is applied to the winnings.)

If the bet is a loser, the house does not charge a commission, but keeps the entire amount. That money, though, goes to pay off winners.

One way to look at the operations of a casino—and it is only one of many ways—is this: Over time a casino makes money only on winning bets.

Even if a player strikes it rich on a particular bet, the casino can count on the law of averages rebuilding the pot over time. Among other things most winners stick around and proceed to lose their winnings.

The worst possible player for a casino is someone who comes in and wins quickly (paying very little commission along the way) and then leaves ahead of the game (contributing little or nothing to the pot for other winners).

THE HOUSE PERCENTAGE

How does a huge and expensive operation like a major casino make much money if it is able to hold on to only a few percentage points of the action at the table?

Well, first of all, there is *a lot* of action at most casinos, and so those nickels on the dollar add up very quickly.

Second, though, and more important, there is the fact that the vast majority of gamblers are just not very good at what they do. They'll play hunches, they'll use faulty "systems," and they'll just plain make costly mistakes at the tables. The costliest error of all for many gamblers is "chasing": throwing good money after bad when they are losing, or perversely throwing away their winnings when they are ahead.

The true winning percentage at most casinos is in the neighborhood of 20 percent.

EVERYBODY HAS A SYSTEM

Some of us like to bet on our age (which in the case of roulette freezes you in time at age thirty-six; the keno game is a bit more accommodating, up to eighty). These schemes are harmless, so long as you realize that the odds of any particular number coming up are the same on each spin of the wheel.

More complex and sometimes dangerous betting systems are those that are based on some sort of betting scheme. The most popular of these is a "doubling" strategy, which sounds logical—and is, over time—but rarely works for most bettors with limited resources.

Put another way, doubling is not a very good strategy unless you have a lot of money and a lot of time. Make that an almost unlimited amount of money or an infinite period of time, unless you run into a nice streak of luck—and luck is not an element of strategy.

Doubling works like this: Let's say your basic bet is $10. If you bet $10 and lose, your next bet is for $20; if you lose again, you double again to $40 and so on. At some time the bettor will win and at that point will be slightly ahead.

Let's assume you are wagering an even-money bet, which means that when you win, your $10 is returned as $20. If you win ten times in a row, you will be $100 ahead of the game.

Now, let's consider what happens when you lose. Remember: You are planning to double your bet with each loss. As any schoolkid who has had to work on math tables can tell you, doubling a simple number can quickly lead to a huge value. For example, if you were to start with a $10 bet and lose ten times in a row, your eleventh bet would have risen to $10,240, and you will be out-of-pocket $20,470 at that moment, which just may be beyond your budget for spending money. And you may run into the table limit, which is yet another way for the casino to increase its chances of cleaning out your wallet.

But let's say you win that even money bet of $10,240. The crowd will gasp, the dealer will smile, and you will feel greatly relieved as you are handed a stack of chips worth $20,480. You and the dealer may be the only ones who realize that the net profit on your huge bet will be $10!

Casinos make out quite well on doublers, because the fact is that sooner or later most run out of money or nerve and drop out before they make their small profit.

Gambling professionals—and remember that there are very few who consistently make money at the "game"—say that the classic doubling scheme is exactly backward. They suggest you increase the size of your bet when you are winning and reduce your bets when you lose. This way you take advantage of your streaks rather than work against them.

In other words, don't chase your losses.

If you just continue to play at the same level without changing the amount you bet, over a period of time, the house's advantage is almost sure to eat away your bankroll.

SLOT MACHINES

At one time the conventional wisdom may have been that table games—from roulette to twenty-one to baccarat—were where the real action was at a casino. The slot machines were looked down upon as the province of the low roller.

Today the average bet at the tables is still considerably higher than at the slot machines, but don't make the mistake of assuming that casinos look down on slot machines as being less interesting than the table games. According to government reports, revenues from slot machines now make up more than two-thirds of gaming income.

Here is the rap on slots: They are dumb, require no skill, and provide no human interaction. They are pure exercises in luck, and like other casino bets, they ask the player to put aside the knowledge that the casino is almost sure to win over time.

The easiest game in town has just two requirements: coins or tokens of the right denomination and a strong arm. Actually most modern slot machines don't even require you to pull the handle; there's a button you can press to let the machine do the work.

The sexy thing about slot machines is that they can pay off with astronomical amounts; the highest of the high—progressive machines—can return millions of dollars on a bet of $3.00 or $5.00.

On slot machines, the house edge is expressed as a "payback" percentage. A particular machine may claim 98 percent payback, meaning that over time the machine pays back 98 percent of the money put into it. The casino keeps 2 percent as its advantage, which can add up to a lot of money over time.

Some casinos will advertise that their machines are "loose," meaning that they pay back higher than others; no casinos I know of will announce that their machines are "tight" with your money. However, in general the small-change machines (nickels and quarters and the rare penny machines) are tighter than the larger denomination slots.

According to the Nevada Gaming Control Board, the average payback on slot machines in the state ranges from about 74 to 85 percent; in other words, over time, the average slot player can expect to lose $15 to $26 out of every $100 bet.

The odds against winning are based on the number of reels (rolling sets of symbols) and the number of symbols on each reel. The highest payoff five-reel machines may work out to a chance of 1 in 3.2 million pulls for the jackpot.

Most slot machines pay better jackpots to bettors who play the maximum number of coins on a pull. So if you are willing to bet about $1.00 per pull, you generally would be better off at a quarter machine putting in five coins at a time ($1.25 per pull) than putting in a single dollar token at a dollar machine.

As I've noted, the biggest payoffs are to be found at "progressive" machines, which are slots tied into an electronic network within the same casino, across a group of casinos under the same ownership, or even as part of a statewide network run by an independent slot company. The potential payoffs are huge—millions of dollars in some cases—but the odds against winning can be astronomical.

One other point to be aware of is the payoff scheme for a particular jackpot. Most systems pay off their huge jackpots with an annuity: If you win what is advertised as a $1 million prize, what you may receive are twenty annual checks of $50,000 each, which costs the casino less and is worth less to you. A few casinos, always seeking some new lure, advertise full payoffs at the time of winning.

■ EVERY SLOT MACHINE IS NOT THE SAME

Understand this: Slot machines are fixed. Technicians can set the rate of payout over time. It's all legal, and it's all under the supervision of state gaming authorities.

Another thing: Not all slot machines in the same state, same city, or even the same casino are set at the same payoff rate.

All things can and do change, but in general it seems that the better slot payoffs are found in downtown Las Vegas, with rates just a bit better than those on the Strip. The worst are probably to be found outside of the casinos—at the airport, in supermarkets (really), and bars.

The best payout percentage is usually found on the higher denomination machines, especially the $5.00 slots.

What does it mean when a machine pays off at a 95.8 percent rate? Well, it could mean that a bettor putting $100 into the machine will walk away with about $95.80 and a sore arm. Or, it could mean that the same bettor could lose every penny of his or her stake, and the next player could leave with $191.60 for a $100 bet. Even more likely, ninety-nine bettors could lose every penny and the one hundredth could hit a $10,000 jackpot. In every case, over time, the house will earn a profit. And over time, every player but the most lucky will lose.

■ PROGRESSIVE SLOTS

Many of the casinos around the state offer megapayoff progressive slot machines that are tied into a central system. On these particular machines your odds of winning are the same whether you are playing at a major casino, at a lesser one, or at a machine in the corner of a Laundromat. (Don't believe me about the

Laundromats? In some parts of Nevada, you'll find machines in airports, drugstores, supermarkets . . . and Laundromats.)

Some of the brand names for progressive games include Megabucks and Quartermania. A recent trend has seen licensing of other entertainment properties to create a brand of machines: Elvis Slots, Sinatra Slots, Jeopardy Video Slots, The Addams Family Slots, and Regis Cash Club Slots among them.

In a progressive system, the jackpot grows as it adds portions of the money bet by players all around the state. When a winner is declared, the jackpot drops to its base level.

VIDEO POKER

Among the hottest types of gambling machines are video poker devices. There are dozens of different formats, but most of them come down to versions of stud poker. The machine will deal you five cards and you can choose to hold any or all of them or draw from one to five new cards. After the second round of cards, the hand is evaluated and winning hands are paid off.

Most machines pay off only on a pair of jacks or better. In addition, the relative payoffs are much higher for the best hands. Therefore, professional video poker players generally recommend throwing away any low hands and always making a play for the high-payoff hands. For example, in standard poker you would almost never draw to an inside straight (seeking to fill out a straight with a gap in the middle, as in 9-10-Q-K), but in video poker it might be worth a chance.

One area worth paying attention to are the listed payouts on video poker machines. Some casinos pay off considerably better than others; there may even be a noticeable disparity between and among machines in the same casino.

ROULETTE

Round and round she goes, where she stops nobody knows. Some historians track the roulette wheel back to the ancient Chinese or Tibetans of 1,000 years ago; the famous French scientist and mathematician Blaise Pascal is credited with adapting the wheel to a casino game in 1655.

Of the four major table games (roulette, craps, blackjack, and baccarat), roulette offers the poorest odds to the player. The American game, as played in Nevada with the 0 and 00 numbers added to the layout, gives the house a 5.26 percent advantage on most bets; the worst gamble for the player is the five-number bet, which gives the house an advantage of more than 7 percent. It is, though, one of the simplest of games to play. In the standard Nevada game, the wheel is divided into alternating red and black compartments that are numbered from one to thirty-six; in addition, one compartment is numbered 0 and another 00. A player can bet on any of the thirty-eight numbers directly and is paid off at 35:1. (Here is the house advantage presented about as clearly as possible:

There is a one in thirty-eight chance of a particular number coming up, and the winning payoff is 35:1.)

The 0 and 00 are excluded from the payoffs on red/black, odd/even, columns, or rows. In other words the casino wins all bets on color, odd/even, or groups of numbers if 0 or 00 comes up. (There are a handful of smaller casinos in Nevada that may offer roulette wheels with only a single 0, which improves the player's odds somewhat.)

The roulette table, usually made of green felt, includes boxes colored and numbered to correspond to the colors and numbers of the compartments of the wheel. The numbers are divided into twelve rows and three columns; there are also betting boxes for group bets including red or black, odd or even, 1–12, 1–18, 13–24, 19–36, and 25–25. There are also betting boxes for each of the three columns. Finally, there are betting boxes for 0 and 00.

After a period of time to place bets, the dealer starts the wheel spinning in a counterclockwise direction and then sends the ball in the opposite direction. Players can continue to place bets until the ball is about to fall off its track and onto the wheel; the dealer will indicate when bets are closed.

At most casinos you will use special chips to play roulette, cashing in your casino markers for a special set of colored chips in various denominations. The reason for the change is the fact that the player is able to place as many bets as he or she wants, all over the table; the color-coded chips allow the dealer to keep track of which bets belong to which player.

Here is the typical payoff schedule for roulette wheels in Nevada. At most casinos you will find the payoffs listed on the felt surface of the table itself.

Single number, Single 0, or Double 00. Played as a straight number bet, pays off 35:1.

0/00 Split. Pays 17:1.

Five Numbers. Covers 0, 00, 1, 2, or 3. Pays 6:1.

Black/Red. Even money bet. Pays 1:1.

Odd/Even. Even money bet. Pays 1:1.

---

1 to 18/19 to 36. Even money bet. Pays 1:1.

Twelve Numbers or Section Bets. Covers all twelve numbers in selected section. Pays 2:1.

Two Numbers/Split. Pays 17:1.

Three Numbers. Covers three numbers across a row. Pays 11:1.

Four Numbers. Covers four numbers touched by the chip. Pays 8:1.

Six Numbers. Covers the six numbers in two rows. Pays 5:1.

Column Bets. Covers all twelve of the numbers in a single column. Pays 2:1.

As I have noted, casinos are not charitable institutions: They're in this for the money. Here are the natural (mathematical) odds and the casino payoff; the difference between the two is the house advantage at roulette:

	Natural Odds	Typical Casino Payoff
Single Number	38:1	35:1
Split	19:1	17:1
Even Money	1.06:1	1:1
Three Numbers	12.67:1	11:1
Four Numbers	9.5:1	8:1
Five Numbers	7.6:1	6:1
Six Numbers	6.33:1	5:1
Section/Column Bets	3.17:1	2:1

At most casinos the house has an edge of 5.26 percent on all roulette bets except for the five-number bet of 0-00-1-2-3, which is even less advantageous to the bettor, with an edge of 7.89 percent. Put another way, the five-number bet, with payoff odds of 6:1, is the worst bet in roulette.

Since no one bet in roulette is theoretically better than another (with the exception of the five-number parlay), it may make sense to concentrate on one type of bet and hope that your luck over the short term is better than the house advantage's chomp at your bankroll.

BLACKJACK (TWENTY-ONE)

Blackjack, also called twenty-one, is one of the more popular casino games and—on one level—one of the easiest to play. All you have to do is request cards from the dealer, one at a time, until you get as close to a card value of twenty-one as you can. If you get closer to twenty-one than the dealer, you win; if you go over twenty-one or if the dealer is closer to that magic number, you lose. If you and the dealer tie, your bet is returned to you.

Betting is relatively simple, too. You are always betting against the dealer, always betting that your card value will be better than his or hers. There are only a few variations in betting schemes, including doubling down and splitting, which I will explain in a moment.

But although blackjack is easy to play, it is not easy to win. It is, though, one of the few games at the casino that can be consistently beaten, or at least fought to a draw, by a well-educated and careful player.

A player who understands the basic strategy and bets conservatively can expect to win about 1 percent of total action over the course of time, which doesn't sound like much but can quickly mount up into serious money. Players who can count cards and adjust the levels of betting and strategies based on the current condition of the deck can expect to win much more.

The line between winning and losing is always slim, and the casino always stands to benefit from a mistake by the player.

Numbered cards, from 2 to 10, are counted at face value. Face cards (jacks, queens, and kings) count as ten. An ace counts as one or eleven, whichever suits your purposes.

Place your bet in front of you prior to the deal. The dealer will then work his or her way around the table twice, dealing two cards to you and two cards to him- or herself. In the standard game, the player's cards are dealt faceup and the dealer's cards are dealt one down and one up.

If you score twenty-one (an ace together with a king, queen, jack, or 10) with your first two cards, turn them over immediately and collect 1½ times your bet. If your first two cards don't total twenty-one, you can either "stand" (refuse additional cards) or request a "hit" (an additional card). You can request as many hits as it takes to either approach a total of twenty-one or be "busted" (exceed twenty-one and lose).

Watch the players at the table, or ask the dealer about the protocol for indicating whether you want to hit or stand. Some casinos are more picky than others about hand signs used at the table. In most casinos you indicate that you want another card by scratching your current cards toward you on the felt or by waving at the dealer with a "come to me" gesture. (Looser dealers will permit you to nod your head "yes" or perform some other positive signal.) To indicate you want to stand, you can slip your cards, facedown, under your bet or give some sort of a "wave off" signal.

The reason casinos are sometimes picky about the signals used is that they don't want a bettor to ask for his money back on a losing bet because of any ambiguity about betting intentions.

Other casino protocol: Handle the cards with one hand only; don't take the cards off the table, and don't touch your bet once cards have been dealt.

If you are busted, turn over all your cards and watch the dealer take away your bet.

If you stand with your current card total, action passes to the next player at the table and so on until it reaches the dealer.

Although you are free to do just about anything at the table, the dealer must follow some very specific rules. The basic rules at most casinos are these:

■ The dealer must stand with cards totaling seventeen or more and must hit for any total under seventeen.

■ At many casinos, the dealer must also hit on a "soft" seventeen, which is a hand that can be valued as seven or seventeen depending on whether the ace is counted as a one or an eleven.

If the dealer busts, all players still in the game win. If the dealer does not bust and your cards are closer to twenty-one than the dealer's, you will win your bet; if the dealer's cards are closer to twenty-one, you will lose your bet. And if your card value is the same as the dealer's, it is a "push" and your bet is returned to you.

That's all there is to the game. Now, of course, you have to figure out the way to stay a step ahead of the dealer. As I have noted, the dealer has no choice in his or her actions.

There are two steps to becoming a good blackjack player. First is to understand basic playing strategies that will change based on the cards you have drawn and the face-up card displayed by the dealer. The second step, which is for only the most advanced players blessed with extraordinary attention to details and memory, is called "card counting."

I'm not going to go into details on card counting—there are many books about the subject if you've got a few years you want to devote to practicing this art. Basically the purpose of card counting is to determine the balance of the deck to improve your chances at figuring whether cards you may draw are likely to be high-value or low-value cards. A good card counter can all but guarantee a winning margin at the table.

Before you give up those years of study, though, you should be aware that most Nevada casinos look very unfavorably on card counters. If the pit boss or the dealer suspects a player is counting cards, he or she may order constant shuffling of the deck, which disrupts the system, or he or she may try other distractions. The Nevada authorities even cooperate with casinos in barring card counters from their casinos. Obviously both the casinos and the state much prefer losing players to those with a fighting chance at winning.

▪ BLACKJACK BETS

The standard payoff for winning hands in blackjack is 1:1 (your bet is returned with an equal winning amount). If you draw a blackjack (two cards that total twenty-one, such as an ace and a jack or other face card or an ace and 10) you will be paid 1.5:1.

There are also a few special bets you can make once play begins. They include the following:

▪ **Doubling Down.** If you think you have a strong hand with the first two cards you draw (usually a pair of cards totaling nine, ten, or eleven), you can double your bet and hope for a winning hand with the third card you are drawn. You will automatically stand with the hand you have.

▪ **Splitting Pairs.** You can split two same-value cards into two hands each with its own bet. The dealer will give you an additional card on each half of the pair, and you can stand or continue drawing on each hand. At most casinos, though, the payoff on a winning split hand is just 1:1.

▪ **Insurance.** If the dealer shows an ace as his "up" card, you can bet half of your original wager as insurance against the chance that the dealer will have a card worth ten as his "hole" card. In other words, protection against the dealer having a blackjack. If the dealer does score twenty-one, you lose your original bet but are paid 2:1 on your insurance bet.

There are entire books on blackjack strategies; I'll only touch the surface in this book with a simple summary.

First of all, you should always draw a card if you have a hand worth eleven or less; there is no possible way to go over twenty-one.

From there on it gets a bit more complex. First let's define two types of hands:

■ A **hard total** is any hand of any number of cards that adds up to twelve or more without an ace, or any hand in which the ace is valued as one and not eleven. (If the ace were valued as an eleven, the hand would go over twenty-one and therefore bust the bet.)

■ A **soft total** is any hand of any number of cards in which an ace can be valued at either one or eleven without busting the hand. When the ace is valued at eleven, the hand is called a soft hand. A soft total can change to a hard total based on the values of other cards drawn. For example, if you held an ace and a 5, the total can be either six or sixteen. If you were to draw a jack or other ten-value card, your hand would now be a hard total of sixteen since counting the ace as an eleven would bust the hand.

The player in blackjack has some significant advantages over the dealer because the dealer must follow the house rules without exception, always drawing on a sixteen and standing on a seventeen. The player can adjust strategy based on the latest run of cards or the up card shown by the dealer. The one advantage held by the dealer, and it is a very large one, is the fact that the dealer goes last. If a player busts before the dealer draws a card—even if the dealer busts—the player loses his or her bet.

The strategies are based on statistical analyses that show that the dealer is most likely to bust his or her hand when he or she has a low-value card, from two to six, showing. This is called a "bust hand." The dealer will have to draw another card unless he or she has a six showing and an ace hidden. When the dealer shows a bust hand and you have a decent hand yourself, you will be best off standing pat and not drawing another card.

At the other end of the scale, the dealer is likely to have a "pat hand" when a 7 through ace is showing, and unless you have a strong hand already, it will be worth taking a chance to draw another card.

Here are two charts that show common strategies for hard and soft totals.

Hard Total	Dealer's Up Card	Strategy
17	Any card	Stand
16, 15, 14, or 13	2, 3, 4, 5, or 6	Stand
16, 15, 14, or 13	7 through ace	Hit
12	2 or 3	Hit
12	4, 5, or 6	Stand
12	7 through ace	Hit

Soft Total	Dealer's Up Card	Strategy
Ace and 9	Any card	Stand
Ace and 8	Any card	Stand
Ace and 7	9 or 10	Hit
Ace and 7	2, 3, 4, 5, 6, 7, 8, or ace	Stand
Ace and 6	Any card	Hit

Why should you always hit against an ace and 6? Blackjack players consider a seventeen a useless hand, as the only way you can win with it is for the dealer to bust his or her hand. You may as well try to improve your hand until it is greater than seventeen or you reach a stand-pat hard total.

CRAPS

Craps is one of the more exciting games at the casino, one where the players and even the various casino employees are encouraged to yell, shout, and otherwise encourage the little cubes of plastic to come up properly.

Dice have been used from antiquity and probably originated in Asia. Dice marked with dots have been recovered from Egyptian tombs, and Greek and Roman literature contain many references to dice playing. Craps is a form of the old English game of hazard.

I'll cover the basic mechanics of the game and how to bet; if you are serious about playing the game, you should read a more specialized gambling book.

The thrower (called the shooter) makes a money bet, covered by one or more opponents. The shooter throws the two dice against the far wall of the craps table. (This is an important rule of the casino; the boxman or pit boss may halt the game if they don't feel you are throwing the dice with enough force to ensure an honest tumble.) If the first throw totals seven or eleven, the player wins, but if two, three, or twelve is thrown, the player loses. In any of these cases, betting and throwing are repeated.

If the throw totals four, five, six, eight, nine, or ten, that number becomes the player's point, and throwing is continued until the same point is made again or a seven is thrown. If the point is made, the player wins, but if a seven is thrown, the player loses both the bet and the right to throw again.

So far, so good: Now let's talk about the betting protocol for craps, which is a bit more difficult to understand than the game itself. First of all, there are some variations from casino to casino; most casinos offer classes at quiet times or may have a printed summary of rules and payoff odds. Some casinos pay off better than others, too.

Pass Line. A bet placed on the Pass Line means you are betting with the dice and the shooter. If the shooter rolls seven or eleven (a natural) on the first roll, you win and are paid even money (one chip for each chip you have bet).

If the shooter rolls two, three, or twelve (craps), you and the shooter lose. Any other number (four, five, six, eight, nine, ten) is a "point" number and the bet rolls over. If the shooter rolls a point number again before a seven, you and the shooter win.

Don't Pass Line. A bet on the Don't Pass Line means you are betting against the dice and the shooter, and the reverse of the pattern for the Pass Line applies.

You will lose your bet on a seven or eleven on the first roll, and will win on a two or three. A twelve is a "standoff" with no winner or loser. If a seven is rolled before the shooter makes his or her point, you win; if a point number is made before a seven is rolled, you lose.

Come. After the shooter has rolled a point number, you can place a bet on the Come line. You will win your bet if the shooter rolls a seven or eleven, and you will lose if a two, three, or twelve

Richard Freeman, a pit manager at the Golden Nugget in downtown Las Vegas, conducts a lesson on craps.

comes up. Any other combination is a "come" point; if the come point appears before a seven, you win.

Don't Come. After the shooter has rolled a point number, you can bet on the Don't Come line. You will win if a two or three is rolled. A seven or eleven is a loser, and twelve is a standoff. If a come point is rolled before a seven, you lose.

Proposition Bets. Most craps tables allow specific bets on the next roll of the dice; consult the stickman for how to place your bets. These include **Any Craps** (two, three, or twelve), which pays 7:1; **Any Seven,** which usually pays 4:1; a bet on **two** or **twelve,** which pays 30:1; or a bet on **three** or **eleven,** paying 15:1. These bets are not recommended by experts.

Place Bets. Ask the dealer for the way to place this bet in one of the numbered boxes on the felt. Before any roll, you can bet on four, five, six, eight, nine, or ten. If your number comes up before a seven, you win. Typical odds are 7:5 for a five or nine, 7:6 on a six or eight, and 9:5 for a four or ten.

Field Bet. Bet on the next roll of the dice by placing a chip in the Field box. You will be paid even money if a three, four, nine, ten, or eleven is rolled; a two pays 2:1 and a twelve pays 3:1.

Big Six or Eight. Some casinos include a separate betting box for this wager; you will be paid even money if a six or eight is rolled before a seven. Craps experts consider this one of the least attractive bets on the table.

Horn Bet. A four-unit bet that the next roll will come up two, three, eleven, or twelve; even if you win, the house will keep three out of the four units as losing bets. An especially unattractive gamble, according to the experts.

For the more casual player, here are a few observations about the odds of particular numbers coming up in play:

Number	Combinations	Ways to Roll
2	1-1	1
3	1-2, 2-1	2
4	1-3, 3-1, 2-2	3
5	1-4, 4-1, 2-3, 3-2	4
6	1-5, 5-1, 2-4, 4-2, 3-3	5
7	1-6, 6-1, 2-5, 5-2, 3-4, 4-3	6
8	2-6, 6-2, 3-5, 5-3, 4-4	5
9	3-6, 6-3, 4-5, 5-4	4
10	4-6, 6-4, 5-5	3
11	5-6, 6-5	2
12	6-6	1

What we have here is a perfect bell curve. It is obvious that seven is the most common number, with six different combinations. The odds, therefore, are against a point number coming up before a seven.

Here is a chart that shows the actual odds against repeating a point number before a seven is rolled:

Number	Ways to Roll	Odds Against Appearing Before a 7 is Rolled
4	3	2:1
5	4	3:2
6	5	6:5
8	5	6:5
9	4	3:2
10	3	2:1

Here are the odds against a single number coming up on a particular roll:

Number	Ways to Roll	True Odds
2	1	35:1
3	2	17:1
7	6	5:1
11	2	17:1
12	1	35:1

BACCARAT

The ancient game of baccarat (pronounced *Bah*-kah-*rah*) is derived from a French card game dating from the fifteenth century. In Europe, a very similar game is called *chemin de fer,* which means "road of iron," better known as a railroad.

Baccarat is a fairly difficult game to understand, but it is very easy to play, since the dealer will handle all of the work. All you need to do is make your bet. And the house advantage is rather low, just over 1 percent on bank and player bets.

In the version of baccarat played in most Nevada casinos, the game is played with a set of eight decks of cards shuffled and placed in a "shoe." At each table the casino will provide a printed copy of the rules or a wall plaque with rules; in any case, it is the dealer who makes all of the decisions.

The object of the game is to wager on the hand that the player believes will come as close to nine as possible (without going over) with two cards (and a possible third). Ties are replayed. The players may bet a total of any amount equal to or less than the amount of the bank.

You can bet at any time on the player's hand or the bank's; you can also bet on a tie. Standard bets are paid even money, minus a 5 percent commission on all winning bank bets. Tie bets pay 9:1 odds.

The player keeps control of the shoe as long as the bank hand wins; when the bank hand loses, the shoe moves to the next player to the right. A player can voluntarily pass the shoe after any hand.

In baccarat banque the banker plays against only two hands, on which all the other players bet, holding the bank until he or she has lost the original stake or voluntarily resigns.

(In *chemin de fer,* the banker plays individually against each of the other players, betting on his or her hand against each of the hands held by the players. The banker retains the bank until losing a bet, and the bank then goes to the winning player.)

Although only two players—the "banker" and the "player"—are actually dealt cards from the shoe by the banker, all players (including the banker) can bet either on the banker's hand or the player's hand. The "player" is the player with the largest bet on the player's side.

The highest hand in baccarat is nine and the lowest zero. An ace counts as one, a deuce as two, and so on. Face cards and tens, or any combination of cards totaling ten, have no value.

The last digit of the total is the hand value; a seven and a seven, for example, may equal fourteen, but the value of the hand is four; the value of a nine and a four is three.

The cards are dealt, facedown, in the following order: player, banker, player, banker. Both the player and banker expose their cards, and there are no options for the player: You must draw a card if the rules demand.

If the first two cards dealt to the player or the bank total eight or nine, it is called a "natural" and neither side may draw any more cards. A nine is the higher natural and is an automatic winner; if another hand totals eight, the higher of the naturals wins. If both hands total eight or nine, it is a tie and neither hand wins.

Rules for each hand are as follows:

PLAYER

If first two cards total:	Action
1-2-3-4-5-10	Player draws card
6-7	Player stands
8-9	Natural (banker cannot draw)

BANKER

If first two cards total:	Must draw when player's third card is:
0-1-2	Always draw (except for Player Natural)
3	1-2-3-4-5-6-7-9-10
4	2-3-4-5-6-7
5	4-5-6-7
6	6-7
7	Stands
8-9	Natural (player cannot draw)

If the player takes no card, banker stands on 6.

KENO

Keno is bingo with gambling on the odds of particular combinations of numbers being called. In some places it is sort of the background music of the casino, with keno cards and display boards almost everywhere, from the casino floor to the restaurants and sports books.

The game consists of gambling on the likelihood of any one to twenty of eighty numbers being drawn at one session. The more numbers you mark, the higher the possible payoff (and the lower the chances of winning).

To play the game, obtain a blank keno ticket from a keno writer or from the tabletop holder in many restaurants or lounges and put an X through the numbers you want to bet on. Give your bet to the runner and retain the duplicate ticket he or she will give to you.

Depending on the time of the day and the size of the casino, the keno game will be conducted as often as two or three times per hour; some casinos even run multiple games at the same time, using color-coded cards.

At the drawing the casino selects twenty of the eighty numbers at random. Compare these with the numbers you selected; it isn't hard to figure out if you've won or lost. There are no guaranteed winners in a game; if all the players lose, the house wins all the money. When there is a large payoff, it will almost certainly be larger than the amount bet in the current game, but it will come out of the pool of money from previous losing sessions.

The simplest bet in keno is just to select a few numbers and bet on them coming up. Be aware that the payoff at various casinos will vary. At some houses the highest payoff is a fixed amount, while at others the top payment is part of a progressive pool shared with other casinos. If the pool is large, the payoff will be large; if someone has tapped it lately, the payoff will be less. You should also be aware that most keno games limit the total payout per game; if you have the good luck to win a high-payoff bet, you might also have the bad luck to do so in the same game as someone else's winning play.

Keno is a game at which the casino has a huge advantage, as much as 40 percent on some bets. The large payoffs for small investments and its slow pace make it a sometimes enjoyable pastime when you are too busy eating dinner to stand at the tables.

Be sure you read and understand the rules of the game at each casino. At most establishments, for example, you must immediately cash in winning tickets before the next game is begun; in other words, a ticket that is worth $250,000 drops to $0 if not collected within minutes. Obviously you don't want to be sitting in a show, up in your room, or otherwise distracted if you have a live keno ticket. Some casinos have introduced series tickets that are valid for extended periods of time across multiple games; study the rules and the fine print.

Among the various types of bets are these:

Straight Bet. Mark from one to fifteen (or twenty at some casinos) and bet any amount at or above the minimum, which is usually $1.00.

Split Bet. This is a means of placing multiple bets from one ticket. The most common method to indicate this type of bet is to place a circle around a group of numbers or to draw a line between two groups of numbers. Make sure the keno writer understands the bet you want to make and marks the card appropriately.

Way Tickets. This is a bet that combines three or more equal-size groups of numbers. For example, you could mark three groups of six numbers, referred to as a three-way six-spot. Once again, be sure that the keno writer understands your intentions and marks your card properly.

Special Tickets. Many casinos will offer special tickets that offer slightly higher payoffs. Be sure you understand the rules for the special games, and be sure that your ticket is marked properly for the special game, or the payoff for a winning card will be made at lower standard odds.

Top and Bottom. Bet that thirteen or more of the twenty numbers drawn in a round of keno will be from the top or bottom of the card (in other words, that thirteen or more of the numbers will be between one and forty or between forty-one and eighty).

BINGO

You know, just like the game the church ladies offer Thursday nights. Some of the low-roller joints offer games with fees as low as 10 cents; anything to bring in a buck. In bingo the house always wins, raking off a percentage of the pot.

You'll find bingo games at many of the downtown and off-Strip casinos; for whatever reason, the game is considered too lowbrow for the megaresorts. Here are some of the bingo rooms in Las Vegas:

Arizona Charlie's, Boulder. Twenty-four-hour action with new sessions beginning on the odd hours. 4575 Boulder Highway. (888) 236–9066. www.arizona charliesboulder.com.

Boulder Station. 9:00 A.M. to 11:00 P.M. with sessions beginning on the odd hours. 4111 Boulder Highway. (702) 432–7777. www.stationcasinos.com.

Fiesta Rancho. 9:00 A.M. to 11:00 P.M. with new sessions on the odd hours. 2400 North Rancho Drive. (702) 631–7000. http://rancho.fiestacasino.com.

Gold Coast. 9:00 A.M. to 11:00 P.M. with new sessions on the odd hours. 4000 West Flamingo Road. (800) 331–5334. www.goldcoastcasino.com.

Palace Station. 11:00 A.M. to 11:00 P.M. with new sessions on the odd hours. 2411 West Sahara Avenue. (702) 367–2411. www.stationcasinos.com.

Sam's Town. 9:00 A.M. to 11:00 P.M. with new sessions on the odd hours. 5111 Boulder Highway. (702) 456–7777, (800) 634–6371. www.samstownlv.com.

Sunset Station. 9:00 A.M. to 11:00 P.M. with new sessions on the odd hours. 1301 West Sunset Road, Henderson. (888) 786–7389. www.stationcasinos.com.

Texas Station. 9:00 A.M. to 11:00 P.M. with new sessions on the odd hours. 2101 Texas Star Lane, North Las Vegas. (702) 631–1000. www.stationcasinos.com.

PAI GOW

A game that originated in ancient China and is sometimes called Chinese dominoes, Pai Gow is increasingly popular in Nevada because of the influx of Asian gamblers. Similar to baccarat, the house collects a commission of 5 percent on all winning bets.

Pai Gow is a rotating bank game that uses a standard set of thirty-two Chinese dominoes. The dealer mixes or shuffles them, and they are then placed in eight stacks of four tiles. The dealer and up to seven players are each given one stack.

The object of the game is to divide the four tiles in your stack into the best two pairs; if your rankings are higher than those of the banker, you win. If the banker's rankings are higher or the same as the player's, the player loses the bet.

The game, then, can be seen as similar to playing two separate hands of baccarat at the same time, with nine being the highest point. There are twenty different combinations of dominoes that are higher than nine, with sixteen of the combinations made up of pairs. The other four combinations of dominoes that are higher than nine are called Wong and Gong.

The position of "banker" is rotated, counterclockwise, among the players and the casino's dealer after each game. To be the banker you must be able to cover all bets or half the bets of all of the players at the table. If you choose to cover half the bets, the house will bank the other half of the bets and will have the right to set the banker's dominoes.

A player can pass the bank to the next player if he or she does not wish the honor (and risk) of being banker. Of course the chance to win multiple bets only happens when you hold the bank.

After bets have been placed, the banker casts three dice that determine which player is given the first stack of dominoes. The players then rank their hands and place the two combinations in front of their bets.

The house dealer will then open the hands of the players and determine the winners and losers.

If you are not already confused, there is a complex ranking of the value of combinations of the dominoes. Each casino should have a printed sheet or a wall poster showing the rankings. If you are serious about this game, see if the casino has any classes available.

PAI GOW POKER

One way in which Pai Gow has been simplified for Western players is Pai Gow poker, which combines elements of the ancient Chinese game with American poker. It is played with a standard deck of fifty-two cards plus a single joker.

The joker is a not a true "wild" card. It can be used only as an ace or as a wild card to complete a straight, flush, or straight flush.

Each player is dealt seven cards. The player's task is to arrange the cards into two hands: a two-card (low) hand and a five-card (high) hand. The object of the game is to arrange your cards so that both of your hands rank higher than both of the banker's two hands.

Rankings are based on standard poker rules. Therefore the highest possible two-card hand would be two aces, and the highest five-card hand would be a royal flush.

The player's two-card (low) hand must rank higher than the banker's two-card (low) hand, and the player's five-card (high) hand must rank higher than the banker's five-card (high) hand. And, finally, the five-card hand must rank higher than the two-card hand. For example, if the two-card hand is a pair of fives, the five-card hand must consist of a pair of sixes or better.

If one of the hands ranks exactly the same as the banker's hand, this is a tie; the banker wins all tie hands.

If the player wins one hand but loses the other, it is called a "push"; when hands push, there is no exchange of money.

Losing hands lose the money wagered. Winning hands are paid even money, minus a 5 percent house commission before paying a winning hand. In other words if you were to bet $100 and win, you would receive your $100 back plus $95 in winnings.

Note: It is the responsibility of the player to set his or her own hand properly. A mistake will cost you the bet.

Pai Gow Poker Rankings
Five aces (using the joker)
Royal flush
Straight flush (A, 2, 3, 4, 5 is highest nonroyal flush)
Four of a kind (four aces highest rank)
Full house
Flush
Straight
Three of a kind
Two pair
One pair
High card

SPORTS AND RACE BOOK

One of the more interesting areas of major casinos is the sports and race book, where you can place bets on almost every major sporting event. Satellite dishes feed multiple TV screens showing horse racing from around the country as well as professional and collegiate basketball, hockey, baseball, and football. You can also bet on far-distant events, such as picking the winner of the Super Bowl, the Stanley Cup, the NBA Championships, or the World Series at the start of a season.

The types of bets for each event vary, as do the payoff schemes.

■ FOOTBALL

To place a bet all you need to do is pick a team and determine how much you want to wager. In order to win a straight football bet, though, your chosen team must "cover the spread" by either winning or not losing by the indicated number of points.

The point spread is determined by oddsmakers, who choose one team as the favorite; then a guess is made of how many more points that team is likely to score than the underdog team. It is then said that the favorite gives a certain number of points to its opponent.

For example, if Team A is listed as a fourteen-point favorite over Team B, to win a bet on Team A, it must be victorious by more than fourteen points. If you bet on Team B, the underdog, you will win if they win or if they lose by less than fourteen points.

Point spreads may change before a game begins and even while the game is under way. However, all bets stand as written; the point spread in effect at the time you place your bet is the one that will be used in determining whether your particular bet wins or loses.

Here is the way an available football bet might appear on the boards:

101	New England Patriots	(ov/un 42)
102	San Francisco 49ers	−14

In this case the teams are identified by a betting number. The bottom team is always the home team, unless indicated. The 49ers are listed here as a fourteen-point favorite, meaning that they must win the game by no less than fifteen points for you to win your bet. If you were to take the Patriots, a fourteen-point underdog, you will win your bet if they win the game or if they lose by no more than thirteen points.

The *ov/un* listing is the estimation of the total number of points that will be scored in the game. You can bet that the final score (including overtime) will add up to more or less than this amount; the point spread has no effect on the bet. This bet pays off at 10:11.

Straight Bet. This is a wager on one event whose outcome for betting purposes is determined by a point spread or money odds. The standard betting odds on a point spread bet are 11:10, meaning that you can win $10 for each $11 you wager. (If you bet $11 and win, you will be paid a total of $21.)

Parlays. Two or more team events or propositions can be tied together to make one wager. All teams must win by the listed point spread. Parlays are more challenging to win than straight bets, but the return on the money is much more attractive. The payout odds progress as the bettor picks more teams. Parlay payoff odds differ from casino to casino; consult the rules of the sports book.

Teasers. Some sports books offer a wager in which additional points are either added to the underdog or subtracted from the favorite. Teaser points and payoff odds are posted.

Halftime Wagers. Some sports books permit wagering at halftime of selected college and professional games. All wagers are against the point spread at odds of 10:11. In halftime wagering, the second half is treated as an entirely new game and each team's slate is wiped clean at the end of the first half.

■ HORSE RACING

You can bet on any horse to win, place (come in first or second), or show (come in first, second, or third) as well as wager on combinations of horses or combinations of races.

Horses are assigned a betting number on the display boards and scratch sheets, and bets are placed by specifying the amount of the bet, the type of the bet, and the horse number.

Winning bets are paid off based on the odds in effect at the time the race begins. You are not betting against the casino but instead against all other bettors in the pari-mutuel pool. Here are the approximate payoffs for horse racing odds, based on a $2.00 bet; multiply the payoff times the appropriate factor for a larger bet:

Odds	Pays on $2 bet	Odds	Pays on $2 bet
1-5	$2.40	8-5	$5.20
2-5	$2.80	9-5	$5.60
1-2	$3.00	2	$6.00
3-5	$3.20	5-2	$7.00
4-5	$3.60	3	$8.00
1	$4.00	7-2	$9.00
6-5	$4.40	4	$10.00
7-5	$4.80	9-2	$11.00
3-2	$5.00	5	$12.00

Check the house rules for payoffs. Here is some of the fine print from Harvey's at Lake Tahoe: Full track mutuels are paid up to $100 across the board on all straight winners; after then the maximum odds are 20:1 to win, 8:1 to place, and 4:1 to show. Daily doubles, exactas, parlays, and house quinellas are subject to a 150:1 maximum limit, not to exceed $5,000 on a single wager.

Straight Wager. A single bet on one horse in one race. Pays off at pari-mutuel odds.

Daily Triple. A single bet in which you attempt to pick the winners of three designated races. Payout is limited to 299:1 at many casinos.

Trifecta. A single bet that predicts the win, place, and show horse in a single race. Payout is limited to 299:1 at many casinos.

Daily Double. Pick the winner of the first two races at a track or (at some tracks) two other races. If one of the horses is scratched, the bet is converted to a straight wager on the remaining horse. Odds are based on the betting pool at the track.

Exacta. Select one horse to win and another to place in a particular race. Paid based on track odds.

BASKETBALL

Similar to football betting, there is both a point spread and an over-under bet available. Here is an example of some betting offerings:

501	New York Knicks	(ov/un 218)
502	Chicago Bulls	−8½

In this case the Bulls are favored by 8½ points, meaning that they must win by nine or more points for the bet to be paid. To win a bet on the Knicks, they must win the game or lose by eight points or less. Bets are paid 10:11.

The over-under bet allows you to wager that the total score will be over or under 218, with a payoff at 10:11.

There are also **basketball parlays** that combine various games; all teams in a parlay must cover the point spread to win the bet.

BASEBALL

There is no point spread in the standard baseball bet; instead, the betting "units" are adjusted to represent the estimation of the oddsmakers of the chances of either of the two teams.

A baseball betting option is presented like this:

601	NY METS	+1.20	7	ov −1.10
602	CHI CUBS	−1.35	7	un −1.10

The minus (−) on the board indicates the favorite, while the plus (+) indicates the underdog.

In the above example, the Cubs are the favorite at −1.35. To bet on the Cubs, you must bet 1.35 units for each one you hope to win; for example, you would have to put up $13.50 to win $10.00 for a total of $23.50. If you bet on the hapless Mets and they win the game, you will be paid 1.20 units for each unit you wager; for example, you would be paid $12 for a $10 bet for a total of $22.

The next number is the total or over/under number, the estimation of the combined score of both teams. Also indicated are the over and under odds, in this case 1.10, meaning you would have to put up $11 in hopes of winning $10 more.

Some casinos will offer a run line bet, which is similar to a point spread in that it requires the favorite to win by the specified number of runs. Or, if you bet on the underdog, that team receives extra runs added to the final score. The run line uses the same sort of unit wagering as other baseball bets.

Some sports books permit you to qualify your bet so that it only applies if the listed pitcher starts the game; if a different pitcher is used, the bet is scratched and your money will be refunded.

HOCKEY

Hockey bets follow the same model as baseball, with a point or "Puck Line" defining the difference in teams, plus an over-under bet for total goals.

BOXING

To bet on a boxing match, you either lay odds or take money odds.

Here is the way a boxing bet might be listed:

101	P. Herman	+4.50
102	Ali	−6.00

In this case Ali is the clear favorite, and bettors must put up six units to win one. For example, a $600 winning bet would return $100 in profit, or a total of $700.

A bet on Peewee Herman would pay off 4.5 units to one unit bet. For example, a $100 winning bet would return $450 in profit for a total of $550.

Other bets on major bouts include wagering on whether a match will go above or below a specified number of rounds.

A LIST OF LAS VEGAS CASINOS, HOTELS, AND MOTELS

LIKE MOST EVERYTHING ELSE in Las Vegas, room rates are subject to the laws of supply and demand. During convention and holiday periods and peak summer periods, a very ordinary motel room can command presidential-suite rates; during quiet periods in the winter, some of the best rooms in town are offered for pocket change. The hotels, motels, and casino-hotels in this section range from acceptable to excellent; I have not included many smaller hotels where I would not personally want to lay my head.

CASINO-HOTELS ON THE STRIP

Arizona Charlie's. 740 South Decatur Blvd. 253 rooms. (702) 258–5200, (800) 342–2695. www.azcharlies.com.

Bally's Las Vegas. 3645 LVBS. 2,814 rooms. (702) 739–4111, (800) 634–3434. www.ballyslv.com.

Barbary Coast Hotel & Casino. 3595 LVBS. 200 rooms. (702) 737–7111, (800) 634–6755. www.barbarycoastcasino.com.

Bellagio. 3600 LVBS. 3,933 rooms. (702) 693–7111, (888) 987–6667. www.bellagio.com.

Caesars Palace. 3570 LVBS. 3,340 rooms. (702) 731–7110, (800) 634–6661. www.caesars.com

Circus Circus Hotel & Casino. 2880 LVBS. 3,770 rooms. (702) 734–0410, (800) 634–3450. www.circuscircus.com.

Excalibur Hotel & Casino. 3850 LVBS. 4,008 rooms. (702) 597–7777, (800) 937–7777. www.excaliburcasino.com.

Key

LVBN = Las Vegas Boulevard North (Downtown)

LVBS = Las Vegas Boulevard South (The Strip)

Flamingo Las Vegas. 3555 LVBS. 3,565 rooms. (702) 733–3111, (800) 732–2111. www.lv-flamingo.com.

Four Seasons Hotel Las Vegas. 3960 LVBS. 424 rooms. (702) 632–5000. www.fourseasons.com/lasvegas.

Harrah's Las Vegas. 3475 LVBS. 2,579 rooms. (702) 369–5000, (800) 634–6765. www.harrahs.com.

Imperial Palace Hotel and Casino. 3535 LVBS. 2,700 rooms. (702) 731–3311, (800) 634–6441. www.imperialpalace.com.

Luxor Hotel/Casino. 3900 LVBS. 4,408 rooms. (702) 262–4000, (800) 288–1000. www.luxor.com.

Mandalay Bay Resort & Casino. 3950 LVBS. 3,700 rooms. (702) 632–7777. www.mandalaybay.com.

MGM Grand Hotel. 3799 LVBS. 5,034 rooms. (702) 891–7777, (800) 929–1111. www.mgmgrand.com or www.mgmmirage.com.

The Mirage. 3400 LVBS. 3,044 rooms. (702) 791–7111, (800) 627–6667. www.themirage.com.

Monte Carlo Resort & Casino. 3770 LVBS. 3,002 rooms. (702) 730–7777, (800) 311–8999. www.monte-carlo.com.

New York–New York Hotel & Casino. 3790 LVBS. 2,024 rooms. (800) 693–6763. www.nynyhotelcasino.com.

Paris Las Vegas. 3655 LVBS. 2,916 rooms. (702) 946–7000, (877) 796–2096. www.parislasvegas.com.

Planet Hollywood Resort and Casino. (Aladdin). 3667 LVBS. 4,000 rooms. (877) 933–9475. www.aladdincasino.com.

Riviera Hotel & Casino. 2901 LVBS. 2,100 rooms. (702) 734–5110, (800) 634–6753. www.theriviera.com.

Sahara Hotel & Casino. 2535 LVBS. 1,720 rooms. (702) 737–2111, (800) 634–6666. www.saharavegas.com.

Stratosphere Casino Hotel & Tower. 2000 LVBS. 2,444 rooms. (702) 380–7777, (800) 998–6937. www.stratospherehotel.com.

Treasure Island. 3300 LVBS. 2,900 rooms. (702) 894–7111, (800) 944–7444. www.treasureisland.com.

Tropicana Resort & Casino. 3801 LVBS. 1,878 rooms. (702) 739–2222, (800) 634–4000. www.tropicanalv.com.

The Venetian Resort Hotel Casino. 3355 LVBS. 4,049 rooms. (702) 414–1000, (877) 883–6423. www.venetian.com.

Wynn Las Vegas. 3131 LVBS. 2,700 rooms. (702) 770–7800, (877) 770–7077. www.wynnlasvegas.com.

CASINO-HOTELS NEAR THE STRIP

Amerisuites Las Vegas/Paradise Road. 4520 Paradise Road. 202 rooms. (702) 369–3366. www.amerisuites.com.

Best Western Mardi Gras Inn. 3500 Paradise Road. 314 rooms. (702) 731–2020, (800) 634–6501. www.bestwestern.com.

Best Western McCarran Inn. 4970 Paradise Road. 100 rooms. (702) 798–5530, (800) 626–7575. www.bestwestern.com.

Bourbon Street Hotel & Casino. 120 East Flamingo Road. 166 rooms. (702) 737–7200, (800) 634–6956. www.bourbonstreethotel.com.

The Carriage House. 105 East Harmon Avenue. 165 rooms. (702) 798–1020. www.carriagehouselasvegas.com.

Courtyard by Marriott Las Vegas. 3275 Paradise Road. 149 rooms. (702) 791–3600. www.courtyard.com.

Crowne Plaza Las Vegas. 4255 South Paradise Road. 201 rooms. (702) 369–4400, (800) 227–6963. www.sixcontinentshotels.com.

Doubletree Club Airport. 7250 Pollock Drive. 190 rooms. (702) 948– 4000. www.doubletree.com.

Embassy Suites Convention Center. 3600 Paradise Road. 286 rooms. (702) 893–8000. www.embassysuites.com.

Embassy Suites Las Vegas. 4315 Swenson Road. 220 rooms. (702) 785–2800. www.embassysuites.com.

Emerald Springs Holiday Inn. 325 East Flamingo Road. 150 rooms. (702) 732–9100.

Fairfield Inn by Marriott. 3850 Paradise Road. 129 rooms. (702) 791–0899, (800) 228–2800. www.marriott.com.

Gold Coast Hotel & Casino. 4000 West Flamingo Road. 711 rooms. (702) 367–7111, (800) 331–5334. www.goldcoastcasino.com.

Hampton Inn Las Vegas/Summerlin. 7100 Cascade Valley Court. 128 rooms. (702) 360–5700. www.hampton-inn.com.

Hampton Inn Tropicana. 4975 Industrial Road. 325 rooms. (702) 948–8100. www.hampton-inn.com.

Hard Rock Hotel and Casino. 4475 Paradise Road. 657 rooms. (702) 693–5000, (800) 473–7625. www.hardrockhotel.com.

Hawthorn Suites Las Vegas Strip. 5051 Duke Ellington Way. 278 rooms. (702) 739–7000. www.hawthorn.com.

Hooters Casino Hotel Las Vegas. 115 East Tropicana Avenue. 711 rooms. (702) 739–9000, (866) 584–6687. www.hooterscasinohotel.com.

La Quinta Inn. 3970 Paradise Road. 228 rooms. (702) 796–9000, (800) 531–5900. www.laquinta.com.

Las Vegas Hilton. 3000 Paradise Road. 3,174 rooms. (702) 732–5155, (800) 732–7117. www.lv-hilton.com.

Marriott Suites. 325 Convention Center Drive. 378 rooms. (702) 650–2000. www.marriott.com.

The Orleans Hotel & Casino. 4500 West Tropicana Avenue. 840 rooms. (702) 365–7111, (800) 675–3267. www.orleanscasino.com.

Palace Station Hotel & Casino. 2411 West Sahara Avenue. 1,029 rooms. (702) 367–2411, (800) 634–3101. www.palacestation.com.

The Palms Casino Resort. 4321 West Flamingo Road. 455 rooms. (702) 942–7777, (866) 942–7770. www.thepalmslasvegas.com.

Residence Inn by Marriott. 3225 Paradise Road. 192 rooms. (702) 796–9300, (800) 331–3131. www.marriott.com.

Rio All-Suite Hotel & Casino. 3700 West Flamingo Road. 2,563 rooms. (702) 252–7777, (800) 888–1808. www.harrahs.com.

St. Tropez All Suite Hotel. 455 East Harmon Avenue. 149 rooms. (702) 369–5400. www.sttropezlasvegas.com.

Santa Fe Station. 4949 North Rancho. 200 rooms. (702) 658–4900, (800) 872–6823. www.santafe.stationcasinos.com.

Terrible's Casino. 4100 Paradise Road. 373 rooms. (702) 733–7000, (800) 640–9777. www.terribleherbst.com/casinos/lasvegas.

Westin Casuarina. 160 East Flamingo Road. 825 rooms. (702) 836-9775. www.westin.com/lasvegas.

DOWNTOWN LAS VEGAS AND AREA CASINO-HOTELS

Best Western Main Street Inn. 1000 North Main Street. Ninety-one rooms. (702) 382–3455, (800) 851–1414. www.bestwestern.com.

Best Western Parkview Inn. 921 LVBN. Forty-two rooms. (702) 385–1213, (800) 528–1234. www.bestwestern.com.

Binion's Gambling Hall & Hotel. 128 East Fremont Street. 354 rooms. (702) 382–1600, (800) 937–6537. www.binions.com.

Boulder Station Hotel & Casino. 4111 Boulder Highway. 306 rooms. (702) 432–7777, (800) 937–6537. www.boulderstation.com.

California Hotel and Casino. 12 Ogden Avenue. 781 rooms. (702) 385–1222, (800) 634–6255. www.thecal.com.

El Cortez Hotel. 600 East Fremont Street. 308 rooms. (702) 385–5200, (800) 634–6703. www.elcortezhotelcasino.com.

Fiesta Rancho. 2400 North Rancho Drive. 100 rooms. (702) 631–7000. http://rancho.fiestacasino.com.

Fitzgeralds Casino Hotel. 301 Fremont Street. 638 rooms. (702) 388–2400, (800) 274–5825. www.fitzgeraldslasvegas.com.

Four Queens Hotel & Casino. 202 East Fremont Street. 690 rooms. (702) 385–4011, (800) 634–6045. www.fourqueens.com.

Fremont Hotel & Casino. 200 East Fremont Street. 452 rooms. (702) 385–3232, (800) 634–6182. www.fremontcasino.com.

Golden Gate Hotel & Casino. 1 East Fremont Street. 106 rooms. (702) 382–6300, (800) 426–1906. www.goldengatecasino.net.

Golden Nugget Hotel & Casino. 129 East Fremont Street. 1,907 rooms. (702) 385–7111, (800) 634–3454. www.goldennugget.com.

Gold Spike Hotel. 400 East Ogden. 107 rooms. (702) 384–8444, (800) 634–6703. www.goldspikehotelcasino.com.

J.W. Marriott Las Vegas Resort, Spa & Golf. 221 North Rampart Boulevard. 541 rooms. (702) 869–7777. www.marriott.com.

Lady Luck Casino Hotel. 206 North Third Street. (Due to reopen in 2007). 792 rooms. (702) 477–3000, (800) 523–9582. www.ladylucklv.com.

Main Street Station. 200 North Main Street. 406 rooms. (702) 387–1896, (800) 713–8933. www.mainstreetcasino.com.

Plaza Hotel & Casino. 1 Main Street. 1,037 rooms. (702) 386–2110, (800) 634–6575. www.plazahotelcasino.com.

Railroad Pass Hotel and Casino. 2800 South Boulder Highway, Henderson. 120 rooms. (702) 294–5000. www.railroadpass.com.

Sam's Town Hotel & Gambling Hall. 5111 Boulder Highway. 648 rooms. (702) 456–7777, (800) 634–6371. www.samstownlv.com.

Suncoast Resort & Casino. 9090 Alta Drive. 432 rooms. (702) 636–7111. www.suncoastcasino.com.

Sunset Station Hotel & Casino. 1301 West Sunset Road, Henderson. 448 rooms. (702) 547–7777. www.sunsetstation.com.

Texas Station Gambling Hall and Hotel. 2101 Texas Star Lane. 202 rooms. (702) 631–1000. www.texasstation.com.

Vegas Club Hotel & Casino. 18 East Fremont Street. 410 rooms. (702) 385–1664, (800) 634–6532. www.vegasclubcasino.net.

MOTELS ON THE STRIP AND SURROUNDING AREA

Budget Suites of America—Paradise. 3684 Paradise Road. 360 rooms. (702) 699–7000. www.budgetsuites.com.

Budget Suites of America—Stardust. 1500 Stardust. 639 rooms. (702) 732–1500. www.budgetsuites.com.

Budget Suites of America—Tropicana. 3655 West Tropicana. 480 rooms. (702) 739–1000. www.budgetsuites.com.

Budget Suites of America—Wynn. 4205 West Tropicana. 414 rooms. (702) 889–1700. www.budgetsuites.com.

Candlewood Suites. 4034 South Paradise Road. 277 rooms. (702) 836–3660. www.candlewoodsuites.com.

Casino Royale Hotel. 3411 LVBS. 150 rooms. (702) 737–3500. www.casinoroyalehotel.com.

Comfort Inn—Central. 211 East Flamingo Road. 121 rooms. (702) 733–7800. www.comfortinn.com.

Days Inn Town Hall Casino and Hotel. 4155 Koval Lane. 360 rooms. (702) 731–2111. www.daysinn.com.

Days Inn Airport. 5125 Swenson. 327 rooms. (702) 740–4040. www.daysinn.com.

Econo Lodge. 1150 LVBS. 124 rooms. (702) 382–6001. www.choicehotels.com.

Holiday Inn Express. 8669 West Sahara Avenue. Fifty-nine rooms. (702) 256–3766. www.holiday-inn.com.

Homestead Village Midtown. 3045 South Maryland Parkway. 123 rooms. (702) 369–1414.

Howard Johnson Hotel & Casino. 3111 West Tropicana Avenue. 150 rooms. (702) 798–1111. www.hojo.com.

Howard Johnson Inn. 1401 LVBS. One hundred rooms. (702) 388–0301. www.hojo.com.

Howard Johnson Inn. 5100 Paradise Road. 146 rooms. (702) 798–2777. www .hojo.com.

La Quinta—Strip. 3782 LVBS. 114 rooms. (702) 739–7457. www.laquinta.com.

Motel 6—Industrial. 5085 Industrial Road. 139 rooms. (702) 739–6747. www.motel6.com.

Motel 6—Tropicana. 195 East Tropicana Avenue. 608 rooms. (702) 798–0728. www.motel6.com.

Rodeway Inn & Suites. 167 East Tropicana Avenue. 262 rooms. (702) 795–3311. www.choicehotels.com.

Somerset House Motel. 294 Convention Center Drive. 104 rooms. (702) 735–4411.

Super 8 Motel. 4250 South Koval Lane. 306 rooms. (702) 794–0888. www .super8.com.

Travelodge Las Vegas Strip. 2830 LVBS. One hundred rooms. (702) 735–4222. www.travelodge.com.

Travelodge South Strip. 3735 LVBS. 126 rooms. (702) 736–3443. www .travelodge.com.

Travelodge West Sahara. 1501 West Sahara Avenue. 223 rooms. (702) 733–0001. www.travelodge.com.

Vagabond Inn. 3265 LVBS. 132 rooms. (702) 735–5102.

Wellesley Inn and Suites. 1550 East Flamingo. 125 rooms. (702) 731–3111. www.wellesleyinnandsuites.com.

Yucca Motel. 1727 LVBS. Twenty-two rooms. (702) 735–2787.

MOTELS IN DOWNTOWN LAS VEGAS AND AREA

Best Western Main Street Inn. 1000 North Main Street. Ninety-one rooms. (702) 382–3455.www.bestwestern.com.

Best Western Nellis Motor Inn. 5330 East Craig Road. Fifty-two rooms. (702) 643–6111. www.bestwestern.com.

Best Western Parkview Inn. 921 LVBN. Forty-one rooms. (702) 385–1213. www.bestwestern.com.

Boulder Palms Luxury Suites. 4350 Boulder Highway. 182 rooms. (702) 434–9900.

Budget Suites of America—Indios. 4625 Boulder Highway. 280 rooms. (702) 454–4625. www.budgetsuites.com.

Budget Suites of America—Nellis. 4855 Boulder Highway. 839 rooms. (702) 433–3644. www.budgetsuites.com.

Budget Suites of America—Rancho. 2219 North Rancho. 704 rooms. (702) 638–1800. www.budgetsuites.com.

Comfort Inn North. 910 East Cheyenne Avenue. Fifty-nine rooms. (702) 399–1500. www.comfortinn.com.

Crest Budget Inn. 207 North Sixth Street. 149 rooms. (702) 382–5642. $30.

Days Inn Downtown. 707 East Fremont Street. 147 rooms. (702) 388–1400. www.daysinn.com.

Downtowner Motel. 129 North Eighth Street. 200 rooms. (702) 384–1441.

Holiday Inn Express North Las Vegas. 4540 Donovan Way. Seventy-four rooms. (702) 649–3000. www.holiday-inn.com.

Motel 6—Boulder Highway. 4125 Boulder Highway. 161 rooms. (702) 457–8051. www.motel6.com.

Mount Charleston Hotel. 2 Kyle Canyon Road. Sixty-three rooms. (702) 872–5500. www.mtcharlestonhotel.com.

Ramada Inn. 3227 Civic Center Drive. 118 rooms. (702) 399–3297. www.ramada.com.

Super 8 Motel. 5288 Boulder Highway. 150 rooms. (702) 435–8888. www.super8.com.

Super 8 Motel—Nellis. 4435 LVBN. 105 rooms. (702) 644–5666. www.super8.com.

Super Suites. 3625 Boulder Highway. 186 rooms. (702) 431–7121.

Town and Country Manor I. 4311 Boulder Highway. 143 rooms. (702) 454–9393.

Town and Country Manor II. 4360 Boulder Highway. Ninety-two rooms. (702) 547–9393.

Travelodge. 2028 East Fremont Street. Fifty-eight rooms. (702) 384–7540. www.travelodge.com.

MOTELS AND RESORTS IN OUTLYING AREAS

Best Western Lake Mead Motel. 85 West Lake Mead Drive, Boulder City. Fifty-nine rooms. (702) 564–1712. www.bestwestern.com.

Best Western Lighthouse Inn and Resort. 110 Ville Drive, Boulder City. Seventy rooms. (702) 293–6444. www.bestwestern.com.

Best Western Northshore Inn at Lake Mead. 520 North Moapa Valley Boulevard, Overton. Forty-three rooms. (702) 397–6000. www.bestwestern.com.

Bonnie Springs Motel. #1 Gunfighter Lane, Old Nevada. Fifty rooms. (702) 875–4400. www.bonniesprings.com/motel.html.

Buffalo Bill's Resort & Casino. 31700 LVBS. 1,285 rooms. (702) 382–1111. www.primmvalleyresorts.com.

Echo Bay Resort. Echo Bay, Overton. Fifty-two rooms. (702) 394–4000. www.echobayresort.com.

Hyatt Regency Lake Las Vegas Resort. 101 Monte Lago Boulevard. 496 rooms. (702) 567–1234.

La Quinta Inn & Suites Las Vegas Northwest. 7101 Cascade Valley Court. 128 rooms. (702) 360–1200.

Primm Valley Resort & Casino. I–15 South at California-Nevada border. 660 rooms. (702) 679–5460. www.primmvalleyresorts.com.

Silverton Hotel Casino. 3333 Blue Diamond Road. 304 rooms. (702) 263–7777.

Whiskey Pete's. I–15 South at California-Nevada border. 777 rooms. (702) 386–7876. www.primmvalleyresorts.com.

INDEX

HOTELS/CASINOS: LAS VEGAS

SHOWS, SHOPPING, AND ATTRACTIONS: LAS VEGAS REGION

About the Author

Corey Sandler is a former newsman and editor for the Associated Press, Gannett Newspapers, Ziff-Davis Publishing, and IDG. He has written more than 160 books on travel, video games, and computers; his titles have been translated into French, Spanish, German, Italian, Portuguese, Polish, Bulgarian, Hebrew, and Chinese. When he's not traveling, he hides out with his wife and two children on the island of Nantucket, 30 miles off the coast of Massachusetts.

Receive Econoguide Updates

You can receive a free subscription to the *Econoguide Newsletter* for updates, announcements, and special offers. To subscribe, go to our Web page at www .econoguide.com and click on the newsletter subscription link. You can also subscribe by sending an e-mail with your name and e-mail address to: newsletter@ econoguide.com.